CANADIAN PENTECOSTALS:
A HISTORY OF
THE PENTECOSTAL ASSEMBLIES OF CANADA

CANADIAN PENTECOSTALS

*A HISTORY OF
THE PENTECOSTAL ASSEMBLIES
OF CANADA*

by

Thomas William Miller

Edited by William A. Griffin

Full Gospel Publishing House
6745 Century Ave, Mississauga, Ontario
Canada L5N 6P7

About the Author

Dr. Thomas William Miller is recognized as one of the leading historians in the Canadian Pentecostal Movement. He was converted as a teenager in a Pentecostal church in Melville, Saskatchewan, where Ian Presley served as pastor. Miller's distinguished academic background includes a diploma from Central Pentecostal College, Saskatoon; BA, University of London; MA (history) and PhD (education), University of Saskatchewan; and MST (theology), Lutheran Theological Seminary, Saskatoon.

He and his wife Dorothy pastored in Leask, Sask.; Maple Ridge and Nelson in B.C.; and for brief stints in Ottawa, Peterborough, and Essex in Ontario. The record of his teaching career begins with a two-year assignment as an instructor at Central Pentecostal College. He also taught for 13 years at Eastern Pentecostal Bible College in Peterborough. Responding to an invitation to go south, Miller served as chairman of the Biblical Studies Department and later as vice-president of the Jimmy Swaggart Bible College in Baton Rouge, Louisiana. Most recently he served as superintendent of Heritage Christian Schools in Calgary.

Dr. Miller is the author of *Ripe For Revival*. Several of his scholarly articles have been published in *Pneuma*, the journal of the Society for Pentecostal Studies. He frequently writes articles for religious magazines such as *The Pentecostal Testimony, Pentecostal Evangel,* and *Christianity Today.*

The Millers have three children — Sheralee, Reginald, and Timothy.

© Full Gospel Publishing House 1994. All rights reserved. No part of this book may be reproduced in any form or by any electronic or mechanical means including information storage and retrieval systems without permission in writing from the publisher.
Published by Full Gospel Publishing House,
The Pentecostal Assemblies of Canada
6745 Century Avenue • Mississauga, Ontario • L5N 6P7
ISBN 1-895168-35-X
Printed in Canada

Dedication

To those Canadian Pentecostal pioneers whose lives of dedication, sacrifice, and heroism will surely merit the Master's highest accolade — "Well done, good and faithful servants . . . enter into the joy of the Lord."

Although few in number and feeble in resources, they succeeded in one generation in covering the Dominion with the Pentecostal message. Bitter hostility, deliberate misrepresentation, and outright persecution failed to restrain them. They were empowered with the supernatural ministry gifts of the Holy Spirit and were convinced that they were living in the closing days of the age of grace.

The price they paid to preach the full gospel cannot be accurately measured by posterity — perhaps because they themselves tended to discount their sacrifices as unworthy of recognition or praise. Nevertheless, they proved that Pentecostalism was not a theological novelty but a genuine work of God. To conserve the fruits of their labors, they established The Pentecostal Assemblies of Canada.

A Representative Group of Pioneers — General Executive, 1933

Back Row: J. H. Blair, John McAlister
Middle Row: James Swanson, W. E. McAlister, C. M. Ward, R. E. McAlister, W. L. Draffin, C. E. Baker
Front Row: D. N. Buntain, A. E. Adams, G. A. Chambers, A. G. Ward, J. W. McKillop.

But you will receive power when the Holy Spirit comes on you; and you will be my witnesses in Jerusalem, and in all Judea and Samaria, and to the ends of the earth.
Acts 1:8

When the Day of Pentecost came, they were all together in one place. Suddenly a sound like the blowing of a violent wind came from heaven and filled the whole house where they were sitting. They saw what seemed to be tongues of fire that separated and came to rest on each of them. All of them were filled with the Holy Spirit and began to speak in other tongues as the Spirit enabled them.
Acts 2:4

Contents

Foreword — James M. MacKnight 9

Editor's Preface — William A. Griffin 10

Acknowledgements — Thomas Wm. Miller 13

Introduction 15

Chapter 1   PENTECOSTAL BEGINNINGS 21

Chapter 2   "THIS IS THE PENTECOST:"
PENTECOSTALISM IN ONTARIO 1906-1919 39

Chapter 3   THE EARLY WORK IN THE WEST 71

Chapter 4   CONFLICT AND CONSOLIDATION 99

Chapter 5   AND HE GAVE SOME 125

Chapter 6   PIONEERING PENTECOST IN EASTERN CANADA .. 155

Chapter 7   CAMP MEETINGS, CONVENTIONS, AND
CONFERENCES 185

Chapter 8   THE REGIONS BEYOND 1907 - 1940 219

Chapter 9   COMING OF AGE 1939-1958 245

Chapter 10   THE THIRD FORCE 267

Chapter 11   "CLASSICAL PENTECOSTALS" IN CANADA 295

Chapter 12   "THE UNBELIEVABLE YEARS" IN OVERSEAS
MISSIONS 325

Chapter 13   ON TRACK! 353

Chapter 14   EXPANDING THE VISION 375

Chapter 15   DECADE OF DESTINY 397

A Note on the Sources 413

Appendices 417

Subject Index 429

Foreword

Spontaneous manifestations of Holy Spirit power were occurring around the world. In Eastern Canada, a three-storey building had been acquired at 651 Queen Street in Toronto by Mr. and Mrs. James Hebden in which they opened a "rescue mission" and "faith healing home" in May of 1906. Ellen Hebden, who had been converted at age 15, was praying in her room for more power in her ministry on November 17, 1906. Suddenly, the Holy Ghost came upon her and her whole being was filled with praise and adoration as she repeated a word in an unknown tongue.

The next morning she announced she had received "the Baptism of the Holy Ghost." While in prayer the following day, she began to *sing* in tongues. For three hours many listeners in attendance at the mission were in awe as Mrs. Hebden prayed and sang in the Spirit. "This is the power of the Holy Ghost," she proclaimed. Within five months, her husband and about 80 others had similar experiences.

From this humble beginning, hundreds of thousands of Canadians have since been filled with the Holy Spirit and have spoken in tongues as the Spirit has given them utterance. The history of The Pentecostal Assemblies of Canada is an incredible story of the Spirit being outpoured upon all flesh. Several have undertaken to record segments of our history with great effect. In *Canadian Pentecostals: A History of The Pentecostal Assemblies of Canada,* Tom Miller has gathered the most extensive account of Canadian Pentecostalism I have ever read. One of Miller's secrets has been his persistent pursuit of many of the pioneers to record their accounts and impressions of what really happened in the beginning of this latter-day outpouring.

As I read through the manuscript, I was caught up and carried along with excitement at the great works of God wrought through the Spirit resting upon fellow Canadians. I am encouraged and challenged to keep praying and expecting God to do it again.

In the author's introduction, he poses a sobering question, "Where do we go from here?" Many of us know where we *should* be going as a Pentecostal Fellowship! The dominant strain coming through in this fascinating chronicle is that the Baptism in the Holy Spirit is foundational to all of our evangelistic efforts to reach the whole world with the liberating power of the gospel. These early Pentecostals were passionate in their desire to reach people for Christ in their Jerusalem, in their Judea, in their Samaria, and in the uttermost parts of the earth.

It is my fervent prayer that this volume will become a dynamic instrument to ignite another Pentecost.

James M. MacKnight
General Superintendent

Editor's Preface

It was time for someone to trace the emergence of one of Canada's most vigorous ecclesiastical entities — The Pentecostal Assemblies of Canada. Dr. Miller has made a major contribution to the entire religious community and particularly to his colleagues in the Fellowship. Generations of Bible college students to come will learn about the McAlisters, Argues, Chawners, Uptons, and many other Pentecostal "saints" from this volume.

But Miller has not only ferreted out the personalities and events which shaped the Pentecostal Movement, he has also endeavored to capture on paper the essential spiritual excitement which permeates the decades of growth. As much as possible, an attempt has been made to preserve the unique terminology which was so meaningful for the pioneers of Pentecostalism in this century. Our children need to hear about the "waves of glory" and being "slain under the power of God."

The attempt to tell the story of the PAOC in Canada and trace its impact around the world has been difficult for one very basic reason — Pentecostals, traditionally, have not been too interested in preserving records. Our fathers preached and lived the "imminent return of Jesus Christ for His Bride." The record of the past did not seem to have great value to our forefathers because any day soon they believed the church would meet the Lord in the air and relocate to the heavenly home.

Miller's task of weaving the bits of information about personalities, reports, clippings, and minutes of business meetings into the historical fabric has been abetted immeasurably by the vivid recollections of some of the surviving seniors. Their encounters with God throughout a life-time in the Fellowship made indelible impressions upon them. Some of them report incidents which happened 50 years ago as if they took place last week. Indeed, the fire of Pentecost still burns fervently in their testimonies.

Obviously, we are not claiming that this volume tells the whole story; we are not even suggesting that it reports on all the important people and events. Often dates are unavailable. Occasionally, it has been virtually impossible to discover the first names or initials of the women who played an equal role with their male counterparts. No doubt there are Pentecostal attics which contain treasures of clippings and correspondence which could correct or add to future reprints of *Canadian Pentecostals: A History of The Pentecostal Assemblies of Canada.*

William A. Griffin
General Secretary

Acknowledgments

I have been interested in history as long as I can remember. As a youth, I found high school history courses fascinating — invariably I read the assigned textbooks before the classes began.

After my Christian conversion and while still a teenager, I was introduced to the "romance" of the early days of Pentecostalism in Canada. The recollections of some of the mature "saints" fuelled my enthusiasm to find out more about the near legendary figures and events which were part of the origin and development of the "Fellowship," as the PAOC has always liked to refer to itself.

Commendable work has been done by various authors in assembling historical details. General Superintendent Walter McAlister solicited letters and data from scores of PAOC pioneer ministers for a proposed history book. Gloria G. Kulbeck was commissioned to compile the data and write the story of the Pentecostal Assemblies of Canada. Her book, *What God Hath Wrought*, was well received.

Another history of the Fellowship which achieved wide recognition was written by PAOC historian and Bible teacher Gordon F. Atter. He was the son of a first-generation Pentecostal and was personally acquainted with most of the leading personalities in the movement. Atter's book, *The Third Force*, was first published in 1962 and has been reprinted in two later editions.

I am grateful for the encouragement which both McAlister and Atter have given me. Their assessments of the urgent need for the Fellowship to understand and appreciate its roots have stimulated my own interests and labors to attempt a more-comprehensive history of Pentecostalism in Canada, with particular focus on the PAOC.

Another motivation for my involvement in this history of the PAOC is related to my interest in revivalism. As a youth in a Pentecostal church, I was familiar with a "revivalistic atmosphere." I personally witnessed a local revival in Melville, Saskatchewan, which stirred the entire community and produced many conversions. From my pastors and visiting evangelists I first heard the names of Wesley, Finney, and Moody. Years later in seminary, I devoured accounts of Finney's theology and ministry. Finney's view on revival and the Oberlin School's teaching on holiness had a profound impact on the late 19th-century Holiness Movement in North America. That religious phenomenon, in turn, greatly affected the Apostolic Faith/Latter Rain/Pentecostal Movement of the early 20th century. I found many references to Finney in my study of PAOC sources — one of his sermons was reprinted in an early issue of *The Pentecostal Testimony*.

So my chief interests in historical, theological, and revivalistic developments in the PAOC came together and coalesced in this book. It is quite clear that the Pentecostalism which emerged in Canada after 1907 was a product of a variety of forces which together produced a dynamic Fellowship of full gospel believers.

It is not possible to list the scores of individuals who have willingly contributed to the task of assembling this history. The data has come from the files of national, district, and local church offices. It has come also from the hearts and minds of dozens of people who "lived" this history and communicated their thoughts by correspondence and personal interviews.

I am also grateful for the Publications Committee of the PAOC who encouraged me to continue with the research and agreed to publish the book. The committee appointed William Griffin to serve as the editor. Griffin has nurtured the manuscript through several drafts and has been helpful with his revisions and additions. Other national officers have read all or parts of the manuscript and offered significant comments. A former director of the Overseas Missions Department, Carman Lynn, has also reviewed the missions portions of the narrative. Douglas Rudd, the PAOC archivist, has played an important role in verifying many of the dates, names, and events in the text. Lillian Cornelius helped compile the list of missionaries in the appendix. Dan Lessard, Allan Leggate, Kevin M. Johnson, Patti Griffin, and members of the Church Ministries staff in the national office have worked diligently on the copy.

Finally, I am most appreciative for the advice, encouragement, and patience of my wife Dorothy. Without her support this arduous project never would have been completed.

Thomas William Miller
Author

Introduction

WHERE DO WE GO FROM HERE?

It may seem strange to begin a book with the query, "Where do we go from here?" But it is a question which late 20th-century Pentecostals ask with increasing frequency. It was posed by R. E. McAlister, a founding father of Canadian Pentecostalism, to his colleagues in 1950.[1] The inquiry has appeared again in recent denominational literature and has prompted a number of self-evaluations by respected spokesmen. One of the most prominent of those calling for a re-examination of the modern role of the Pentecostal Assemblies of Canada (PAOC), the largest Pentecostal organization in the nation, has been its General Superintendent, James M. MacKnight. In his 1991 Report to the PAOC District Conferences, MacKnight called for a realistic appraisal of the Fellowship — as credential holders of the PAOC are wont to call their denomination — and a renewed emphasis on evangelism.[2] This trend to self-analysis and recommitment has resulted from a growing awareness in the PAOC of its historical development from the status of a Canadian revivalist sect to that of a nationally recognized denomination.

The developmental process generally followed by revival groups has been documented in a study by David O. Moberg. It defines five phases of development from the origin of a sect to denominational status and then to spiritual decline. Moberg concludes that revivalist associations rarely have retained their primary religious emphases past the third or fourth generation.[3] A considerable number of self-examining Pentecostals are of the opinion that the PAOC is now facing a crucial period in its development. For example, PAOC historian Gordon F. Atter, after 60 years in the Fellowship, has warned of the dangers of "over-organization." In his view the PAOC has matured to the point where it is now confronted with that threat:

> As organizations get older and become concerned with self-perpetuation, organization can become a threat. Of necessity, organization must become more detailed as the Fellowship grows, but a time comes when it becomes top-heavy with organization. I think we're at the crossroads in that respect now.[4]

The Pentecostal Assemblies of Canada, about which such concerns have been expressed, is part of a worldwide movement which is now approaching 400 million participants. It is the largest charismatic denomination in Canada with members and adherents numbering approximately 231,000 in 1994.[5] The PAOC and the other established Pentecostal organizations witnessed the emergence of charismatic groups in the Roman Catholic Church and some of the older Protestant denominations during the 1970s. The Pentecostals were quick to offer fellowship but found difficulty in achieving any structural unity because of significant doctrinal and lifestyle differences. A similar process marked American Pentecostalism in that same decade. These new groups which emerged came to be designated "Neo-Pentecostals," or "Charismatics." In time, some spokesmen for these Neo-Pentecostals began to refer to the older Pentecostal associations as the "Classical Pentecostals." Most of the Charismatics in Canada have remained within their traditional organizations and it is difficult to estimate their numbers.

Researcher Grant McClung claims the membership of Pentecostal and charismatic churches worldwide to be 382 million. These churches gain 19 million members each year and give 34 billion dollars to Christian causes. There are some 3,000 independent charismatic denominations worldwide. Their impact overseas has been considerable, but has been less noticeable in Canada. Little space will be devoted to them in this focus on the history of the PAOC.[6]

The number of Pentecostals in Canada as a percentage of the population is relatively small. It has grown from 0.5 per cent of the population in 1941 to about 1.6 per cent by 1991.[7] While the percentages seem small, it must be noted that the total of all evangelical Protestants in Canada has been in the seven per cent range for several years. The influence of Pentecostals on Canadian culture, economics, politics, and religion has been proportionately greater than their numerical size. PAOC adherents may be found in every segment of national life, from the halls of Parliament to the classrooms of the universities and the frontiers of the Northland.

Hundreds of young men and women are training in PAOC colleges for varied ministries. Canadian Pentecostals may be found on the mission field in nearly 40 countries. Ministers in more than 1,050 churches proclaim the gospel in the homeland where the number of credential holders exceeds 3,500. The Fellowship raises more than 12 million dollars annually for all forms of outreach. PAOC evangelism in Quebec has been so successful that more than one-third of all evangelical ministries in that province were Pentecostal by the beginning of the '90s.

Pentecostalism in Canada, from its inception, has been a revivalistic, holiness, and charismatic movement. The first known instance of the Baptism in the Holy Spirit,[8] with the phenomenon of tongues-speaking, occurred in Toronto in 1906. This event took place only a few months after the outbreak of glossolalia at the Azusa Street Mission in Los Angeles. The earliest converts to the Pentecostal revival in Canada were drawn largely from the ranks of evangelical denominations, such as the Baptists, the Methodists, the Christian and Missionary Alliance, the New Brethren in Christ, the Mennonites, and the Salvation Army. A sprinkling of adherents came from the mainline groups such as the Anglicans, the Presbyterians, and the Congregational Church. They brought with them a commitment to sound orthodox doctrine and zealous evangelism. Many also were loyal to the principles of the late 19th-century Holiness Movement which had infiltrated most of these denominations.

As a result of the frequent occurrences of supernatural healing among the early Pentecostals, they added "Divine Healing" to their fundamental dogma. The doctrine of the "Second Coming" had received renewed interest among the Holiness groups which emerged in the final quarter of the 19th century. It quickly assumed great significance among early Pentecostals. When the dramatic religious awakening at the turn of the century spread over North America and the world, Pentecostals generally concluded that the return of Jesus Christ was imminent.[9] And so "Salvation, Baptism in the Holy Spirit, Divine Healing, and the Second Coming" became the four cardinal doctrines of the fledgling Pentecostal Fellowship in Canada. The Pentecostal distinctives were commonly referred to as "the full gospel."

The original members of the Fellowship were subject to an intense barrage of public criticism, deliberate misrepresentation, and outright persecution. Pentecostal meetings often were disrupted and preachers threatened with personal injury. Nonetheless, the new groups prospered and carried the message to every part of the Dominion. In 1919, just a few years after Azusa Street, the believers had acquired a federal government charter as The Pentecostal Assemblies of Canada.

At the time of writing, the PAOC has enjoyed eight decades of uninterrupted growth. Even during the disastrous years of the Great Depression in the 1930s, the Fellowship was one of the fastest-growing religious bodies in the country. In that difficult decade of the '30s, the number of PAOC churches rose from 65 to 300. By any commonly accepted standards of organizational success, the PAOC has been uncommonly successful. Pentecostals attribute their achievements to the ministry of the Holy Spirit among them, and to their acceptance of the Bible as the sole source of authority in doctrine and practice.

But the extraordinary accomplishments of the past 80 years have, in themselves, led some thoughtful observers to ask penetrating questions about the future. It remains to be seen whether the PAOC will follow the historical pattern from origin to decline observed by Moberg, or be an exception. The hopeful indications of the Fellowship's "exception" status are the expressions by the leadership of their awareness of the critical stages of development and their determination to maintain the distinctive spiritual emphases. As relevant and interesting as questions about the future may be, it is time to turn to the business at hand — the origins and development of the Pentecostal Movement in Canada with particular reference to The Pentecostal Assemblies of Canada.

Endnotes

1. Taken from the title of a sermon by R. E. McAlister.
2. James M. MacKnight, "Report of the General Superintendent to the District Conferences," *1991 National Office Reports,* PAOC Archives.
3. David O. Moberg, *The Church as a Social Institution: The Sociology of American Religion* (Grand Rapids: Baker, 2nd ed. rev., 1984), pp. 118-23.
4. Thomas Wm. Miller, taped interview with Gordon F. Atter, April 30, 1984. Similar concerns for the future welfare of the Fellowship were expressed in taped interviews by Walter E. McAlister, May 1, 1981 and Tom Johnstone, April 29, 1984.
5. William Griffin, "Report of the General Secretary," *1994 National Office Reports,* PAOC Archives.
6. Statistics cited in "World View Update" (July 1991), published by the Overseas Missions Department, PAOC.
7. The total number of people declaring themselves Pentecostal (not necessarily PAOC) in the 1991 Canadian census was 436,435 or 1.6 per cent of the nation's population. PAOC statistics indicated that its members and adherents totalled 206,172 in 1991 which means that it represented about 47 per cent of the Pentecostal population. In the period between the 1981 census and 1991, the number of Pentecostals in the nation increased 28.8 per cent; PAOC growth in the same period was 51.1 per cent. Pentecostal researcher Kevin Shanahan points out that Pentecostals are the sixth largest group of Protestants in Canada -- the top five all suffered significant decreases during the '81-'91 period; see Shanahan, "StatsCan Counts Heads," *Eastern Journal of Practical Theology,* 7:2 (Fall 1993), 17-33.
8. Many expressions occur in the literature to categorize the experience which makes Pentecostalism a distinctive religious movement. The most common are: Baptism of the Holy Ghost, Baptism in the Holy Spirit, Baptism of the Spirit, the Infilling, Filled with the Spirit, and, more recently, Spirit Baptism. This latter term, which was popularized by the Charismatics of the 1970s and '80s, has found its way into the current writings of Classic Pentecostals. In this volume I have used the same terminology adopted by pioneer Pentecostals wherever this enhances accuracy or reflects the "flavor" of the times. However, for the sake of clarity, when referring to the Pentecostal experience in PAOC history, I will confine

myself to the expression "Baptism in the Holy Spirit," or for brevity, "the Baptism." With respect to baptism in water, PAOC theology is identical to that of Baptists who view that ordinance as a public acknowledgment of a personal conversion experience.

9. The perception of early Pentecostals that their revival was evidence that the Second Coming was imminent has been demonstrated by Edith L. Blumhofer, *Pentecost in My Soul: Exploration in the Meaning of Pentecostal Experience in the Early Assemblies of God* (Springfield: Gospel Publishing House, 1989), pp. 27-28. Many of the titles adopted by the early Pentecostals, in the USA and Canada, reflected this self-conscious awareness that they were involved in a revival which heralded the Second Coming of Christ. Among such self-chosen labels were Apostolic Faith, Full Gospel, Latter Rain, Pentecostal Revival, Fellowship, and Pentecostal Movement. Generally, the terms "Pentecostal Revival" and "Pentecostal Movement" were used to identify this new religious phenomenon on a North American or worldwide basis. In Canada, the early Pentecostal/Apostolic Faith/Latter Rain believers gradually came to consider themselves part of the "Fellowship." The usage of the above terms will be readily apparent from the context in which they appear, but the "Fellowship" is a designation specific to the PAOC throughout this volume.

Chapter 1

PENTECOSTAL BEGINNINGS

Pentecostals in Canada have always pointed to the outpouring of the Spirit on the Day of Pentecost (Acts 1-2) as the origin of their basic doctrines and practices. Their more recent precursors, however, have been the great revivalists since the time of Wesley and the Holiness Movement of the 19th century. Indeed, revivalistic and holiness teachings and methods were among the chief factors in the emergence of modern Pentecostalism. With few exceptions, the worldwide Pentecostal Movement betrays striking evidences of its religious parentage, and nowhere is this more true than in Canada.

The Methodism of John and Charles Wesley, strengthened by the itinerant evangelism of George Whitfield, was carried at an early period from the British Isles to North America. The rediscovery of the necessity for a born-again experience was highlighted by the revivals under the leadership of Gilbert Tennent and Jonathan Edwards in New England. From there, a powerful surge of religious renewal swept over Nova Scotia. Still later, the Methodist circuit riders of the Northern States brought their doctrines to Upper Canada (now Ontario).

The innovative evangelism that made the camp meetings such a success in frontier Kentucky at the turn of the 19th century resulted in the technique being imported to Canada. The first Methodist camp meeting was held at Hay Bay, near Napanee, in 1805. Camp meetings ever since have been a marked feature of Canadian evangelism and were used most effectively by the Pentecostal pioneers to promote their distinctive doctrines. By the 1830s, the revivalistic successes of Charles Grandison Finney had inaugurated a new type of evangelism in which protracted prayer meetings and the altar call became prominent features. These methods were also incorporated in the ministries of the Canadian Pentecostals.

1 / PENTECOSTAL BEGINNINGS

Out of the great Laymen's Revival of 1857-59 came a renewed emphasis upon prayer as an essential part of evangelism, and this too resurfaced in Pentecostalism. The renewed emphasis among Methodists in the late 19th century on Wesley's doctrine of sanctification gave rise to the Holiness Movement. The Canadian evangelical denominations of the time — Baptist, Christian and Missionary Alliance, Methodist, Presbyterian, and Wesleyan — were among the first to adopt Holiness teachings. It is significant that many early Pentecostals were drawn from the ranks of these denominations.

John Wesley's piety was deeply influenced by the Moravians who had been instrumental in his conversion. The Moravians were a product of 17th-century Pietism in Germany and the Hussite Movement of the former Czechoslovakia. A persecuted remnant settled on the estate of Count Zinzendorf where, in 1727, a mighty tide of revival swept the community. For two months a wave of spiritual ecstasy led many into the infilling of the Spirit. Thereafter, the Moravians emphasized the need for a constant indwelling of the Spirit.[1] Wesley was initially repelled by the "enthusiasm" of these people, but soon witnessed in his own meetings some similar phenomena. In one service near Bristol, hundreds of people fell to the ground, crying out in an agony of contrition and seeking salvation. There also were reports of believers giving prophecies and having visions. It is clear that Wesley believed in the presence of miracles.[2]

From the first, Wesley sought to control noisy outbursts. He also rigorously excluded from his Methodist societies those who exhibited mental instability or spiritual decline. Nonetheless, he acknowledged the genuineness of religious phenomena. Through his long life and ministry, he gradually developed his views on sanctification as both an obligation and a privilege of born-again believers. These views were spread widely towards the end of the 17th century and reappeared among evangelicals late in the next century.

Unusual physical manifestations occurred during the First Great Awakening in New England in 1734. While preaching in Northampton, Massachusetts, Jonathan Edwards saw people grasp the pillars of the church, crying out that they were sliding into hell. As he put it, "the Spirit began extraordinarily to set in and wonderfully to work among us."[3] Within six months there were over 300 converts in the community, and the awakening spread throughout New England. Its progress was marked by voluble praying, weeping over sin, and shouts of victory from the converted. Some professed to have experienced visions or trances. An estimated 50,000 people came into the churches as a result of this move of God, and the doctrine of the "New Birth" was firmly established as an absolute necessity for church membership.

The revivalistic ministry of James McGready and others on the Kentucky frontier at the end of that century resulted in an extraordinary awakening. Because of the great distances people had to travel to attend religious services, camp meetings were sometimes scheduled where a series of services would be held over a period of several days or, in some cases, several weeks. The most famous of these camp meetings was at Cane Ridge, in August 1801. With thousands present, there were many unusual physical manifestations as people came under conviction of sin. They fell to the ground, cried out for mercy, shouted for joy, leaped and danced — and the critics had a field day. In fact, revivalism was stereotyped from that time onwards as essentially a mass outpouring of emotion and religious fanaticism. More objective assessments of the Cane Ridge meetings, however, found that the entire frontier was civilized and transformed.[4]

The revival campaigns of Charles Finney had a more pervasive impact on modern evangelicalism than any other 19th-century event. Beginning around 1820, Finney engaged in a ministry so powerful that entire communities were stirred and large numbers were converted to Christ. At Rochester, New York, in 1830-31, about 1,200 in a population of 10,000 were converted in a few months. The local revival produced a general religious awakening as an estimated 500,000 were converted in the Eastern States. Finney preached for an immediate conversion and holiness of life. His "new measures," as they then were derisively called, included publicly praying for sinners, personal witnessing, and preaching. He popularized the "altar call" and used trained young men to assist him in counseling the inquirers. His methods were adopted by the next generation of preachers and have been an essential part of evangelical and Pentecostal preaching ever since.

Since Finney's meetings were often characterized by emotional outbursts among the people, there was a willingness to accept these phenomena as normal by-products of the Spirit's work. Since over 85 per cent of his converts remained in the churches, there existed a strong incentive to accept his views. Finney also played a prominent role in the emergence of the renewed emphasis on the "Entire Sanctification" teachings of the late 19th century. He used the term "Baptism of the Holy Ghost" often, and professed to have had such an experience in his own life.[5]

The revivalistic successes of Edwards and Finney had their counterparts in the maritime colonies of Nova Scotia and Prince Edward Island in Canada through the ministries of Henry Alline and Donald McDonald. The "New Light" evangelist, Henry Alline (1748-1784), emigrated from New England about the time of the First Great Awakening. After his

1 / PENTECOSTAL BEGINNINGS

conversion, he became an itinerant evangelist preaching the need for a new birth. So great was his influence that he came to be called "the Apostle of Nova Scotia." Though he had many converts, Alline was not an organizer and his disciples eventually became the nucleus of the infant Baptist denomination in the colony. As a result of Alline's ministry, the doctrines of a conversion experience and water baptism became established in Canadian evangelicalism.[6]

A similar revival movement was initiated in 1826 on Prince Edward Island by Donald McDonald (1783-1867). McDonald was a Scottish Presbyterian clergyman, converted out of alcoholism, who became a fiery evangelist. By the time of his death, he had 14 churches and 5,000 converts under his supervision. Again, the "New Birth" doctrine was strongly supported by McDonald. A notable feature of McDonald's meetings was the presence of physical manifestations among those under deep conviction of sin. Some fell down, some cried for mercy, and others shouted for joy at deliverance. Some critics derided the McDonald meetings, but other competent observers concluded that the Holy Spirit was the source of his unrivaled successes.[7] The impact of this revival lasted several generations and probably had a beneficial influence on J. E. Purdie, the "Father of Canadian Pentecostal Bible Colleges." Purdie was born, educated, and converted on Prince Edward Island.

In the last half of the 19th century a new religious force emerged in North America which was to profoundly influence Pentecostalism. It arose out of a renewed interest among Methodists (and some other evangelicals) in John Wesley's views on "Perfection," or "Sanctification." And it received a great impetus from scores of Christian leaders concerned about the spiritual impotence of the church. The Oberlin theologians, Finney and Asa Mahan, helped popularize such expressions as sanctification and Baptism of the Holy Ghost. Finney's teachings in his *Memoirs* and *The Oberlin Evangelist* were supplemented by Mahan in his books.[8] There was keen interest among the Baptists and Methodists of Canada West (southwestern Ontario) in these publications, especially in the Hamilton region. A host of Holiness advocates arose in both the USA and Canada to promulgate the renewed emphasis on personal holiness. James Caughey, a Finney convert, preached several times in Quebec, and Phoebe Palmer held meetings in Hamilton, Eastern Ontario, and the Maritime provinces.

One of the services was reported in *The Christian Guardian*:

> For weeks previous to the meeting, fervent prayer from many an anxious heart had been ascending to God ... Our hearts were cheered by the arrival of Brother and Sister Palmer who were, as usual, eminently successful in their efforts to turn men to

righteousness ... the effect was really awfully glorious: some three hundred persons under the Divine influence seemed moved as with a rushing mighty wind: some shouted "glory to God in the highest." Scores prostrate before their Maker cried aloud for mercy, while others stood aghast and could only say: "How dreadful is this place."[9]

The Palmers later reported over 100 conversions and noted that some 90 people had the experience of "entire sanctification." The summer camp meeting was the usual venue for promoting Holiness teachings. These became so popular that eventually there developed a series of regular conferences known as The National Camp Meeting for the Promotion of Holiness. This association played a large part in producing a new blend of Pietism, Wesleyan Perfectionism, and American Revivalism.[10]

One unexpected result of the spread of Holiness principles throughout Canada was a number of schisms in the older evangelical denominations. Church history in this country usually has been written by scholars financially supported by their own denominations. The denominational perspective on revivalistic groups thus tended to be biased and negative.[11] As a result, these groups without exception began under a cloud of suspicion and often faced bitter persecution. This happened in the Maritimes where the infant Baptist church was vilified by the Anglican political/religious establishment.[12]

The Methodists in Ontario sought to limit the influence of Ralph C. Horner and eventually "Bishop" Horner founded the Holiness Movement Church.[13] Some "Hornerites" were among the first to respond to the Pentecostal message when it reached Ontario, the most notable of which was R. E. McAlister, a charter member of the PAOC. Even when Methodists adopted revival techniques, like the cross-Canada team ministry of H. T. Crossley and J. E. Hunter, they did not satisfy those in the church committed to Holiness teachings.[14]

The Anglicans sought to minimize the impact of the new revivalism by establishing their own evangelical branch, the Church Army. But they still lost members to groups like the Salvation Army, which was at the forefront of the revivalistic surge. The Army itself faced a schism in 1891 when P. W. Philpott led a large number of officers in protest against the Army's supposed surrender to a "social welfare gospel."[15] About the same time, the various branches of Canadian Mennonites were experiencing internal strife and some fragmentation. The strife arose from differing views about the benefits of the Finney/Moody type of revivalism. There also was a conflict over the introduction of Sunday schools to Mennonite churches. Solomon Eby eventually emerged as the leader of a faction which founded the Mennonite Brethren in Christ in 1883. This group was

1 / PENTECOSTAL BEGINNINGS

committed to fervent revivalism and acquired support from sympathetic groups on both sides of the Canada-USA border.[16]

The impact of the Holiness Movement on early Pentecostalism in Canada is apparent in a review of the religious backgrounds of the pioneer leaders. The list includes Ellen Hebden, A. H. Argue, A. G. Ward, R. E. Sternall, J. D. Saunders, and D. N. Buntain. Aimee Semple McPherson was influenced through her early membership in the Salvation Army at Ingersoll, Ontario. Solomon Eby became a Pentecostal leader in 1908.

Two other rediscovered Christian doctrines came into prominence among evangelicals during the late 19th century. These were the Baptism in the Holy Spirit, evidenced by glossolalia, and divine healing. The former has become the distinctive doctrine of the worldwide Pentecostal Movement, but divine healing also has figured prominently in its teaching and preaching. There were more incidents of glossolalia, commonly referred to as speaking in tongues, in the past century than is commonly believed.

Edward Irving, a Presbyterian clergyman in London, England, joined with his church in praying for a restoration of apostolic powers. A local revival occurred in 1830 in which tongues-speaking was common. There also were prophecies, visions, and a number of miraculous healings. Persecution was so intense that Irving and his people formed the Catholic Apostolic Church. After Irving's premature death, doctrinal errors emerged and the organization finally disintegrated, but not before it had given a high profile to the gift ministries of the Holy Spirit.[17] At its height, the Irvingite church had 10,000 members, some of whom emigrated to North America. Church historian Philip Schaff was personally acquainted with one of their churches in New York state and had heard the "unknown tongues."[18] An Irvingite congregation was established in Kingston, Ontario, among whom tongues-speaking was common.[19]

Many instances of glossolalia were known among the early workers in the Salvation Army. General Booth often told his officers that they needed "the Baptism of Fire." His son Bramwell witnessed what he called "the power of the Holy Ghost" in the all-night prayer meetings. He noted that many received visions and dreams from God, some were supernaturally healed, and others literally danced for joy. He even witnessed what he called bodily "levitations" in which some worshippers were actually lifted off their feet! There also were instances of tongues-speaking.[20]

As the 19th century neared its close, there were ever-increasing reports of the phenomenon of tongues-speaking and divine healing among

PENTECOSTAL BEGINNINGS / 1

evangelicals. In one of D. L. Moody's meetings at a YMCA in Britain, a number of young men were baptized in the Spirit and spoke in tongues. Moody himself professed to have received a Baptism of the Spirit, although he did not provide any details of the experience, believing it "too sacred." A remarkable revival took place among the widows and orphans in the mission of Pandita Ramabai in Mukti, India. Scores were filled with the Spirit, and there were visions, prophecies, and healings. Many spoke in tongues and news of the outpouring spread all over the world. It even reached the Argue family in Winnipeg.[21]

Another outburst of glossolalia occurred at Providence, Rhode Island, in 1875 in the church of Elder R. B. Swann. Remarkable healings resulted from the prayers of these people and they came to be known as "the Gift People." In 1879 a Holiness Baptist preacher named W. Jethro Walthall received the Spirit and spoke in tongues. Similar groups of charismatic believers were known to exist at the time in New York State, Massachusetts, and Georgia. In Delaware, Ohio, in 1891, Daniel Awrey was filled with the Spirit and became a prominent early leader among what was coming to be called the "Pentecostal" sects. An outpouring of the Spirit took place in the Swedish Mission Church in Moorhead, Minnesota, in 1892. It was marked by numerous miracles of healing, tongues-speaking, and interpretations. This revival spread to North Carolina where the phenomena came under the official censure of the Methodist Episcopal Church. Similar reports could be adduced to prove that the close of the century witnessed an ever-growing frequency of charismata among evangelical believers.[22]

The sporadic occurrence of bodily healings gradually led to a renewed emphasis on healing as a heritage of believers. Divine healing had been known to the early Methodists and was practised by an English sect known as "the Peculiar People." General Booth included what he called "faith healing" in the tenets of the Salvation Army. The early *War Cry* papers contained reports of supernatural deliverances.[23] The "Gift People" of New England witnessed remarkable healings after prayer. One of the chief proponents of divine healing was Mrs. Maria Woodworth-Etter. During a five-month preaching campaign in St. Louis, Missouri, in 1890, some 600 people were healed. There were healings of the blind, deaf, mute, crippled, and other victims of various diseases, including some given up to die by the medical profession. Other remarkable healings took place during her meetings in Los Angeles in 1893. So frequent were these phenomena that Mrs. Woodworth-Etter was once tried for practising medicine without a license.[24]

An eccentric preacher named John Alexander Dowie acquired fame as a healer at the turn of the century. Dowie founded the community of

1 / PENTECOSTAL BEGINNINGS

"Zion" near Chicago, where the sick could come for prayer. He fell into doctrinal errors which led to his eventual demise, but his teachings on healing gained wide acceptance throughout North America. One example will suffice to demonstrate the impact of this rediscovered apostolic doctrine. In the Dowie Mission in Toronto in 1900, a man with a broken back was instantly healed after prayer. The healing was witnessed by the parents of J. Roswell Flower, for many years a leader of the Assemblies of God.[25]

Thus the late 19th century provided a fertile seedbed for the Pentecostal Movement and gave the fledgling charismatic groups their distinctive doctrines: Salvation, Baptism in the Spirit, and Divine Healing. A fourth distinctive, the Second Coming of Jesus Christ, was a product of the outpouring of the Spirit that received its greatest impetus from the Azusa Street revival of 1906-09 in Los Angeles.

It was at the Azusa Street Mission that all these strands of "Pentecostal" theology coalesced to form a basis for 20th-century Pentecostalism. All branches of the new movement, including the Canadian, were shaped by the events of "the thousand day revival" in Los Angeles. But there were several significant events that specifically contributed to the extraordinary manifestations of the Spirit in 1906. One was the short-term winter Bible school conducted in 1899 by Charles F. Parham in Topeka, Kansas. Parham was a Methodist evangelist who had adopted the teachings of Alexander Dowie and A. B. Simpson on divine healing. When he opened his second winter school in 1900, the students examined the scriptural evidence for the Baptism in the Holy Spirit. They concluded it was "speaking in tongues" and began to seek the experience. On New Year's Day, 1901, Agnes Ozman was first to receive the Baptism and speak in unknown tongues. Other manifestations included prophesying, ecstasies, and great joy. A local newspaper investigated and reported:

> The Rev. Charles F. Parham and his Bible students from Bethel College, Topeka, held a revival meeting last night.... These comprise a new sect who believe that the "gift of tongues" mentioned in the Scriptures has come to them, and that under the complete influence of prayer they are able to talk in languages they themselves do not understand.[26]

From Topeka, Parham and small bands of believers fanned out over nearby states to share their testimonies. The result was that many came into the experience and great interest was expressed in holding further meetings. Howard Goss, who until 1903 by his own admission was an infidel, was converted and filled with the Spirit. He attended the Parham Bible school in Houston, Texas, and gave the following report:

> ... a revival was carried on in the city in connection with the school and a great work was done in the streets. Many more were saved and filled with the Spirit and spoke in tongues. Mr. Parham taught that all would speak in tongues when filled with the Spirit.[27]

Another series of Pentecostal meetings were held in Orchard, Texas, in which many more received the Baptism in the Spirit.

According to Goss' account, there were at least 60 preachers and workers in Texas alone who claimed the Baptism by the time the still-greater work began in Los Angeles. Zealous workers had taken the new doctrine to Dowie's "Zion" in Chicago, and hundreds of Texas residents had received their personal Pentecost. But it was at Azusa Street that a work began which captured the imagination of the evangelical church world. It also became the focus of a campaign of misrepresentation, vituperation, and outright persecution.

The chief figure in the origin of the Apostolic Faith work in Los Angeles was William Seymour, a black Holiness preacher who first heard the Pentecostal message at Parham's Houston conference. Seymour was invited to preach in a cottage on Bonnie Brae Street in Los Angeles and there the modern Pentecostal Movement began to acquire both national and international prominence. According to Frank Bartleman, an eyewitness of the meetings, Seymour had not yet received the Baptism in the Spirit when he arrived in California. It was in a prayer meeting "on the ninth of April, 1906, that the Spirit was first poured out."[28]

Frank Bartleman was an itinerant evangelist who had settled in Los Angeles in 1903. He was deeply stirred by news of the revival in Wales, in 1904, and wrote to Evan Roberts for information. A Baptist pastor in the city, a Rev. Smale, also visited Wales and returned with glowing reports of the work of God. Bartleman, who was a skillful and prolific writer of religious tracts and magazines articles, began exhorting many to pray for another "Pentecost." When the great revival broke out in the Azusa Street Mission, Bartleman attended and wrote numerous reports which spread widely the news of the extraordinary events.

Another trustworthy observer was A. W. Orwig, who for weeks attended services in which multitudes were converted, scores of healings took place, and the phenomenon of tongues-speaking became very familiar. Orwig cited many instances in which believers spoke in languages they had never learned, and of cases in which people were converted when hearing such messages. The services lasted "day and night" for three years, promoting the coining of the term "the thousand day revival." There also was an outpouring of calumny, persecution, and deliberate misrepresentation by the Los Angeles press. Orwig cited an

1 / PENTECOSTAL BEGINNINGS

incident in which a reporter at the Mission was changed from a bitter opponent into a zealous supporter by the scenes he witnessed, and, as a consequence, lost his job.[29]

William Seymour always claimed that Charles Parham was the father of what he called the "Apostolic Faith Movement," but it was Seymour who was the acknowledged leader at Azusa Street. He was a very humble man, often sitting on the platform with his head bowed as "the Spirit took control," but he gave effective leadership to the meetings. He put out an occasional newspaper, beginning in September 1906, titled *The Apostolic Faith*, in which he proclaimed, "The Pentecost Has Come." Seymour's paper was read and re-read by thousands of believers eager for news of the "Latter Rain Outpouring." It was a very effective means of introducing multitudes to such phrases as "the Pentecostal Baptism," "the evidence of speaking in tongues" and "the Promised Latter Rain."[30]

Seymour's *Apostolic Faith* paper reflected, from its very first edition, the Holiness and Dispensational convictions of its editor. This was of great significance for the infant Pentecostal Movement, since his journal had a great influence in shaping the views of many pioneer Pentecostals. Seymour's "Statement of Faith" is an unmistakable reflection of the commonly shared views of a number of evangelical and revivalistic sects of the time.

THE APOSTOLIC FAITH MOVEMENT

Stands for the restoration of the faith once delivered unto the saints — the old-time religion, camp meetings, revivals, missions, street and prison work and Christian Unity everywhere.

Teaching on Repentance — Mark 1:14,15.
Godly sorrow for Sin, Example — Matt. 9:13, 2 Cor. 7:9, 11, Acts 3:19, Acts 17:30, 31.
Of Confession of Sins — Luke 15:21 and Luke 18:13.
Forsaking Sinful Ways — Isa. 55:7, Jonah 3:8, Prov. 28:13.
Restitution — Ezek. 33:15, Luke 19:8
And Faith in Jesus Christ.

First Work — Justification is that act of God's free grace by which we receive remission of sins. Acts 10:42,43, Rom. 3:25.

Second Work — Sanctification is the second work of grace and the last work of grace. Sanctification is that act of God's free grace by which He makes us holy. John 17:15,17 — "Sanctify them through Thy truth; Thy word is truth!" 1 Thess. 4:3, 1 Thess. 5:23, Heb. 13:12, Heb. 2:11, Heb. 12:14. Sanctification is cleansing to make holy. The Disciples were sanctified before the Day of Pentecost. By a careful study of Scripture you will find it is so now "Ye are clean through the word which I have spoken unto you" (John 15:3, 13:10) and Jesus had breathed on them the Holy Ghost (John 20:21,22). You know that they could not receive the Spirit if they were not clean. Jesus cleansed and got all doubt out of His Church before He went back to glory.

The Baptism with the Holy Ghost is a gift of power upon the sanctified life; so when we get it we have the same evidence as the Disciples received on the Day of Pentecost (Acts 2:3,4) in speaking in new tongues. See also Acts 10:45,46, Acts 19:6, 1 Cor. 14:21 — "For I will work a work in your days which ye will not believe, though it be told you" (Hab. 1:5).

Seeking Healing — He must believe that God is able to heal — Ex. 15:26 "I am the Lord that healeth thee" James 5:14, Psa., 103:3, 2 Kings 20:5, Matt. 8:16, 17, Mark 16:16, 17, 18. He must believe God is able to heal "Behold I am the Lord, the God of all flesh, is there anything too hard to Me?" Jer. 32:27. [31]

The doctrine of sanctification was preeminent among the Holiness groups at the turn of the century. William Seymour made a clear distinction between it and the Baptism in the Spirit:

Too many have confused the grace of Sanctification with the enduement of Power, or the Baptism with the Holy Ghost; others have taken "the anointing that abideth" for the Baptism and failed to reach the glory and power of a true Pentecost.[32]

He revealed his Dispensational views in an article on the rediscovery of the apostolic gifts. The appearance of the charismata was proof, for Seymour, that long-lost ministries were being restored to the Church of Christ. The Pentecostal Baptism was one such renewed doctrinal emphasis:

THE PENTECOSTAL BAPTISM RESTORED

The Promised Latter Rain Now Being Poured Out on God's Humble People.

All along the ages men have been preaching a partial Gospel. A part of the Gospel remained when the world went into the dark ages. God has from time to time raised up men to bring back the truth to the church. He raised up Luther to bring back to the world the doctrine of justification by faith. He raised up another reformer in John Wesley to establish Bible holiness in the church. Then he raised up Dr. Cullis who brought back to the world the wonderful doctrine of divine healing. Now He is bringing back the Pentecostal Baptism to the church.[33]

1 / PENTECOSTAL BEGINNINGS

Whether Seymour had skilled assistance in the editing of his paper or not, it is evident that his accounts of the Azusa Street meetings caught the attention of evangelicals throughout North America. In fact, his paper was one of the first to proclaim that the Los Angeles revival was a harbinger of numerous similar outpourings of the Spirit worldwide. The following selected extracts from *The Apostolic Faith* bear all the marks of a genuine, as well as enthusiastic, eyewitness report. The very first edition of *The Apostolic Faith* included a statement of faith which clearly reflected the Holiness convictions of Seymour. The third edition revealed a Dispensational theology which viewed the outpouring of the Spirit as a precursor of "the last days."

BIBLE PENTECOST

Gracious Pentecostal Showers Continue to Fall

The news has spread far and wide that Los Angeles is being visited with a "rushing, mighty wind from heaven." The how and why of it is to be found in the very opposite of those conditions that are usually thought necessary for a big revival. No instruments of music are used, none are needed. No choir — but bands of angels have been heard by some in the spirit and there is a heavenly singing that is inspired by the Holy Ghost. No collections are taken. No bills have been posted to advertise the meetings. No church or organization is back of it all. All who are in touch with God realize as soon as they enter the meetings that the Holy Ghost is the leader. One brother said that even before his train entered the city he felt the power of the revival.

Travellers from afar wend their way to the headquarters at Azusa Street. As they enquire their way to the Apostolic Faith Mission, perhaps they are asked "O, you mean the Holy Rollers," or, "It is the Colored church you mean?" In the vicinity of a tombstone shop, stables and lumber yard (a fortunate vicinity because no one complains of all-night meetings) you find a two-storey, white-washed old building ... here you find a mighty Pentecostal revival going on from ten o'clock in the morning till about twelve at night....

As soon as it is announced that the altar is open for seekers for pardon, sanctification, the baptism with the Holy Ghost and healing of the body, the people rise and flock to the altar. There is no urging. What kind of preaching is it that brings them? Why, the simple declaring of the Word of God. There is such power in the preaching of the Word in the Spirit that people are shaken on the benches. Coming to the altar, many fall prostrate under the power of God, and often come out speaking in tongues. Sometimes the power falls on people and they are wrought upon by the Spirit during testimony or preaching and receive Bible experiences.

The testimony meetings which precede the preaching often continue for two hours or more and people are standing waiting to testify all the time. . . . Hundreds testify that they received the Bible evidence of speaking in a new tongue that they never knew before. Some have received the "gift of tongues" or "divers tongues" and the interpretation. . . . The demonstrations are not the shouting, clapping or jumping so often seen in camp meetings. There is a shaking such as the early Quakers had and which the old Methodists called the "jerks." It is while under the power of the Spirit you see the hands raised and hear speaking in tongues. . . . Many receive the Spirit through the laying on of hands, as they did through Paul at Ephesus. Little children from eight years to twelve stand up on the altar bench and testify to the baptism with the Holy Ghost and speak in tongues. . . .

It is noticeable how free all nationalities feel. If a Mexican or German cannot speak in English, he gets up and speaks in his own tongue and feels quite at home for the spirit interprets through the face and the people say amen. No instrument that God can use is rejected on account of color or dress or lack of education. This is why God has so built up the work. . . . Seekers for healing are usually taken upstairs and prayed for in the prayer room and many have been healed there. . . . The sweetest thing of all is the loving harmony. Every church where this has gone is like a part of the family. . . . The Lord is saving drunkards and taking the appetite for liquor and tobacco completely away. Reports have come from Denver that forty souls have received the Pentecost and are speaking in tongues.[34]

By the end of 1906 Seymour was receiving reports of a worldwide occurrence of tongues-speaking in Pentecostal meetings. He reprinted these accounts in *The Apostolic Faith* and thus gave the fledgling Pentecostal Movement its first characterization as an international religious awakening.

Pentecost in India

News comes from India that the baptism with the Holy Ghost and gift of tongues is being received there by natives who are simply taught of God. The India Alliance says, "Some of the gifts which have been scarcely heard of in the church for many centuries are now being given by the Holy Ghost to simple, unlearned members of the body of Christ, and communities are being stirred and transformed by the wonderful grace of God. Healing, the gift of tongues, visions and dreams, discernment of spirits, the power to prophesy and to pray the prayer of faith, all have a place in the present revival."[35]

1 / PENTECOSTAL BEGINNINGS

As the acknowledged leader at the Azusa Street Mission, Seymour received reports from many lands concerning the spread of the new Pentecostal teachings. He reprinted these reports with titles which clearly reflected his view of Pentecostalism as an international religious movement.

Later editions of the Mission journal incorporated glowing accounts of international progress under such titles as "Beginning of Worldwide Revival." Another collection of eyewitness accounts sent to Los Angeles was reprinted under the title "Pentecost Both Sides The Ocean." A selection from this lengthy article gives some indication of the scope of the revival:

PENTECOST BOTH SIDES THE OCEAN

> The Pentecost has crossed the water on both sides to the Hawaiian Islands on the west, and England, Norway, Sweden and India on the east. . . . We rejoice to hear that Pentecost has fallen in Calcutta, India. . . . We have letters from China, Germany, Switzerland, Norway, Sweden, England, Ireland, Australia and other countries from hungry souls that want their Pentecost. . . . In Stockholm, Sweden . . . The first soul came through tonight, receiving the baptism with the Holy Ghost and Bible evidence. . . . In Christiana, Norway, — God is wonderfully demonstrating His power. . . . T.B. Barratt.

New Scandinavian Revival

> The Witness of "Tongues" Manifested in Christiana.

> The following report of the Pentecostal revival in Norway is from the Vicar of All Saints, Sunderland, England, Bro. A. A. Boddy. He had been to Christiana, Norway, visiting Bro. Barratt's meeting.
> My four days in Christiana cannot easily be forgotten. I remember well the scenes two years ago, when I stood with Evan Roberts . . . but wonderful as such scenes in Wales were, the scenes in the Torvegadon Mission Room and other places were more supernatural. I believe that very soon we shall witness the same in England. . . . Boys and girls around me from seven to twenty years of age, were seeing visions and speaking in tongues, as well as older folk. . . . All this time perhaps a dozen are speaking or praying in Tongues, or prophesying and prayer and praise "in the Spirit" is going on all over. People of course ridicule, but those meetings go on every day, and twice a day, and not in one place of meeting only nor in one single town. . . .[36]

Similar reports of Pentecostal phenomena around the world were reprinted in *The Apostolic Faith* paper as long as it was published by Seymour.

As the revival progressed, its early leaders became still more convinced that the evidence of the Baptism in the Holy Spirit was the "speaking in tongues." They regularly sent reports to Seymour of additional instances of revival and charismatic occurrences. Evangelist G. B. Cashwell told of a group of Holiness people in South Carolina, called "The Church of God," which had accepted his teaching on the Baptism. Cashwell reported:

> Twenty-three received the baptism with the Spirit and all spoke with tongues. . . . All do not have the gift of tongues as taught in 1 Cor. 12, but . . . all that I have heard and seen receive the Holy Ghost have spoken in tongues.[37]

Another prominent leader was Florence Crawford, an itinerant preacher, who took an active part in the Azusa Street meetings. She travelled throughout the Western States and eventually became founder of the Apostolic Faith of Portland, Oregon. Crawford was one pioneer who adopted the position that the infilling of the Spirit was, as she put it, "evidenced" by the speaking in tongues. This has been the unaltered position of the oldest and most prominent branches of North American Pentecostalism.[38]

The first generation of Pentecostals in Canada developed a fraternal relationship with their counterparts in the United States. Long before there was a PAOC or an Assemblies of God, there was a good deal of border crossing for ministry and visitation by leaders and lay people alike. The widely scattered congregations in both countries had a great diversity of theological backgrounds, but they shared one deeply held conviction about the ministry of the Holy Spirit. They believed that the apostolic gifts of the Spirit were available to all 20th-century believers. They also affirmed that the evidence of the Baptism in the Spirit was the speaking in tongues "as the Spirit gave utterance."

The Azusa Street Revival in Los Angeles had a profound effect upon the early history of Pentecostalism in Canada. Its chief impact was felt in Winnipeg through the early ministry of Andrew Harvey Argue and in the Ottawa region through the preaching of Robert E. McAlister. A separate and uniquely Canadian form of Pentecostalism emerged at a very early date in Toronto in a small mission run by James and Ellen Hebden. The varied strands of the Pentecostal Movement in Canada are traced in considerable detail in later chapters of this book. It is evident that

1 / PENTECOSTAL BEGINNINGS

Canadians, true to their national character, have insisted upon their own course. While being careful not to lose their distinctive identity, Canadians have maintained very close ties to the American Assemblies of God, a body of believers often described in the early literature as a "sister organization."

Another Pentecostal organization with which the PAOC has a special relationship is the Pentecostal Assemblies of Newfoundland (PAON). Although Newfoundland was a British Crown Colony until it joined Canada in the middle of the century and has its own history of the origins of the Pentecostal message, it was affected to some extent by several early Canadian Pentecostals. At one time in the late 1920s, the Pentecostals in Newfoundland were affiliated as a "District Council with the PAOC."[39] In some respects there has been a parallel development in the two organizations as they have cooperated in overseas missions, Bible college training, and several church ministry programs. Appropriate attention is given to the history of the PAON later in this volume.

Endnotes

1. John Greenfield, *When the Spirit Came* (Minneapolis: Bethany Fellowship, 1967 reprint of *Power from on High*, 1928).

2. W. B. Selbie, *Evangelical Christianity: Its History and Witness* (London: Hodder and Stoughton, 1911), p. 202.

3. Ola E. Winslow, ed., *Jonathan Edwards: Basic Writings* (New York: New American Library, 1966), p. 99.

4. John B. Boles, *The Great Revival: 1787-1805* (Lexington: University of Kentucky Press, 1972), pp. 54-69.

5. Charles G. Finney, *Memoirs of Rev. Charles G. Finney* (New York: Barnes, 1876), pp. 20-21.

6. James Beverly and Barry Moody, eds., *The Journal of Henry Alline* (Hantsport, NS: Lancelot Press, 1982); J. M. Bumstead, *Henry Alline, 1748-1784* (Toronto: University of Toronto Press, 1971); Edward M. Saunders, *History of the Baptists of the Maritime Provinces* (Halifax: John Burgoyne Press, 1902), pp. 22-23.

7. M. Lamount, *Rev. Donald McDonald: Glimpses of His Life and Times* (Charlottetown: Murley and Garnhum, 1902); Ewen Lamont, *A Biographical Sketch of the Late Rev. Donald McDonald* (Charlottetown: John Coombs, 1892), pp. 19-20.

8. Finney's views in *The Oberlin Evangelist* have been compiled by Louis G. Parkhurst, Jr. in *Charles F. Finney: Principles of Holiness* (Minneapolis: Bethany House Publishers, 1984). See also John L. Gresham, *Charles G. Finney's Doctrine of the Baptism of the Holy Spirit* (Peabody: Hendrickson Publishers, 1987). Asa Mahan set forth his view clearly in his *Autobiography Intellectual, Moral and Spiritual* (London: for the author, 1882).

PENTECOSTAL BEGINNINGS / 1

9. Joshua Reynolds, "Augusta," *Christian Guardian*, 29:4 (October 28, 1857), 2; see also Phoebe Palmer, "Revival Extraordinary," *Christian Advocate and Journal* (November 5, 1857).
10. Melvin E. Dieter, *The Holiness Revival of the Nineteenth Century* (Metuchen, NJ: Scarecrow Press, 1980).
11. S. D. Clark, *The Developing Canadian Community* (Toronto: University of Toronto Press, 2nd ed., 1968).
12. Maurice W. Armstrong, "Backgrounds of Religious Liberty in Nova Scotia," *Collections of the Nova Scotia Historical Society*, vol. 7 (Halifax: Ross Print, 1947), 17-32; see also Robert S. Wilson, "Isaiah Wallace and Revivals Among the Maritime Baptists: 1850-1905," paper read at the Evangelical Theological Society of Canada, Toronto, March 1981.
13. Ralph C. Horner, *Wesley on Prostration* (Toronto: Wm. Briggs); and Mrs. A. E. Horner, *Ralph C. Horner; evangelist* (Brockville: Standard Book Room).
14. H. T. Crossley, *Practical Talks on Important Themes* (Toronto: Briggs, 1895).
15. H. H. Walsh, *The Christian Church in Canada* (Toronto: Ryerson Press, 1956), pp. 312-313.
16. Frank Epp, *Mennonites in Canada, 1786-1920* (Toronto: MacMillan, 1974), pp. 144-153.
17. See K. R. Hagenback, *History of the Church in the Eighteenth and Nineteenth Centuries*, J. F. Hurst, trans., vol. 2 (New York: Carlton and Lanadhan, 1869), 1064; Gordon Strachan, *The Pentecostal Theology of Edward Irving* (London: Darton, Longmand and Todd, 1973); Larry Christenson, "The 1830 Apostolic Movement," *New Wine*, 12:6 (June 1980), 22-25; and Arnold Dallimore, *Forerunner of the Charismatic Movement: The Life of Edward Irving* (Chicago: Moody, 1983).
18. P. Schaff, *History of the Christian Church,* vol. 2 (Grand Rapids, Eerdmans, 1952), 237.
19. Gordon F. Atter, *The Third Force* (Peterborough, Ontario: for the author, 3rd ed. rev., 1970), p. 35.
20. R. G. Moyles, *The Blood and Fire in Canada: A History of the Salvation Army in the Dominion, 1882-1976* (Toronto: Peter Martin Associates, 1977), p. 15; Bramwell Booth, *Echoes and Memories* (London: Hodder and Stoughton, 1977 reprint of 1925 ed.), pp. 65-72; and Bramwell Booth, *These Fifty Years* (London: Cassell, 1929), pp. 11ff.
21. Helen S. Dyer, *Pandita Ramabai: A Great Life in Indian Missions* (London: Pickering and Inglis); and Zelma Argue, *What Meaneth This? The Argue Evangelistic Party* (Winnipeg: for the author).
22. Bennett F. Lawrence, *The Apostolic Faith Restored* (Springfield: Gospel Publishing House, 1916).

1 / PENTECOSTAL BEGINNINGS

23. Mark Sorrell, *The Peculiar People* (Exeter: Paternoster Press, 1979); Thomas F. G. Coates, *The Prophet of the Poor: The Life Story of General Booth* (London: Hodder and Stoughton, 1905); see also note 20.

24. Maria B. Woodworth-Etter, *Acts of the Holy Ghost, or, The Life, Work and Experience of Mrs. M.B. Woodworth-Etter, Evangelist* (Dallas: Worley Printing, 1913).

25. Carl Brumback, *Suddenly . . . From Heaven: A History of the Assemblies of God* (Springfield: Gospel Publishing House, 1961), pp. 10-11.

26. *Kansas City Star* (January 30, 1901).

27. Quoted in Lawrence, *The Apostolic Faith Restored*, pp. 64-65.

28. Ibid. pp. 66-76; see also Frank Bartleman, *My Story* (Columbia, South Carolina: J. M. Pike, 1909).

29. Quoted in Lawrence, *The Apostolic Faith Restored*, pp. 77-87.

30. William Seymour, ed., *The Apostolic Faith*, 1:1 (Sept. 1906). Altogether, he published several editions, the latest of which was in May of 1908. These were collected many years later and published under the title *Like as of Fire: A Reprint of the Old Azusa Street Papers* (Wilmington, Mass.: Fred T. Corum, 1981).

31. Ibid.

32. *The Apostolic Faith*, 1:1 (September 1906), 2.

33. *The Apostolic Faith*, 1:2 (October. 1906), 1.

34. *The Apostolic Faith*, 1:3 (November 1906), 1.

35. Ibid.

36. *The Apostolic Faith*, 1:5 (January 1907), 1.

37. *The Apostolic Faith*, 1:6, (February-March 1907), 2-3.

38. *A Historical Account of the Apostolic Faith* (Portland, Oregon: Apostolic Faith Publishing House, 1965); see also John T. Nicholl, *The Pentecostals* (Plainsfield: Logos, 1966), pp. 94-122.

39. See the "1932 Yearbook of the PAOC," PAOC Archives, p. 6.

Chapter 2

"THIS IS THE PENTECOST" PENTECOSTALISM IN ONTARIO 1906-1919

Enthusiastic proponents of the Pentecostal revival in Los Angeles referred to that city as "the American Jerusalem." For three years the Apostolic Faith Mission on Azusa Street was the magnet for believers from all parts of the United States and many countries of the world. In that same period of time, a number of other focal points for the "Latter Rain" people — a designation used synonymously with "Pentecostal" for some years — developed in a number of American cities. The most important of these, from a Canadian point of view, was the W. H. Durham Mission in Chicago.

A similar situation arose in Canada, where two cities — Toronto and Winnipeg — became the earliest hubs of the renewal movement. Pentecost made its first appearance in Toronto late in 1906 and in Winnipeg in 1907. Both centres became resorts for hundreds of clergy, lay workers, and spiritually thirsty believers who were seeking more power for their lives and ministries. From the two cities there went out a steady stream of Pentecostal witnesses to spread throughout the nation, what then was called, "the full gospel."[1] Given the fact that the first account of a Canadian receiving the Baptism in the Spirit, accompanied by speaking in tongues, occurred in Toronto, the history of the new religious movement in Ontario is of the greatest significance.

The origins of Eastern Canadian Pentecostalism can be traced to the East End Mission (often called the Hebden Mission) directed by Mrs. Ellen K. Hebden. So great was the impact of this earliest revival centre that it is appropriate to refer to it as "the Canadian Azusa." The first Canadian to receive the experience of speaking in tongues was Mrs. Hebden.[2] She was an independent evangelist who had recently emigrated from England to Canada. It has been speculated that Hebden first heard of

2 / "THIS IS THE PENTECOST"

the outpouring of the Spirit in Los Angeles through some tracts, but she gave no indication in her early writings about her sources. One thing she has made clear, however, is that initially she was opposed to tongues-speaking and resisted it.

Ellen Hebden had been converted at the age of fifteen. After marrying James Hebden, the couple moved to Toronto. They acquired a three-storey building at 651 Queen street, in which they opened a "rescue mission" and "faith healing home" in May 1906. By all accounts given about her by her contemporaries, she was a woman of strong convictions and, according to G. F. Atter, a better preacher than her husband. Her Baptism in the Spirit, with tongues-speaking, was to have a profound impact on the early days of the Pentecostal Movement in Canada.

Mrs. Hebden was praying in her room for more power in her ministry, on November 17, 1906, when she sensed an unusual moving of the Spirit of God. Her report of her subsequent Baptism and speaking in tongues was later sent to Seymour and published in his paper. A fuller account was reprinted by Hebden in the periodical she founded early in 1907, *The Promise*. As she noted, it was "without any expectation" of such an experience that the Spirit filled her to overflowing. An abbreviated version of her report reads as follows:

> Suddenly, the Holy Ghost fell upon me.... My whole being seemed to be filled with praise and adoration ... I was praising Jesus all the time, and yet it did not appear to be me but the power within that was praising Him.... I said to the Lord, "What does this mean?" and a very quiet, yet distinct, voice said, "Tongues." I said, "No Lord, not Tongues." Then followed a moment of deathlike silence, when the voice again uttered the word "Tongues." This time I felt afraid of grieving the Lord and I said, "Tongues, or anything that will please Thee and bring glory to Thy Name." One unknown word was repeated several times, and I thought that must be Tongues.[3]

Soon she began to sing in tongues and for three hours was listened to with awe by many at the Mission. Later she proclaimed, "This is the power of the Holy Ghost; this is the day of Pentecost." Within five months her husband and about 80 others had similar experiences.

There remains one possibility that another Canadian had the Pentecostal experience before Mrs. Hebden. John Loney of Snowflake, Manitoba, wrote to William Seymour in 1906:

> I am in sympathy with your work, am baptized with the Holy Ghost and fire, and have received the gift of some as yet unknown tongue or tongues. It first came two years ago, and is proving more distinct

and real. Believe God is preparing me for some special work in some part of His vineyard.[4]

Loney's account was reprinted in Seymour's *Apostolic Faith* paper in December. At this date, it is impossible to ascertain whether he was in fact a Canadian or possibly an American immigrant. Snowflake is near the border and many thousands came north at the turn of the century to take up homesteads on the Canadian Prairies. Since Loney's name does not appear in any available records of the PAOC nor is there any other evidence of his Canadian citizenship, it seems safe to claim Ellen Hebden as the first Canadian recipient of the Baptism in this century. Certainly she was considered by many in southern Ontario to have been the first. George C. Slager was converted to Christ at the East End Mission in the summer of 1908. He attended the early Latter Rain meetings and took part in the first Pentecostal convention in Toronto in the autumn of 1908. Slager later wrote that "Mrs. Hebden was the first to receive the baptism in the Holy Spirit accompanied by the initial evidence of speaking in other tongues . . . in fact, they claimed that she was the first to receive this experience in Toronto."[5]

Reports of the events in Toronto spread throughout southern Ontario and as far as Los Angeles. It was another example of those apparently spontaneous manifestations of Holy Spirit power which were occurring all over the world. Stanley H. Frodsham, author of *With Signs Following*, has referred to the East End Mission as a remarkable example of this process.[6] Toronto became a "Canadian Jerusalem" as early Pentecostal leaders made the city a key stopping point.

George Chambers reported that he met many "workers from all over the world who had come to see and experience what God was doing for hundreds of others."[7] There he met some missionaries on furlough, the Randalls and Lawlers, who later took the Pentecostal message to eastern Ontario. Frank Bartleman, of Azusa Street fame, visited Toronto on one of his world tours to promote the movement. Another prominent American leader, Daniel Awrey, visited the East End Mission at that time. A report in Seymour's paper states that a "Bro. O. Adams" of Los Angeles was in Toronto in 1906 to investigate the outbreak of glossolalia there. He reported that a number had received the experience according to Acts 2:4. From Ohio came A. S. Copley and his observations also found publication in *The Apostolic Faith*. Copley reported three services a day at the Hebden Mission and special prayers for healings. He concluded that "Pentecost has begun in Toronto."[8]

Some of the evangelical leaders in Toronto were vigorously opposed to the unusual meetings. By a curious twist of fate, one of the most

2 / "THIS IS THE PENTECOST"

outspoken was George Chambers, who at a later date became a founding father of the Pentecostal Assemblies of Canada and its first General Superintendent. Chambers then was pastoring a Mennonite Brethren in Christ congregation just six blocks from the Hebden's work. In early 1907 he was deeply concerned lest his people be "infected with the Hebden errors." He had read some tracts on the outpouring of the Spirit in Los Angeles and welcomed the news of revival. However, he rejected the claim that believers, after their Baptisms, spoke in languages they had never learned. His congregation had been praying for a revival, but this "put a damper on our ardent praying." In his handwritten memoirs he declared:

> When we heard of such strange doings we asked the Lord not to allow such to come to us in Toronto. . . . How terrified we were when we heard that the things we had feared had come.[9]

As Chambers ruefully noted, God heard their prayers and the local revival bypassed his congregation. Later on, he received his personal Pentecost, accompanied with tongues-speaking, and apologized to the Hebdens for "the many harsh things" he had said.

Within a short period of time there were at least six Latter Rain/ Pentecostal congregations in Toronto. George Fisher led a full gospel work on College Street and a Pastor Craig opened a mission in the centre of the city. Mr. and Mrs. George Murray (Mrs. Murray was referred to as the "blind missionary" from India) had a church on Concord Avenue on the west side of the city. From these small assemblies a number of workers went throughout North America, and some to overseas lands, with the story of Pentecost rediscovered. The Hebden Mission continued for some time to be the focal point of the new religious movement. Mrs. Hebden's reports in *The Promise*, and to Seymour, were not exaggerated. Corroboration came from George Slager who was a regular attendant at the meetings in 1908:

> It was all so new and wonderful to us in those early days. One felt the Presence of God as soon as one entered the place. There was such variety in the meetings. Something happened in every meeting. Sinners were convicted and prayed through to salvation; and it seemed so easy to receive the baptism of the Spirit. The reason being that folk were really spiritually hungry. There were also remarkable healings. Brother R. Spillenaar and myself were saved in the same meeting there . . . and later baptized in the Holy Ghost. . . . In a short time some of the baptized believers were called of God and sent to the various mission fields of the world. The work was unorganized in

"THIS IS THE PENTECOST" / 2

those days, so these went out without financial backing other than God's promises.[10]

Among those who left the Mission for the foreign field were Charles and Emma Chawner. Chawner was a Toronto house painter who attended the Queen Street meetings after his wife was miraculously healed in 1905. Another pioneer couple were Arthur and Jessie Atter of Abingdon, near Hamilton.[11]

For a few years Toronto remained the hub of the revival movement in Central Canada. Pentecostal adherents so increased in numbers that the city became the scene of the first Pentecostal Workers' Convention in September 1908. The meetings were held in a hall on Concord Avenue, where the Murrays were pastors. Some of the best-known of the early workers were the Slagers, the Hebdens, John Salmon, Mr. and Mrs. D. W. Kerr, Mr. and Mrs. W. E. Moody, George Fisher, A. G. Ward, and G. A. Chambers. Also present was J. T. Boddy of Ohio.[12] Another convention was held in the Hebden Mission in 1909. The Slagers attended and wrote:

> Three services each day was the rule. . . . Again and again the tender, melting presence of the Holy Spirit was discernible . . . Many were baptized with the Holy Ghost. The only way we knew it to be so with them was because we heard them speak with other tongues and magnify God. Many sick ones recovered as the brethren anointed them in the name of the Lord. . . . From early morning till late in the night the burden was foreign fields.[13]

A third workers' convention was held at 651 Queen Street in 1910. Present were "Bro. Scott" and "Bro. McAlister from Winnipeg." In addition, Robert and Aimee Semple, who had just concluded meetings with W. H. Durham at London, brought reports of success. Robert Semple had renewed his consecration to preach the gospel after he was healed of tuberculosis. He also received the Baptism at the East End Mission and took the Pentecostal message to Ingersoll. It was there that Aimee Kennedy was filled with the Spirit and married Semple. They had worked for a time pioneering churches in Ontario, then assisted Durham at his Chicago mission. After the meetings in London were over, Durham joined the group in Toronto.[14]

Some of the conference speakers and itinerant workers may have resided for a time in the Pentecostal Workers' Home on Borden Avenue. This facility was operated by a Mrs. Builder, who also opened her doors to spiritually hungry believers so they could stay in the city while seeking the Baptism. Her home no doubt sheltered some of the early workers who left Toronto for overseas mission fields. George Chambers once made up a list of those who had gone to Africa, China, Egypt, Hong Kong, and

43

2 / "THIS IS THE PENTECOST"

Mongolia in the decade before the PAOC was organized. The list included 15 names, all associated, at least briefly, with the East End Mission. In addition, there were two missionaries from Kitchener and five from Parry Sound.[15]

The Hebden Mission was clearly the leading Pentecostal work in eastern Canada before 1919. By the end of 1910, there were 14 congregations in the country, most of which had some connection with the Hebdens. For example, a man named S. T. Odegaard of Brownlee, Saskatchewan, read a tract about their ministry, came to Toronto in 1907, and received the Baptism with tongues. On his return, Odegaard opened a Pentecostal mission in Moose Jaw.[16] Besides this type of widespread influence, the Hebdens knew most of the pioneer leaders in Ontario and had cordial relations with A. H. Argue of Winnipeg. Two missionaries from the Argue Mission in the Manitoba capital seem to have been channeled through Toronto on route to their new fields.

The Hebden work was acknowledged to be the scene of the first known "Latter Rain Outpouring" in 20th-century Canada. Since Toronto was the scene of the first three workers' conventions, it seems curious that the Hebden Mission failed to become the headquarters of Canadian Pentecostalism. After a few years of prominence, the Mission ceased to exercise any real influence over the Pentecostal Movement in Canada. The answer to the mystery probably lies in the Hebdens' vigorous opposition to any form of organization. Leaders like A. G. Ward and G. A. Chambers soon realized that some structure was indispensable to preserve the fruits of the revival and to protect the believers against false teachers. Thus, when a group of pioneers gathered in Ottawa to seek incorporation for the PAOC, the Hebdens were not present.

One other factor contributed to the demise of their work: a steadily increasing emphasis on a "prophetic" ministry by Mrs. Hebden. Eventually, it appears, she directed people to specific fields of ministry by this method. When most of the early Pentecostal leaders recognized the threat to orthodox Christianity, Ellen Hebden lost her preeminence in the movement. Though services at her mission continued at least until 1914, the moral and legislative leadership had passed to those men who united in 1919 to form the Pentecostal Assemblies of Canada.[17] By this time other workers, such as A. G. Ward, G. A. Chambers, John T. Ball, R. E. Sternall, R. E. McAlister, and A. H. Argue, had emerged as recognized leaders of Pentecostalism in Canada. Several of the first generation Pentecostals have fondly recalled those glorious, early years at the Hebden Mission and have acknowledged the contribution it made in their historical writings.[18]

Many of the new Pentecostal groups in Ontario were the by-product of local opposition. At Vineland, in the Niagara Peninsula, Mrs. Henry Snyder and Mrs. George Stewart heard of the Toronto outpouring and came to join in the blessings. When they tried to share their experiences with their pastor and congregation at home, they were expelled. Prayer meetings were held in local homes until David Fretz donated an unused school building. The group thus formed the nucleus of one of the earliest Pentecostal churches in the country. A. G. Ward served as their pastor in 1908 and 1909.[19]

This pattern — reception of the Baptism in the Holy Spirit with tongues and subsequent testimony to others, followed by persecution and expulsion — was followed many times in the decade after the Toronto outpouring of 1906. PAOC historian Gordon Atter has noted that it characterized the way in which many Pentecostal congregations began. It was not the newly baptized believers, but their former religious associates, who precipitated the schism in the old-line denominations.[20] On the other hand, the Latter Rain Christians refused to keep quiet about their glorious experiences, or to refrain from pointing out the "deadness" of their pastors and churches. So the process of separation rarely was one-sided. Those who emerged as splinter groups frequently adopted the name "Pentecostal Church of God," "Apostolic Faith," or "Latter Rain" as a distinguishing mark. At a later period, when controversy and error arose, most of these groups in Canada retained only the term "Pentecostal."

Like all revival movements before it, the Pentecostal phenomenon in Canada appeared schismatic and divisive to many observers. Nonetheless, there were very marked benefits for the new charismatic groups in having deep roots in the older evangelistic denominations. The Mennonite Brethren in Christ (MBC) association in Ontario was a particular source of strength for early Pentecostalism. The MBC was a product of several revivals and mergers among the "Old" Mennonites in Ontario and the Northern States. Solomon Eby was a leading revivalist for the denomination (now The Missionary Church) and was its Ontario superintendent until his retirement in 1906. Eby was present at a church convention in 1908 in Kitchener when A. G. Ward of Winnipeg preached on the Holy Spirit. The convention was mightily moved by a spiritual outpouring and a number received the Baptism with tongues.[21]

The unusual phenomena among the people of the MBC gave promise of a new surge of Pentecostalism, but denominational leaders began to oppose the new doctrine. The issue was discussed and then voted upon in the assembly of ministers. It was September, the church windows were open, and a dove (Gordon Atter said it was probably a pigeon) flew into the church. The bird sat above the convention delegates until a decision was made to reject the charismatic experience and Pentecostal teaching as

2 / "THIS IS THE PENTECOST"

"heresy" and not a part of the MBC Articles of Faith. Then the "dove" flew out the window. To what extent the denominational leaders opposed the new teaching is difficult to determine. In any event, their actions led to the rejection of Pentecostal views among the MBC adherents. About 90 people who refused to renounce their experience and convictions were expelled. Eight MBC clergymen, including G. A. Chambers, thus came into the fledgling Pentecostal Movement.[22]

Chambers, like the leaders at the MBC conference, was unaware that A. G. Ward had received the Baptism while in Winnipeg. But Ward was a personal friend and his testimony and sermons left a lasting impact on Chambers. Ward was a native of Toronto where Anglican and Methodist influences made an impact on his life. As a young man, he became a "field evangelist" for the Christian and Missionary Alliance in Western Canada. Reports of the outpouring in Los Angeles, and the extraordinary events at the Hebden Mission, moved him to seek for a personal Pentecostal encounter with God. "My heart," he later wrote, "became very hungry for God's best in my life." He was director of the Alliance Mission in Winnipeg in 1907 when he received his personal Baptism in the Holy Spirit. He prayed, "Oh Lord, make me as holy as a pardoned sinner can be made, and fill me as full of Thyself as Thou art willing to fill me." Then the Spirit came and "Waves of glory swept through my soul and my lips uttered His praise in an unknown tongue." He learned afterwards that he gave messages in "German, Indian, Scandinavian and Polish." The Bible became a new book, he claimed, and it became easier to exercise faith in God after his Pentecostal experience.[23]

It was only a short while later that A. G. Ward spoke about his experience at the Kitchener conference. In the years that followed he itinerated throughout Ontario, helping Pentecostal workers build up their congregations or founding new assemblies himself. His observations on the sacrifices entailed in such pioneering are revealing.

> It is never easy to pioneer any work for God, and the Pentecostal work in Ontario was no exception to this rule. . . . In some places I received for my services the sum of two dollars, in other places, nothing at all. Still, God helped us to carry on, and daily we were encouraged in the Lord.[24]

Ward organized one of the first Pentecostal camp meetings in Ontario, at Markham, in the summer of 1909. It was there that he and his wife dedicated their son Morse (C. M. Ward) to the Lord for foreign service, if the Lord so willed. A. G. Ward became a Bible conference speaker, a teacher in Bible schools, an author of several books, and a renowned pastor. He was also an effective General Secretary for the PAOC.

Before his death in Toronto in 1960, Ward wrote a brief, personal perspective on the impact of 20th-century Pentecostalism in Canada. His observations provide an insight into this pioneer's concept of vision, faith, and worship:

> What a change almost overnight. There was no more struggling to make our meetings "go" — no more burning of midnight oil to discover something to say to the people. No more wondering if any strangers would be in the service. The crowds were coming. Sinners were awestruck as they listened to the fiery, God-inspired message that poured from the lips of His freshly-anointed ministers. The saints were being revived; sick people were taking on new courage; many were touching the hem of His garment, and resurrection life was flowing into frail, diseased bodies.
>
> The vision of a lost world and of millions sitting in darkness waiting for the life-giving gospel became so real. We must go — the urge of the Holy Spirit was upon us. We discovered that the "Go ye" of the risen Lord meant us — that the whole business of the whole Church was to give the whole Gospel to the whole world, no matter what the cost of sacrifice might be. Missionaries went out by the score. Soon there were hundreds. Today there are more than a thousand. The Pentecostal Movement has already made a substantial contribution to the evangelization of the world.
>
> The Pentecostal Movement has brought many of God's dear people into a new realm of faith. I thank God for the lessons He has taught us concerning the simplicity of faith and of our privilege to believe Him for things both small and great. We have found that it is never a venture to step out in faith and to dare to believe God for anything He has promised once we are convinced that it is His will to grant the same. Thus closed doors have been opened, "mountains" have been removed, mighty things have been accomplished, multitudes of sick people have been healed, the seemingly impossible has been done, and our heavenly Father has been glorified.
>
> Furthermore, the Pentecostal Movement has called the people of God back to real worship. It is so easy to become absorbed with forms, ceremonies, external trappings — with the things that appeal to the intellect or that stir man's emotional nature forgetting that Jesus said, "God is a Spirit, and they that worship Him must worship Him in Spirit and in truth." It was a glad day when we learned to be still in His presence; when we allowed ourselves to be immersed in God — lost to everything and everyone but Him. Then hours seemed like minutes while we revelled in things sublime.[25]

George Augustus Chambers attended Bible School in Cincinnati with A. G. Ward before either had heard of the Los Angeles revival. Chambers

2 / "THIS IS THE PENTECOST"

was reared in a Methodist home on a farm near Lindsay, Ontario. He was converted during his teens while working in Toronto. His call to the ministry came while working on a ranch in Manitoba. Chambers was awakened from sleep by a voice saying, "George Chambers! Will you be willing to preach My gospel?" He resisted the call until a serious accident prompted him to obey God. After attending Ohio Bible School, he became affiliated with the MBC denomination.

A discouraging year's labor as a pastor in Guelph prompted Chambers to return to secular work for a short period of time. Yielding once again to the insistent call from God, he took charge of a small mission in Toronto where he first came into contact with the Pentecostal message. His initial rejection of the Hebdens' ministry was modified somewhat by the influence of "Holy Ann" Preston. One Sunday the renowned saint declared, with great joy, "Revival is coming! Revival is coming!" Chambers was one of five clergymen who officiated at Preston's funeral, attended by about 3,000 people.[26]

Chambers visited the Elim Bible school in Rochester, New York, operated by a Mrs. Baker, where the emphasis was on seeking more spiritual power for service. After a few months in Toronto, he accepted a call to Elkland, Pennsylvania. It was there, during a local revival, that he finally received his Pentecostal experience. His son also was supernaturally healed after prayer. Thus, when he came to pastor the little Pentecostal group at Vineland, G. A. Chambers was a devout believer in divine healing and a committed Pentecostal preacher.

In 1911, the Vineland congregation experienced a revival and over twenty families joined the church. The impact of the Pentecostal message on individual lives can be imagined from the following letter, dated March 15, 1911. It was from Effie Moyer (née Brewer) to her sister Mamie McPherson:

> You will be surprised to get such a letter from me. But God wants me to write. For some time . . . I have been praying and searching the Scriptures. Then I went to the Mission. I have been watching those that left our church and after being persecuted they had something that I did not have, and when the Invitation was given I went to the altar and felt the Power of God upon my body. . . . I fell under the Power of God and I commenced to shake. I had always been opposed to the shaking. . . . I soon commenced to speak in an unknown Tongue . . . The next evening . . . the Power came over me and I commenced to give messages to the cold, careless church members, also some of the unsaved. God spoke through me for about one hour like that, telling the people Jesus was coming soon. . . . Oh Mamie, it was more real than my own life. God . . . wanted me to give the same message to you. . . . The ministers anointed me and

laid their hands on me, and prayed and I was instantly healed (of heart trouble). Read this prayerfully.

Your unworthy sister, Effie.[27]

The work at Vineland progressed so well that Chambers arranged for a summer camp meeting in 1912 at nearby Jordan Station. Mighty signs and wonders were manifested during the camp, including the reported sound of an angelic chorus. After an entire night of prayer,

> They witnessed a visitation of angels who seemed to hover over the camp while singing and playing heavenly music . . . Mrs. Zaltzman of Kitchener said that she was caught up to heaven in the Spirit, and heard and saw things too sacred to utter.[28]

This phenomenon has been verified by R. E. Sternall, one of the founding fathers of the PAOC, who was present at the 1912 camp. He wrote that about two o'clock one morning the people were praying in the central tent when the Spirit began extraordinarily to move them to prophetic utterance. A great outpouring of love and praise was so intense that the believers began to worship with a melodious sound that was "almost beyond this world." Then, he added, "We heard an angelic host descending upon us with rapturous song." Sternall's account was supported by a Mrs. Pepper of Stratford, who was also present in the camp.[29]

There also were humorous events at the Jordan Valley camp which stood out in the memory of the participants. It had been arranged that a firm in Toronto would ship out extra blankets as needed. When these arrived they were packed in twelve casket boxes, giving rise to a rumor in the community that the Pentecostals planned to raise the dead and were shipping in bodies!

One of the pioneer Pentecostals, John T. Ball, was renowned in the early days for his success in establishing new assemblies. Ball was one of the MBC clergymen who left the denomination after the Kitchener convention. He also attended the 1912 camp. He first heard of the Pentecostal revival while pastoring five churches on the Markham circuit. A missionary told Ball of his own reception of the Spirit and added, "When you get your baptism you will speak in tongues." John Ball was a diligent student of the Word, and his thorough searches convinced him of the truth of the new teaching. He spoke in tongues when he was baptized in the Spirit. He was given an ultimatum that he must refrain from proclaiming this message or he would have to leave the circuit. However, when his parishioners demanded that he stay and preach Pentecost to

2 / "THIS IS THE PENTECOST"

them, Ball opened up a work in the village of Markham.[30] In a remarkable manner a lot in the centre of the village was provided where he erected a church and served as pastor for eight years. Then came a stint of pastoring in Toronto. Afterwards, he opened a church in Mount Forest and another in Owen Sound in 1917. A revival in Owen Sound produced numerous converts: one of whom was W. Clifford Nelson, later a pastor in Kitchener and a Pentecostal administrator in Western Canada.

Cottage prayer meetings throughout the region resulted in many more conversions and scores were filled with the Spirit. Outstanding miracles of healing took place.[31] The post-war influenza epidemic which took thousands of lives reached Owen Sound at that time. Much prayer, however, was offered and not one of the Pentecostal adherents in the region died. The physical preservation of the Pentecostal people during the epidemic created great interest in their message. As Ball remarked, "They were very impressed . . . They wanted to know if this baptism was for everybody . . . and why didn't other churches have it?" His response was that the experience came by faith, and people did not have it because it was not preached. The process was the same, he added, for receiving divine healing.

During that winter, he held meetings in five locations throughout the community. Once a local lawyer remarked to Ball that "the people of this city are dying of respectability." Not only were converts added to the young assembly, but recruits for the Pentecostal ministry came out of John Ball's Owen Sound meetings. Besides W. C. Nelson, already noted, there were Earley King and John Lynn, who became PAOC missionaries; J. H. Blair, a long-time district superintendent of Western Ontario; and H. H. Barber, later to become pastor of Calvary Temple in Winnipeg. J. Harold Blair had been converted in a tent meeting in the Ottawa Valley conducted by R. E. McAlister. He was a lay preacher in Mount Forest when John Ball took him as an assistant at Owen Sound. Blair once summarized Ball's ministry: "When John Ball gave an altar call, he expected people to come to Christ. He had faith, and God honored his faith."[32]

After eight fruitful years in Owen Sound, the Balls held meetings in Southampton and in Pembroke. In the latter town, a mighty outpouring of the Spirit occurred during a campaign with A. H. Argue, his daughter Zelma, and son Watson. Crowds of over 500 attended nightly meetings and a large number of young people were converted. An eyewitness wrote an enthusiastic report of those days:

> The power of God was falling, people were getting saved and healed and baptized with the Holy Spirit. Whole families were saved and

filled with the Spirit sometimes. The Pembroke revival was a God-sent revival. Never shall we forget how God manifested His power. ... For five months, there were three services on Sunday and four nights in the week.[33]

Ball pioneered Pentecostalism in Oshawa where a third strong assembly resulted from his labors. His successes in this most difficult form of evangelism earned the highest respect of his colleagues.

Ball's effective preaching no doubt resulted from his diligent preparation in prayer and study. Many hours were spent daily in such activity, even to the point where he wrote out his sermons in longhand. While he preached, "People were known to have fallen from their seats while others, who entered the service unconverted, would rise to their feet to give praise to God."[34] In spite of his strenuous labors in pioneer evangelism and church planting, John T. Ball preached the gospel for over 50 years. He died November 10, 1955.

To the northeast of Owen Sound, across Georgian Bay, lies the port community of Parry Sound. The Pentecostal message reached that area around 1909, but the way in which it was introduced is unknown. Two women, Mrs. Martha Perry and her daughter, Mrs. Olive Peterkin, appears to have been the first to practise the Pentecostal faith in the community. They were zealous in witnessing and praying that God would raise up local leaders. They distributed literature to many people. Mrs. Susan Marshall and her family responded to the gospel. Among others whose interest was stirred were two milkmen, Dan and Fred Michaelis. Dan was one of the first to believe and receive his Baptism in the Holy Spirit with the evidence of tongues. He and Fred helped with services in a local home. Fred and Martha Michaelis had been told by a doctor that they could have no more children, but, after prayer, Martha delivered another daughter. They left in 1921 to begin Pentecostal meetings at Maple Lake. Another worker raised up from the Parry Sound congregation was Sarah Weller, who went in 1911 as a missionary to India. In 1918, Sarah contracted malaria, died on the field, and was buried on the mission station.

The persecution and opposition faced by the first group of Pentecostals is a common denominator in the histories of most of the early assemblies. At Parry Sound, it took a particularly violent turn. The congregation had erected a church building in 1912, and Rev. and Mrs. George Will had become pastors. One night during the meeting someone poured kerosene on the building and set it on fire. When the fire brigade arrived, the chief refused to turn on the water hoses. Instead, he said, "Let it burn, then we will get rid of these crazy people." The believers were looking on and

2 / "THIS IS THE PENTECOST"

praying. Peter Weller lifted his face to heaven and prayed, "Oh Lord, if You will put this fire out, I will pay for the shingles." Suddenly, out of a clear sky, rain began to pour down and within minutes the fire was out.[35] Out of this small group the Lord raised up a number of faithful workers, including Marian Weller, a sister to Sarah. Marian was filled with the Spirit at Parry Sound in 1911, and later went to the Elim Bible school in Rochester, N.Y., where she met her husband, Karl Wittich. After graduation in 1913, they went to Itiger in German East Africa to start a Pentecostal mission work.

The Pentecostal message was taken by a layman from Parry Sound to North Seguin (then called Orange Valley). This work was continued by Arthur Atter and his wife after their return from China. They fixed up an abandoned loggers' shack as a home, and Atter walked the entire valley inviting people to cottage meetings. The first service, on a Christmas night, resulted in a revival in which scores of Orange Valley inhabitants were converted. About 40 received the Baptism in the Holy Spirit and spoke in tongues. One of the most resistant to the gospel was A. E. Adams, who was known to have "made it rough" on his wife, a believer. One night, however, the church was thrilled to see Adams bow in repentance and, in a very fine voice, sing "Jesus, Lover of my Soul" as his confession. Adams became a preacher and pioneered the work in Bristol Ridge, Quebec. For a number of years he served as superintendent of the Eastern Ontario and Quebec District of the PAOC.

The story of Pentecostal foundations in London reflects once again the sacrificial spirit of the pioneers. The key workers were Robert and Aimee Semple and W. H. Durham. Robert Semple went from Toronto to Ingersoll to hold the first Pentecostal meetings in that community. There he presented the full gospel message for a number of months in 1907. One who heard him eagerly was a youthful Salvation Army woman named Aimee Kennedy. By the end of the year, she had received the Baptism in the Spirit. In August of 1908 she and Semple were married. They began meetings in London, in the home of a Mrs. Armstrong, and then in a bigger house where large crowds attended. Over 100 received the Baptism with tongues within a year. The Semples assisted W. H. Durham in his Chicago mission for some months, but Aimee's role was relatively minor. She assisted chiefly in playing the piano and praying with the converts. The Semples returned with Durham to London for meetings during the winter of 1909-1910:

> The Spirit was manifested immediately, and within the first week of the mission, approximately seventy believers were filled. Pentecost had come to London. Durham left in 1910, and meetings of the

fledgling, Spirit-filled congregation were held in the home of Mr. and Mrs. W. H. Wortman at 546 Dundas Street. By 1912, more suitable quarters were desired, property was purchased at 557 Dundas Street, and the existing building renovated to hold services.[36]

During the next decade, there was no permanent pastor in London. Ministry was carried on by visiting evangelists and members of the congregation. Nonetheless, their numbers increased steadily and they even had the joy of seeing three of their number go to the mission field: Dr. and Mrs. C. M. Wortman to Argentina, and Lettie Ward to China. After an eighteen-year career on the mission field, Dr. Wortman became the Secretary-Treasurer of the PAOC in 1939. R. E. McAlister arrived in 1922 as the first full-time pastor in London. As for Durham, he returned to his North Avenue Mission in Chicago where he played a prominent role in the spreading of the Pentecostal message through the Northern States. His influence extended to the Western Canadian Prairies as well, through A. H. Argue of Winnipeg who went to Durham's mission to seek the Baptism.

The Semples received a call to the overseas field and left Canada in 1910 for China. They stopped on route for meetings at the Hebden Mission in Toronto. By that date, Aimee Semple was beginning to manifest her God-given talent for public ministry. Ellen Hebden reported that Aimee's "gift of interpretation was such a blessing in giving to us the very words in given tongues that it made the presence of God very manifest to all."[37]

According to G. A. Chambers, the early work at Kitchener (then called Berlin), began in much the same way as in London. Kitchener, as the site of the MBC conference which provided so decisive a step for Chambers and other Pentecostal workers, immediately provided a nucleus of believers. The "Pentecostal Mission at Berlin," as the assembly was called, recorded its formal establishment "by a Pentecostal convention, Jan., 1909." The next year an evangelist named Brother Edmonds conducted tent meetings in the community and remained for a time to minister to the congregation. But there was no permanent clergyman until R. E. Sternall came in 1911. In the interim, the affairs of the assembly were directed by a group of elders and deacons. These men were selected by the congregation only after fervent prayer. As one of the Kitchener church's record books reports,

> Under the date of September 30, 1910, we read, "Resolved that October 1 be set apart as a day of fasting and prayer, for the purpose of getting the mind of the Lord for the appointment of Deacons and Elders."[38]

2 / "THIS IS THE PENTECOST"

It is not surprising that the Kitchener congregation enjoyed steady growth in numbers and influence, even in the absence of a full-time pastor. The assembly was also blessed with the presence of a few older men who had ministerial experience with the MBC. The advice of brethren like Solomon Eby, Amos Eby, and C. R. Miller was available for the people before the arrival of Sternall.

Reuben Eby Sternall was one of the seven leaders who applied, in 1919, for a charter from the Canadian federal government to give a legal framework to the young Pentecostal Movement. He was born at Chippewa Hill, in the Bruce Peninsula of Ontario, and was converted at the age of 16 in a local revival. He attended Nyack Bible College in New York and was baptized in the Spirit during meetings at nearby Rochelle. Among his colleagues at Nyack were Frank Boyd, E. S. Williams, J. Roswell Flower, and William Evans, all men who later figured prominently in the development of the American Assemblies of God. Sternall was quite impressed with the teaching ministry and spiritual perception of A. B. Simpson, then at Nyack. While still at the college, Sternall married Ella (Sunshine) Hostetler. He began his long and fruitful career in the Pentecostal ministry by taking up the pastorate in Kitchener in 1911.

One of the early methods for reaching the community with the Pentecostal message was the "convention" — a special time set apart for seeking spiritual refreshing and for reaching sinners with the good news of salvation. In addition, many in Kitchener and nearby communities were reached through the camp meetings which were held each summer. Some participants came from as far away as Montreal. The custom of the time was to erect a large tent for the meetings and for dining. Visitors came equipped with their own tents for living accommodations. In many respects, it was the old-time Methodist camp meeting with a Pentecostal flavor.[39]

Following their ministry at London, the Sternalls pastored at Kinburn, Kingston, St. Catharines, and other centres in Ontario. In some of these areas, Sternall was the first to introduce what the Pentecostals called "the full gospel." While he pastored in Kingston, he became familiar with the few remaining members of an Irvingite church. Because of his charismatic message, he was permitted to rent the local church and later purchase it. The Irvingites had a firm rule not to sell the property to any group that did not acknowledge the Baptism in the Holy Spirit as a present reality. It also was in Kingston that God performed a miracle in keeping the family from freezing one winter. Aleta Piper, Sternall's daughter, recalled that only two tons of coal were available for fuel, but the house always needed five tons each winter. Somehow, no one could explain how, the meagre store of coal kept the house warm in spite of an especially severe winter. Although Sternall suffered for years from ill health, he trusted God to sustain him, and lived to the age of 97 years.[40] After his retirement from active ministry, he became a kind of "pastor's pastor" to younger workers. He once summed up his philosophy of the Christian life in an article titled, "If I Had My Life to Live Over:"

> If I had my life to live over again, I would not want to live my own life at all. I would choose to let 'Christ in me' be in complete control, with none of self to hinder Christ at all. . . . the devil . . . has planted an evil seed of pride in human nature that has grown into two ugly branches. They are self-sufficiency and insufficiency. . . . If God's people yield to either disposition they refuse to let the Victor take over in their lives. . . . With Christ in control, I would fear men and devils so little because I would be fearing God so much, loving God so much, and obeying God so much.[41]

When George and Ida Chambers went to Kitchener in 1912, they did so in what they believed to be the leading of the Lord. While in prayer, Ida was impressed by the words "Ye shall hear a voice behind you, saying, 'This is the way, walk ye in it.'" Then came the invitation to Kitchener where they labored during the difficult years of the First World War. It was in that period of hostilities that the city fathers re-named the city (previously Berlin) in honor of one of the leading generals of the allied forces. Chambers began camp meetings near London which came under bitter persecution from Roman Catholics in the area. When these meetings were over, the large, but dilapidated, tent was sold to Aimee Semple. She had been widowed while in China, and had returned to Ontario with an infant daughter. Here she launched out into the ministry with her unique gifts of preaching and praying for the sick. It was a ministry that led her throughout Canada and the United States and made her one of the leading evangelists of the 1920s.

During the war in Europe, the fledgling Pentecostal Movement, composed of many who were mainly pacifist in sentiment, "took a strong stand against going to war," as George Chambers recalled. This attitude was influenced no doubt by the Mennonite heritage of some of the early Pentecostal leaders. Some young believers were incarcerated in the federal prison at Kingston for refusing to bear arms. One man's imprisonment even resulted in his death:

> In the First World War, the Canadian government granted conscientious objector (or C.O.) status only to those who belonged to certain religious groups, such as Mennonites and Quakers — and

2 / "THIS IS THE PENTECOST"

even then, only with great difficulty. Many of the other religious groups were treated harshly. About 130 C.O.s were imprisoned; some Jehovah's Witnesses were treated brutally, and one Pentecostal C.O. in Manitoba died three weeks after being sent to prison. There is strong speculation that his death was the result of torture.[42]

Other Pentecostals enlisted, but managed to be assigned to non-combat duties. In spite of their personal difficulties, they succeeded in spreading still further the full gospel message.

The First World War placed enormous demands on the resources of all Canadians, but the Kitchener church, under Chambers' able leadership, continued to expand in numbers and in community influence. During one of the overseas mission conventions which he had organized, the believers donated the sum of $8,000. It represented a huge sum for the time, and was reported in the daily papers. Local clergymen expressed amazement, especially as the money was designated for missionaries. At the time, no PAOC organization existed to support overseas workers; these courageous souls went out by faith in the Lord with only their local congregations aware of their work.

In 1916, the Chambers moved to Ottawa to pastor an assembly established by R. E. McAlister. Congregations were being set up in rapid order in the decade following the Baptism of Mrs. Hebden, but there was a shortage of qualified pastors. The need often was met by the recruitment of a younger man to assist one of the pioneer leaders. John T. Ball had done this successfully; G. A. Chambers and R. E. McAlister, among others, made use of the same method. The shortage of trained pastors meant that considerable movement took place among the churches. An examination of some early church records indicates that the average stay of a pastor was three years. As brief as they were, these periods of pastoral oversight contributed to the establishment and growth of the pioneer congregations. Frequent moves, however, exacted a heavy toll on the wives and families of the pastors.

Viola Spaetzel, in a tribute to her parents, George and Ida Chambers, gives a vivid account of life in the home of an early Pentecostal preacher:

> It has been my observation that preachers' kids, of the Pentecostal variety, live comparatively free today of the snubs, bumps and ridicule that bruised the tender hearts of children of ministers of my day. It was not easy to leave the shelter of home and mother's love to go off to school each morning, and to be left alone on the side-lines to watch the children play while you nursed a deep hurt, and hungrily wished to be included in the game.
>
> Nor was it easy to be uprooted every three or four years

and leave the friends you had made in the assembly, and go off to start all over again adjusting to a new assembly and new school, here to be accepted briefly with the children until it became known that you were a Pentecostal preacher's kid, and then to be made fun of again. A move such as this usually affected one's school work too, and resulted in your getting behind.

Mother Never Complained

As I grew older I was to learn that what was difficult for a minister's child was also hard on the parents. Although I never heard my mother complain, I've seen tears come to her eyes and roll down her cheeks as she once again packed up and prepared to leave old friends and face with Dad, a new assignment.

I can still see the old patch-bag as Mother sorted over piece after piece to try to match a blouse or dress to patch a worn spot or lengthen a hem, for "we must look our best in a new church, and we can't afford new ones." As the older children outgrew the garments they were handed down to the younger ones and nothing was ever discarded until it was no longer wearable.

Shoes were passed on in the same manner and we often looked enviously at our Sunday school friends who sported new clothes. But while our wants weren't all supplied, our needs were, according to His promise....

It was a great time for the preacher's kids when the family was invited to a farm home for dinner. Some of the good things that graced those tables in abundance never found their way to ours at home. These were occasions for object lessons by my father when we returned home, to the effect that the Lord sometimes provides extras for us along the way.

In at least two pastorates my father held, the preacher's children were church janitors, and my Saturday afternoons were spent cleaning and dusting the mission hall in readiness for the Sunday services — unremunerated, of course. I never questioned this or wondered why we had to do it. I just took it for granted it came with the job. I wonder if this is still a practice anywhere.

Marvelous Answers to Prayer

I wasn't to appreciate till later years some of the marvelous answers to prayer we experienced in those early days, some of which I vividly remember and some of which were told to me by my parents.

On more than one occasion, when our cupboard was so nearly empty that Mother wondered what she would give her family for their next meal, Dad would gather the family around and we would take the need to the Lord in prayer. Before we arose from

2 / "THIS IS THE PENTECOST"

> our knees a box of groceries or a bag of potatoes was placed at our door. Or someone would call at the house with a cheque or a gift of money the Lord had laid on their heart to take to the pastor.
>
> When it looked as though my younger sister would die from pneumonia in the days before antibiotics, Dad shut himself in an upstairs room and asked not to be disturbed. He told the Lord he would not leave the room until the child was healed. Before many hours the change came and she was completely healed. Oh glory be to God! My heart goes out in praise and worship as I recall the goodness of the Lord in our home in those early days.
>
> **Father Was General Superintendent**
>
> In later years my father spent eighteen years as General Superintendent of The Pentecostal Assemblies of Canada. It was my privilege at times when Dad could spend a while at home, to be his secretary. In those days his office included being missionary secretary. His business office was our kitchen and his desk the kitchen table. Here I typed many, many letters to missionaries. That was when I learned to love and appreciate them and became familiar with many of their problems.
>
> It was my privilege to be church pianist for many years, a service which took me back in memory to my very early years when Mother, as a preacher's wife, was expected to be at every service to play the piano.
>
> Baby sitters were not in vogue then, so the four children were taken to the service and placed on the front row benches. Stretched out on the seats, I slept out many a good sermon preached by my dear father. And many a night I recall being carried home over his shoulder.
>
> I have merely touched on a very few experiences as I look back on my life as a Pentecostal preacher's daughter. I thank God for a home where prayer was the essential ingredient to every day living and where God was honored.[43]

The worldwide influenza epidemic following the War reached eastern Ontario by August of 1918. Chambers was pastoring in Ottawa and was kept busy visiting the sick and praying with the dying. Altogether, one in six were affected by the disease and some 30,000 Canadians died. But the Chambers family invoked divine protection in prayer each morning; and not one of them became ill from the "flu." Throughout the terrible three-month epidemic, the work in the capital city expanded and Ottawa became the focal point for Pentecostalism in the Ottawa Valley.

Chambers began services in 1918 at Mille Roches, near Cornwall, out of which came a local revival. In his own estimation, "The Book of Acts was never more literally repeated than it was in Mille Roches . . . As far as I know, there was not one prayer that we offered to God that was not answered."[44] Later that year, he held more meetings in the community, assisted by W. L. Draffin, an Ottawa layman. Draffin distributed tracts and announcements about the upcoming service and Chambers did the preaching. He felt a "burden for Mille Roches (that) so gripped my heart that my interests were no longer limited to Ottawa." Because the people were so ignorant of the basics of the gospel, he preached for six weeks before giving an altar call. At his first invitation, 48 people responded and one lady, who could not get out into the aisle, actually climbed over the seats to get to the altar.

In retrospect, Chambers observed, "Never was there a better small revival than that." When he returned to Ottawa, he left William Draffin as pastor of the new assembly. The Mille Roches meetings were especially notable because it had been a quarter of a century since any attempt at revival work had been attempted in the village. Chambers gave a glowing account of the revival:

> I was pastor at Ottawa at that time and Brother Draffin was feeling the urge of the Spirit to get out into the Lord's work, when some who were interested in Mille Roches requested that we go down and hold a few meetings somewhere in the village. The home of Mr. Fred Young was opened to us to entertain for a time any one who would come; so with a supply of tracts, and announcement cards, Brother Draffin and Brother Wilson left for Mille Roches to try to secure some place for services.
> This was one of the biggest revivals in a small place I had ever witnessed. The entire community was stirred for miles; the very atmosphere seemed charged with God. From the very commencement God began to answer prayer. The hall that had been engaged for services had formerly been used for a dance hall, and once or twice a week for a theatre. We could not definitely count on it permanently, so we went to prayer, with the result that the theatre company became disgusted because of small crowds and they never did return or any others attempt it. The dancing crowd became disinterested because of the revival that had broken out, so that for weeks there were no dances. By that time the landlord decided to rent it to us as long as we wanted it. In answer to prayer the pool gang was broken up when the leader of the gang was saved and several others. This attracted the rest to the services through curiosity and conviction. In answer to prayer the hotel was closed and the proprietor moved out of town. The St. Lawrence paper mill was the place of livelihood of many in the town who had started to come to the meetings and some of whom were

2 / "THIS IS THE PENTECOST"

under deep conviction. We had an all night prayer in which we asked God definitely in some way to save those attending who were employed there; even if He had to cause the mill to break down or cease operation till they got saved; the next day the main shaft in one of the departments, where a number were employed, broke, giving us a chance to visit and pray in homes of a number. We had asked God to take sleep from the people and give them a vision of Himself. This He did in several cases that resulted in their salvation.

On Easter Sunday morning we were invited to the Methodist church to assist in the service, as we had no morning service in the hall as yet. Being called on by the pastor of the church to lead in prayer, as I stood to pray, I placed my hand on the shoulder of the brother just in front of me, feeling led to do so. Immediately he began to shake, and kick his feet, and cried out, "Oh Lord save me, Oh Lord, save me." Immediately after this between ten and twelve stood up expressing their desire to be saved. That night at the hall there were around forty-eight young and old at the altar seeking salvation. Every one either left the hall or came for salvation. This went on night after night for months.

After a few weeks people began to receive the Baptism of the Holy Ghost, and for several months the revival went on unabated. People were definitely healed in their homes, and in the services marvelous healings took place.

The outstanding miracle of the revival was, and is, Brother John Manson. He was a man in weight of over two hundred pounds and had developed tubercular trouble of the spine, leaving him absolutely helpless from his hips down. His feet and legs were as though they were dead, and had dwindled away to the size of that of a schoolboy's limbs. At his request, after being given up by Montreal specialists, and sent home to die, his wife asked us to come over and pray for him. After dealing with him regarding his soul, and his acceptance of Christ, we anointed him and laid hands upon his head, when instantly, like a bolt from the blue, he commenced to shout, shake and kick with those poor helpless legs which he had stretched out in front of him on an invalid's chair. This continued until he had been shaken to the floor and there he lay for several hours. From that minute he was healed, the disease was cured and stayed. Life began to return to his limbs and though not fully restored so as to be able to walk without a cane, yet he is well as he ever was and drives his car and has carried on his business. He and his wife, and their boy then age ten were all gloriously saved and filled with the Holy Ghost.[45]

Chambers and Draffin went forty miles up the valley to "spy out" the town of Arnprior. They tried to rent the town hall for meetings, but the police chief opposed them. After they obtained permission from the mayor to hold street meetings, the chief ordered them to leave, alleging the meeting would block the traffic. When Chambers protested that he had official permission, the chief sought to arrest him. A crowd of men, however, who had been listening with interest forced the chief to desist. From that time on they were unmolested. They finally rented the town hall; from the first meeting there was keen interest in their message. An Arnprior matron named Mrs. Aikins had prayed for a long time for God to send someone with the message of Pentecost. There had been no revival meetings in the region for years. Chambers noted that "the spiritual condition was ripe for God to work."

For two weeks they preached every night and twice on Sundays, and visited people in their homes during the day. At the end of six weeks many had been saved, healed, and filled with the Spirit, and over 60 were baptized in the first water baptismal service. But not without continued opposition, for one resident threatened to shoot the preachers if his wife were baptized. More hindrances appeared when Chambers and Draffin tried to buy property for a church building, but a local businessman secretly purchased a desirable lot and then conveyed it by deed to the new Pentecostal congregation. The first formal meeting of the assembly took place on July 4, 1918.[46]

Arnprior was a community where feelings ran strong on the issue of Pentecost. Families sometimes were divided in their views. A town official, whose daughter was a youth leader in the church, opposed the work. When he committed suicide soon after, his death was, in Chamber's view, a tragic consequence of men opposing God. On the other hand, the town magistrate and his wife were soon converted and became faithful supporters of the work. The small group of believers erected a church building and began holding services in the autumn of 1920. It was at this time that the preacher suffered a broken wrist while cranking what he called "a musical Ford." Since he had been preaching on divine healing and felt he could not seek medical aid, he called on God for assistance in his dire need. "All of a sudden," he exclaimed, "I felt my wrist snap into place and pain cease." Later, while suffering excruciating pain from an attack of kidney stones, he again trusted God and was healed.

One form of outreach the preachers used was a summer camp meeting to which people came who otherwise would not enter their church. Souls were saved, bodies healed, many baptized in the Spirit, and visitors took the full gospel message back to their home communities. In this manner Pembroke residents came into contact with Pentecostal teachings and prepared the way for John T. Ball to begin meetings in that community.

George Chambers and William Draffin were lovingly remembered by the Arnprior church for decades after they moved on to other communities. But they had many dedicated lay assistants, as Chambers'

2 / "THIS IS THE PENTECOST"

wife Ida once observed: "The dear saints who sowed and watered with us ... will share in the reward."[47]

Robert Edward McAlister (just R.E. to those who knew him well) played a pivotal role in the establishment of early Pentecostalism in Ontario and throughout Canada. His life story is one of the outstanding biographies of the Canadian Pentecostal revival. He was born in 1880, near Cobden, Ontario. His Scottish Presbyterian ancestors had been part of the Holiness Movement which was known for its lifestyle of "separation from the world." McAlister's niece, Lila Skinner, once wrote of the strict rules that governed their behavior. Women were expected to wear

> full skirts to the ankle, a high neckline on dresses, and sleeves to the wrist. The hair was pulled back and done up in a knot. . . . All social frivolity and like behavior was frowned upon and life was a serious affair.[48]

The rules for men were equally demanding: they were to dress plainly, even to the extent of eschewing special mourning clothes at funerals. "Showy white shirt fronts," and even neckties were denounced as prideful and wasteful of the Lord's money. Preachers were to live within their means "by fasting at least once a week." Holiness people were to avoid church entertainments, secret societies, games of chance, and buying life insurance; this latter proscription was aimed at the failure to trust God for life protection.[49] This stern morality and personal self-denial was an integral part of McAlister's home life. It played a significant part in his theological and ideological position when he later became a Pentecostal.

McAlister was converted at the age of 21 and soon thereafter went to a Bible school in Cincinnati to prepare for the ministry. It was later, while engaged in evangelistic work in Western Canada, that he first heard of the Azusa Street outpouring. He went to Los Angeles, determined to see for himself whether the work was genuine. He arrived at the Mission on December 11, 1906, soon received his personal Pentecost, and was on the way home a few hours later.[50]

He shared his experience with family members in the Westmeath area of Ontario and wrote to his sister Jessie in Montreal and his brother John in Manitoba. John, who had already read a tract by A. H. Argue, carefully examined the Scriptures to see if the experience was both biblical and available in the 20th century. John went to the Argue Mission in Winnipeg where he, his son Walter, and daughter Lila received their own Pentecostal experience. All three family members became significant workers in the new movement: John as a pastor in Alberta, Walter as

General Superintendent of the PAOC, and Lila as wife of long-time missionary James Skinner.

R. E. McAlister began working in the nation's capital early in 1908 and had formed a small congregation by the autumn. He also itinerated through Ontario and Western Canada holding meetings. In January of 1910 he returned to Toronto to share in a Pentecostal convention. Mrs. Hebden was quite impressed by his ministry, as evidenced by comments she made in *The Promise*:

> Bro. McAlister from Winnipeg just opened his mouth and out of his inner being flowed rivers indeed of living water till the vessels in the household of God were filled again and again with bread and wine of the kingdom of God. It was just the pure Word of God administered in season to many, accompanied by the Holy Ghost.[51]

During the winter of 1910-11, McAlister teamed up in Ottawa with two missionaries on furlough, H. L. Lawler and H. E. Randall. A. H. Argue and Harvey McAlister also contributed to effective meetings which were conducted in the city. At the time, the workers in Ottawa referred to themselves as the "Apostolic Faith," a title they likely adopted from Seymour's work in Los Angeles.

At a Pentecostal convention held in March in the Queen's Hall, there were some people in attendance from nearby Kinburn. Greatly impressed, they took the new message home with them. A local revival began in which about 60 people were converted and a number healed. In later services, another 21 came to the Lord. With the additions, the Kinburn congregation now was so large it needed a church building. By the end of 1911, Kinburn had a Pentecostal church, the first building in Canadian history erected specifically as an "Assembly of God."[52] This structure continued to be used for Pentecostal worship until the 1980s. McAlister and his wife gave oversight to this new assembly. The first full-time pastor was Elder M. F. Eby of Kitchener, who came in 1914.

R. E. McAlister's association with Ottawa spanned the decade after 1911, during which he both pastored in the city and travelled extensively to promote the full gospel. He also organized camp meetings, one of which resulted in the establishment of a church at Edwards, Ontario. Services were held in that town during the winter of 1912-13 and the following summer at a nearby site called "Shirley's Bush." McAlister was the main speaker whom "the Lord blessed and used in a wonderful way." The whole community was stirred, and scores were converted and filled with the Spirit. Another McAlister camp meeting the next year led to the erection of a Pentecostal "tabernacle" at Edwards.[53]

In May 1911, McAlister launched his first publishing venture, *The*

2 / "THIS IS THE PENTECOST"

Good Report, which gave information on upcoming meetings as well as testimonies and reports. The magazine characterized the services as repetitions of the Day of Pentecost, accompanied by healing. Perhaps the most outstanding incident concerned the healing of Mrs. Charles E. Baker. Mrs. Baker had cancer and was facing a second operation when she went to the "Apostolic Faith" meetings. Her testimony was printed by McAlister as she had given it:

> I came here for healing . . . they laid hands on me and prayed, and Jesus healed me, praise His name. I left the meeting and walked home, and did not feel tired. . . . Since then I have been tarrying for the baptism of the Holy Ghost. . . . On the 6th of April, in the Mission, I received with the sign following, as in Acts 2:4, speaking in other tongues. . . . My way has been sunshine and happiness ever since.[54]

As a result of his wife's healing, C. E. Baker gave up his Ottawa business and entered the Pentecostal ministry. He labored at Kinburn, then in the Ottawa Valley, and finally in Montreal where he pioneered a work. The church he built and pastored in Montreal until his death in 1947 became one of the most influential Pentecostal centres in Eastern Canada.

While in Ottawa, several issues of *The Good Report* detailing the progress of the Pentecostal Movement were published and distributed, but it is impossible to say how many. The early press runs totaled 45,000 copies which were distributed without charge. McAlister trusted the Lord to provide the funds as needed. He also prepared another periodical, entitled *The Morning Star*, which was sent to Herbert Randall in Egypt for translation and publication. One result of the first distribution of this paper was the conversion of 50 readers.

The most significant contribution which McAlister made in the publishing field was the creation of *The Pentecostal Testimony*, still the official publication of the PAOC. The *Testimony* played a seminal role in the development of Canadian Pentecostalism, for it was the chief means of spreading the news of evangelistic campaigns, camp meetings, church openings, business conferences, missions conventions, and information from the foreign field. McAlister contributed to the establishment of the first full-fledged Pentecostal Bible school in Canada by advertising its curriculum in the *Testimony*, urging young believers to seek formal training in preparation for the ministry. The magazine was an important unifying agent for the thin band of Pentecostal groups which stretched from coast to coast. McAlister's keen perception of the value of the press in disseminating the full gospel was a mark of the man's astuteness.

R. E. McAlister had another unique characteristic — one to which he seldom referred in his works but which his colleagues admired with great sincerity. He was gifted with a photographic memory. McAlister once noted that if he read a passage of Scripture three times, he forever retained it in his memory. He used this rare gift to great advantage in preaching; indeed, he could quote an entire book of the Bible during his discourses.

Gordon Atter, who knew McAlister very well, considered him to be one of the greatest of the first generation of Pentecostal preachers in Canada. At that time, according to Atter, a preacher who did not move about in a vigorous style on the platform was considered a "dud." McAlister, however, rarely moved. He had a rather monotonous type of delivery and tended to preach long sermons. Yet,

> he was one of the greatest preachers we had because of his material. He never went into the pulpit but what he was completely prepared. As an example, he could preach 30 sermons on the Book of Revelation and never open the Bible. He could quote it verbatim.... When he was through, you would remember that sermon, and his altar calls were tremendous. A logical expositor, almost like a lawyer.[55]

Dr. C. M. Wortman expressed great admiration for McAlister's preaching abilities, noting, "He had a way of marshalling the truths of the Bible so as to overwhelm the listener." Often his sermons were interrupted by spontaneous praises to God. J. H. Blair, who was led to the Lord by McAlister in 1915 at Metcalfe, Ontario, was equally impressed by the man's skill. It was "his logical presentation of the truth that appealed to me; also his sane and well-ordered type of religious service."[56]

Like a number of other early leaders, McAlister was for a short time associated with the so-called "Jesus Only" group. The indefatigable evangelist managed to attend the World-Wide Camp Meeting of 1913 in Arroyo Seco near Los Angeles. The camp became famous as the scene of the introduction of the "Jesus Only" doctrine among early Pentecostals. McAlister was associated also, at various times, with Frank Ewart and Franklin Small, both advocates of the "Jesus Only" teachings. For example, he shared preaching duties with them between 1913 and 1917 at Los Angeles, Toronto, and Winnipeg. By that latter date, the heretical tendencies of their doctrine began to become more evident and thus to come under increasing attack.

It was not until after the formal organization of the PAOC in 1919 that McAlister formally renounced the "Oneness" doctrine. That he was involved at all can be attributed to the lack, among the pioneer ministers,

2 / "THIS IS THE PENTECOST"

of any systematic statement of their cardinal doctrines. Another factor was the lack of any form of Pentecostal organization until 1914 in the United States and 1919 in Canada. Furthermore, the number of Pentecostals relative to the population in Canada was quite small, and even that small number (only 513 Pentecostals in 1911) was scattered over the whole country. The most important reason, however, was that the earliest form of the "Jesus Only" teaching was primarily an emphasis on worship of Christ. None of the pioneers could fault a teaching which exalted Jesus as Lord, and only gradually did doctrinal aberrations develop. When they did, R. E. McAlister took a prominent role in denouncing them. In fact, he became a champion of orthodox trinitarianism among Canadian Pentecostals. Though lacking advanced formal education, McAlister was a pastor, evangelist, author, theologian, financier, administrator, and a promoter of missions both at home and abroad. He was for many years the acknowledged constitutional expert for the denomination, and served for years as its secretary-treasurer. His colleagues considered him a man with God-given wisdom. Many a thorny issue on the conference floor was solved by his counsel. When a serious schism, which had its origins in Saskatchewan in the 1940s, posed a deadly threat to the Fellowship throughout Canada, McAlister was instrumental in stopping its spread. He helped to minimize its impact by travelling through the affected areas and presenting solid, biblical teaching in many of the churches.

He was a prime mover in the organizational activities from 1917 to 1919 which resulted in the granting of a federal charter for the PAOC. Although he and his colleagues were loath to set up another denomination, they were determined, through the chartering of this new religious movement in Canada, to "protect doctrine" and to preserve the fruits of the great apostolic revival sweeping over the land. To this end, they were successful. As G. A. Chambers put it, "A spontaneous spiritual movement continued for many years" after the outpourings at Azusa Street and at the Hebden Mission.

Chambers' summary of the course of the Pentecostal renewal in its first decade in the Dominion reads like a repetition of the Book of Acts. He claimed that thousands had been saved, filled with the Holy Ghost, and healed. As for early Pentecostal meetings, he wrote:

> Services would run all night, for weeks at a time. People would be slain under the power of God, sometimes for days, and frequently for hours. Supernatural manifestations were the order of the day. Services did not depend on a leader. . . . Supernatural signs were witnessed by many. . . . People have been lifted bodily into mid-air by the power of the Holy Spirit. Literal tongues of fire have been

seen sitting on the heads of the worshippers. . . . Those were days of Heaven on Earth, days for which the church is praying that they will return again.[57]

Chambers' glowing account had reference to the Pentecostal Movement throughout Canada. More restrained reports of those extraordinary meetings have been given by A. G. Ward and R. E. McAlister. All these leaders made the point that the work of the Spirit was independent of any human leadership. It became a truism among the pioneers that the revivalistic movement had "no human founder" in Canada. This theme of divine origins appeared repeatedly in their sermons and writings.

Another prominent theme was, as Ward put it, "at long last the 'end time' is upon us." So deeply committed to the concept of an imminent return of Jesus Christ were these early 20th-century Pentecostals that they tended to ignore the economic, political, and social issues of their day. Curiously, their chiliasm did not blind them to the potential for fanaticism and doctrinal error that existed in the absence of any formal denominational structure.

Certainly, R. E. McAlister played a seminal role in the organizational process. Another portrait, from one who knew him well, aptly summarizes his early contributions in this regard:

> Wherever he went, he left a trail of Pentecostal blessing. From his pen flowed forth a constant stream of Pentecostal literature . . . He became a tower of strength in shaping the Canadian Fellowship in its early organization, in its missionary program, and especially in its sound doctrinal development.[58]

Endnotes

1. The emphasis was placed on the word "full" in the expression, "the full gospel." The inference was that the gospel should include not only Salvation, but also the Baptism in the Holy Spirit, Divine Healing, and the Second Coming of Christ.
2. Thomas Wm. Miller, "The Canadian 'Azusa': The Hebden Mission in Toronto," *Pneuma*, 8:1 (Spring 1986), 5-29.
3. E. Hebden, "How Pentecost Came to Toronto," *The Promise*, 1, (May 1907); see also *The Apostolic Faith*, 1:6 (February-March 1907), 4. Mrs. Hebden's comments seem to indicate that she was unacquainted at the time with the work of the Azusa Street Mission.
4. William Seymour, ed., *The Apostolic Faith*, 1:4 (December 1906), 3.
5. George C. Slager, letter to W. E. McAlister, March 24, 1954, typed copy in PAOC Archives.
6. Stanley H. Frodsham, *With Signs Following* (Springfield: Gospel Publishing House, 1946), p. 53.

2 / "THIS IS THE PENTECOST"

7. G. A. Chambers, "Fifty Years Ago," *The Pentecostal Testimony* (May 1956), 6.
8. *The Apostolic Faith*, 1:6 (January 1907), 1; see also A. S. Copley, "Pentecost in Toronto," p. 4 of the same edition.
9. George A. Chambers, "History of the Pentecostal Assemblies of Canada," handwritten memoirs, PAOC Archives.
10. See note 5.
11. "A Trip to Abingdon," *The Promise*, 12 (February 1909), 3; Mrs. J. Atter, "Reminiscences of Pioneer Days," *Western Ontario Full Gospel Advocate*, 1:4 (February 1, 1944); and Gordon F. Atter, *Down Memory's Lane* (Port Colborne: for the author, 1974), pp. 5-8.
12. See note 3.
13. "Convention," *The Promise*, 14 (October 1909), 2.
14. *The Promise*, 15 (March 1910).
15. Data derived from a summary of Pentecostal overseas missionaries, PAOC Archives, c. 1956.
16. *The Promise*, 15 (March 1910), 8; see also *Songs of the Reaper: The Story of the Pentecostal Assemblies of Saskatchewan* (Saskatoon: PAOC Sask. District, 1985), p. 75.
17. See note 2.
18. G. A. Chambers, *50 Years in the Service of the King, 1907-1957* (Toronto: Full Gospel Publishing House, 1960); Gloria G. Kulbeck, *What God Hath Wrought: A History of the Pentecostal Assemblies of Canada* (Toronto: PAOC, 1958), p. 107; and James Montgomery, "The Pentecostal Assemblies of Canada: Canada's Oldest Pentecostal Denomination: 1919-1969," *Jubilee Souvenir* (Toronto: PAOC, 1969).
19. "Memories: the Story of 75 Years in Vineland," anniversary brochure, Vineland Pentecostal Church, 1983.
20. Thomas Wm. Miller, taped interview with Gordon F. Atter, April 30, 1984.
21. Roy Clifford Spaetzel, *History of the Kitchener Gospel Temple, 1909-1974* (Kitchener: for the author, 1974), pp. 5-16.
22. Gordon F. Atter, *The Third Force* (Peterborough: College Press, 3rd ed. rev. 1970), p. 39; see also George A Chambers, *50 Years in the Service of the King 1907-1957*.
23. A. G. Ward, "My Personal Experience of Pentecost," *The Pentecostal Testimony* (May 1956) , 7.
24. A. G. Ward, "How the Pentecostal Experience Came to Canada," typed copy of letter, PAOC Archives.

25. A. G. Ward, "Hitherto Hath the Lord Helped Us," *The Pentecostal Testimony* (October 1956), 10-11; see also C. M. Ward, "Yet Once More," *The Pentecostal Testimony* (May 1956), 4, 5, 13.
26. Chambers, *50 Years in the Service of the King 1907 -1957,*. pp. 8-9; see also Helen E. Bingham, *An Irish Saint: the Life Story of Ann Preston* (Toronto: Evangelical Publishers, 1927).
27. Letter of Effie Moyer to Mamie McPherson, March 15, 1911. Used by permission.
28. Chambers, *50 Years in the Service of the King,* p. 20.
29. R. E. Sternall, "Angels Join in Singing With the Saints," *The Pentecostal Testimony* (May 1956), 8.
30. John T. Ball, "Early Days of Pentecost," typescript, PAOC Archives; see also G. A. Chambers, "A Tribute to John T. Ball," *The Pentecostal Testimony* (April 1956), 26; and R. J. Irvine (J. T. Ball's daughter) correspondence to Thomas Wm. Miller, April 11, 1982.
31. William Clifford Nelson, *From Plow Handles to Pulpit,* autobiographical booklet.
32. John T. Ball, note 30; Thomas Wm. Miller, taped interview with G. B. Griffin, August 5, 1984; Jack West and Harold Davis, *They Call Him Mr. Braeside: The Life Story of J. H. Blair* (Toronto: Harmony Printing), pp. 27-28.
33. John T. Ball, note 30.
34. G. A. Chambers, note 30; and W. E. McAlister, "Rev. John T. Ball Called Home," *Pentecostal Testimony* (February 1956), 9.
35. Valone Sly, Eunice Morris, and Viola Hasking, eds., *Parry Sound Pentecostal Tabernacle: Sixty Years of Service* (Parry Sound: Parry Sound Printing, 1972); and Mrs. A. E. Adams, letter to W. E. McAlister, April 1, 1954, PAOC Archives.
36. Aimee Semple McPherson, *This is That* (Los Angeles: Echo Park Evangelistic Assoc., 1923), pp. 57-58; *Aimee, The Life Story of Aimee Semple McPherson* (Los Angeles: Foursquare Publications, 1979), pp. 23, 37, 40; and "70 Years at London Gospel Temple" (London Gospel Temple, 1980), pp. 9, 11.
37. *The Promise*, 15 (March 1910), 1.
38. "The Celebration of the Golden Jubilee 1909-1959" (Kitchener: Kitchener Pentecostal Temple, 1959).
39. Aleta Piper, letter to Thomas Wm. Miller, 1983.
40. Ibid.
41. R. E. Sternall, "If I Had My Life to Live Over," *The Pentecostal Testimony* (October 1956), 15.

2 / "THIS IS THE PENTECOST"

42. Chambers, *50 Years in the Service of the King*, p. 23; and John Longhurst, "Conscientious Objectors Worked But Didn't Fight," *Abbotsford, Sumas & Matsqui News* (October 11, 1989), C11.

43. Viola Chambers Spaetzel, "A Tribute To My Mother," *The Pentecostal Testimony* (May 1967), 3, 33.

44. G. A. Chambers, "The Mille Roches Revival of 1918," *The Pentecostal Testimony* (June 1, 1943), 9.

45. Ibid.

46. Chambers, *50 Years in the Service of the King*, p. 32.

47. Mrs. G. A. Chambers, "Greetings," *Fortieth Anniversary, Glad Tidings Pentecostal Church, 1919-1958* (Arnprior: for the church, 1958), p. 5.

48. Lila McAlister Skinner, "The McAlister Family Tree," handwritten memoirs, March 1978. Used by permission.

49. *The Doctrine and Discipline of the Holiness Movement* (Ottawa: Holiness Movement Publishing House, 1907).

50. A. G. Ward, "Tributes of Fellow Ministers to R. E. McAlister," *The Pentecostal Testimony* (November 1953), 12.

51. *The Promise* 15, (March 1910), 1.

52. The Kinburn Church Minute Book has inscribed on its frontispiece: "The 9th Line Tabernacle of the Assembly of God. Dedicated May 28th, 1911."

53. "History of the Edwards Pentecostal Church," anonymous handwritten report, PAOC Archives.

54. Mrs. C. E. Baker, "Baptized and Healed," *The Good Report*, 1 (May 1911), 1.

55. Thomas Wm. Miller, taped interview with G. F. Atter, April 30, 1984.

56. See C. M. Wortman and J. H. Blair in "Tributes," note 50.

57. G. A. Chambers, "History of the PAOC," handwritten manuscript, PAOC Archives.

58. G. F. Atter, *The Third Force* (Peterborough, ON: College Press, 3rd ed. rev., 1962), p. 74.

Chapter 3

THE EARLY WORK IN THE WEST

The Pentecostal work in Western Canada is forever associated with the name of A. H. Argue and the city of Winnipeg. Although Argue was not the first in Winnipeg to receive the Baptism in the Spirit, he quickly emerged as the most prominent among the early workers. The Manitoba capital had a number of vigorous independent evangelical missions and a congregation of the Christian and Missionary Alliance. A. G. Ward was a field supervisor for the Alliance in Manitoba when he first heard of the Pentecostal outpouring. Ward's Winnipeg mission was sponsored by evangelicals such as former mayor Thomas Ryan, William Gibson, and Archdeacon Phair. His meeting hall was used also by four lady Mennonite workers: Emma Hostetler, Mary Dresch, Martha Hisey, and Mary Markle. The former three later went as Pentecostal missionaries to Africa, while Mary Markle became the wife of A. G. Ward.

Another evangelical recruit to the new revivalistic group was R. J. Scott who, having learned of the Azusa Street event, moved his family to Los Angeles late in 1906 to share in the meetings. In the reports which Scott sent back to Winnipeg, he reminded his readers that he was a skeptical type of man but that he was convinced of the validity of tongues-speaking when he heard a woman sing a Native Indian song. Scott knew the woman "never was closer than 1,200 miles from the Natives and had never been taught by anyone." Later he heard her speak in the Armenian language. Subsequently, Scott tarried in prayer for nine days and received "the Bible evidence of speaking and singing in tongues."[1]

Scott became active in Seymour's mission in Los Angeles and helped organize the first convention of Pentecostal workers in North America. A tabernacle seating 1,000 was erected outside the city and thousands came when the camp began on June 1, 1907. Scott apparently stayed in California for years; he was present in the meetings held there by the healing evangelist Maria Woodworth-Etter. He also took a leading role in the so-called World-Wide Camp Meeting at Los Angeles in 1913.[2]

A. G. Ward outlined the sequence of events which first introduced the Pentecostal experience to Winnipeg residents. A young man named John Graves, a member of a local prosperous family, "got under the burden for a national revival. He gave himself to almost unceasing prayer." During the winter of 1906-07, Graves prayed from 6 a.m. each day until 3 p.m. For 11 weeks he prayed at the Home and Foreign Mission (Alliance), then prayed another five weeks in the Wesley Methodist church. The first break, as Ward recalled, came during an all-night prayer meeting for the outpouring of the Latter Rain.

A number were baptized in the Spirit, including Graves and Ward, and a Pentecostal revival movement was inaugurated. Ward attended the first meetings held in the Argue home, but did not remain long in the West. He went to Ontario early in 1908 for meetings with the Mennonite Brethren in Christ and began a pioneering Pentecostal ministry in that part of the country. Ward made very complimentary remarks about A. H. Argue and acknowledged him as the local leader:

> Almost immediately after I received the Baptism in the Spirit, Mr. A. H. Argue, at that time a well-known and highly respected business man in Winnipeg — the man of whom it was said that God and he were the two persons who could be trusted — and who had gone to Chicago to tarry for the Holy Ghost Baptism, and who had received, returned to Winnipeg. His heart was all aflame with this new experience, and at once he opened his home for "tarrying meetings." Under his earnest and able leadership the work went forward . . . until . . . possibly thousands of people in Winnipeg and throughout Manitoba came under the mighty Latter Rain outpouring of the Spirit.[3]

His appreciation for the life work of A. H. Argue led Ward to describe him as "The Grand Old Man of Canadian Pentecostalism." A later assessment of Argue's ministry, by G. F. Atter, described him as "the greatest Pentecostal evangelist Canada produced."[4]

Andrew Harvey Argue was born in 1868 at Fitzroy Harbor, near Ottawa, the grandson of a Methodist layman who had come to Canada from Ireland in 1821. After building their first log home in the wilderness, the elder Argue invited neighbors for the first Methodist meetings in that area. His son John was a Methodist lay preacher, or "exhorter," who moved his family, which by then included Andrew, to a farm in North

THE EARLY WORK IN THE WEST / 3

Dakota. It was there that A. H. Argue was converted during revival services conducted by the Salvation Army. He was not an unruly young man, but had been determined, against his father's wishes, to play his violin at the local dances. The night he was saved, he walked only halfway to the altar before he received an assurance of sins forgiven. Another result of the revival meetings was that Argue met a Canadian girl named Eva who had been assisting in the services. They were soon married and began a five-year stint as farmers in North Dakota. Their first two children, Zelma and Harvey, who later were to assist their father in Pentecostal meetings, were born there before the Argue family moved to Winnipeg.

It was an astute move, for the city was then at the heart of the great economic boom of the Canadian West. Together with his brothers, Argue launched a successful real estate business. Winnipeg was the gateway to the new homestead lands opening up in the West, and many thousands of European immigrants came through the city. In the decade after 1900, while the city increased to a population of 450,000, land and housing were in great demand. The Argue firm prospered for several reasons, certainly not the least of which was the saying in the region that "God and A. H. Argue are the only two persons who can be trusted."

A. H. Argue had a keen interest in gospel work, having himself served as a Methodist exhorter. He used his resources to support various local ministries, and travelled, at his own expense, to preach at camp meetings in Ontario. He also was involved in the Holiness Movement, and became a close friend of Dr. George Watson, who preached "the deeper truths" in Winnipeg. In fact, Argue named his son Watson after his friend. Through his Holiness contacts and the Alliance Mission in Winnipeg, Argue met Anglican Archdeacon Phair, who later became an enthusiastic Pentecostal. Another friend was the American bishop, J. H. King, of the Fire-Baptized Holiness Church, with whom he worked in Ontario church meetings. King later became a prominent Pentecostal pioneer in Georgia. Winnipeg was the scene of Argue's meeting with A. B. Simpson, the founder of the Christian and Missionary Alliance. When Simpson preached divine healing during the winter of 1906, Argue went for prayer and was healed of "a chronic internal trouble" which he had suffered for many years.[5]

The beginning of the 20th century was marked by an unusual manifestation of spiritual hunger among a multitude of evangelical believers in North America. Even before the Pentecostal experience arrived in Winnipeg, there had come news of extraordinary movings of the Holy Spirit around the world. Information on the outpouring of the Spirit, in Topeka, Kansas in 1900-01, was followed by news of the 1904

3 / THE EARLY WORK IN THE WEST

Welsh Revival. There was a similar move of God in Pandita Ramabai's mission in India and the Door of Hope Mission in China. Finally, there was the Azusa Street Revival of 1906 in Los Angeles, with a similar move of the Lord in the Hebden Mission in Toronto. Zelma Argue has commented on the urgent prayers of Winnipeg believers at that time for a divine effusion of the Spirit in their city. Another student of Pentecostalism in the West was W. J. Taylor, former superintendent of the Manitoba and Northwestern Ontario District of the PAOC. In his early history of that district, he noted that "This hunger seemed to be a worldwide phenomenon . . . Groups of people in Manitoba had been in continuous prayer for revival, and for a mighty visitation from God." Reports sent in 1907 to Seymour in Los Angeles confirmed that "the saints" in Winnipeg had long been praying for "an outpouring of His Spirit . . . and especially for a revival . . ."[6]

A. H. Argue was preaching at a camp meeting at Thornbury, Ontario, when he first read in a tract about the Azusa Street meetings. He showed it to Bishop J. H. King, also at the camp. King's reply was that it "could be possible" that people could speak in unknown tongues. Argue went back to Winnipeg, learned all he could about the Latter Rain revival, then travelled to Chicago to W. H. Durham's North Avenue Mission. Durham had recently received the Baptism in the Holy Spirit in Los Angeles and had turned his Chicago mission into a Pentecostal centre. Curiously, there seemed to be no contact at that time between Argue and Mrs. Hebden in Toronto. In the Windy City, Argue sought for the Baptism in an atmosphere of excitement and religious phenomena. The mission was so full of divine power, according to eyewitnesses, that "a thick haze . . . like blue smoke" filled its upper region. When this haze was present, some people entering the building fell down in the aisles before reaching the pews. Many received the Baptism in the Spirit as well as supernatural healing of various diseases. A. H. Argue witnessed some of these events:

> . . . I waited on God for 21 days. . . . During this time I had a wonderful vision of Jesus. . . . I was filled with the Holy Ghost, speaking with other tongues as the Spirit gave utterance.[7]

When Argue entered into the Pentecostal experience, he was nearly 40 years of age, not a time of life when men usually enter the ministry. Yet he was soon to begin a 20-year career as one of the leading Pentecostal evangelists in North America. His background as a Methodist exhorter and a supporter of various mission works in Winnipeg, his supernatural healing, and his Baptism in the Holy Spirit with tongues-speaking were characteristics shared by many of the early Pentecostal leaders. Argue now had practical experience, an evangelical theology, and a charismatic encounter with God. Coupled with these were his natural gifts as a speaker and his platform skills. He was over six feet in height, ruggedly handsome, with a powerful voice and an energetic delivery.

All that Argue needed to complete his doctrinal system, and fulfil the model of a first-generation Canadian Pentecostal preacher, was a conviction that the Second Coming of Christ was imminent. This theological certainty was quick in coming, as the Rapture of the Church was almost immediately highlighted among the Latter Rain believers. In fact, the very term "Latter Rain" signified their conviction that they were the forerunners of the last great move of God on earth prior to the Second Coming. Thus A. H. Argue started his full-time ministry as an evangelist with what became the four cardinal doctrines of Pentecostalism enshrined in his theology: Salvation, Divine Healing, Baptism in the Holy Spirit, and the Second Coming.

After Argue received his personal Pentecost, he sent a telegram to his wife Eva which read, "Received Baptism in Holy Spirit. Coming home on first train." His daughter Zelma described how awed her mother was at the prospect of a Spirit-filled husband:

> Filled with the Holy Ghost, and now coming home! When the door opened and . . . in walked father, she actually stood back at the other end of the room, uncertain how to greet one who had received this sacred experience. We have smiled over it since.[8]

Immediately upon his return, he opened his home for so-called "tarrying meetings" in which earnest seekers prayed for the Baptism in the Holy Ghost. He quickly became the acknowledged leader of the new religious group. Argue had once held revival meetings in North Dakota in which over 50 people were saved, but the meetings in Winnipeg soon outstripped all previous achievements. He withdrew from the real estate business, invested his money in income-producing property, and thus became financially independent. So wise were his investments that he was able to provide for his own necessities until his death in his 91st year. After he began itinerating throughout America as an evangelist, he often gave the "love offering" back to the pastor of some struggling Pentecostal mission.

Other meetings were held in the home of a Mrs. Lockhart in the Manitoba capital. But the first to receive the Baptism in the Spirit, after meetings began in the Argue home, were Emil Schwab, followed by Mrs. Lockhart, and then a Mrs. Campbell. This historic "first" occurred either

3 / THE EARLY WORK IN THE WEST

on May 2 or May 3. Argue's own account used the former date, which may be considered the birthday of the Pentecostal Movement in Western Canada. Other Pentecostal meetings began about the same time in Vancouver, British Columbia, through the ministry of workers from nearby Portland, Oregon. However, their efforts were sporadic and their successes minimal.

The Winnipeg work was the earliest full-time Pentecostal ministry in the West. When the Spirit fell upon believers in the Argue home, the news spread like wildfire and scores came to the meetings. A Winnipeg Pentecostal thought them important enough to report the first meetings to Seymour in Los Angeles. The writer referred to Argue's sermon on that auspicious occasion, when local believers first spoke in tongues. The text was Acts 10:44-46. The Winnipeg meetings also were significant for their eventual impact on the Assemblies of God in the United States. Stanley Horton, an AG preacher and Bible College instructor, reported that his father Harry had received a "mighty baptism . . . in cottage prayer meetings in Winnipeg."[9]

News of the unusual meetings attracted hundreds of people from various Manitoba communities. Some of these were destined to become prominent later in the new movement. Franklin Small had arrived from Ontario in 1900 and was converted in Winnipeg. He and his mother attended the Argue Mission at 501 Alexander Avenue. She told her son, Franklin, the meetings "were the nearest thing to old-fashioned Methodism" she had seen since childhood. For a time Small assisted Argue, acquiring the practical experience needed by a full gospel preacher. Later he began itinerating throughout North America and still later became one of the prime movers in the establishment of the PAOC. Small left the Fellowship when it rejected the "Jesus Only" doctrine.[10]

A. G. Ward's involvement in the Winnipeg revival was a brief one, though he spent some time preaching on northern Manitoba Native reserves. He was once preaching through a Native interpreter when, to his astonishment, he found himself preaching in an unknown language. The interpreter told him he had spoken in a local Native dialect. John McAlister, a skilled harness-maker in Winnipeg, was filled with the Spirit in the Argue meetings, as was his son Walter. John later settled in Edmonton where he became a lay preacher of the full gospel. Walter eventually became the General Superintendent of the PAOC. His own account of his Baptism is full of poignant interest:

> I received the Baptism of the Spirit in his mission at 501 Alexander Avenue. . . . A. H. Argue was a very godly man. As a young boy in his mission I looked up to him as the most saintly man I'd ever seen. His face just seemed to glow with the glory of God.[11]

THE EARLY WORK IN THE WEST / 3

Early Pentecostalism spread in a spontaneous manner throughout the province of Manitoba. Many of those filled with the Spirit in Winnipeg became zealous Pentecostal proclaimers in their home areas. For example, an elderly believer from Poplar Point testified to his friends when he returned home. About 20 received the Baptism, with accompanying tongues, and a Latter Rain/Pentecostal assembly was established. Other communities quickly reached with the full gospel were Elmwood, Dauphin, Portage la Prairie, Brandon, Fort Frances, and the Rainy River district. From the Argue Mission (at first called "The Apostolic Faith Mission") the Pentecostal message spread to southern Manitoba and to the northern Native reserves. The southern centres included Cartwright, Mather, Milner, and Neelin. From the reserves, Natives came by dog sled and train, in the middle of winter, to the Winnipeg mission, and returned to spark local revivals throughout the North. Even well-known American leaders visited the city. Among them was Mrs. Florence Crawford who had been one of the main workers at the Azusa Street Mission before she began itinerating in the western states. Eventually, she founded a Pentecostal association called the Apostolic Faith with headquarters in Portland, Oregon. Mrs. Crawford was present when A. H. Argue held a Pentecostal convention in Winnipeg in November of 1907.[12]

The Argue meetings attracted a significant number of people from the better-educated classes in the city. Although persecution often was experienced in the form of disruptive and mocking spectators, broken windows, and abusive shouting, the work was not seriously affected. Despite such opposition, prominent businessmen, leading citizens, and even clergymen were brought into the Pentecostal experience. One of the best known was Archdeacon Phair, for 40 years an Anglican minister and a college professor. Initially, he condemned the meetings, but later was himself filled with the Spirit. Another respected convert to Pentecostalism was Professor A. D. Baker of St. John's College in Winnipeg. These clergy recruits were all the more extraordinary because they were joining ranks with Argue, a man who had only a grade-six education (average for that time) and was a self-taught theologian.

Argue excelled as a preacher and evangelist. A family member said that after his Baptism in the Spirit, "he just lived in the Bible. He memorized the New Testament, especially the Book of Acts." Historian Gordon Atter was greatly impressed by Argue's evangelistic talents. He was very energetic on the platform, moved about a great deal, and had a powerful delivery. To illustrate this point, Atter told of a time when a famous Cincinnati preacher was dismally failing in his pulpit ministry. Argue was present, was called upon to preach, and "in five minutes he had 29 sinners at the altar."[13]

3 / THE EARLY WORK IN THE WEST

In 1908, Argue went on a tour of Eastern United States and visited Toronto en route. It is interesting that he sent an account of the meetings to Seymour in Los Angeles. His report is proof of the cordial relationship that long existed between the Winnipeg and the Los Angeles believers. In Toronto, Argue shared briefly in pioneering ministry with the workers in that area.[14] The next stop was New York City where 25 people received the Baptism. More meetings were held in Philadelphia, Baltimore, Washington; and then in Chicago, where there already were about 14 Pentecostal missions. Stops at Zion City, St. Paul, and Minneapolis witnessed similar moves of the Spirit upon eager crowds of listeners.

After returning to Winnipeg, the indefatigable preacher launched a publishing ministry to spread the news of the Latter Rain revival. He prepared a summary of the Canadian work in a little paper called *The Promise of Pentecost*. It was published in Egypt (it appears he was in contact with the missionaries Lawler and Randall) in both Arabic and English. Argue's message was spread widely in North America by his own paper, titled *The Apostolic Messenger*. Some issues ran to over 40,000 copies which he distributed without charge. This paper was so popular among early Pentecostals that it was requested in 1911 by a missionary in El Salvador. In its pages, Argue wrote very effectively about the worldwide move of God, citing more than 40 countries where the Pentecostal Movement had begun. He also used its pages to defend the Pentecostal doctrines, explaining why the charismata had disappeared by his day, and citing John Wesley to explain how the gifts could be recovered.[15]

Argue desired to become better acquainted with the Pentecostal work in Los Angeles and moved his family there in 1912. He left responsibility for the Winnipeg congregation to a group of five laymen. Franklin Small and other acknowledged speakers were assigned the preaching tasks. The family moved back to Manitoba in 1916, but not before Argue had distinguished himself as one of the leading evangelists of the North American Pentecostal Movement. While the children continued their education, an important part of which was acquiring skill in playing musical instruments, Argue travelled in evangelism. His goal, even at that early date, was to associate his children, Watson and Zelma, with him in evangelistic work.

His interest in divine healing led Argue to establish a close connection with Mrs. Woodworth-Etter, the famous healing evangelist. He shared in the dedication service for her new tabernacle in Indianapolis, then assisted her at the 1913 World-Wide Camp Meeting at Los Angeles. He witnessed "some most marvellous healings" and noted that many had been filled with the Spirit and had spoken in tongues. People attended from many parts of the USA, Canada, and even from foreign lands. Subsequently, the Canadian evangelist itinerated throughout America preaching in camp meetings, religious conventions, and evangelistic campaigns. His reputation was such that he was invited by American Pentecostals to share in discussions that led to the eventual formation of the Assemblies of God in 1914.

A. H. Argue was a trusted associate of such early American leaders as W. H. Durham, E. N. Bell, and H. G. Rogers. Each of these leaders recognized the growing need for some form of organization to preserve and perpetuate the Pentecostal revival. Many had called themselves the "Apostolic Faith" people, but this proved less satisfactory after Florence Crawford founded a church organization in Portland, Oregon, and titled it "The Apostolic Faith." Discontent arose with this latter designation because of the "many regrettable things" which had taken place under the "Apostolic Faith" label.[16] H. G. Rogers and about 50 other full gospel workers selected a new title for themselves — "The Church of God," but it was too similar to that of another, earlier organization. In 1913, this body of ministers, by then numbering about 350 workers, met to draw up a list of recognized Pentecostal individuals and to set up criteria for holding credentials.

Further organizational work was done at the Interstate Camp Meeting in Eureka Springs, Arkansas, in 1913. That same year, E. N. Bell called for a "Bureau of Information" to supply "authentic information from the field." The "bureau" which was formed included "A. H. Argue of Long Beach, California." This group was active in subsequent meetings which led to the establishment of the Assemblies of God at Hot Springs, Arkansas, in 1914. The new body was to be an "association," not a new denomination. Hierarchal forms of church government had been one of the chief sources of the reproach and opposition they had encountered since Azusa Street. Another factor contributing to the emergence of a loosely-knit association was the threat of doctrinal error posed by the "New Issue" teachings.

The "New Issue," later called "Jesus Only" or the "Oneness" doctrine, was known to the Latter Rain and Apostolic Faith groups from the inception of the 20th-century Pentecostal Movement. Its origins lie far back in the history of the Church, but its modern manifestation was a source of constant disagreement among early Pentecostals. Two of the best-known early evangelists, Andrew Urshan and Jack D. Saunders, debated the Jesus Only doctrine in Los Angeles in 1909 and attracted a large crowd. At the World-Wide Camp Meeting of 1913 near Los Angeles, R. E. McAlister noted, while preaching, that the baptismal formula in Acts was not the same as the one in the gospels. That night, a

3 / THE EARLY WORK IN THE WEST

man named John Scheppe had a "revelation" about the name of Jesus in which was combined all the fullness of God. Revelations were difficult to refute; besides, how could anyone oppose a teaching that so greatly exalted the Lord Jesus?

Only gradually did the threat to the historic Christian faith become apparent. A. H. Argue was one of the first to take a resolute stand against the Jesus Only teaching. In his ministry as an evangelist, however, he sought to avoid controversy by baptizing converts with the formula, "In the Name of the Lord Jesus Christ, I baptize you into the Father, Son and Holy Ghost."[17] After his return to Canada in 1916, Argue was joined by John McAlister in resisting attempts to implant the Oneness teaching as a doctrinal plank in the theology of the Pentecostal believers.

Argue made Winnipeg his headquarters for his wide-ranging evangelistic ministry after 1916. C. O. Benham was pastor of the Winnipeg assembly from 1916 to 1919. Argue assisted in the services while in the city between evangelistic meetings. The local assembly was troubled by "problems," as Argue referred to them, in connection with the work of Franklin Small. Small had adopted the Jesus Only doctrine and had founded a rival church in that city. In spite of the problems, the mission experienced steady growth. In meetings in 1917, about 75 received the Baptism with tongues-speaking. Since larger quarters were needed, the old Wesley church was acquired. A noteworthy convert in 1917 was J. Rutherford Spence, who later became a missionary to China.

The Winnipeg church from its inception had been missions-minded as well as evangelistically oriented, largely because of the leadership of A. H. Argue. His zeal for evangelism both at home and overseas was motivated by a belief that the Lord could return at any time — possibly, as he noted, even within "five years." Though he never made the mistake of setting a day, Argue lived with the conviction that the "parousia" could take place at any moment. His preaching reflected that view. His favorite book, next to the Bible, was a volume titled, *Forty Future Wonders: Predicted in Daniel and Revelation*. Robert Smith, a Pentecostal pastor and grandson of Argue, reports that he rarely saw his grandfather without this book.[18] Other prominent features of his early ministry were his conviction that God still heals today and that every believer should receive the Baptism in the Spirit. In fact, it was said of A. H. Argue, by many of his contemporaries, that he could start preaching at any point in the Bible and would always end in Acts 2:4!

Between 1916 and 1920, Argue's chief contribution to the fledging Pentecostal Movement lay in making Winnipeg a centre for evangelism and discipleship for Western Canada. He was primarily an evangelist, not an administrator, but his tireless labors helped establish new congregations in the faith. For example, in 1917 he assisted W. L. Draffin in his Pentecostal mission in Toronto. Many were converted and about 200 received the Pentecostal experience. It was in this assembly that Willard and Christine Pierce acquired training for the ministry. Another notable recruit was Beatrice Sims, who herself became an effective evangelist. The Winnipeg church provided Pentecostalism with a number of other preachers and evangelists, as well as overseas workers. Archdeacon Phair became active in outreach after his personal Pentecost. H. E. Robinson itinerated, like the early Methodists, among assemblies of believers in the Rainy River district. A Native named George Rumble from the Fisher Reserve, who had been converted in the Argue Mission, took the full gospel to his people in northern Manitoba.

Another effective lay worker influenced by Argue was Elmer Cantelon, a very successful businessman and owner-operator of a custom threshing outfit. After his conversion in Manitoba, Cantelon met A. J. Lankin, a man who had been plagued with sickness before being miraculously healed in answer to prayer. Lankin, who had assisted Argue for a time, encouraged Cantelon to engage in lay ministry. As a result, Cantelon acquired an empty church in Cartwright and founded a Pentecostal assembly. The area was notorious for drunkenness, but so many were converted in a revival in the town that the whiskey trade dwindled away to nothing. Later, Elmer Cantelon combined forces with Emil Schwab, the first to receive the Baptism in the Argue Mission, to establish the Pentecostal camp at Rock Lake, Manitoba in 1919.[19]

The impact that the "grand old man of Canadian Pentecostalism" had on the movement extended throughout Western Canada. The work done in Alberta by John McAlister could not have taken place before his personal Pentecostal experience in the Argue Mission. It was that encounter with God that gave him the power and ability to preach. George Taylor and his wife, who came into Pentecost through the Argue Mission, became pioneers of Pentecost in Red Deer, Alberta, in 1911. The full gospel message also was established in Eston, Saskatchewan, by a lay worker from Argue's church. This rapid spread of Pentecostalism throughout Canada was extraordinary for the times, given the sparse population scattered over vast distances.

The Prairie Provinces were not fully settled until after the turn of the century. They were originally developed by the Ottawa government as an outlet for the manufacturing products of Ontario industries and as a source of raw materials. Manitoba had a head-start in population growth because of its Métis communities and the early establishment of Hudson Bay posts which prospered through the fur trade. After its incorporation as a province in 1870, Manitoba was quickly filled with thousands of

3 / THE EARLY WORK IN THE WEST

immigrants who came to take up the government's offer of free land. Since many came from Ontario and the eastern provinces and a considerable number from Europe, the population base was largely Anglo-Saxon and French-Canadian with a mixture of Germans, Icelanders, and other Europeans.

By contrast, Saskatchewan did not achieve provincial status until 1905, and it had a more heterogeneous population mix. Thousands came from the nearby Dakotas and other northern states, and many thousands more from Europe. These latter groups tended to settle in communities where race, language, and religious characteristics could be preserved. To this day, the highway from Prince Albert to Lloydminster passes through communities which are mainly one ethnic grouping — Swedish, Hungarian, French-Canadian, Russian, German, and English. Typically, these groups retained their mother tongues for three generations. As a result, cross-cultural communication proved difficult for the early Pentecostal evangelists.

Another hindrance to the rapid spread of Pentecostalism on the Prairies was the lack of familiarity of many of the newcomers with American Revivalism or the late 19th-century Holiness Movement. Both of these elements were prominent in the religious heritage of the first generation of Pentecostals in North America. A third limitation in the growth of the Pentecostal Movement was the difficulty of travel throughout the Prairies. Winters were long and very cold. Roads were often just dirt tracks in the new settlements. It was not until after the Second World War that the major highways in Saskatchewan were finally paved. Despite these hindrances, the news of the outpouring of the Spirit, both in Los Angeles and Toronto, had reached some Prairie residents as early as 1907.

S. T. Odegaard, of Brownlee, Saskatchewan, long had felt that his religious experience was unsatisfactory; he desired more power to live for God. A little paper from Seattle, Washington, with teachings on the Baptism came into his possession. When he visited the Hebden Mission in Toronto, he received his personal Pentecost. Upon his return he founded a Pentecostal assembly in Moose Jaw, although he remained primarily a lay preacher all his life. He supported this work financially for many years. In 1920 his name appeared in a list of pastors in the first issue of *The Pentecostal Testimony*. An autumn convention was held in his church in 1921.[20]

The Pentecostal message reached Melfort in north-central Saskatchewan sometime in 1907. Joseph Grainger had visited the Seymour mission in Los Angeles and had taken the full gospel message back to his friends and neighbors. He reported, in a letter to Seymour, that "I can report victory in my soul and have been joined by my precious wife on the upward march. . . . There are many hungry souls here eager for the Gospel."[21] Another resident of the province who was influenced by the Azusa work was E. W. Johnson of Stockholm. Around the middle of 1907, he wrote to Los Angeles to report a miraculous healing through prayer.

Healed By The Lord

I feel led by the Holy Spirit to testify to the glory of God. . . . The Lord has wonderfully healed me from cataract of nine years' standing. . . . Just before this, my wife was very sick, as near death as I have ever seen . . . but we got some of the saints to pray for her and He wonderfully came and healed her. . . . So she pitched her medicine out once and for all and took Jesus as her only Doctor.[22]

The letter from Johnson is evidence of the existence of a group in Stockholm who believed in divine healing and who had contact with the full gospel message within a few months of the outpouring of the Spirit in Los Angeles.

Pentecostalism in southern Saskatchewan is associated with the ministries of Franklin Small and C. A. C. Story. Small's sister lived in the Eston district, where prayer meetings had been held for some time before his arrival in 1914. He held a few meetings, but the crowds were small and his duties in Winnipeg obliged him to leave. Two female workers continued with meetings among the local farmers. Plans were laid for a camp meeting at Trossachs in July of 1914, at which Small and A. H. Argue were to preach. A local assembly resulted from these efforts, but more success attended the ministry of an Assemblies of God evangelist, Hugh Cadwalder. He came to Manitoba for meetings in Winnipeg, then moved to Eston for a few weeks. For two months there was no outward response to his full gospel message. Then a break came in a prayer meeting in which 14 people were converted and some began to speak in tongues. Stories of these unusual events circulated rapidly throughout the region and brought many curious, and spiritually hungry, observers. Among them were Sammy Wilson, a Presbyterian student-minister, and C. A. C. Story, a godly homesteader.

The Pentecostal meetings were foreign to Wilson's experience and training, but he soon became convinced that the work was genuine and of God. After his stint as a student-minister, he completed his theological training and later became a Pentecostal clergyman. Story had taken up a homestead in 1910 near Swift Current. He and his brother F. G. M. (Gus) Story brought five horses with them, an expensive commodity at the time, and dedicated one animal to be used exclusively to carry on a lay ministry

3 / THE EARLY WORK IN THE WEST

among the new settlers. When he heard of the extraordinary meetings at Eston, he attended and soon joined with the group. Story was chosen to serve as pastor for the full gospel assembly in Eston and a new church at Hughton, about 40 miles distant. Believers in both towns provided the finances for the Story brothers (for Gus came to help him). They bought a car and evangelized other communities, including Swift Current. Story pastored in Saskatchewan for several years, then moved to British Columbia where he later became the district superintendent.[23]

The meetings at Eston attracted the attention of D. N. Buntain to the Pentecostal message. Buntain, who was converted in Prince Edward Island, had moved west to seek work. Feeling a call to the ministry, he joined the Methodist church and pastored a congregation near Doddsland, Saskatchewan. A saintly old lady in his church asked once if he "had been baptized in the Holy Ghost." Her language baffled him, but he understood it better after the Eston meetings. However, it was not until he had seen the results of Dr. Charles Price's 1920 meetings in Winnipeg that Buntain joined the Pentecostals.[24]

In a similar manner, another prominent early leader was recruited in Saskatoon. Pentecostal services were held from 1917 onward in the home of Orville Hetherington, an employee of the Canadian National Railway. Hetherington kept his secular job so he could finance his activities as a lay preacher. He rented a building in the centre of the city, fitted up the back part for living quarters, and held public meetings in the front part. Converts were few and progress was slow in Saskatoon, but 1919 saw the introduction into Pentecostal ranks of a man whose services to Canadian Pentecostalism are incalculable, J. Eustace Purdie.

Purdie was the rector of St. James' Anglican church in Saskatoon when he received the Baptism in the Spirit with speaking in tongues. His first exposure to the Pentecostal Movement had occurred in Campbellton, New Brunswick, in 1911. But it was not until after he completed his theological studies in Toronto, and moved to Saskatoon, that he entered into a similar experience. His own account is reprinted below:

> ... two Pentecostal evangelists, Brother and Sister Crouch from the USA ... had a marvellous prayer meeting in the rectory when hands were laid upon me ... the power of God swept me off my seat. ... Since those days I have anointed hundreds for healing and prayed with as many seekers for the infilling of the Holy Spirit, and in nearly every case the Spirit manifested Himself in me by tongues flowing from my lips.[25]

On another occasion, when recalling that event, Purdie spoke of the coming of the evangelists as providential. Since both had a Holiness background, they found immediate acceptance with the young rector who had been much influenced by reading Phoebe Palmer's *Guide to Holiness* magazine. He added, "God was . . . most anxious that I meet these two servants of the Lord."[26]

The evidence of Divine Providence in Purdie's life was clear to all who knew him as the founder of the first permanent Canadian Pentecostal Bible school, and as its principal for a quarter-century. Many of the first generation of full gospel workers in the Dominion, who rose to positions of leadership in The Pentecostal Assemblies of Canada, were products of this college. Even his boyhood days on Prince Edward Island were significant, in retrospect, in leading him to a vital role in Pentecostal education. After his conversion in Charlottetown in 1889, he became a zealous lay worker in the evangelical "low church" branch of the Anglican Church. In 1902, he began studies in Wycliffe College in Toronto, an institution founded to combat the "high church" sacramentalism then becoming so dominant in Canadian Anglicanism. The evangelical professors there had a lasting impact on Purdie's life and views. When he founded the Pentecostal Bible school in Winnipeg in 1925, he based its whole curriculum on the model he had admired at Wycliffe.

Purdie pastored several churches in the United States and in St. John, New Brunswick. It was there he acquired experience in revival work by assisting Evangelist Reuben Torrey in a 1920 campaign. He thereafter employed the revivalistic terminology of Torrey in his own services. He also witnessed the conversion of 250 people at meetings in Fredericton, New Brunswick, when Bishop Richardson preached in local churches. So the young Anglican preacher developed a high regard for the revival technique as well as a keen interest in the doctrines of the Holiness Movement. These experiences helped make him receptive to the Pentecostal message when it came to Saskatoon.

The city then had a population of about 35,000. Purdie's church, St. James, was one of the finest structures in the community. Purdie was concerned about the impact of new doctrines on his people. New theological liberalism, known as "modernism," was sweeping through the mainline denominations of North America with disastrous effects. Fortunately for Purdie, his local bishop was evangelical in his views, and supportive of all that his rector sought to do to guard his congregation from error. One such effort involved a preaching mission with Dr. William Evans of Moody Bible Institute as the speaker. The salvation messages led to the conversion of about 45 people. Similar meetings were held in the church, one of which featured the famous Congregational clergyman, G. Campbell Morgan. Bearing in mind that he had an

3 / THE EARLY WORK IN THE WEST

Anglican assembly, Purdie adopted a method "the Lord gave me for Anglican people." After his sermon, he invited any who wished more instruction on the Scripture to remain for counselling. He used lay assistants to instruct the inquirers on the way to salvation. People came from over 100 miles away to attend these meetings. Although Purdie was talented in this work, he was convinced that his Baptism in the Spirit had infused his ministry with increased spiritual power.

When young Walter McAlister was just beginning his life-long Pentecostal ministry, he came to Saskatoon, about 1919, and preached in Purdie's church. Dr. Purdie recalled his impressions of McAlister:

> He was only about 21 then . . . and he was really remarkable for a young man, the people thought his messages were so deeply spiritual and so true to the Cross and to the Holy Spirit.[27]

The response to McAlister's ministry in the city was good, but the Pentecostal work, centred in the Hetherington mission downtown, continued to be relatively weak. After his own Pentecostal experience, Purdie led his congregation into the Baptism in the Spirit with the evidence of tongues. Some seekers, like a Brethren church member living in the countryside, came to Purdie specifically to receive the Baptism. After instruction and prayer, the Brethren man received, and spoke in tongues for over an hour. Then he and Purdie prayed for another seeker:

> We just held our hands over him and he went out full length on the floor, and when he struck the floor he was speaking in tongues. And they simply rolled out of him.[28]

The Purdie meetings in Saskatoon were characterized also by unusual healings. Arthur Lincoln, a lay evangelist, was both healed and filled with the Spirit. Mrs. William Calderbank, a parishioner, was healed of an internal hemorrhage through prayer. A Lutheran clergyman, who had received the Baptism in the Spirit in Europe, held meetings for Purdie in which people received the Baptism in a very simple manner. As Purdie recounted the event, the clergyman addressed a seeker,

> "Do you want the infilling of the Holy Ghost?"
> He said, "I do."
> "Do you want it now?"
> He said, "Yes."
> And they both stood there in faith and he said, "Be filled with the Holy Ghost now." And down he went. The Lutheran clergyman never touched him, just spoke the words, and he spoke for 40 minutes in tongues.[29]

THE EARLY WORK IN THE WEST / 3

Purdie's Pentecostal ministry in Saskatoon was unfettered by any denominational restrictions because he had the firm support of his bishop. Gradually, however, he was drawn more fully into the burgeoning Pentecostal Movement in Canada as he became well-known and highly respected by the early leaders. The St. James congregation never became fully charismatic and the main Pentecostal work in Saskatoon was established by others, such as Walter McAlister. McAlister had settled in the city after a very successful evangelistic campaign in Spruce Lake. It was his ministry that led to the firm establishment of Pentecostalism throughout the Saskatchewan district.

John McAlister stayed in Winnipeg for two years after his Baptism in the Spirit, then moved his family to Camrose, Alberta, settling soon after in Edmonton. His family attended the independent Beulah Mission, a small Holiness assembly. When the people wanted John to teach them about the Pentecostal experience, he complied with their request and ministered regularly to a small group of about 15 people. This was the nucleus of the numerous Pentecostal churches which came to be established in that region. John, who was a harness-maker, not a clergyman, relied as much as possible on guest preachers, one of the first of whom was R. E. McAlister. When McAlister had finished a successful evangelistic campaign, John was left with an increased congregation. He decided to give up his secular employment and became a Pentecostal pastor. He rented a store for $15 a month and held meetings which brought a number of people to the Lord.[30] One of the most notable results of his work was the conversion, in 1918, of a man from St. Walburg, Saskatchewan. The convert had come to the Edmonton Exhibition for a time of excitement, but went home saved and filled with the Spirit. He returned later with several friends who also were converted in the McAlister meetings. Before their return to Saskatchewan, they begged John to come and hold meetings in St. Walburg.

Walter McAlister was just then getting established as a real estate agent with a promising future in the city. But he felt great concern over the plight of the new converts and their lack of spiritual leadership. He offered to go to St. Walburg to assist in any way he could, but the men insisted they needed the elder McAlister's ministry. They were thresher-men whose skill and hard work brought them very substantial incomes. But they also were widely known in the area as hard-drinking and foul-mouthed characters. The transformation in their lives astounded their friends and relatives and disposed many residents to attend meetings when John and Walter arrived in the autumn of 1918. Services were held in the Emmaville schoolhouse. John preached for four nights before giving an altar call. When he finally gave an invitation, many flocked to

3 / THE EARLY WORK IN THE WEST

the front for salvation. John returned to Edmonton, while his son stayed on to preach at the request of the new assembly.

Walter McAlister's experience was perhaps typical of many of the first generation of Pentecostal preachers who had no formal theological training before entering the ministry. He recounted, in a humorous vein, his first sermon:

> I'd only made two attempts to preach, and failed both times. I was left in charge with no experience whatever. I had a weeknight service — it didn't go well, and I wondered what the rest of my life was going to be. . . . Sunday evening . . . the schoolhouse filled with people, and I hadn't even had the sense to make notes. . . . I'd just been reading my Bible . . . but walked up to the front, knelt down at the school-teacher's desk and prayed, "Oh God, if You don't help me now, I'm going to make the greatest failure that's ever been made." . . . We sang a few hymns, then had a little prayer, then opened the Bible and read . . . and as I looked into their faces, God gave me a love for them, and that night I preached my heart out.[31]

In the busy months that followed, Walter's ministry proved successful. Within a year about 50 had received the Baptism in the Holy Spirit with tongues. When the railroad was built through the region, the Emmaville schoolhouse was replaced by a church building erected by his congregation in the new town of Spruce Lake. The work was not without opposition. One night, all the lumber stockpiled on the building site was removed and thrown into the lake. But the believers patiently salvaged the materials and the work went on unabated. At a July 1919 convention in Edmonton, Walter was ordained with the Assemblies of God. Among those who laid hands on him and prayed were his father, H. M. Cadwalder, and A. H. Argue.

Pentecostal meetings were held in the Cut Knife area shortly after the Emmaville services began. Initially, John McAlister preached in both communities, and two local assemblies were established. After this evangelistic interlude, John returned to his own church in Edmonton. Meetings in Moose Jaw were conducted in 1919 by Walter McAlister and his younger brother Hugh. G. A. Chambers and W. L. Draffin came from the East to assist them and about 60 people received their Pentecost at that time. Many of the recipients had come from Cut Knife. When they returned home, they formed a solid nucleus for the local congregation. It was at the Moose Jaw meetings that Walter met a gentleman from Parkside, who invited him to hold meetings for a small group of Pentecostal believers in his community. He started to conduct the services in Parkside in the early 1920s. The story of those meetings is given later in this narrative.

Evangelical efforts in the town of Canwood, Saskatchewan, began with the establishment of a Baptist congregation around 1913. A lay preacher named Paul Anderson, who had received the Baptism, came from Winnipeg to hold meetings sometime prior to 1919. Through Anderson's ministry a number of Canwood residents came into the Pentecostal experience. Pastor and Mrs. Lamb led the congregation in the construction of a new Pentecostal church and a parsonage in 1919. In spite of considerable resistance in the community, people were saved, healed, and filled with the Spirit.

The Pentecostal message was taken to Maxim by lay workers Charles and Mabel Hurlbut. Mrs. Hurlbut formerly worked with Carrie Judd Montgomery, a California preacher who had a healing ministry. When they moved to Maxim, the Hurlbuts asked for the use of the school house for prayer meetings. It was about 1917 when a young rancher by the name of Leif Erickson was recruited in a rather unusual way. Erickson was hunting some stray horses and stopped in Maxim to make inquiries. Invited to the prayer meetings, he consented, but was reluctant to go into the building because of his rough riding clothes. Finally, he joined the meeting and responded to the altar call. Then he told his brothers, Arthur and Walter. All three were converted to Christ. The Hurlbuts were very missionary-minded; in fact, they farmed at Maxim solely to grow wheat which could be sold for missionary support. Through their influence, the Erickson boys went to Pentecostal Bible schools in the United States and eventually to the mission field of Peru.

Another prominent pioneer worker was brought into the PAOC through the witness of lay workers in Craik, Saskatchewan. George R. Upton, a Baptist from Ontario, travelled to the West to secure employment on a farm. His employers, who were Pentecostals, took him to gospel services in Craik where he first became acquainted with the Pentecostal message. Later, while on the way to visit his family in Ontario, young George stopped off in Winnipeg. He experienced his personal Pentecost in that city in 1919. Upton returned to his farm employment in Saskatchewan for a few months, then assisted A. J. Lankin to introduce the Pentecostal message to Regina. Another assistant to Lankin, a female evangelist, eventually became Upton's wife. In due course, Upton gave up secular work and entered full-time ministry as the pastor at Weldon.[32] It was the beginning of a very productive career in ministry which would culminate in his long stint as Missionary Secretary for The Pentecostal Assemblies of Canada.

Early outreaches in Alberta had introduced Pentecostalism to the people in Calgary around 1908. Possibly the influx of American settlers from

3 / THE EARLY WORK IN THE WEST

southwestern states provided close contacts with the Azusa Street Mission. At any rate, a family named Kelly was one of the first in Calgary to espouse the full gospel teachings. John McAlister took the Pentecostal message to Edmonton in 1917. Alberta also attracted a number of pioneering American Pentecostals, both as evangelists and as short-term pastors. In 1919, the Chicago evangelist, Philip Wittich, conducted a successful campaign in Edmonton. Hugh Cadwalder, an American preacher who greatly assisted in Pentecostal work in Saskatchewan, came to pastor the Edmonton congregation in 1919. John McAlister left the city to engage in evangelistic ministry. Later, McAlister became the superintendent of the district of Alberta and British Columbia, prior to their separation into two administrative regions.

Calgary was for a time the scene of labor for Dr. Lillian Yeomans, an American physician who had been supernaturally healed of a drug addiction. Yeomans travelled extensively throughout Alberta, and other parts of Canada, preaching on divine healing and the Baptism in the Holy Spirit. It would appear that she herself received the Baptism with tongues about 1907. From various accounts, Yeomans was preaching "in the Pentecostal Mission in a Western Canadian city" in 1909 when an extraordinary event took place. During the meetings at the mission a "woman of the streets," with venereal disease, was saved, healed, and filled with the Spirit. A bachelor farmer in the church decided to marry her, against the strenuous objections of his family. The young man stated that his fiancee's sordid past was not on trial, but rather "the blood of Jesus Christ." If the woman was not totally saved and cleaned up, he averred, then no one present was saved! To which Dr. Yeomans heartily responded with, "Preach it son, I'm with you." The result was a wedding and a married life in which the woman gave ample evidence of being "a new creation in Christ."[33]

The doctor itinerated for years in rural Alberta, preaching even in hay lofts, and praying for the sick. In one community, where she proclaimed the Pentecostal Baptism, the spectators expected a certain woman to be first to receive. She was accounted by all as most deserving, but her husband, who was considered a "bad" man, was the first. The man was so ashamed of his sins that he knelt alone, in a dark corner of the hayloft, and there was saved and broke out in tongues. His wife was dumbfounded and remarked, "He's got the Baptism before me, and he is *so* bad. Perhaps I need to be saved from my goodness more than he needed to be saved from his badness." Then the new convert arose and preached what Yeomans called "the most wonderful sermon on Calvary I ever heard." Soon, others came into Pentecost; one woman sang and praised God in Gaelic, which soon changed into High German, a language known to the doctor. At another tent meeting, held "in Western Canada," a five-year-old girl, deaf as a result of scarlet fever, was anointed and prayed for. Both her parents were converted and publicly took Jesus as their "family Physician." Yeomans left the area, but later received a letter from the family announcing the complete healing of the girl: she now "could hear a pin fall."[34]

Red Deer, Alberta, received the Pentecostal message in 1911 when George Taylor moved there from Cartwright, Manitoba. Taylor, who received the Baptism in the Holy Spirit at the Argue meetings in 1910, had ministerial experience as a Methodist lay preacher, or "exhorter." He held meetings in his home where many of his friends and neighbors were introduced to the full gospel message, but no strong work was established in that community until the 1920s.

Other dedicated laymen carried the message to Alberta towns and cities with great diligence and at their own expense. Victor Nystedt was a recent immigrant who had the Pentecostal Baptism before his departure from Sweden. He told the Swedish pastors and people of the Wetaskiwin and Metiskow Baptist churches of his experience. A number of the church people received the Baptism, including both pastors. By 1912, the new message was being proclaimed to the nearby homesteaders by Nystedt and another lay worker, H. H. Sellin. Sellin became a pastor of one of the new assemblies that resulted from their labors. For 20 years he proved to be a faithful leader of his congregation.

At Lethbridge, in the southern part of the province, meetings began as early as 1912 under the direction of C. M. Neve. A layman named Simonette spearheaded an outreach to surrounding communities. Coalhurst was reached in 1917 with the Johnson family being the first in that town to respond to the full gospel. A congregation was soon established with Simonette serving as pastor. So successful did this work become that at one time, when the older Lethbridge work was languishing, the Coalhurst assembly provided support for it. Other meetings were held in Turner Valley around 1917, but nothing more is known of the advancement of Pentecost in that area.

Laymen from Lethbridge introduced the Pentecostal teachings to the Hughenden district sometime before 1918. Many were attracted to these early gatherings, some travelling up to 20 miles by horse and buggy in summer, or by sleigh in winter. As automobiles became more numerous, visitors attended these meetings from further afield — Amisk, Metiskow, Veteran, and Wainwright. The work at Lethbridge received a strong boost with the arrival in 1919 of Walter McAlister as pastor. It was there McAlister met Ruth Manley, his future bride. The arrival of George Schneider also helped to strengthen the new assemblies. Schneider had

3 / THE EARLY WORK IN THE WEST

received the Baptism in the Spirit in Saskatchewan and had preached for a time in Saskatoon. Most of his ministry thereafter was in Alberta, where he was particularly successful in spreading Pentecostalism among the German-speaking people of the province. Many other Pentecostal congregations were established at a relatively early date in Alberta. Little information on their origin has survived in a documentary form. It is clear, however, from the personal accounts available that lay workers played a crucial role[35]— a role which followed the familiar pattern established in Ontario, Manitoba, and Saskatchewan, and one which was to be repeated in British Columbia.

Several attempts have been made to establish the date of the introduction of Pentecostal teaching to British Columbia. According to researcher Donald Klan, the date appears to be 1907, when tent meetings were held in Vancouver. Rev. and Mrs. C. L. Cross, and their assistants, Mr. and Mrs. A. G. Garr, came up from Los Angeles that year and ministered in the Vancouver area.[36] The Crosses disappeared from Canadian history, but the Garrs worked in Canada for a few years. They were present at a 1909 camp meeting in Ontario, and were recipients of the first missionary offering ever taken at a Canadian Pentecostal camp meeting. A. G. Ward met them and described them as "southerners of a refined type. They are good-looking, well-made young people, set to move in any society." He noted that Mrs. Garr had a voice for preaching that "would carry a great distance in the open air."[37]

The tent meetings of these early workers were located near a Methodist church, and many of the members came to their services. The doctrines proclaimed were salvation, sanctification, and Baptism in the Holy Spirit. A nucleus of believers was established when a number were converted and came into the Pentecostal experience. This group may have used the name, "Apostolic Faith Mission." It held meetings in an unused church in the Mount Pleasant district. In January of 1908, the assembly invited George S. Paul of Winnipeg to be its pastor. Paul had once held a supervisory position with the Holiness Movement in Winnipeg. The Holiness influence permeated the new Pentecostal group from the start. The group was augmented by the influx of newcomers such as Mrs. E. Butler, who, before moving to Vancouver in 1910, had been a member of a Holiness church in Winnipeg.

The work in Vancouver was considerably enlarged by a local revival in 1908 in which quite a number of Methodist families were recruited. In spite of considerable opposition, these Pentecostal believers succeeded in acquiring their own church building in 1910. This congregation may also have received new recruits from the ranks of Canadians who went to Portland, Oregon, to attend the services of Mrs. Florence Crawford.

Crawford exerted a significant influence on British Columbia Pentecostals. She was a strong personality who assumed leadership of a new full gospel group in Portland, late in 1906. She and a band of followers went to Winnipeg in 1907 to assist A. H. Argue in one of his early conventions. Her own summer camp meetings near Portland attracted many Canadians. One of them was a wealthy lumberman who was healed of heart trouble in the 1908 camp meeting. Another Canadian brought into Pentecost in Portland was A. V. McPherson. He had been converted in Canada in 1902, but found his personal Pentecost in Crawford's meetings. He remained in the city and eventually became a preacher with her Apostolic Faith denomination. The 1910 summer camp services resulted in an additional number of British Columbians experiencing the Pentecostal Baptism before returning home.[38]

A spirit of cooperation developed between the Portland workers and Pastor Paul in Vancouver, but they do not appear to have conducted any joint meetings in B.C. The reason the Canadian workers did not become a part of the Apostolic Faith of Portland possibly had its source in Crawford's method of church government, which some thought to be authoritarian. Evidence that other young assemblies were discontent with her style of governing may be seen in the defection of three Apostolic Faith groups which broke away to form a new association, The Pacific Coast Missionary Society. Paul's Vancouver church was a member of this association for some time.[39]

A separate source for Pentecostalism was the cottage prayer meeting which began in 1910 in Vancouver in the home of a Mr. and Mrs. Black. These people had received the Holy Spirit infilling in Los Angeles. Another early mission, whose founding date is unknown, was established by Elder William Jackson on Dunlevy Avenue, in the Japanese section of the city. This work may have grown out of prayer meetings held in the home of Mrs. Annie Brown in the Collingwood district about 1910-12. Jackson, who had worked with Brown, later held meetings in an upstairs hall on Cordova Street. It was in this hall that F. R. Maddaford accepted the Pentecostal teachings. This family had a Presbyterian background, but came into Pentecost soon after Mrs. Maddaford's healing of an illness that six medical specialists had pronounced incurable. Maddaford became a Pentecostal preacher and later was elected superintendent of the British Columbia District at its first conference in 1928.[40]

Both Paul and Jackson concentrated their early evangelistic efforts on the "down-and-outs" in Vancouver's inner city. The Pauls established several branch missions in the suburbs where they ministered on weekends, but the bulk of their work was among the drunkards, transients, and the unemployed that gathered on Cordova Street. To

3 / THE EARLY WORK IN THE WEST

increase the effectiveness of their street meetings, they designed a truck with a folding platform which could hold a pump organ and several seats. The gospel truck became a familiar sight on numerous street corners during the warm summer months.

The Pauls sought to reach other nearby towns and cities, and in 1916 conducted a most successful campaign in Chilliwack. A number of people, largely drawn from Methodist ranks, were converted in this way and drawn into the Pentecostal Movement. Keenly interested in overseas missions, the Pauls assisted a couple to go to China in 1910. Another worker was sent out to join the first couple in 1917. During the short lifetime of the Pacific Coast Missionary Society, ten workers were sent overseas and most of their support came from the churches pastored by the Pauls. Unfortunately, they were never successful in establishing a strong, self-propagating form of Pentecostalism in British Columbia. Donald Klan has concluded that one reason for this failure was the position taken by Mrs. Paul. After her husband's death, she headed the original mission work and was intolerant of any effort to start other missions in the city.[41]

Another reason for the short-lived impact of the Pauls' work was the nature of the congregation they had gathered around them — transients, the unemployed, and the outcasts of society. In its 30 years of operation, the Paul mission ministered to thousands of Vancouver residents, but failed to build a base composed of families. Thus the Paul's pioneer work did little more than introduce Pentecostal teachings to British Columbians. By contrast, the Dunlevy mission, while also working with transients and outcasts in Vancouver, managed the transition from downtown "rescue mission" status to that of a family-based church.

By 1916, the Dunlevy group was meeting in a hall at the corner of Hastings and Columbia. Early evangelism was directed by a young layperson named Alva Walker, who held street meetings each Friday night. The young people of the assembly assisted Walker in this weekly endeavor, a practice which was of great value in providing new leaders. Harry Eggleton was one of the group who thus gained experience in various forms of ministry. When Harry's father had been raised up from a death bed through prayer by Pentecostals in Toronto, the whole family joined the new movement. After moving to Vancouver, the family members became quite involved in the Dunlevy work. Harry, though only 18 at the time, was made deacon and treasurer. His chief responsibilities were to find the funds to pay the rent, to see that visiting preachers were paid, and to keep the church hall clean.

These responsibilities were onerous for such a young a man, but they proved extremely important later when Eggleton went to the mission field.

Some of the difficulties he faced can best be visualized by reading his personal account:

> As often as possible Frank Gram of Tacoma would send up a special speaker who would stay for two or three weeks, and it was up to me as treasurer to see that they were well paid. The rent for the place was $60.00 a month and more than once the Lord had to work a miracle to get us enough money to pay it. . . . I had gone to the Mission to clean the place up . . . and I found a man half drunk in the doorway. . . . I talked to him about Salvation and managed to get him . . . to the altar where he prayed through to a real good experience. God had sobered him up in the meantime. When he went to go, he put a hand in his pocket and pulled out a roll of bills and insisted that I take it. . . . That month had been a bad one and I lacked $35.00 of having the rent and it was due the next day. After he was gone I unrolled the bills and found exactly the $35.00 needed for the rent. I'll tell you, I had me a real little Camp meeting all by myself . . . that morning.[42]

Harry Eggleton went on to become a Pentecostal preacher and served several pastorates in the lower B.C. mainland. With his wife Marguerite he went to the West Indies where for 30 years they labored as missionaries.

Robert Gillespie, formerly a successful businessman in Winnipeg, came to pastor the Dunlevy congregation. As was common among Pentecostal churches before the 1940s, there were few programs aimed specifically at children or youth. But frequent meetings, involving participation by all ages, made up for the lack at that time.[43] Two services were held during the week and three meetings on Sundays. Gillespie and his flock practised foot-washing, an uncommon ritual among early Canadian Pentecostals. The custom may have developed out of the relative proximity of Vancouver to Los Angeles and the frequent travel of early leaders between the two points. William Seymour had a regular foot-washing observance in his Azusa Street Mission. Whatever its origin, foot-washing did not long remain as a ritual among B.C. Pentecostals. The main doctrinal emphases were the same in the West as in the East — Salvation, Divine Healing, Baptism in the Holy Spirit, and the Second Coming.

No doubt other efforts were made to establish Pentecostalism in the lower mainland before 1920, but apart from one exception, no records have survived. In 1915 a Mrs. Adams and her son Leslie opened a small mission work on Lonsdale Avenue, near the ferry wharf in North Vancouver.[44] It probably was the nucleus of what eventually became a Pentecostal community of believers in that centre. Despite the zealous

3 / THE EARLY WORK IN THE WEST

labors of such lay workers, and the sacrifices of dedicated preachers, Pentecostalism did not establish itself very firmly nor widely in British Columbia in the decades before 1920. That was to change, however, with the advent of the salvation-healing ministry of Dr. Charles S. Price throughout Western Canada, a thrilling story that is related later in this narrative.

Endnotes

1. *The Apostolic Faith*, 1:6 (February-March 1907), 7.
2. Ibid., 1:8 (May 1907), 1-2; Maria B. Woodworth-Etter, *Acts of the Holy Ghost, or Life Work and Experience of Mrs. M. B. Woodworth-Etter, Evangelist* (Dallas: John F. Worley Printing, 1913), p. 250.
3. A. G. Ward, "How the Pentecostal Experience Came to Canada," typed copy of letter, PAOC Archives.
4. Thomas Wm. Miller, "The Significance of A. H. Argue for Pentecostal Historiography," *Pneuma*, 8:2 (Fall 1986), 120-158.
5. Zelma Argue, *What Meaneth This?* (Winnipeg, 1923), pp. 6-7, 10, 14-16, 29; see also C. M. Ward, "Yet Once More," *The Pentecostal Testimony* (May 1956), 4-5, 13.
6. Zelma Argue, "Memories of Fifty Years Ago," *Pentecostal Evangel* (April 22, 1956), 6-7, 29; W. J. Taylor, "History of the First 50 Years of the Manitoba & N.W. Ontario District, 1927-1977;" *The Apostolic Faith*, 1:9 (June-September 1907).
7. A. H. Argue, "Azusa Street Revival Reaches Winnipeg," *The Pentecostal Testimony* (May 1956), 9.
8. Zelma Argue, note 5.
9. Stanley M. Horton, "Twentieth Century Acts of the Holy Spirit," *Pentecostal Evangel* (October 21, 1962), 19; see also Argue, note 7; and *The Apostolic Faith*, 1:9 (June-September 1907), 1.
10. Robert A. Larden, *Our Apostolic Heritage: An Official History of the Apostolic Church of Pentecost of Canada Incorporated* (Calgary: Apostolic Church of Pentecost of Canada, 1971), pp. 25-35.
11. Thomas Wm. Miller, taped interview with Walter E. McAlister, May 3, 1984.
12. *The Apostolic Faith*, 1:12 (January 1908), 1.
13. Thomas Wm. Miller, taped interview with Gordon F. Atter, April 30, 1984; and taped interview with Beulah Argue Smith and Eva Argue Robinson, July 29, 1984.
14. A. H. Argue, note 7.

15. *The Apostolic Faith*, 2:13 (May 1908), 4; and Zelma Argue, *What Meaneth This?* note 5.

16. Ethel Goss, *The Winds of God: The Story of the Early Pentecostal Days (1901-1914) in the Life of Howard A. Goss* (New York: Comet Press, 1958), pp. 167-168.

17. Thomas Wm. Miller, taped interview with Beulah Argue Smith and Eva Argue Robinson, July 29, 1984.

18. Reported in conversations with the writer; Smith has the book: M. Baxter, *Forty Future Wonders: Predicted in Daniel and Revelation* (London: Christian Herald Office, 1903, 11th ed.).

19. See Elmer J. Cantelon, *Harvester of the North* (Toronto: Full Gospel Publishing House, 1969).

20. *The Promise* (March 1910), 8; Gloria G. Kulbeck, *What God Hath Wrought: A History of the Pentecostal Assemblies of Canada* (Toronto: PAOC, 1958), pp. 153-154.

21. *The Apostolic Faith*, 1:12 (January 1908), 4.

22. *The Apostolic Faith*, 1:9 (June-September 1907), 3.

23. C. A. C. Story, "Pentecostalism in Saskatchewan," handwritten memoirs, 1954, PAOC Archives; see also Robert A. Larden, *Our Apostolic Heritage* . . . , pp. 33-34, 115-116.

24. D. Mark Buntain, *Why He is a Pentecostal Preacher* (Toronto: Full Gospel Publishing House, 1944), pp. 9ff.

25. J. Eustace Purdie, "My Own Pentecost," *The Pentecostal Testimony* (June 1970), 4, 9.

26. Gordon K. Franklin, typed copy of taped interview with J. E. Purdie, Saskatoon, 1973, p. 139. Used by permission.

27. Ibid., p. 75.

28. Ibid., p. 73.

29. Ibid., p. 75.

30. Lila McAlister Skinner, "The McAlister Family Tree," handwritten memoirs, March 1978. Used by permission.

31. See note 11.

32. Paul Hawkes, *Songs of the Reaper; the Story of The Pentecostal Assemblies of Canada in Saskatchewan* (Altona, MB: PAOC Sask. District, 1985); and George R. Upton, letter to Thomas Wm. Miller, August 1, 1983.

33. Lillian B. Yeomans, *Divine Healing Diamonds* (Springfield: Gospel Publishing House, 1933), p. 6.

3 / THE EARLY WORK IN THE WEST

34. Lillian B. Yeomans, *Healing from Heaven* (Springfield: Gospel Publishing House, 1926), pp. 119-124, 137-138.
35. *Rejoice: A History of the Pentecostal Assemblies of Alberta and the Northwest Territories* (Altona, MB: PAOC, Alberta and N.W.T. (Mackenzie) District, 1983), pp. 1-13.
36. Donald T. Klan, "Pentecostal Assemblies of Canada Growth in British Columbia from Origins until 1953," unpublished MCS thesis, Regent College, Vancouver, B.C., 1979. Used by permission.
37. A. G. Ward, note 3.
38. Klan, 40-42, 60; see also *A Historical Account of the Apostolic Faith* (Portland: Apostolic Faith Mission, 1965), pp. 76, 80.
39. Klan, 43-45.
40. Lionel R. Maddaford and Lynda Tennant, "A Chronology of Broadway Tabernacle," booklet, Vancouver, 1977; and Klan, pp. 63-65.
41. Klan, 45-47, 52-59.
42. Harry Eggleton, typescript memoirs, January 25, 1954. No other data available, but likely copied from a letter with information solicited by W. E. McAlister for a "history" of the PAOC, PAOC Archives; see also Marguerite Eggleton, "History of the Nelson Church, 1924-1974," typewritten account, corrected and updated by Mrs. Eggleton, Nelson, B.C., September 1990.
43. See also Gloria G. Kulbeck, *What God hath Wrought: A History of the Pentecostal Assemblies of Canada* (Toronto: Full Gospel Publishing House, 1958), p. 174.
44. Klan, 66-67.

Chapter 4

CONFLICT AND CONSOLIDATION

The first 20 years after the outpouring of the Spirit in Parham's Bible school in Topeka, Kansas, were marked by vigorous evangelism by the Pentecostals. Whatever their label at the time — Full Gospel, Apostolic Faith, Latter Rain, Church of God, or Pentecostal — the pioneers were remarkable for their zeal and their self-denying sacrifice in spreading their message. Seymour's paper, published in Los Angeles, reported a worldwide spread of the new teachings and the establishment of Latter Rain groups at a phenomenal rate. This growth occurred despite the lack of organization, financial resources, and ecclesiastical support. The eye-witness accounts and early histories of men such as Howard Goss, B. F. Lawrence, A. H. Argue, and R. E. McAlister reflect an extraordinary devotion to their Lord and an enormous energy in propagating their basic themes — Salvation, Baptism in the Holy Spirit, Divine Healing, and the Second Coming.

When the conflict between the full gospel message and the accepted theologies and ecclesiastical organizations of the day could not be contained, Pentecostalism began to emerge as a distinctive religious force. In this respect, the modern Pentecostal Movement experienced the historic religious cycle of revival movements. The process, for centuries, has been one of the revival, followed by rapid growth, then institutionalization and bureaucratization, and, finally, a departure from the original Biblical and denominational distinctives.[1] Then another renewal movement would arrive on the scene.

The Wesleyan Awakening provides a well-known example of this process. John Wesley always considered himself to be an Anglican priest, whose theology could be found, as he put it, in the "Thirty-nine Articles" of the Established Church. However, the practical realities of his revival

4 / CONFLICT AND CONSOLIDATION

forced him to found the Methodist denomination as a means of preserving its fruits. The Anglican Establishment remained closed to his converts. The later revivals and awakenings in America under George Whitfield, Jonathan Edwards, and Charles Finney led to similar results. The ecclesiastical hierarchies of the day rejected the doctrine of the necessity of a conversion experience. Some opposed the methods of the revivalists, and other issues arose which led to division and schism.

Even the Maritime Colonies of Canada were affected: there was a division there between the "Old Lights" who rejected a conversion theology and the "New Lights" who proclaimed its necessity. As the 19th century drew to a close, the impact of the great revivals lessened and dedicated church people became progressively dissatisfied with their denominations. One result was the reappearance of the old Wesleyan teachings on sanctification (Holiness), and the emergence of more than 20 Holiness sects between 1890 and 1900. By the end of the century, an estimated 100,000 Methodists had left their denominations for the new Holiness bodies of North America.[2]

With the decline of revivalistic impulses in America, and widespread dissatisfaction with the quality of spiritual life in many denominations, a third factor can be discerned behind the emergence of the present-day Pentecostal Movement. A new, and entirely corrosive, stream of theological thought arose late in the last century known now as "Modernism" or "Liberalism." Its roots lay in the writings of Hegel, Marx, and Nietzsche. Their influence on seminarians who generally went to Europe, especially Germany, for advanced studies in the 19th century, had devastating results for the North American churches.

When Darwin's evolutionary theories came into vogue among religious leaders, men like H. E. Fosdick, Shailer Mathews, and H. N. Wieman sought to combine Biblical teachings with Darwinian assumptions.[3] Thus there developed a so-called "evolutionary theism" or "theistic evolution" in many denominations. Many earnest believers profoundly disapproved. They perceived a spiritual decline which was accompanied by gross doctrinal digressions from historic Christianity. Their dissatisfaction made them ripe candidates for a message based on the Word of God. The outbreak of Pentecostalism at the turn of the century appeared to multitudes to be God's answer to the desperate needs of the churches.

Once again, the history of Revivalism was repeated in the experiences of the early Pentecostals in America. Rejection of their beliefs, ecclesiastical resistance, and outright physical persecution became common. Although they denied wanting to divide the churches, Pentecostals were considered schismatics because they proclaimed "new and heretical teachings" among their denominational colleagues. Often, though they sought to remain within their churches, they were made unwelcome or officially excommunicated. Seymour printed in his little paper one such story: an elderly lady, after her Baptism in the Spirit and speaking in tongues, was forced to leave a life-long association. As she walked down the road, she commented, "Yonder is the meeting house, here goes the church."[4]

It was this concept of themselves as being divinely enlightened, filled with God's Spirit and sanctified to God's use, that animated this first generation of Latter Rain saints. William Seymour maintained, through the pages of the *Apostolic Faith*, that his was not just another erratic, heretical cult. He claimed it was in the mainstream of genuine Christianity and at the forefront of God's reviving work among the churches. Mrs. Hebden, of the East End Mission in Toronto, made a similar claim: "That this work is of God, we have no doubt, nor have we anything else to seek than His glory."[5] When the PAOC was founded in 1919, it was intended, wrote George Chambers,[6] to be a cooperative fellowship of Pentecostal believers and in no way was designed to become another denomination.

In spite of such disclaimers, the Pentecostals were, in fact, disturbers of the old order in the churches. It always has been a fact of revivalism that it breaks with hoary old methods, superficial sanctity, and ecclesiastical formalism. Early Pentecostal leaders were frowned upon, or entirely rejected. Their new-found convictions of conversion and Baptism in the Spirit were condemned. Thousands of believers became, as it was so quaintly put at the time, "come-outers." A. G. Ward, who had ministered in Western Canada with the Methodists and the Christian and Missionary Alliance, left both groups to become a freelance Pentecostal preacher. G. A. Chambers and eight other clergymen in the Mennonite Brethren in Christ group were ordered by church leaders to renounce the Baptism in the Spirit and tongues-speaking, or leave the denomination. When they declined to surrender their Pentecostal views, they left the MBC with about 80 church members following them.

Many of the earliest Pentecostal lay people at Abingdon and Vineland were excommunicated for their espousal of the Latter Rain teachings. J. E. Purdie's experience was unusual in that his Anglican bishop was sympathetic and did not insist on his expulsion. Even large segments of the Holiness Movement rejected Pentecostalism. Many Holiness people were obliged to forsake their former associations when they refused to renounce their Pentecostal experience. It must be admitted, too, that at times the zealous advocates of this latest religious awakening were excessive in their denunciations of the "old-line" and "dead" denominations. As a rule, however, Pentecostal leaders devoted themselves to

4 / CONFLICT AND CONSOLIDATION

propagating the full gospel, rather than to religious infighting.

The early days of this great religious awakening were notable also for an almost universal opposition from the press. Both religious and secular papers condemned the charismatic manifestations among Pentecostals. So scurrilous and so continuous were the attacks that Pentecostalism acquired a stereotyped image as a seedbed for heresy, schism, fanaticism, and ignorance. That impression fastened so firmly on the public consciousness that, for decades, Pentecostals were despised and maligned. Many persecutors and opponents felt they were doing God a service by burning down the Pentecostals' tents, assaulting their preachers, and persecuting even their children. From the first, at Azusa Street, newspaper reports grossly distorted the facts. A. W. Orwig, who was present at the meetings, commented:

> The daily papers of the city had characterized them (the meetings) as scenes of wild fanaticism, enacted by ignorant and crazy people. Especially was the reputed speaking in unknown tongues bitterly denounced as a fraud and was sacrilegiously caricatured.[7]

Frank Bartleman made frequent reference to the deliberate misrepresentation of the Azusa Street meetings in the newspapers. One exception, he noted, was a Los Angeles reporter whose attendance at the services convinced him it was all from God. The reporter's attempt to write an impartial account was rejected by his editors and the man was dismissed. In this respect also, the Pentecostal awakening was similar to those great revival movements of the past.

The phenomenon of speaking in tongues was the most misunderstood and most vigorously condemned of all the features of early Pentecostalism. Divine Healing came in for its share of condemnation, but was less easily disposed of because of the numerous instances of irrefutable healings. The doctrine of the Second Coming was, to many critics, merely a religious novelty. The so-called "social theologians" of that time rejected any supernaturalism in the Bible. They taught that mankind would create its own "heaven" on earth and ridiculed this doctrine as a delusion, or "pie-in-the-sky," for the unhappy masses.

Other sources of criticism in that early period concerned the role permitted women in the Pentecostal Movement. Leaders like Maria Woodworth-Etter, Florence Crawford, Aimee Semple McPherson, and Ellen Hebden were very active from the start of the revival. The religious culture of North America was not then favorable to the idea of women in the pulpit. Even someone as successful and famous as Aimee Semple McPherson was obliged, after 20 years of ministry, to defend her right to preach in some of the union campaigns she held in the United States.[8]

One very frequent criticism involved the perception that Pentecostals were drawn from the lowest classes of society. Seymour was a case in point: he was an uneducated Negro, his meetings were in a shabby part of Los Angeles, and his adherents were presumably all uncultured and ignorant. This is another aspect of the stereotype that was affixed to early Pentecostalism that has only recently been dispelled. Even so, some critics still seek to present what has been entirely a religious revival as a "social protest" phenomenon.[9] As is often the case, there may be an element of truth in these charges: the bulk of early Pentecostals were from the lower social classes. What is overlooked, however, is that this was true of the total demographic profile of North America. The great "middle class" known to us now is the product of a later stage of economic development. Before 1920, the vast majority of North Americans lived on farms and in villages or small towns. Judging from eyewitness reports from both Azusa Street and the Argue Mission in Winnipeg, the Pentecostals had members of the social elite attending the meetings. That was true as well for the Hebden Mission in Toronto. Former General Superintendent Tom Johnstone, who came into the movement near the start, reported that some early Pentecostals were both spiritual and highly educated.

Nonetheless, it is true that the bulk of the believers were not well educated. But one must not evaluate the socio-economic level of the early Pentecostals by the standards of the present. In the tumultuous years of farm settlement and industrialization underway prior to 1920, relatively few North Americans got even a grade eight education. The Great Depression of the 1930s deprived millions of educational opportunities. Despite the limitations imposed upon them by persecution and lack of resources, the Canadian Pentecostals established short-term Bible schools in the early 1920s. In 1925, a Bible college was established in Winnipeg which provided a three-year curriculum of theological studies.[10] Contrary to the stereotypical image of Pentecostals which prevailed for decades, it is clear that they were fairly representative of North American society as a whole.

It was not "social protest" nor "economic deprivation" that motivated the early 20th-century believers to carry out a worldwide program of evangelization. It was their strong conviction that God was reviving His Church in "the last days" in preparation for the "soon return of Jesus." Their protests were against denominations and churches that succumbed to the prevailing theological Liberalism/Modernism. They decried the "higher criticism" which invaded the seminaries and emasculated the gospel of all relevance for modern man. Pentecostals denounced the then-popular view of churchmen that "education" and "social reform" would

4 / CONFLICT AND CONSOLIDATION

improve society and transform human nature. The horrors of the First World War helped to dispel these mistaken philosophies and gave credence to the position taken by Pentecostals. Formalism and tradition had so permeated many of the formerly-evangelical denominations as to make worship for many an unsatisfactory ritual. In contrast, Pentecostals advocated a vigorous pulpit style, exuberant worship modes, and vocal prayer, both for the individual worshipper and the corporate body of believers. An integral part of their proclamation was the availability of supernatural healing, through faith and prayer, and the apostolic gift of the Baptism in the Holy Spirit. From the first, the overwhelming majority accepted speaking in tongues as the "initial, physical evidence" of that Baptism.

Early Pentecostals repudiated forms of church governance which perpetuated a religious hierarchy at the expense of populist decision-making. Thus early Pentecostal assemblies usually were of the self-governing, democratic type, perhaps closest in form to the 19th-century Congregational system of church government. Revival philosophy and the sanctification ethic of the 19th-century Holiness Movement were prominent features of their public ministry. Their rejection of the then-popular anti-biblical theologies of some other denominations, misrepresentations by the press, and persecution by the public resulted in enormous obstacles in propagating the new Movement. Another, and more serious, problem which the pioneers had to cope with was the threat of theological error within their own ranks. There was the risk of strong personalities developing a "cult following." It was to preserve doctrinal purity and to eliminate the risks of cultism that steps were taken to establish a form of church government acceptable to the majority of Pentecostals in Canada.

Most of the first generation of Latter Rain/Pentecostal/Apostolic Faith people came into the movement from the evangelical denominations. They were quite aware of the risks posed by sects and cults. The Methodists and Baptists, for example, had witnessed numerous groups "hiving off" in the late 19th century. No doubt some of the first Pentecostal leaders were aware of the 1913 prediction by a prominent professor in an American seminary. He claimed that the early demise of the entire movement was inevitable.[11]

A. G. Ward, R. E. McAlister, and A. H. Argue were among the first to undertake the organization of the scattered assemblies across the Dominion. Ward was a speaker at a June, 1909 camp meeting at Markham, Ontario, when the initial attempt was made to develop some type of organization among the pioneering pastors. The camp was a blessing to those who attended and was significant for its emphasis on overseas missions. A. G. Garr and his wife, Lillian, were in attendance and a large offering was collected for their fare to India. The keen interest in missions prompted men like Ward to seek some means of systematically providing financial support for workers like the Garrs. In addition, Pentecostal churches had suddenly emerged on the Canadian scene in widely scattered communities and it was extremely difficult to keep in contact with each other. Some rudimentary form of association seemed essential, in Ward's view.

There was another, potentially destructive, problem: of the itinerant teachers, preachers, and evangelists criss-crossing the country, a few had been proven to be unsatisfactory in theology or conduct. Arthur Atter, before going as missionary to China, had a visit from a man claiming to be collecting funds for a leper colony near Shanghai. Atter was wary, but had no factual information until he himself reached China. Then he discovered that his suspect was a "con man" and was wanted by American authorities. Fortunately, on information from Atter, the fraudulent fund-raiser was apprehended and imprisoned.[12]

Such problems were known to Ward. Besides, his background in the Christian and Missionary Alliance and the Methodist denominations left him with an appreciation for the safeguards provided by organization. So it was he, along with A. A. Boddy, a visiting Pentecostal who was a vicar in the Church of England, who first tried to develop a Canadian Pentecostal association. His own account of that action is most illuminating as to its purposes. It also is significant that the name chosen for the proposed organization was modeled after similar bodies in the United States and England.

> At this camp meeting it was thought wise, and to be the mind of the Lord, to form the simplest kind of an organization possible, for we felt as the work grew it would be difficult to carry on either at home or on the mission field without some headquarters to which workers might refer their problems, and seek counsel. During the Camp we formed what was to be known as the "P.M.U." — the Pentecostal Missionary Union. We chose this name in order to conform with a similar organization formed the same year by some of the American brethren in a Camp at Alliance, Ohio, and also with a British organization which had taken the same name. Perhaps we were premature in this undertaking. In any case, it soon met with great opposition from some Canadian workers, particularly the Hebdens, who seemed to feel that God had called us away from all organization and that we ought never again to become identified with anything "man-made." Rather than engage in a controversy, and thus endanger the spiritual state of this new Movement, we decided not to lay any stress upon the infant organization.[13]

4 / CONFLICT AND CONSOLIDATION

The opposition from the Hebdens was immediate and vigorous. Mrs. Hebden's renunciations of a professional clergy and of church organization were set forth in no uncertain terms in her publication *The Promise*. In 1907, she wrote an article condemning the use of the title "Reverend" by gospel workers.[14] Following the actions taken at the Markham camp meeting, she wrote another very critical article in the autumn of 1909 titled "Organization".

> We desire to state most emphatically that in the Lord's work at 651 Queen Street and at 191 George Street, Toronto, we have no connection whatever with any general organization of the Pentecostal people in Canada. As a "missionary church" we stand alone in God's divine order, and extend the right hand of fellowship to every member of the body of Christ . . . and we decline absolutely all responsibility for any so-called representatives of the Pentecostal work in Canada.[15]

Canadian historian Gloria Kulbeck has suggested that the Hebdens' view on organization may have moderated after a few months.[16] But in a later article in *The Promise*, Ellen Hebden issued an even-stronger denunciation of organizational efforts among Pentecostals. It is evident that she blamed "organization" for division and conflict among the Pentecostals.

> In Pentecostal circles there is some agitation and what appears to be contention, but which is mostly the tumult of truth over the question of organization. Many who innocently take sides in the conflict of opinion are not yet grounded on the Word of God regarding it, and thus innocently promote division . . . Some few of those who organize do so with the prospect of receiving honors from men, but the great majority are no doubt endeavoring honestly to promote the cause so dear to their hearts . . . organizations have been in existence during the dark ages, but under the outpouring of the latter rain, there is no place for conformation to the world. . . . Not only is the free leading of the Spirit against man-made organizations, but the unity of that Spirit demands its abolition and . . . organization intensifies and perpetuates division. See the denominations of today and you have a self-evident reason against organizations of men. . . . The Word gives the local Church in many places . . . but nothing higher than the local Church. . . . There is . . . absolutely no room for incorporated Presbyteries, Boards, Synods or Pentecostal Missionary Unions.[17]

That kind of anti-organization expression was plain. It is understandable that Ward and his associates drew back from precipitating conflict with the acknowledged pioneer of Pentecostalism in Ontario. Nonetheless, there still remained a need for some structural plan for the fledging movement in Canada as the number of churches and adherents continually increased in the decade that followed. The Pentecostal Missionary Union, favored by Ward and Boddy, would have provided some framework for cooperation and for dealing with several very serious theological controversies which troubled the pioneers. These issues have since come to be known as the "Finished Work," the "Jesus Only," and the "Initial Evidence" controversies.

Much of the controversy can be credited to the cultural and theological climate at the turn of the century. Believers were eager to get all the "light" possible on Scripture, especially on various facets of the Baptism in the Spirit, Divine Healing, and the Second Coming. Howard Goss noted that preachers feared compromising their message more than anything else at the beginning of the movement — to be labelled a "compromiser" meant the end of ministry. Consequently, reported Goss, a preacher who failed to dig up a new slant on Scripture, or get some new revelation, was considered "slow, stupid and unspiritual."[18] Pentecostals sometimes inclined towards an undue subjectivism in doctrine and in practice. One of J. E. Purdie's chief aims, in establishing the Bible school in Winnipeg, was to combat this tendency among Canadian believers.

The first issue, the "Finished Work," arose out of the experiences of W. H. Durham in his Chicago North Avenue Mission. Durham visited Los Angeles and was baptized in the Spirit at Azusa Street. William Seymour published an account of Durham's experience, but apparently was unaware that Durham would soon abandon his views on "sanctification as a second work of grace." Both leaders had advocated a "three-stage" process as the norm for all believers — Salvation, Sanctification, and then Baptism in the Holy Spirit with tongues. Seymour used the pages of *The Apostolic Faith* to advance the thesis that believers had to be sanctified *before* receiving the Holy Spirit. Out of this viewpoint came a popular slogan that "the Lord will not fill an unclean vessel."[19] Many early Pentecostals shared this view, including Charles F. Parham, J. H. King, and, for a time, A. H. Argue.

This teaching had its origins in the Holiness heritage of thousands of pioneer Pentecostals. The 19th century witnessed a debate in the Holiness Movement about sanctification as either "instantaneous," or "progressive," or both. Thus many believers came to look upon their Baptism in the Holy Spirit as "a third work of grace."[20] By degrees, it came to be insisted by some leaders that sanctification was an indispensable qualification for the Baptism in the Spirit. Durham, a gifted speaker and a capable student of the Word, found upon his return to Chicago that the

4 / CONFLICT AND CONSOLIDATION

theory did not fit the facts in his mission. Many who came to receive the Spirit in his meetings had recently been converted, some the very day they received the Spirit and spoke in tongues.

Durham abandoned the doctrine of sanctification as a "second work of grace" as a result of his own Baptism in March of 1907, and from observations in his own mission. Possibly Durham was influenced by a theology shaped by his earlier Baptist connections. In any case, he became a zealous advocate of what came to be called "The Finished Work of Christ." He proclaimed this teaching at a convention of workers in Chicago in 1910, and in his mission paper, *The Pentecostal Testimony*, in June of 1911. He denounced a doctrine which, in his view, meant that a man could be born again and yet be left with a heart still unclean and full of enmity to God. Durham argued that salvation was a complete work of the Spirit that changed the nature of the converted. Therefore, a "second work of grace" was totally unnecessary.[21]

Durham preached his revised theology in Los Angeles in February, 1911, but found opposition from Seymour and one or two other Pentecostal leaders. Durham went back to Chicago, where he died of a fever the next year.[22] His "two-stage theory" — Salvation and Baptism in the Spirit — was widely discussed throughout North America and very quickly came to be accepted by the majority of early Pentecostals. A major result of the controversy, however, was the division of the Pentecostal Movement into what Synan has called the "Wesleyan" and the "non-Wesleyan" branches. Another set of definitive terms employed by Vinson Synan was "Holiness-Pentecostal" and "Baptistic-Pentecostal." Eventually, a third group arose, out of the Jesus Only controversy, which he titled the "Unitarian-Pentecostals."[23]

It is interesting to note that pioneer Pentecostal Frank Ewart, who was Durham's assistant in Chicago, became an advocate of the Jesus Only doctrine — or, as some prefer, "Oneness Pentecostalism." On the other hand, A. H. Argue who attended Durham's meetings and received the Baptism there, adopted the Finished Work teaching and rejected the Jesus Only position.[24]

Durham's Finished Work teachings were particularly acceptable to Pentecostals with a Baptist background, but many Canadians originally subscribed to the three-stage theory. That is clearly evident in books of sermons by pioneers like Franklin Small and G. A. Chambers. The result was, as Walter McAlister recalled, that the teachings of Durham "caused division for a time — some immediately accepted that position, others did not."[25] Pastor George Paul of Vancouver rejected Durham's doctrine and affirmed his commitment to the idea that the "unclean vessel" could not be baptized in the Spirit. According to researcher Donald Klan:

The Pauls referred to the "one-work of grace" theory as a delusive heresy contrary to the plain teaching of the Bible. They reacted sharply against William Durham's teaching that a convert could receive the baptism of the Holy Spirit without previously experiencing a second, definite work of cleansing. They maintained that the Lord would not send his Holy Spirit to inhabit an unclean vessel.[26]

By 1916, the Assemblies of God had adopted Durham's view and incorporated it in its Statement of Faith. A reference to "Entire Sanctification" was employed in the Statement "apparently to mollify advocates of a stronger Wesleyan position." However, it left a number of theological ambiguities that needed further revision in the years that followed.[27]

Canadian Pentecostal leaders were as much involved in the Finished Work controversy as the American pioneers, but had no official organization before 1919. As a result, the process towards adoption of the two-stage view consisted of informal discussions. Nonetheless, after the incorporation of the PAOC, and the formation of its first Statement of Faith, the predominant position among Canadians was against sanctification as a second, distinctive work of grace. Instead, it was viewed as instantaneous in reference to divine action and progressive in practical Christian experience. And this doctrine has remained virtually unchanged in all subsequent editions of the PAOC *Statement of Fundamental and Essential Truths.*

What has not been so easily settled among North American Pentecostals has been the complex dispute over the Trinity which emerged at an early date. Differences have been so great as to separate them into orthodox trinitarian and Jesus Only branches. Other terms for this latter group were "New Issue" and "One Name". The advocates of this doctrine prefer being called "Oneness Pentecostals". The "Jesus Only" teaching had circulated in various evangelical groups shortly after the turn of the century. It did not pose a serious threat until the 1913 World-Wide Camp Meeting near Los Angeles at which thousands of people were present from America, Canada, and around the world. Over two hundred clergymen sat on the platform, among them R. E. McAlister. The featured speaker was Mrs. Woodworth-Etter.

The meetings were remarkable for the number and nature of the healing miracles that occurred. Woodworth-Etter commented on the meetings:

> The world-wide camp meeting was no doubt the largest gathering of baptized saints in these last days . . . the power of God was poured out so wonderfully. . . . Hundreds were healed in soul and body. . . .

4 / CONFLICT AND CONSOLIDATION

> Many miracles of healing were wrought, people were saved and baptized.[28]

Among the healings were reported cases of cancer, tumors, Bright's disease, dropsy, tapeworm, consumption, and heart trouble. People felt themselves to be on the borderline of Heaven. It was in such circumstances that the "New Issue" became a more serious controversy among the pioneer Pentecostals.

One of the camp preachers delivered a sermon based on Jeremiah 31:31, leaving in the minds of the people the idea that God was going to do "a new thing." Later, R. E. McAlister, in his sermon, drew attention to the different baptismal formulas in Acts and in the Gospels. When he commented that the apostles baptized converts in the name of Jesus, a "great distress" swept over the congregation. Another preacher immediately took McAlister aside and warned him his remarks might be interpreted as supporting the false teachings then being propagated by a certain independent preacher. McAlister explained he had not intended to teach that the Acts formula was the only correct one.[29] The next morning, however, a zealous believer named John Scheppe, after having spent the night in prayer, ran through the camp shouting that he had received a revelation of the power of the name of Jesus. In the emotional climate of the camp, Scheppe's claim received some favorable response. When a woman soon afterward was marvelously healed of cancer, some took it to be confirmation of the "revelation," including Frank J. Ewart. One immediate result was that "two itinerant evangelists went to the Pacific Ocean where they were re-baptized in Jesus Name."[30]

For a time R. E. McAlister was interested in the New Issue, teaching and assisting Frank Ewart in the Los Angeles meetings. Franklin Small embraced the doctrine and did his utmost to have it adopted by the Pentecostal churches in Canada. At the first, the New Issue did not assume threatening proportions for early Pentecostalism. It was, after all, very difficult to fault a teaching that so greatly exalted the Lordship of Jesus Christ. Then there was the absence of doctrinal formulations among the Pentecostals and an openness to "new light" on old truths. Some theologically untrained believers argued that the baptismal formula in Acts was necessarily a later revelation from God, since it came *after* the Gospels in the order of New Testament books. Fairly soon, however, perceptive leaders recognized the dangers to Christian orthodoxy and to the doctrine of the Trinity.

One year after the 1914 formation of the Assemblies of God, the New Issue came up for debate at the St. Louis Council. It was again the subject of debate at the 1916 General Council. A statement was drawn up that "became unacceptable to those who had embraced the One Name doctrine." Of the 585 ministers present, 156 withdrew to found rival associations. Soon afterward, the list of clergymen with the Assemblies of God had increased to 429. AG historian Carl Brumback attributed such growth to the perception of many independent Pentecostals that the Assemblies of God had acquired greater stability.[31]

AG leaders issued an elaborate doctrinal statement on the Trinity and "person, as related to the Godhead." The split, however, was never mended and it became necessary at various times to reaffirm the orthodox position of the Assemblies.[32] The PAOC adopted the AG position *in total* after its incorporation, although disagreement marred even the founding convention of the Canadian denomination. The two chief proponents of "Jesus Only" in Canada were Frank Small and Howard Goss. Small became the pastor of a Pentecostal work in Winnipeg before he went to Los Angeles for the 1913 World-Wide Camp Meeting. Upon his return to the Manitoba capital he established a New Issue congregation and began re-baptizing believers. He brought up Frank Ewart from California to preach at a camp meeting near Winnipeg in 1916 and also at his new campground at Trossachs, in southern Saskatchewan.

Small argued that the Jesus Only formula must be the right one because God had healed, and filled with the Spirit, many who were re-baptized. Small and his people sought to recruit people from the original Argue Mission in Winnipeg. A number of Oneness workers went to Vancouver in 1919 in an unsuccessful attempt to enlist the Pentecostals in the Columbia Street Mission to their views. On the Prairies, several of the early assemblies joined Small and his new association, the Apostolic Church of Pentecost of Canada, after its founding in 1921. In Eastern Canada, the Jesus Only groups were located mostly in New Brunswick. Eventually these eastern disciples joined the United Pentecostal Church of the USA. PAOC historian G. F. Atter has described Small as a man of deep convictions and strong personality; he was frequently a controversial figure, but "one of the leading Canadian Pentecostal pioneers."[33]

Howard Goss helped organize the 1914 conference that led to the establishment of the Assemblies of God. After he adopted Oneness views, he joined the Pentecostal Assemblies of the World, headquartered in Indianapolis. This group also merged, at a later date, with the United Pentecostals, with offices at St. Louis, Missouri. While ministering in Canada, Goss assisted in organizing the Pentecostal Assemblies of the World in Canada to which some prominent leaders belonged. This title, in 1919, was shortened to The Pentecostal Assemblies of Canada.[34]

Despite his flair for organization, Goss was unsuccessful in enlisting many Canadians in his cause. Pioneer leaders like A. E. Adams, C. E.

4 / CONFLICT AND CONSOLIDATION

Baker, G. A. Chambers, W. L. Draffin, and R. E. McAlister initially were sympathetic to the Jesus Only views. They came fairly soon to perceive the dangers inherent in the doctrine and renounced it. McAlister wrote an article titled "Confessedly, Great is the Mystery of Godliness" in which he tried to correct the earlier misunderstanding of the nature of the Godhead. As his nephew W. E. McAlister noted, it was a painful thing for his uncle and others to do, for they had thought that the New Issue was a divine revelation. C. E. Baker, while pastoring in Montreal, found that the Jesus Only preachers who came to evangelize had little success until they dropped the doctrine. The subsequent blessings in terms of conversions, healings and baptisms convinced "Daddy Baker" that he had been wrong to espouse the New Issue.[35]

The third of the major theological disputes to trouble the early Canadian Pentecostals revolved around the question of speaking in tongues. Was the tongues phenomenon the primary evidence of the Baptism in the Spirit, or merely one of several possible signs? The debate came to be known as the "Initial Evidence Controversy," shortly after its appearance in Waco, Texas. At a short-term Bible school in that city, the issue was given considerable study. Some held a view of tongues as "one evidence" of the Baptism in the Spirit, but W. F. Carrothers presented so convincing a case for the "initial physical evidence" position that the majority present were satisfied.[36] To put theology to the test, it was agreed to preach the Baptism in the Spirit, without mentioning tongues at all, at upcoming evangelistic meetings in San Antonio. This was done, and still people came through to the Baptism with tongues. The position, therefore, adopted by Charles Parham and his followers at the Topeka Bible school in 1900-01 was reaffirmed.

The bulk of Pentecostals at the Azusa Street Mission also looked upon tongues as the evidence for the Baptism, although William Seymour's writings on the topic were somewhat ambiguous. In 1907, he referred to tongues as "one of the signs that go with every baptized person, but it is not the real evidence of the baptism in the every day life." In the same edition of *The Apostolic Faith*, he wrote:

> The Baptism with the Holy Ghost is a gift of power . . . so when we get it we have the same evidence as the Disciples received on the Day of Pentecost (Acts 2:4) in speaking in new tongues.[37]

A later article by Seymour called the evidence of the Baptism "Divine love, which is charity." It must be remembered that although this man was greatly used of God in the Los Angeles revival, he was uneducated and theologically untrained. His rather contradictory statements help to explain the eventual demise of his Azusa Street Mission as the American headquarters of the fledgling movement. The focus of debate quickly shifted to the first leaders of the Assemblies who once more discussed whether tongues was the Biblical evidence.

F. F. Bosworth, an admirer of Charles G. Finney, could find no specific reference to tongues-speaking in the famous revivalist's writings. Bosworth, therefore, came to question tongues as the evidence and raised the issue at the 1918 AG convention. One spokesman noted, in response, that Finney was referring to a Baptism of the Holy Ghost, and possibly tongues, when he noted in his *Memoirs* that he had "literally bellowed out the unutterable gushings of his heart." Another AG leader clinched the argument by reminding Bosworth and his few supporters that it was Scripture, not the experience of famous Christians, that was the basis for correct belief. The Council overwhelmingly opted for tongues as the initial physical evidence. One by-product of this gathering was the publication of various tracts on the difference between the evidence and the gift of tongues. Bosworth left the AG and joined the Christian and Missionary Alliance.[38]

In Canada, the Initial Evidence controversy was not as disruptive for early Pentecostalism, although it has resurfaced on occasion. The view that any gift is evidence of the Baptism in the Spirit has consistently been rejected by the great majority in the Canadian Fellowship. PAOC historian Gordon Atter has observed that a failure to maintain the view of tongues as the primary evidence for the Baptism in the Holy Spirit has led to a decline in its expression among believers. After studying Pentecostalism in several countries, he noted, "In almost every case, those who have reverted to the other view have, for all practical purposes, soon lost all signs of this supernatural visitation."[39]

The problems that arose from these three doctrinal disputes, in addition to several less-threatening issues, gave a strong motivation to many pioneer leaders to view organization more favorably. The first moves in that direction, by A. G. Ward and Vicar Boddy, were repelled by a number of acknowledged spokesmen, notably Mrs. Hebden and G. A. Chambers. Chambers' view at that early period was, "After all, God has taken us out of organized churches, why bind ourselves up?"[40] Ward wished to avoid controversy among the first assemblies and allowed his Pentecostal Missionary Union of 1909 to die. But the need for some form of self-government was pressing and could not long be avoided. For one thing, the number of adherents was steadily increasing. The Canadian census of 1911 reported 513 citizens who were identified as Pentecostal in belief. A decade later, that number had increased to some 7,000.[41]

There was the need for some means of validating the ministries of the

4 / CONFLICT AND CONSOLIDATION

early workers in a vast land with slow means of communication. And there was the practical problem of finances. Only ordained clergymen could travel on Canadian railroads for half-fare. Inexpensive travel was very important at a time when automobiles were costly and highways were slow. To meet the need, some men, like Arthur M. Atter, took out papers with an American body, the Pentecostal Assemblies of the World. At one time, Atter held credentials with three North American religious associations. The growth in the number of congregations meant that more clergymen were needed. R. E. McAlister met the need on one occasion by ordaining A. E. Adams in 1917,[42] but that was an irregular procedure, even for the unorganized bodies of believers.

A rapid shift in attitude was evident by 1917 when the next round of organizing activities took place. By that time, George Chambers had altered his view:

> We took the position that God was forever through with organization, so for a number of years the movement in Canada, like that in other countries, did not feel our need of system and order, but every man was a sort of law unto himself. . . . After years of battling along, each man for himself (some calling it the faith life), seeing and doing some quite foolish things, we finally woke up to the fact that some order and system was needed and right.[43]

Chambers played a prominent role in the establishment of The Pentecostal Assemblies of Canada and gave it many years of capable leadership as its first Chairman. But R. E. McAlister can properly be considered the architect of what has come to be Canada's largest Pentecostal denomination. McAlister was widely respected as a preacher, church planter, and writer. His skill in organization already had been demonstrated by some of the early camp meetings he had supervised. His personal integrity and devotion to the Pentecostal message were unquestioned.

There is some confusion of dates in the reminiscences and unsophisticated handwritten "histories" of some early Pentecostals. One date given for the earliest organizational meeting was 1916. The initial meetings, however, which resulted eventually in the formation of the PAOC, were held in May of 1917 in Montreal.[44] Those present included R. E. McAlister, G. A. Chambers, R. E. Sternall, Frank Small, A. M. Pattison, Harvey McAlister, and W. L. Draffin. More meetings were held that summer during the camp meeting at Charleston Lake, near Lansdowne, a short distance from Ottawa. It is likely that McAlister had arranged for the camp meetings, since he made Ottawa his headquarters at the time and had utilized camp meetings before in his itinerant evangelism.

The workers at the Lansdowne camp who met to consider a national association were C. E. Baker, G. A. Chambers, C. L. Cross (camp manager), W. L. Draffin, H. A. Goss, R. E. McAlister, and R. E. Sternall. Goss did his utmost at the time to promote the Jesus Only doctrine as an integral part of their theology. He also tried to get them to affiliate with the Pentecostal Assemblies of the World, an American association. Both he and Small favored adopting the name "Pentecostal Assemblies of the World in Canada." The title was rejected, although an abbreviated form came to be used later when the application was made for a federal charter. By this time, the Oneness teachings were becoming more controversial in Canada and they emerged as a side issue at these founding conferences.

Gordon Atter, who was personally familiar with the principals in these conferences, has studied the documents involved. His account differs in some particulars from that of Gloria G. Kulbeck,[45] but they are essentially the same. An additional exploratory meeting was held in Mille Roches, Ontario, in November, 1918, and then two more meetings in Montreal during the winter that followed. Some of the leading men from the West attended several of these meetings, including A. H. Argue and Frank Small. Eventually, it was decided to seek incorporation for the congregations in Eastern Canada and for the Argue church in Winnipeg.

The federal government issued a charter for The Pentecostal Assemblies of Canada on May 17th, 1919, under the Companies Act. The first trustees were William Lloyd Draffin, Reuben Eby Sternall, George Augustus Chambers, Robert Edward McAlister, Harvey McAlister, Arthur Miles Pattison, and Frank Small.

In the Letters Patent, for the PAOC, the new body defined "the following purposes and objects, namely:

(a) To conduct a place or places of worship;
(b) To organize and conduct schools of religious instruction;
(c) To carry on home and foreign missionary work for the spread of the gospel;
(d) To carry on charitable and philanthropic work;
(e) To publish, sell and distribute Christian literature and papers;
(f) To collect, solicit and accept funds or other subscriptions for the carrying on of the work of the co-operative body and for any other religious, charitable or benevolent purpose;
(g) To exercise any of the powers usually conferred on duly incorporated benevolent societies by either Dominion or Provincial authority;
(h) To dispose of the entire undertaking of the corporation."[46]

The first meeting of the Board of Trustees took place in Ottawa on May 26, 1919, with all signatories but W. L. Draffin and Frank Small present.

4 / CONFLICT AND CONSOLIDATION

A constitution was adopted, with a preamble which made explicit the exact nature of the new organization. It was to be a "fellowship" of cooperating churches and not a religious hierarchy.

> WHEREAS the Pentecostal ministers representing a number of assemblies in Canada met together for the purpose of consultation and prayer and to adopt necessary means whereby they could better cooperate for the furtherance of the gospel, and after prayer and consideration, unanimous agreement was reached that a cooperative body was necessary, and
>
> WHEREAS we deem it advisable to avoid creating unscriptural lines of fellowship, to affiliate on the basic principles of love and righteousness and truth with due recognition for each other, allowing for the liberty of conscience for matters pertaining to personal conviction,
>
> THEREFORE BE IT RESOLVED that we, as representative ministers from the Pentecostal assemblies in various parts of Canada, shall henceforth be known as The Pentecostal Assemblies of Canada whose purpose is neither to legislate laws of government nor to usurp authority over the various local assemblies, nor to deprive them of their scripturally recognized local rights and privileges but to cooperate with them and assist them by all legitimate means consistent with New Testament principles of Christian conduct, and
>
> Be it further resolved that we disapprove of making a doctrinal statement a basis of fellowship and cooperation but that we accept the Word of God in its entirety, conducting ourselves in harmony with its divine principles and Apostolic example, endeavoring to keep the unity of the Spirit in the bond of peace until "we all come in the unity of the faith." [47]

The young Fellowship had only 27 assemblies affiliated with it in 1919. In Eastern Canada there were groups at Alliston, Arnprior, Barrie, Bristol Ridge, Edwards, Hamilton, Kinburn, Kingston, Kitchener, Markham, Mille Roches, Montreal, McBain, North Seguin, Ottawa, Owen Sound, Russel, and Sandtown. Winnipeg was the only congregation at the time in Manitoba but there were assemblies at Edmonton, Eston, Lethbridge, Moose Jaw, Prince Rupert, Saskatoon, Spruce Lake, and Vancouver in the three western provinces. Some of the western workers had taken a keen interest in the founding of the PAOC, especially A. H. Argue, although he was not a signatory to the Charter.

One of the first official acts to follow was the holding of a "General Assembly" at Kitchener, November 25-28, 1919. There was a total of 31 clergy and lay delegates present; a number of most important decisions were taken.[48] One by-law (No. 6) adopted at the conference ensured that the PAOC would always have a democratic form of church government. The legislation granted to any layman, appointed as an official delegate by a local congregation, the right to speak in, and vote at, all national meetings. Other decisions were made on ordination, the proper baptismal formula, and the work of overseas missionaries. The rite of ordination was to be performed by senior men already in possession of some form of certification from one of the branches of the Pentecostal Movement. Two or more men could ordain to the ministry by the imposition of hands and prayer, but the candidates must first be approved by the delegates in conference.[49]

The matter of the baptismal formula and the funding of overseas missions were solved in a very practical way. The policy for water baptisms was to be left to individual choice:

> Much contention and confusion has been caused over the issue of One God and Trinitarian views, also the Baptismal Formula. . . . Be it resolved to disapprove . . . all such issues that divide and confuse God's people to no profit, and that aggressive evangelism be our motto. Whereas we recognize a three-fold relationship of Father, Son and Holy Ghost being clearly taught in the New Testament, Be it resolved that we express ourselves in harmony with this truth. . . . As to baptism, we feel like leaving the matter of formula with the individual.[50]

Clearly, personal choice was to be allowed for the baptismal formula, but there was to be no doubt about the orthodox trinitarian theology of the PAOC from its inception. As for missions, the solution was equally practical: the delegates simply adopted a practice already in vogue among a number of congregations. These assemblies had been collecting funds for missionaries and had distributed two-thirds of the collections for overseas work and one-third for missions in the homeland. The decision to incorporate this financing arrangement into the structure of the PAOC was made at this first "national" conference. It was to be "recommended" to the affiliated churches, not imposed on them. A letter subsequently was sent to all assemblies acquainting them with the Kitchener decisions, and outlining the goals of the PAOC.

The Oneness doctrine, espoused by Frank Small and Howard Goss, was rejected at the founding conference of 1919. Further attempts by Small to get the teaching adopted by the PAOC met with the same results. Soon afterwards, Small left the Fellowship and founded another Pentecostal body dedicated to the Jesus Only viewpoint, with headquarters in Western

4 / CONFLICT AND CONSOLIDATION

Canada. Early leaders such as John McAlister and A. H. Argue had opposed the New Issue from its first appearance. They also were conscious of the need for some form of organization for the West. At a meeting in Moose Jaw in 1919, a decision was made to affiliate with the Americans as the Western Canada District Council of the Assemblies of God. The U.S. evangelist Hugh Cadwalder was involved in these deliberations and was elected the first chairman of the new district.

The leaders of the eastern churches took the further action in 1920 of uniting with the AG as the Eastern Canada District Council. This brought both groups into a cooperative relationship, strengthened by some churches having membership in both the PAOC and the AG. Initially, the new arrangement promised to provide stability and continuity for the Canadians, but eventually a number of problems developed which made affiliation with the American organization less attractive. There was a difference of policy between the AG and the PAOC in the direction of their overseas missions work. A second factor was, as Gordon Atter put it, "national influence": Canadians simply wished to govern their own affairs. The ties with the AG were severed by mutual agreement, and the churches in the West came into the PAOC in 1922 under the legal framework already existing with the federal charter. A cooperative international relationship has continued to exist between the AG and the PAOC to this day.[51]

G. A. Chambers and R. E. McAlister played pivotal roles in these organizational and administrative decisions. Chambers was elected first Chairman of the Fellowship and he travelled extensively promoting the work. He had been pastoring at Arnprior prior to the first conference. His work took him from Newfoundland to Vancouver and he was away from home a great deal of the time. He recognized the difficulties his travels caused for his wife:

> Sometimes I wondered if it was right for me to be away so much from home. However, the hand of the Lord leading, and many blessed experiences, more than compensated for all the privations which we were called upon to endure.[52]

During the very difficult days following the economic collapse of 1929, Chambers found it impossible to find a pastor for the young assembly in Peterborough. Finally, he moved his family there and pastored the church while continuing his duties as General Superintendent. This was possible only because R. E. McAlister handled the great bulk of PAOC administration. George Chambers was a tireless advocate of Pentecostalism across the Dominion and a zealous promoter of worldwide missions. He was the chief force behind the development of a district campground at Cobourg, and one of the main advocates for the establishment of the Bible school in Winnipeg. As General Superintendent, he attended most of the District Conferences which, by the time of his retirement in 1934, had increased from two to seven. His leadership in the development of the PAOC will be described later in this narrative.

R. E. McAlister had an equally seminal role in the founding and the growth of Canadian Pentecostalism. In the estimation of A. G. Ward, McAlister and Chambers were the most influential personalities in the organization of the Fellowship. Where Chambers gave overall leadership by attending conferences, camps, and conventions across the country, McAlister provided legislative and administrative skills at the head office. He was elected first Secretary-Treasurer and carried out his duties in addition to pastoring. He was sent as an official representative of the eastern churches to the early conferences in the West, demonstrating his wide acceptability to the adherents across the country. For many years, the administrative centre of Canadian Pentecostalism was wherever McAlister was pastoring: at first in Ottawa, later in London.

McAlister also launched *The Pentecostal Testimony* in 1920 and was editor, publisher, and distributor for 15 years. The first issue in December was put together, with the help of his wife Laura, in a little mission hall in Ottawa. His editorial facilities consisted of a hand-set printing plant with an old door suspended over two boxes for a table. He called the periodical *The Canadian Pentecostal Testimony* and used it to promote the theological, governmental, and missionary views of the PAOC. Its first edition contained articles by him on "The Baptism of the Holy Ghost" and "The Unity of God." This latter was designed to prove that "Plurality is implied in the use of the pronouns referring to God in the Old Testament." The rest of the four-page magazine was devoted to news of revival in Canada and the solicitation of funds for the eight missionaries already on the foreign field. McAlister was officially appointed editor at the second annual conference meeting in Montreal in November, 1920.[53]

The contribution the *Testimony* was to make to the unifying and the growth of the young Fellowship cannot adequately be calculated. McAlister had the foresight to envision something of the magazine's impact when he put out the first issue.

The Paper

> The publishing of a Canadian Pentecostal paper has been a keen felt need for a long time, as there is not a Canadian paper in the Dominion. Workers have given expression to this from coast to

4 / CONFLICT AND CONSOLIDATION

coast. It will not only be of interest and upbuilding to all Assemblies but it will always be kept clean-cut from all contentious issues, and will be safe to hand out to anyone at any time and at all times.

It will have the effect of stimulating the Missionary spirit, as well as the spirit of cooperation, and now that a missionary treasury is established at the head office, which will be in touch with all the foreign fields, as well as all the distributing centres, it will gather together hundreds of dollars for the mission work from isolated places where no regular assemblies are established, and where no missionary avenues have yet been opened

It will be an advertisement medium for any Assembly desiring to take advantage of in the announcement of special meetings and convictions.

Now, friends, here is your opportunity if you really desire a Canadian paper. Get behind it at once. We absolutely need finances to get a start and get it into the field. Come across now! If there is any reason why this paper should not be published, speak now, or forever hold your peace. Every Assembly should distribute a large roll each month. Now we will be anxious to know how this paper is received and we will be glad to hear from any who have words of appreciation, comments or suggestions. If there is any way you feel that it can be improved, let us hear from you.[54]

R. E. McAlister was the prime mover in the development of a new constitution and a statement of faith for the PAOC. A decision was made at the seventh General Conference of 1927 to adopt a doctrinal statement of The Pentecostal Assemblies of Canada which would be "separate from the statement used by the General Council at Springfield, Mo."[55] It was McAlister who carried out the preliminary work and got both the *Statement of Fundamental and Essential Truths* and the *General Constitution* adopted by the Canadian Fellowship. He claimed, in a 1946 letter to C. B. Smith (then General Superintendent), that it was he who "wrote our doctrinal statement of Fundamental and Essential Truths" and that it was he who "got out our present Constitution."[56]

Walter McAlister has noted that "the original Charter made no reference to doctrine," but that the need for a systematic presentation of Pentecostal distinctives very soon became apparent.[57] The initiative for a made-in-Canada doctrinal statement appears to have come from R. E. McAlister through his publication of the AG Statement of Faith in the February, 1926 edition of the *Testimony*. The next step would have been approval at the 1927 General Conference.

It also is likely that McAlister played a significant part in the development of the PAOC form of government, which both Gordon Atter and Tom Johnstone have described as "Presbygational." By this term, they meant an amalgam of both Congregational and Presbyterian principles of church government. R. E. McAlister had a Holiness Movement and a Methodist background. Many of the first group of Canadian leaders were recruited from the Baptist, Christian and Missionary Alliance, Mennonite, and Methodist denominations. These groups were committed to a philosophy of local church government, and the principle was carried over into Pentecost. Congregational policy was very much insisted upon by the early leaders, and the independence of each congregation was carefully guarded. The pages of the *Testimony* in the 1920s reveal a constant awareness, on the part of the editor, of the sovereignty of the local church. But the gradual development of church government at the national level, and later the provincial, led to the adoption of some elements of Presbyterianism. The resulting "Presbygational" system was adapted early to serve the unique needs of Canadian Pentecostalism and has continued in operation until this day. That reflects most favorably on R. E. McAlister, who had so intimate an involvement in its adoption and its development over the years.

Men like R. E. McAlister, G. A. Chambers, and A. G. Ward were providentially used of God in the establishment of the PAOC. There were also scores of other Spirit-filled workers whose labors and sacrifices brought Pentecostal congregations into existence. Unfortunately, the story of many of these first generation pioneers will never be known: indeed, they often neglected even to record some of their major achievements, lest they receive the glory they felt due to their Lord. According to Walter McAlister, the Pentecostal awakening in North America was the result of much prayer and a deep longing on the part of multitudes for more of God and more of His power in their lives. It led to what he called "a spontaneous spiritual movement (that) continued for many years."

Perceptive men like Ward, Chambers, and McAlister realized very soon that the benefits of the Pentecostal revival could only be preserved by some type of organization. They realized that the distinctive doctrines of 20th-century Pentecostalism had to be identified and enunciated in some formal manner in order to maintain them. The legislative and administrative work they did laid the basis for the continuation of the Pentecostal Fellowship in Canada and for its evangelistic outreach around the world. Even these notable leaders, however, could never have anticipated, before 1920, the extent to which the work would grow. A. G. Ward acknowledged that his colleagues were men of great faith and courage, but could never, in their dreams, have envisioned the extraordinary progress of Pentecostalism in Canada and around the world.

4 / CONFLICT AND CONSOLIDATION

Endnotes

1. Thomas Wm. Miller, *Ripe for Revival: The Church at The Crossroads* (Burlington: Welch Publishing, 1984), p. 187.
2. Vinson Synan, *The Holiness-Pentecostal Movement in the United States* (Grand Rapids: Eerdmans, 1971), pp. 53-54.
3. Lefferts A. Loetscher, ed., *Twentieth Century Encyclopedia of Religious Knowledge*, vol. 2 (Grand Rapids: Baker, 1955), 660-663; and Van A. Harvey, *A Handbook of Theological Terms* (New York: MacMillan, 1964), pp. 152-154.
4. *The Apostolic Faith*, 1:2 (October 1906), 3.
5. *The Promise*, 1 (May 1907), 1.
6. George A. Chambers, "In Retrospect," *The Pentecostal Testimony* (November 1934), 7.
7. Orwig's eyewitness account was reprinted in B. F. Lawrence, *The Apostolic Faith Restored* (Springfield: Gospel Publishing House, 1916), p. 77.
8. Aimee Semple McPherson, *This is That* (Los Angeles: Echo Park Evangelistic Assoc., 1923).
9. For example, see Robert M. Anderson, *Vision of the Disinherited: The Making of American Pentecostalism* (New York: Oxford University Press, 1979).
10. Thomas Wm. Miller, taped interview with W. E. McAlister, May 3, 1984.
11. John T. Nichol, *The Pentecostals* (Plainfield: Logos, 1966), p. xi.
12. Thomas Wm. Miller, taped interview with Gordon F. Atter, April 30, 1984.
13. A. G. Ward, "How the Pentecostal Experience Came To Canada," typescript copy of memoirs, PAOC Archives.
14. *The Promise*, 2 (June 1907), 2.
15. *The Promise*, 14 (October 1909), 1.
16. Gloria G. Kulbeck, *What God Hath Wrought: A History of The Pentecostal Assemblies of Canada* (Toronto: Full Gospel Publishing House, 1958), pp. 35-36.
17. *The Promise*, 15 (March 1910), 1.
18. Ethel Goss, *The Winds of God: The Story of the Early Pentecostal Days (1901-1914) in the Life of Howard A. Goss* (New York: Comet Press, 1958), pp. 155-156.
19. *The Apostolic Faith*, 1:5 (January 1907), 2; 1:7 (April 1907), 3; and 1:10 (September 1907), 3.
20. See Melvin Dieter, *The Holiness Revival of the Nineteenth Century* (Metuchen: Scarecrow Press, 1980).
21. Carl Brumback, *Suddenly from Heaven: A History of the Assemblies of God* (Springfield; Gospel Publishing House, 1961), pp. 98-99.

22. Frank Bartleman, *Another Wave Rolls In* (Northside, Cal.: Voice Publications, 1970), pp. 106-112; formerly published as *What Really Happened at Azusa Street* (1925).
23. Vinson Synan, *Charismatic Bridges* (Ann Arbor: Word of Life, 1974), pp. 10-13.
24. Walter J. Hollenweger, *The Pentecostals: The Charismatic Movement in the Churches* (Minneapolis: Augsburg, 1973), p. 25; see also Robert A. Larden, *Our Apostolic Heritage* (Calgary: Kyle Printing, 1971), p. 30.
25. Thomas Wm. Miller, note 10; see also G. A. Chambers, *The New Testament Church: Its Ministers and Ministries* (Peterborough: College Press), p. 25.
26. Donald T. Klan, "Pentecostal Assemblies of Canada Church Growth in British Columbia from Origins Until 1953," unpublished MCS thesis, Regent College, Vancouver, B.C., 1979, 47.
27. William W. Menzies, *Anointed to Serve: The Story of The Assemblies of God* (Springfield: Gospel Publishing House, 1971), p. 318.
28. Maria B. Woodworth-Etter, *Signs and Wonders* (Indianapolis: for the author, 1916, 7th ed. rev.), pp. 250-252.
29. J. Roswell Flower, "History of the Assemblies of God," typescript copy of classroom notes, Assemblies of God Archives; used by permission. See also Frank J. Ewart, *The Phenomenon of Pentecost* (Hazelwood Word Aflame Press, 1975, rev. ed. of 1947 book), pp. 105-106.
30. Flower, *op cit.* For a summary of Oneness theology, see David Arthur Reid, "Origins and Development of the Theology of Oneness Pentecostalism in the United States," *Pneuma*, 1:1 (Spring 1980), 31-37.
31. Brumback, *Suddenly From Heaven*, pp. 204-210.
32. See Article V, of the Constitution of the Assemblies of God, September 1927; cited in Irwin Winehouse, *The Assemblies of God: A Popular Survey* (New York: Vantage Press, 1959), pp. 204-205.
33. Gordon F. Atter, *The Third Force* (Peterborough: College Press, 1962, 3rd ed. rev.), pp. 76, 204.
34. Ibid., pp. 60, 94, 95.
35. Thomas Wm. Miller, taped interview with Gordon F. Atter, note 12; also taped interviews with Walter E. McAlister, May 1, 1981 and May 3, 1984.
36. Bennett F. Lawrence, *The Apostolic Faith Restored* (Springfield: Gospel Publishing House, 1916), p. 67.
37. *The Apostolic Faith*, 1:9 (June-September 1907), 2.
38. Brumback, *Suddenly From Heaven*, pp. 216-225.
39. Atter, *The Third Force*, p. 149.
40. Thomas Wm. Miller, taped interview with Gordon Atter, note 12.

4 / CONFLICT AND CONSOLIDATION

41. *Canada Year Book* (Ottawa: Statistics Canada, 1978).
42. Atter, *The Third Force*, p. 67; and Kulbeck, *What God Has Wrought*, p. 115.
43. George A. Chambers, "In Retrospect," *The Pentecostal Testimony* (November 1934), 7.
44. Chambers (note 43) gave the date as 1916. G. F. Atter (note 12) is a more reliable source.
45. See notes 12 and 16.
46. From the original Letters Patent document on file at PAOC Archives; see also James MacKnight, "Pentecostal Assemblies," Spirit Of Toronto, ed. by M. L. Holton (Toronto: Image Publishing Inc.), pp. 115-127.
47. "Minute Book, Pentecostal Assemblies of Canada," May 26, 1919, PAOC Archives.
48. See first issue of *The Pentecostal Testimony* (December 1920).
49. "PAOC Minute Book, General Assembly of the PAOC at Kitchener, November 25-28, 1919," 1.
50. Ibid., 4.
51. Atter, *The Third Force*, p. 96.
52. George A. Chambers, *50 Years in the Service of the King* (Toronto: Testimony Press, 1960), p. 39. Roy C. Spaetzel of Kitchener has researched the history of the Kitchener Pentecostal Church as well as the formative period of the PAOC. He reported that G. A. Chambers, as General Chairman, attended a Saskatoon meeting about September 1922. Also present were Hugh Cadwalder and Elder E. N. Bell, who represented the Assemblies of God. Spaetzel claimed there was "a meeting of Minds" among these three leaders which led to the November 1922 amalgamation of the two Canadian districts and their genial separation from the AG; see Roy C Spaetzel, "How Pentecost Came to Ontario During January 1908," typewritten monograph, Kitchener.
53. "Minute Book, 2nd General Conference, Montreal, Nov. 23-25, 1920," 1. For an analysis of R. E. McAlister's role, see Thomas Wm. Miller, "Robert E. McAlister: The Architect of Canadian Pentecostalism," *The Pentecostal Testimony* (May 1989), 7-9, 40; (June 1989), 11-13, 24; (July 1989), 9-11; (August 1989), 28-30.
54. *The Canadian Pentecostal Testimony* (December 1920), Ottawa: reprinted in *The Pentecostal Testimony, Supplement* (January 1970).
55. The Assemblies of God doctrinal statement had been printed earlier in the February 1926 issue of *The Pentecostal Testimony*.
56. R. E. McAlister, letter to C. B. Smith, January 22, 1946, PAOC Archives.
57. See note 10.

Chapter 5

AND HE GAVE SOME...

The decade of the '20s was a momentous period in the religious history of North America. In business, customs, and styles, it was "The Roaring Twenties," but in religion it was an era of vehement assault on historic Christianity, especially on its evangelical branch. Liberal theologies, having infiltrated many of the seminaries after 1890, made inroads at the parish and church levels. Modernist churchmen issued what was known as the *Auburn Affirmation*, a document so far-reaching as to threaten the foundations of the Christian faith as generally held by most North American denominations.

A number of responses to this threat were made before 1920, one of which was the publication of a series of booklets entitled *The Fundamentals: A Testimony to the Truth*. These booklets were distributed in the thousands through the support of well-to-do businessmen. They emphasized historic Christian affirmations about God, fallen mankind, the supernatural, and the real existence of heaven and hell. Theological controversy reached a peak in the famous Scopes Monkey Trial of 1925 in Tennessee. A school teacher named John Scopes was put on trial for teaching evolution. The legal arguments made international headlines for several months and helped to publicize the issues. A most regrettable result of the trial was the portrayal of the Fundamentalists in America as bigoted, ignorant, and hostile to modern science.

Fundamentalism acquired a stereotyped image that was extremely negative in the eyes of the public. When Pentecostalism made its appearance, it was associated in the minds of many with this image. Even though the Fundamentalists on the whole rejected the Pentecostal distinctive, and repudiated the "holy rollers," Pentecostals continued to face prejudice and rejection in many quarters. This poor public image was

5 / AND HE GAVE SOME...

increased by the hostile press which reported on the Azusa Street meetings.

By 1920 there were only 27 PAOC churches in Canada. The number of members of those assemblies is unknown, although census statistics indicated that only 7,000 Canadians had identified themselves as Pentecostal. Obviously, Pentecostals had little impact on the general public. The decade that followed, however, was characterized by a relatively rapid advance in the number of converts, PAOC churches established, and religious institutions set up.[1]

Pentecostals were vigorous opponents of the "new theological insights" being propagated by the Modernists and Liberals. Aimee Semple McPherson, for example, denounced the preachers who not only failed to condemn the irreligious views of men like Robert Ingersoll, but gave them tacit support by including these radical precepts in some of their sermons:

> Mr. Ingersoll lectured for years against the Bible. The admission fee was always one dollar. Eventually Mr. Ingersoll ceased. A man asked him one day: "Bob, why don't you keep up your lectures against the Bible?" "Well," he said, "I don't need to ... I now have a million dollars, and I don't need any more money; and a lot of preachers nowadays ... are making the same criticisms exactly against the Bible that I have been making, and they have an audience that I can't get and an influence that I never had."[2]

It was the ministries of workers like McPherson, Charles Price, J. D. Saunders, J. H. Blair, and the earlier recruits to Pentecostalism — A. H. Argue, G. A. Chambers, R. E. McAlister, and his nephew W. E. McAlister — that helped to counter theological Modernism in the 1920s in Canada.

The decade was one of consolidating already established Pentecostal churches, pioneering new assemblies, reaching the masses through healing campaigns, and entering areas of the country previously untouched by the full gospel message. For example, James Montgomery helped introduce Pentecostal teachings in the Maritimes. A number of attempts were made at a relatively early date to evangelize the remote Canadian North. The foreign missions program, which had begun in a spontaneous fashion, came under the aegis of the PAOC in this decade and was greatly expanded.

Continual expansion on every front required development and frequent adjustments to the denomination's legislative machinery. The number of districts increased, campgrounds were set up, and several short-term Bible school programs were conducted. During this period, a three-year

Bible college program was established in Winnipeg. By the end of the '20s, the PAOC had become a truly national religious organization.[3] In G. A. Chambers' opinion, the Fellowship in Canada had made phenomenal progress by 1929. Receipts to the national office had increased from $1,000 in 1920 to $83,000 in 1929; membership had expanded from 7,000 to more than 26,000.[4]

The economic boom of the '20s culminated in a stock market crash which precipitated the Great Depression. George Chambers looked upon 1929 as "our banner year," but predicted great difficulties in the future for the Pentecostal work in Canada. As it is now known, the effects of the Depression were greatly magnified by a long-lasting drought which devastated the Prairie communities. The economic sufferings and deprivation did not end until the advent of the Second World War in 1939, which, of course, brought the introduction of even more difficulties. Young men were taken into the Armed Forces, the Bible schools had mainly female students, and shortages of construction materials hampered the building of church facilities. The war cut off some PAOC missionaries from the homeland during the conflict — a few were made prisoners-of-war.

It was the work of the church-planting pioneers and the salvation-healing evangelists that made the 1920s such a successful period for Canadian Pentecostalism. One of the most noteworthy representatives of the latter category was Aimee Semple McPherson. McPherson, a resident of Ingersoll, Ontario, had been converted and filled with the Spirit there, before going to China as a missionary. The tragic death of her first husband led to her return to Ontario, where she launched into tent evangelism. By 1921, when she arrived in Winnipeg to hold meetings, she was one of the best-known Pentecostal preachers in North America.

Evangelist A .H. Argue, Pastor W. E. Moody, and many of the believers gave unstinting support to her campaign. Still, only small crowds came to the first services. When McPherson discovered that thousands of Winnipeg citizens were enthusiastic dancers, she personally visited the dance halls, spoke to receptive groups, and then invited them to her church meetings. In one dance hall McPherson addressed about 2,000 people, some of whom were later converted to Christ. When she visited the notorious "red light" district, with police protection, the Winnipeg press gave wide coverage to her talks to the "fallen women." The crowds at her meetings became so large that police had to close off the roads several blocks away from the church. A. H. Argue later reported:

> It was estimated that nearly 1700 were crowded into the main Auditorium of the church. The large basement was turned into a

5 / AND HE GAVE SOME . . .

prayer room and seekers and workers would quickly fill it. The altar upstairs also would fill up night after night with sinners, sometimes two and three rows all across the front, seeking God. It was wonderful to see the old-time conviction rest so mightily upon the people that they would rush to the altar and weep their way to Jesus. It was impossible to keep account of the numbers being saved and coming through to the baptism. One week . . . our count ran to between 40 and 50 who received the Holy Ghost . . . Numbers saw visions. There were surely marvelous Bible signs in our midst. At the healing meetings one would be reminded of the time Jesus was upon earth, by the way the people thronged to the altar for prayer. Some very remarkable testimonies of healing were given: tumors, ruptures, rheumatism and gall stones being removed; in fact the many various cases of healing were too numerous to mention. Sister McPherson made her messages so simple that they were both easily understood and very impressive. Numbers of ministers . . . attended, and some received the baptism of the Spirit. The community has been stirred as never before by any other single spiritual effort in our city . . . The three daily papers took an active interest . . . so that Winnipeg and the country surrounding were kept informed as to the progress of the Revival.[5]

The McPherson meetings made Pentecostalism a well-known religious movement in Manitoba and helped create a favorable attitude to it. Her meetings about that time in Alberta had similar results. The services were held in Lethbridge at the request of Pastor John McAlister. When the building secured for the campaign burned down, they moved to the curling rink, even though the weather was cold and the ground damp. Still, large crowds came and many were saved and healed. McPherson found the meetings difficult because of the effect of the dampness on her health, but it "was heaven on earth to the dear, starving saints of the great Northwest; and so great was the financial struggle that we were happy to donate our time as a missionary work."

According to the pastor, some 300 people were converted and at least 60 filled with the Spirit in just two weeks. The report gave the meetings a very high rating: "It is the unanimous opinion, expressed everywhere, that this has been the greatest spiritual awakening that the City of Lethbridge has ever known." The small prayer room was crowded with over 150 at a time; people from other churches received the Baptism with tongues, and "sick ones came and were healed by the mighty power of God." People came from as far east as Winnipeg, and from as far west as Prince Rupert. Some came from the northern American states and even from California. The Lethbridge church subsequently enjoyed steady growth enabling Pastor McAlister to lead the congregation in the purchase and renovation of a church building.[6]

AND HE GAVE SOME... / 5

C. E. Baker invited McPherson to Montreal, where he had been working since 1916. He had a mission hall on McGill College Avenue, but he secured the old St. Andrew's Church on Beaver Hall Hill for the McPherson campaign. Baker's enthusiasm for the meetings was evident in his report that "Canada's largest city is visited with floods of the Latter Rain." Prayer meetings in homes and the church preceded the services. The very first altar call given saw many fall to their knees and cry for mercy, seeking forgiveness of sins. Many were filled with the Spirit and spoke in tongues in that first meeting.

The blind were given sight, the lame walked, the sick rose up and leaped and ran, praising God. Police were unable to cope with the crowds. Ministers in Montreal referred to it all as "the real, old time Religion."[7] Hundreds were converted, including French-speaking folk who knew not one word of English. Soon the building, seating 2,000, was too small. One eyewitness, Reuben P. Spurrell, reported hundreds of conversions, and, as a consequence, later became a Pentecostal preacher himself. People attended from Toronto, Ottawa, Chicago, Winnipeg, Kingston, New York, Newfoundland, New Hampshire, and other regions. Such revival-healing services did much to establish Pentecostalism in the Dominion during the 1920s.[8]

Even Mrs. McPherson's ministry in California had a beneficial effect in Canada. One of her converts was a young Canadian by the name of George B. Griffin who attended meetings in Angelus Temple while his family was temporarily living in Los Angeles. After the family returned to Canada, Griffin became a PAOC pastor and Bible college teacher. Several Canadians also were among the 300 students in her first Bible school, conducted in Angelus Temple in 1924-25.

McPherson was largely responsible for the inauguration of another revival-healing ministry that greatly advanced Pentecostalism in Canada. Dr. Charles S. Price, a prominent liberal clergyman in Lodi, California, was a skeptic with respect to the supernatural. When he visited McPherson's meetings, he was converted and soon received the Baptism in the Spirit. His testimony in his home church led many others to seek salvation and a number also received the Baptism.[9] Price preached with great effectiveness and began to pray for the sick. From this small beginning in California came a sensational salvation-healing ministry which Price exercised throughout Canada and the United States.

After visiting the Price meetings to investigate, Dr. W. J. Sipprell, pastor of the Metropolitan Methodist Church in Victoria, British Columbia, invited Price for special meetings in April 1923. The crowds soon increased to 3,000. After a number of notable healings, so many people were attracted to the services that it was necessary to move to the

5 / AND HE GAVE SOME . . .

city hockey arena where the crowds swelled past the 6,000 mark. On the last day of the meetings in Victoria, 9,000 were in attendance. Sipprell reported that at least 500 people testified to him of bodily healing. Among the most noteworthy was that of a deaf and dumb man who was able to hear and speak after prayer. Another was Rev. W. J. Knott of Victoria who was healed on April 17 after suffering 20 years from headaches, stomach pains, and a goitre on his neck. Perhaps the most dramatic of the healings was that of 21-year-old Ruby Dimmick. Ruby's father was the pastor of a local Methodist church. He reported that Ruby, from the age of 13, had developed severe curvature of the spine, causing one leg to be one and a half inches shorter than the other. Surgery in a Toronto hospital was of no avail. Ruby was sitting beside her father in a Price meeting when, according to reports, the power of God touched her, lengthened her leg, straightened her spine, and reshaped her deformed foot. Ruby ran through the auditorium praising God for her healing. Thousands of people attending the meeting witnessed the miraculous event. One eyewitness, Mrs. E. Hazel Mussen of Abbotsford, B.C., reported in correspondence that she was present in 1923 when Ruby Dimmick and W. J. Knott were healed and could verify the marvellous impact of the miracles. It was said that the power of God was so powerful in the services that great conviction of sin seized hundreds of people and scores of conversions occurred in every meeting. At times, there were 700 to 1,000 people at the altar seeking God.[10]

Dr. Price gave prominence to the spiritual needs of his listeners. His preaching was in the Pentecostal Revival tradition — with emphasis on sanctification, the gift of tongues as evidence of the Baptism in the Spirit, divine healing, and the imminent return of Jesus Christ. Price also made a clear distinction between man's agency and God's power. It was Jesus who was the healer, he insisted, and only Jesus. Canadian historian James Gray called it "hell fire and brimstone" preaching and noted that heaven and hell were real places to Price. Gray added that the evangelist had no use for "the ethereal claptrap" of the modernist preachers who spoke as if the two places did not exist.[11] The fact that Price had training in law, before choosing the ministry as a vocation, may have added to the effectiveness of his sermons. His contemporaries considered him to be a fluent but not particularly eloquent speaker. They observed that the key to his success was the anointing of the Holy Spirit on his ministry.

The salvation-healing ministries of both McPherson and Price came under frequent attack from theologically liberal clergymen and sometimes the secular press. The negative impact, however, was minimal and was often balanced by positive comments. One secular paper, the *Victoria Daily Colonist*, reported: "In the history of the concerted Christian efforts in an evangelistic way, there has never before been the tremendous interest aroused as was manifest in the campaign." The Victoria Ministerial Association, on May 11, 1923, published a "Resolution of Commendation" for the Price meetings. After the campaign ended, large crowds continued to attend numerous local churches. Metropolitan Methodist Church had up to 1,200 at its Wednesday prayer meetings. The older evangelical churches experienced a "marked improvement" in their previously declining fortunes. The Pentecostals in Victoria received a great boost from the Price meetings. The attendance at their own prayer meetings for some weeks following increased to about 1,000 a week.[12]

The Greater Vancouver Ministerial invited Price for meetings in May 1923, in the 8,000-seat Georgia Street Arena. Local Pentecostals gave enthusiastic support. Many Baptist congregations in the city also supported the Price campaign. One enthusiastic layman even took out newspaper advertisements to report, "Folks are being healed in body and soul, put in for your share." Crowds were so large that at times an estimated 5,000 were unable to gain admission. Even the stairways were packed, to the dismay of fire department officials. The owner of the arena, Frank Patrick, estimated that in three weeks of meetings about a quarter-million people had been in attendance. Both salvation and healing again were given prominence. One unusual conversion was that of a Vancouver woman who was a well-known revolutionary socialist. The altar worker who prayed with her was Elsie Brooks, who later became a Pentecostal evangelist.

Despite the enormous crowds, the many healings, and the hundreds of conversions, some members of the Vancouver clergy denounced Price's meetings as a "faith healing campaign which exploited human suffering." Several Modernist clergymen issued a statement claiming that the healings had been induced by "emotional excitement, strongly reinforced by hypnotism and mass suggestion." However, scores of other preachers defended the meetings as blessed by God and the healings as genuine. Sixteen members of the Baptist Ministerial Association of Vancouver issued a public statement of total endorsement of the Price campaign of May 1923. The significant results of these meetings gave great prominence to the Pentecostal doctrines of Salvation and Divine Healing. Many of the converts found their way to the Sixth Avenue Pentecostal Tabernacle. A Vancouver correspondent to *The Pentecostal Testimony* reported great satisfaction with the advancement of Pentecostalism through the recent meetings in the arena.[13]

Price began another series of meetings in Calgary in 1923. Drawn by the healings, large crowds attended from the start. The Alberta Medical Association charged Price with practising medicine without a licence. When the case reached court, the magistrate dismissed the charge. The

5 / AND HE GAVE SOME...

AMA then rented a lecture hall and gave presentations denouncing the work. While a small crowd attended these lectures, thousands were listening to Price. After the Calgary meetings, he moved on to Edmonton, where in 24 days over 10,000 people were counted at the altars.

It was in the Edmonton meetings that Lorne F. Fox was introduced to the full gospel. His father was scheduled for major surgery for gall stones, hernia, and possible cancer. One night the senior Fox was healed at a Price service. Fox's sister, Ethel, was healed of tuberculosis and near-blindness. As for Lorne Fox, he had had three lesions of the heart and 19 recorded heart attacks. Nine doctors had concluded that nothing more could be done for the young man. In the Price meetings Lorne Fox was totally healed. The family physician declared all three to be "totally healed by direct intervention of Divine Providence."[14] Lorne Fox later launched a worldwide evangelism-healing ministry which was highly regarded by Pentecostals everywhere.

Price held a salvation-healing campaign in Brandon, Manitoba, in 1923. This was the scene of another remarkable healing. Mrs. E. Lang had been injured in an auto accident in 1918 and had undergone surgery twice. In constant pain, she went to the Price meetings and was completely healed. The next year she married a preacher and spent the rest of her life in Pentecostal ministry. Equally extraordinary healings occurred the next year during the Toronto campaign. The medical fraternity there could not deny the fact of the healings, but attributed them to the "science of mental healings or psychotherapy."

A series of campaigns with Price were held in Winnipeg in the '20s and '30s where thousands were reached with the full gospel message. In Winnipeg the crowds sometimes marched to the meeting hall led by a brass band. With Watson Argue's involvement in some of the services, Pentecostalism was clearly identified with the divine healing message. Under Argue's leadership, a large church building was acquired for the enlarged Winnipeg assembly. It was re-named "Calvary Temple" at Dr. Price's suggestion. It was the first of many Pentecostal churches so named in the decades that followed.[15]

Charles Price was best-known to the Canadian public as a healing evangelist. His own views of ministry, however, gave equal emphasis to the message of salvation and the Baptism in the Holy Spirit. He repeatedly told his audiences that Jesus alone was the healer and to "look away to Christ, in whom alone they could find deliverance from all their sufferings." He also warned that it was possible to lose a healing once obtained. He often quoted the results of a 1928 conference of bishops of the Protestant Episcopal Church in Oklahoma. Several medical men were present, including the famous Dr. Charles H. Mayo of Rochester. The conference delegates concluded that "Christian healing has passed beyond the age of experiment and its value cannot be questioned."

Price sometimes taunted the people who chose those parts of his message which appealed to them, but rejected other portions. Among these were the Fundamentalist leaders of America who accepted his teachings on healing but rejected the Baptism in the Spirit with tongues. Price sometimes mocked such leaders with the phrase, "Our friends the Fundamentalists are fundamental on only part of the fundamentals." On the Baptism in the Spirit, he wrote:

> The Baptism of the Spirit must be preceded by a conviction of its necessity just as strongly as when earlier convinced of the need of a Savior — therefore one must hunger for it, and such hunger exists only in hearts entirely consecrated.[16]

The campaigns of Aimee Semple McPherson and Charles S. Price helped to publicize and gain acceptance for the Pentecostal Fellowship in Canada. A number of Canadians also had ministries which were powerfully effective, though not as widely known across the nation. A. H. Argue, after his return to Winnipeg from California, became one of the most prominent Canadian evangelists with a salvation-healing emphasis in his preaching. His early ministry in Toronto in 1917 resulted in the establishment of a congregation which eventually became Evangel Temple. In 1927 the assembly purchased a large church building which for 50 years was a centre of evangelism in the city's core. Argue's message had a strong divine healing component:

> "Have your faith backed up by action!!! — That is, have an active faith." In praying for the sick, he strongly emphasized, with unction, active scriptures such as "Stretch forth thine hand!!", "Lay hands on the sick and they shall recover!"[17]

He was equally emphatic in his sermons on prophecy, for he lived in the constant expectation that the Lord was soon to return. His chief love, however, was preaching on the Baptism in the Holy Spirit with tongues as the evidence. His sermon "The Baptism of the Holy Ghost" was heard by many thousands in scores of meetings in Canada and the United States.

When Zelma, Watson, and Beulah were old enough, they began to accompany their father on his travels. Zelma became his full-time assistant in the 1920 meetings in C. E. Baker's church in Montreal. The pastor reported:

> In the large St. Andrew's Church, many were saved, healed, baptized. Some had very striking visions and God's mighty power

5 / AND HE GAVE SOME . . .

was manifested in a wonderful way. This was Miss Argue's first evangelistic trip with her father, and God has truly made her a blessing to young and old.[18]

Then followed meetings in Kitchener, attended by some local Mennonites who entered in fully "when the glory fell." A meeting in Arnprior with pastor G. A. Chambers brought forth enthusiastic praise. A "cloud of glory" was said to rest on the tabernacle and each service seemed to surpass the preceding one. About 35 received the Baptism in the Spirit and a considerable number were saved. At the last service, 2,000 people stood in the rain to hear Argue's sermon. Zelma assisted with prayer, counseling, and some musical selections.

A campaign in Ottawa late in 1920 was memorable for its results. Pastor R. E. McAlister reported that "from the first meeting, God's mighty power was in the place, saving, healing and baptizing." He added that "Divine Healing was God's Trump Card for this city."

One healing of a 16-year-old girl with spinal meningitis had a profound effect upon the people. After prayer, she was able to move her limbs for the first time since infancy, and then, finally, to walk. Strong men wept like babies as they watched her. A woman, who had seven operations on her knee, removed the cast after prayer and was able to walk a mile home. Two ladies with running sores were healed; one of them had gone to England for a skin graft which had failed. Many were healed while sitting in the pews before prayer was offered. Two Catholic ladies brought a baby with a humpback for prayer, and two days later the hump disappeared. Argue called it "the greatest visitation of God's healing power" that he had ever witnessed.

The Argue meetings in Ottawa made an impact upon the highest social levels in Ottawa. The wife of Commander R. M. T. Stephens of the Royal Canadian Navy had suffered for years from a bladder and kidney disease. When she saw the Argue "Healing Mission" advertised, she decided to attend. Mrs. Stephens remarked that the Pentecostals "seemed to know the Lord in a way we did not." She heard the sermon, joined in the hymn, and then, suddenly, was free of all pain and fever. Commander Stephens went to all the meetings and soon received the Baptism in the Spirit. The Stephens later ministered in the United States, England, and Switzerland where they saw additional healings, Pentecostal Baptisms, and souls saved.[19]

A second Argue campaign in Montreal resulted in the healing of a 28-year-old man who had been deaf and dumb since childhood. The miracle was attested as genuine by a doctor from Owen Sound, Ontario, who was present in the Montreal service when the healing occurred. Services with Pastor J. T. Ball in Owen Sound brought more healings and quite a number of people received the Baptism. For four weeks the altar was crowded every night. The pastor reported that more than 30 people received the Baptism in the Holy Spirit according to Acts 2:4.

The Argue meetings shortly afterwards in Vancouver received a glowing testimonial from Pastor C. Orville Benham:

> ... the supernatural power of God was demonstrated in the healing of the sick and in the manifestation of the gifts of the Spirit. ... Perhaps 200 souls were saved ... more than one hundred were known to be baptized in the Spirit as per Acts 2:4.[20]

Throughout the early 1920s, the Argues itinerated mainly in the United States, but with frequent campaigns in Canada. At Findlay, Ohio, Watson Argue led song services with his trombone playing and Zelma gave him musical support. Scores were filled with the Spirit and many were saved and baptized in water. A long drought then threatened the surrounding farming community with economic disaster. One day the people at the Argue services joined in fervent prayer for rain. The Findlay *Courier* reported the results:

> ... a cloud no larger than a man's hand scudded up from the Southwest over the horizon ... the advance guard of a fleet of clouds that brought blessed rain ... there has been no such downpour for many weary and feverish weeks.[21]

A. H. Argue and his family assistants made Winnipeg the headquarters for their evangelistic ministries which extended over decades. The list of places where they held campaigns covered the major centres where the Pentecostal message had been firmly planted during the early years of the Movement's history. Their itinerations took them to dozens of American locations, such as Oberlin, Seattle, St. Louis, Granite City, New York City, and throughout the states of Pennsylvania, Texas, Illinois, Washington, Minnesota, and California. Argue also preached in Aimee Semple McPherson's new Angelus Temple in Los Angeles.

A. H. Argue's contribution to the establishment of North American Pentecostalism is difficult to assess simply because it was so extensive. He was a pioneering pastor, evangelist, author, publisher, and denominational organizer. He played important roles in the founding of both the Assemblies of God and The Pentecostal Assemblies of Canada. His sermonic themes of Salvation, Divine Healing, Baptism in the Holy Spirit, and the Second Coming were powerfully confirmed by undeniable miracles. This emphasis was extremely important in getting those cardinal doctrines firmly fixed as the characteristic teachings of the Pentecostal

5 / AND HE GAVE SOME...

Movement. His ministry in Winnipeg substantially assisted in the formation of what was ultimately to become the largest Pentecostal assembly in Canada. He was the key speaker at the first Braeside Camp Meeting in Western Ontario in 1935. Even the overseas missions program of the PAOC received a great impetus from Argue's work in Manitoba.

Argue continued his effective work as an evangelist until illness confined him to a wheelchair. He spent the remaining years of his very fruitful life in prayer for the Pentecostal Fellowship and the next generation of full gospel workers. His influence on the second generation of Canadian Pentecostals may be gauged by the comment of Walter McAlister, who was baptized in the Spirit as a child in the Argue Mission. McAlister said, "I looked upon him as the most saintly man I'd ever seen — his face just seemed to glow with the glory of God."[22] Gordon Atter's personal assessment, after Argue's death in 1959, was that he was "probably the greatest Pentecostal evangelist Canada has produced."[23]

After they had acquired some experience, the Argue children launched into various ministries of their own. Illustrative of the kind of success which Beulah and Eva had were their meetings in Terre Haute where the membership of a struggling Pentecostal congregation increased from 30 to over 90 people. When the Pentecostal Bible college opened in 1925 in Winnipeg, Beulah enrolled. After graduation, she married C. B. Smith, who was eventually to become General Superintendent of the PAOC. Zelma continued as an evangelist for many years until her retirement in California. Watson also launched into evangelism on his own. Often he was advertised as the "athlete preacher" because of the laurels he had won as a swimmer. Young people, especially, responded to his ministry and his athletic accomplishments. He itinerated for some time in the United States and briefly filled the pulpit for Aimee McPherson at Angelus Temple. In 1937, he became pastor of Calvary Temple in Winnipeg.

One of the most colorful of the Pentecostal evangelists who crisscrossed Canada in the 1920s and '30s was J. D. "Jack" Saunders. His Canadian ministry began around 1919 at a convention in Winnipeg. He was the featured speaker at the Rock Lake Camp in Manitoba on several occasions from 1922 to 1932. Saunders held campaigns in such cities as Lethbridge, Edmonton, and Vancouver in the West, and London, Montreal, and Ottawa in the East.

Saunders had been a United States Navy man and was something of a hero in the fleet because of his boxing prowess. While in San Francisco, he wandered into a gospel meeting where he was converted and filled with the Spirit. When he began his work as a Pentecostal evangelist, his wife vigorously opposed his sermons on the Baptism in the Spirit with tongues, and sometimes publicly denounced his message. After her death, he married a woman whose support contributed to his effective ministry for many years. One rather unique recollection, provided by a close acquaintance of the Saunders, referred to the manner in which Saunders second wife would give a message in tongues accompanied with certain body movements. Often when Saunders would give the interpretation, according to the reporter, he would exhibit the same body movements, apparently without being conscious of doing so.[24] Another clergyman, familiar with Saunders' work, remembered an occasion when a bully threatened to break up Saunders' street meeting. The unruly critic called all preachers cowards and cheats and challenged Saunders to a fight. Saunders agreed on the condition that boxing gloves would be used. After soundly thrashing the loudmouth challenger, Saunders was filled with remorse and vowed never to put the gloves on again.

Needless to say, his former career as a navy man and boxer, and his naturally colorful character, made him a favorite with the crowds who came to hear him. Jack Saunders was primarily a preacher of Salvation, but he also gave prominence to the Pentecostal doctrine of Divine Healing. Once, while preaching in Edmonton, in a largely Roman Catholic district, some outstanding healings occurred and quite a number were converted. It was here that a miracle took place that Saunders considered one of the most extraordinary in his long career:

> Just as we were commencing to pray for the sick, the church door opened and four men walked in carrying a man crippled with arthritis, sent by the Roman Catholic priest. They brought the man to the altar, put him down and said to the pastor, "Here, Minister, is something to start on." I took the oil and was about to anoint this man, but before I did, the power of God struck him and he jumped to his feet shaking his hands and dancing around perfectly healed, and the men who brought him were so terrified they ran out of the church as fast as they could go.[25]

A young married woman also was healed: she was so badly swollen from two tumors that she weighed over 250 pounds. After prayer, there was no immediate change, but several days later she passed both tumors and was totally healed.

Saunders had another unusual experience during a second campaign in Edmonton. While preaching on his theme of "Crossing the Deadline," he was suddenly stopped by the Spirit with the words, inwardly heard, "That is enough, someone has said 'No'." Saunders went to a man he knew and asked, "Brother, did you say 'No'?" The man was ashen. With saliva dripping from his mouth, he nodded his head. The man, a member of a

5 / AND HE GAVE SOME . . .

Pentecostal family, left the meeting and never entered a church again. As Saunders related the story, he said it taught him that "there is a place to which the human heart may go in his dealings with God where he will reject the overtures of God's mercy and cross the deadline beyond which there is no hope."

In a Sunday morning meeting in Lethbridge, Saunders prayed for a young woman named Katie Steele who was suffering from a tubercular leg which was six inches shorter than the other. After prayer, Katie fell to the floor under the power of God and lay prostrate from 11 a.m. to 4 p.m. When she regained her composure, she had the leg brace removed. By 5 p.m. Katie Steele was walking again. At a Winnipeg service, the evangelist was asked to pray again for a woman he had previously anointed and prayed over. Doctors had suggested that the woman had only about two weeks to live. Saunders was initially uncertain about what he should do, but he believed God gave him direction. He proceeded to write a message on a piece of paper for the woman: "They that put their trust in God shall never be confounded." Three years later he met the same woman in Ottawa and discovered that she was completely healed.

Once, while preaching in Fort Frances, Saunders found it impossible to continue because harassers were throwing rocks on the tin roof of the meeting hall. He called the believers to an early morning prayer meeting and the rock-throwing stopped. Soon, the wife of the instigator of the disturbance was converted and then many others came for salvation. A Pentecostal assembly was the result. Saunders sometimes used the story of the rock-throwing incident in his sermons to encourage more prayer among the believers. During meetings in Montreal, another remarkable answer to prayer occurred. After 29 young people volunteered to pray all night for souls, the next service saw 29 converts come into the church.[26]

Pentecostalism in Canada in the 1920s and '30s seemed to have a plethora of highly individualistic characters. One of them was a fiery Irishman named John McConnell whose salvation-healing ministry was highly regarded across the land. McConnell had meetings in Calgary in 1922 in which scores were converted and many were healed. About 50 were filled with the Spirit and enough money was pledged to build a church. Perhaps his best-known meetings were those held in London in 1924, where R. E. McAlister was pastor. A First World War veteran named George Dent had been paralyzed in one leg; several operations had deprived him of the further use of an arm. Following prayer, Dent was totally healed, according to the story carried in the *London Free Press*. Mrs. John Wright of London, a cripple for 10 years, was one of many others who were healed through prayer. McConnell, disclaiming any power in himself, told the papers that "we try to get the patient's soul in harmony with God. God will not cooperate with sin, and this sin must be driven from the souls of the sick before they can hope for any cures." During these meetings, the altars were crowded with seekers, as many as 100 at a time. Many received the Baptism in the Spirit, with tongues, and over 100 were baptized in water. The burgeoning London congregation found it necessary to secure a larger tabernacle. In one of the concluding services a total of $2,000 was collected for overseas missions.[27]

There often were unusual manifestations of divine power in local Pentecostal assemblies, even without the presence of the more famous evangelists. During the tenure of R. E. Sternall as pastor at St. Catharines, there was a heavenly visitation that astounded the church members. While praying in the mission hall, the Spirit fell upon the believers, and then, suddenly, to their surprise, the hall was filled with strangers and firemen. Many people, who had reported seeing flames of fire race along the roof of the hall, had rushed to help the volunteer fire department. Sternall's response to the puzzled spectators, who found no literal fire but a "fired-up" congregation, was that "the only fire around was the fire of the Holy Ghost and they couldn't put that out."

The work in St. Catharines was helped by the lay ministry of Mabel Cunningham. Mabel, reared as an Anglican and converted in a Baptist meeting, was filled with the Holy Spirit during meetings conducted by Pentecostal evangelist David Wellard. Her husband was healed of heart disease and entered the full gospel ministry in Parry Sound. After the death of Mabel's husband, the little congregation in Parry Sound requested her to assume the duties of pastor. Although she pastored several other assemblies, her chief contribution to the Canadian Fellowship lay in her work with Evangelists Ray and Joyce Watson in the Maritimes. Many were healed through her prayers. According to her daughters, people sometimes referred to Mabel Cunningham as "the Aimee Semple McPherson of Canada."[28]

Many of the early evangelists interspersed their itinerant ministries with periods of pastoring. J. D. Saunders, for example, would sometimes remain two or three years in a church before returning to the evangelistic field. Other workers were church-founders, staying long enough in a community to get a nucleus of Pentecostal believers in place, and then moving on to plant another congregation. And some, like R. E. McAlister, who had administrative positions to fill along with their preaching duties, gradually settled down to a chiefly pastoral ministry. George A. Chambers, while acting as the first General Superintendent, moved to Peterborough in 1929 to pastor a small group of about 20 people which had been gathered by an evangelist. They had been meeting in what Chambers called the "ostler's" residence — the rooms of a man who

5 / AND HE GAVE SOME...

cared for horses in a local stable. When Chambers held his first meeting with them, a number received the Baptism in the Holy Spirit. He stated he could not leave them without pastoral care:

> I realized that I would have to remain for at least a time, suspending all my other duties. The hungry people would not hear of my leaving until someone else could come to minister to them.[29]

After he secured the use of a theatre on George Street for Sunday services, the crowds grew until about 400 were in attendance. Mrs. William Sutherland, who previously had received a vision of the Pentecostal outpouring, was one of the first to receive the Baptism in the old theatre. The success of these meetings, and the economic effects of the Depression, convinced Chambers to make Peterborough his home.

The General Conference of the PAOC had provided salaries of $50 weekly for Chambers and R. E. McAlister, but those sums had to be reduced to $10 a week during the 1930s. The condition of his health obliged Chambers to resign his national office position in 1934 after he had settled in Peterborough. His love for evangelism, however, resulted in the spread of the full gospel to many of the nearby communities. Groups of believers travelled by bus or truck each Saturday evening to hold meetings in Campbellford, Havelock, Lindsay, Marmora, and Omemee. Some of the 30 to 50 people in each group would sing, others witnessed, some gave out tracts, and some preached. A slide show, which was a novelty in these towns and villages, and a public address system enabled those watching and listening at a distance to share in the excitement. In this way, Pentecostal congregations were founded in these communities which have continued to the present time.

The rapid spread of Pentecostalism across the country was seriously hampered by the Great Depression of the 1930s. It is well-nigh impossible for younger Canadians to comprehend the personal hardship endured by a whole generation during the "dirty thirties." Statistical data are not very meaningful, but a look at the drop in wages conveys something of the problems then faced. This writer's father, for example, who was a railroad worker in 1929 earning $300 monthly, had his income reduced in the '30s to $25 a month — and that was in the form of government relief! School teachers, the ones who could find employment, often worked for only $8.50 a month plus board.

The Prairies suffered even more because of a long drought and a drastic drop in commodity prices which literally forced farmers off the land. Wheat dropped in less than three years from $1.60 a bushel to 38 cents. Naturally, the finances of the Canadian Fellowship dropped. Missions offerings slid precipitously from $8,000 in January of 1930 to $4,000 the following April. A. G. Ward called on *Testimony* readers to pray for the Fellowship because "Dark days are upon us and darker days lie just ahead."

Not until 1937-38 did the rains return to the West. In the interim, thousands of young men left home and took to travelling the country in search of work. They were called "hoboes" and their method of travelling on the freight trains was called "riding the rods." Although Pentecostal evangelism was greatly hampered by the difficult times, dedicated workers who willing to make personal sacrifices and to endure hardships continued to proclaim the full gospel.

Saskatchewan was primarily a farming region and, therefore, was particularly hard-hit by the drought and the Depression. However, since it had providentially received the Pentecostal message earlier, a number of strong assemblies had been established which managed to weather the economic storms. Walter and Hugh McAlister began meetings at Parkside in the winter of 1922. The people in this mainly Swedish settlement responded with open hearts to the Pentecostal message. In spite of bitterly cold January nights, the meetings held in an old store were packed to the door. In three weeks over 80 were saved. One of the notable converts was John Martin, an alcoholic who was delivered through prayer from any craving for liquor or tobacco.

Walter McAlister recalled later, "We didn't preach any better or pray more fervently, but a few godly people had prayed much before the meetings." One of them was an old man who had long interceded with God for a revival. Now that it had come, he declared to McAlister his conviction that his life-work was ended. He passed away a short time afterwards. When the McAlisters moved on to other pioneering efforts, two young women, Ruth Manley and Alice Wilson, came to preach. Soon another 40 Parkside people were won to Christ. Within a year of the first meetings, a Pentecostal church had been erected in the town. The work was so effective in the community that the local pool hall, dance hall, and beer parlor had to close down for lack of business.[30]

The Pentecostal Movement in Canada has been characterized by its rapid growth through the work of zealous laymen. The local revival in Parkside, Saskatchewan, is a notable example of the way in which successful evangelism resulted in "spin-off" effects. A Pentecostal assembly was formed at Garrick, Saskatchewan, as a result of the witnessing and labors of Rolla Richmond. This man, by 1926, had become deeply dissatisfied with his intense pursuit of pleasure. He visited a number of churches, but only found what his heart desired when he attended the Parkside church. At that time, J. Rutherford Spence, a

5 / AND HE GAVE SOME...

missionary to China then on furlough, was serving as pastor at Parkside. Spence was instrumental in the conversion of Rolla and his family. Shortly afterwards, Rolla contracted pleurisy and developed a goitre, but was healed of both ailments after prayer. This dedicated layman acquired a vision for a Pentecostal church at Garrick. He began meetings with the assistance of a young farmer named Eric Hornby. Hornby was later to enter full-time ministry with the PAOC. Rolla and his wife also helped get meetings started at White Fox where they worked with Evangelist Clinton Ward during the winter of 1936-37.[31] Another layman named Gus Story introduced Pentecost to the town of Herschell.

Pentecostal pioneer Walter McAlister fondly recalled the story of Gus going to the secretary of the Canadian Bible Society in Saskatoon and asking him which was the "hardest" community in the province. When told it was Herschell, Gus went there, visited all the homes and farms, invited people to meetings, and began to preach. As McAlister put it, "Gus was more a farmer than a preacher himself, but he had a great desire to see souls saved." One of the converts from those meetings was Jim Routley, whose family considered him the "black sheep." Jim Routley afterwards entered the Pentecostal ministry.[32]

Zealous lay workers also introduced the full gospel to Naicam. Sam and Ida Geiger settled in the town in the early '30s and opened a business with the specific intention of establishing a Pentecostal church. They gave financial aid to the workers whom Saskatchewan Superintendent J. W. McKillop sent out. Ida paid the rent on the town hall for six months. The meetings with evangelist Todd Cantelon were packed out with over 200 in the hall. Sinners came under conviction and some, like Bennie Anderson, were converted *outside* the hall. Bennie would not enter but stood outside the hall and listened to the convicting messages. One day he simply knelt down in a farm field and gave his life to Christ. Ernie Parker missed all the church services until the day he buried his son. Then he started to attend the meetings and on the third night he was saved.

Although the evangelists had to leave, meetings continued with local leadership, interspersed with the ministry of itinerant preachers. By dint of much sacrifice and labor, the congregation erected a new church building in 1932 under the leadership of layman Mervil C. Jackson. To save expenses while building, the Jacksons lived in a granary. One man cashed in his life insurance policy and gave the proceeds for the church building. Another donated the land, and a woman gave 10,000 board feet of lumber. In this fashion, a Pentecostal church was erected in spite of the economic dislocations of the Great Depression.[33]

W. Clifford Nelson was a layman who came into the Pentecostal Fellowship through the ministry of John Ball in Owen Sound in 1918.

AND HE GAVE SOME . . . / 5

Following a "call" to the work, he went to Lethbridge to assist pastor John McAlister, but soon started preaching on his own in Swift Current. Later, while pastoring in Weldon, Saskatchewan, he took on young Clare Scratch as a helper. Clare, a former bank employee, eventually was to become a long-time missionary in China. From the congregation at Weldon came the young woman, Marie Larson, who was to become the wife of George R. Upton. Nellie Hendrickson, who later served for many years in educational work in Africa, also was a product of the church in Weldon.

Nelson took up a pastorate in Metcalfe, Ontario. He recalled, with humor, the loss of his $25 gold tooth while preaching there one day. At that time, however, it was a serious matter to replace the tooth on his $2.25 weekly salary! In 1929, the Nelsons moved to Lethbridge and began a gospel radio broadcast, "The Sunshine Evangel Hour" — a dramatic venture for those days. This broadcast was so popular it was continued for 25 years by succeeding pastors. In the early '30s the Nelsons moved to Edmonton to help mend a split in the local church — an uncommon but nonetheless sad spectacle in that period of strong personalities and strongly-held doctrines. Through the inspired leadership of Nelson, the congregation moved out of a rented basement auditorium into a new church building in 1933. Although it was the height of the Depression and many thousands were unemployed, the church was completed. Donald Gee of England was the dedicatory speaker. In the years that followed, the Edmonton assembly gave considerable support to the establishment of other Alberta churches.[34]

Gordon F. Atter knew what it was, as a youth, to be the son of a Pentecostal pastor. His father, A. M. Atter, went to China early in the century. When ill health brought the family home, the elder Atter pioneered a number of churches in the eastern area of Ontario. Although Gordon had experienced the ridicule of schoolmates for his Pentecostal faith, he responded to the call of God in 1922 and began a long ministry with the PAOC as preacher, teacher, and author. After attending a short-term Bible school in Montreal, he assisted his father and other pastors at Westmeath, near Pembroke. Meetings with Evangelist John McConnell in that town produced more than 50 converts. A church building was acquired for the new congregation.

After attending the short-term Montreal Bible school, Gordon Atter took up his first pastorate at Orange Valley, near Parry Sound. Atter made pastoral visits on skis in the winter and rode a bicycle in the summer. His first Sunday offering, he recalled with a laugh, was about 50 cents. But his hard work and dedication paid off in other ways. In 1927 a revival broke out which lasted for nearly a year. Many were restored to God, a

5 / AND HE GAVE SOME...

number were saved, and several were healed. It all proved to be a mark of divine approval for the young man whose ministry was to stretch over the next 50 years.[35]

One of the most prominent of the Pentecostal workers to arise in the 1920s was J. Harold Blair. The Blair family came into Pentecost during the meetings held by R. E. McAlister and Harvey McAlister at Metcalfe in 1915. J. H. Blair entered the ministry as an assistant to John Ball at Owen Sound, and was ordained in 1920. Although the little church he took over at Southampton had been struggling, under Blair's dynamic leadership it began to move forward. With the aid of his new bride, he began a program of evangelism which led to the conversion of over 40 people. So exuberant were his meetings, and so loud the prayers, that complaints were made to the police. However, the meetings continued unabated. The Blairs planted a church in Mount Forest, then pastored in Owen Sound where they erected a new church.

In 1927, the Blairs moved to Hamilton where they built up a very strong assembly. Some of the young workers enlisted over the years for ministry under Blair's supervision in Hamilton included Allan Mallory, Allan Saunders, and Jack West. It was in that city that Blair formed the plan to establish a district camp at nearby Paris — now known as Braeside Camp. Blair (affectionately called "J.H.") also served for many years as Western Ontario district superintendent.[36]

One of the remarkable aspects of the pioneer Pentecostals was their innovativeness and willingness to experiment with new ways of spreading the gospel. In the 1920s radio was in its infancy, but farsighted men recognized its potential for reaching the masses. Clifford Nelson's work in Alberta already has been mentioned. Dr. Charles Price's Sunday sermons were broadcast when he visited Winnipeg in 1924. The next year, Pastor Watson Argue and his young people conducted regular services over a local station at a cost of $10 per airing. Intermittent broadcasting from Winnipeg continued until 1936, when religious programs were transmitted from the church over a five-station hookup.

Churches were sometimes founded as a result of these imaginative Pentecostal outreaches. R. E. McAlister's radio program from London reached into the southwestern Ontario community of Bothwell which responded with a request for spiritual leadership. When Rev. and Mrs. Sammy Wilson were sent to Bothwell, their first street meeting attracted hundreds of listeners. Many were saved and a congregation was formed in the town. Radio also was helpful in getting the full gospel into the nearby communities in Blenheim, Dresden, and Ridgetown. Pentecostal preaching on the radio from a Saskatoon station, during the pastorate of C. B. Smith, led to the conversion of young Tom McNair of Asquith, a nearby village.

AND HE GAVE SOME . . . / 5

Subsequently, Smith, assisted by McNair, established a Pentecostal assembly in the area. Tom McNair later went into full-time ministry.

When Pentecostal meetings began at Onion Lake, near Lloydminster, in 1927, they had to be held in a tent. A small group of believers was formed under the leadership of Nellie Hendrickson and Ivy Sparks. W. B. Greenwood later became pastor and lived in a small tent during the winter months. He had to chop wood each day for his stove and slept with his clothes on to keep from freezing. Eventually, Greenwood moved into a house with a young couple who assisted him. The three of them lived on $6 a month with "lots of cracked wheat (but) not much milk or sugar."[37]

Clarence and Harvey McAlister began work in the Camrose district in the '30s. The growing congregation rented a building from the Seventh Day Adventists for $9 per month for a period of seven years. Eventually, they bought the building for $1,000 and used it until 1977.

At Burdett, Pentecostal meetings were conducted in several homes in 1939. Students from the Saskatoon Bible school who had summer jobs in the area gave the young church a boost in its early years. Two graduates, Ernest Hawtin and Albert Schindel, helped the church get organized after it purchased the old Mormon church.

One epic tale of privation concerns the evangelistic ministry of Julius Schatkoske who travelled throughout the swamp and muskeg country around Newbrook, north of Edmonton. Roads were so poor that settlers used the railroad bed for their transportation. Schatkoske did the same, walking many miles a week to reach scattered settlements. Schatkoske was known to his far-flung parishioners as the "walking Bible." This rare talent, coupled with great dedication, made him a very effective evangelist.

Among the first to be reached in northern Alberta were the German-speaking homesteaders. One congregation was established among them as early as 1933. A second assembly was founded at Ellscott, where a refugee from Siberia, E. Drisner, provided hospitality for the itinerant Pentecostal workers. Conditions among the settlers were primitive. Their furniture was made from the trees on their land. One account of their introduction to the modern breakfast cereal of corn flakes is rather humorous. The homesteaders, unaware of how the cereal should be eaten, served it dry as a special treat! The important observation is that they had a hunger for the gospel. Believers from several small communities combined to erect a Pentecostal church at Newbrook. Adeline Emde recalls walking the railroad tracks with her shoes in her hand, then washing her feet and wearing the shoes in church.

Out of such self-denying ministry and such devotion to the gospel came a host of German-speaking assemblies in Alberta. Tent meetings in the early 1930s at Hughenden by Rev. C. Peterson brought many into

5 / AND HE GAVE SOME . . .

Pentecost, including the local pool hall owner. After his conversion, he shut down his business because he considered it an unacceptable enterprise for a Pentecostal believer.

A visiting evangelist had a notable effect in that same community. He warned that unrepentant residents faced some kind of disaster unless they turned to God. A short time later, a man set fire to his buildings and then shot himself. A powerful wind fanned the flames and threatened the whole town. A Pentecostal believer by the name of Mrs. Dixon stood in the road and prayed to God to intervene. The wind suddenly changed and Hughenden was saved. More converts came into the church when Ernie Robinson and Clifford Nelson held tent meetings there in 1935. These two men helped organize the nearby Czar Lake Camp. When all camp construction costs were paid, the $800 which was still left from a fundraising effort was used to build a church in Hughenden.[38]

Pioneering work in British Columbia required the same degree of dedication and innovativeness. Evangelist J. E. Barnes was the means of the 1929 conversion of Hugh Fraser, former welterweight boxing champion of Canada. Fraser's testimony was a great attraction to large numbers of people who could not otherwise be reached.

Arthur Townsend was a pioneering pastor with a special love for the British Columbia northland. He founded a number of Pentecostal congregations under the most difficult circumstances. Once he used an entire bequest which was left to him to build a new church building in a northern town. He was himself an exponent of hard work, sacrificial service, and living by faith. Townsend often warned the people against those false teachers who travelled about proclaiming their great faith, but also advertising their need for funds. In his book, *Sod-Buster*, he declared, "When one tells by letter . . . or by any other medium whatever, that he is doing a work of faith, that work no longer becomes a faith work."[39]

Pentecostal work in the lower mainland of B.C. received an impetus from the young people's group at Sixth Avenue Tabernacle in Vancouver. This group supported a team, composed of Cecil and Molly Perks, Alva Walker, and Percy Crawford, in opening up Nanaimo to the full gospel. Their ministry, which began in 1922, resulted in a number of converts — the most notable of whom was Tom Johnstone. After his conversion in a prayer meeting, Johnstone received the Baptism in the Holy Spirit and spoke in other tongues. He assisted the pastor in the Nanaimo church for about two years. Then he launched out into full-time ministry in Ontario, Quebec, and the Maritimes. As an evangelist, Tom Johnstone had his unique and characteristic methods. His experiences as an amateur boxer provided some effective illustrations for his sermons.

AND HE GAVE SOME . . . / 5

In the interests of historical accuracy, one unhappy division in the young assembly in Vancouver must be recorded. A split arose out of a dispute over local leadership. One group, led by Pastor Robert Gillespie, continued services on the corner of Columbia and Hastings street. The second group, including Harry Eggleton, began a new mission on Hastings Street. The separation was brief and the parties were reconciled in a most unusual manner. Eggleton reported the rather amazing circumstances which led to the reconciliation:

> In 1920, our Assembly decided to call Brother W. E. McAlister to come for special services, and at the same time, unknown to us, Brother Gillespie had called Brother C. O. Benham for special meetings. The two of them met on the train on the way to B.C. They decided to try to get the two Assemblies together, and after three weeks of special meetings (which consisted of prayer meetings every night) we were ready for the proposal for uniting the two Assemblies. It was celebrated by a united picnic to Stanley Park, and the next Sunday we all met together in the Columbia and Hastings Mission.[40]

Benham remained as pastor and called Evangelist Jack Saunders for a campaign. There was some initial shock when Benham rented the old burlesque theatre for the meetings, but crowds soon filled the building and dozens were converted. Soon the congregation had to seek larger quarters, eventually settling down on Sixth Avenue. The down payment for the tabernacle came from Frank Maddaford; it represented his entire financial resources of $100. From this church, many consecrated young workers ventured out to start churches in Abbotsford and Salmo. Harry Eggleton went to Nanaimo, Nelson, Penticton, and, some years later, to the British West Indies. Another young worker, Alva Walker, became an Assemblies of God missionary in Cuba after developing his ministry talents in pioneer work in B.C.

The progress of Pentecostalism in the province was difficult and expensive: the mere existence of the imposing mountain ranges guaranteed that! Finances were in short supply in the 1930s, trained pastors were not available, and experienced leadership was spread thin over the province. British Columbia had no district superintendent until 1927. Prior to that date, the work was supervised by the Alberta district office. Nonetheless, the work prospered.

Especially effective were the evangelistic campaigns of Dr. Price, A. H. Argue with Watson and Zelma, Rev. and Mrs. "Billie" Black, Dr. E. E. Hall, Willard Pierce, Smith Wigglesworth, Dr. J. Australia, and Mary T. Miller. The reunited congregation of Sixth Avenue Tabernacle

5 / AND HE GAVE SOME . . .

"mothered" several assemblies in Vancouver. It also supplied a number of dedicated lay workers for Canadian and overseas ministries. The Tabernacle had receipts of over $12,000 in 1922, a sum which enabled it to finance other assemblies and to help workers who "went out in faith." A Mr. Pelkey and his wife went to Alberta to found a church. Alice Wilson left Vancouver to begin an evangelistic ministry in the USA. W. R. Collings opened up a mission in North Vancouver. John W. Knight and his wife began a church in Prince Rupert. Alex and Gwen Munroe went to Japan as missionaries where they were joined later by Ray and Jean McNaughton from the Vancouver main church. Fred and Rhoda Clarke went to Kenya. Wilfred and Ruby Morris began work in Peru and then moved to Venezuela.

One of the most successful of these early church planters was J. E. Barnes. When John Barnes began in B.C. in 1926, there were about seven Pentecostal churches. He pioneered assemblies in the B.C. interior. In Grand Forks he began meetings in a millinery shop, and in Fernie he started Pentecostal services in a funeral parlor. Even after his election as district superintendent, in 1929, he continued his itinerant evangelism. At Kimberly, Barnes held meetings which soon established another Pentecostal group. At Kelowna, he had his first meetings in a café. In Merritt, he made use of another funeral parlor for Pentecostal services. In 1931 he pioneered at Kamloops. His love for the ground-breaking type of evangelism continued until he resigned his administrative post in 1935. Thereafter, he travelled extensively across Canada and the United States. He ended his life's work with several terms of teaching in the B.C. Bible school. Winifred Barnes continued in the ministry in British Columbia after her husband's death.[41]

One of the most challenging tasks facing the Pentecostal workers in British Columbia has been to reach the thousands of people scattered along the Pacific coast. If the length of all tidal waters reaching inland were taken into account, the gospel workers had a parish 7,000 miles long. These unreached people lived in logging camps, fishing camps, mining towns, and Native reservations. There were few roads and no railways near the coast in that early period. One of the couples to catch a vision for the spiritual needs of these unreached groups was Frank and Mabel Harford. When their vision was presented to the District Conference in 1939, both leaders and laymen responded generously with financial support. A grant from PAOC headquarters in Toronto enabled the Harfords to purchase a 32-foot fishpacker which they converted into a "Gospel Boat." Harford became the "Skipper" who took the full gospel to needy souls along the West Coast.

It was a difficult and often dangerous task. North Pacific weather is rightly respected for its ferocity, and many times the gospel boat workers were in serious danger. Despite facing hazards too numerous to list, none of the Pentecostal maritime evangelists have been lost at sea. B.C. District Superintendent P. S. Jones was in the best position to assess the dedication of the boat workers:

> The Gospel Boat navigators have fought many a battle against riptides, sloppy seas, high winds and blanket fogs. They have been mercilessly thrown around by mighty, rolling seas, trying to make port. Their boats were comparatively small, their equipment was not of the best, and their living quarters were cramped, yet while there was one lost soul to be rescued, the men and women who manned the Gospel Boats would put out to sea.[42]

Percy S. Jones had himself come into the Pentecostal Movement through the 1923 campaign of Charles S. Price in Victoria. Jones had served in the Army Medical Corps during the First World War. His wartime experience made him an unsettled and searching man. After his conversion, he was filled with the Spirit and recalled the event with typical English humor:

> I lifted up my head and began to pray. I shall never know in this life what I said, for as I began to pray I was suddenly overwhelmed with a strange, awe-inspiring power that was entirely foreign to me . . . a streak of seeming electricity shot from my toe to my head. . . . I was a stiff and starchy Englishman, taught always to stifle my feelings and emotions. God evidently found it necessary to shake me loose from such a hide-bound life and my whole being shook with the power of God. . . . I have never been the same man since that tremendous upheaval.[43]

In a short time, Jones prayed for healing from diabetes and an abdominal illness, and was completely healed. He knew little about the principles of Divine Healing, but healing through prayer became one of his chief sermon themes as a Pentecostal pastor. He gave up a good job and launched into the Pentecostal work, with only God to supply the needs of his family. After a short ministry at Vegreville, in Alberta, he returned to B.C. where he spent most of his remaining years in pastoral and administrative work.

In his unpublished autobiography, P. S. Jones paid tribute to the salvation-healing evangelists and pastors who laid the foundations of modern Pentecostalism in Canada. His keen observations about the men and the times provide a valuable insight into the conditions under which pioneer work was carried on in the decades leading up to the Second

5 / AND HE GAVE SOME...

World War. Jones noted that the success of evangelists was directly proportional to their humility and their prayer life. He maintained that the gifts of God came chiefly though "tarrying" at the altar:

> We learned . . . that some of the best revivals were the result of more or less unknown evangelists who had a passion for souls and who gave themselves unreservedly to the . . . ministry. Some of these tarry meetings were precious beyond compare. We often tarried before the Lord until the wee hours of the morning. Some of our people have come to the conclusion that there is an easier way to receive God's best than that of tarrying, but in our experience we have come to know the rugged road is the God-appointed road; the best things are hidden from those who are not willing to spend time and energy to receive them. People of the world must work for what they get, and the same process is true in the Kingdom of God.[44]

After his election as district superintendent, Jones sought to plant Pentecost in every part of the province. He was gratified by the responses of young men and women who willingly sacrificed all to win souls and found churches. He once recalled with delight the young worker from Victoria who went north and built three churches in three communities known for their wickedness and hardness towards the gospel. To a young man who asked, with tears in his eyes, where he could work for God, Jones suggested an isolated lumber town. The dedicated worker went there, supported himself by labor, and built a thriving congregation.

It was such pioneering, claimed Jones, that laid the foundations for Pentecostal assemblies both in the homeland and the foreign fields. The superintendent sometimes found himself under attack from "poor, deluded souls (who) used to reproach us in those days for permitting young people . . . to go through such hardship." They knew little, he opined, about the great joy which comes to those who perform sacrificial labors for their Lord. Jones also astutely observed that without the spirit of sacrifice among Pentecostal workers in Canada, the work overseas would suffer:

> Nothing is more precious to a consecrated worker than to endure all things for His dear sake. The true vision for worldwide missions must be ever dependent upon the advancement of the home base.[45]

Endnotes

1. G. A. Chambers, "In Retrospect," *The Pentecostal Testimony* (November 1934), 7.
2. Aimee Semple McPherson, *This is That* (Los Angeles: Echo Park Evangelistic Assoc., 1923), p. 218.
3. Newfoundland did not become a part of Canada until 1949. The Pentecostal message was carried to St. John's, Newfoundland, by Alice Garrigus and took root independently of what was happening on the mainland. During the 1920s the Pentecostal Movement experienced revival and steady growth throughout the entire island. The Pentecostal Assemblies of Newfoundland retain a separate identity from the PAOC but participate in a fraternal relationship, especially in the area of foreign missions.
4. See note 1; and *Canada Year Book* (Ottawa: Statistics Canada, 1945).
5. Quoted in McPherson, *This is That*, p. 220.
6. John McAlister, "Reports From Western Canada," *The Pentecostal Testimony* (December 1920).
7. C. E. Baker, "Canada's Largest City Is Visited With Floods Of The 'Latter Rain'," *The Pentecostal Testimony* (January 1921), 2.
8. R. P. Spurrell, letter to Thomas Wm. Miller, October 27, 1983.
9. Thomas Wm. Miller, taped interview with George B. Griffin, August 5, 1984; *The Bridal Call Foursquare* (October 1924), 21-22; and Charles S. Price, *The Story of My Life* (Pasadena: for the author, 1935), pp. 19-36.
10. Mrs. E. Hazel Mussen, in letter to the author, May 6, 1990; Price, *The Story of My Life*, pp. 41-42; Charles S. Price, (ed.), *Golden Grain*, 1:10 (December 1926), 21; and Charles S. Price, *The Great Physician* (Winnipeg: DeMontford Press, 1924), pp. 62-80.
11. James H. Gray, *The Roar of the Twenties* (Toronto: MacMillan, 1975), p. 223.
12. *Victoria Daily Colonist*, April 13, May 1, 1923, quoted in "60th Anniversary, 1923-1983, Glad Tidings Pentecostal Church, Victoria, B.C.;" see also Price, *Story of My Life*, pp. 46-47; Donald T. Klan, "PAOC Church Growth in British Columbia From Origins Until 1953," unpublished M.C.S. thesis, Regent College, Vancouver, 1979, 89; and R. E. Upton, "Victoria's Glad Tidings Tabernacle Celebrates 45th Anniversary," *The Pentecostal Testimony* (March 1968), 8.
13. *The Pentecostal Testimony* (June 1923), 5; also *Golden Grain*, 3:9 (November 1928), 6; and 5:1 (March 1930); and Klan, 94-100.
14. Lorne F. Fox, "The Charles S. Price Story," *World Pentecost*, 3 (1973), 10, 11-14; and Ethel M. Fox, *Bless The Lord O My Soul: The Story of the Fox Evangelistic Party* (Phoenix: for the author, 1973).
15. Conveyed to the author in conversation with Rev. H. H. Barber, pastor of Calvary Temple, Winnipeg, September 1984.

5 / AND HE GAVE SOME . . .

16. "The Special Committee's Report on the Dr. C. S. Price's Healing Campaign," *The Christian Guardian* (Toronto: Methodist Church of Canada, January 16, 1924), 14-16; Price, *Story of My Life*, p. 51; C. S. Price, *The Great Physician* (Oakland: C. S. Price Pub., 1923), p. 45; see also his *Golden Grain*, 3:9 (November 1928), 29; 4:1 (March 1929), 23; and 8:1 (April 1933), 32.

17. Zelma Argue, "This is My Dad," *TEAM*, 3:3 (July-September 1956), 3-6; A. H. Argue, "Closing Scenes in Prophecy," *The Pentecostal Testimony* (October 1955), 7, 26; "Jesus the Great Physician," *The Pentecostal Testimony* (August 1957), 5, 28; and "The Baptism of the Holy Ghost," *The Pentecostal Testimony* (April 1931), 10, 16.

18. Zelma Argue, *What Meaneth This?* (Winnipeg: for the author, 1923), p. 30.

19. Zelma Argue, pp. 31-33; and A. H. Argue, ed., *The Revival Broadcast*, 1:1 (Midwinter 1923-1924), 4.

20. Zelma Argue, p. 40.

21. Ibid., p. 60.

22. Thomas Wm. Miller, taped interview with Walter E. McAlister, May 3, 1984. For a fuller account of A. H. Argue's importance for the North American Pentecostal Movement, see Miller, "The Significance of A. H. Argue for Pentecostal Historiography," *Pneuma*, 8:2 (Fall 1986), 120-158.

23. Thomas Wm. Miller, taped interview with G. F. Atter, April 4, 1984.

24. G. F. Atter, in conversation with the author, August 21, 1976.

25. J. D. Saunders, "35 Years of Ministry," *The Pentecostal Testimony* (August 1956), 8.

26. Ibid., 21

27. *The Pentecostal Testimony* (August 1924), 7; and *The Pentecostal Testimony* (September 1924), 7.

28. R. E. Sternall, "When God's Fire Brought the Fire Dept. to Church," *The Pentecostal Testimony* (May 1956), 8; and letter to the author from Aleta (Sternall) Piper, March 10, 1980.

29. George A. Chambers, *50 Years in the Service of the King, 1907-1957* (Toronto: Testimony Press, 1960), pp. 40-45.

30. Thomas Wm. Miller, taped interview with W. E. McAlister, May 1, 1981.

31. George R. Upton, *Pioneer of the North: The Story of Rolla and Elsie Richmond* (Victoria: Morris Printing), pp. 13-30.

32. Miller, note 30.

33. Gordon K. Franklin, *Forty Years with God: The History of the Pentecostal Church in Naicam* (booklet, 1971).

34. Wm. Clifford Nelson, *From Plow Handles to Pulpit* (autobiographical booklet, for the author).
35. Gordon F. Atter, *Down Memory's Lane: An Autobiography* (Port Colborne, ON: for the author, 1974), pp. 15-23.
36. J. H. Blair, "History of the Ministry of J. H. Blair in the Pentecostal Assemblies of Canada," typed copy of memoirs in PAOC Archives, 1955; Jack West and Harold Davis, *They Call Him Mr. Braeside: the Life Story of Rev. J. H. Blair* (Toronto: Harmony Printing).
37. *Rejoice: A History of the Pentecostal Assemblies in Alberta and the Northwest Territories* (Edmonton: Alberta and N.W.T. District, 1983), p. 63.
38. Ibid., pp. 9-10, 53-55, 67-68, 145-147.
39. Arthur Townsend, *Sod-Buster* (Toronto: Vantage press, 1975), pp. 104-105.
40. Harry Eggleton, "History of the PAOC in B.C.," typed copy of personal memoirs, PAOC Archives.
41. Mrs. J. E. Barnes, letter to P. S. Jones, PAOC Archives, 1956; and Thomas Wm. Miller, interview with Winifred M. Barnes, February 26, 1991; see also Lionel R. Maddaford and Lynda Tennant, "A Chronology of Broadway Tabernacle," booklet, 1977.
42. Quoted in Gloria Grace Kulbeck, *What God Hath Wrought* (Toronto: Full Gospel Publishing House, 1958), pp. 184-185; see also Frank Harford, "Pentecost Along the Canadian Pacific Coast Line," typed copy of handwritten reminiscences, PAOC Archives.
43. Percy S. Jones, typed copy of autobiography in possession of his daughter Joyce. Used by permission.
44. Ibid.
45. Ibid.

The James McAlister Family

Back Row: *Robert, Mary, Harvey, Jessie*
Front Row: *Lizzie, John, Margaret, James;* **Inset Left:** *David;* **Right:** *Gavin*

The A. H. Argue Family

Back Row: *Elwin, Zelma, Wilbur, Eva*
Front Row: *Beulah, A. H. Argue, Eva, Watson*

The James Swanson Family

Left to Right: James (General Superintendent 1935-36); Gordon, Mac, Hazel, James Jr.

The Otto Keller Family

Otto, Marian, and son Weldon (about 1922). The Kellers were missionaries in Africa in the 1920s.

A. G. Ward

Charles and Annie Baker, and Leva

Robert E. McAlister

Laura McAlister

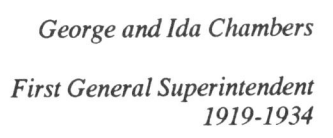

Fourth Annual Meeting of The General Assembly of The Pentecostal Assemblies of Canada, held in Kitchener, Ontario, October 9-14, 1922.

Arthur and Jessie Atter and son Gordon

Missionaries to China 1908

George and Ida Chambers

First General Superintendent 1919-1934

Locations of The National Office of The Pentecostal Assemblies of Canada

740 Queens Street
London, Ontario

362 Danforth Avenue
Toronto, Ontario

50 Euston Avenue
Toronto, Ontario

Below left: C. H. Stiller, *General Secretary-Treasurer, 1967-1971*
Below Right: R. W. Taitinger, *General Superintendent, 1969-1982*

10 Overlea Boulevard, Toronto, Ontario

6745 Century Avenue, Mississauga, Ontario

1950 General Conference in Saskatoon, Saskatchewan

Left to Right: G. R. Upton, Missionary Secretary; C. M. Wortman, General Secretary-Treasurer; and C. B. Smith, General Superintendent.

Executive Officers in Session, 1960

Left to Right: James Montgomery, Director of Sunday School and Youth Department; C. M. Wortman, General Secretary-Treasurer; W. E. McAlister, General Superintendent; George R. Upton, Missionary Secretary; and Tom Johnstone, Director of Home Missions and Bible Colleges.

First Joint Session of Officers
The Assemblies of God, USA and the PAOC, 1962

Standing, Left to Right: *Gayle F. Lewis, Howard Bush, C. M. Wortman, and M. B. Netzel.*
Sitting, Left to Right: *Bert Webb, James Montgomery, Charles H. Scott, George R. Upton, Barlett Petersen, Thomas F. Zimmerman, Tom Johnstone, C. H. Stiller, and J. Philip Hogan.*

Goodbye Jack!

E. N. O. Kulbeck, and his camera, with Clare Scratch saying goodbye to Missionary Jack Lynn.

First Pentecostal church building, Kinburn, Ontario, 1911.

East End Mission 651 Queen Street East Toronto, Ontario, 1906. Also known as The Hebden Mission.

Mille Roches — site of the formation meeting of the PAOC in 1918.

The new Winnipeg Calvary Temple with the historic steeple from the orginal building.

Kennedy Road Tabernacle and the senior citizens' Heritage, Brampton, Ontario.

The sanctuary of Queensway Cathedral, Toronto, Ontario.

Left to Right: J. H. Blair, W. H. Found, W. B. Greenwood, C. H. Ratz.

Dr. J. E. Purdie

H. D. Honsinger

Central Pentecostal College Faculty – 1964

Left to Right: Karel Marek, Joyce Bartos, A. C. Schindel, May English, G. N. Fulford, Grace Brown, and W. A. Griffin.

C. M. Ward
Revivaltime Speaker

H. H. Barber
*Calvary Temple
Winnipeg*

*David Mainse
100 Huntley Street*

*Allon Hornby
1980 General Conference Speaker*

*Maud Ellis
Lakeshore Pentecostal Camp, 1978*

*R. E. Sternall, one of the
PAOC founders, at age 96*

1974 General Conference
Executive Officers

Left to Right: S. D. Feltmate, Executive Director of Christian Education and Youth; Charles Yates, General Secretary; C. W. Lynn, Executive Director of Overseas Missions; R. W. Taitinger, General Superintendent; A. G. Richards, General Treasurer; and R. M. Argue, Executive Director of Home Missions and Bible Colleges.

1982 General Conference
Members of the General Executive

Standing Left to Right: J. H. Faught, V. W. Taylor, Oscar Masseau, Jack Counsell, R. L. Schmunk, H. H. Barber, I. A. Roset, A. D. Moore, M. P. Horban. *Sitting Left to Right:* Paul Hawkes, G. R. Upton, W. C. Cornelius, Charles Yates, J. M. MacKnight, A. G. Richards, W. A. Griffin, H. J. Cantelon (absent Allon E. Hornby).

Missions Convention in Ottawa – 1951

Men, Left to Right: J. Lynn, G. R. Upton, H. Kerr, F. Myer, C. Barker, J. R. Spence, R. J. Jamieson, H. Underhill, and J. E. Morrison.
Women, Left to Right: Salome Cressman, Ethel Bingeman, Renata Siemens, Coralee Haist, Edna Lynn, Kay Kerr, Lenora Myer, Myrtle Barker, Florence Spence, and Verna Underhill.

National Women's Ministries Committee – 1993

Left to Right: Viola Pennoyer, Della Innes, Carol Parks, Nina Shoemaker, Eileen Stewart, Guylaine Chouinard, Donna Thorne, Mary Campbell, and Hilda Sigglekow.

Executive Officers – 1993

James M. MacKnight
General Superintendent

William A. Griffin
General Secretary

Reuban L. Shmunk
General Treasurer

Lester E. Markham
Overseas Missions

Keith H. Parks
Church Ministries

Kenneth B. Birch
Home Missions and
Bible Colleges

Chapter 6

PIONEERING PENTECOST IN EASTERN CANADA

The 20th-century Pentecostal Movement encountered great obstacles when it advanced from the Eastern Townships to the East Coast. From the first settlement of Europeans in Canada (at Sable Island, 1598), the chief communications route was along the St. Lawrence Valley. French Canadian communities sprang up on both sides of the river and two great cities — Quebec and Montreal — became, respectively, the military and commercial centres of the region.

As a result of the British conquest of 1760, a new province named Upper Canada (Ontario) was created. The territory occupied by the French population was known as Lower Canada and became the largest province in the country, covering an area of almost 600,000 square miles. After the American Revolutionary War, and later the War of 1812, thousands of English-speaking immigrants came to Upper Canada and the Montreal area. The domination of the commerce of Montreal by "les Anglais" led to some resentment and a perception that French-Canadian culture was in danger of disappearing.[1]

Although the 1867 Confederation of the East and West created the Dominion of Canada, there remained what historians have called "the two solitudes." The commercial and communications network that developed along the St. Lawrence greatly assisted the process of political integration, but was not able to bridge the gap between the two Canadas. French-speaking, Roman Catholic Quebec maintained its distinctiveness beside English-speaking, largely Protestant Ontario. The roots of the divisions have been traced by a Pentecostal pioneer in Quebec who had a keen interest in the history of early Protestantism. E. L. Lassègues noted that a conflict of religions in France itself had created a long-standing opposition to all things Protestant — and hence to

6 / PIONEERING PENTECOST IN EASTERN CANADA

Pentecostalism — for generations in Quebec. In a tract entitled "Pentecost in Quebec," he wrote:

> It is a fact little known but nonetheless true that early settlers from France were largely Protestant, not Catholic. The country they left had slaughtered the Huguenots by the thousands. The new King, Henry IV of Navarre, ... declared religious liberty for his people. Nonetheless, many Protestants, weary of persecution and fearing its recurrence, sought in Canada, a possession of France, the opportunity of pursuing the practice of their religion unmolested ...
> The hardships of the country caused them untold suffering and near extinction, yet repeated expeditions finally succeeded in establishing a flourishing colony with declared religious liberty. ... Then in France ... the Huguenots were again crushed ... in New France ... monks sent a deputation to Paris with an appeal to expel all Protestants from Canada ... thus the Protestants of Canada were deprived of strong leadership. ... When Wolfe came ... the once-strong colony was practically extinct. ...
> Compromises and treaties were made ... with a view to appeasing the French majority, which ... was vastly Roman Catholic. ... The clergy seized the liberties granted them and firmly drew the curtains of segregation about them, setting up their undisputed control in government, education, law, business, religion, *et cetera*. The French set about to re-capture Canada, not by the sword, but through the "revenge of the cradle."[2]

The nature of this so-called "revenge" was to encourage the "Habitants" to have large families. Under the electoral system in the Dominion, it was hoped that a French-Canadian populace would be large enough to control the entire country. In this objective, the Roman Catholic Church was unsuccessful, but the birth rate was so high for generations that French Canadians totalled about one-third of the population. Church membership throughout Canada was further augmented by immigration from traditionally Catholic regions of Europe. Thus the province of Quebec has been a bastion of Catholicism and a serious challenge to evangelical missions for two centuries.

Language, culture, religion, and even the legal system helped perpetuate the divisions between "la belle province" and the rest of the country. Not until the 1970s was the supremacy of Catholicism seriously challenged. The advent of television played a large role in opening up the region to the secular influences of modern North America. A grass roots resistance to religious traditions and a rejection of the old classical education system — long under church aegis — accelerated the pace of cultural, religious, and social change in Quebec. But the province remained a challenge for Evangelicals. One Pentecostal leader described it as "one of the greatest mission fields of the world."[3]

Early attempts to evangelize Quebec were made by revivalists like Methodist James Caughey, who made several visits to Montreal between 1827 and 1841. Over 600 converts were recorded in these meetings, but they appear to have been drawn largely from English-speaking residents.[4] The Baptists made numerous attempts to establish churches, with some success, but the bulk of Quebecers were untouched by the few evangelical organizations that entered the province. Considerably more success followed the work of Pentecostal missionaries since the turn of the century.

During R. E. McAlister's ministry in Ottawa, C. E. Baker and his wife were converted and brought into the Latter Rain Revival. Mrs. Baker's miraculous healing from cancer convinced Charles Baker that this was God's work. He became a lay helper for several Pentecostal clergymen at Ottawa and nearby Kinburn. After McAlister moved on to another field of service, J. L. Hart provided leadership for a brief period. The Bakers assumed the pastorate late in 1912 and began a vigorous program of evangelistic outreach. They had such famous early Pentecostal leaders as G. T. Haywood come for meetings. On one occasion, Mrs. Baker dedicated herself to the Lord's work in a very dramatic manner:

> As the people marched around (a table) with their offerings, Sister Baker remained by the offering plate with her hand on the table, there consecrating herself and her husband to God's work.[5]

The Bakers held several preaching and healing campaigns in the Howick Pavilion at the Ottawa Exhibition Grounds. It was there that Mrs. J. L. Hart was healed of tuberculosis. When the young congregation at Kinburn was in need of supervision, the Bakers took on the added responsibility. The Kinburn people were enthusiastic, devoted, and determined to move ahead with a church building of their own. The outpouring of the Holy Spirit in the winter of 1911 was followed by the erection of a church building the next spring.

The first service in the new sanctuary occurred on the very day a cyclone hit Kinburn. The church members and the building escaped unscathed. The church trustees who directed the activities of the congregation until a pastor could be secured were H. Gilchrist, R. G. Baird, Wm. Laughlin, T. Fulford, A. Peever, and S. G. Stevenson. This building was the first in Canada erected specifically for Pentecostal worship. It was originally known as The 9th Line Tabernacle of the Assembly of God.

6 / PIONEERING PENTECOST IN EASTERN CANADA

The form of church government was democratic in the full sense of the word. All business was transacted by means of resolutions, debated and adopted, at the quarterly business meeting. Each family in the church was canvassed to determine its ability to contribute to pastoral support. No public offerings were taken at first, but the practice of passing the collection plate during the service eventually became the method of raising funds. A parsonage had been secured, but Baker remained in Ottawa while he oversaw the work of the Kinburn church. He maintained these responsibilities until he moved to Montreal in 1916. Meticulous records of the Kinburn assembly were kept by volunteer church secretaries. One page in the Minute Book shows that in February of 1914 the sum of $14.79 had been put into the "Offering Box" and $13.50 had been disbursed, leaving a balance of $1.29. Brother Eby of Berlin (now Kitchener) came as pastor about that time, and his monthly salary was $9.00.[6] It seems that C. E. Baker acted as a supervisor of the work done by Eby in Kinburn, while he carried on his own pastoral and evangelistic ministry in Ottawa.

The first attempt to take the Pentecostal message to Quebec occurred in 1913 when the Bakers went to the Gatineau River community of McBean. They were assisted by A. W. Otto. The workers felt that God had been preparing the way through the prayers of some local believers. Hundreds of lives for miles around were reached with the full gospel message. Otto reported that he

> . . . had never before seen people so hungry for the Gospel, nor who were so easily led to Christ. Conversions took place so rapidly that . . . a little over a week after the meetings began, 28 believers, men, women and children, were baptized in the River. . . . Whole families . . . were saved. The Lord confirmed the word by signs following, and a number of remarkable instances of healing were reported.[7]

After the meetings concluded, Otto remained to give leadership while the Bakers moved on to Montreal. They began a ministry in 1916 which continued unabated until Charles Baker's death in 1947. The Bakers began in Montreal with cottage prayer meetings and public services in rented halls in various parts of the city. Eventually, they settled into a hall on Van Horne Avenue. A. H. Argue and members of his family on one occasion provided them some very effective evangelistic meetings. It was during those decades that the Bakers witnessed the conversion of thousands of unbelievers, the Baptism in the Spirit of hundreds, and the appointment of numerous workers to overseas mission fields. Not surprisingly, he was lovingly called "Daddy" Baker by colleagues and parishioners alike.

The most spectacular period of growth in Montreal followed the series of meetings held by Aimee Semple McPherson in 1920. At Baker's invitation, "Sister" McPherson held many days of special meetings in St. Andrew's Church on Beaver Hall Hill. The place was packed every day for weeks on end. Special police forces had to be assigned to control the huge crowds. On several occasions the streets near the hall were so packed with people that the traffic was halted. Some commentators believe it was the greatest religious revival in the city's history. One eye witness to the many healings was R. P. Spurrell. He recalled accounts of remarkable healings which resulted in the conversion of hundreds of people to Christ. Spurrell, overwhelmed with what he saw, was moved to enter the Pentecostal ministry where he served faithfully for 50 years — a life time of work which he claimed was motivated by what he witnessed in Montreal.[8]

Baker also found the McPherson meetings to be extraordinary, although he was not unfamiliar with the phenomenon of divine healing. He wrote a report which he titled "Canada's Largest City Is Visited With Floods of the Latter Rain." A selection of his enthusiastic statements reflects, even at this late date, something of Baker's excitement over the McPherson services:

> How shall we begin to lay before you the wonderful things that took place . . . the saints of God were with one accord; night after night they met together . . . to reach through to God on behalf of this city. Afternoon prayer meetings were held in different homes. . . . Sunday came . . . Altar call was given at the close of the address . . . those who had been living at a distance from God . . . were the first to lead the way, then . . . others, weeping and crying for mercy, asking that their sins might be forgiven. The Spirit fell and souls came through to the Baptism in the first service.
> The first evening meeting revealed an altar filled with sinners seeking salvation, with a prayer room below filled with hungry children of God seeking the Baptism. . . . Thursday was set apart for healing and prayer for the sick. . . . After a glowing talk from our sister . . . all eyes were turned on a young girl with crutches. . . . Prayer was offered, she arose to her feet and to the amazement of the crowded house she walked across the platform . . . and there was . . . great exclamations of joy and praises to God . . . The people could no longer keep their seats but stood to their feet and in one volume there arose the sound of many hands clapping together for joy. . . . Many other cases . . . that I wish I could tell, but space is limited . . . shortly the building, seating 2,000, was too small. Many from Toronto, Ottawa, Chicago, Winnipeg, Kingston, New York, Newfoundland, New Hampshire, and others. . . . By this time the press were bringing before the public the things that God was doing

in our midst. Reporters . . . were amazed at what they saw and heard and at times would almost forget their task . . . looking on in wonder and amazement. . . .

Policemen were nearly taken off their feet by those seeking to just get in . . . many blind, halt and lame, suffering from many diseases . . . and then would come the sight of those who were completely delivered walking back and forth over the platform praising God for what He had done. I cannot do justice to these services, nor am I able to touch on the emotion and high spiritual tide that was felt so keenly in the meetings. Ministers of the city confessed that this was nothing else than the real "old time Religion;" this resulted in churches and ministers feeling their need of more power. . . . Blind were made to see, lame to walk straight, sick rising up and leaping and praising God. . . . The crowds were intense, policemen unable to cope with them at times . . . hundreds thronged the altar.

Strong men throw themselves on the platform as they responded to the call, weeping and calling on God to save them from their sins. . . . Our closing day . . . Many more seeking salvation, and the prayer room was not to be forgotten; men and women . . . some kneeling, some lying prostrate under the power of God. . . . God's presence was real the moment you entered the place, the air being charged as it were with His Spirit. . . . Scores of young men and women . . . praying to God for salvation. As the burdens rolled away young men would be seen emptying out of their pockets cigarette cases and tobacco, getting cleaned up, ready to join the mighty army of redeemed soldiers.[9]

The salvation-healing meetings gave Pentecostalism a high profile in Montreal and led to a substantial increase in church membership. Baker led the congregation in the purchase and renovation of a theatre on Drummond Street. This was the key outpost of the Pentecostal Movement in Quebec. The church enjoyed steady growth and eventually moved in 1954 to a new facility — Evangel — at the corner of Tupper and Closse streets.

In his several decades of leadership at Evangel, "Daddy" Baker was the spiritual father to hundreds of new converts. Baker took a lively interest as well in expanding the local outreach of the church, and Evangel "mothered" several Montreal congregations. He had a keen interest in overseas missions. The congregation sent a number of workers to the foreign field and provided generous financial support for the steadily developing missions program of the PAOC. The wide-ranging interests of the pastor were reflected also in the fact that the Baker home was the scene of the meeting in 1917 of the founding fathers of the denomination. It was there they first decided to apply to Ottawa for a federal government charter. Although it cannot be documented, it has been said that it was Baker and two other Pentecostal pastors who applied for a provincial charter. By an Act of the Quebec Legislature the PAOC was recognized as "an ecclesiastical corporation in the Province of Quebec."

Since there were no Bible school facilities for Pentecostals in Canada at the time, workers acquired training and developed skills through ministries in the central church. Among the earliest of such locally-trained workers in Baker's Montreal church was a noted bass singer, Fred Carter, who turned his musical talents to good use in church meetings. His brother Ed became the leader of the Evangel orchestra. Charles W. H. Scott, a convert who had been miraculously healed of lockjaw, later became a prominent leader in the Assemblies of God in the United States. Elmor and Laura Morrison went to China with the support of this church. When they were forced by revolution overseas to return to the city, the Morrisons were employed in directing the Upper Room Mission in Montreal. Later, when they were able to return to the land of their calling, the members in the mother church provided the funds. Indeed, Evangel Church steadily increased its contribution to missionary outreach until the annual total soon amounted to more than $100,000.

Members of the congregation, led by Gordon Presley, sought to secure a foothold for the Pentecostal message in Verdun in 1925. A work eventually was established in that place with a couple by the name of Cole as pastors. Baker was assisted at various times by George Griffin, Paul Kauffman, Arnold Kalamen, Beatrice Sims, and William Kautz. When Griffin arrived in 1937, he inaugurated an expanded teaching ministry in the church.

As a result of Evangel's zealous support for missions, both at home and overseas, it came to be called "Montreal's Centre of Evangelism."[10] The church was strategically located to reach the eastern regions of Canada. A stream of visitors attended the church while en route to the West or the northern United States. Frequently the result was the conversion of the unsaved, or the Baptism in the Spirit of the spiritually thirsty. These people usually became eager advocates of Pentecostal doctrine wherever they went. One notable example was Eugene Vaters of Newfoundland. As a young Methodist pastor, Vaters travelled to the West seeking a deeper experience with God. When he heard of the unusual meetings in Montreal, he decided to attend some of the services. Although he did not then completely understand the doctrines preached, he was favorably impressed by what he heard and saw. Vaters continued his journey westward, but began actively to seek for the Baptism in the Holy Spirit. After he and his wife had experienced Pentecost for themselves, they felt impressed to return to their home in Newfoundland with the full gospel message. On the way, they stopped off in Montreal, and for some time gave various forms of assistance to the work there. Vaters became a friend of "Daddy" Baker. He was asked to assist Christopher Swann who then was working in The Upper Room Mission.[11] In this manner, the influence of the Montreal Pentecostals was carried over to Newfoundland, where Pastor Vaters spent the rest of his life in the establishment of the movement on the island.

In addition to Roman Catholicism, to which reference has been made, another major obstacle for the Pentecostals in Quebec was the disastrous consequences of the Great Depression. Still, the zeal of the early workers did not abate, and a number of towns and cities were reached during that period. Cottage prayer meetings opened up Greenfield Park in 1930. Tom and Doris Johnstone, while pastoring at Verdun, also gave leadership to this group. Johnstone occasionally engaged in evangelistic ministry in other areas of Quebec, notably as a speaker at the Magog camp meeting. Charles and Margaret Day also pastored in Montreal. In 1938 they led their people in purchasing and renovating a building on Rosemount. Although they had only a $100 down payment, the congregation was able to dedicate their new church the next spring.

In 1943, the Pentecostals in Greenfield Park bought a store and remodeled it into a sanctuary. The pastor at the time was W. F. Rourke. It was Rourke who organized the first Men's Fellowship group in Quebec. He and his wife Elizabeth, while pioneering in the Maritimes, had proven the value of enlisting the men of the church for outreach and evangelism.

The Pentecostal work among the Italian-speaking residents of Montreal had its inception around 1920. It received a great boost from the extraordinary impact of the McPherson meetings. A lay Methodist church worker named G. A. Distaulo was ministering to his own people in Montreal at the time. He was already an able preacher of the Word, but became interested in the Pentecostal experience when he saw its impact on lives. Together with some friends, Distaulo met to pray for the Baptism; all experienced a personal Pentecost. Thereafter, his small cottage prayer meetings were crowded. Soon a vacant store was acquired and redecorated for worship. Distaulo became the spokesman for Italian Pentecostals in the city and over a twenty-year period oversaw the establishment of other Italian language churches.

A sacrificial spirit was a common characteristic among these early Pentecostals. When a new church was being built, much of the labor was undertaken without charge by the members. One man gave his entire bank balance to purchase construction materials. Both men and women labored on the excavation of the site. When this first church was completed, the members turned their attention to sponsoring another congregation in the

Ville Emard district. Today, there is an Italian conference of churches which maintains a fraternal relationship with the PAOC.

The groundwork for a French-speaking Pentecostal work in Quebec had been prepared providentially a short time before the Bakers arrived in Montreal. Around the turn of the century, a family of French Methodists had emigrated from the Channel Islands to Canada. One son, Philip Lebrocq, having heard of the Baptism in the Holy Spirit and tongues-speaking, began to search for someone to instruct him. In 1913, he met a couple by the name of Sydenham who had come into Pentecost through meetings in Ontario. A friend named Bertha Smiley joined the Sydenhams in assisting Lebrocq to understand and receive the desired Baptism in the Spirit. Lebrocq also received much encouragement from the Bakers. He married Smiley and together they engaged in a Pentecostal ministry in the province that lasted for half a century. They established a church for French-speaking Pentecostals, which in turn later helped other congregations to get started.

French-Canadian Pentecostalism received another boost from the recruitment of L. R. Dutaud, a Baptist pastor. At the McPherson meetings of 1920, his wife was healed of tuberculosis of the throat, cancer, and other serious ailments. Mrs. Dutaud, though a pastor's wife, confessed to being a sinner. She was converted, healed, and then baptized in the Spirit. This demonstration of the power of God so close to home removed all prejudice and opposition from Dutaud. He was baptized in the Spirit and became an active Pentecostal worker in Quebec.

One of the unusual aspects of these 1920 meetings, which helped inaugurate the Pentecostal revival among the French, was that many who did not understand English were converted. One chronicler of these events later reported:

> ... many French folk had been saved, healed and filled with the Spirit in these meetings, although most of them understood little, if any, English.... Pastor Baker asked Pastor Dutaud to open meetings for them. It may seem strange to say that many met God in these meetings without understanding that which was preached. Mrs. Dutaud tells me that her father ... who never did understand a word of English ... had a crippled arm for years. Medical help availed nothing. As Mrs. McPherson preached, and he watched her without understanding a word, he said; "She has the face of an angel, not that of a woman," and the power of God went through him and his crippled arm became whole as the other. I have met others here who tell me the same story.... Madame Vinet ... who understood very little English, but she could "feel God in the meetings," was healed of cancer of the breast. A Roman Catholic all of her previous life, she was saved, filled with the Spirit ... and while still prostrate on the floor receiving her baptism, the cancer dropped out of her breast, leaving three holes which later filled up.[12]

6 / PIONEERING PENTECOST IN EASTERN CANADA

The Dutauds opened their first French-speaking church in the north section of Montreal in April 1921. The hall, which had only two rooms, was so packed with people that the orchestra was moved into a closet. However, there was no problem in hearing their enthusiastic playing. The Sunday school was located in the basement where an occasional rat scurried across the floor while school was in progress. But no one seemed to care when so many were being saved, healed, and filled with the Spirit in almost every meeting. Even demons were cast out through prayer: one man was so possessed that he rolled and writhed on the floor until he was delivered through prayer. He subsequently became a very useful church lay worker.

Dutaud later began religious services in Quebec City and in Trois-Rivières, although these two works ceased upon his death. Just before he died, he rallied and exclaimed "La gloire de l'Eternel est ici" (The glory of the Eternal is here). As the work he founded grew, it became necessary to move to a larger hall on St. Lawrence Street and then into still larger facilities on Papineau Street in 1948. The Depression years naturally hampered the evangelistic efforts of the Dutaud assembly, but it nonetheless enjoyed a steady growth in membership. Prayer was the key, as Lebrocq reported:

> There was no need for an evangelist. It was during the depression, few people were working, and as many as 50 and 60 would come to the afternoon prayer meeting.[13]

Many of the best known families in French Pentecostal circles were active in those early meetings — the Archambaults, Bastaraches, Bergerons, Gagnons, Turgeons, Villeneuves, and Vinets. But progress had to be made in the face of persecution and various forms of opposition. As Roland Bergeron observed, the Quebecer has been taught since infancy that there is no salvation outside the Roman Catholic Church. Anyone leaving that denomination came under censure and sometimes rejection by family members. Nonetheless, the great transformation in lives often led to the conversion of others in the family. Such was the case for the Desmarais family. In 1939, 12 members of this St-Hyacinthe family were led to Christ.

The "Act of Quebec" in 1774 ceded all educational rights to the Roman Catholic Church. This old parochial system made it very difficult for Pentecostals to secure suitable education for their children. To meet this need, a French-language day school, Montreal Christian Academy, was opened in 1943. A former nun, Madame Tassé, and her husband Louis took charge of this enterprise. Over the years it has met a critical need for Pentecostal families in the province. A need for a home for the aged was met by the establishment of the "House of Welcome" at Montfort. This site later became the location of the provincial Pentecostal camp meeting.

Another of the great needs for the burgeoning assemblies was a French-language training school for church leaders. Under the leadership of W. L. Bouchard, Berea Bible Institute was founded in 1941 in Montreal. For the next 30 years, most of the ministers in Pentecostal churches in Quebec received training at Berea. In fact, for a long time, it was the only French Pentecostal Bible school in the world.[14]

The potential for evangelism offered by radio was recognized by E. L. Lassègues. In 1942 he launched the first French-language Pentecostal gospel program in the history of the province. The broadcasts reached people otherwise untouched by the Pentecostal message. It provided practical assistance for those lay workers who were seeking to open new evangelistic centres. Members of the Leboeuf family were converted about that time. Through the influence and efforts of the Leboefs, other families were brought into the Pentecostal experience. Mme. Gaudet, a deaconess, pastored this group for some years before the Second World War.

The French-speaking assembly in St-Hyacinthe began in 1939 with the arrival of lay preacher Arthur Samson. After his conversion in a Pentecostal church in Montreal, Samson gave up his trade as a shoemaker and became a full gospel worker. It was a decision that cost him much in personal suffering because it was opposed by members of his family. Samson's pioneering efforts in St-Hyacinthe were vigorously resisted by the local religious leaders. Growth was slow and the new believers were often the targets of public persecution in the form of rock-throwing and fusillades of rotten eggs as they walked in the streets. Sometimes they had to cope with dismissal from employment because of their loyalty to Pentecostal views. From its first humble meeting in a warehouse, the congregation moved to better facilities and eventually to its own building. Pastor Samson gave leadership to the St-Hyacinthe assembly for more than 35 years. When he retired in 1978, his associate, Roger Daigneault, succeeded him as the senior pastor of Centre Evangélique de St-Hyacinthe.

Following his conversion, Ovila Bergeron began ministry in Senneterre and evangelized the Abitibi area. He started in Senneterre with house-to-house visitation. Meetings later were held in the town by Lucien Chouinard and Roland Bergeron. They managed to purchase a house and renovated it for church use. Armand Gagné expanded the work and graduates of Berea Bible Institute gave assistance. The Pentecostal message also was introduced to Chomedey through home visitation. Many families were converted and a number of supernatural healings took place.

The work in Quebec so prospered and increased in membership that a separate French Conference was organized in 1949. It worked in cooperation with the English Eastern Ontario and Quebec District of the PAOC.[15] This arrangement continued for about twenty years with only minor changes in administrative structure of the PAOC in Quebec. Revival and new evangelism techniques in the early-70s produced such growth that new forms of supervision evolved. Details of these alterations are discussed in a later chapter.

Pentecostalism first reached the Maritimes around 1923 where it encountered a revivalist tradition that helped in the establishment of the new movement. Both Nova Scotia and Prince Edward Island had been blessed by 18th and 19th-century revivals which were in some respects precursors of later Pentecostalism. A layman named Henry Alline became a powerful itinerant evangelist in Nova Scotia after his conversion in 1775. Although his efforts met with much opposition from the British colonial authorities and the Anglican Church, Alline was successful in leading many people into a born-again experience. Alline's converts formed a loose federation, but he never attempted to incorporate them in any kind of church or denominational structure. Many of his converts, however, later became leaders of the Baptist and Methodist churches which were founded late in the 18th century.[16] Perhaps Alline's most enduring legacy to Nova Scotia was his doctrine of the "New Birth." It left an imprint on the social consciousness that was of obvious benefit when Pentecostal teachings were introduced.

The chief revival personality on Prince Edward Island in the 19th century was Donald McDonald, a Scottish clergyman. McDonald left Scotland in shame because of an addiction to alcohol. It was on P.E.I. that McDonald came into a born-again experience and subsequently became a "flaming evangelist." Like Alline, he faced considerable resistance from Island officials and church leaders, both for his emphasis on the New Birth and for his revival methods. Extraordinary emotional and physical responses marked his meetings.

Following the "Great Revival" of 1830, McDonald became the acknowledged leader of a revivalistic sect known as the McDonaldites.[17] His teachings were taken by lay workers to some regions of New Brunswick, but with less success attending them than on P.E.I. It is possible that the ancestors of J. E. Purdie, the noted Canadian Pentecostal educator, came under McDonaldite influences. A powerful local revival in 1859 in Restigouche, New Brunswick, made a lasting impact on that region, and perhaps helped create a climate favorable to the later introduction of 20th-century Pentecostalism.[18]

In its initial form, the Pentecostal awakening followed the historic pattern of all revivalist movements in history. The full gospel message was taken to New Brunswick by two sisters from Macon, Georgia. Carro and Susan Davis were school teachers and members of the city's social elite when they were converted. After hearing of the outpouring of the Holy Spirit at Chicago, they went there and came into a personal Pentecost at a mission run by the Urshan brothers. After being engaged in lay ministry in Macon, they set out for Fredericton around 1923 in response to a "call" from the Lord. They founded the first full gospel mission in that city.

The next year they moved to Saint John where their preaching resulted in a local revival. Here the Davis sisters began to emphasize the chief doctrines of early Pentecostalism — "Jesus Christ is Saviour, Baptizer, Healer and Coming King."[19] As a result of the revival, a second full gospel assembly was established in the province. Through the ministry of the sisters in Moncton still another Pentecostal congregation appeared. As the church in Saint John developed under the leadership of the Davis sisters it "mothered" branch assemblies around the city. Other dedicated workers later established Pentecostal congregations throughout the Maritimes.[20]

It was early in the 1920s when Pentecostal workers came to Halifax, Nova Scotia. Again women played a prominent role. A doctor's wife and the wife of a judge, who had attended Aimee Semple McPherson's meetings, brought news of the great awakening in the United States to their home in Halifax. Not long afterwards, a Baptist evangelist named Mattie Crawford, who had come into a personal Pentecostal experience, held a two-week campaign in the city in 1925. Thousands attended her services and many were converted, healed, and baptized in the Spirit. After she left, there was no one to give leadership and the work languished until the arrival of Evangelist Ray Watson in 1929. Watson had been a bank robber before his conversion and his testimony attracted large crowds to his meetings in the old Mayflower Rink in Halifax. A local newspaper reported:

> He is a forceful speaker and brings his message in simple gospel language to the people. He is assisted by Mrs. Watson, whose skill as a violinist, and rare sweet singing voice, adds greatly to the services.[21]

Joyce Watson was a Saskatoon girl who had been converted and filled with the Spirit during the ministry in that city of W. E. McAlister. The Watsons began a half-hour gospel radio ministry in Halifax, a novelty for the community and an attention-getter for the evangelists. By the time of their departure for meetings elsewhere, there was a local congregation of Pentecostal believers meeting in a downtown hall. Clare and Lydia Scratch came to pastor this group.

Ray Watson's spectacular career as a bank robber (which resulted in a 25-year prison sentence), and his conversion, made him a "natural" as an evangelist. He had considerable success in the Maritime provinces in the 1920s. Watson and his wife were assisted in their meetings by workers from Western Canada, some of whom came from the newly established Pentecostal Bible school in Winnipeg. A woman named Mrs. Eddy, in Bathurst, New Brunswick, had prayed earnestly for Pentecostal meetings in her community, and gave much help to the Watsons after their arrival. Bathurst then had a population of about 4,000. The evangelist put up a large banner reading "From Bank Robber to Pulpit" and rented an empty store. The local clergy refused to cooperate, but the services soon became the talk of people in the shops, the mills, and even on the streets. Numbers of curious listeners were soon converted, filled with the Spirit, and baptized in water. Altogether, there were an estimated 150 converts in the city as result of the two-week campaign.

Tom and Doris Johnstone came from the West to assist the Watsons. Later, when Ray and Joyce Watson moved to Campbellton for meetings, the Johnstones stayed on to pastor the Bathurst assembly. By early 1929, they had acquired a hall seating about 250 and had about 47 students in Sunday school. Tom Johnstone discovered his congregation consisted largely of people who after having received the Baptism had been expelled from their former churches. It was evident that these people desperately needed teaching on the biblical principles of the work and gifts of the Holy Spirit.

One of his most unusual experiences involved a vision a young woman convert had concerning the Marriage Supper of Christ. The woman was totally ignorant of the Bible teachings on the subject. In her vision, she reported seeing several notorious sinners of Bathurst present at the Supper. Johnstone knew these people to be immoral, drunkards, and bootleggers. But without exception, within a short time, all those the girl saw in her vision were brought into the church.[22]

In the years following, the Bathurst congregation purchased a building and renovated it for their church, later named Evangel Tabernacle. Two branch works were developed at New Bandon and on Miscou Island under the leadership of M. S Winger. Some of the assistants at Bathurst were graduates of the Winnipeg Bible school — Carolyn Thaler, Beulah Hamilton, and Elsie Grierson. These pioneer efforts cost the workers much in terms of self-denial and personal sacrifice. The Watsons trusted God completely for their needs, although at times they let the leaders in Ontario and Western Canada know of their problems. In a note to R. E. McAlister in London, Watson noted that from any funds received, "Not one cent will be used for our personal uses, as we have always, and will always, trust God for our own expenses."

The Campbellton campaign conducted by the Watsons was very successful with the "Bank Robber" banner again attracting large crowds. Hundreds could not get into the packed meetings in the Orange Hall. In one week over 50 were converted. Soon there was a congregation of 85 with a Sunday school of about 200 students. In five weeks of meetings, there were 150 saved and three or four were filled with the Spirit in each meeting. Mabel Cunningham, a lay worker, came from St. Thomas, Ontario to assist for a time in the work. Carolyn Thaler and Beulah Hamilton came from Bathurst in 1929 to act as pastors of the Campbellton assembly. Among the early converts were the entire Underhill family, and Annie MacKnight, the mother of James MacKnight, who became General Superintendent of the PAOC. When J. E. Purdie travelled from Winnipeg in the summer of 1930 to his family home on Prince Edward Island, he stopped off and preached to the Pentecostal congregations in both Bathurst and Campbellton.[23] Later, James Montgomery became pastor at Campbellton, beginning a career that led to his election as Maritime district superintendent and later as a national executive officer of the PAOC.

The Watsons moved on to Glace Bay in Nova Scotia where they found themselves in the midst of a phenomenal revival. A Pentecostal lay worker named Claude Jones, who had begun meetings earlier, already had a small group of converts. Six mines at Glace Bay drew workers from many surrounding communities, and as far away as Newfoundland. The town had a reputation of being a "rough place." Despite the frontier community environment, the Watsons loved ministering to the people. They rented a large hall where huge crowds assembled — often out of curiosity but later to hear the full gospel. Joyce Watson reported the sense of conviction for sin which rested on those who attended:

> Those folk would actually hold on to their seats — some were lifted right off their seats by the power of God, only they didn't know why. They would sit still till "It" would "hit" them, as they said, and then would run to the altar, get saved, then get up and testify like an older Christian.[24]

Another account of the Glace Bay meetings referred to them as an "old time revival" with dozens saved, and the altars full of people crying out for mercy. Under conviction of sin, men ran out of the building, while others were left shaking by the power of God upon them. The Watsons held meetings also in North Sydney and at New Glasgow. After the Watsons left the Maritimes, they spent most of their remaining years in the ministry in the United States.

William and Elizabeth Rourke began both their married life and their ministry at the same time, in the early 1930s. They drove to the town of Bath on the banks of the St. John River in their 1928 "Chevie." The vehicle had been purchased for $175 with the small legacy Elizabeth had received from her grandmother. They immediately started holding meetings in Bath and two nearby communities, New Denmark and Fielding. An elderly gentleman at Bath arose at 5 a.m. each day to pray for a visitation from heaven; his prayers were answered. In one meeting, as Rourke spoke on the Second Coming, conviction seized the audience and a number came forward for salvation. Within a short period of time, there were 23 converts in the young assembly. As in all pioneering work, there were sacrifices to be made.

Not only were the Maritimes hard hit by the Great Depression, Pentecostal preachers were not greatly supported by the people. However, as Elizabeth Rourke recalled, God always met their needs:

> One day we had some calling to do and all we had was one dollar for gas. We purchased four gallons with it. My husband always kept close watch on the tires and this particular time he found four one dollar bills by the back wheel. . . . We drove a short ways down the road when something went wrong with the car right in front of a garage. It cost $2.95. Those were difficult days financially. No home mission support. No WM groups to send a parcel.[25]

The sacrificial labors of workers like the Rourkes, Johnstones, and Watsons resulted in the establishment of a number of Pentecostal congregations in the Maritimes. For a brief period of time, Ray Watson was the leading Pentecostal in the region. After his departure, however, it was felt by the workers that some organization was needed to conserve the work and to continue evangelism in the area. As a consequence, the first Maritime District Conference was convened in Halifax in 1930 with 24 delegates present. Also on hand was G. A. Chambers, the General Superintendent of the PAOC. The delegates officially adopted the PAOC *Constitution and By-laws*. At the 1931 Conference they elected James Montgomery as their first district superintendent.

Montgomery had been converted as a youth in Northern Ireland. He had a Pentecostal experience while praying one day with an elderly Methodist layman. Although he did not fully understand the experience, he clung tenaciously to it in the face of bitter opposition from his father. Eventually, he was given an ultimatum to forsake his charismatic experience or leave home forever. When he refused to comply with his father's demands, young James was physically forced out of the house. On the street, rejected by his family, and soaked by the rain, he heard a voice in his mind say, "Fear not my child, when thy father and thy mother forsake thee, then I the Lord will be with thee." Awed by the message, James lifted his hand to Heaven and said, "Father, take my hand and lead me and I'll go all the way with Thee."[26]

Impressed by the preaching of the famed English Pentecostal pioneer George Jeffreys, Montgomery started his own preaching career by assisting local workers. He was only 15 years of age at the time. Feeling led of the Lord, he emigrated to Canada and assisted in the work of the Upper Room Mission in Montreal. After short stints as an evangelist, he pastored at Arnprior and St. Catharines in Ontario. Later, he moved to the Maritimes. As Montgomery recalled, the hostility he met in that region was similar to the opposition encountered by Pentecostals in Northern Ireland. The local priests drove listeners away from the Pentecostal street meetings, but people followed the preacher to a schoolhouse where numbers were converted.

Once, while preaching, Montgomery noted a rather bizarre response to his ministry. As he moved forwards, numbers of people left the schoolhouse; when he moved backwards, the people returned. Later, when he asked the reason for their actions, the people said the power of God in the ministry of the Word was so great they could not bear to stay in the building, and had to move outside. They could go back inside when the preacher moved back from the doorway. These schoolhouse meetings led to the conversion of several people, who were to become lay assistants for Montgomery. Others later became full-fledged Pentecostal preachers and evangelists to other Maritime communities.

The onset of the Depression in the early-30s severely hampered evangelistic progress in the region. District Pentecostal officials had few financial resources with which to assist the workers. At one District Conference of that period, it was reported that annual income had been only $79, while yearly expenditures had totaled $82. In an effort to alleviate their financial difficulties, the Maritime workers moved towards an affiliate status with the Eastern Ontario and Quebec District. This arrangement proved rather unsatisfactory and the action was reversed in 1934.

6 / PIONEERING PENTECOST IN EASTERN CANADA

Concerted efforts were made to open new assemblies throughout New Brunswick, Nova Scotia, and Prince Edward Island. In 1936, M. S. Winger became district superintendent. Winger also served as president of the Maritimes Bible Institute when it was founded in 1944. The school began in Halifax but was moved to Truro where it continued until 1947. A site near Truro became the home of the first district campground, named Camp Evangeline. Eventually, Truro became the headquarters of the Maritime District of the PAOC. After Ivan Raymer became superintendent in 1948, the district appointed leaders for Sunday schools, Christ's Ambassadors, and Women's Missionary Council activities.

Two sisters from the United States, Emily and Gertrude Thomas, were led by the Lord to start a church on the island of Bermuda in 1935. Under the leadership of Harold Thomas, the church, known as Evening Light Pentecostal, joined the Maritime District of the PAOC in 1947.[27] Eventually two more Pentecostal congregations were formed in Bermuda which also became affiliated with the Maritime District.

The Pentecostal message found fertile soil in Newfoundland. The island has a long history of evangelical missions since the early 18th century. As a colony of Great Britain from 1583 until its confederation with Canada in 1949, Newfoundland had been the target of a number of British missionary endeavors. Church of England missionaries arrived in the 1720s. Missionary evangelism, however, was made difficult by laws which prohibited permanent settlement on the island for many years. Settlers circumvented these regulations by choosing to live in isolated communities known as "out-ports."

Methodist clergyman Lawrence Coughlan came in 1765. The entire population of the island then was estimated at 12,000, most of whom were illiterate and unacquainted with the gospel. After three years labor, Coughlan had a revival with hundreds along the shores of Conception Bay being converted. As in England, the Methodist workers in Newfoundland witnessed unusual physical prostrations among the people deeply convicted of sin. Coughlan reported that the people

> were pricked to the heart, and cried, "What must we do to be saved?" Some prayed aloud, others shouted for joy, telling what God had done for their souls. . . . Under almost every sermon and exhortation, some were cut to the heart, and others rejoiced in loud songs of praise.[28]

Methodists went to the Labrador coast to evangelize the Inuit and the Amerindians in 1824. They also worked among the many Newfoundlanders who sailed each summer to the northern fishing grounds. A mission was founded by the Moravians in 1771 near

Hopedale, but the extent of their work was limited by the nomadic ways of the Native peoples.[29] Another powerful influence for religion in Labrador and Newfoundland was the medical mission of Wilfred Grenfell. It was Evangelist D. L. Moody's influence, during a preaching tour in Britain, which led young Grenfell to dedicate his life to the northeast coast of Canada. Grenfell's hospital at St. Anthony and a small hospital ship provided both medical and religious benefits to the outports.[30]

The Salvation Army came to Newfoundland in 1885 with the arrival of Captain Emma Churchill. Meetings began at Portugal Cove, near St. John's. Their work in the city met with fierce opposition from those who regarded them to be "the queer religionists." On one occasion, Army officers were besieged in their St. John's headquarters by a howling mob. By the time General Booth made his only visit to Newfoundland in 1894, he found the Army had established "citadels" — as they called their church halls — in 25 island communities. In 1920, there were as many Salvationists in Newfoundland as in all of Eastern Canada.[31] The Army was to play a significant role in the establishment of Pentecostalism on the island.

The chief pioneer Pentecostal worker was Alice Garrigus, a spinster who arrived in Newfoundland in 1910. Garrigus was over 50 years of age when she left her native United States, directed by God to a place about which she knew nothing. She was a school teacher and a public speaker of recognized skills when she joined a devout Christian group that was praying for spiritual renewal. After she heard of the Welsh Revival and the outpouring of the Spirit in Los Angles, Garrigus sought and received a Pentecostal experience. It was a prophetic message in the church in New Hampshire in 1908 which first raised in her mind the word "Newfoundland." An inner conviction confirmed for her that this was the place where God wanted her to serve, but she had to look at an atlas to find the location of the island. Although she was still drawn by an earlier desire to go to China, she believed that a second message from God settled the call to Newfoundland:

> ... the Holy Spirit said "You are looking too far, go to Newfoundland." She had to get a map and see where Newfoundland was ... but she ... did not arrive ... until December 1, 1910. Easter Sunday, 1911, she opened Bethesda Mission. Miss Garrigus was then 52 years of age.[32]

In the opinion of PAOC leader George Chambers, the task she had undertaken was "a great deal harder than some of our foreign missionaries have to face."[33]

6 / PIONEERING PENTECOST IN EASTERN CANADA

The first Pentecostal meetings, on New Gower Street in St. John's, were held in a hall renovated to hold about 250 people, with living quarters upstairs. The walls were adorned with Scripture texts and a table and organ filled most of the platform. Behind the dais was a room soon known to all who attended as "the Pentecostal Room," where earnest seekers for the Baptism in the Holy Spirit gathered for prayer. From the first, as former PAON Superintendent Eugene Vaters noted, the stamp of divine approval was on the work:

> God came forth in mighty power, saving, baptizing, and healing . . . and many were the miracles of healing in those days. Sister Garrigus built her work on "holiness" teaching, and it went deep.[34]

Steady growth in membership made it necessary to enlarge the mission premises. After the need was made the subject of prayer, a gift of $500 came for this purpose from people completely unknown to Garrigus.

Although she never entertained doubts about her personal mission work in Newfoundland, Garrigus believed firmly that men ought to give leadership in church functions. To this end, she arranged for male assistants to help with water baptisms. Baptismal candidates would testify to curious crowds of onlookers before their immersion; many gave testimonies of supernatural healings. A number of individuals given up to die were healed in answer to prayer. On one occasion, two little girls, with touching faith, brought their blind sister to Garrigus for prayer; the child eventually recovered her sight. A woman on crutches, facing the amputation of her legs, came to Bethesda Mission just before going to hospital. When the believers went to prayer, the woman suddenly was running around the hall totally healed.

Naturally, these dramatic healings attracted still larger crowds, among them a Mrs. Smallwood, whose son Joseph was later to become Prime Minister and lead Newfoundland into the Canadian confederation. In his memoirs, *I Chose Canada*, Smallwood recounted his mother's conversion at the Bethesda Mission and described the impression Miss Garrigus had made on him when he was a young boy.[35]

For the first decade of her work in Newfoundland, Garrigus confined her ministry to the capital city where, in her view, no other mission was presenting the "full gospel." Her message consisted of the four major doctrinal emphases which marked the mainstream Pentecostal Movement in mainland Canada — Salvation, the Baptism in the Holy Spirit, Divine Healing, and the Second Coming. Her Bethesda Mission received a boost from a visit to St. John's by the great-granddaughter of General Booth. The relative of the founder of the Salvation Army, a Mrs. Demarest, gave prominence in her preaching to the doctrine of the Baptism in the Spirit. Some of the estimated 2,000 converts from her Newfoundland campaign found their way to the Bethesda Mission. Among the visitors to the mission was Robert English, a local businessman who had held gospel services in his home. When Garrigus met him, she recognized they had much in common and invited English to become her co-pastor. In this way, Robert English eventually became the superintendent of the growing work on the Island.[36] Garrigus highly valued the charismatic phenomena and miraculous healings which characterized the meetings at Bethesda, but she valued equally the grounding of the converts in the Word of God. For this reason, she occasionally invited Pentecostal leaders, such as R. J. Jamieson and C. E. Baker, to provide doctrinal instruction for the growing numbers of lay workers. One of the earliest of these lay assistants was Lucy Raines, a former Salvation Army officer. Other lay workers travelled to nearby communities on the shores of Conception Bay, but the St. John's Mission lacked the resources to support permanent works in these localities.

There were ample opportunities for outreach among the sailors whose ships visited the city for supplies. Many curious seamen came to Bethesda, some to mock and others to be converted. One notable case involved a man who was a bitter critic of the tongues-speaking phenomenon. In a service at the Mission, the critic heard a humble believer, incapable of reading or writing, speak in fluent Portuguese under the direction of the Holy Spirit. The critic was convinced and became a believer. Another convert was C. L. March, who was crippled in both legs and had to be carried into the meeting. After being healed through the prayers of the believers, he was converted and later became a lay worker.

By the mid-1920s, as lay preachers moved to other centres, Pentecostalism began its final outreach to all parts of Newfoundland. A revival at Humbermouth (now Corner Brook) led to the recruitment of men who were to become prominent Pentecostal preachers — such as Arthur Winsor and William Gillett. Work at Humbermouth began when two laymen, C. L. March and Herbert Eddy, arrived and erected a two-storey building. One half of the structure was used as a furniture store and the other half for full gospel meetings. The locals called it "the Ark."

William Gillett was a fearless man who later testified that the only time in his life when he ever felt afraid was when he first attended these services. He once remarked, "It was the great manifestation of God's power in the services that convicted me." Although only 19 years of age at the time, Gillett was selected to go with other lay workers to Deer Lake. He proved his effectiveness and was ordained to full-time ministry in 1927. He and his wife Matilda pastored for some time at Springdale before travelling to Labrador where they conducted an itinerant ministry among the Eskimos and Newfoundlanders.

Bert Parsons carried the same concern for the people living in Labrador. On several occasions Parsons had spoken in an Eskimo dialect, under the direction of the Spirit, although he had never even met an Eskimo. Claude Young and his wife joined Pastor Gillett in pioneering the north coast with the Pentecostal message. Although they had no financial resources, they were able to build a boat with lumber which was provided quite providentially. After praying for a motor for their boat, Gillett was informed one day that an engine had arrived at a nearby port with his name on the bill of lading. The engine exactly fitted the needs of their gospel boat.

The "Gospel Messenger" sailed north in 1932 as far as Rigolet without finding a single person on the way who could claim a salvation experience. On one summer trip north, the boat ran out of gas forcing them to sail into White Bay. Landing at the village of Griquet, they held the first Pentecostal meetings in the area. Eventually a church was founded, which the Gilletts later pastored. The "Gospel Messenger" also was used to transport lay workers, often under dangerous conditions, to many isolated communities in Newfoundland. Evelyn Forsey, who came into Pentecost at the age of 13 and spent over 30 years of her life in full gospel ministry, was one of 17 gospel workers who nearly drowned when the boat was almost wrecked on the Muddy Shag Rocks. Only fervent prayer, and Gillett's skill, avoided a terrible calamity for the infant Pentecostal Movement in Newfoundland. Such dangers and self-denial were constant elements in the early work. Claude Young, for example, had 12 family members to provide for on his pastor's income which sometimes totaled only $3 a week.[37]

Arthur S. Winsor helped to evangelize Deer Lake in the face of heavy opposition from the townspeople. Garrigus visited the community and remarked that rarely had she seen gospel meetings carried on under such difficult conditions. God intervened, however, in a way that powerfully impressed the people. A fire broke out and destroyed many buildings, but when it neared the Pentecostal meeting hall, it suddenly veered away.

Pastor Winsor, joined by Thomas Mitchell, C. L. March, and Herbert Eddy, held meetings in Grand Falls Station (now Windsor) in the summer of 1926. March provided funds for lumber and a new Pentecostal church building was erected. They went on to Springdale, a journey of 35 miles on foot, and began preaching in the school house and in homes. At the end of two weeks, they baptized five converts in water. Some months later they reached out to the small village of Port Anson, where numbers were saved and filled with the Spirit, speaking in tongues. Then a full-fledged revival broke out and scores were converted and baptized in the Spirit during a two-week period. As Pastor Winsor described the move of God,

> It was a Holy Ghost revival. We don't know of anyone who attended the meetings who did not get saved. Before the meetings were over, some who were over 70 years of age turned to the Lord. ... We had no music of any kind. ... When we would start to sing "Lord send the power," the Spirit would just rest on the people. That's when they would come to that altar and be saved ... right from the beginning of the service, they would turn to the Lord. Many nights we would not get a chance to preach at all. The house would be filled with the glory of God.[38]

Pastors Winsor, Mitchell, March, and Eddy held meetings at Twillingate, then again in Springdale in 1927. At that time, young Philip Butt was converted: he would subsequently give over 40 years to Pentecostal ministry. Still, there were lingering forces of opposition. At Springdale, Winsor was arrested on a charge of high treason — "speaking against the Crown." On inquiry, when the magistrate discovered the charge had been made by critics who had never been in the Pentecostal meetings, Winsor was released. Although he was urged to prosecute the critics who had so maliciously slandered him, Winsor refused to do so. As he put it, "We were in a revival and did not have time for small matters." In one later meeting, 10 people were converted, among them Jonas Noble, father of Pastor G. E. Noble.

Winsor and Gillett had an unusual experience on their way to preach at Springdale. Gillett had a vision in which he saw a jug with a broken side. Although puzzled by the meaning of the experience, the men went on to Springdale, where, to their surprise, the exact figure of the jug seen in the vision was sitting in a shop window. This was taken by the workers as confirmation that the Lord had led them to that community. Numbers of Springdale people came into the Pentecostal experience and a strong church was established in Springdale.

The itinerant Pentecostal evangelists were concerned at that early date chiefly with the proclamation of the full gospel. Although they established numerous new congregations, they gave scant attention to organization and administration. Alice Belle Garrigus was viewed as the founder of the work, but the man who organized and consolidated Pentecostalism in Newfoundland was Eugene Vaters. Before his own Baptism in the Spirit, Vaters had been a devout Methodist living in the community of Victoria. Vaters was troubled at the time by what he perceived as a drift to Modernism in the Methodist Church. He decided to go to Chicago to acquire a sound theological education for himself. He also felt a need for more reality and power in his religious life. First, however, he visited Garrigus' Bethesda Mission in St. John's. By his own admission, he was greatly impressed by what he called "those queer people" who met in "a hole-in-the-wall" meeting place. On the way to Chicago, Vaters stopped in Montreal to visit Charles Baker's assembly. There he received additional favorable impressions of the Pentecostal Movement.

Shortly after his arrival in Chicago, Vaters decided to seek out a "Pentecostal Bible school." This quest took him to the Elim Bible school in Rochester, N.Y. There, he and his young wife Sarah sought for, and received, the Baptism in the Holy Spirit. Once again, after a time of theological study and prayer, Vaters felt led to make another move — one that would lead him into full-time ministry in Newfoundland. On the return journey, the Vaters once again visited the Baker assembly in Montreal. They remained for a time in that city to assist the Baker outreach mission halls before heading back to the island.

The Vaters began a Pentecostal ministry in Victoria in 1924. At that time, Vaters declared that he had only five cents to his name. But God greatly prospered their efforts and many were converted and filled with the Spirit with the evidence of tongues. In a short while, funds were collected and a new church building was erected. It was in the new church that God gave the young congregation what Vaters considered to be a mighty outpouring of the Holy Spirit:

> A woman near the altar . . . saw in a vision, as it were, a cloud hanging over the altar. Suddenly it burst. At the instant the power fell. Some were thrown to the floor, others remained with upright hands, while one after another began to speak in "other tongues" and magnify God. Most of those baptized at the time were men in the prime of life.[39]

Through these Victoria meetings, Eugene Vaters became acquainted with Alice Garrigus, with whom he enjoyed a cooperative relationship in the work. In 1927, Vaters became General Superintendent of all Pentecostal ministries in Newfoundland. He held that post for over a quarter-century, during which time he knit together the disparate elements of the young movement. Under his leadership, membership in the churches increased until by 1935 there were some 3,700 adherents. He also pioneered the establishment of a Pentecostal day school system in the region. His successor as General Superintendent, A. Stanley Bursey, summarized Vaters' ministry:

He led the movement, under God, through times of testing, times of victory, and gave wise leadership to the young movement, when it was easy to side-step in doctrine, in practice and in commitment.[40]

Organization enabled the young denomination in Newfoundland to assist in worldwide missionary endeavors. Garrigus sent funds in 1934 to A. G. Ward, the Missions Secretary of the PAOC, to support the work in Lucknow, India.[41] It is possible that she had furnished money at an earlier date as well. Newfoundlander Newman J. LeShana was supported on the field by Garrigus in the amount of $60 a month — a not inconsiderable sum at the height of the Great Depression. Ward later reported that about 300 people had been converted to Christ through this mission work. The Newfoundland Pentecostals also sent funds to Toronto for the work of the early Canadian missionaries in Liberia. Later, Newfoundland believers took on the challenge of nearby Labrador as a mission field on their own doorstep.

Newfoundland profited from the labors of Canadian Pentecostals from the mainland in the formative years of the work. Botwood was first reached by Pastor Winsor and his lay assistant, Thomas Mitchell, in 1926. A congregation was established and a church erected within two months, but there was no settled pastor for some time, Finally, two graduates from the Winnipeg Bible college, Irene Morris and Viola Wilson, arrived to provide leadership. In a 1930 report in *The Gleaner*, these two women described their difficulties in reaching the 900 inhabitants of Botwood:

> The people are so religious about Sabbath-keeping, etc., that the biggest sinner is very self-righteous. Nearly every winter there would be a revival and every summer many of them would backslide. One brother actually was at the altar twenty-five times before he got anything real, but now he is baptized with the Spirit and on fire for God. Five have received their Baptism, twenty have been saved and are going on.[42]

Late in the 1920s, Thomas Mitchell held meetings at Middle Arm on Green Bay. He was a humble man, declaring that he was unfit to preach, but would carry the bags of anyone called of God. At Middle Arm the Lord blessed him and used his ministry in the conversion of several people in the area. At Bishop's Falls around 1930 two young men, who had just returned from the Canadian mainland after receiving the Baptism in the Spirit, were instrumental in founding a Pentecostal church. It was pastored for a time by Sarkis Alexanian, a graduate of the Bible college in Winnipeg.

6 / PIONEERING PENTECOST IN EASTERN CANADA

Pentecostalism in Newfoundland also benefited greatly from the recruitment of former Salvation Army officers who had received their personal Pentecost. Captain E. R. Pelley took the Pentecostal message to Black Island in 1929, a place which, in his opinion, was in a sad spiritual state. When A. S. Bursey arrived some months later, a congregation was set in order on Black Island. Another former Salvationist, E. R. Milley of Exploits, in Notre Dame Bay, joined the Pentecostals in 1938 and pastored at Bay Roberts. While pastoring at Roddickton, he was asked to pray for a woman who was paralyzed from the waist down. Prayer for the sick was unfamiliar to Milley, but he complied and the lady was healed. Another remarkable incident in his ministry involved the raising of a dead woman. The body already had been washed and dressed for burial when he arrived on the scene. As he stood there, uncertain what to do, he raised his hands and prayed. What his words were he could never afterwards recall, but the woman arose and lived another 40 years.[43]

The Pentecostal Movement in Newfoundland was unique in its development of an elaborate primary and secondary school system. This day school system was necessary largely because of the historical development of education in the region. The first educational programs on the island were church-related. As the various denominations grew, each formed its own parochial school system. Since the children of the Pentecostals appeared to be unwelcome in other denominational schools, they determined to establish their own Pentecostal schools. The first school opened in 1933. Many non-Pentecostal families who wanted a sound academic and strong religious education program chose to send their children to the Pentecostal schools. In this fashion, the PAON parochial school system became a means of evangelism. At its first request for official recognition in 1936, the Pentecostal system was rejected by the government's ministry of education, but later the coveted approval was given. By the time full recognition was accorded in 1954, the PAON had 13 schools and over 750 students. Its subsequent expansion was supervised by Geoffrey Shaw who encouraged every effort to bring the system to the highest level of efficiency and academic excellence.

One of the effective ways of spreading the Pentecostal message throughout Newfoundland was by the printed page. Early efforts were under the leadership of Eugene Vaters who published a small magazine called *The Independent Communion*. Later, Vaters and Garrigus jointly published the *Elim Pentecostal Evangel*. Another brief venture birthed *The Pentecostal Herald*, but this periodical ceased when the workers voted in 1929 to make *The Pentecostal Testimony* of the PAOC their official magazine. In 1935, the *Good Tidings* magazine was introduced in

Newfoundland and became the official voice of the PAON.

Alice Belle Garrigus could hardly have imagined, when she began preaching in 1911, the extent to which Pentecostalism would pervade Newfoundland. Although she retired from active leadership in her later years, she continued to preach well into her 80s. When she died in 1949 at the age of 91, her life had spanned the entire history of Pentecostalism on the island. Grateful pastors and people erected a monument to her memory inscribed:

Alice B. Garrigus
1858-1949
Founding Mother
Pentecostal Assemblies of Newfoundland.

Endnotes

1. A. R M. Lower, *Colony to Nation: A History of Canada* (Toronto: Longmans, 1946), pp. 119-125, 181ff.
2. E. L. Lassègues, "Pentecost in Quebec," tract, PAOC Archives.
3. Gordon R. Upton, "Mission Canada: The Changing Face of Missions," *The Pentecostal Testimony* (November 1985), 29.
4. James Caughey, *Revival Miscellanies* (Boston: Magee, 1852), pp. 252-253.
5. G. A. Chambers, "History of the PAOC," handwritten manuscript, PAOC Archives.
6. *Minute Book of the 9th Line Tabernacle of the Assembly of God, Kinburn, Ontario,* handwritten record of the church by various recording secretaries, original in the church files. Used by permission.
7. "Revival at McBean, Quebec," typed copy of original paper by A. W. Otto, PAOC Archives.
8. R. P Spurrell, letter to Thomas Wm. Miller, October 27, 1983.
9. C. E. Baker, "Canada's Largest City Is Visited With Floods of the Latter Rain," *Canadian Pentecostal Testimony,* 2 (January 1921), 2.
10. W. E. McAlister, letter to E. J. Carter, June 7, 1956; and Salome Cressman, "A Half Century of Pentecost in Quebec," *The Pentecostal Testimony* (September 1964), 4-7, 33; see also French translation by G. Gagnon, *Le Mouvement De Pentecôte Au Québec* (booklet) and *Perspective,* bulletin of the District of Eastern Ontario and Quebec, February 1982.
11. Eugene Vaters, *Reminiscences* (St. John's: PAON, 1983), pp. 80, 107.
12. Ethel Logan, letter to W. E. McAlister, June 14, 1956, PAOC Archives.

6 / PIONEERING PENTECOST IN EASTERN CANADA

13. Cressman, "A Half Century of Pentecost in Quebec," *The Pentecostal Testimony* (September 1964), 6.
14. E. L. Lassègues, letter to J. E. Purdie, December 1954, PAOC Archives.
15. Cressman, "A Half Century of Pentecost in Quebec," *The Pentecostal Testimony* (September 1964), 7.
16. Thomas Wm. Miller, *Ripe for Revival* (Burlington: Welch, 1984), pp. 61-63; see also J. M. Bumstead, *Henry Alline, 1748-1784* (Toronto: University of Toronto Press, 1971), p. 28.
17. David Emrys Weale, "The Ministry of the Reverend Donald McDonald on Prince Edward Island, 1826-1867," unpublished PhD thesis, Queen's University, Kingston, 1976.
18. James Eustace Purdie, "Purdie Papers," Central Pentecostal College Library Archives, Saskatoon, Saskatchewan.
19. Fred H. Parlee, "Carro and Susie Davis," *The Pentecostal Testimony* (December 1987), 16.
20. Ibid., 17
21. "Faith Tabernacle, 40th Anniversary, 1929-1969," booklet, Faith Tabernacle, Halifax, 1969.
22. Thomas Wm. Miller, taped interview with Tom Johnstone, April 29, 1984.
23. Various accounts of these meeting were published in the bulletin of the Winnipeg Bible school, *The Gleaner*, 1 (December 1929); 2 (February 1930); and *The Pentecostal Testimony* (April 1929), 11, and (May 1929), 13, 15.
24. Essie Watson, letter to W. E. McAlister, February 15, 1954, PAOC Archives; see also *The Pentecostal Testimony* (May 1930).
25. Elizabeth Rourke, letter to Thomas Wm. Miller, March 1, 1985.
26. Thomas Wm, Miller, taped interview with James Montgomery, July 29, 1984; see also "Maritime Workers' Convention," *The Pentecostal Testimony* (April 1, 1932), 11.
27. C. M. Morton, letter to D. N. Buntain, January 5, 1946, PAOC Archives; see also *To God Be The Glory*, 50th anniversary booklet published by the Evening Light Church, Hamilton, Bermuda.
28. Alexander Sutherland, *The Methodist Church and Missions in Canada and Newfoundland* (Toronto: Methodist Church, 1906), p. 71ff; and J. E. Sanderson, *The First Century of Methodism in Canada*, vol. 1 (Toronto: Briggs, 1908-1910), 13-15.
29. Arminius Young, *One Hundred Years of Mission Work in the Wilds of Labrador* (London: Stockwell); *A Methodist Missionary in Labrador* (Toronto: Methodist Church, 1916); see also Young, "Moravians in Canada," *Canadian Heritage* (October-November 1983), pp. 13-19.
30. Wilfred T. Grenfell, *What Christ Means to Me* (Boston: Pilgrim Press, 1927).

31. R. G. Moyles, *The Blood and Fire in Canada: A History of the Salvation Army in the Dominion, 1882-1976* (Toronto: Peter Martin, 1977), pp. 79-87, 180.
32. For the early story of Miss Garrigus in Newfoundland, see Burton Janes, *The Lady Who Came* (St. John's: Glad Tidings Press, 1982). The quotation is from A. S. Winsor, in a series of six articles on early Pentecostalism titled "Things Seen and Heard," in *Good Tidings*, vols. 28 and 29 (May-June 1972 to July-August 1973). Used by permission.
33. G. A. Chambers, "History of the PAOC," handwritten manuscript, PAOC Archives.
34. Another general history of Pentecostalism in Newfoundland is John W. Hammond, *The Joyful Sound: A History of the Pentecostal Assemblies of Newfoundland and Labrador* (St. Stephens, NB: for the author, 1982). The quotation is from Eugene Vaters, "Pentecostal Work in Newfoundland: the Story Told for the First Time," *The Pentecostal Testimony* (May 1936), 19.
35. Hammond, *The Joyful Sound: A History of the Pentecostal Assemblies of Newfoundland and Labrador*, pp. 46-57.
36. Burton Janes, *The Lady Who Stayed* (St. John's: Glad Tidings Press, 1983), p. 221.
37. Thomas Wm. Miller, personal interview with Pastor Claude Young; accounts of these evangelistic campaigns are in Winsor's six-part series in *Good Tidings* and in Hammond, pp. 123-124; see also Evelyn Forsey, "Gratitude and Praise," *Good Tidings*, 36:6 (November-December 1980).
38. A. S. Winsor, "Things Seen and Heard," *Good Tidings* (May-June 1973).
39. Vaters, "Pentecostal Work in Newfoundland: the Story Told for the First Time," *The Pentecostal Testimony* (May 1936), 19-20; see also Vaters, *I Reminisce* (St. John's: Glad Tidings Press, 1983), pp. 62, 96, 120ff.
40. A. S. Bursey, "Pastor Eugene Vaters . . . a cohesive force" *Good Tidings*, 38:1 (January-February 1982).
41. Alice B. Garrigus, letter to A. G. Ward, January 18, 1934, PAOC Archives.
42. *The Gleaner*, 2 (February 1930), 4; see also Hammond, p. 90.
43. Garry E. Milley, ed., "Journal of Pastor E. R. Milley," unpublished. Used by permission.

Chapter 7

CAMP MEETINGS, CONVENTIONS, AND COLLEGES

The evangelistic/healing campaigns of the early Canadian Pentecostals made a major contribution to the spread of the full gospel message across the nation. Camp meetings and Bible colleges were two other useful tools in the establishment of the Pentecostal Movement, especially in Western Canada.[1] Still another important factor was the practice of holding conventions (conferences) at which denominational organization could be developed and measures taken to preserve doctrinal distinctives. These methods came naturally to many of the Pentecostal pioneers since they were schooled in such practices in their former denominations and because they seemed to have a instinct for employing things that worked.

Pentecostals with a Methodist or Baptist background inherited a love for camp meetings which had been popular with those older denominations since the great revivals of the 18th century. The most famous was the Cane Ridge camp meeting of 1801 in Kentucky. In August of that year crowds of up to 25,000 gathered by wagon, on horseback, or on foot for several weeks of preaching and spiritual renewal. The crowd was enormous for the time, considering that the largest city on the Kentucky frontier then had a population of less than 1,800. With as many as seven preachers at a time exhorting the crowds, thousands were converted. Extraordinary physical manifestations, such as falling to the ground, crying out under conviction, and shouting praises to God were frequent phenomena.

So successful was this particular camp meeting that scores more were held in other places. This method of evangelism became a regular fixture among the Baptists, Disciples, and Methodists. The camp meeting was held in high regard, especially among the Methodists, as a powerful means of reaching the settlers on the remote frontiers. S. C. Swallow, a

7 / CAMP MEETINGS, CONVENTIONS, AND COLLEGES

Methodist clergyman with over 50 years of camp meeting experience, outlined its many benefits for evangelizing the unchurched masses:

> In America, camp meetings served to introduce and give homogeneity to a membership otherwise estranged and heterogeneous. They supplied the place of large churches. ... They drew the masses ... and leavened them with a new theology. ... Justification, adoption, the witness of the Spirit, sanctification — immediate, clear, satisfactory — here found most enthusiastic advocates and faithful adherents.[2]

The first Canadian camp meeting was held by Methodists at Hay Bay, near Napanee, Ontario, in 1805. Thereafter it became a regular feature of Methodist evangelism in Upper Canada.[3] When the Empire Loyalists arrived from the United States after the revolutionary war, they joined thousands of Dutch and German settlers in Ontario. The Methodists extended their outreach among these people with the circuit rider and the camp meeting.[4] The Native tribes also were evangelized by this method: in 1823, for example, both Natives and whites gathered for a camp meeting at Rice Lake, Ontario.[5]

Canadian Methodism began to be affected negatively by the "Social Gospel" around 1860. The emphasis on personal conversion declined and the camp meetings lost some of their popularity.[6] Occasional periods of religious revival like that which swept over North America from 1857 to 1859 brought rejuvenation to the denomination and kept alive its evangelical traditions for another generation. Significantly, the camp meeting was the method used for reviving the Methodist Church, particularly in the Hamilton region. Phoebe Palmer, the noted Holiness teacher, held meetings at nearby Spencerville at "the Great Union Camp Meeting" which produced dramatic results:

> For weeks ... fervent prayer ... had been ascending to God. ... Our hearts were cheered by "Spirit of glory and of God" [which] rested upon the people in such a powerful manner as but few present ever before witnessed ... some three hundred persons under the Divine influence seemed moved as with a rushing mighty wind: some shouted "Glory to God in the highest." Scores prostrated before their Maker cried aloud for mercy, while others ... could only say "How dreadful is this place." ... 103 had professed conversion during the meeting and 92 entire sanctification.[7]

Crowds of 6,000 were in attendance and the churches enjoyed a period of renewed vitality and respect. That was the heritage of many first-generation Canadian Pentecostals at the turn of the century, especially

CAMP MEETINGS, CONVENTIONS, AND COLLEGES / 7

those with Baptist and Methodist backgrounds. The first specifically "Pentecostal" camp meetings were held as early as 1908, within a year or two of the Holy Spirit infilling of such leaders as A. H. Argue, Ellen Hebden, R. E. McAlister, and A. G. Ward. McAlister reported in May 1911 that the "4th Annual Camp Meeting of the Pentecostal Saints of Sand Bay" would be held on the shore of Lake Singleton near Lindhurst Station in the Ottawa area.[8] One report indicates that there was a camp meeting in 1908 near Simcoe in a sheltered spot known as Post's Cove. There is no evidence that it was ever repeated.

A. G. Ward was the chief organizer for a camp meeting at Markham, Ontario, in 1909, and again in 1910. The second camp in 1910 had 3,000 people on its closing day. Ward and interested friends had raised funds for a tent. After using it for the two summers at Markham, they sold it to a rising young preacher, Aimee Semple, known as "The Girl Evangelist." Semple's meetings were crowded out at Mount Forest and the tent was used with great effect there and in other evangelistic campaigns.[9] From Canada she went to the United States where she ultimately founded The Church of the Foursquare Gospel in California.

The Markham Camp of 1910 was notable for the number of prominent early Pentecostal leaders it attracted. A. G. Ward, already a nationally-recognized spokesman for the Pentecostal Movement, and Vicar A. A. Boddy of Sutherland, England, were present. Boddy, on a worldwide tour to promote Pentecostalism, preached several times at the 1910 meetings. Various early leaders came from the United States, among them A. G. Garr and his wife Lillian. Mrs. Garr was an impressive speaker. At one memorable meeting, after she had spoken on reaching the world with the full gospel, she called on the people to give generously for missions. Then, according to the oft-repeated story, she placed her hand on an offering plate as a symbol of her personal dedication to overseas evangelism. It made a powerful impact on the viewers. The Garrs later moved to India for gospel work. Their successes were reported to North American Pentecostals through the pages of the Azusa Street Mission paper. Markham thus was the site in 1910 of the first special "Missionary Offering" and the first special "Missionary Commissioning Ceremony" among Canadian Pentecostals. It also was the scene of the earliest attempts to develop a simple organizational structure for the fledgling movement. Regrettably, when these first halting steps were met with some prejudice and misunderstanding, A. G. Ward decided to drop the scheme.[10]

The Pentecostal message received considerable public attention as a result of two camp meetings in 1911 and 1912 at Jordan Station, near Vineland, Ontario. George Chambers took the lead in organizing these camps, which he often described as "heaven on earth." Hundreds of

7 / CAMP MEETINGS, CONVENTIONS, AND COLLEGES

spiritually thirsty believers gathered to learn more about the Baptism in the Holy Spirit with the evidence of speaking in tongues. Hundreds more of the curious onlookers came only to be entertained, but quite often they were brought under deep conviction of their sin. Among the visitors were earnest Christians from London, including W. H. Wortman, whose son Dr. Charles Wortman later became a PAOC missionary. Well-known American Pentecostals such as Dr. Yokum, Frank Bartleman, and Daniel Awrey attended and ministered.

Prayer was offered for the sick and many testimonies were given about healings. So common was the practice among these early believers, and so frequent were the answers to prayer, that the outsiders seemed ready to believe almost anything was possible for the Pentecostals. A rumor once swept through the area that prayer was to be made at the Jordan Valley Camp to raise the dead, and that bodies were being shipped in for this purpose! The truth was that when the large crowds necessitated more cots and mattresses than were on hand, George Chambers ordered more from a firm in Toronto. When the materials arrived, they had been packed in casket boxes. Nonetheless, the rumor served to attract hundreds more to the meetings.[11]

G. A. Chambers and R. E. McAlister utilized the camp meeting as a regular part of their evangelistic outreach in the formative period of the movement in Ontario. McAlister supervised meetings in the summers at Lansdowne and Mille Roches in the Ottawa region. Chambers preached at camps at London, Kitchener, and Arnprior. The 1919 meetings at Arnprior were remarkable for the display of divine power in the services. Many were baptized in the Spirit, others were freed from demonic powers, some were healed, and a considerable number were converted. One memorable event was described by Chambers:

> ... a strange, supernatural light appeared to light up the various tents with a celestial brightness. A holy Awe fell on the entire camp. God wrought in a wonderful and unusual way until many were led to exclaim that God was truly in our midst.[12]

This use of the camp meeting to spread Pentecostalism was enormously successful and scores of such meetings were held in several parts of Canada. A camp meeting was held by J. H. Blair at Walkerton in 1923, the "first real Pentecostal camp meeting ever held in this part of the country." An advertisement in the *Testimony* advised campers to bring their own bedding, tents, and a straw tick on which to sleep. Straw would be provided at the camp.[13] G. A. Chambers and J. D. Saunders were the featured speakers. Chambers even used the camp meeting as an evangelistic device when he pastored at Peterborough during the

Depression. A vacant lot in the centre of the city was secured, a tent erected, and a loudspeaker conveyed the singing and the message to curious bystanders and people in parked cars, as well as to those in the tent. When Tom Johnstone pastored in Quebec, he and C. F. Day, of the Upper Room Mission in Montreal, held a successful two-day camp meeting at Magog.

The camp meetings in the various communities proved to be, in the words of Johnstone, chiefly "forerunners of the larger district camps" which gradually evolved. The increasing numbers of converts, the advent of the mass-produced automobile, like Henry Ford's "Model T," and the rapid improvement in the highway system made it possible to attract people from greater distances. This increase in the number of interested people and their new ability to travel prompted the pioneer leaders to organize regional camp meetings.

The first permanent camp in Western Ontario was established by J. H. Blair when he served as district superintendent. Blair had held a fall camp meeting in 1934 near Woodstock, but sought a more suitable site. He found it near Paris along the banks of the Grand River. Having only $50 for a down payment on the $2,500 property, Blair believed God would miraculously provide the balance. He was motivated by a conviction that the camp meeting would bring unity to the district and growth in its affairs. The new campground was called "Braeside" — a Scottish term that meant "a hill alongside a river." Acquainted with the history of Methodism, Blair once observed that "as long as the Methodists had camp meetings, their churches were alive. When the camp meeting died among the Methodists, their churches died."[14]

Evangelists A. H. Argue and Zelma Argue were the first speakers and Asa Miller of Michigan was the first Bible teacher at Braeside Camp. A large tent seating 1,000 was used the first summer, then work began on more permanent facilities. But the first summer justified the sacrifice and effort. About 2,300 people attended the final service, and over 100 were baptized in the Spirit. Argue's final words of advice to J. H. Blair were indelible: "Brother Blair, keep your meeting Pentecostal and your altar alive."[15] Most of the construction work for the permanent building was done by the superintendent and volunteers from his assembly at Hamilton.

As the camp continued for decades, it acquired a reputation for having some of the best national and international Pentecostal leaders as speakers. Crowds grew to 5,000 at times, and many thousands could testify to salvation, healing, and Baptism in the Spirit at Braeside. One early famous evangelist was A. A. Wilson of Kansas City, Missouri, whose recollections of the 1937 camp are instructive:

7 / CAMP MEETINGS, CONVENTIONS, AND COLLEGES

> Throngs of people overflowed the big tabernacle nightly, and the power of God was ever present to transform and deliver. . . . Great miracles of healing were seen that have withstood the ravages of time. But the memory of seeing over one hundred and fifty receive the mighty Baptism in the Holy Ghost . . . Hallelujah. The service would continue . . . often to the early hours of the morning. . . . There are men and women today, in all parts of the world, who are preaching the Gospel because of Braeside Camp. . . . In recalling those fleeting moments, I can only say "they were days of Heaven on Earth."[16]

Dr. Charles Price preached his first Canadian camp meeting at Braeside. His view of its effectiveness in bringing unity to the scattered congregations was similar to that of Blair. The camp meeting, he wrote,

> can be a tremendous factor in bringing about the solidarity of the district. It ties the preachers together in the bonds of fellowship far more effectively than the business meeting or a conference.[17]

These goals were in view when Blair and Gordon Atter established a regional campground at Spring Bay on Manitoulin Island. An old Mennonite camp site was acquired in 1941 and the first meetings were held the next year. Since then, the facilities have been greatly expanded. Atter has been one of the mainstays in both assisting in the supervision of the camp and preaching at the services. Again, Blair and Atter were instrumental in the organization of Silver Birches Camp Ground in 1949. The camp was set up on a beautiful site near the Northern Ontario community of Kirkland Lake. Although the camp is under the supervision of the Western Ontario District, regional Pentecostal churches have accepted responsibility for its operation. Both Spring Bay and Silver Birches provided a format of preaching and teaching similar to Braeside, the larger camp near Paris.[18]

The largest of the camps in the Eastern Ontario and Quebec District was set up on the north shore of Lake Ontario, near Cobourg, in 1935. The Pentecostal preacher in that town, Allen Mallory, found the site, which was owned by an American who had used it for a horse-racing farm. After a survey by George Chambers, then the district superintendent and pastor in Peterborough, the land was acquired and plans made for a camp meeting. That first winter, Mallory shovelled snow for about two kilometers from the highway into the campsite in order to do work on the buildings. Much of the labor on the grounds, and a portion of the $2,800 purchase price for the farm, was provided by volunteers from Peterborough.

The first services at the Cobourg camp, in the summer of 1936, were held in the old barn which had been renovated by removing the horse stalls and putting sawdust on the floor. People lived in small tents and food was provided on site at a cost of 25 cents per meal. The first camp speakers were Otto Klink and W. I. Evans. Donald Gee of Britain was one of the early Bible teachers. One stalwart, W. B. Greenwood, attended every camp from its inception.

Chambers was an indefatigable promoter of the Cobourg camp, as one of his advertisements in the *Testimony* reveals:

> Sleeping cottages . . . ready for use . . . for $75 and $100. . . . To mention a few attractions . . . playground for children . . . plenty of parking space with watchmen in charge . . . half-mile of the finest beach. . . . all buildings will be lighted by Hydro . . . all camp drinking water is government tested . . . the new dining pavilion is entirely screened . . . cool lake breezes without discomfort.[19]

People began to erect cottages on the campgrounds and live there through the summer months. When W. B. Greenwood became district superintendent (1950 - 1964), he promoted the continual development of Lakeshore Pentecostal Camp, as it came to be known. Further improvements were made to the camp during the tenures of Richard Bombay and Gordon Upton as district superintendent. Hundreds of Pentecostals and large numbers of curious people gathered at the camp from the start. The ministries of well-known preachers, missionaries, and evangelists left a lasting impact on the listeners. Many present-day Pentecostal clergymen and denominational leaders, such as Cal Bombay and William Griffin, trace their decision for gospel ministry to the influence of Cobourg camp. When Lakeshore Camp celebrated its 50th anniversary in 1986, the camp tabernacle could seat 1,800 people and the grounds accommodated about 150 private cottages.

The forerunner of the modern Manitoba district camp was launched in 1919 at Rock Lake through the efforts of laymen like Elmer Cantelon. Cantelon, a successful prairie harvester, had the financial ability along with the interest to secure suitable property on the lakeshore to hold a camp meeting. He invited Jack Saunders as the first camp evangelist. Before his conversion, Saunders had been a boxer known to his colleagues as "Wild Jack." But the transforming power of the gospel turned the boxer into a powerful preacher. Scores of people were converted and many filled with the Spirit at these first meetings.

Saunders returned summer after summer, and always ministered with great effectiveness. At one water baptismal service, a crowd of scoffers and roughnecks made mocking remarks, but their attitude turned to tears and solemn quietness as they observed the sincerity of the worshippers.[20] Others who spoke at the Rock Lake Camp included Donald Gee from England, Canadians A. H. Argue and W. E. Moody, and W. T. Gaston

7 / CAMP MEETINGS, CONVENTIONS, AND COLLEGES

from the USA. Meetings were held each summer, with the exception of 1927. The Rock Lake Camp was later replaced by the Manhattan Beach Camp on Pelican Lake near Ninette.

Like its predecessor, the Manhattan Camp became a source of blessing to thousands of Manitobans and out-of-province visitors. Its establishment was due largely to the energy and foresight of W. C. Nelson, the district superintendent. From 1938 to 1943, Nelson carried on a program of continuous improvement to the campground, often laboring himself with other volunteers. He had been in the habit of preaching at some of the smaller regional camps at Rock Lake, Emo, and Gilbert Plains, but believed that Manhattan Beach Camp could provide a central meeting place for the believers each summer. It was the custom in the early days for each camp meeting to be held successively for two-week periods. Nelson found this to be an exhausting ordeal the first year when he spoke at all the camps. As he later recalled,

> They worked their camp speakers hard in those days, so that during the three camps that first year, I preached 96 sermons, and lost eighteen pounds in the line of duty.[21]

He preached the three camps again the next summer, then was elected superintendent. Not surprisingly, he soon took steps to develop a larger, central camp for the whole district at Manhattan Beach.

The first camp meetings in Saskatchewan were held in 1923. One was held at Brock under the direction of Pastor Freeman Hamilton, and another at Saskatoon in July. The latter site became the place for several years of a province-wide gathering of the Pentecostal workers and adherents. The tent in Saskatoon was set up first on the grounds of the Bedford Road Collegiate with D. W. Kerr as the featured speaker. This man has been described by pioneer leader H. M. Cadwalder as "the father of missionaries." G. A. Chambers, representing Eastern Canada at this camp, observed that the services were characterized by a marked sense of the presence of God. Some outstanding healings took place, including cases of deafness and the restoration of a crippled woman.[22]

While pastoring at Parkside, Walter McAlister held a camp meeting for Natives on the nearby Mistewassis Reserve in 1925. Believers from Canwood and Shell Lake also attended, but it was a short-lived effort. In 1942, the District Executive bought a former health resort on the shores of Lake Manitou, near Watrous. This site, with its famous salt deposits, served as the district campground for decades.

As early as 1931, a proposal was made by John McAlister for a permanent camp location in Alberta, but several years passed before it became a reality. In 1935, the district, under the leadership of

Superintendent George Upton and with the cooperation of Pastor A. Dalby, sponsored a summer camp meeting in a large tent pitched on the church lawn at Mayton. The meetings attracted crowds of 300. An interesting historical note relates to two young boys who committed their lives to the Lord at that camp meeting — Roy and Gordon Upton, who would become ministers and make significant contributions to the work of the PAOC. The following year, the camp meetings were held at Czar Lake Camp, a resort area east of Wetaskiwin. Pastors Ernie Robinson and W. C. Nelson helped to organize the meetings. Local farm families provided the food and the church ladies cooked the meals. A. G. Ward was the preacher. Many recalled one of Ward's meetings when a sense of awe pervaded the congregation and a spontaneous chorus of praise swept over the crowded tent.

The first permanent district camp in Alberta was the product of the vision and labor of George Upton. He found and negotiated the purchase of a property on Sylvan Lake, now the site of Sunnyside Camp, which was ideal. The first services were held in 1937 under two tents joined to form a large canopy. A tabernacle was put up within three years. Among the earliest speakers were Dr. Charles Price, J. D. Saunders, Lorne Fox, and Watson Argue. Other camps were established in Alberta to meet the distinctive needs of some of the ethnic conferences. The German Branch of the PAOC conducted an annual camp at Alberta Beach, and the Slavic Branch campground was located at Moose Lake.[23]

In British Columbia, the camp meeting was a relatively late development, largely because of the barriers imposed by the mountainous terrain and the smaller population of Pentecostals on the West Coast. When Gordon Atter and Wesley O'Brien were students in the Winnipeg Bible school, they held a summer camp meeting in Nelson in 1927. C. M. Ward, while pastoring in Victoria, organized a camp meeting at Chilliwack. As former District Superintendent P. S. Jones described the 1933 camp, it was

> a daring act of faith, because the work in B.C. at that time was in its infancy, but God set His seal upon the venture. Many ... remember ... the blessing of the Lord .... The ministries of Rev. Donald Gee and Rev. A. G. Ward are still remembered.[24]

The increasing interest in summer camps prompted pastor P. A. Gaglardi, of Langley Prairie, to organize a camp in 1941. He secured Dr. Charles Price as the speaker. Large crowds attended despite the primitive condition of the campground. Later, land was secured for a permanent campground near Abbotsford where a tabernacle seating 2,000 people was erected.

7 / CAMP MEETINGS, CONVENTIONS, AND COLLEGES

Another effective form of evangelism and church growth was the local church "convention," which drew together both pastors and people for inspiration and instruction. The early camp meetings were designed to reach large groups of unevangelized people. They also served to unify and indoctrinate the early Pentecostals, but they were demanding in terms of time, labor, and money. Conventions could be organized at any time of the year and were less demanding on their organizers. They were a feature of Canadian Pentecostalism from the beginning, as G. A. Chambers noted:

> ... in the early days of our church, "Conventions" were held quite frequently. These were not simply "Missionary" Conventions but a time set apart for Ministers and others to gather together for a time of spiritual refreshing.[25]

Since trained Pentecostal clergymen were in short supply, lay people eagerly attended the conventions where they were able to listen to noted preachers and teachers. These convocations were common in the first decade of the history of the Canadian Fellowship, especially at the Hebden Mission and other locations in the Toronto area. From the start, they attracted interested spectators, confirmed the convictions of believers, developed denominational strength, and recruited many more converts.

A. H. Argue attended some of the earliest conventions in Toronto. He organized a fall convention in his own church in Winnipeg in 1907, shortly after his Baptism in the Spirit. One of the special speakers was Mrs. Florence Crawford of Portland, Oregon, who came with an entourage of assistants and lay people. Argue was so pleased with the results that fall conventions became a regular feature in the Winnipeg assembly. These events attracted many of the best-known Pentecostal spokesmen of the time. People and preachers came to the Winnipeg conventions from across the prairie provinces and from the United States. Argue summarized the 1910 convention:

> ... 147 were baptized in water and the wonderful works of God were much in evidence.... Cree Indians from the ... north would come [and] a genuine revival broke out among these dear souls.... How fervently they sought the Lord! Some of these, returning to their own people made effective preachers and missionaries. People came from ... across the border. A great company were baptized in the Spirit, many carrying revival fires to their homes. New works started in a number of places.[26]

R. E. McAlister held several successful conventions in Ottawa during his brief pastorate in the city. Since his church hall was small, he generally scheduled the meetings in the local Exhibition buildings.

In Moose Jaw, Saskatchewan, a convention in 1921 featured G. A. Chambers and W. L. Draffin as speakers. It was preceded and accompanied by much prayer:

> ... from the standpoint of spiritual results, it was possibly one of the greatest Conventions in our Fellowship in Western Canada. Sixty people received the Baptism of the Holy Spirit.[27]

Among the seekers was a group of 15 from Cut Knife who came for the primary purpose of being filled with the Spirit. All but one "came through."

Walter McAlister held a convention in Saskatoon in 1924 in an attempt to revive the local congregation. At the convention, several people experienced their personal Pentecost. The impact on the 95 delegates helped solidify the Saskatoon church. Thomas Bunting later came to pastor the Saskatoon congregation. Within a short time of his arrival the assembly raised the funds for its own building.

The Pentecostal pioneers in the Leduc region of Alberta came together in that community in 1934 specifically for the purpose of spiritual renewal. Under the direction of Pastor and Mrs. W. Frederick, the workers enjoyed several days of blessing and acquired a fresh sense of mission. One of the emphases at the Leduc convention was the urgency of "getting the job done."[28]

Such gatherings proved enormously beneficial for those workers who often labored in hostile situations, with small financial resources and no umbrella organization to provide counseling and moral support. Percy Jones, while serving as superintendent of the B.C. District, often paid tribute to those self-sacrificing pioneers. He called them "brave, courageous, loving and able ministers" who often seemed forgotten by their colleagues in more prosperous surroundings.[29] Thus it is easy to understand why the conventions assumed such an important role in the first two decades of the Pentecostal Movement in Canada.

The practice of holding conventions underwent gradual changes as Pentecostalism developed. Just as the small, regional camp meeting was supplanted by the large, centralized district camp, so was the convention replaced eventually by the District Conference. Initially, denominational business was transacted during the early camp meetings (what there was of it to transact in that formative period), but continuous growth required a more systematic approach to church government. In a similar manner, church business often was carried on in conjunction with the local convention, but this practice proved too limited in scope to meet the needs of a multitude of churches.

7 / CAMP MEETINGS, CONVENTIONS, AND COLLEGES

This transition is clearly evident in the history of the Saskatchewan region. A camp meeting/conference was held in Saskatoon in 1923. The *Testimony* advertisement called it a "Western Canada Conference and Camp Meeting." The camp was scheduled for the period July 1 - 15, and the conference to be held concurrently July 2 - 6. E. N. Bell, representing the Assemblies of God, and G. A. Chambers, representing the eastern churches, were to be the "Special Workers." The meetings were characterized by times of fasting and prayer, business sessions and elections, and worship and praise. Evangelistic meetings were held each night for the general public.

This dual-purpose type of camp meeting eventually was dropped in favor of two separate kinds of gatherings. The term "convention" came to refer to a special-purpose meeting — for example, the "Missionary Convention." G. A. Chambers, during his tenure as General Superintendent of the PAOC, placed a high priority on overseas missions. Indeed, Chambers' vigorous promotion of missions conventions undoubtedly had an effect on maintaining the missions orientation which the PAOC has had from its origin. In this emphasis, he was joined by R. E. McAlister, who advertised such gatherings in the pages of the *Testimony* and held frequent missions conventions in his years as pastor in London, Ontario. The "convention" terminology also came to be applied to other special-purposes meetings for the advancement of such things as Christian education, youth work, and women's ministries.

After the incorporation of the PAOC in May 1919, the use of the word "conference" came to be associated primarily with the District and General Conference. The ministers and lay representatives from the churches met regionally at District Conference held annually, and nationally at General Conference held biennially. At these conferences the structure and by-laws were formulated for the Fellowship. Extensive research in the documents filed in the PAOC archives has failed to uncover any early rationale for the forms of church government adopted by the charter members. Nor has personal interviews or letters of inquiry elicited from surviving members of the pioneer leadership provided any information on the legislative antecedents of the movement in Canada. There can be no doubt, however, that the democratic aspects of Methodism were present from the beginning.

On May 26, 1919, the "first meeting of the Trustees of the Pentecostal Assemblies of Canada" was held in Ottawa. R. E. Sternall, G. A. Chambers, R. E. McAlister, Harvey McAlister, A. M. Pattison, W. L. Draffin, and Frank Small elected, "till the first annual meeting of the General Assembly," three men as officers. Those first officers were

G. A. Chambers as Chairman, C. A. Baker as Treasurer, and R. E. McAlister as Secretary. At its first "General Assembly" at Kitchener in November 1919, there were 31 delegates present, both laymen and ministers. Clergymen were referred to as "Elders" and the term also was applied to lay preachers — an unmistakable custom of the Methodists. One of the first by-laws passed (No. 6) recognized any layman appointed by a local assembly as entitled to a voice and a vote in the proceedings.[30]

Whatever their religious and ecclesiastical heritage, the charter members were practical and flexible in dealing with any organizational problems which arose. Since there were only about 30 workers in the country in 1919, and clergymen were especially in short supply, there was a need to ordain more men to the ministry. In an unusual move, G. A. Chambers, R. E. Sternall, and R. E. McAlister ordained each other. Thereafter, ordinations were of a more traditional nature and were performed at the official conferences.[31] After applicants for ordination were examined by district leaders, their names were presented for approval at the annual conferences to the voting delegates.

Until 1927, the country was divided into two large districts, the West and the East. But Ontario and Quebec in the East were too large, and the church was growing too rapidly, to continue this practice. A vote by delegates at a conference at London in 1927 divided the original Eastern Canada region into the Western Ontario District with W. L. Draffin as superintendent, and Eastern Ontario and Quebec District with A. E. Adams in the leadership role. Western Canada was slower in developing its legislative structures, but there were eventually to be four western districts. In most cases the districts parallel provincial boundaries, with the exception noted above which joins Eastern Ontario with Quebec and also the provinces of Nova Scotia, New Brunswick, and Prince Edward Island which are combined in the Maritime District. The seven districts operate as self-governing entities whose constitutions take their form and substance from the General Constitution of the PAOC.

Pioneer Pentecostals were in general agreement about their doctrinal distinctives long before they had any form of ecclesiastical organization. These were primarily the four cardinal beliefs, namely, Salvation, the Baptism in the Holy Spirit, Divine Healing, and the Second Coming of Christ. Some early leaders, because of their previous theological convictions, would have added a "holiness" emphasis to this list. It was at the conferences that the practical implications of the Pentecostal distinctives were worked out. For example, the 1921 Eastern District Conference ruled that no credentials were to be issued "to anyone who has been divorced, and remarried, while their first companion is still living." Several grades of clerical status were outlined whereby pastors

7 / CAMP MEETINGS, CONVENTIONS, AND COLLEGES

had levels of official sanction, ranging from a "Letter of Recommendation" to ordination. Those without any theological training were to be "under the care of some pastor or, if possible, [were] to attend a Bible school." Since at the time no such school existed in Canada, prospective students were urged to attend the Central Bible Institute in Springfield, Missouri.

At the fourth annual General Conference of the PAOC at Kitchener in October 1922, delegates approved a plan to recruit "local officers to care for district business." The next year, it was decided to hold biennial general assemblies and to elect officers for two-year terms. Another significant decision was the resolution at the 1924 Eastern Conference which directed the increasing overseas missions funds to be disbursed through the PAOC national office. Missionary funds no longer were to be sent directly from the donors to the foreign field.[32]

The Pentecostal Fellowship in Canada did not develop in isolation. Canadian delegates participated in the "Great Unity Conference of the Pentecostal Movement of North America" at St. Louis in late 1922. More noteworthy was the association which the PAOC had with the Assemblies of God in the United States. For a short period in the early years of its history, the Canadian Pentecostals operated in loose association with the Assemblies of God as AG District Councils. But steady church growth in Eastern and Western Canada made many Canadian leaders realize the awkwardness of the situation. The first step towards dissolution of formal ties with the AG were taken in 1922 when a special committee met in Kitchener with representatives from both eastern and western churches. It was agreed that the Canadian District Councils of the Assemblies of God should be dissolved and both East and West should unite under the name, The Pentecostal Assemblies of Canada.

The recommendation was confirmed in the 1925 Western District Conference. Delegates called for a distinctively Canadian system in which East and West would consist of "one body with Provincial Districts with equal representation in the General body." They also elected provincial superintendents for Saskatchewan and Alberta. Superintendents for Manitoba and British Columbia were to be appointed temporarily until conditions in those two areas warranted self-chosen leaders. Since similar sentiments arose at the 1925 Eastern District Conference, there was overwhelming support for cutting formal ties with the American Assemblies. The critical decision to separate was taken at the General Conference in Winnipeg in 1925. The leaders of the Assemblies of God quickly complied with the request for separation.[33]

The first united conference of all Canadian delegates was held in 1927 in Saskatoon. One of the history-making events of that conference was the approval of a resolution calling for "a doctrinal statement of the Pentecostal Assemblies of Canada" that was separate from that of the Assemblies of God. The desired doctrinal summary subsequently was drafted by R. E. McAlister and printed in *The Pentecostal Testimony*. This General Conference concluded with the election of G. A. Chambers as Chairman of a nation-wide, and entirely Canadian, PAOC.

Conferences continued to be the venue in which early leaders carried on denominational business: activities which ranged from ordination procedures, missions matters, legislative functions, evangelistic methods, and even disciplinary regulations. Missions funds were to be solicited across the entire Fellowship, and administered through the national office. Ordination, as decided at the 1928 General Conference in Montreal, was restricted to applicants already approved at the district level. The actual ordination could take place when two or more regularly ordained ministers in good standing, by the imposition of hands and prayer, gave formal recognition to those with a call to ministry who gave proof of their gift by two or more years of successful ministry. Plans were initiated in 1932 to establish the Full Gospel Publishing House which provided a Canadian supply of Pentecostal literature,

The General Executive was given the authority to divide Canada into suitable districts, in which superintendents were to be elected for two-years terms. By virtue of their offices, the district superintendents were to sit as members for the same two-year period on the General Executive. Discipline was to be exercised in cases of doctrinal aberration, or "unacceptable practice, of a serious nature," on the testimony of "not less then five witnesses," the case being heard by both district superintendent and general superintendent. If the decision was unsatisfactory to the accused, there was provision for an appeal to re-consider. Regulations were adopted respecting the use of "worldly and unsaved people" in PAOC meetings, and on incorrect advertising and "unscriptural methods in evangelistic services."

The organizational phase of the PAOC was completed largely within two decades of its incorporation in 1919. In 1932, for example, it was ruled that a two-thirds General Conference vote was needed to add to or amend the official constitution and by-laws. There were, however, many issues to be settled later at the district level. For several years, Pentecostals in mainland Canada were associated with either the Eastern or the Western District. The Newfoundland churches which grew out of the Bethesda Mission of Alice Garrigus maintained a cooperative relationship with the PAOC. The two bodies retained separate corporate identities, but the PAON was allowed to send two official delegates to PAOC General Conferences.[34] The Eastern District was comprised of

7 / CAMP MEETINGS, CONVENTIONS, AND COLLEGES

Ontario, Quebec, and the Maritimes. The Western District included all those living in the four western provinces. The Chairman of this region was Hugh Cadwalder, an Assemblies of God pioneer who was pastoring at Swift Current at the time of his election. The first Canadian to hold the post was pastor Walter McAlister of Saskatoon, who was chosen in 1925.

In Alberta, there was no formal organization until 1924, the year in which John McAlister was elected district superintendent. German Pentecostals in the province looked to George Schneider for leadership. Before his Baptism in the Holy Spirit in 1918, Schneider had been a clergyman with the Evangelical Church.

Manitoba had its first District Conference in 1926 and elected D. N. Buntain, a former Methodist preacher, as superintendent. The work in British Columbia lacked formal supervision until 1928, when F. R. Maddaford became superintendent. In all cases, these men were full-time pastors and carried on the work of supervision as best they could. As progress and development took place, the need for the time and energy of full-time leaders became more obvious. The first person to devote himself exclusively to the role of district superintendent was P. S. Jones in British Columbia when he was elected in 1944. Although he preferred the pastoral ministry, Jones handled his new duties with skill. He recognized the potential dangers of excessive denominational machinery and legislation:

> District conferences of necessity must deal with business and (the) legal side of organization, but spiritual anointing always oils machinery and makes less necessary so much that is purely and solely of legalism. The nature of our fellowship was clearly defined at its inauguration. . . . It was intended to be essentially voluntary, cooperative . . . and its future would depend upon a continuance of that primary vision. . . . Business methods are essential; constitution and by-laws are necessary for the promotion of effort, but it is wonderful how few resolutions are needed at conferences when the Holy Ghost falls upon those attending.[35]

When the work in Eastern Canada became too large to administer effectively, it was divided into Western Ontario, Eastern Ontario and Quebec, and the Maritimes. Growth was steady. James Montgomery sometimes recounted how he and other clergymen, en route to a meeting, travelled along Highway 2 in Ontario and claimed, by faith, a Pentecostal church in every town and city they passed. In years to come, their prayers were fully answered.[36]

The Maritime ministers met in Halifax in 1930 and asked W. R. Watson, an evangelist, to provide leadership for the work. Less than two years later, James Montgomery became the district superintendent. Pentecostal churches in New Brunswick, Nova Scotia, and Prince Edward Island were relatively few in number — and in each province there were a number of congregations who chose for a long time to remain independent of any formal organization.

Language differences prompted various ethnic groups to develop their own conferences within the general framework of the PAOC. These included the Slavic Conference set up in 1931, the Finnish Conference organized about 1939, the German Conference in 1940, and the French Conference in 1949. The work among Italian-speaking Pentecostals was centred mainly in Toronto and Montreal. The Italian Pentecostals have maintained a close relationship with the PAOC but have continued as a separate entity.

With these developments in ecclesiastical structure, the PAOC had moved from the status of a religious sect to a fully accredited denomination. But one further element was essential to its perpetuation — the establishment of training institutions for its clergy and missionaries which would both preserve and propagate its distinctive theology. That essential element was the Bible school.

There were no permanent Pentecostal training institutions in Canada before 1925. Those interested in religious education most often attended one of the evangelical schools in the USA. In fact, a number of students in A. B. Simpson's school at Nyack, New York, were filled with the Spirit in the period around 1907. The Christian and Missionary Alliance leaders were ambivalent about the outpouring of the Spirit among their ministerial students and their pastors. Eventually, however, they chose not to formally sanction the experience, but also not to condemn it, an attitude summed up in the phrase "Seek not and forbid not."

A more receptive attitude was evident in a "faith Bible school" operated by several Pentecostal women at Rochester, New York. Here believers were taught the doctrine of Baptism in the Spirit and encouraged to seek the experience. Among those who attended was Eugene Vaters of Newfoundland. Another evangelical school in Cincinnati, Ohio, provided a training opportunity for R. E. McAlister. Most Canadian leaders, however, did not have the resources to attend these schools.

A considerable number of the early leaders had some formal training in their former denominations; men such as A. G. Ward, D. N. Buntain, and J. E. Purdie.[37] Thus the first leaders of the Fellowship were men with varying degrees of theological training and many others without any formal instruction. As a result, there arose two prevailing views on religious education which have characterized Pentecostalism for its entire history.

7 / CAMP MEETINGS, CONVENTIONS, AND COLLEGES

Many zealous workers believed the coming of the Lord was so close at hand that time could not be "wasted" in formal training. Some had unhappy recollections of their former denominations, where they perceived that the churches had "lost out with God" because the clergy had been educated out of spirituality into what they called "deadness." A popular catch-phrase of the time was the quotation of Paul's words about the "letter" killing while "the Spirit giveth life." Another slogan was based on Paul's presumed denigration of human wisdom in 1 Corinthians. Other workers, who believed they had benefited from formal education, wished to make it available to young candidates for the ministry. And so an ambivalent attitude developed which for decades marked the PAOC as both wary about, and supportive toward, Bible schools. J. E. Purdie described the dominant attitude quite properly:

> The ministers and people in the early . . . Pentecostal church were so occupied with the salvation of souls and the building up of the household of faith, together with days and nights of prayer, that with great victories in the spiritual realm they had not become conscious for a considerable time of higher education . . . the Pentecostal church . . . amid all the revivals. . . .(was) cautious as to how far she should go in exalting the intellectual . . . this church was not opposed to any ministers of other churches that had intellectual attainments in higher education and degrees, as long as (they) adhered to the Bible as the highest authority. . . . Pentecostals were not opposed to education when it was sound and true to the great theological settlement of the Reformation . . . Therefore they gradually saw the need of Bible colleges.[38]

As early as 1921 there was a recognition of the need for some type of formal training for ministerial candidates. R. E. McAlister, in the *Testimony* that year, urged young workers to go to the new AG Central Bible Institute in Springfield, Missouri. The Eastern District Conference in 1923 approved setting up "Itinerary Bible Schools in Eastern Canada." A competent teacher was to be sought to hold one-month schools in various localities. Although this strategy was never carried out successfully and details are sparse, one short-term course with classes both during the day and in the evening was conducted in Montreal by D. W. Kerr in 1924; another course, with George B. Griffin as the teacher, was held at the Cobourg camp in 1937. Gordon Atter attended the course in Montreal and then, as did many others, opted for the new Bible school which opened in Winnipeg.[39]

A decision was reached at the General Conference in Winnipeg in 1925 to establish a permanent school in that city which could offer three years of training for the ministry. Initially, the Winnipeg institution was thought of as "a temporary Bible school for one or two years," with the understanding that both East and West could set up their own regional schools later. Emil Schwab, G. A. Chambers, R. E. McAlister, A. G. Ward, and Dr. Howard Geddes were named as faculty, but Chambers and Ward were unable to stay in Winnipeg because of their responsibilities in Eastern Canada. Eventually, Dr. J. E. Purdie became the principal and directed the new school from 1925 to 1950.[40]

The church in Vancouver proposed a short-course school in 1922, but was unable to carry out its plans. The Victoria assembly began holding classes in rented facilities in the winter of 1924. Rev. and Mrs. H. Wesley Cooksey oversaw the program, from which about 40 students graduated. Approximately 30 of these people entered full-time ministry. Notable among the graduates were P. S. Jones and J. E. Barnes, both of whom served later as the district superintendent. Cooksey also held a short-term school in Saskatoon in February of 1924 with the help of George Schneider and John McAlister. About 40 attended these first sessions and then returned for classes during the January-March period the following year. Many of these students went to the Winnipeg school when it opened in the fall of 1925.[41]

J. E. Purdie was in Prince Edward Island when the General Conference delegates appointed him principal of the Winnipeg school. Purdie had sensed for some time the need of formal training for Canadian Pentecostals in order to overcome the excessively subjective elements which surfaced in doctrine and preaching of the 1920s. A graduate of the Anglican Wycliffe College in Toronto, he pastored several churches where he developed a keen interest in evangelism. It was while he was rector at St. James Anglican Church in Saskatoon that he received the Baptism in the Holy Spirit. Purdie combined his conservative heritage from Wycliffe with a vibrant Pentecostal experience and an effective expository preaching style. His theology was influenced by his Anglican education; his contacts with Methodist, Holiness, and Standard churches; and his Baptism in the Holy Spirit with the evidence of speaking in tongues. All these elements shaped his ministry and, in turn, the direction of the Bible college which operated in Winnipeg over a 25-year period.

Perhaps no man in all of Canada was better suited at that time to inaugurate a Pentecostal Bible college program. Purdie was viewed by his peers as one of the outstanding theologians in the Fellowship. He was trusted by the PAOC leaders, was well-known and respected by evangelical leaders in other evangelical circles, such as Reuben A. Torrey and Aimee Semple McPherson, and was particularly successful in relating to young people. His clear perception of the weaknesses inherent in the young Pentecostal Movement because of the shortage of trained

7 / CAMP MEETINGS, CONVENTIONS, AND COLLEGES

clergymen compelled him to move into this strategic role. The essence of his educational philosophy may be gleaned from his own words:

> The history of the Church proves that the majority of Ministers who were most spiritual and most used in the salvation of souls were those who had tremendous doctrinal and theological convictions. . . . Applying the foregoing to the present day evangelistic groups, we discover many colorless preachers who are earnest but who have a "zeal without knowledge" . . . Because they lack the true understanding of what they believe, their congregations suffer . . . If we would stem the tide of Traditionalism, Rationalism and Mysticism, it behooves the Minister to be thoroughly prepared for his work. Hence the value of the . . . Christian Colleges.[42]

In pursuit of his academic and spiritual goals, Purdie developed the curriculum of the new Canadian Pentecostal Bible College along the lines of that offered by his alma mater — Wycliffe College. He wanted graduates to be both intellectually prepared and empowered by the Holy Spirit to become "soul-winners and teachers of the Word." He advertised in the *Testimony* that the Bible college was offering such subjects as:

> . . . the Bible by Books; Church History; English; Missions Study; Music; Homiletics; Pastoral Theology; Bible Doctrines; Bible History and Geography; Prophecy; Dispensations; the Four-Fold Gospel; Public Reading of the Bible and Voice Culture.[43]

Within a year of its commencement, the college offered, to those who could not attend classes, a "Home Study Course on the Bible." As many as 600 were enrolled in these correspondence courses.

In 1925, Purdie had collected 47 volumes of reference works on Romans for student use. His great appreciation for this Pauline epistle was transmitted to his students. Charles Ratz, for example, attended Purdie's classes, and later wrote his own book on Romans which he used for many years while teaching at Eastern Pentecostal Bible College. Ratz often commented with warm appreciation on the influence which Purdie had on his spiritual and academic development.

The dangers facing the young revivalistic Fellowship in Canada seemed to be constantly before Purdie. He frequently warned colleagues of the risk of a lapse into fanaticism or unscriptural organization. He believed the Pentecost Movement could best be established by sound doctrine and competent preaching. The goals of the Bible college, in his words, were to lay a "rock-bed in things Biblical, Doctrinal, Theological and Historical, upon which the preacher's experience may rest." No preacher could be "made" by study alone, declared Purdie, but the best training was needed, in addition to the anointing of the Holy Ghost, to reach Canada for Christ. Both evangelistic and teaching ministries, he noted, were outlined in the New Testament as essential for the success of the Church. In his opinion, there were seven "Factors that Make a Divinity College." He summarized them as follows:

- a Doctrinal Statement;
- a faculty of trained teachers who accepted the statement;
- the very best curriculum;
- a saved, Spirit-led student body;
- devotional life among both faculty and students;
- a missionary vision; and
- a good library.[44]

When Purdie first began to implement his philosophy in the first term in 1925, the Canadian Pentecostal Bible College had a student body of 33 and a faculty of three. Purdie was the principal and was assisted by Miss K. I. Reid, who had a Master of Arts degree, and D. N. Buntain, the local PAOC pastor. Students were encouraged to engage in evangelism during the summer months; about 18 devoted themselves to that task the first year. For the second term, the enrollment increased to 60 and the faculty to five. The third school year attracted 96 students, which meant that the classrooms in the basement of Buntain's church were crowded. Another church was purchased, plus two houses rented, at a cost of $9,000, and CPBC continued to show steady growth.

From the start, a monthly day of fasting and prayer was observed. Purdie credited the success of the school to the prayers of students and faculty. During the 1927-28 term, there was, what many called, a gracious visitation from heaven. One morning in the dining hall, when 160 were present, a man led out in prayer:

> He just seemed to touch the Throne and the Power came down ... inside five minutes all were laid out on the floor ... it was a sovereign move of God ... A number just walked into the Infilling and quite a number received their call to the mission field.[45]

Two men working on the furnace in the basement were so affected that they were converted on the spot.

Many of the students were to become leaders in the Fellowship and missionary pioneers. Beulah Argue, for example, a graduate from the first class of 1925, established her own ministry and then married C. B. Smith, another graduate. After years of effective pastoral ministry, Smith would be elected General Superintendent of the PAOC and still later serve as

7 / CAMP MEETINGS, CONVENTIONS, AND COLLEGES

president of Eastern Pentecostal Bible College. People like Gladys Lemon (national director of the Women's Missionary Council), W. B. Greenwood (superintendent of Eastern Ontario and Quebec), Earl Kulbeck (editor of *The Pentecostal Testimony*), and Earley King (missionary) are only a few names on the list of graduates who made significant contributions to the Fellowship. G. Raymond Carlson, General Superintendent of the Assemblies of God in the United States, has testified that the year he spent in the school in 1934 had a major impact on his life and ministry.

Some faculty members and students played a role in the establishment or operation of other regional PAOC schools when they later made their appearance. Among these were D. N. Buntain, J. C. Cooke, C. A. Ratz, E. W. Robinson, L. T. Holdcroft, and A. C. Schindel. Others entered a variety of ministries in the educational field: for example, Bernard Embree became a professor in a seminary in Taiwan and E. Earle Cairns a professor at Wheaton College.

During its 25 years of operation (1925-1950), the school in Winnipeg, renamed Western Bible College, was the nearest thing to a national theological training school in the formative years of the PAOC. It produced over 500 graduates. The great majority of men and women who attended the school went into full-time ministry; over 40 went to various mission fields.

Dr. Purdie retired from Bible college work when the school in Winnipeg closed in 1950. He remained active in ministry, however, for many years with preaching and teaching assignments in the churches. He produced a catechism for the PAOC, titled *Concerning The Faith*, which preserved the doctrinal views which received such widespread acceptance. Long before his death in 1977, recognition was given to the foundational role which Purdie had played in building the theological base for the Fellowship. A tribute from Willard C. Pierce serves to illustrate the point:

> The young movement was most fortunate in securing . . . this consecrated minister, teacher and theologian. . . . he contributed to the . . . Assemblies a solidity and strength which has left an indelible mark on . . . hundreds of its ministers and missionaries . . . during his early years in Western Bible College, Dr. Purdie met with the opposition of many who felt there was no need of training.[46]

Both C. B. Smith and D. N. Buntain spoke of the "tremendous influence upon the PAOC" of Purdie's school and noted that WBC had been the model for other regional Bible colleges. He is regarded appropriately as the "Father of Canadian Pentecostal Bible Colleges."[47]

Although Dr. Purdie and his faculty did an admirable job in training a generation of leaders, there remained in the minds of many a desire for regional Bible schools in both the East and the West. As early as 1931, the PAOC set up the National Bible College Committee to be responsible for all matters involving any Bible colleges endorsed by the denomination. This action was precipitated by the temporary closing of the Winnipeg college in 1930 and its transfer to Toronto where Purdie and many of his students relocated. The Toronto school, located in an old hotel on the southwest corner of Danforth and Dawes Road, operated for only two years before the effects of the Great Depression, the enrollment of a relatively small student body, and some tension between Purdie and prominent leaders, such as A. G. Ward, R. E. McAlister, and G. A. Chambers, brought the experiment to a close. With the closing of the school in Toronto, Purdie was requested to return to Manitoba and take up his former post as principal. Dr. H. C. Sweet, who had resigned from the Winnipeg Bible Institute as a protest to the expulsion of students who were speaking in tongues and who was then conducting some classes in the basement of Buntain's church in Winnipeg, joined forces with Purdie.

Another attempt was made to establish a Bible school in the East in 1939. Classes were started in Bethel Pentecostal Tabernacle (later named Danforth Gospel Temple), when it was located at 50 Euston Avenue in Toronto, with an initial enrollment of 45. James Swanson served as principal in this school which was known as Ontario Pentecostal Bible School. C. B. Smith and Tom Johnstone also served stints as principal. When the facilities at Euston Avenue were outgrown, the school moved to Evangel Temple in 1946, and then to Peterborough in 1951.

The old Nicholl's Hospital in Peterborough was acquired at a cost of $70,000 by a committee headed by J. H. Blair and renovated for classroom and dormitory use. Prior to the move to Peterborough, the school was renamed Eastern Pentecostal Bible College to reflect the fact that it served all of the churches in Eastern Canada, including the Pentecostal Assemblies of Newfoundland. The funds expended then seem to be minuscule, by current standards, but they were a heavy drain on the school's supporters. Part of the purchase price was secured by 40 committed Pentecostal people who each signed a bond in order to raise $40,000. Another $30,000 was raised at the Braeside Camp. Scores of volunteer laborers gave thousands of hours to the task of renovation.[48]

W. H. Found was the first president of the college on the new campus in Peterborough. C. A. Ratz, who came to assist Smith in 1941, was a dominant figure for the next 32 years. Others who served on the faculty during the first years in Peterborough included May Swanson; Mrs. R. E. McAlister; Bernard Embree; Norman Schlarbaum; Morris Zeidman, guest

7 / CAMP MEETINGS, CONVENTIONS, AND COLLEGES

lecturer from Toronto; and Fred Parlee, the pastor of Dublin Street Church. Early additions were C. H. Bronsdon, G. B. Griffin, Beulah Smith, and Gordon Atter. Special mention must be made of Emma Hann, a graduate of the Toronto school in 1947, who joined the staff in 1952 and virtually looked after registration and office matters for more than 35 years. C. B. Smith assumed the presidency in 1958 and upon his tragic death, in a car accident in 1961, was succeeded by C. H. Bronsdon. President Bronsdon resigned in 1979 when he moved to Winnipeg to pastor Fort Garry Pentecostal Assembly.

EPBC reached the end of an era when Ratz stepped down as Academic Dean in 1973. The new dean, William A. Griffin, a graduate of EPBC who had taught at Central Pentecostal College in Saskatoon for 10 years, was the first of what became an influx of teachers and graduates from Central — Alvin Schindel, Gordon Fulford, Tom Miller, Gordon Bjorgan, Carol Sirett, Betty Funk, and Ron Kydd. The cross pollination of colleges helped produce an excellent quality of education.

According to available records, during its first 30 years of operations, Eastern Pentecostal Bible College provided instruction to more than 4,000 students and graduated about 2,200 from its three-year course. Over 170 graduates have served in 35 foreign countries.[49]

Like other PAOC regional colleges, EPBC has expanded its curriculum to include four-year degree courses and has acquired accreditation from the American Association of Bible Colleges. Modern facilities, a well-equipped library and dining hall, and a well-qualified faculty now enable the college to enrol 500 students a year. At the time of writing, Carl Verge serves as president and David Boyd as academic dean.

Central Pentecostal College in Saskatoon began as a local church institute in Star City, Saskatchewan. In 1935, Pastor G. R. Hawtin opened the school with only eight students. Soon afterwards it was moved to Saskatoon and housed in rented facilities. Known at first as Bethel Bible Institute, it was approved by the PAOC and became a regionally operated school in 1942, under the direction of the Saskatchewan District Executive. Male students were in short supply during the Second World War, but a large, post-war influx necessitated renovations and additions to the collection of buildings on the Avenue A North campus. When Western Bible College in Winnipeg closed in 1950, the Manitoba and Northwestern Ontario District directed its students to Saskatoon. Faculty members included George Hawtin, Percy Hunt, W. H. Found, Peter Walker, and Don Emmons, the pastor of Elim Tabernacle. Regrettably, the history of BBI is connected with a theological controversy which developed into one of the most serious schisms in PAOC history. The Latter Rain Movement, as it was known, shook both the Institute and the

Saskatchewan District to their foundations in 1947. With the dismissal of Hawtin and Hunt, and the loss of most of the students, the school came close to extinction. Robert M. Argue, who had been pastor of the church in Regina, accepted the appointment as principal and served in that position until the fall of 1956. He was assisted by Ed Austin, Alvin Schindel, May English, and Grace Brown. Argue's leadership and the sacrificial labors of the faculty saved the school from disintegration during very difficult years. Carl H. Stiller, the district superintendent of Saskatchewan, acted as president and gave the school good support until his election in 1962 to a national post, Executive Director of Home Missions and Bible Colleges.

In 1961, the school was renamed Central Pentecostal College and formally placed under the sponsorship of both the Saskatchewan and Manitoba and Northwestern Ontario districts. Karel Marek joined the faculty and served for over 25 years. William Griffin arrived in 1962 and taught systematic theology until he transferred to EPBC in 1972. Alvin Schindel, after performing the duties of dean of education for a number of years, became the president in 1964. He held this post until 1974, when he also moved to the Peterborough college where he taught Old Testament courses. Ken Birch moved from an executive assistant's job in the national office to assume the president's duties in that same year. A new campus was acquired on the former site of the Lutheran Seminary in Saskatoon in 1972. Ron Kadyschuk serves as acting president at the time of writing.

A large percentage of the school's graduates have gone into ministry in Canada and the overseas missions fields. Among the latter were two graduates of the class of 1935 — Nellie Hendrickson and Clara Siegrist. Other notable graduates include Howard Honsinger (district superintendent of Western Ontario), William Cornelius (Executive Director of Overseas Missions), and Brian Stiller (Executive Director of the Evangelical Fellowship of Canada). The writer also numbers himself among the graduates. CPC has been an indispensable factor in the provision of young Pentecostal workers for the prairie provinces. Not only has it provided a number of teachers for EPBC as reported above, but it has made a significant contribution to Northwest Bible College in Edmonton in the form of two presidents, Marvin Dynna and Gordon Franklin, and an academic dean, Ron Kadyschuk.

There was some discussion about establishing a regional school at the 1929 Alberta District Conference, but finances did not permit. Short-term Bible schools were held for some years in Calgary, Edmonton, and Lethbridge, but no full-time school was available until D. N. Buntain arrived in the district in 1946. Convinced that the province needed a Bible

7 / CAMP MEETINGS, CONVENTIONS, AND COLLEGES

school, he began to plan for its opening in the facilities provided by his own church in Edmonton. As Buntain saw it, the need was paramount:

> ... young people were growing up throughout the area with little or no full gospel opportunities ... As we came to Edmonton ... the burden and vision of a Bible Institute possessed my soul. At first we met with stiff opposition ... Edmonton Tabernacle wholeheartedly supported the idea from the start and gladly placed... the tabernacle at our disposal.[50]

The first term began late in 1947 with 47 students enrolled. Buntain was the principal, assisted by his wife Kathleen, John and Ida Cooke, Ruth Schoen, Dorothy Plastow, and Lila Dickinson. The curriculum was similar to that of other PAOC schools — a combination of Bible and theological instruction plus considerable practical experience through student involvement in local churches and missions. After Buntain's death, the leadership of NBC passed to John Cooke, and in turn to Ernie Francis, Marvin Dynna, Gordon Franklin, and Gerald Johnson.

In its first 40 years of operation, the Canadian Northwest Bible Institute (now called Northwest Bible College) provided training for over 1,600 students and graduated about 600 from its three-year course. One of its best known alumnus is Robert Taitinger, former General Superintendent of the PAOC and president of EPBC. Other prominent graduates are Jack Keys and Ken Gaetz. Keys was an effective missionary in the West Indies for a number of years and is, at the time of writing, the district superintendent of Alberta and Northwest Territories. Ken Gaetz led in the development of the far-flung network of The Pentecostal Sub-Arctic Mission in the Canadian North. A small nursing station which he established eventually became the H. H. Williams Memorial Hospital in Hay River, Northwest Territories.

The short-term Bible school which started in Victoria in 1924, known as Faith Bible School, did not survive more than one year. Although there was no direct link between this school and British Columbia Bible Institute which was founded in 1941, the early school "definitely proved that Victoria was fertile ground for planting a Pentecostal Bible school."[51] The decision to establish the permanent school was made at the 15th annual conference of the B.C. District in July of 1941. P. S. Jones, a graduate of the earlier school in Victoria, was a member of the five-man Bible School Committee which was set up to implement the conference decision.

BCBI opened in October 1941 in Victoria. Pastor E. W. Robinson, who was a graduate of Purdie's Winnipeg school, was appointed principal. Much of the curriculum was based on classroom notes taken in Purdie's lecture periods. Formal instruction began with about 75 students in evening classes and seven in day-time courses. The following year there were 22 full time students — 20 women and two men, a ratio which reflected the effects of the Second World War. When the number of students increased, the leaders purchased a building adjacent to Glad Tidings Tabernacle for use as a dormitory. After the war an influx of veterans swamped the facilities.

In 1951 the school was transferred to a site in North Vancouver which formerly had been a boy's residential school. Robinson for a time commuted to Victoria to continue his pastoral duties. In 1956, Robinson concluded 15 years of ministry at the Bible college. Tom Johnstone became president that same year. Some of the faculty members during the early-50s were W. J. Friesen, Arthur and Betty Schindel, James Purse, Florence Spence, and Olive Shipton.

In its first 15 years of operation British Columbia Bible Institute provided instruction to some 800 students and graduated nearly 200 from its three-year theological program. Of that number, 44 became pastors, 28 became deaconesses and lay workers, and three went to the mission field.[52]

In 1962 the school was renamed Western Pentecostal Bible College, with former missionary Vernon Morrison as president. When L. T. Holdcroft succeeded him in 1968, the school again had outgrown its facilities. In 1974 the college was moved to its present site near Abbotsford. An ambitious program of campus improvement and upgrading of the facilities produced a new library, college chapel, classrooms, and dormitories. After receiving permission to grant degrees by the provincial cabinet in 1981, the college conferred degrees upon 21 four-year graduates in 1982. It was a first for PAOC Bible colleges. At the time of writing, the president and academic dean are James Richards and Roger Stronstad respectively.

The Maritimes Bible school which was founded in 1944 in Halifax operated for only three years. Its goal was to provide training for young people who, for financial reasons, could not make the long trip to the Toronto school. Principal Cyrus Myhre was assisted by M. S. Winger, F. Chorley, W. H. Found, I. D. Raymer, and their wives. In that brief period of operation, the school sent several graduates into pastoral work and Raymond and Lillian McKillop as missionaries to the West Indies. Since 1947, students from the Maritime Pentecostal churches have attended the Bible college in Ontario.

Another school launched under difficult circumstances was the Berea Bible Institute (Institut Biblique Bérée) in Montreal. Following a revival in the area, it was realized that training must be offered in the French

7 / CAMP MEETINGS, CONVENTIONS, AND COLLEGES

language to the lay workers. Mme. L. Bellemare of Montreal and W. L. Bouchard, who had come to assist from Providence, Rhode Island, set up Berea in 1941. For a number of years, it was the only francophone Bible school in North America. Its three-year curriculum was modelled on that of the English-speaking Bible colleges of Canada. When E. L. Lassègues became president in 1953, his faculty included René Robert, formerly of Switzerland, Salome Cressman, Marie-Paule Gagnon, and Gerald Morris. In its first few years, Berea graduated over 40 students, most of whom became pastors in Quebec.[53]

Pentecostal theological education in Quebec took a new course when Berea opened a new three-storey building in 1956 and expanded its curriculum to include non-French-speaking students. Religious persecution in Quebec put many obstacles in the way of Pentecostal leaders. Lay people often were fired from jobs because of their involvement with the PAOC. The school has performed a critical role in the recruitment and preparation of workers for the province. In a letter to Dr. Purdie in 1954, Lassègues noted both the difficulties and the triumphs:

> The enrollment has never been high. Our entire constituency is small compared to her English-speaking contemporaries. Its students often have been recently saved . . . but its labours have not been in vain. Graduates from this school have been instrumental in opening up works in Rouen, Senneterre, Tiblemont, Granby, Sherbrooke, Megantic, Magog, St-Calixte, to say nothing of the help they have been in the local churches and schools.[54]

Officials of the PAOC have been keenly aware of the special problems associated with evangelizing Quebec. A new strategy, named FLITE, was launched in 1969, under the direction of Robert Argue, the Executive Director of Home Missions and Bible Colleges. The acronym stands for "French Language Intensive Training for Evangelism." The FLITE program enlisted graduates of the English-speaking Bible schools and gave them an intensive course in French-language skills. Upon graduation, these students had sufficient proficiency to pioneer and pastor French-speaking churches. Within just a few years FLITE graduates were pastoring 10 new assemblies in Quebec and New Brunswick. Some graduates moved into established pastorates and thus greatly strengthened the work throughout the province.

A second innovative program of studies, known as Formation Timothée, has made a significant contribution to the growth of the PAOC in Quebec. The Timothée program, based in Quebec City, provides specialized instruction, including the use of video tapes, for French-speaking lay workers who are pastoring churches and unable to take time off for long periods of formal study. The off-campus program offers both Greek and Hebrew as part of the 40 courses of study which extend over a four-year period.[55]

One of the most difficult areas to evangelize has been the great Canadian Northland, stretching thousands of miles across the vast tundra. Of almost equal challenge have been the Native reservations which long were the preserve of the Roman Catholic and Anglican churches. John Spillenaar, "the flying missionary," helped publicize the plight of Canada's Native peoples — Native and Inuit — and the necessity of training them to evangelize their own races. Varying schemes and programs have been undertaken for Native evangelism, but always the need for Native workers has been paramount.

A Native Bible school was set up at Senneterre, Quebec in 1965 by Richard Zabriskie, assisted by Arthur Lemmert and Marcia McCorkle. The school offered the lay workers and interested people several four-week short courses during the year. Annual camp meetings were held to consolidate the progress among the 30,000 Natives who inhabit the region. This instructional program was taken over by the Northland Mission, a project of the Western Ontario District. The new school was located at Moosonee, which has a history of PAOC outreach stretching back to 1955. Students were brought in by plane for periods of concentrated study, over two-month periods, and then returned to give leadership in their own home areas.

By 1969, the instructional program was being offered at Nakina, Ontario. Dale Cummins, former missionary and teacher at Eastern Pentecostal Bible College, and his wife Alberta provided leadership. For a time Brian Steed, pilot and Pentecostal pastor, flew in the students to the teaching centre. Ian Winter, also a pilot and a pastor, took on the transportation responsibility when he became director of the Northland Mission. In the early 1980s, Guy Campeau became pastor at Pickle Lake and principal of the Native school for evangelism. During his tenure, he set up a challenging curriculum which ensured thorough instruction in the Bible. Samuel Beardi of Bearskin Lake was the first to graduate from this new program in 1985.[56] The school was subsequently moved to Sioux Lookout, Ontario.

Numerous evangelistic efforts in the rest of Canada have sought to reach Native peoples, but only in recent years have systematic programs been developed to bring them theological training. Much of this delay was due to the low level of education among Natives living on the reserves, and to legal problems in setting up training schools on Native

7 / CAMP MEETINGS, CONVENTIONS, AND COLLEGES

lands. One of the most ambitious evangelistic programs began in 1965 when Immanuel Jensen (known to the Natives as "Indian Jensen") held two-week study courses on Manitoba reserves. Jensen was the first, full-time director of Native work in the PAOC. In a short time, he was assisted in evangelism by Native workers trained in his short-term schools.

Work among Saskatchewan Natives was initiated in the 1960s by individual pastors and lay workers, such as Ivar Roset, Carson Latimer, and Wilson Waterhouse. After Sam Biro was appointed Saskatchewan District Director of Native Evangelism, the work developed to the point where a Native Bible school was opened at Canwood. One of its first graduates was Burton Ahenakew, who became an evangelist to his own people at Hay River in 1970.

In British Columbia, the Native peoples have been the subject of various church-originated outreach programs. The most unique program, however, has been the "Gospel Boat" evangelism along the rugged B.C. coast. One result of this form of outreach was a request in 1965 by the Natives of the Alberni Reserve to be affiliated with the PAOC. Charles Whaley of the Mission for Canadian Natives in Vancouver set up a "West Coast Indian Pentecostal Bible School" in 1967. It was aimed chiefly at Native fishermen, who were free during the winter months to attend. There were eight students in the first class.[57]

The development of the PAOC from the status of a revivalistic sect to denominational stature was largely accomplished within two decades of its incorporation. The outpouring of the Holy Spirit, in 1906 in Toronto and in 1907 in Winnipeg, was followed by a rapid spread of the Pentecostal Movement throughout the nation. There were relatively few trained clergymen at the start, and only a minuscule number of believers, to spread the message.

The summer camp meeting and the church convention were methods employed with great success by the pioneer leaders. The camp meeting served to publicize Pentecostal doctrines on the one hand, and to overcome deep-seated hostility and widespread misunderstanding on the other. As local assemblies were established and pastors settled down to a more traditional form of preaching/teaching ministry, the local convention assumed a very important role. Evangelism, indoctrination, and a modification of public attitudes to the movement were key goals. As these objectives were being steadily realized, the benefits of formal theological training for Pentecostal workers led to the formation of Bible colleges. Graduates of the colleges in turn helped expand the outreach to every corner of Canada. By the time of the Second World War, the number of Pentecostals had increased from 513, in 1911, to over 57,000. The

CAMP MEETINGS, CONVENTIONS, AND COLLEGES / 7

number of PAOC churches had grown to 300, with 190 ordained ministers and 52 missionaries. In spite of dire predictions by hostile observers that "the whole thing will blow over soon," the Pentecostal Assemblies of Canada had become an established entity.

Endnotes

1. Cornelius John Jaenen, "The Pentecostal Movement," unpublished MA thesis, University of Manitoba, 1950, 38-42.
2. S. C. Swallow, *Camp Meetings: Their Origin, History and Utility* (New York: Nelson and Phillips, 1899), pp. 10-11.
3. Arthur Kewley, "The Beginning of the Camp Meeting Movement in Upper Canada," *Canadian Journal of Theology*, 9:3 (1964), 192-202.
4. W. H. Withrow, et al, eds., *The Nineteenth Century Series*, vol. 9 (Toronto: Linscott, 1900), pp. 39, 45.
5. George F. Playter, *The History of Methodism in Canada* (Toronto: for the author, 1862), pp. 218, 279, 286.
6. Neil Semple, "The Impact of Urbanization in the Methodist Church in Central Canada, 1854-1884," unpublished PhD thesis, University of Toronto, 1979.
7. "Augusta," *Christian Guardian*, 29:4 (Oct. 28, 1857), 2.
8. R. E. McAlister, *The Good Report*, 1 (May 1911), 4.
9. Aimee Semple McPherson, *This is That* (Los Angeles: Echo Park Evangelistic Assoc., 1923), p. 95.
10. A. G. Ward, "How the Pentecostal Experience Came to Canada," typescript copy of handwritten report, PAOC Archives; see also Thomas Wm. Miller, "The Canadian Azusa: The Hebden Mission in Toronto," *Pneuma*, 8:1 (Spring 1986), 5-29.
11. G. A. Chambers, *50 Years in the Service of the King, 1907-1957* (Toronto: Full Gospel Publishing House, 1960), p. 20.
12. Ibid., p. 34.
13. *The Pentecostal Testimony* (August 1923), 7.
14. Quoted by Gordon F. Atter, in conversation with Thomas Wm. Miller, 1984.
15. Ibid.
16. Quoted by Jack West and Harold Davis, *They Call Him Mr. Braeside* (Toronto: Harmony Printing), pp. 92-93.
17. Reprinted from the *Golden Grain* (1939) by West and Davis, *They Call Him Mr. Braeside*, p. 94.

7 / CAMP MEETINGS, CONVENTIONS, AND COLLEGES

18. Gordon Atter, *Down Memory's Lane* (Port Colborne: Moss Press, 1974), p. 47.

19. G. A. Chambers, *The Pentecostal Testimony* (May 1936), 16; see also Chambers, *50 Years in the Service of the King, 1907 - 1957*, p. 44; and Thomas Wm. Miller, "Half a Century at Cobourg Camp," *The Pentecostal Testimony* (July 1986), 10-11; .

20. Elmer J. Cantelon, *Harvester of the North* (Toronto: Full Gospel Publishing House, 1969), pp. 80-84; see also Cantelon in *The Pentecostal Testimony* (September 1923), 1

21. Wm. Clifford Nelson, *From Plow Handles to Pulpit*, autobiographical booklet for the author, p. 15.

22. H. M. Cadwalder in *The Pentecostal Testimony* (August 1923), 7.

23. George R. Upton, *My Search for Reality* (for the author, 1987), pp. 33-34; and *Rejoice: A History of the Pentecostal Assemblies of Alberta and the Northwest Territories* (Edmonton: Alberta and Northwest Territories District, 1983), pp. 120-125.

24. P. S. Jones, "History of the Pentecostal Assemblies of Canada: B.C. District," typescript copy of Jones' personal report, PAOC Archives.

25. Quoted in *Souvenir of the Golden Jubilee, 1909-1959* (Kitchener: The Pentecostal Tabernacle, 1959).

26. A. H. Argue, "History of the PAOC," typed copy of handwritten memoirs, PAOC Archives, ca. 1955.

27. W. E. McAlister, "Our First General Superintendent Promoted to Glory," *The Pentecostal Testimony* (February 1958), 5; McAlister reported the actual event about 37 years earlier in *The Pentecostal Testimony* (December 1921), 1.

28. *The Pentecostal Testimony* (May 1934), 11.

29. Percy S. Jones, typed copy of his handwritten memoirs prepared by his daughter Joyce Watts. Used by permission.

30. Data abstracted from the original *Minute Book of the PAOC*.

31. R. E. Sternall considered the mutual ordinations as unusual, even for the formative period of the Canadian Fellowship. The incident has been confirmed for the writer by Sternall's daughter, Aleta (Sternall) Piper, November 26, 1979.

32. *Minute Book of the PAOC*, see reports for District and General Conferences in 1921, 1922, 1924.

33. *Minute Book of the PAOC*, "Eastern District Conference, Toronto, July 29 - Aug. 1, 1924;" "Western District Conference, Winnipeg, Aug. 12-16, 1925;" "General Conference, Winnipeg, Aug. 14-17, 1925;" "General Conference, Winnipeg, July 30 - Aug. 5, 1927;" and Paul Hawkes, *Pentecostalism in Canada: A History With Implications For The Future*, dissertation for San Francisco Theological Seminary, 1982, pp. 135-136."

CAMP MEETINGS, CONVENTIONS, AND COLLEGES / 7

34. *Minute Book of the PAOC*, "General Conference Minutes, London, August 1932;" a 1929 report on a Newfoundland conference describes it as the "Fourth annual conference of The Pentecostal Assemblies of Newfoundland, District Council of Pentecostal Assemblies of Canada," *The Pentecostal Testimony* (June 1929), 3.
35. P. S. Jones, memoirs, note 29.
36. James Montgomery, *Memoirs*, mimeographed copy, PAOC Archives.
37. A more systematic analysis of education among PAOC leaders may be found in Ronald Kydd, "The Contribution of Denominationally Trained Clergymen in the Emerging Pentecostal Movement in Canada," *Pneuma*, 5:1 (Spring 1983), 17-33.
38. Quoted by Erna Alma Peters, *The Contribution to Education by the Pentecostal Assemblies of Canada* (Altona, MB: for the author, 1971).
39. G. F. Atter, note 18; *The Pentecostal Testimony* (November 1923); and *The Gleaner* (May 1938), 5.
40. *Minute Book of the PAOC*, "Eastern District Conference, Arnprior, Aug. 27-31, 1923"; also at "Toronto, July 29-Aug. 1, 1924; and at "London, Aug. 4-9, 1925;" see also "Western District Conference, Winnipeg, Aug. 12-16, 1925"; and "General Conference, Winnipeg, Aug. 14-17, 1925."
41. John W. Knights, "History of the PAOC: Vancouver," typed copy of Knights' handwritten *Reminiscences*, PAOC Archives; "60th Anniversary, 1923-1983, Glad Tidings" (Victoria: Glad Tidings Pentecostal Church, 1983), pp. 5-6; and C. A. C. Story, "History of the PAOC," typed copy of his personal recollections, PAOC Archives.
42. *The Portal*, yearbook of Western Bible College, Winnipeg, 1939; see also Gordon K. Franklin, taped interview with Dr. J. E. Purdie, typed copy in Central Pentecostal College Library Archives, Saskatoon, 1973. Used by permission.
43. J. E. Purdie in *The Pentecostal Testimony* (July 1929), 15.
44. *The Portal*, 1947.
45. Gordon K. Franklin, interview with Purdie, pp. 111-115.
46. Willard C. Pierce in *The Gleaner* 11:1 (April 1950), 12.
47. Thomas Wm. Miller, "Portraits of Pentecostal Pioneers: J. E. Purdie," *The Pentecostal Testimony* (February 1987), 22-24.
48. Emma Hann, *Reflections of Eastern Pentecostal Bible College*, mimeographed booklet, Peterborough, 1982; and Carman W. Lynn, *Truth Aflame: A History of Eastern Pentecostal Bible College* (Peterborough: EPBC, 1989).
49. Hann pp. 20-21; see also Peters, note 38, pp. 44-49.

7 / CAMP MEETINGS, CONVENTIONS, AND COLLEGES

50. *Rejoice*, note 23, pp. 134-139; and D. N. Buntain, letter to J. E. Purdie, January 29, 1924, PAOC Archives.

51. *Jubilation: Five Decades in the Life of Western Pentecostal Bible College* (Abbotsford, B.C.: Western Pentecostal Bible College, 1991), p. 9.

52. O. Shipton, "British Columbia Bible Institute," typed copy of an undated letter, PAOC Archives); see also Lawrence Van Kleek, "BCBI and WPC Libraries, 1941-1970," a paper prepared for Fraser Valley College, Abbotsford, B.C., 1980, p. 4.

53. E. L. Lassègues, "Pentecost in Quebec," tract, PAOC Archives.

54. Lassègues, letter to J. E. Purdie, December 1954, PAOC Archives.

55. David R. Boyd, "Quebec: Canada's Samaria," *The Pentecostal Testimony* (September 1984), 25.

56. Peters, note 38, pp. 62-67, 70-71; "Ni Ki No Na — God's Call," booklet of the silver anniversary of the Northland Mission, 1950-1975, Port Colborne: Northland Mission, 1975; "Northland Mission Report," in annual conference report, Western Ontario District, Niagara Falls, April 29 - May 2, 1985; "Vision North," mimeographed publication of the Northland Mission, Burlington, April-May 1985.

57. Peters, note 38, pp. 68-73.

Chapter 8

THE REGIONS BEYOND 1907-1940

A. B. Simpson's hymn, "The Regions Beyond," was a favorite of evangelicals at the turn of the 20th century. It motivated groups like the Christian and Missionary Alliance to send volunteers with the gospel to foreign lands. It also expressed perfectly the commitment of Canadian Pentecostals to missionary endeavor. In the tradition of all genuine revivals, the outpouring of the Holy Spirit in Los Angeles, Toronto, and Winnipeg sparked an immediate concern for missions. William Seymour's *Apostolic Faith* journals recorded the overseas departure of many workers, both clergy and lay, in the first three years after 1906.

In Toronto, the Hebden Mission witnessed a similar spontaneous move to reach the masses with the full gospel. These attempts were made, it must be remembered, in the complete absence of any form of ecclesiastical structure or regular financial support. Overseas missions was entirely "a faith work," as George Slager noted. Present from the first days of the East End Mission, Slager reported that "these (missionaries) went out without financial backing other than God's promises," because "the work was completely unorganized in those days."[1]

George Chambers once made up a list of all the missionaries who had gone from Toronto to foreign fields before the PAOC was chartered in 1919. It read as follows:

    Brother & Sister Chas. Chawner — Africa
    Brother & Sister A. Atter — China
    Brother & Sister Hindle & Grace Fordham — Mongolia
    Brother Edgar Scurrah — South Africa
    Brother & Sister Slager — China
    Brother & Sister Semple — Hong Kong
    Brother & Sister Lawler — North China
    Brother Randall — Egypt.[2]

8 / THE REGIONS BEYOND: 1907-1940

In addition, Chambers noted that a number of Pentecostals from other communities went to Africa before 1919: two from Kitchener and five from Parry Sound. Randall and the Lawlers had worked with Chambers in pioneering the Ottawa region for Pentecost while they were in Canada on furlough.

There is little doubt that Charles W. Chawner was the first from Canada to carry the Pentecostal message to a foreign land. He was a painter in Toronto when he and his wife Emma, who was miraculously healed through prayer, became involved with the East End Mission. The Chawners became active lay workers in Toronto and in nearby Ontario communities. Historian Gordon Atter, who knew Chawner personally, described him as "a saintly man — a great man — his prayers were the simplest thing in the world, just like a child addressing a father."[3]

Soon after his Pentecostal experience in February 1907, Chawner received a remarkable vision of his future missions assignment in South Africa. He believed God gave him explicit instructions about his journey:

> He made it plain that I should leave all and follow him to Zululand, and having drawn me aside one day He told me it was time to go. He led brother Hebden in such a way that he secured the ticket much more reasonable than we expected, and so laid it on the hearts of the friends of the Mission that sufficient money was contributed, most of it in one night, all of it within about one month, to supply me with some needed clothes, pay the passage over the water, and the railways right to Weenen, Natal, S.A.[4]

Chawner did not leave Toronto for another year. He found it difficult to leave Emma and the children in Toronto without having any means to support them in his absence. Yet the burden increased while in prayer. Sometimes when he would visualize dark faces, the words, "Natal, go, go, Zulus, Zulus," would burst from his lips. He also was given the promise of Jeremiah 49:11, "Leave thy fatherless children, I will preserve them alive — let thy widows trust in Me." The Lord also spoke to Emma Chawner, as she once testified, saying, "You haven't given up all." Finally, she came to the place of "full trust in God and willing to let go that His will might be done." Just before Chawner left Toronto, on February 12, 1908, the Lord provided sufficient money and supplies to meet his family's needs.[5] With the exception of a few furloughs, he was to spend the rest of his life in Africa.

Chawner arrived at Capetown in March and was directed while in prayer to Weenen, the end of the railway line. After a year of travel, most of it by foot on rough and sometimes dangerous terrain, sharing the Pentecostal experience with other missionaries and preaching to the natives, he returned to Canada for Emma and the children. When they left Toronto in the spring of 1909, it was again with the prayers of the believers but with no promise of financial support. Ellen Hebden reprinted his early letters home in her magazine, *The Promise*, and some funds reached him from time to time. The bulk of his support, however, appears to have come from the generous and committed operators of a furniture store in the Toronto area, Mr. and Mrs. W. J. Brown.

The Chawners reached Zululand and began a study of the language. Before his studies were completed, Chawner itinerated as a Pentecostal evangelist, using interpreters wherever necessary. He made an interesting observation about the people to whom he ministered:

> The Zulus will never decide anything at once. It must be weighed, and weighed carefully. Still, they will come, thank God, back again.[6]

After finding a suitable location about 30 miles from Vryheid, he established a mission compound which he named "Bethel." Edgar Scurrah came in 1910 to assist Chawner, then moved on to another field. John and Georgie Guthrie arrived in 1915. They took over Bethel's operation so the Chawners could itinerate throughout Zululand – by ox cart no less! Sometimes the wagon required as many as 12 donkeys because of the rough terrain.

Although the Chawners met with considerable opposition from the people and their tribal leaders, they reported that the miraculous intervention of God always vindicated their ministry. Once, native leaders asked him to pray to his God to send rain to end a disastrous drought. The day after Chawner prayed an abundant rain storm brought desperately needed water. On these preaching itinerations, many came to the Lord. The first convert was a man of 90 whom they renamed Abraham. On one occasion during a meeting, Chawner felt impressed to call on a native woman to lead in prayer. She did so with such fervor and grace that Zulus all around her began to call on God for mercy. Many needy people were converted on the spot.

During the First World War, the Chawners were on furlough in Canada and involved themselves in the work at home. It was during the war years and the early 1920s that the Hebden Mission in Toronto lost its predominance in the early Pentecostal Movement. An undue emphasis by Ellen Hebden on the prophetic gift led to doctrinal problems. Chawner, Arthur Atter, and some other pioneers disassociated themselves from Hebden's leadership. Most of them aligned with the fledgling PAOC. In fact, Chawner attended one of the planning meetings in Montreal that led to the incorporation of the Canadian Fellowship. Thereafter, he was a

8 / THE REGIONS BEYOND: 1907-1940

welcome speaker at Pentecostal camp meetings and conventions where he impressed all with the quality of his childlike faith. Walter McAlister travelled to meetings with Chawner and reported the high esteem he had for him:

> A very deeply spiritual man . . . Charles Chawner had a coat on a peg in the train and, every few minutes, would open the coat, put his face inside, and pray to God . . . He was one of those unique, pioneer missionaries. Hardships meant nothing to him . . . he just lived for God.[7]

Back in Africa, evangelistic outreaches targeted the miners in the Rand, in Swaziland, and in the city of Durban. Missions work among the Zulus steadily expanded. Chawner's long ministry among his beloved Zulus was characterized by many remarkable instances of divine protection. On one occasion, when miles from the mission station and facing a long journey through lion-infested country, he hurried to get to the station before nightfall. He reported that the adventurous trip home included a trail down a mountain, a river crossing via leaps from boulder to boulder, and a steep path up to his home — all the while "praising God for the privilege of telling the Zulus the Glad Tidings." To his amazement, he arrived at the station in the early evening, having covered "quite a few miles of rough terrain within half an hour."

Throughout his years of missionary service, Chawner rose at 5 a.m. to pray, a practice which he maintained until his death in Africa in 1949. His deep devotional life left a lasting impression on his fellow Pentecostal missionaries and leaders in the homeland. His sacrificial labors in opening up Zululand to the full gospel inspired one Pentecostal author to dub him "the Apostle to the Zulus."[8]

Chawner had believed for years that God was calling his son Austin to succeed him. Content in praying that God would reach Austin's heart, he wisely left the decision to the young man without exerting any pressure on him. Austin had often witnessed the mighty works of God in his father's ministry, but planned on a commercial career for himself. However, after a personal spiritual encounter with God, he made the decision to prepare for ministry. The younger Chawner travelled to Canada to seek employment in a bank to finance his theological studies. Subsequently, he enrolled in Bethel Bible Training School in Newark, New Jersey, where he experienced the double blessing of being baptized in the Holy Spirit and also finding his wife Carrie.

Upon their return to South Africa, Austin and Carrie assisted the senior Chawner for a time before seeking entry to the Portuguese-ruled colony of Mozambique. When permission was refused, Austin began ministry among the natives from Mozambique who worked in the South African gold mines. Later, with permission secured, he evangelized among the Tsonga tribes, travelling the rough paths by bicycle and on foot. Chawner's ministry in Mozambique began in May 1927, but permission to establish a permanent mission site was still refused by government officials. The immediate remedy was to set up a new station at Shingwedzi, just over the border from Mozambique and still within reach of the Tsongas. The PAOC provided funds for this project. October 2, 1927 was a day of rejoicing when Austin baptized the first convert.

In spite of several personal bouts with malaria, within two years Austin overcame the opposition of some tribesmen who resisted his ministry and assembled a significant number of new Christians in a church. He began a program of religious education with the aid of a small printing press sent from Canada. The Bible studies and hymn sheets which he printed in the Tsonga language helped stabilize the believers in the Christian faith. Eventually, his Tsonga hymn book went to six editions, the last totalling 50,000 copies. After a number of men had learned to read and write and had acquired some basic training, they spread out to evangelize among their own people.

The national Bible school functioned well and appeared to have a secure future when the PAOC registered it with the colonial government in 1933. Unfortunately, the school had to be closed in 1936 when the widespread financial effects of the Depression took their toll.[9]

The history of Chawner's missionary service is filled with trials and heartaches. His wife Carrie and his mother both died on the field. Altogether, nine early Pentecostal workers laid down their lives during the '30s on the Mozambique border. Austin himself nearly died from malaria and on another occasion faced death as a result of an insect bite. Death for white people bitten by the "magroda" was virtually a certainty, but he was spared through the prayers of his national helpers. Another test of faith involved plagues of locusts when all the food was consumed by hordes of insects blanketing territory up to four miles wide and 25 miles long. Some heat spells drove the temperature as high as 145 degrees Fahrenheit.

Chawner's second marriage to Ingrid Lokken provided him not only with a wife but also a very effective co-worker. Ingrid, a Norwegian Pentecostal, arrived in Africa in 1922 and sought permission to enter Mozambique. The authorities attempted to deter her by requesting that she apply each week for an entry permit. Convinced that she had a mandate from God to evangelize the colony, she persisted with her application until it was granted four years later. The marriage of Austin and Ingrid was the union of two hearts who had a passion for Mozambique. The Chawners made the city of Loureco Marques the centre for their work. By 1935 the couple had pioneered 14 assemblies in the colony, enlisted 30 African ministers, and produced a good number of Christian publications.

Austin Chawner was a spokesman for the PAOC in its dealings with the governments of Mozambique and South Africa. A gifted linguist with a diploma in the Tsonga language, Chawner assisted the British and Foreign Bible Society in its translation work. He earned the degrees of BA and B.Th. and was awarded a Doctor of Divinity by an appreciative educational institution. This was no small accomplishment for a man who spent his entire life in mission evangelization among primitive peoples.

By 1960, the number of churches in the former Portuguese colony exceeded 300 and the mission work had expanded to many other regions. When he died in 1963, thousands of Pentecostals throughout Africa and Canada mourned his death. His last recorded words were, "Thank God we live for a purpose — an eternal purpose." Ingrid Chawner continued ministry in Mozambique until her death in 1976.[10]

The rapid growth of the first Pentecostal missions in Africa required a steady stream of recruits from the homeland. The availability of a relatively large number of early Pentecostals to overseas fields is proof that the Canadian Fellowship was imbued from the start with a missionary zeal. Delegates at the first PAOC General Conference in 1919 approved the mission work in the Congo "in which J. K. Blakeney and wife are interested." They also urged local assemblies to adopt a program of missions support. Regular offerings were to be received, one-third of which was for home expansion and two-thirds for overseas needs.

Within a year the PAOC assemblies had raised $2,359.82, of which $1,900 was sent to foreign lands. By 1921, annual PAOC receipts totalled $12,000 with $9,000 of that amount going to the missionaries. A policy was adopted which directed missions funds to the national office for distribution to the foreign fields. A landmark decision which still characterizes PAOC missions policy was taken in 1933 at the Toronto General Conference: it involved the adoption of "the indigenous church idea" which was to be recommended "to all our missionaries on the field." The goal overseas was to develop a "self-governing, self-propagating and self-supporting native church." The source of this philosophic concept of missions in PAOC ranks is difficult to locate, but it is evident that the Fellowship was decades ahead of many other evangelical denominations in its approach to world evangelization.[11]

The PAOC, like so many other organizations, faced one of its gravest challenges when the disastrous decade known as the "hungry thirties" (or the "dirty thirties") began. It was precipitated by the stock market collapse on "Black Tuesday," October 29, 1929. Millions were left unemployed and homeless; thousands of businesses went bankrupt. Farm prices dropped so low that planting the seed became unprofitable. For instance, wheat dropped from $1.60 a bushel in 1929 to 40 cents within two years. The Pentecostals in Canada did not escape the economic consequences.

Missions Secretary A. G. Ward wrote prophetically when he urged prayer as "the greatest need in the Pentecostal Fellowship," for "dark days are upon us and darker days lie just ahead." Missionary offerings dropped from nearly $8,000 in January of 1930 to less than $4,000 the following April. Despite these setbacks, the PAOC not only managed to keep most of its 33 workers on the mission fields but placed two additional missionaries under appointment in 1933. At this time there were only 26,301 Pentecostals in the whole of Canada, not all of whom were in the PAOC. One of the positive factors which bolstered the Pentecostals during this difficult era was the growing relationship with Pentecostal organizations in other countries. Donald Gee of Great Britain was only one of the many who made international tours. He visited Canada in 1933.[12]

Among the missionary recruits sent out in 1937 and 1938 were Fred and Rhoda Clarke and Vernon and Gertrude Morrison. The hardships which the Clarkes experienced while supervising a mission in Vancouver prepared them well for the work in Africa. For 30 years they ministered at mission stations in South Africa, such as Louis Trichardt, as well as throughout Kenya and Uganda.[13] The Morrisons labored for a term in Liberia, but illness forced them to return home. After several years of pastoring in Canada, they returned to South Africa. When Otto Keller died, Morrison transferred to Kenya and opened the Bible school. His son Leroy assisted him for a time and later managed the Evangel Press.

The South African missionaries reached nationals from Mozambique who came there seeking work, thus continuing the type of evangelism pioneered by Austin Chawner. When the Clarkes moved to assist in Kenya, Earley and Pearl King arrived from Canada to take over the Shingwedzi Mission. Later the Kings went to the Rand to direct the work of evangelizing the migrant workers from other African countries. King worked in the mining compounds where the men lived and Pearl held meetings in the townships and in hospitals. Many of the converts reached in the mines became lay evangelists to their own tribes after completing their labor contracts in the South African gold mines and returning home.

As the number of converts steadily increased, the need for Christian education became ever more pressing. Canadian Pentecostals excelled in launching basic education programs in British East Africa. This work began as a by-product of one of the most heroic missionary endeavors in modern history. Marian Weller of Parry Sound, Ontario, was one of the chief instruments used by God in both evangelizing and educating the Kenyans. She was living in Toronto when she first heard of the Baptism in the Holy Spirit from her sister Sarah. In 1911, Sarah went to India where she met and married missionary J. H. Royce. The Royces served in India for several years before Sarah succumbed to malaria.

Marian was baptized in the Holy Spirit in meetings in North Seguin, near Parry Sound. One night, in prayer, the words "Oh Africa, dark Africa" burst from her lips. She regarded this experience as her call to Africa. Although she had business school training, Marian determined to get more Bible instruction and went to the Elim Bible school in Rochester, N.Y. From the beginning, she expressed a childlike confidence in the Lord's ability to supply her needs:

> I re-consecrated my life to God and went forward by faith in Him. While crossing the border between Canada and the United States and going through the immigration office, I was asked . . . "Where are you going?" I replied "To Bible School." "How much money do you have with you?" "Six dollars," I answered. "Who is going to support you while in school?" "The Lord" was my reply. With that, the officials allowed me to pass, saying, "If you have that kind of faith we will let you go."[14]

In Rochester, she met her husband Karl Wittich, a Baptist who had received the Baptism in the Holy Spirit. In 1913, they set out for ministry to what then was known as German East Africa. When the couple went overseas they took Clarence Grothaus with them as an assistant. After settling at Itiger, Wittich soon mastered the local language and preached with some success. Tragically, Wittich and Grothaus died within a few months, victims of the malaria which was ravaging the region. When the news reached Wittich's father in New Bremen, Ohio, he responded:

> . . . we (cannot) comprehend God's ways in their so untimely demise. . . . God has taken the pioneers from this new field to Himself, but He has not abandoned his mission, nor the lonely sister in the midst of hungry souls.[15]

Marian herself fell ill with malaria for six weeks and nearly died. When she recovered from the sickness and resumed her duties, she found that all the mission supplies had been stolen.

Refusing to return to Canada, Marian Wittich labored for four years at other mission stations. Because of the war then raging in Europe, the German authorities in Tanganyika imprisoned her. After she was released, in answer to prayer, she felt led to travel to the coast, many miles away, to catch a ship for Canada. Although movement was forbidden by the colonial government, and she had no money, she travelled on foot in the company of a team of porters and managed to reach the coast. It was a gruelling journey of 240 miles.

At the end of the First World War, Marian Wittich returned to the field where she met and married Otto Keller, a missionary from the United States. When they first arrived, government regulations prohibited their purchase of land. After praying about the need, they were able to acquire a 99-acre estate with funds sent from the homeland. The Kisumu site became the home of the Nyang'ori Mission Station. A church was built, as well as a school, workshop, dormitories, and a guest house for missionaries. By 1923, the Kellers had established 25 district schools in a region inhabited by 60,000 nationals.

In this way the Kenyans were first taught to read and write their own languages and the basic educational system of the colony was established. National workers who were trained at Nyang'ori later helped to evangelize their tribes. As the gospel and education impacted the pagan societies, the nationals gradually gave up some of their traditional customs. One practical result of the introduction of Christian standards was the dress-making classes for women and girls as they became interested in clothes to cover themselves. At first, tribal elders vigorously resisted educating women and girls, but found to their amazement that such females were highly sought after by the bachelors and brought a much higher dowry price — in cows.

Otto Keller's two-fold approach of evangelism and education was amply justified, but he realized that the mission could not continue on an independent basis because of government regulations. When they made overtures to the PAOC, the Kellers were received into "cooperative fellowship" at the General Conference of 1923.[16] These ties were strengthened by the arrival of more missionaries from Canada. A revival broke out on the station in 1929 and scores were converted and filled with the Spirit. The revival spread to 12 different tribes and greatly advanced the Pentecostal work. By the time Otto died in 1942, the Kenya work had three main mission stations at Nyang'ori, Goibei, and Awasi. The field office supervised over 200 branch churches, a group of missionaries, and more than 500 African pastors, teachers, and evangelists.

Marian Keller continued on the field after her husband's death until poor health forced her to return in Canada. Words which she penned in 1933 describing her first 20 years in Africa provide an insight of her courage and commitment:

> Twenty years of happy service in Africa! The first ten years were full of hardships, suffering, sorrow and sacrifice. But what does that matter in comparison to what He endured for us? . . . Had I only more lives to give Him, gladly would I surrender them all.[17]

She died in 1953 in Victoria. Her obituary concluded appropriately with the words, "May her example inspire others to like precious faith."

Educational work among Kenyan Christians was further expanded when Nellie Hendrickson reached the field in 1929. Hendrickson was a teacher and a graduate of the Winnipeg Bible school. She provided advanced instruction in Bible studies and inaugurated a course in pedagogy for national teacher candidates. Eventually, she became the founder and principal of the Teachers' Training School. In the opinion of Carman Lynn, former Executive Director of the PAOC Overseas Missions Department, Nellie Hendrickson could be considered the "mother" of the Pentecostal Assemblies of God school system in Kenya.[18]

The significance of Hendrickson's contribution cannot be overestimated. She had a very significant influence on the progress of the Pentecostal message as well as the economic-political development of the colony. It was from the PAOC school systems that many future church and secular leaders emerged. The budding church leaders assumed directors roles for the Pentecostal Assemblies of God in Kenya; some of the students who followed the political route became the governing leaders of Kenya after it secured independence from Britain. Just as Hendrickson's work expanded PAOC national education from the original base laid down by the Kellers, so her own work was further developed by the ministries of James and Lila Skinner and John and Ella McBride.

Skinner was a school teacher at Parkside, Saskatchewan, when he was converted and baptized in the Spirit. Turning away from his teaching career in 1936, he and his wife accepted the appointment to assist Otto Keller in Kenya. After serving effectively for 12 years in this role, Skinner moved on to other mission fields where his experience and skills as an educator were in great demand. Among their accomplishments was the founding of the mission station at Marhumbini in southern Rhodesia, where the Skinners devoted 12 years of service. The construction of such a station finally made it possible to secure government recognition for the PAOC in the region.

Their itinerant work among the tribes they sought to evangelize, and their travels in the interests of Christian education, were severely limited by the poor roads and by the lack of suitable transportation. When news of these problems reached Canada, Pentecostal youth across the nation raised funds for a vehicle for the Skinners. Out of this initial project developed the now-familiar "Wing the Word" program which supplies vehicles for missionaries.[19]

Skinner's work included teaching, writing, and preaching, in addition to the supervision of the PAOC educational program in Kenya and

Rhodesia. After 40 years of ministry in Africa, he took up the post of Overseas Missions Promotion Secretary in the national office of the PAOC in Toronto.

About the time the Skinners had enlarged the education work in Kenya, there was a parallel development in the provision of medical services. Marion Munro and Renata Siemens set up a medical dispensary where both the gospel and medicine were administered to the nationals. By 1939, medical missions began to assume a larger role in PAOC overseas evangelism.

The spontaneous missions outreach which followed the outpouring of the Holy Spirit at Toronto and Winnipeg is nowhere better illustrated than in the country of Liberia. A party of eight Pentecostals — both American and Canadian — landed at Cape Palmas late in 1908. During the first 10 years over 20 missionaries died from tropical fevers. Liberia justly earned its nickname, "the white man's grave." Few details are available, but among those who succumbed to the fevers were a Miss Morrison and a Mr. Ross of Toronto, a Miss Scutt of Winnipeg, Martha Marr, Fred Knoll, and Mrs. J. M. L. Harrow. Survivors Martha Hisey of Winnipeg and Mr. and Mrs. J. Perkins began the development of the Liberian Pentecostal Mission. Stations were built at Newaka and Gropaka. Among the large number of converts from the great revival in 1913 was a tribal chief and a witch doctor. For three years a remarkable spiritual work continued at the stations. Help came in 1915 with the arrival of Laura Arnold and Ethel Bingeman.

Sophie Nygaard came to Liberia in 1919; it would be her home and place of service for the next 40 years. She worked from the station at Putu at a time when that whole region was not completely under the control of the government at Monrovia. A brief anecdote gives a wonderful glimpse of this woman's faith. The story involves a customs official whom she was trying to persuade to release to her a package sent from Canada containing some needed food. Since she did not have a bill of lading, the official would not give her the package unless she could name the contents in the package. Nygaard knew that the package was supposed to contain cans of meat, but the official insisted on her stating the number of cans. Breathing a prayer to the Lord for guidance, Sophie said "Thirty-seven." When the box was opened and there were 37 cans inside, Nygaard got her supplies.[20]

Endeavoring to evangelize the remotest tribes, she made numerous treks throughout the interior with Liberian helpers. On one such journey, Nygaard's party was caught in the forest at the height of a torrential storm and trees were falling everywhere. She prayed for divine protection. The nationals with her later reported that as they moved along the forest path, the storm raged on both sides and behind them, but ahead of them always lay a dry safe path until they reached their destination.

As the work in Liberia was enlarged by the sacrificial labors of these early missionaries, it became evident that the mission needed more formal ties with the Pentecostal Fellowship in Canada. In this respect, Liberian missions followed the pattern established by pioneer Pentecostal missionaries elsewhere in Africa. As the mission programs expanded, more finances and more workers were constantly needed, and relationships with the PAOC came to be more formalized. For example, the 1919 Conference formally approved Laura Arnold's application for missionary credentials four years *after* she first went to Liberia. Others who responded to the challenge in that land were Ethel Bingeman, Vernon and Gertrude Morrison, Ruth Le Pers, and Edith Bronsdon. Later recruits included Kenneth Stevenson, Frank and Winnifred Schwartz, William and Viola Brown, Immanuel and Isabel Jensen, Joy Hansell, and Gerald and Ruth Morrison.

Liberia remained one of the most dangerous fields for missionaries. Ruth Le Pers described it as

> a land which combines in its own small territory nearly all the plagues and pestilences of the entire continent. Its animals are dangerous, its reptiles venomous, its insects poisonous, its fevers deadly, and its diseases loathsome.[21]

For many years after the arrival of the first workers in 1908, there was only one primitive five-mile road joining the interior with the coast. But Canadian Pentecostals continued to arrive: Margaret Wadge in 1937 and Annie Cressman in 1941. Wadge worked with Sophie Nygaard at the Putu Station, while Cressman worked among the Tchien people in the interior of the country. Cressman's call to Liberia came while reading a report in *The Pentecostal Testimony* submitted by Nygaard. She recalled the event in a conversation with the writer:

> While reading the letter . . . I said to myself, "When the young people of the Elmira church read that letter, they'll get ready and go. It seemed that simple. And God said, "Annie, you go." And it was never the same again.[22]

Nygaard retired from Liberia in 1959 and lived in Vancouver until her death in 1976. Even in retirement she depended upon the Lord for the necessities of life. Her lifelong motto was, "Nothing But My Best Is Good Enough For Jesus." That motto undoubtedly characterized the dedication of many other missionaries — both Canadian and American — who have served in Liberia.

Several decades of Pentecostal ministry resulted in the establishment of day schools and Bible schools. A large leprosarium was founded to treat sufferers with that terrible disease. A notable achievement was the reduction of the Tchien dialect to writing and subsequently the translation of parts of the New Testament into that language. Eventually, the work on that field was organized as the Liberian Assemblies of God.

One of the many examples of early Pentecostal zeal for missions is the story of the Arthur M. Atter family. Atter was a prosperous farmer living at Abingdon, near Hamilton, when he first heard of the Pentecostal revival. An uncle named William Manley, a Free Methodist clergyman, had received the Baptism in the Holy Spirit in Los Angeles. This man shared his charismatic experience with the Atters and also prayed for Arthur, who then was dying of tuberculosis. After Arthur's supernatural healing, the family became involved with the Hebden Mission in Toronto.

Atter later became the recognized leader of about 40 Pentecostals at Abingdon. But there was growing in the hearts of the Atters a conviction that the Lord had called them to win souls in China. In a letter to Ellen Hebden, Jessie Atter testified, "How I love Him and His dear saints, and have such a longing for souls to be saved." In 1909, the Atters sold their belongings and, with their young son Gordon, sailed for China. They also took along a young convert named Will Burns of Toronto who later died in China while fulfilling the Great Commission. The Atters had no one to provide them with regular financial support, but they were driven by a belief that the coming of the Lord was so near that there could be no delay in reaching the nations. Their first preaching meetings were held on the coast near Shanghai, usually two or three times each day.

During the hot season in China young Gordon became deathly ill. When their own prayers seemed to bring no relief, the parents prayed that the boy would be laid on the heart of someone in Canada to intercede for his healing. Suddenly, the lad began to improve. A letter afterward from home revealed that an aunt had been awakened from sleep and had been impressed to pray for him. The dates corresponded.[23]

Although there was much progress in China which provided a foundation for Canadian Pentecostal work in that field, the Atters were compelled to return to Canada because of illness. For a number of years they pioneered new assemblies in Ontario. Arthur Atter was known as a capable Bible teacher. He took part in some of the discussions that led to the formation of the PAOC in 1919.

The work which the Atters started in China was continued by Lettie Ward of London, Ontario. Ward was one of about 50 people from the London assembly who went into full-time Pentecostal ministry. She arrived in China in 1914 and worked on that field until the Second World

8 / THE REGIONS BEYOND: 1907-1940

War forced her to return to Canada in 1940. Like all the pioneers, she faced great privation and had numerous trials of her faith. During her first Christmas in China, she had nothing to eat but two bread crusts and a bit of jam. In spite of the complete absence of any organization to support her, she managed to learn the language, carry on evangelism, and give leadership to Chinese believers.

Ward was astonished to learn in 1917 that only 70 out of every 10,000 Chinese women could read. To enable the women to better understand and spread the gospel, she and an American woman founded China's first Pentecostal school for women. From this humble beginning came some dedicated Chinese workers and biblically literate women. At least a couple of the graduates later became teachers in the Ecclesia Bible Institute when it was set up in Hong Kong. Lettie Ward died in 1961.

Another Ontario Pentecostal called to China was a devout young Christian from Berlin (now Kitchener). Coralee Haist received her "call" when she first came into the Pentecostal experience. She was strongly influenced by a Pentecostal school teacher named Laura who later married R. E. McAlister. Coralee's Pentecostal experience soon led to a temporary ejection from home by her mother. She prayed earnestly for her family, most of whom came into the Pentecostal Fellowship before she went to China. Leaving home for a distant unknown land with only $25 in her purse was a traumatic experience for the young missionary. She especially suffered over the look of anguish on her father's face as her train left the Kitchener station.

A long boat journey from Vancouver brought her to China in 1917 where she labored in evangelism for the next 25 years. Haist was mainly involved in village evangelism until the Japanese invasion of Mainland China forced her to flee to Hong Kong. After the formation of the PAOC, she affiliated with the Canadian body and carried on evangelism and "roof-top" primary school outreach in the crowded crown colony until her retirement from active ministry.[24]

China has been blessed by some of the most devoted gospel workers which Canada has produced. John Rutherford Spence fits into that category of missionary. Spence emigrated from Scotland to Canada and worked for a time with the Salvation Army in Winnipeg. After receiving the Baptism in the Holy Spirit, he was called by God to China. But Spence was middle-aged and suffered from a speech impediment. After being healed in answer to prayer, he was directed to China in 1919. There he met Phoebe Holmes, an American who had worked a short time with Robert and Aimee Semple in Hong Kong.

Phoebe Holmes opened the first Pentecostal mission station in Wang Kong, near Canton, in 1912. The area was infested with robbers and opium dens, but Holmes and an assistant held meetings each night and crowds came to hear the gospel. Soon, there was a nucleus of believers and hundreds eventually were saved, including some who later became leaders of the Chinese national church. Holmes later moved to the Sz Wui district and founded another prosperous assembly. Part of her evangelistic outreach was accomplished through the operation of a girls' school. By this means she was able to reach into the upper-class homes. In 1920, when her chapel and school were burned during a local civil uprising, Holmes was rescued by a party which included J. R. Spence. They were married a year later and labored in China until their furlough in Canada.[25]

The Spences hoped to return to China, but ill health forced them to stay in Canada for several years. They pastored at Gilbert Plains, Manitoba, where the Lord gave them a revival and many were converted. Eventually, the family returned to China and labored in itinerant evangelism in the remote, unreached regions. Tent evangelism was a great novelty at the time. The Spences had a tent which could seat 800. They used the tent to make new contacts with great success and established several Pentecostal congregations through this method. In one city, they discovered a Christian academy with 900 male students. The school, unfortunately, was filled with men who favored revolutionary Bolshevism and had little interest in the gospel. As Spence put it, "Not the Gospel but modern Christianity had failed in China."

In spite of the opposition, Spence held a series of meetings in the school in 1928 and many came to Christ. The missionary made a point of preaching the full range of Pentecostal doctrines. Many young believers experienced the Baptism in the Holy Spirit with speaking in tongues.

This pioneering work, which was rewarding but physically exhausting, took its toll on Phoebe who died in 1939. A short time later the Japanese invaded China and Spence was interned in a prison camp until 1943. Chinese believers, at the risk of their lives, smuggled eggs to the incarcerated missionary. As he once recalled, the eggs, though eaten raw, were the perfect food for even the shells provided him with nutrients. Nonetheless, when he was repatriated to Canada, he weighed a mere 116 pounds.

After returning to Canada, John Spence married Florence Sanders. When the Second World War ended he and his bride set out for China to engage in missionary work. The Communist takeover later forced them to flee to Hong Kong, where for years both taught in the Ecclesia Bible Institute. Spence retired in 1970 and spent his remaining years in Canada where he died in 1976. His ministry had spanned half of a century. The long years in China both blessed the Chinese and inspired a generation of

8 / THE REGIONS BEYOND: 1907-1940

young Canadians. His pioneering work in China had been similar in many respects to that of Ivan Kauffman.

Ivan and Frances Kauffman first went to China in 1907 with the Christian and Missionary Alliance. While on furlough, they came into the Pentecostal Movement and returned to China as full gospel missionaries. They tried at an early date to enter the forbidden region of Tibet, but when their efforts proved fruitless, they determined in 1923 to concentrate on China. They settled at Tsingtao where one of their initial contacts, a Mr. Chou, became the first Chinese in Shantung province to receive the Pentecostal Baptism. After Kauffman and his national believers gave themselves to intercessory prayer, a remarkable revival in 1925 swept over the community. Over 80 were saved and about 20 filled with the Spirit. Although a cholera epidemic swept through Shantung at this period and about 150 died each day, not one of the believers died from cholera.[26]

The Kauffmans moved to Shanghai and held tent meetings in the late '20s with considerable success in winning converts. When the congregation outgrew its first building, a large downtown theatre was secured for meetings. Another revival came in 1930 and crowds grew to 700 in each service. In one nine-day period, 130 were saved and 70 filled with the Spirit. Five new churches were founded as a result. The great interest that the revival spawned in other denominations provided numerous opportunities to share the Pentecostal experience. Consequently, hundreds more received the Baptism in the Spirit with speaking in tongues. By the end of 1933, Kauffman could write to the homeland, "Never was China better prepared for the Gospel than now." Unfortunately, this great Pentecostal missionary pioneer died the next year. His two sons, Don and Paul, later became effective missionaries in the Orient. The influence of Ivan Kauffman was felt in the hearts and lives of many Canadians, as well as his Chinese converts. R. E. McAlister testified that "His missionary zeal, together with a spirit of unselfishness, was always an inspiration to me."[27]

When news of the death of Ivan Kauffman reached Canada, Clare and Lydia Scratch volunteered to go as replacements. Scratch, who was then district superintendent of Alberta, possessed ministry qualifications which were needed for the work in China. The couple arrived in 1935 and gave many years of sacrificial labor for the Lord. Together with J. R. Spence, Clare Scratch was imprisoned during the Second World War and then repatriated to Canada. Lydia had previously returned to Canada with their daughter Lorraine and their infant son Gordon. Like other missionaries who returned to China after the war, the Scratches were given only a brief period to minister before the Communist seizure of power in 1949 brought gospel work to a complete halt. But their influence continued through their converts in remote areas and the orphanage they established in Foochow.

Scratch's missionary zeal compelled him, after his expulsion from China, to work for the Christian Children's Fund in Travancore, India. In 1953, he accepted the position of Missionary Promotional Secretary for the PAOC. His wife Lydia died in 1959. Later Scratch married Elma Barber and the couple spent two years in missionary work in China during the mid-60s. Although he retired in 1969 he did not settle for an inactive role. In March 1970, he joined the pastoral staff of Calvary Temple in Denver, Colorado. After serving the Lord in ministry for 53 years, Clare Scratch died in 1974. His life as a missionary and pastor was characterized by a special gentleness and courtesy which endeared him to all who met him.[28]

While J. Elmor Morrison and his wife, Laura, pastored in Montreal and some Ontario centres, they had their hearts set on carrying the gospel to China. The primary obstacle was a lack of funds. A miracle arrived in 1923 when a faithful believer provided the needed money — $500 — in the mail. Like those who went before them, the Morrisons found China to be a land tormented by roving bands of robbers, oppressive landlords, numerous civil wars, and gross ignorance among the people. Not only did this dedicated couple have to face the problems arising from the filth and disease encountered in everyday life, they occasionally had to flee from their home station into the country to escape vicious mobs and bandits. The hostile conditions were a constant challenge during their first term. Upon their return in 1928, however, they experienced considerable success and were able to open a mission station in the Tsing Yuen district, plus two other outstations. With the cooperation of the American Assemblies of God, a Bible school was established in Canton where Morrison served as principal.

This thriving mission work was interrupted by the Japanese invasion which was a prelude to the Second World War. The family was sent to Australia and later returned to Canada, but Elmor Morrison stayed at his post in China. He avoided capture by constantly moving into areas deep behind Japanese lines where he continued his evangelistic activities. For four years there was no information on his fate. The end of the war brought exciting news of his survival.

China missions began anew in 1945, but the Communist conquest in 1949 forced the Morrisons to relocate in Hong Kong. There both Elmor and Laura ministered in the Bible school where scores of young Pentecostal preachers were trained for work among the Chinese. In 1960, they retired to Canada. One of their sons, Keith, became a teacher in

8 / THE REGIONS BEYOND: 1907-1940

Kenya and later received appointment as executive assistant in the Overseas Missions Department of the PAOC's national office. It is impossible to estimate adequately the work the Morrisons accomplished in sending trained full gospel workers from Hong Kong back into China. Nor can the impact of the Chinese Pentecostals on the "underground" church in that vast land be gauged properly. Recent reports suggest the rapid growth of the Chinese national church is related, at least in a measure, to these devoted Canadians.[29]

The career of another important Canadian Pentecostal missionary was inaugurated in an unusual manner through the supernatural healing of a British sailor. When Will Butcher joined the navy in 1929 at the age of 16, he planned to make it a life-long career. While posted with the "China Fleet," he was one of several young sailors attacked by a Chinese mob. Butcher vowed never to return to that land. After his conversion in a Pentecostal church while on leave at home, he believed he received a divine call to minister in China. But there was a complication: he was legally bound for one more year to serve in the British navy. His release from the legal restriction came in a roundabout fashion. When Butcher fell ill, doctors diagnosed a life-threatening brain tumor which precipitated his discharge from the navy. Later, in an Assembly of God church, he was totally healed.

After a time of preparation in a Bible school, he and his bride (Elsie Welsteed) went to China. Butcher's earlier training in oriental languages, which earned him a Master of Arts degree from London University, prepared him providentially for his new career of missionary evangelism. When they encountered difficulties in China, the Butchers spent one term in Japan before settling at Shanghai. From this centre, Butcher ranged far out into the countryside on evangelistic forays. He perfected his language skills by talking to patients as he pulled teeth, dressed wounds, and prayed for the sick.

Butcher sought to identify as closely as possible with those to whom he was preaching by itinerating "Chinese style." He wore the clothes of the common people, slept on hard pallets in the country inns, and ate the coarse fare of the peasants. This approach allowed him to contact classes of Chinese, such as Taoist priests, otherwise not accessible to European missionaries. Once he met a priest to whom he said,

> "I have come to tell you about the Way to God." The old man's eyes brightened, "We have a common quest, I see. We both are seekers after the Way." "But I am not a seeker," Will put in eagerly, "I have found the Way." "Impossible," said the aged priest ... "My ancestors for generations have sought the Way. You are young. What you are talking about must be something new."[30]

THE REGIONS BEYOND: 1907-1940 / 8

In response, Butcher read to him from his Mandarin Bible and led the Taoist priest to a confession of Christ as Savior. Later, when he told the man's family about the "Way," all of them became Christians.

Will and Elsie Butcher ministered in China until the 1949 Communist seizure of power. Following their return to Canada, they pastored a church in Swan River, Manitoba. When the PAOC missions department made a decision to enter the needy field of Thailand, the man chosen to spearhead that evangelistic endeavor was Will Butcher. The chapter of his ministry in Thailand is told later in this narrative.

The history of modern Pentecostalism in India began with the outpouring of the Spirit, at the turn of the 20th century, in Pandita Ramabai's mission. A. H. Argue, who had been stirred by the news from India, shared the reports with those who read his early Pentecostal publications. Among the Canadians who went to India before the 1919 formation of the PAOC were Sarah Weller of Parry Sound and three workers from Kitchener — Miss C. B. Herron and Mr. and Mrs. Alex Lindsay. Some earnest full gospel workers connected with the Hebden Mission in Toronto had gone to India around 1909. Barbara Johnson, one of the Hebden group, married Rev. J. Nortons, whom she met in India. Together they operated a Pentecostal home for boys at Dhoud. Another early mission was supervised by Paul and Olga Andreasen in Lucknow. Later, N. J. LeShana of Newfoundland went to Lucknow. The 1934 PAOC General Conference commissioned another missionary, Ilene Edwards of Toronto, to assist in the work. Other Canadian missionaries to India were Alfred and Mary Cawston and Harold and Verna Underhill.

The difficulties occasioned by the Great Depression, and the fact that the American Assemblies of God already had firmly established mission works in India, led to a decision by the PAOC to withdraw from India and leave the territory to the Americans. It was a difficult decision, for Canadians had long held a keen interest in the progress of the Pentecostal Movement in India.[31]

Canadian representatives of the PAOC began to enter various fields in South America soon after the establishment of the organization in 1919. The first to reach Argentina were Charles and Margaret Wortman. Dr. Wortman had been a specialist in obstetrics in London, Ontario. His parents were brought into the Pentecostal Fellowship through the ministry of George Chambers. They had been profoundly impressed by the supernatural manifestations of the Spirit at the famous Jordan Valley Camp Meeting. Upon their return to London, they began to conduct services in their home. Dr. Wortman, impacted by the gospel, turned from a medical career to commit his life to evangelism in Argentina. The Wortmans settled in Buenos Aires in 1921 and within two years had built up a thriving congregation.

8 / THE REGIONS BEYOND: 1907-1940

When the Wortmans began to reach out to other nearby communities, they met Niels and Annina Sorensen in the city of Bolivar. The Sorensens, who had received the Pentecostal infilling while visiting the United States, were eager to unite with Dr. Wortman under the aegis of the PAOC. Thus the full gospel was proclaimed from two key centres. A powerful revival swept the mission churches in 1926 and brought in about 100 new converts. When Wortman went on furlough to Canada, he enlisted Fred and Susan Clements of London.[32] Louise Layman was another recruit for the work in Argentina.

The Clements were especially successful in recruiting national workers. Soon there were at least 500 Pentecostals gathering at the annual Easter meetings in the cities of Bolivar and Daireaux. The ranks of the missionaries had corresponding growth with the coming of a Norwegian couple — Erling and Alvina Andresen. The Andresens worked first in Bolivar and then opened up the Rio Tercero region. This promising work was temporarily hampered by the death in 1939 of Clements and the return of his family to Canada. The Wortmans also left for the homeland, where Dr. Wortman took up the post of General Secretary-Treasurer of the PAOC — a post he held with distinction until his death in 1967.

Andresen was named as the supervisor of the Bolivar field. Pentecostal evangelism continued to expand throughout Argentina. The number of workers was increased by the arrival of several female missionaries from the Assemblies of God and from Pentecostal Holiness groups in the USA. No other Canadians were sent out until the 1940s. However, the seed planted and watered by these pioneer Pentecostals produced a bountiful harvest a generation later when a mighty tide of revival swept over Argentina.

The Pentecostal work in Brazil did not get underway in earnest until the close of the Second World War. The delay in evangelizing South American countries may be attributed to several causes: the shortage of workers and financial resources in the sending countries, the Great Depression, and the vigorous opposition from the Roman Catholic Church. In spite of the progress made in the decades before the war, South America could be characterized generally, in the words of James Skinner, as "the Neglected Continent."[33]

One geographical region, abutting South America, which was not neglected was the West Indies. Pentecostal missions work was undertaken on the islands early in this century. Robert and Elizabeth Jamieson went to the area in 1905 as Holiness missionaries. When the Jamiesons left their home in Mansfield, Massachusetts, the only funds they had were the proceeds from the sale of their furniture. Miraculously, a shipowner offered to transport their missions supplies at no cost to their new home on the island of St. Croix. People in the little Holiness mission in Massachusetts had promised to help, but Jamieson recollected that "we were well aware that we had embarked on a life of faith in the promise of God: and never once during all the years did our Father fail us." The services were held on the street and two souls were saved the first night. Later meetings were frequently disrupted by wild and drunken rowdies, sometimes urged on by the local priest. Once a man assaulted Jamieson with a horsewhip. He was rescued when a friendly storekeeper — a powerful man — sheltered him in his store and threatened to beat any one who touched the missionary. In the face of this kind of persecution, the Jamiesons persevered and built a church on St. Croix in 1906 which held 400 people.

Spiritual victories were still accompanied by tests of their faith. On one occasion the Jamiesons had only a few crusts of bread to eat. After prayer, Jamieson was led by God to a beehive under his cottage floor — now they had bread and honey. Several evangelistic trips to other islands helped to establish groups of believers. At Montserrat, a national was converted and later ordained for the Pentecostal ministry. He was the first of many islanders who helped to evangelize the West Indies. It was on Montserrat that the missionary was arrested for preaching and his congregation forcibly dispersed by the police. Undaunted, the people simply returned to the meeting tent and crawled under the flaps. The police were not only obliged to release the preacher, but the police inspector himself later requested Jamieson's forgiveness for the actions taken against him. By the time the Jamiesons went home on their first furlough in 1910, they had founded churches on several islands. Their converts formed the nucleus of what later came to be the Pilgrim Holiness Church of the West Indies.

One of the chief reasons for the Jamiesons' furlough was to inquire more fully into the Pentecostal Movement, about which they had been reading. While at a camp meeting in Vermont, they both received the Baptism in the Holy Spirit and spoke in tongues. With their new-found experience, the couple returned to the West Indies. When the Jamiesons testified about their Pentecostal Baptism to the officials of the Holiness Church, they were dismissed. To avoid controversy, they moved to Montserrat in 1912 and began Pentecostal meetings. Church officials on that island attempted to dissuade people from associating with the missionary couple. One spokesman, who had accepted the message brought by the Jamiesons, verbalized his response to the church officials in rather blunt language: "We know what you have, and we know what we have now, and we don't want you." This was the beginning of a very effective outreach on the island. A later outpouring of the Holy Spirit saw

8 / THE REGIONS BEYOND: 1907-1940

men and women receive the Pentecostal fullness in their homes, in the church, and even in the fields.

The scene of action for Jamieson shifted to Newfoundland for a brief period when Alice Garrigus, the founder of the Pentecostal work in that region, invited him to assist her. For seven months he labored in St. John's where he sometimes faced physical danger as a Pentecostal preacher. Once, the husband of a woman he was to baptize vowed to shoot the preacher. Jamieson simply arranged first to baptize all the other candidates, and then the woman in question. He reasoned, with childlike faith and heroic courage, that by baptizing the others before the wife of the threatening husband, he would have finished his God-given work before he was shot. The record shows that the husband was suddenly seized with violent pains about the time of the baptismal service and never showed up![34]

After returning to the West Indies, the Jamiesons engaged in constant evangelism. Ruth Pemberton and Clara Siemens arrived from Canada in 1918 and settled as pastors in St. Kitts. The Jamiesons moved on to Barbados and held meetings in an undertaker's warehouse. Coffins were simply pushed aside for the meetings. In 1923, they conducted services in Trinidad where Jamieson was attacked and nearly killed by a man insane with rage over the work of the Pentecostal church. The missionary recovered from his injuries, but refused to press charges against his assailant. The man later lost all his wealth, saw his wife go blind, and was reduced to abject poverty. Such possible consequences did not go unnoticed by other would-be persecutors.

The work went forward with such success that Jamieson realized the time had come for some form of religious organization. In 1926 he affiliated with the PAOC and in turn became the first Canadian-appointed director of the West Indies mission. The PAOC provided $300 a month for support and took steps to set up a local training centre for national workers.[35] A new outreach was initiated in Diego Martin where the first service saw the entire congregation move to the altar to seek God. A church building was later purchased and renovated through funds provided from Canada as a memorial to the late husband of Mabel Cunningham of Ontario.

Some of the earliest Canadian recruits for missions work on the islands were Harry and Marguerite Eggleton, who arrived from Vancouver in 1927. They took over the church in Woodbrook so the Jamiesons could continue as itinerant evangelists. It was some years later, when more missionaries were available, and when advancing age made frequent travelling difficult, that Jamieson gave up his beloved preaching tours. Harry Eggleton had pastored several churches in British Columbia and had witnessed the healing power of God in the meetings of Dr. Charles S. Price. He put his experience to good use in the West Indies. For 30 years, he and his wife provided ministry and supervision for the national workers. By the time the Second World War was over, the West Indies field had developed to the point where a district superintendent was needed. Harry Eggleton was chosen for the post.

Kenneth and Edith Stevenson came from Ontario to assist in the 1930s and for a time pastored a large Pentecostal assembly in Trinidad. But Liberia was the land of their calling, and when that field was again open to them, they returned to it.

At various times during the 1940s, the West Indies had up to 26 Canadian missionaries. Eventually, the work which the Jamiesons founded became a self-governing denomination, in cooperative fellowship with the PAOC, with headquarters in Trinidad. Although his wife died in 1948, Jamieson carried on a few more years until poor health ended his active ministry. He died in 1961. His passing marked the end of an era in pioneering by Pentecostal missions.

Endnotes

1. G. C. Slager, letter to W. E. McAlister, March 29, 1954, typed copy in PAOC Archives.
2. "Historical Sketch of the Beginnings, 1905-1925," a summary of early missions activities, undated and unsigned, but probably compiled by G. A. Chambers, typed copy in PAOC Archives.
3. Thomas Wm. Miller, taped interview with Gordon F. Atter, April 30, 1984, tape on file in Eastern Pentecostal Bible College library, Peterborough, ON.
4. Charles W. Chawner, "A Cry from the Dark Continent", *The Promise*, 12 (February 1909), 4-5.
5. Charles and Emma Chawner, *Called to Zululand: A Story of God's Leading* (Toronto: for the author, 1923).
6. Charles W. Chawner, *The Promise*, 15 (March 1910), 6.
7. Thomas Wm. Miller, taped interview with W. E. McAlister, May 3, 1984, tape on file in EPBC library, Peterborough, ON).
8. Gloria Grace Kulbeck, "C. W. Chawner: Apostle to the Zulus," *The Pentecostal Testimony* (December 1959), 9-10; see also Mrs. C. A. (Ingrid) Chawner, "A Great Man Hath Fallen in Israel," *The Pentecostal Testimony* (March 15, 1949), 7,14; .
9. "Called Into His Vineyard," *The Pentecostal Testimony* (April 1927); C. Austin Chawner, *Have You Heard About Mozambique?* PAOC Archives; see funeral eulogy, "In Memory of Dr. Charles Austin Chawner, BA, B.Th., DD, October 20, 1963, PAOC Archives; and George Upton, *The Miracle of Mozambique* (Toronto: PAOC, 1980).

8 / THE REGIONS BEYOND: 1907-1940

10. Thomas Wm. Miller, "Austin and Ingrid Chawner: Pioneers in Northern Transvaal and Mozambique," *The Pentecostal Testimony* (August 1988), 10-11, 24.

11. "2nd Annual Meeting, PAOC Montreal, Nov. 23-25, 1920," *Minute Book,* PAOC Archives; see also the "General Assemblies of the PAOC at Kitchener, Nov. 25-28, 1919;" "Special Meeting of the General Assembly of the PAOC at Montreal, Sept 21, 1928;" and report on the "Eastern District Conference, Toronto, July 29-Aug. 1, 1924." All sources in the *PAOC Minute Book.*

12. Two interesting studies of the Great Depression are Barry Broadfoot, *Ten Lost Years, 1929-39* (Don Mills: General Publishing, 1975), and James H. Gray, *The Roar of the Twenties* (Toronto: MacMillan, 1975); "What God Hath Wrought," *The Pentecostal Testimony* (April 1932), 4-7; and Donald Gee, *Upon All Flesh: A Pentecostal World Tour* (Springfield: Gospel Publishing House, 1935), pp. 104-107.

13. "Looking Back on 60 Years of Missions," *The Pentecostal Testimony* (September 1974), 12-13.

14. Marian Keller, *Twenty Years in Africa, 1913 - 1933: Retrospect and Prospect* (Toronto: Full Gospel Publishing House, 1933), pp. 13-14; see also Valone Sly and others, compilers and editors of *Parry Sound Pentecostal Tabernacle: Sixty Years of Service.*

15. "Death of Rev. Karl Wittich and Rev. Clarence Grothaus in German East Africa," *The Christian Evangel*, 2:19 (May 9, 1914), 2, reprinted in *Pentecostal Evangel* (August 19, 1973); see also Sly, note 14.

16. "Minutes of the General Conference and Eastern District Conference, Arnprior, Aug. 27-31, 1923," *The Pentecostal Testimony* (September 1923), 7.

17. Marian Keller, *Twenty Years in Africa*, p. 45.

18. Carman Lynn, in conversation with Thomas Wm. Miller, May 1986.

19. "The James Skinners — thirty-eight years service," *The Pentecostal Testimony* (September 1974), 8-9; and Lila Skinner, "Memoirs of the McAlister Family," handwritten manuscript, March 1978.

20. Annie Cressman, "A Tribute to Miss Sophie Nygaard, 1885-1976," incorporated in her eulogy, July 4, 1976.

21. Ruth E. Le Pers, *Living in the Land of the White Man's Grave* (Winnipeg: Wesley Press, 1933), p. 7.

22. Thomas Wm. Miller, taped interview with Annie Cressman, January 31, 1986.

23. "A Trip to Abingdon," *The Promise*, 12 (February 1909), 3-6; *The Promise*, 14 (October 1909), 2; and Gordon F. Atter, *Down Memory's Lane: An Autobiography* (Port Colborne, for the author, 1986).

24. Coralee Haist, *How Great Oh God Thou Art* (Hong Kong: Yee Tin Tong Printing Press, 1969).

25. George R. Upton, "John Rutherford Spence Called Home," PAOC Archives, 1976); see also "Last Mile of the Way," *The Pentecostal Testimony* (August 1976); "Pen Portraits of Pioneers: Rev. J. Rutherford Spence," *The Pentecostal Testimony* (July 1960), 10, 33; and "J. Rutherford Spence: Birthday Biography," *The Pentecostal Testimony* (October 1970), 5, 26. Spence also wrote a small booklet on his prison experiences, "Behind Barbed Wires," PAOC Archives; Don Kauffman, "China Receives the Full Gospel: Phoebe Holmes Spence," *The Pentecostal Testimony* (July 1988), 14-15.

26. Thomas Wm. Miller, "Portraits of Pentecostal Pioneers: Ivan Kauffman, Clare Scratch," The Pentecostal Testimony (July 1987), 20-21.

27. Quoted by Miller, "Portraits of Pentecostal Pioneers," 21.

28. Ibid.; "Pastor Carman Clare Scratch," *Temple Times*, 13:47 (November 22, 1974); and "In Memoriam: Pastor Carman Clare Scratch," order of service for funeral, PAOC Archives.

29. "Rev. and Mrs. J. E. Morrison," mimeographed biographical sketch, author unknown, PAOC Archives; Roy Clifford Spaetzel, *History of the Kitchener Gospel Temple, 1909-1974* (Kitchener: Kitchener Gospel Temple, 1974).

30. M. Grace Brown, *The Orient Calls: The Story of William Butcher* (Saskatoon: for the author), p. 15.

31. See *The Promise*, 12 (February 1909), 7; 15 (March 1910), 2; and *The Pentecostal Testimony* (October 1926), 8, and (November 1934), 1.

32. *The Pentecostal Testimony* (October 1926), 8; and *70 Years at London Gospel Temple* (London: London Gospel Temple, 1980), pp. 9, 14.

33. J. W. Skinner, *Golden Harvest,* (Toronto: PAOC, 1970), p. 3.

34. Myrtle Barker, *The Jamiesons: As Told to Myrtle Barker* (Mississauga, ON: PAOC), pp. 15, 35-36.

35. See Barker, note 34, pp. 43-44. For an early perspective on PAOC missions policy, see "Missionary Policy," *The Pentecostal Testimony* (October 1926), 7-9.

Chapter 9

COMING OF AGE
1939-1958

The 20-year period beginning with the Second World War was one of great importance for the Pentecostal Assemblies of Canada. It marked the commencement of a global conflict which reshaped the world and also the start of the long cold war between the USA and the USSR. What is especially remarkable for the PAOC is that the development of denominational maturity and institutional efficiency evolved throughout the years of international tension. Indeed, these two decades witnessed the development of the Fellowship to its highest level of administrative efficiency since its establishment in 1919.

The disastrous social and economic impact of the Depression was just beginning to decline toward the end of the '30s when Canada became embroiled in the Second World War. Hitler's rise to prominence as chancellor of Germany led to the annexation of Austria, an assault on Czechoslovakia, and the invasion of Poland. Within a few month's time, the nations of Germany, Italy, and Japan were aligned against the Allies — Britain, France, and members of the British Commonwealth, including Canada. Hundreds of thousands of men were recruited for the Armed Forces with two Canadian divisions heading overseas very soon after the onset of the war. Canada, in a relatively short period of time, shifted from the pain of the Depression to the difficulties associated with a wartime economy.

The first major action involving Canadians was the 1942 Dieppe Raid, a disastrous offensive which resulted in 3,300 losing their lives or being taken prisoners at the hands of the Germans. Later, Canadians fought with the British Eighth Army in North Africa, in Italy, and on the Continent after the D Day Invasion of 1943. Canadians were particularly effective during the battle of the Falaise Gap in 1944. They played a key role in the liberation of the Netherlands. When the newly liberated Dutch faced

9 / COMING OF AGE: 1939-1958

starvation, the Canadian army rushed in supplies in a rescue operation which was never forgotten by the host country.

The Canadians ("Canucks"), a part of the multinational force which invaded Germany, helped bring about the unconditional surrender of the Nazi regime — one of the most infamous and godless powers in world history. During the war years, over six million Jews were exterminated in Nazi death camps like Dachau and Buchenwald. Pentecostals in the Armed Forces were motivated by the biblical promise respecting Israel in Genesis 12:3, "I will bless those who bless you, and whoever curses you, I will curse."

The war against Japan in the Pacific arena was brought to an end by the atomic bomb attacks on Hiroshima and Nagasaki in August of 1945. Canadian troops were prepared to transfer to the Far East after the defeat of Germany, but instead were able to return home to be demobilized. The tragic consequences of war left nearly 50,000 Canadians dead and thousands more wounded out of the one million men and women from Canada who served in the military ranks.

As part of its defense effort, Canada financed its own wartime production. The national debt rose by 10 billion dollars. Huge quantities of war materials were shipped overseas, as well as the foods and grains to sustain the civilian population. From 1939 to 1945 an estimated 60 per cent of Canada's national expenditure was for the war effort.[1] This focus required the strict domestic rationing of all the necessities of life in the homeland by the Wartime Prices and Trade Board. Construction materials and gasoline were nearly non-existent for civilian use. The effects upon churches and pastoral ministries can be easily imagined.

Less easily understood was the impact the war had on the social fabric of Canada during six years of total commitment to an international conflict. The Pentecostal Movement was profoundly affected as thousands of its young adherents went into the services. Churches in some places were left with only teenagers, women, and older male members. The Bible schools had chiefly female students. Great difficulties were encountered in all the areas of PAOC evangelism.

When the First World War occurred between 1914 and 1918, the infant Pentecostal Movement was relatively unaffected: its membership was very small and it had no formal organization. Consequently, there were few Pentecostals in the Armed Forces. Besides, there was a rather strong anti-war sentiment among most evangelicals, including Pentecostals during that period. Pacifism was a very powerful force at the turn of the century. It was not until 1917 that the United States was able to neutralize sufficiently its anti-war stance to permit participation in the conflict.

Some radical changes, with reference to the PAOC, had taken place by

COMING OF AGE: 1939-1958 / 9

the time of the second global conflict. In the 1940s, the Fellowship had about 45,000 regular attenders in its churches and nearly 1,300 credential holders.[2] Large numbers of its young people enlisted in what was perceived by the PAOC generally to be a "crusade in Europe" against oppression and evil. Although the Nazi atrocities only gradually came to light near the end of the war, there had been little doubt from the outset that fascism was antithetical to Christianity. The American Assemblies of God had the resources to put Pentecostal chaplains into the armed services, but this was not possible in Canada.

Some preachers thought the war could be the beginning of the "Great Tribulation" foretold in Scripture, but most seemed to recognize it as a desperate struggle against both a human and spiritual enemy. In 1941, a young minister by the name of Mark Buntain wrote in the *Testimony* that young believers should enlist in the army of the Lord as well as in the armed forces of their country. Gradually, the official magazine came to feature articles of special interest to military men and women, with such titles as "Attention Christian Youth! Have You Enlisted?" "Soldier Boys at Home and Abroad;" "What Can We Do for the Soldiers?" "Servicemen's Department;" and "Overseas News." One article gave the following list of Pentecostal men already in England: Walter and Phil Wragg of Radium, Sask.; John Blakely of Maxwell, Ont.; Bob Wilson of Merritt, B.C.; Maurice Johnston of Lindsay, Ont.; Bill Stanley and Dan Cucheron of Vernon, B.C.; Morley Evans of Toronto; Gordon Barres of Portage La Prairie, Man.; and Leslie Rafuse of Montreal.

One example which demonstrates the involvement of Pentecostals is the record of 39 men from Calvary Temple in Winnipeg who were engaged in 1943 in the war overseas. Copies of *The Pentecostal Testimony* were regularly mailed to the personnel in the forces.[3] Other gospel literature was also sent to them. Letters home, thought to be censored by the authorities, were often read from the pulpits and sometimes reprinted in the *Testimony*.

Earnest prayer was made for the success of the Allies in the great conflict, and especially for the safety and spiritual welfare of sons and daughters. Letters home told not only of needs but of victories won by faithful Christian witnesses. A letter from Lloyd McFarlene, to his friends in the Winnipeg Bible school, recounted how McFarlene recuperated from his wounds in a hospital in Newfoundland. At the same time, he and some friends were holding meetings for other soldiers. Another letter from Jake Fehr, written while he was convalescing in England after being wounded in action, appealed for the prayerful interest of the believers, "All the boys stress the great need of your prayers that they may be kept strong and true and used in bringing others to Christ." Ivar Wendelbo

247

9 / COMING OF AGE: 1939-1958

reported on his work at an evangelistic mission hall in England. Miles Sturliff, then stationed at Prince George, B.C., was directing two Sunday schools and a fellowship lodge.

Various editions of *The Gleaner*, the Western Bible College paper, included accounts of the efforts being made by Pentecostal servicemen in evangelism, both in Canada and overseas. Many young men were active in preaching, witnessing, and working for the Lord in a variety of ways and places: to name a few, Peter Sly was stationed with the navy at Prince Rupert, B.C., and Robert Hoover and Don Roulston were in England. Some letters home told of dramatic deliverances from injury and death; for example, Dave Sadler, serving with the navy during the invasion of Europe, was transferred from his ship, H.M.C.S. Fraser, just before it sank in 1945.

Many of these young Pentecostal people matured and had their values refined during the heat of conflict. Sgt. E. B. Barry noted that four years in the forces meant meeting men of every race, religion, and culture with opportunities to discuss the issues of life. He added, "For such times as these, study is necessary to enlarge the field of thought and to illuminate the mind to truth." When the war ended there was a great influx of veterans into the Bible schools after 1945. There also was a devastating period of counting the cost paid by Canadians in the process of fighting for basic freedoms: the church at Victoria, B.C., for example, lost four out of its 24 members who were sent to the war.[4]

Enrollment in the PAOC Bible schools, which had been understandably low during the conflict, took a sudden jump in the later months of 1944 and in 1945. Some statistics for the Bible college in Toronto, the largest of the PAOC institutions, reflected this development. In 1941, the school had 90 students, nearly two-thirds of whom were women. Enrollment rose to 180 in 1944 and to 209 in 1945. By the time the first post-war class graduated in 1948, there were 29 female and 30 male graduates — a dramatic shift in the ratio from earlier years.[5] The war veterans were eligible for relocation benefits, including education, and many Pentecostals used these grants to pay for their Bible school training in preparation for full-time ministry.

Despite the dislocations caused by the war and its aftermath, the two decades under review marked the "coming of age" of The Pentecostal Assemblies of Canada. In this regard, the PAOC was following the historic pattern of revivalistic movements: from the first phase of beginnings, through the second phase of formal organization, to a third phase of maximum efficiency. These three developments have been charted by David O. Moberg in his sociological study of churches (*The Church as a Social Institution*) and by this writer in his analysis of revival movements in history (*Ripe for Revival*).[6] Moberg's study of American denominations found that there are typically five phases of development in every organization. The first three listed above are invariably followed by fourth and fifth stages of increased institutionalization. In the end, the organization usually becomes formal, bureaucratic, and obsolescent.

In *Ripe for Revival* a similar pattern was identified in church history. A renewal movement would bring new vitality to earnest believers and a revivalistic sect would be born. Zealous evangelism then brought an increase in membership, development of informal organization, and improvements in operational efficiency. This historic process can be discerned in the development of the PAOC from its inception as a revivalistic movement in 1906 through to 1958.

The elaboration of denominational legislative machinery went on swiftly during and after the tumultuous war years. These two decades — the '40s and '50s — marked the transition of the PAOC from the status of an evangelistic sect to that of a denomination.[7] To the seven legislative regions into which Canada earlier had been divided by the PAOC, there were added in this period a number of Branch Conferences. German Pentecostal churches, for example, organized a conference in Leduc, Alberta, in 1940 at which the nine delegates chose Wilhelm Kowalski to be their first superintendent. Their intention was to establish a formal relationship with the PAOC. At the 1944 General Conference in Hamilton, when the question of a working relationship with the German and Slavic Pentecostal Assemblies in Canada came on the floor, the delegates assigned the General Executive the responsibility of granting to "the various foreign speaking groups recognition as a branch" of the PAOC. The "Official List of Ministers and Missionaries Together with a Directory Of Assemblies" (revised to May 1, 1947) referred to five "Foreign-speaking Branch Conferences:" namely, German, French, Slavic, Finnish, and Italian. The report of the General Secretary-Treasurer to the 1954 General Conference stated there were at that time "11 French-speaking assemblies, 26 German, 20 Slavic, 8 Finnish and 8 Italian." In 1960, the criteria for Branch Conference status stipulated that the branch should have at least twelve churches which would conduct services in the language of the group. It should be noted that the Italian churches did not function as a Branch Conference and later, while maintaining a fraternal relationship with the PAOC, established their own organization.

Special reference should be made to the status of the French-speaking churches. At a time when terms were not used with the same precision, the French-speaking churches were lumped unfortunately with "foreign-speaking" groups. The work in Quebec had for some years been conducted under the aegis of the Eastern Ontario and Quebec District.

9 / COMING OF AGE: 1939-1958

When French-speaking believers first applied to the PAOC for formal recognition as a separate entity, the General Executive voted in April of 1949 to endorse the formation of a French-speaking conference. Under conditions then prevailing, it was decided that this new conference should function as part of the PAOC Overseas Missions Department.

In the 1950s, the superintendents of these language groups were invited to sit on the General Executive, although the formal adoption of this proposal did not come until a later date. By 1958, the national governing body of the PAOC had grown from its initial membership of three ordained men to include five national officers, three members-at-large, seven district superintendents, Branch Conference superintendents, and the superintendent of the French Conference.

National conferences were held biennially and district conferences annually, with officers in both jurisdictions elected for two-year periods. Delegates to the 1946 General Conference voted to enlarge representation to include as voting members -- at both district and national conferences -- all ordained ministers, missionaries, women workers with the ministerial license for women, and official lay delegates. The number of such lay delegates depended upon the size of the membership of each congregation. While it became technically possible for the conferences to be controlled by the votes of lay delegates because of their potential numbers, in practice this has never happened. Indeed, PAOC officials have continually urged local churches to send lay representatives to the conferences.

Other steps were taken in this period to make the operations of the General Executive as efficient as possible. The ever-increasing workload of the General Superintendent led, in 1952, to the election of two district superintendents to act as assistant general superintendents, one in the East and one in the West. In practice, the role of the assistants has been confined to largely ceremonial exercises. All of these structural developments in the policy-making and administrative bodies of the Fellowship occurred during the terms of three consecutive General Superintendents: D. N. Buntain (1936-1944), C. B. Smith (1944-1952), and W. E. McAlister (1952-1962). Modifications and alterations of national and district legislative machinery were made in the years following, but the fundamental organizational structure of the PAOC was completed by 1958.[8]

In the period under study, the number of Pentecostals in the country had grown to 144,000. There were then about 140 missionaries, 1,350 clergy and licensed lay workers, and about 650 PAOC churches. The steady increase in membership, resources, and responsibilities led to the expansion of the administrative infrastructure which has been officially described as "departmentalization."[9]

An increased number of missionaries and new mission fields demanded more refined modes of operation. While overseas missions had always occupied the attention of the leadership of the developing Fellowship, a decision was made in 1944 to set up the Overseas Missions Department. Prior to this time, the General Secretary-Treasurer (R. E. McAlister, 1919-32; A. G. Ward, 1932-38; and C. M. Wortman, 1939-44) had also served as Missionary Secretary. G. R. Upton was elected to be the first full-time Missionary Secretary in 1944.

Identifiable groups within the local church had developed and demanded special attention. Children and young people in the churches needed systematic instruction in the Bible and organized activities appropriate to their age groups. The introduction of national Sunday school and youth departments was the response to this need. Women and men also had unique requirements — they not only needed to be ministered to but also needed challenges which would employ their special talents and interests in ministry to others. The formation of national departments to supervise women's and men's activities occurred in due time.

The five operating Bible schools needed direction, financial support, and development of faculty and facilities. It was natural for a national department to emerge. As national home missions endeavors received more attention, there was a trend to separate these ministries from overseas missions and to place the oversight of them with the Home Missions Committee. Administratively, the home missions emphasis came to be linked with the Bible college portfolio.

The process of "departmentalization" merits closer examination. Of particular interest is the development in this period of a religious education program for children and youth. At the beginning of the Second World War, there were about 10,000 pupils in attendance at PAOC Sunday schools, but there was no systematic approach to biblical instruction at the local level and no national organization to provide any guidance. Teaching the children was often a sideline for pastors; sometimes it was aimed merely at keeping the youngsters from disrupting the adult meetings. But it was quickly recognized by perceptive men and women that the Sunday school was an excellent means of providing religious education for the children of church members and opportunities for evangelism among children of non-churched families. Wartime shortages made enlargement of church facilities impossible. With the arrival of peace and more favorable economic factors, congregations began to renovate their buildings and erect new ones. Many of the churches made provision for Sunday schools in their building programs.

9 / COMING OF AGE: 1939-1958

Nationally, the PAOC encouraged growth in this field of ministry by establishing the National Sunday School Department in 1940. Lorne C. Honderick served as part-time director. He was a zealous promoter of child evangelism and education and wrote numerous promotional articles for the *Testimony*, such as, "Have You a Missionary Heart? We Need Your Help to Reach Children of Untouched Areas with the Gospel Story," "Bible Truth Crusade for Children," "Better Sunday School Department," and "Thirty Reasons Why The Early Conversion of Children Should Engage The Attention of Every True Christian."[10]

The 1940s witnessed the growth in attendance at some PAOC church schools to 200 and 300 students each Sunday. Regional conventions sprung up to promote the Sunday school program and provide pastors with guidelines in directing these schools and in recruiting staff. Contests were held and awards given for successful growth. Vacation Bible schools were organized as an effective means of summer evangelism among children. From 1943 to 1945, for example, there were about 160 evangelistic summer programs, with an enrollment of almost 15,000 children. Honderick faithfully directed the department until he was succeeded by James Montgomery as full-time director in 1947.

Montgomery brought a vision of an expanded program. His own background in Northern Ireland, which was closely connected with religious education, gave him a keen personal interest in the work. Montgomery noted that one of the weaknesses of the Sunday schools in the 1940s was the lack of training among the teachers. Montgomery travelled constantly across Canada promoting the concept of "a trained teacher in every classroom." He organized the first National Sunday School Convention in Toronto in 1949, with 116 delegates in attendance.

By the '50s, it was realized that one hour a week was not enough to properly instruct children and to build Christian character. The 1954 General Conference called for the development of "a definite program for mid-week activities and training for Junior and Teenage boys and girls." A program entitled "Pentecostal Crusaders" was designed for children ages 7 to 14. Montgomery directed the program, ably assisted by Edgar O'Brien and Bernard Parkinson. The basic goals of the Crusader program were to develop Christian character, to impart religious knowledge, and to provide wholesome recreation. By 1958 there were over 600 children involved in the program in 50 local units.

Curiously, the same 1954 General Conference gave recognition to another program for girls, known as "Missionary Action Girls," and authorized the establishment of a department under the direction of the WMC. Later the name would change to "Canadian Missionettes." The existence of two effective mid-week programs — Missionettes for girls only and Pentecostal Crusaders for boys and girls — would be a source of some tension for years to come.

Early evidence of the Fellowship's interest in social concerns shows up in a ministry to unwed mothers and their children. Mabel and Joseph Hutchinson founded Bethel Home for Girls in their own home in June 1928. The work grew steadily over the years as the Hutchinsons ministered to hundreds of young women in need. After the death of "Mother" Hutchinson in 1959, the PAOC agreed to take over the management of the home and brought it under the umbrella of the Pentecostal Benevolent Association. Pearl Hutchinson took over the reins as administrator after the death of her mother-in-law. Bethel was a place of refuge for girls in trouble but it was also a place to find God. Some of its graduates enrolled in Bible school and a number have entered the ministry both in the homeland and overseas.[11]

The youth program, known as "Christ's Ambassadors" and borrowed from the American Assemblies of God, was set up in 1949 at the instigation of Montgomery, who had the direction of youth ministries added to his Sunday school responsibilities. The emphasis on evangelism and missions was evident from the beginning:

> The organization was designed to minister not only to the needs of Canadian Youth, but also to give them an objective to do something worthwhile — to reach the world's millions with the Gospel.[12]

The C.A. program caught on immediately. Regular weekly youth services become a feature in most Pentecostal assemblies. The themes of such meetings were identified as "the four Cs — Christ, Companionship, Courtship, and Careers." C.A. services typically were held on Fridays in the local church.

Pentecostal youth long had demonstrated an interest in evangelistic outreach, but had been given little direction at the national level. Maritime young people, for example, had paid for three tents to be used in summer evangelism in 1946. And young people in British Columbia, led by Pastor M. E. Kirkpatrick, raised $3,000 to construct a mobile church. It was a "tabernacle on wheels" which could be taken to new areas, and set up quickly as a small church hall.

Canadian young people were mobilized to donate the money to buy a vehicle for a missionary in Africa. Out of this initial purchase emerged the "Speed the Light" (another American title) program. Since its inauguration, funds have been collected to send Canadian missionaries trucks, cars, motorbikes, bicycles, public address systems, tents, lighting equipment, books, and tracts. The program has been extremely successful

9 / COMING OF AGE: 1939-1958

in "putting wheels under every PAOC missionary family" and in giving Pentecostal youth an insight into world missions. It has been Canadianized and renamed "Wing the Word."[13]

Youth rallies, modelled after those sponsored by the Youth For Christ organization, proved popular. However, Pentecostal youth rallies reflected, in their conduct and their aims, the same emphases as the conventions and camp meetings held for their seniors. The PAOC youth rally played a very significant role in the spiritual development of thousands of young people. Many of these teenagers were in small churches, with few peers with whom to fellowship. The area-wide rallies provided these youth with social contact among a larger assembly of committed Pentecostals.

The two decades before 1958 marked a period of lingering hostility towards the Pentecostal message: persecution and prejudice had not entirely died out. Young people were subjected to these pressures, and the youth rallies provided them with encouragement and opportunities for reconsecration to their Lord. A system of regional rallies was developed. Soon, youth rallies were appearing in each district across Canada, and were vigorously promoted by the *Testimony* with such articles as "Why Young People Need a Service of Their Own." One of the first of these Pentecostal gatherings specifically for youth took place in British Columbia in 1949. From these cooperative efforts came further developments — the organization of the district "C.A. Convention," the appointment of individuals to give overall supervision to youth work at the district level, and youth camps.

The organization of the women of the Fellowship into groups known as the Women's Missionary Society is a fascinating story. When the first Pentecostal workers went overseas, there was no formal organization to support them. Their chief source of funds were friends in their former local assemblies. The keen interest in foreign missions that characterized the PAOC from its earliest days led a number of church congregations to make attempts to supply the missionaries with money and supplies. A rudimentary program thus developed at the local level, spontaneous in nature and not thought of as anything more elaborate than a congregational involvement in missions. But the groundwork was laid for the development, after 1919, of a program of systematic and efficient support of the PAOC missions in overseas countries. It seems that the women were the earliest local group to voluntarily take on the task of missionary support throughout Canada.

This pattern of *ad hoc* development of support programs was typical of the early Canadian approach. Over several decades there emerged a continuous process of development and organization among the women at the local, regional, and national levels. As the sheer number of functioning women's groups revealed the need for a national organization, the Women's Missionary Society was set up at the national office in Toronto. The first national director appointed was Ethel Bingeman. The women's organization was placed under the general supervision of Missionary Secretary George Upton in 1944. Directors were appointed for each district and eventually there were directors for each local group as well. The 1950 General Conference in Saskatoon approved a constitution and changed the name to Women's Missionary Council. The object of the organization was to encourage women to pray for the missionaries and to cooperate in support of any mission work endorsed by the PAOC. Twenty-nine years later as the objectives of the organization broadened to include a variety of ministries for women, the name would change again — Women's Ministries.

A number of periodicals for women were produced at both the district and the national level to tie these groups together and to make their individual efforts more efficient. One magazine, *News and Views*, was published for many years. It provided information on women's activities in local churches and their contributions to both local and foreign needs.

Ethel Bingeman offered 10 years of inspired leadership to the national WMC and saw its membership increase to about 35,000 women by 1953. The women were organized into 320 local associations. Their contributions to worldwide evangelism, both in prayer and material support, were very significant. When Bingeman retired to become the wife of missionary Robert Jamieson, she was succeeded by Gladys Lemmon.

Lemmon, who had for years taught the "Missions" course at Western Bible College in Winnipeg, brought a lifelong devotion to home and overseas ministries to her new post. Under her direction, the number of WMC groups grew to over 400 in Canada, 26 in the West Indies, and two in Bermuda. She once described the progress of WMC work up to 1957 as follows:

> ... thousands of our Christian women are praying, visiting hospitals and shut-ins, doing house-to-house visitations, wrapping thousands of pounds of literature, distributing thousands of tracts and standing back of all our Christian workers at home and abroad.[14]

The organization of the Pentecostal men was, once again, the product of a spontaneous effort to assist in evangelism at home and abroad. The personal involvement of laymen in church work may be traced to the very beginning of Pentecostalism in Canada. The efforts of Elmer Cantelon

9 / COMING OF AGE: 1939-1958

and Emil Schwab to set up the first camp meeting in Manitoba is a notable example. But no male-oriented organizations, similar to the Women's Missionary Council, appeared until about 1950. A number of men at Calvary Temple in Winnipeg that year set up what they called a "Men's Missionary Council." Its goal was to correspond directly with the missionaries, pray for them, and try to assist with practical support. One of the unique features of this group was its self-assessment of a yearly fee for each member. Initially, the program was directed to home missionaries in Manitoba, but its interests widened to include mission efforts worldwide.

Widespread interest in such programs prompted the national office to establish a men's organization in 1955, under the direction of James Montgomery, the national officer in charge of Sunday schools and Christ's Ambassadors. Two of its stated goals involved evangelism by men among their own communities, and further development of the ties among men in the entire Canadian fellowship. Soon there were over 30 groups in operation and many novel ways were found for involvement in church-related work. One such innovation was the undertaking of construction projects in the local churches and at the district camps. Later, the Men's Fellowship would participate in a ministry known as "Work Force," which involved teams of men going to home and foreign mission locations to carry out construction and renovation projects. To coordinate the activities of the early men's groups, a number of periodicals were published by the national office.

The rapid influx of war veterans to the Bible schools brought to the forefront the need for national direction in the coordination of ministerial education. As early as 1931 at the General Conference in London, a National Bible College Committee was put in place "for the supervision of all Bible School matters, including the curriculum, and general policy of all Canadian Bible Schools." In 1946, the national committee on Bible schools and colleges was activated with Dr. Purdie as chairman, Charles Ratz as secretary, and the Bible college principals as the other members. Subsequent development in this area resulted in the appointment of a National Bible College Committee in 1956 which would formulate and administer the "National Standard for Canadian Bible Colleges." The members of the '56 NBCC were H. H. Barber, John M. Watts, and Ralph Hornby. The number of national officers increased from four to five with the election in 1958 of Tom Johnstone as the first officer in charge of Home Missions and Bible Colleges.

The original constitution and by-laws of the PAOC had been revised in 1932. Further revision was undertaken in 1946 to keep pace with denominational growth. At the request of delegates at a General

Conference, a constitution for use of the various districts was formulated and adopted in 1946. The needs of the local church for some type of self-directing legislation was met in 1950 with the design of a "Local Church Constitution." This document, when adopted by individual churches, provided for a combined congregational-presbyterial form of government. It was congregational in that sovereignty in the fields of local government, finances, elections of officers, and choosing of pastors was in the hands of the congregation. It was presbyterial in that its self-government was delegated by the congregation to a board of deacons, working in cooperation with the pastor. This "presbygational" system, as former General Superintendent Tom Johnstone called it, was extended to the district and the national levels of government.

Pastors and lay delegates elected, from among their own number, those officials who would direct the affairs of the PAOC at the district and the national administrative centres. All regulations, respecting ordination and the holding of credentials, were formed by majority decisions of delegates at a General Conference. Since the foundational decisions have been made by the rank-and-file credential holders and lay delegates, government by a detached ecclesiastical bureaucracy has been avoided by the PAOC.

Tom Johnstone, who participated in the deliberations of the conferences which brought many of the above-described developments to a final form by the late-50s, was well qualified to draw conclusions about the makeup of the Fellowship. In an interview in 1984, Johnstone noted:

> The danger of organization is that it introduces coercive measures as substitutes for voluntary and cooperative action. . . . You cause concern when you look upon your equals as unequals and set up rules to keep them in specified bounds.... The original structure of the PAOC put great stress upon the sovereignty of the local church... cooperation was voluntary. . . . All of us related to God in the same way — as a family, not a business. I think that some of the genius of the early PAOC inhered in that fact.[15]

Johnstone emphasized, in his recollection of the years of legislative and administrative development prior to 1958, that the process was not a "conscious one." It arose from the varying denominational backgrounds of the first two generations of PAOC leaders. The organizational structure of the Canadian Pentecostal Movement thus was the product of a pragmatic, adaptive mentality that drew on many types of theological concepts and ecclesiastical experiences. No doubt this approach shaped the kinds of ministerial qualifications that came to be the standard in the PAOC by 1958. There were then six categories of official ministerial standing, plus a certificate which was issued to lay workers.

9 / COMING OF AGE: 1939-1958

The "voice" for the Fellowship had been, from its start, *The Pentecostal Testimony*, founded by R. E. McAlister while he was pastoring in Ottawa. He used an old storm door suspended on two boxes for his composition table, and a handset press for printing. The first issue was distributed free of charge in December of 1920. Although funding was always uncertain, McAlister turned out the periodical for many years which served as a "cement" for the burgeoning Canadian Fellowship. His skills as a writer, editor, and publisher were of inestimable value to the growth of Pentecostalism. He helped shape the views of an entire generation of believers with respect to the organization of the PAOC, evangelism in the homeland, and missions overseas. The circulation of the *Testimony* grew steadily, reaching 12,000 subscriptions by 1958.

A logical development of McAlister's magazine venture was the establishment of a publishing department. The Full Gospel Publishing House was formed in 1927. Initially, it supplied Bibles and gospel literature to Canadian Pentecostals, most of which were imported from the Assemblies of God publishers in Springfield. Gradually, however, the FGPH became a publishing and distribution enterprise in its own right. Early receipts of $6,000 annually grew to nearly $200,000 in 1958.

One PAOC publishing project deserves special attention, for it represents an attempt by national leaders to provide the whole Fellowship with an historical and a theological rationale for its existence. The project was the printing in 1951 of Dr. J. E. Purdie's catechism, *Concerning The Faith*, which contained about 300 questions and answers to be used in the formal instruction of Pentecostals. Purdie's Anglican heritage was evident in his systematic approach to this method of religious indoctrination, but his Pentecostal position also was clear in his philosophical preface to the book. His object was to prove that Pentecostalism flowed out of the historic and orthodox principles of the Bible and the Early Church.

Half of a century after the outpouring of the Holy Spirit in Canada (1906-1958), the Pentecostal Fellowship had assumed a definite form with firmly held convictions. With the organizational process largely completed in that period, the PAOC emerged as a full-fledged denomination. In its seven District Conferences there were 671 assemblies, 500 ordained ministers, over 500 female workers and deaconesses, and 120 missionaries on foreign fields. In addition there were 81 congregations in its French and Branch Conferences and more than 80 churches in the Pentecostal Assemblies of Newfoundland which was in a fraternal relationship with the PAOC. Newfoundland Pentecostals numbered more than 15,000 on an island with a population of 420,000. Thus Newfoundland was, on a per capita basis, the "most

Pentecostal" part of Canada. By 1958, the PAOC had 15 regional camp meeting sites, and could boast of 632 Sunday schools with an enrollment of 68,000 students. The vast bulk of the membership in this Canadian Fellowship was under 30 years of age.

The numerical size and the relative youthful age are significant facts, given the rigorous standards of membership that were enforced throughout this period. Even the letdown in public morality that accompanied the Second World War was not permitted to influence PAOC standards of conduct. Leaders and preachers, youth workers and Sunday school teachers alike were unanimous in demanding a "separation from the world." The old Holiness Movement principles were deeply ingrained in the Canadian Fellowship. Members were abjured to abstain from tobacco, alcohol, dancing, theatre-going, and card-playing.[16] Critics of Pentecostalism frequently seized upon this aspect of the Fellowship to condemn its leaders as narrow-minded and intolerant. But such views did not prevail with all of the Canadian public for the number of Pentecostals grew from just over 5,000 in 1911 to 143,887 in 1961. Those statistics represented phenomenal growth for a religious group which had been so minuscule as to be nearly invisible. The federal census figures for 1961 indicated that all Pentecostals combined made up 0.8 per cent of the population.

The history of the PAOC, however, was not one of trouble-free development and continuous growth. In the late-40s and early-50s, the Fellowship faced a doctrinal threat so serious that its very existence was in question. That threat consisted of the so-called "New Order of the Latter Rain." The theological controversy had its origins in Saskatchewan, but spread its influence over much of North America and infected even the much larger Assemblies of God. AG historian Carl Brumback attributed the appearance of this sect within Pentecostalism as an almost inevitable consequence of rapid growth. He theorized that development had been so swift and growth so prodigious as to create a set of "secondary problems." Brumback thought that the concentration by leaders on the solution to growth problems may have led to "a deadness of soul." To buttress his argument, Brumback noted that the gifts of the Spirit (so much in evidence in the earlier decades) were less prominent in the '30s and '40s.[18]

There obviously was a great concern in Canada about the apparent decline in spiritual fervency. The *Testimony* in the 1940s printed numerous articles expressing alarm over the "settling down" of the movement and the need for more prayer for revival among the churches. It was in this climate that the "New Order of the Latter Rain" made its appearance. Its initial success can be attributed to the widespread perception that the Pentecostal Movement was then in need of spiritual renewal.

9 / COMING OF AGE: 1939-1958

The first evidence of a significant theological aberration in PAOC ranks emerged in the Bethel Bible Institute in Saskatoon in 1947. It was related to a form of ministry which had an honorable history among Pentecostals — the salvation-healing campaigns. Among the most prominent evangelists in the group at that time were men such as William Branham, Oral Roberts, T. L. Osborn, and A. A. Allen. A Canadian researcher, Richard Riss, has concluded from his studies that the earliest leaders of the Saskatchewan sect were deeply impressed by the 1947 Branham healing campaign in Vancouver.[19] The PAOC had always maintained Divine Healing as one of its distinctive doctrines: the effective salvation-healing ministries of A. H. Argue, Aimee Semple McPherson, and Dr. Charles Price in Canada were proof of their appreciation of such emphases. But the "Branham-style" approach to divine healing had a new dimension.

William Branham claimed that an angel visited him early in 1946 and commanded him to take the gift of divine healing to the world. Starting with healing meetings in St. Louis, he soon had huge crowds in attendance. A year later, Oral Roberts began a similar type of ministry. In a short period of time there were a number of "healing evangelists" crisscrossing the continent. Their activities were chronicled in Gordon Lindsay's new magazine, *The Voice of Healing*, which proved to be an effective vehicle in acquainting multitudes with the teachings and the practices of these evangelists.

Branham was especially influential in Canada where he held meetings in various major cities such as Vancouver and Regina. At Branham's meetings in Regina, an extraordinary positive response from the huge crowd was apparent after prayer for the sick produced some remarkable healings. But the impact of men like Branham was not the only cause for the theological schism which rocked the Saskatchewan assemblies of the PAOC and touched dozens of other Pentecostal congregations throughout Canada and the United States. The New Order of the Latter Rain was, as L. Thomas Holdcroft most correctly described it, "an organizational schism before it was a spiritual cause."

This "organizational" problem first surfaced at Saskatchewan's Bethel Bible Institute. The school was founded by George Hawtin in Star City, Saskatchewan. Hawtin moved the school to Saskatoon without any official sanction by district officials. Although he operated the school independently without PAOC supervision, school representatives solicited support from the district churches and recruited students from them. A disagreement arose between the District Executive and the school officials over the curriculum and some of its controversial teachings on demonology and fasting. The school was advocating a

40-day fast as the ideal. Such a fast, it was contended, would endow the believer with greater spiritual powers.

To all of these problems was added a conflict over the construction of a new building for BBI which did not have the approval of the district leaders. At the summer District Conference in 1947, the Saskatchewan officials were vindicated by the delegates when a stand was taken against the school's leadership. As a result, the key figures in the BBI controversy left Saskatoon and established themselves and the bulk of the student body in a new school in North Battleford. The principal figures from the school involved in the conflict were George and Ernest Hawtin and Percy Hunt. Soon they combined forces with Herrick Holt, the pastor of the Foursquare Church in North Battleford, in the establishing of Sharon Bible School, a high school, an orphanage, and a technical institute.[20]

The Saskatchewan PAOC District Executive was left with the task of picking up the pieces. The buildings of the Institute were unfinished and unpaid for, the files and records had been removed to North Battleford, and the remaining student body was very small. District Superintendent C. H. Stiller and Robert Argue, the new principal, worked tirelessly to rebuild Bethel Bible Institute. Within three years, the school was graduating workers who went into PAOC churches and to the mission field. This writer graduated from the school in 1952, and can recall to this day the huge problems faced by Argue and his newly recruited staff. He also recollects the hardships endured by students in dormitories improperly built and unfinished, as well as the meals of a rather monotonous and non-nutritious nature. Gradually, however, even these problems were surmounted.

Canadian Pentecostal leaders drew back in dismay from some of the practices associated with the "Latter Rain Movement" as it expanded throughout the country. The new sect gave what appeared to be an undue and exaggerated importance to the gifts of the Spirit — elevating them to equal status with the Bible itself. Concern also arose in the PAOC over what seemed to be the exploitation of zealous Christians by some Latter Rain evangelists and teachers. It was "a situation quite unlike the pre-World War II era," as one Pentecostal historian described it.[21] The radical movement found considerable sympathy among Pentecostals because it presented itself as a persecuted body of spiritual people who were interested only in reviving moribund Pentecostalism.

Latter Rain workers often approached PAOC churches for the purpose of diverting them into affiliation with the North Battleford organization. Indeed, they published a guide for their workers entitled "How to Take a PAOC Church." The PAOC, for a time, lost the allegiance of twelve churches in Saskatchewan and one in British Columbia. The Latter Rain Movement also spread to Eastern Canada and to parts of the United States, turning some Pentecostal denominations into theological battlegrounds in the process.

Extreme claims and bizarre doctrines surfaced among the Latter Rain teachers. An exaggerated emphasis on the role of the prophet and the spiritual gifts led inevitably into heresy. Many Pentecostals were at first attracted to what appeared to be a fresh surge of power and vitality in the Fellowship. They had, after all, been reading in the PAOC *Testimony* many exhortations to seek spiritual renewal. Only by degrees did the excesses of the Latter Rain leaders, and the unscriptural nature of their claims, become evident to the ordinary believer. This was a particularly painful problem for the Assemblies of God.[22] In Canada, the leaders of the New Order of the Latter Rain, or "New Thing" as it sometimes was called, claimed that Joel's prophecies about the "former rain" and the "latter rain" applied to the PAOC/AG and to themselves. The PAOC/AG were the result of the "former" outpouring of the Spirit at the turn of the century, and the New Order was obviously the "latter" outpouring of the late-40s.

The AG responded to these teachings in 1949 by condemning an "overemphasis relative to . . . gifts," and the "erroneous teaching that the Church is built on . . . present-day apostles and prophets." Another Latter Rain doctrine rejected was "the extreme teaching . . . regarding the confession of sin to man." The PAOC leadership, at both the Saskatchewan and the national level, endorsed the negative evaluations offered by the Assemblies of God, and had the AG statement reprinted in the *Testimony*.[23]

C. B. Smith, then both General Superintendent and editor of the *Testimony*, dealt with the topic in his editorial, "An Explanation Of Our Position Relative To Spiritual Gifts." Smith identified three chief points of concern:

1. It is being taught that people may receive all manner of gifts by the laying on of hands and prophecy. . . . People are being called out of the audience by name and given gifts by prophecy. . . . We do not believe this to be safe practice; but fear that it will lead to further extremes, if not disaster.

2. It also is claimed that the gift of tongues is the gift of languages; and that those who are directed to foreign fields through prophecy will never have to learn the language.

3. Some people claim to have the gift of healing in their right hand. Their knowledge of the possession of such a gift seems to be

determined by a burning sensation in the hand. Does it not seem dangerous to judge such important matters as the possession of spiritual gifts by an ecstatic experience.[24]

The chief characteristics of the New Order of the Latter Rain of the late-40s and early-50s have been listed by L. T. Holdcroft as a rejection of established churches, an authoritarian leadership style, a great emphasis upon prophecy, and a neglect of the role of Scripture as the final authority in doctrine.[25] The practical result of these aberrations was much in evidence at a New Order meeting attended by PAOC pastor Richard A. Bombay and his wife Olive. Hearing reports of wonderful meetings in a church in Detroit, the Bombays made a trip from Ontario to investigate. In his *Memoirs*, Bombay recorded his observations of some Latter Rain teachings and practices which he believed were in direct contravention of the Bible:

> It was like a continual convention with prayer, singing, preaching, and many professed prophecies, most of them promising that God was going to do a "new thing" that was away beyond the Pentecostal outpouring. I was acquainted with many who were there. . . . One of the first things that came to my notice was the great number of "independents" present. Were they dissatisfied with their independence? It was also very apparent that there was a "power struggle" for recognition as "the apostle of the Latter Rain." I was aware that one of them had angled for leadership among the PAOC. Here he appeared to be the "prophet" who "called out" those who were to have hands laid upon them for the imparting of "gifts."[26]

Bombay was himself "called out" and the "prophet" proposed laying hands on him so he would receive "the gift of an apostle." When he declined by saying that the "prophet" could add nothing to his PAOC ordination, the onlookers were shocked. After this experience, Bombay made a point of following the careers of these "Latter Rain prophets." One had been in and out of the ministry repeatedly; another acquired wealth and lived like a prince. Many others, he noted, lost out with God and went into secular employment. Some New Order followers in Saskatchewan and British Columbia lapsed into extremism, heresy, and even immorality. Some fell away entirely from the faith. This result was more common than is realized, but has been documented by researchers such as C. J. Jaenen.[27]

Tom Johnstone also was very familiar with the development of the New Order. He calculated that its primary failure was its departure from the principle of final biblical authority for 20th-century Pentecostals. His

9 / COMING OF AGE: 1939-1958

observation was accurate, for New Order leaders considered the Book of Acts to be "unfinished," and themselves to be inspired by the Spirit to receive new revelations. These new insights and teachings could not be questioned, it was alleged, because they had originated with the Holy Spirit. A logical result of this conduct was the rejection of all "organization," although they seemed unaware of the incongruity of their establishment of a new organization at North Battleford.

The PAOC managed to cope, over a period of time, with the problems created by this schism. Some local pastors came to understand the heretical nature of the Latter Rain and drew back from their initial enthusiasm for it as a renewal movement. R. E. McAlister wrote a booklet entitled "The Manifestation of the Spirit" which did much to dispel false teachings among PAOC people. The booklet emphasized that only the Holy Spirit conferred the gifts, not self-appointed prophets. McAlister travelled throughout Western Canada preaching on the gifts and their proper use. His reputation as "the Walking Bible" made him a formidable opponent for the New Order.

Besides these strategies, the PAOC was assisted in re-establishing itself in Saskatchewan by the growing awareness among Pentecostals of the errors and incipient heresies in the schismatic movement. The practice of telling young couples by "prophecy" whom they should marry could only lead to disaster. And some misguided individuals who were "called" to overseas fields arrived there and found, to their dismay, that they had not received a miraculously-conferred foreign language. Some Latter Rain people had gone further and claimed that they would be supernaturally transported to the foreign field, but that claim was too bizarre to be tolerated for very long. Although the New Order leaders rejected PAOC authority, they exercised an autocratic control over their own disciples, and that too generated eventual discontent. Gradually, as most of the separated churches in Saskatchewan began to reject the schismatic leaders, they applied for reinstatement in the PAOC. By the late-50s, most of them were in full fellowship once more with the district and national offices of The Pentecostal Assemblies of Canada.

The fact that the New Order was nurtured in a Bible school was not lost on the Canadian Fellowship. Steps were taken to ensure that more direct control of all PAOC clerical training institutions should be placed in the hands of the National Bible College Committee. The critical importance of the Bible schools was re-emphasized for all Pentecostals in Canada. One result was a greater willingness to provide financial support for the schools. This funding addressed, at least in a measure, what has always been one of the chief weaknesses in the PAOC organizational structure. Another result was a fresh realization of the widespread hunger among

COMING OF AGE: 1939-1958 / 9

believers for a genuine move of the Spirit and for a fresh awakening of love and joy in their church services. The laity wanted a continued emphasis on the charismata, but one that was properly balanced with correct practice and sound theology. The PAOC had been committed, from its inception, to such views and practices, but 40 years is a long time in revivalistic circles. It was difficult to maintain the original fervor that animated the first-generation Pentecostals. The New Order of the Latter Rain, although it produced schism and error, had at least one virtue — it reminded the Fellowship throughout Canada that Pentecostalism could survive only by perpetuating *both* its biblical and charismatic distinctives. As for the New Order, it eventually faded into obscurity. For a few years several hundred followers continued to gather for annual camp meetings at North Battleford, but this too finally ceased. The schools and organizations associated with the movement have disappeared. By contrast, the PAOC has survived the traumatic war years, the post-war adjustment period, and a decade of division and schism in its ranks. And during the whole period, it was gearing itself for the future. By 1958, it had come of age!

Endnotes

1. C. P. Stacey, "Second World War," *Encyclopedia Canadiana*, vol. 10 (Ottawa: Canadiana Co., 1965), 376-383.

2. C. M. Wortman, "Pentecost on the Move!" *The Pentecostal Testimony* (November 1952), 6.

3. *The Pentecostal Testimony* (February 1943), 14, provides just one sample of such communications.

4. See *The Gleaner*, 5:3 (December 1941), 9; 6:1 (February 1945), 7; 6:3 (December 1945), 12; and "60th Anniversary, 1923-1983, Glad Tidings Pentecostal Church," (Victoria: Glad Tidings, 1983), p. 13.

5. Data on enrollment is rare and often incomplete for the war years. EPBC statistics are from Emma E. Hann, "Reflections of Eastern Pentecostal Bible College," mimeographed booklet, 1982, p. 5.

6. David O. Moberg, *The Church as a Social Institution: The Sociology of American Religion* (Grand Rapids: Baker, 1984, 2nd ed.); Thomas Wm. Miller, *Ripe for Revival: The Churches at the Crossroads of Renewal or Decline* (Burlington: Welch, 1984); see also Bryan R. Wilson, "An Analysis of Sect Development," *American Sociological Review*, 24 (1959).

7. Further elaboration of the sect-to-denomination process is in E. T. Clark, *The Small Sects in America* (Nashville: Abingdon, 1937); and S. D. Clark, *Church and Sect in Canada* (Toronto, 1948).

9 / COMING OF AGE: 1939-1958

8. For more detail about PAOC legislative development, see Paul Hawkes, "Pentecostalism in Canada: A History with Implications for the Future," unpublished D.Min. dissertation project for San Francisco Theological Seminary, 1982.
9. *The Pentecostal Assemblies of Canada: A Brief History,* booklet, PAOC Archives, p. 11.
10. *The Pentecostal Testimony* (February 15, 1943), 12-13.
11. "Bethel Home Newsletter: 65th Anniversary Edition," 1993; and W. M. Kilburn, "Bethel Rescue Home," *The Pentecostal Testimony* (April 1953), 4.
12. Thomas Wm. Miller, taped Interview with James Montgomery, July 29, 1984).
13. Gloria Kulbeck, *"What God Hath Wrought,"* (Toronto: The Pentecostal Assemblies of Canada, 1958), p. 46.
14. Gladys Lemmon, "The Women's Missionary Council and Evangelism," *The Pentecostal Testimony* (February 1957), 20.
15. Thomas Wm. Miller, taped interview with Tom Johnstone, April 29, 1984.
16. Gordon F. Atter, *The Pentecostal Movement: Who We Are and What We Believe* (Peterborough: for the author, 1957, revised and enlarged edition of the 1937 original).
17. *Canada Year Book* (Ottawa: Information Canada, 1974).
18. Carl Brumback, *Suddenly . . . From Heaven: A History of the Assemblies of God* (Springfield: Gospel Publishing House, 1961), pp. 330-331.
19. Richard Michael Riss, *Latter Rain: The Latter Rain Movement of 1948 and the Mid-Twentieth Century Evangelical Awakening* (Etobicoke, ON: Kingdom Flagships Foundation, 1987); see also Richard Riss, "The Latter Rain and Healing Revivals," *New Wine,* 12:9 (October 1980), 30-32; and his "The Latter Rain Movement of 1948," *Pneuma,* 4:1 (Spring 1982), 32-45.
20. L. Thomas Holdcroft, "The New Order of the Latter Rain," *Paraclete,* 14:2 (Spring 1980), 18-22; see also C. B. Smith, "An Explanation Concerning Bethel Bible Institute," *The Pentecostal Testimony* (November 15, 1947), 9.
21. William W. Menzies, *Anointed to Serve: The Story of the Assemblies of God* (Springfield: Gospel Publishing House, 1971), p. 330.
22. See Menzies, note 21.
23. C. B. Smith, "A Resolution," *The Pentecostal Testimony* (November 15, 1949), 2.
24. C. B. Smith, "An Explanation of Our Position Relative to Spiritual Gifts," *The Pentecostal Testimony* (June 15, 1949), 2.
25. See Holdcroft, note 20.
26. Richard A. Bombay, Sr., "Memoirs," typed manuscript, 1974.
27. Cornelius John Jaenen, "The Pentecostal Movement," unpublished MA thesis, University of Manitoba, 1950.

Chapter 10

THE THIRD FORCE

The Pentecostal awakening of the early 20th century began in such obscurity that it was virtually unknown to leaders of the established denominations. When noticed at all, it was reckoned a "storefront" and a "wrong-side-of-the-tracks" kind of religion. Some scholarly observers considered this revival movement to be a theological aberration which would disappear in a few years. Those of the mainline denominations who bothered to notice the religious upstart usually condemned it as a fanatical sect. More generous observers accepted Pentecostalism as a genuine revivalistic movement, but expected it to decline on schedule as so many others before it.

Students of revivalism put the life expectancy of religious renewal movements at 30 to 50 years before they degenerate into formalistic denominations. Time has proven the critics wrong. The worldwide Pentecostal Movement has had eight decades of constant increase in numbers and influence. Its members and adherents have been estimated at nearly 400 million — with some observers claiming over 50 million in China alone.

In Canada, the PAOC, the largest Pentecostal body in the country, had become a firmly rooted and fast-growing organization by the end of the 1950s. It had extended its influence beyond Canadian borders through its successful overseas missions endeavors. It had also augmented its vision by means of a new involvement in both North American and international religious associations. The PAOC was one of the charter members at the first World Pentecostal Conference which assembled in Zurich in 1947. Pentecostal representatives from seven countries met to map out a strategy for reaching the post-war world and providing emergency assistance for believers in Europe. Donald Gee of England, an

10 / THE THIRD FORCE

acknowledged international spokesman for the Movement, assured the conference delegates that Pentecostalism would not cease after 30 years as some had predicted.

Canadians E. W. Robinson and C. B. Smith sent back reports to Canada on the goals of the first international gathering of Pentecostals in Zurich. One objective, on which the delegates of all seven countries agreed, was to avoid competition among themselves and to promote cooperation on the mission fields. Robinson and Smith concluded after their experience at Zurich that "fellowship was strengthened and it was felt by a great many that the conference was a success."[1] Subsequent conferences were held in Paris (1949), London (1952), Stockholm (1955), and then in Canada where the PAOC hosted the World Pentecostal Conference in 1958. By that time, there were an estimated 15 million Pentecostals in the world.[2]

Pentecostals at the fifth world conference in Toronto took satisfaction in the reports given of rapid growth worldwide. Their Movement had attracted much favorable publicity from the media, but that was superseded by an extraordinary assessment from conservative scholar Dr. Henry P. Van Dusen, the president of Union Theological Seminary in New York. Van Dusen described Pentecostalism as the "Third Force" in Christendom. It was deserving, he wrote, of a special place alongside historic Roman Catholicism and Protestantism. His views were set forth in a 1958 cover-story in *Life* magazine. Van Dusen noted that Pentecostals then comprised about half of all the evangelical sects in America and were reaching multitudes of people worldwide. He opined that it was a religious revolution comparable in importance to the spiritual movements which had brought into existence both the first century apostolic church and the Protestant Reformation. Van Dusen also suggested that the last half of this century would be remembered in church history as the age of Pentecostal, charismatic Christianity.[3] By the time Van Dusen made this significant statement, the rapid growth and continuous development of Pentecostalism was an established fact.

Evidence of the growth was the emergence in the 1940s and '50s of new national Pentecostal organizations. Both Canadians and Americans participated in the establishment of the Pentecostal Fellowship of North America in 1948. With the establishment in 1952 of the Full Gospel Businessmen's Fellowship International, Pentecostal men shared a meeting territory where they could express and practise their faith. Founded by wealthy businessman and Pentecostal layman Demos Shakarian, the FGBMFI was professedly interdenominational but unashamedly charismatic from the start.[4]

There was also a new acceptance of Pentecostals in parachurch bodies such as Youth For Christ. The 1940s saw the founding of the National

Association of Evangelicals and the National Association of Religious Broadcasters, in both of which the Pentecostals were welcomed.

Even the World Council of Churches, considered theologically liberal and socialistic by many Pentecostals, was contacted in that period. A South African Pentecostal, David du Plessis, attended the 1951 WCC convention as an observer. He also was invited to attend an assembly of the International Missionary Council in Willingen, Germany. This marked the beginning of a very cautious reassessment of Pentecostal relationships with mainline denominations.

Gee was correct in his prediction, for the worldwide Pentecostal Movement has enjoyed continuous growth in the four decades since the Zurich conference. Not only in numbers, but also in social and economic influence, Pentecostalism has spiralled to new plateaus. In Canada, the years before 1960 saw an increase in the number of Pentecostals who could be considered middle and upper-middle class. The stereotyped image of the early adherents, fashioned by less than charitable critics, which suggested that the Pentecostals were recruited from the lowest socio-economic levels contained a measure of truth but was grossly unfair. This distorted sociological view persisted for many years, but the fact was that early Pentecostals had about the same social composition as other evangelical denominations in the early 20th century.

By the late 1950s, the PAOC membership had an unmistakable upwardly mobile character. A new respectability became evident in the election of PAOC members to government offices. Among them, Phil Gaglardi, an ordained minister, and Everett Wood were appointed to cabinet posts in provincial legislatures. In the universities, PAOC students began to move up the academic ladders, through the graduate schools, and on to college and university faculties. The PAOC had "come of age" and its achievements became known to many others besides Van Dusen.

The 1958 World Conference in Toronto brought a considerable amount of favorable publicity to the Canadian Fellowship.[5] The PAOC used the occasion to reaffirm publicly its commitment to the Bible as "the all-sufficient rule for faith and practice." The Bible was to remain the final religious authority. The occurrence of "signs and wonders" was truly Pentecostal, but was only "incidental, and to confirm, the Word." General Superintendent Walter McAlister, in his welcoming address to the international delegates, reiterated the PAOC commitment to world evangelism. His remarks, and the conference deliberations, were reported in the Toronto newspapers and were circulated by the media to many parts of the world.

McAlister's public pronouncement was no idle boast, for the Canadians had carried on an ever-expanding missions program. The thrilling story of

10 / THE THIRD FORCE

early missionary activity described in Chapter 8 (The Regions Beyond: 1907-1940) continued in the record of the next two decades. Throughout the Second World War and up to the 1958 gathering, the PAOC had sent out an increasing number of missionaries and opened up new fields. The roster of overseas workers was enlarged until there were about 135 on the field in the '50s.

Although the Pentecostals had acquired considerable experience in missions, the task did not get easier. In Kenya, for example, the work of the missionaries was adversely affected throughout the 1940s by what missionary James Skinner called "tribal troubles." Despite the unsettled conditions and persecution of the believers, a new Pentecostal Bible school was opened at Goibei, a new mission station was set up among the Luo tribe, and Sunday Schools were organized in 120 churches. In one year, 750 Kenyan converts were baptized in water.

More new missionaries arrived to take up the challenge in Kenya. John and Sophia Kitts, formerly of the Belgian Congo mission, came in 1943 to work with the Kikuyku and Kisii tribes and to establish a new station at Itobo. Sophia Kitts produced translations of selected Biblical passages and also a hymn book for the use of the natives. John and Ella McBride also arrived in Kenya in 1943, after McBride was discharged from the army in Canada. He considered his release to be an act of Divine providence and a confirmation of his call to Africa. The McBrides devoted themselves to missions work among the Nyang'ori tribe and to the supervision of the PAOC educational program in Kenya. Florence Fleming, a native of Vineland, Ontario, went to Africa after pioneering churches in Western Canada. She served on the Labaka and Shingwedzi stations in South Africa and assisted at Emmanuel Press. At the end of the Second World War, she married Henry Koopman and together they opened up the Marhumbini region of southern Rhodesia. The region was infested with malaria, but the Koopmans persevered and the missions work prospered.

Austin and Ingrid Chawner (familiar names in Chapter 8) conducted Bible conferences in various regions. Chawner reported on one such meeting in 1943 at Mangweyana where a crowd of young men came to scoff at the missionaries. When God touched a native worker, the man, speaking like a person with Divine authority, rebuked the scoffers for their blasphemy. Chawner reported that the "warning and exhortation was so directly from Heaven that shame could be read on the faces of the idle scoffers." He added that the power of God came down and there was a general crying out to God for mercy.[6]

Lawrence and Lois Delport arrived in the early-40s to assist Fred Clarke and Earley King in South Africa. The Delports ministered among the Shangana tribespeople and among the Vendas, then considered one of the most primitive groups in Africa. There was a pressing need for evangelistic literature and training for the converts. The situation was alleviated during the war years by moving the small printing press from Shingwedzi to Nelspruit and expanding its operation. Its capacity was constantly increased until it eventually became one of the largest printing establishments in Africa.

The work in Liberia was strengthened with the arrival of fresh missionaries: Annie Cressman in 1941, and Immanuel and Isabel Jensen and William and Viola Brown in 1944. Literature again proved to be an effective means of evangelism and discipleship. In compliance with a Liberian government directive that all educational work must be carried on in the English language, the missionaries were able to use all the printed material they could acquire. There was also a great need, however, for literature in the vernacular languages. In response to this need, Jensen produced a vernacular translation of the Gospel of John and a number of tracts. Annie Cressman continued this specialized type of evangelism with simplified translations of Bible portions for the Tchien people. During her furloughs, Cressman took several courses in linguistics, and by 1946 had completed the first Tchien Gospel of Mark. She was faithfully assisted in the arduous labor of translation by Joy Hansell, who later was to become an editor of *The Pentecostal Testimony*.

Canadian Pentecostal workers in South America were spared the worst effects of the global conflict of the Second World War, but their work was hampered by a lack of trained missionaries. Samuel Sorensen, a son of pioneer N. C. Sorensen, completed his theological studies in Canada and returned to Argentina in 1942. Together with his new wife Esther, they pioneered in La Plata and set up a printing plant to produce Pentecostal literature. The leadership of the Bible school was assumed by E. Howard Kerr. Pentecostal theological education was carried on without interruption during the war. For several years Sorensen served as field director during which time he saw a steady increase in the number of trained national workers. Later, another Sorensen family, Paul and Dorothy, joined the missionary staff and engaged in evangelism and in the production and distribution of literature.

The work in the West Indies enjoyed continual enlargement under the direction of R. J. Jamieson, despite his advancing years and declining health. The work was hampered, however, during the war years because of the tragic loss of a promising missionary recruit. Robert and Marion Parkinson sailed in the ocean-liner "Lady Hawkins" in 1942 for the islands. When the ship was torpedoed by a German submarine, only a few of the 250 passengers on board survived. Robert was drowned, but

Marion was one of those rescued. After her recovery, she continued on to Trinidad and served in the newly-founded West Indies School of Theology.[7] This school was chiefly the result of a dream of a missionary, A. T. Jacobson, who wanted to provide local instruction to West Indian natives so they could minister to their own people.

PAOC evangelism in the Far East was seriously affected by the war and the advent of communism in China. Most of the Western missionaries were forced to evacuate the region, or were interned in prison camps by the Japanese invaders. At war's end, some Canadian Pentecostals were able to labor in China until the communist takeover, but finally were confined to evangelism in Hong Kong and Taiwan. The PAOC work in Japan, which had shown very little growth, came to a halt during the war years. Afterwards, by mutual agreement with the Assemblies of God, missions among the Japanese became a joint venture for a brief period before being completely taken over by the Americans. General MacArthur's call for "twenty thousand missionaries" to evangelize Japan met with a good response in the USA, although the numbers sent to the islands never remotely approached the goals set by the general.

While these advances and adjustments were being made on the PAOC mission fields, the work in Canada was undergoing continuous expansion. North America was not physically affected by the war, although a few air raids were threatened on the West Coast and there were some ship-sinkings off the East Coast. Much of the legislative development of the Canadian Fellowship, described earlier in this narrative, had resulted in a high level of efficiency by 1958. Due credit should be given to the General Superintendents who guided the Fellowship during these eventful years: D. N. Buntain (1936-1944), C. B. Smith (1944-1952), and W. E. McAlister (1952-1962).

Growth in the national organization was paralleled at the district level, as district superintendents led their workers in successful evangelism and church planting. It is not the purpose of this chronicle to present a comprehensive record of the remarkable growth across the nation. Selected accounts from the various regions, however, do illustrate the dedication of the workers and their sense of dependency on the Holy Spirit.

The first PAOC leaders in the British Columbia region — J. E. Barnes, A. J. Hughes, Tom Johnstone and C. A. C. Story — served in dual roles as both pastor of a local church and superintendent of the district. The first full-time superintendent in B.C. was Percy S. Jones, whose term of office was from 1944 to 1952. He took over responsibilities for a vast district with some 8,000 miles of coastline and three main mountain ranges. Except for a few major urban centres, much of the population was engaged in the resource industries — fishing, logging, and mining — and many were located in isolated communities. For these reasons, evangelism by the Pentecostal pioneers in B.C. has been especially difficult. The early pioneers found a variety of ways to reach remote communities.

When Frank and Mabel Harford presented the spiritual needs of the coastal villages to the B.C. District Conference, funds were raised for the purchase of a boat to transport the ministering couple to the coastal communities. The financial support from district sources was supplemented by a grant from the national office. In 1940 the Gospel Light was launched; a second vessel was added in 1943. Pender Harbour became their home port. The Harfords were assisted by John and Mary Shannon, John and Elizabeth Nygaard, and Mr. and Mrs. W. Ackroyd. Throughout the '40s and '50s, the gospel boat work was maintained and expanded through the labors of Robert and Evelyn Starrett, Ingemar Tingstad and his wife, and the Deardens, who provided overall leadership after the Harfords retired in 1952.

Coastal evangelism resulted in the founding of Pentecostal congregations at Bella Bella, Bella Coola, Coal Harbour, Gibson's Landing, Fort Rupert, Port Hardy, Powell River, and Quatsino. The Nygaards, working from a base at Alert Bay, had under their direction a dozen Native congregations totalling about 300 members. The reports given by these workers to their Conferences were modest in their claims and self-effacing regarding their sacrifices. Superintendent Jones, however, was keenly aware of what it had cost them to take the full gospel up and down the Pacific Coast:

> The inland waters along the British Columbia coast are treacherous. Many a boat has foundered on these stormy seas. The Gospel Boat navigators have fought many a battle against riptides, sloppy seas, high winds and blanket fogs. They have been mercilessly thrown about by mighty, rolling seas, trying to make port. Their boats were comparatively small, their equipment was not of the best, and their living quarters were cramped. Yet, while there was one lost soul to be rescued, the men and women who manned the Gospel Boats would put out to sea.[8]

Jones was equally positive about the progress made by self-denying pioneers in the British Columbia hinterland. During his tenure as superintendent, Jones fired up his workers with the slogan, "A Pentecostal church in every city, town and hamlet." To further this aim, the B.C. District established the Revolving Building Fund. It was announced that the superintendent was trusting God to provide $10,000 as initial capital in this fund for church planting — and the sum came in.

Many of the workers had graduated from the district's Bible school. Because of the critical importance of that institution to evangelism throughout the province and the Yukon, the superintendent gave it his wholehearted support. He also paid tribute to its self-sacrificing faculty members for setting an example for the youthful preachers under their tutelage. Graduates from the Bible school were assisted by dedicated lay workers in pioneering new assemblies with financial support from the fund. For example, one young man left a beautiful environment in Victoria to go to a remote northern community. Despite much persecution, he was able to found a congregation, and, with lay helpers, to renovate an old building as a church. Then he built another tabernacle in a neighboring centre and a third church at a former Hudson's Bay outpost. Such pioneering endeavors had the full support of the District Executive.

A portable tabernacle was utilized at Castlegar, in the Kootenays, but with few permanent results until Frances Clemo and Jean Pennoyer began working in that community in 1952. Although there was the common public hostility to Pentecostalism, the two women ministers, confident of their divine call, were undaunted. They rented temporary facilities, purchased a building lot, constructed a church, and assembled a good congregation. The Castlegar Sunday school increased from two pupils to over 80.

Older congregations were expanding their facilities and mothering new assemblies throughout the 1950s. The Abbotsford congregation, for example, began services in its new church, seating 200, in 1940, and thereafter enjoyed a steady increase in membership. When C. B. Smith came as pastor to Victoria, he led the Pentecostal assembly in various outreach ministries as well as the development of programs within the church. In the early-50s an orchestra and brass band were organized and were used for evangelism throughout Vancouver Island. A Missionettes program and a Men's Fellowship ministry also were inaugurated. The steady growth in membership led to the employment of an assistant pastor — somewhat of a novelty in Pentecostal circles in the 1950s. A number of civic and provincial government leaders began to attend the services. One of the latter group was Phil Gaglardi, pastor of the PAOC church at Kamloops and also Minister of Highways in the B.C. government. A new home missions outreach was launched in 1952 among the Chinese in Vancouver. James and Marion House soon had 50 in attendance at their meetings. The work among Chinese-Canadians spread across the country and took root in several metropolitan centres.

It was also in this period that a number of regional campgrounds were set up to better serve the needs of believers. While pastoring at Nelson, Ian Presley led in the development of a campground which would serve the needs of the 14 churches in the Kootenay region. Another campground was established at Nanoose Bay, near Nanaimo, and still others soon appeared in the north of the province.

A new assembly was established in Prince Rupert by the mid-50s. Another new tabernacle was erected to house the congregation in Terrace. Rapid growth was recorded for Sunday schools in Hazelton, Smithers, Burns Lake, and Vanderhoof. Home missions work among the Natives living between Prince Rupert and Prince George was conducted in the English language. The Natives responded to the message and quickly proved themselves capable of assuming indigenous leadership.

One of the most colorful of the pioneer pastors of the day was Art Bell. He reported to the 1953 B.C. Conference that God was graciously moving among the northern Natives. He also spoke of his desire to start Pentecostal meetings in some of the new townsites, such as Kitimat. During the construction of this new community, no one was allowed on the site without the permission of officials. Bell's request to enter was denied, not because of any animosity against him, but because the site was deemed to be safe only for qualified construction workers. Bell was not easily dissuaded: since he could not enter Kitimat by boat, he would trek in overland. In bitterly cold weather, Bell hiked over mountains, crossed icy rivers, and one day appeared in the town. Local officials were so impressed by his feat of determination and endurance that they gave him permission to begin a Pentecostal church.

Another story of sacrificial labor relates to the planting of a PAOC church in Whitehorse, in the Yukon, in 1954. Gordon and Beatrice Richmond, ably assisted by Gloria Wachnuik, took over a small, struggling group and led them in a program of constant growth. Within five months of their arrival, and with the support of two churches in Eastern Canada and one in B.C., the Richmonds erected a lovely chapel. Their Sunday school had 90 pupils. Soon, a branch work was begun at Atlin, about 120 miles away. Whitehorse was also the home base for other evangelistic outreaches throughout the Yukon.

By the start of the Second World War, there were Pentecostal churches in all regions of British Columbia, although not yet in all the larger centres. By 1958, the number of Pentecostals in the province had grown from about 5,000 to approximately 20,000.[9] Less rapid progress was made in the Mackenzie region immediately to the east of the Yukon, but the work there eventually surpassed expectations. The vast region drained by the Mackenzie River has been reached chiefly by workers from Alberta.

In many respects, Alberta experienced the same problems as the rest of the Prairies during the Depression and the war years, but the Pentecostal message took root throughout the province and the Territories during the '40s and '50s. The foundation laid by George R. Upton as Alberta district superintendent (1934-1943) was enlarged during the tenures of W. S. Frederick (1943-1944), A. A. Lewis (1944-1946 and 1948-1950), D. N. Buntain (1946-1948 and 1950-1952), and S. R. Tilton (1952-1968).

The number of Pentecostals in the province had increased from about 1,200 in 1931 to around 5,000 at the end of the war. The Sylvan Lake Camp had an unusually large attendance in the summer of 1943 during the ministry of Dr. Charles Price. The meetings had a lasting impact on the district. Another positive factor was the rapid urbanization of the main population areas which brought thousands of people more easily within the reach of the preachers and evangelists. From 1940 to 1958 there were 16 new congregations established in Alberta.

One of the cities that experienced rapid growth in industry and population was Calgary. The oil boom brought thousands of new residents. When the Pentecostal church, First Assembly, became overcrowded in the early-40s, a new addition was built. During the '50s, under the leadership of John Watts, First Assembly "mothered" three new churches at Montgomery, Capital Hill, and Ogden. A Sunday school venture in a Calgary suburb in 1952 led to the founding of the Montgomery Pentecostal Tabernacle. Harry and Mildred Nettleton, recent Bible school graduates, pioneered this assembly. By 1955, the Montgomery church was self-supporting. In the same year, the First Assembly congregation sponsored construction of a new branch church seating 400 in the Capital Hill district. James Hazlett pastored the new congregation for one year before Charles Yates began a 12-year tenure. Another Sunday school ministry produced the New Life Community Church in Ogden in 1958. Under the leadership of Reuben and Shirley Drisner, the group of believers soon outgrew their rented quarters. The Calmar Christian Assembly began in 1948 when two young women, Alice Shevkenek and Katherine Thiessen, held a Daily Vacation Bible School in the community. After a number of converts were assembled, they were able to buy and renovate an empty church for Pentecostal services.

Rev. and Mrs. George Gullackson started the work in Cold Lake out of a deep love for children and their spiritual needs. They supported themselves by secular employment and began a fund for a church building in Cold Lake. A similar story of self-sacrifice relates to the establishment of a church at Fairview. Charles Howey worked at construction jobs to provide his family's needs while he also ministered to a growing congregation.

When Art Rosenau returned from the mission field in Kenya, he taught school at Forestburg and began Bible studies in the area. The group of believers there combined to buy an old church building, moved it to the town, and renovated it for full gospel services. The first full-time pastors were Ken and Velma Ness.

An evangelist from Minneapolis, Paul Olson, was instrumental in the establishment of a congregation at Lacombe in 1956. Meetings were continued by local lay leaders and students from the Bible school in Edmonton until Jack and Daisy Keys arrived to lead in a building program. Similar reports could be given of church planting programs by dedicated workers in the communities of Peace River, Provost, St. Albert, Stettler, Wainwright, and Westlock.[10]

Pentecostal expansion in Alberta took place among three groups of people: the English-speaking residents such as those mentioned above, the various ethnic minorities, and the Natives in the North. Pentecostal evangelism among ethnic groups has been very successful in Alberta, especially among the Slavs and the Germans. The Prairie revivals of the '30s resulted in the emergence of several congregations composed of Russian and Ukrainian residents. One of their number, K. Haycank, who received ordination from the PAOC in 1932, became a recognized leader in the development of the Western and Eastern Slavic Conferences.

By 1946, J. D. Harbarenko was able to give the PAOC General Conference a glowing report of the progress of Pentecostalism among the Russian, Ukrainian, and Polish people on the Prairies. A Rev. Gardziliwich started Ukrainian-language services for recent immigrants in 1955 in the Clareview suburb of Edmonton. Two years later the assembly began construction of a church as its membership experienced steady growth. Gradually, its evangelistic outreach brought in so many English-speaking residents that an assistant was hired specifically to minister to their needs. In the 1950s, William Melnychuck served both as superintendent of the Western Slavic Conference and as pastor of a congregation on 97th Avenue in Edmonton.

A similar tale of progress applied to the growth of German development in the province in these two decades under review. Thousands of German immigrants settled in Alberta at the turn of the century. Many had connections with the Mennonites, Evangelical United Brethren, and other evangelical groups. When the pernicious effects of theological liberalism infected their denominations, many were attracted to the fundamentalist and charismatic Pentecostal Movement in Canada. The earliest-known outpouring of the Spirit took place among the German-speaking settlers at Wiesenthal, near Leduc in 1919. George Schneider was engaged to become the preacher for this new Pentecostal congregation. The revival made a remarkable impact. As one of the original church members recalled, "We worked on our farms all day and then went to the services in the evening and prayed all night."[11] From Weisenthal the full gospel message was carried to other German groups in the province by men such as Ludwig Posein, a young Baptist farmer. Although he had little formal education, Posein became a successful pastor-evangelist. God confirmed his ministry with numerous healings and many converts.

The Holy Spirit was working among the Germans of Eastern and Southern Europe in the period between the two world wars. A number of leaders emerged such as Oskar Jeske. A great revival occurred in Riga, Latvia, in which thousands were brought to Christ and supernatural miracles and speaking in tongues occurred. When this work was ended by the outbreak of war, some of the preachers came to Canada. One such was Julius Schatkoske who became a spiritual father to the German immigrants north of Edmonton. Schatkoske had the opportunity to preach in a largely Baptist community where, to avoid controversy, he refrained from speaking about the Pentecostal Baptism. Nevertheless, many of his converts were filled with the Spirit and spoke in tongues. There were 10 German congregations in Alberta by the mid-30s. Ludwig Posein served as district director, later to be succeeded by Julius Schatkoske. After the war, the German churches acquired 85 acres at Alberta Beach and developed a modern campground facility.

The Southside Assembly in Edmonton began in 1940 with only 22 members. Daniel Baker provided inspired pastoral leadership. So intense was his love of souls that he expected at least one convert each Sunday and would spend whole nights praying for the salvation of people in the area. Rapid growth in this congregation prompted the erection of a church capable of seating 800 people.

Wilhelm Kowalski had arrived in Canada in 1937. His special talent for teaching and administration led to his selection as the first superintendent of the German Branch when it was formed in 1940. In the years that followed, German-speaking Pentecostals working in cooperation with the PAOC sent out missionaries Don and Evelyne Clements to Japan and Gus and Doris Wentland to Tanganyika (now Tanzania). Other were sent to Argentina and Brazil where strong works were established.[12]

In 1949, a young graduate of the Bible school in Edmonton, Ken Gaetz, travelled 800 miles north to Hay River to begin full gospel work. He was informed, upon his arrival, that no preachers were desired and it would be best if he returned to the South. But Gaetz was determined to stay. Among all the white residents of the community, Gaetz found only one professing believer. The moral conditions of the community reflected the fact that some of the residents were the outcasts of southern society who had gone north to escape all restraints.

Gaetz's first home was a 6 x 12-foot trailer. After his first difficult winter, he built a two-room cabin and began holding services. Few adults came, but he garnered community interest by starting a Boy Scout program and a Sunday school. Several healings through prayer led to more interest and the work grew slowly but steadily. After his marriage to Sarah Solomonson, the couple began gospel broadcasts over the Canadian Army Signal Corps facilities at Hay River. Gaetz also travelled by dog team to remote communities, often camping out at night in temperatures down to 30 degrees below zero — Fahrenheit! He was able to erect a little church in 1950.

Living costs in the area were astronomical. Long distances and extreme weather also made transportation costly. But financial support came faithfully from churches in Alberta and the National Home Missions Department in Toronto as people responded enthusiastically to the challenge which faced Gaetz. When Alberta District Superintendent D. N. Buntain visited Hay River, he reported, "In all my years in the Christian ministry, I never contacted more consecrated, conscientious workers than these folks."[13] The accounts of Gaetz's ministry led other young people to go north to assist, among them Grace Veale and Lila Kreiger.

The entire northern region was to open up to the full gospel in a most unusual manner. With the need for medical services so acute, Gaetz began a nursing station which was gradually expanded. The first nurse was Beatrice Purdy, a graduate from the Bible school in Saskatoon. The station later became a 12-bed hospital, with funding from the Alberta government, the Alberta Pentecostal churches, and the town of Hay River. A large sum of money came through a bequest from the estate of PAOC layman H. H. Williams, a Toronto realtor. By 1958, the hospital building was too small and plans were made for its enlargement. When a flood from Great Slave Lake virtually destroyed the town, it was moved to a new site on which the new H. H. Williams Memorial Hospital was built.[14]

The fully qualified staff donated large portions of their salaries to fund full gospel outreach to other northern communities. In this way, Howard and Wilma Peever were able to begin services at Fort Resolution. Jim and Doris Tyler, who came in 1955, erected a new church and parsonage. Then the Tylers moved to Fort Simpson and led in the construction of another church building. To unify these scattered congregations a campground was established along the shore of Great Slave Lake, about seven miles from Hay River — a first for the North. Progress was made at enormous cost both in financial and personal terms, particularly for the women workers. In her excellent survey of the PAOC Mackenzie mission, Grace Brown commented appropriately:

10 / THE THIRD FORCE

> No account of Pentecostal missions would be complete without paying tribute to the women . . . (who) have displayed unusual courage and steadfastness as well as creativity in their service to God.[15]

Grace Veale and Lily Kreiger graduated from the Northwest Bible College in 1951 and immediately went to work in Hay River, supporting themselves while assisting in the Gaetz mission. Veale engaged in the study of the Slavey Indian language so she could hold Vacation Bible Schools for the children in a number of areas. Travelling by canoe, generally paddled by herself, she engaged in effective itinerant evangelism. Her contributions were so impressive that Chief Lamalice permitted her to hold meetings in his home, where a number of converts were made. Although the white man's culture had led the Natives to depend on the government dole, Veale shared with the Native converts that the Bible teaches that the disciples of Jesus should work and support themselves. One of the proofs that these Natives were genuinely transformed by the gospel was that they began to tithe their incomes for the support of the mission.

Soon there were other women to assist in the ever-growing number of mission outposts in the Territories — gospel heroines like Eva Nichol, Mae Christianson, and Eunice Myrah. The latter two graduated from Bethel Bible Institute in Saskatoon. On arrival at Fort Simpson, they began a half-hour children's radio broadcast and provided religious instruction in the public school. Christianson later spent several winters nursing in the Hay River Hospital.

A layman named Robert Schneider settled at Fort Norman and introduced the full gospel to the community. He played an accordion and the novelty helped to attract crowds to his meetings. He used his own limited resources to buy a house and a store building. These facilities were made available to the first full-time workers who arrived in the town — Dan and Grace Priest. When the Priests settled at Fort Norman in 1958, Schneider paddled off to find another community needing the Word of God. Dan and Grace also itinerated to many other centres by means of a river scow and a freighter canoe. They travelled up to 5,000 miles each summer. Eventually, they opened a new work at Coppermine, a town of 700 people within the Arctic Circle. Now there was a Pentecostal church literally at "the top of the world."

Saskatchewan and Manitoba had been particularly hard-hit by the devastating drought that arrived about the same time as the Great Depression. Consequently, home mission work in that region was carried on under great difficulties. The end of the Second World War and the return of good-growing weather brought increasing prosperity. The Pentecostal workers had both the opportunities and the financial resources to reach out to new communities. Unfortunately, many of the Prairie centres had lost thousands of townspeople and farmers in the preceding decade. Church growth in the '50s was steady, but rather slow. The PAOC made its greatest strides in the populated urban areas where employment was more available.

A congregation had been established at Dundurn, the location of a military camp, in 1946. In the same year, the church at Hague managed to erect a new building, despite the wartime shortages which existed for a time after the conflict ended. Pentecostal services began in Leroy in 1945. While the struggling congregation grew, Pastor Peter Giesbrecht supported his ministry in that town by working as a carpenter. With the encouragement of District Superintendent C. H. Stiller (1948-1962), the Leroy congregation paid off the church debt within two years.

Allan McGie had a vision for gospel outreach in Glaslyn. He began by acquiring a house in the town in 1948, in which he lived and conducted religious services. The congregation grew, moving several times to different locations for its meetings, until a new church building was erected. Construction costs were kept to a minimum by using salvaged (but excellent) building materials and volunteer labor. In total, five new assemblies were established in Saskatchewan in the '50s, despite the unhappy consequences of the "New Order of the Latter Rain" controversy.[16]

One very effective means of revitalizing the spiritual life of the churches was the establishment of a district campground on the shores of Manitou Lake, near the town of Watrous. Living Waters Camp proved to be a source of untold blessings to thousands of believers. Many young people were called into the ministry at the camp meetings and hundreds were saved and filled with the Spirit. Among the Saskatchewan Pentecostals who attended every summer session was Wilson Waterhouse who attended the camp faithfully for nearly 50 years.

The history of Pentecostalism in Manitoba originated with the ministry of A. H. Argue in Winnipeg and has featured the ministry of its most significant church — Calvary Temple. This great church has been one of the chief models for the entire Fellowship in Canada. Its focus on evangelism at home and missions overseas has had a major impact. Through the years, Calvary Temple has had some noted evangelists and preachers grace its pulpit, including Dr. Charles Price who originally suggested the name of the assembly. It may be more than a coincidence that the name "Calvary Temple" has been adopted by many Pentecostal churches across the country.

10 / THE THIRD FORCE

One remarkable campaign which has been long remembered by the senior members of the Winnipeg Calvary Temple took place in the '40s with evangelist Edith Pennington of Louisiana. Over 50 were baptized in the Spirit in nine weeks. According to reports, there was an extraordinary manifestation of the gifts of the Spirit during the meetings. Part of the aggressive evangelism program in the early-40s featured a radio ministry directed by Pastor Watson Argue. The program carried the full gospel message to many parts of the province.[17] By 1957 — the 50th anniversary of its founding — Calvary Temple's budget was over $90,000, Sunday School attendance averaged nearly 600, and two branch churches were being supported by the congregation.

An unusual move of the Holy Ghost occurred in the town of Swan River in the '50s. Evangelist W. J. Gamble had been engaged for two weeks, but his stay was extended to four weeks because of the moving of the Spirit. There were numerous instances of healings and baptisms in the Holy Spirit. This kind of outreach was enthusiastically supported by the district superintendents of that era: W. C. Nelson (1938-1943), W. J. Taylor (1944-1949) and Clarence Walker (1950-1962). The election of Walker in 1950 marked the first time that the Manitoba and Northwestern Ontario district had a full-time superintendent. Walker chose Winnipeg as his headquarters and zealously promoted the work in all regions under his direction.

In the 1960s, some Manitoba churches began sponsoring drive-in church meetings during the summer season, one of the novel evangelistic methods of the decade, both in Canada and the United States. The assembly at St. Vital launched its drive-in services with a unique advantage — the church was located alongside a giant supermarket in the city. A drive-in restaurant, frequented by hundreds of teenagers, also provided a steady stream of listeners to the church's ministry on the weekends. A number of these young people were won to the Lord during these services as thousands of tracts were distributed.

Special "Kids' Crusades" were popular at that time. One of the most successful in Manitoba was held at Dauphin in 1963 with evangelists Peter and Edith Tarling. Many of the hundreds of children in attendance at the meetings were won to the Lord as well as some parents.

This period also witnessed another phase of the remarkable ministry of Dr. J. E. Purdie. Although Purdie had retired from Bible school work some years earlier, he and Mrs. Purdie travelled to a number of Manitoba churches and saw both conversions and healings take place as a result of their ministry.

The famous evangelist Hyman Appleman came to Calvary Temple in Winnipeg in the summer of 1963. About 170, of the 300 who signed decision cards, were received into the church as members. One of the highlights of the Appleman Crusade was the evangelist's pre-service, half-hour lectures on the ministry of the Holy Spirit. Calvary Temple also was the site of an innovative TV ministry in the early-60s. This new media ministry complemented the radio broadcast which dated back to the 1920s. *Faith To Live By*, with Pastor Herb Barber as the featured speaker, quickly found a responsive audience in Manitoba and other provinces.

A new church was founded in the '60s at Kinosota, on the shores of Lake Manitoba. Volunteer labor kept construction costs to a low $5,500. The pastor, E. C. Mitchell, led in the opening of a new branch work at Crane River, about 100 kilometres away. By the time General Conference was held in Winnipeg in 1966, there were a number of new assemblies established in the city's suburbs. These included the churches in Weston, Charleswood, and Sherwood.

Since Manitoba had a large Native population, the district sponsored an aggressive outreach to the Natives throughout the decade. Immanuel Jensen directed 17 credentialed Native workers who ministered among their own people in many locations. Three new chapels were built during the summer of 1967, while the older Native works showed steady, if slow, progress. At Fairford that summer, a crowd of 2,000 gathered on the banks of the river to witness a Pentecostal baptismal service and to hear 20 converts testify to their new faith in the Lord. Special short-term Bible study programs also were developed to train local Native leaders and to establish the believers in their faith.[18]

The Western Ontario district had the distinction of having one man — J. H. Blair — as its superintendent for over 30 years (1933-1966). Thus his leadership spanned the Depression, the war years, and the post-war expansion period in Ontario. The rapid progress of Pentecostalism in this region was fostered by the establishment of a Bible school to serve Eastern Canada. More than 30 new congregations were established in both large urban centres and in smaller communities.

The northern area of the province was reached with the founding of many new assemblies. John Spillenaar's vision for the northern settlements led to his appointment at the 1943 District Conference as a PAOC Northland missionary. He was instrumental in the establishment of churches in Kirkland Lake, Cochrane, and Haileybury. There had been small groups of Pentecostals in each community, but they were unorganized and without pastors at the time. Another church was opened in Hornepayne in 1948 under Spillenaar's direction. Its initial membership totaled about 100. The Northland missionary at first financed himself by secular employment, but gradually the Ontario churches rallied to his support. The Stone Church in Toronto raised $10,000 in

10 / THE THIRD FORCE

1951 to provide Spillenaar with an aircraft and flying lessons so he could reach the remote regions of the province. Out of this man's vision and labor emerged a loosely knit collection of Pentecostal groups across the Ontario Northland and on Native reservations. Other lay workers and preachers assumed leadership in these pioneering efforts until there were Pentecostal congregations in places like Fort Severn, Pagwa River, and Moosonee. Throughout the '50s, Pentecostal works were inaugurated at Churchill, Manitoba; Manitouwadge, Ontario; and on the Native Reserves at Sandy Lake, Sachigo, Round Lake, and Big Trout Lake.[19]

As in other provinces, the work in Ontario benefited greatly from a constant stream of Bible school graduates. One of them was David Mainse, who began services in Chalk River in 1955, a town made famous as a centre for the Canadian nuclear power industry. Mainse found little religious interest in the area among adult residents, but a Sunday School program gave promise of fruitful results. When evangelist Jack Shrier held meetings with Mainse in the town, a group of eight adults responded to the message and became the nucleus for a growing assembly. Mainse made his first venture into gospel broadcasting in Chalk River. He later expanded his evangelistic ministry with both radio and television programs, the best known of which is the "100 Huntley Street" telecast. Crossroads Christian Communications is the corporate name of the ministry.

There was a small group of Pentecostals in Collingwood, on the shore of Georgian Bay, in the early 1940s. Without a church building it was difficult to keep the group together. When Ernest Smythe arrived in 1948 to pastor the group, a number of converts entered into the Pentecostal experience. A new church building was erected with funds provided from the annual "Penny Day" offering received at Braeside Camp in 1955 by the Women's Missionary Council of Western Ontario. The offering, which amounted to $1,500, assisted the Collingwood congregation to erect a building seating 125 in the auditorium with an adjoining six-room apartment for the pastor.

An entirely new congregation was developed in Toronto in 1945 when Graydon Richards ministered to a small group in a rented hall. Within three years the assembly began the construction of the Weston church. Later, the congregation moved to a new site on Dixon Road and the church, pastored by George and Ruth Tunks, was renamed the Abundant Life Assembly.

On the western outskirts of Toronto, Edwin Martin began meetings in the Brampton Legion Hall in 1953. With district financial aid, property was acquired and a church built three years later. Under the leadership of the next pastor, Ron Stevens, the assembly built new facilities on a vacant piece of property on the corner of Kennedy Road and Vodden Street. In addition to the church, known as Kennedy Road Tabernacle, the congregation established the Heritage, a senior citizen's residence, and Kiddies Kollege, a day care centre for pre-school children. KRT, as it was popularly known, was a leader in the burgeoning bus ministries of the '50s. At the peak of its Sunday school ministry, KRT's fleet of buses transported hundreds of children weekly to its Sunday school which often numbered over 2,000 in attendance.

It also was in the post-war period that pastors of settled congregations undertook to "mother" new congregations in their own communities. J. H. Blair's congregation bought property on the Hamilton mountain in 1951 for the purpose of launching another church in that city. About 25 families left the older group to form the nucleus of this new assembly, known as Bethel Gospel Tabernacle. Rae Stewart was the first pastor. Eventually, Hamilton was to have five Pentecostal churches within its borders. Other new PAOC churches which were established before 1958 were in the communities of Acton, Bright, Burlington, Courtwright, Elora, Fergus, Innisfil, Listowel, London, Milton, Pelee Island, Rodney, Watford, Welland, Willowdale, and Wingham. District officials carried out a series of legislative and administrative changes in the two decades before 1960 which facilitated the progress of Pentecostalism in Ontario.

One noteworthy advance was in the area of Christian education. Both established and newer congregations benefited from promotional programs such as the Sunday school visitation strategy. Gordon F. Atter was appointed the district Sunday School supervisor — a new post — and by 1954 there were nearly 140 schools in operation. Special children's summer camps were held in the 1950s and Vacation Bible Schools became regular annual events at most churches. W. H. Moody took over supervision of the Sunday school department on a full-time basis and witnessed a steady increase in the schools and an improvement in their curricula during his tenure which lasted until 1975.

The Christ's Ambassadors work took on a district structure with the election in 1947 of Victor G. Brown as supervisor. C.A. rallies and conventions attracted thousands of Pentecostal youth and served to encourage and challenge them in their devotion to the Lord. It was in the early-50s that Western Ontario youth began to participate in the "Wing the Word" program to raise funds for missionary vehicles and equipment.

With the appointment in 1946 of Mabel Montgomery as director, the Women's Missionary Council began to operate along distinctively district lines. In the following years, the women's organization has provided extensive support for home missions programs and considerable finances for outreach of many kinds, both in Ontario and overseas. Most of these activities were promoted and reported in the district publication, *The Challenge*, a periodical introduced in the 1930s.

10 / THE THIRD FORCE

One distinctive venture into charitable work in this period was the establishment in 1945 of the Pentecostal Benevolent Association. It was the outgrowth of a vision by Walter McAlister to give oversight to such Toronto-area ministries as Shepherd Lodge, Shepherd Manor, Bethel Home For Girls, and Teen Challenge. Some of these benevolent programs began after the period under review, but were later incorporated in the Pentecostal Benevolent Association. Originally, the corporation was the sole responsibility of all the Toronto pastors and a number of laypersons. Eventually, the district superintendents of Western Ontario and Eastern Ontario and Quebec became involved in the oversight of its activities.

In the far north, Western Ontario district leadership has long supported a Native training school to provide indigenous workers for the Native communities. An eight-week training session was inaugurated at Moosonee in 1955. The training program was later transferred to a new site at Nakina, and still later to Pickle Lake. After attempts to train Natives on their home reservation proved unsatisfactory, a scheme was developed whereby students were transported by the district airplane from various locations to a centralized short-term Bible school. This strategy allowed the district to better develop the school facilities and to provide a challenging curriculum for the Native workers. The results throughout the '50s were encouraging, but work among Canada's indigenous peoples has always been attended by special problems relating to Native cultures and government regulations.[20]

Similar stories of rapid growth marked the history of the PAOC in Eastern Ontario and Quebec in the '40s and '50s. The superintendents in that era were C. B. Smith (1938-1942), H. J. McAlister (1942-1945), W. G. McPherson (1945-1946), and W. B. Greenwood (1949-1964). In these two decades, churches were established at Belleville, Brockville, Coboconk, Cobourg, Cornwall, Deseronto, Gananoque, Kingston, Long Sault, Napanee, Port Hope, and Trenton. Local Pentecostal revivals, which strengthened the churches in the area, were reported in the early-40s at Bancroft, Peterborough, and Sharbot Lake.

In Oshawa, a number of new assemblies were mothered by the congregation of Pastor Richard Bombay. It was an enlightened and ambitious program of expansion which historian Gloria Kulbeck called the "Divide and Grow" strategy.[21] Bombay had come into the Pentecostal Fellowship as a youth at Bracebridge through the instantaneous healing of his sister following prayer by itinerant Pentecostal workers. As a young man of 17, he became the pastor of a small congregation and embarked on a lifetime of ministry which perhaps reached its most effective phase while he was pastoring at Oshawa.

Bombay began "mothering" new assemblies by using the talents of dedicated lay men and women. The King Street Pentecostal Church, for example, was started when layman Frank Danzey organized a Sunday school and held "gospel sing-a-longs" in his home. Bombay called for volunteers from his assembly to assist in the King Street Sunday school and to evangelize in that area. With Bombay's encouragement, 37 members of the older congregation transferred membership to the new assembly which allowed it to become self-supporting. A similar process brought into being the Byng Avenue church in the north end of the city. Eventually, there was a Pentecostal group in every major suburb of Oshawa.

Pentecostal evangelism in Quebec has been severely hampered by cultural and language differences with English Canada, as well as by the antagonism of the Roman Catholic Church. Although Pentecostalism was introduced to Quebec early in the 20th century, there were only 19 French-speaking Pentecostal congregations by 1958. There was also an equal number of English-speaking Pentecostal groups in the province at that date. By one estimate, there were still over 100 towns with populations over 5,000 that had not yet been reached by the PAOC.

One method to help overcome the enormous obstacles to evangelism was the training of native Québecois to reach their own people. The Berea Bible Institute was set up in 1941 to help achieve this goal. W. L. Bouchard served as the first principal. E. L. Lassègues assumed leadership of the school in 1953 and was assisted by Salome Cressman from Ontario and by a number of Quebec teachers. Two of the earliest graduates of BBI went north in 1942 to Senneterre, where they founded the first congregation of French-speaking Pentecostals in the Abitibi region. Two young deaconesses, Marie-Paule Gagnon and a Miss Goyette, began full gospel meetings in Granby where they laid the foundations for a new church. Other Bible school graduates began meetings in Ville Jacques Cartier on the South Shore of the St. Lawrence. A church building was constructed in 1953 and a Sunday School program developed which enrolled over 100 students.

Meetings in 1956 in the Dorval area produced a new Montreal-area congregation. Still another group was founded the following year when Marie-Paule Gagnon began services in a private home in Val d'Or. Literature played a vital role in the dissemination of Pentecostalism in the province. The early material in the French language was imported from France and Switzerland. A small printing press at BBI provided literature for evangelism in the province. An advance was made in 1950 when the Quebec Literature Crusade was launched under the leadership of René Robert.

The growth of the French-language work was such that in 1949 the Eastern Ontario District Executive recommended the establishment of a

10 / THE THIRD FORCE

French Conference, with its own elected leaders. The first three superintendents of the French Conference were W. L. Bouchard (1949-1952), René Robert (1953-1954), and E. L. Lassègues (1955-1961). With these men giving the work the immediate supervision it needed, continued growth was recorded throughout the period. The English-speaking congregations, which remained under the direction of the Eastern Ontario and Quebec district, also exhibited steady development. After the death of C. E. Baker in 1947, the Evangel Church congregation in Montreal was pastored by W. H. Kautz. The assembly moved from Drummond Street to new facilities on Closse Street in 1954 where it experienced a remarkable revival. Many cases of supernatural healings were recorded and large numbers of people were baptized in the Holy Spirit. Along with French-Canadians and Natives, people of several ethnic groups were brought into the Pentecostal Fellowship in this revival, including Jews, Greeks, and Italians. Altogether, about 400 were converted.[22] Evangel also was a keen supporter of world missions. During the pastorate of Robert M. Argue, generous sums of money were raised for the work of PAOC missionaries.

Apart from English and French-speaking assemblies, there were several Pentecostal congregations in Quebec composed of people of Ukrainian, German, Finnish, and Italian background. Altogether, there were an estimated 5,700 Pentecostals in the province in 1958, about 60 per cent of whom were located in the Montreal region.

Pentecostalism in the Maritimes suffered for years from the severe economic disadvantages of the region. But steady spiritual progress was made under the leadership of district superintendents M. S. Winger (1936-1047), Claude Jones (1947-1948), and Ivan D. Raymer (1948-1974). The district established its first office complex at Truro in 1945. It also developed a campground, Camp Evangeline, on a beautiful 10-acre site at Debert, Nova Scotia, in 1950. These two properties were then worth about $50,000.

District administrative advances resulted in the formation of departments to promote and organize the ministries of WMC, youth, and Sunday school. The Sunday school program especially was employed to spawn several new assemblies. Regional radio broadcasts were also used effectively by a number of local churches to introduce the full gospel to thousands of Maritimers.

Results were encouraging for district officials in several parts of the constituency. A small group of Pentecostals at Campbellton, New Brunswick, put up a new church building in 1948. The members of Faith Tabernacle in Halifax witnessed steady growth in the '40s under the ministries of W. H. Found, William Rourke, and Arnold Kalamen. Faith

Tabernacle's commitment to world missions was illustrated by the $5,000 offering which its members raised at a single World Missions Convention in 1957. Later, the assembly "mothered" another congregation at nearby Dartmouth, with a dozen of its families forming the nucleus of the new church. Work in the Gaspé region (geographically and culturally a part of Quebec) has been the responsibility of the Maritime District. Roland and Cecile Bergeron began ministry in the Gaspé in 1956 and were able to build a church suitable for both French and English services.

The work on Prince Edward Island began with the ministry of Sheldon and Agnus Myers at Charlottetown in 1956. Sponsorship by the Maritime District helped the work go forward rapidly. The assembly soon was self-supporting. After a church building was put up in Charlottetown, two other Pentecostal congregations were established at strategic locations on the island.

The steady progress which the Pentecostal Assemblies of Newfoundland had demonstrated since its formation on the island continued through the '40s and '50s. By 1958, the PAON had established 20 new assemblies under the direction of its long-time superintendent, Eugene Vaters (1927-1962). Many of these new works were underwritten with central finances. Most of them soon became self-supporting, with some in turn mothering other congregations. Camp Emmanuel, the first campground, was opened at Long Pond in 1947. A new tabernacle, in memory of the founding ministry of Alice Belle Garrigus, was erected on the site in 1955.

Pentecostal evangelism in Newfoundland has in many ways paralleled that of the PAOC, with one significant difference. That distinctive feature was the development by the PAON of a denominational day school system. This system evolved from the many handicaps faced by early Pentecostals in the education of their children. With its long ties to England as a Crown colony, Newfoundland's school programs were all church-related and governed by various ecclesiastical bodies. When the Pentecostal revival swept over the island, the numerous converts found themselves unwelcome both in their former churches and in the church schools. Of necessity, the PAON formed its own educational branch, which has since grown into a network of schools with trained teaching staff and competent administrators. By the mid-50s, the PAON program included 13 schools with 22 teachers and 750 pupils.[23] By 1990, the academic professionalism of the PAON school division was comparable to that of any other in Newfoundland and was fully accredited by the provincial government.

In other respects, the Pentecostal leaders on the island administered their Sunday schools, Christ's Ambassadors, women's programs, and

10 / THE THIRD FORCE

men's programs similar to the PAOC and its constituent districts. In the boys' and girls' mid-week ministries, namely Pentecostal Crusaders and Missionettes, the PAON integrated with the PAOC administration.

The PAON has for some years published a denominational magazine, called *Good Tidings*, which has served an important role in unifying the many groups in the outports. A religious publishing plant and retail outlet was established at the PAON headquarters building in St. John's which has provided high quality literature and church supplies.

Rather than attempting to operate its own theological training institution, Newfoundland Pentecostal leaders combined with eastern districts of the PAOC to support and maintain Eastern Pentecostal Bible College in Peterborough. Newfoundland students composed a significant percentage of the student population at EPBC. In a similar manner, the PAON channelled its overseas missions support through the PAOC missions department in Toronto. By the end of the '50s, several Newfoundlanders were on the overseas fields with their total financial support coming from the Newfoundland churches.

This impressive progress and development of Pentecostalism was made possible only through the vision and dedication of thousands of ministers and lay workers. They viewed themselves as being in the forefront of worldwide evangelism in preparation for the return of Jesus Christ. This self-image, and the rapid progress of Pentecostalism, has been noted by both sympathetic and hostile observers. Dr. Frank Gigliotti of the Presbyterian Church wrote of the "almost phenomenal growth" of Pentecostalism in North America in the '40s. He suggested that "within the next ten years they would possibly lead in number all the evangelical churches in the United States." He commented also on the worship style of Pentecostal services, and added that, in practical terms, wherever the movement had touched the "humbler classes of society" it had made them better citizens.[24]

A Methodist observer thought his denomination was making the same mistakes in the 1950s, respecting Pentecostalism, as had been made in the 18th century by Anglicans about the original Methodists of John Wesley. He added that several evangelical denominations had failed to keep pace with the Pentecostals who were "building little churches everywhere" with people "kneeling at their altars."[25]

A Canadian Presbyterian cleric, Rev. L. H. Fowler, wrote a glowing testimonial to the movement in an article, titled "Salute to Pentecostals," published in the *Toronto Star* in 1959:

> . . . we are witnessing something apostolic in its nature. . . . The Pentecostal Movement has had close and interesting parallels with

the early days of John Wesley and the beginnings of sundry other movements, all of which had great fervor and zeal and single-heartedness.... In a quarter-century's acquaintance with Pentecostal pastors, I find them men of faith and courage.... I don't think they used the word "ecumenicity".... But they are really ecumenical.... They have not time to rant against the rest of us.... The Pentecostal people deserve a salute.[26]

The designation of Pentecostalism by Dr. Van Dusen in 1958 as "The Third Force" in Christendom was merely a recognition by a competent witness of the extraordinary work of the Holy Spirit in the 20th century. Pentecostals themselves were keenly aware of the fact that the movement had no human founder, although many prominent spokesmen and leaders had emerged from within its ranks. They also were aware that they had to safeguard their achievements from religious bureaucracy on the one hand and spiritual decline on the other. Their new-found respectability should not blind them to the goal of world evangelism, as J. A. Synan reminded delegates to the 1958 World Pentecostal Conference in Toronto:

> They say that Pentecost is the third great force in Christendom. But it is really the first great force.... (This) latter rain outpouring of the Holy Spirit is God's final great movement of power to provide a strong witness to the Church and the world before the coming of the Lord Jesus Christ.[27]

One PAOC speaker at the Conference, Tom Johnstone, reminded the delegates that the chief theme of the apostles — Jesus Christ as Lord — must remain the primary element in his colleagues' preaching. It was this theme that brought Pentecostalism to worldwide influence and it must be continued. Johnstone declared that only in this way could the PAOC and all Pentecostal denominations remain a part of "the Third Force."[28]

Endnotes

1. "A Symposium of the World Conference at Zurich, Switzerland," *The Pentecostal Testimony* (July 1, 1947) 2, 18; E. W. Robinson, "The Record of the First Pentecostal World Conference at Zurich, Switzerland, May 6-9, 1947," a mimeographed conference report in Western Pentecostal College library, Clayburn, B.C.

2. Gordon F. Atter, *The Pentecostal Movement* (Peterborough: College Press, 2nd ed., rev. 1957), pp. 9-11; Russell Chandler, "Pentecostals: The Fastest Growing Church," *Kitchener-Waterloo Record* (January 17, 1976).

3. Henry P. Van Dusen, "The Third Force," *Life* (June 9, 1958), 122-124.

291

10 / THE THIRD FORCE

4. Harold Bredesen, "The Second Wave of Pentecost," *Logos* (March-April 1961), 14-16.

5. See the special World Conference souvenir edition of *The Pentecostal Testimony* (October 1958). One interesting incidental point is that Toronto travel agent Joseph Gideon has taken a personal interest in the PAOC and has arranged for Canadian Pentecostals to attend every World Conference since 1961.

6. "More News from Mozambique," *The Pentecostal Testimony* (February 1, 1943), 11.

7. For a biography of Marion Parkinson's life, see George R. Upton, *Plucked From the Sea* (Toronto: PAOC, 1977).

8. Gloria G. Kulbeck, *What God Hath Wrought: The Story of The Pentecostal Assemblies of Canada* (Toronto: PAOC, 1958), pp. 184-185.

9. "Minutes of the Pentecostal Assemblies of Canada, B.C. District," May 19-22, 1953; Carman W. Lynn, "In the Land of the Midnight Sun," *The Pentecostal Testimony* (February 1955), 6; and Donald T. Klan, "Pentecostal Assemblies of Canada Church Growth in British Columbia From Origins Until 1953," unpublished MCS thesis, Regent College, Vancouver, 1979, 193.

10. For Alberta church histories see *Rejoice: A History of the Pentecostal Assemblies of Alberta and the Northwest Territories* (Edmonton: Alberta and NWT District, PAOC, 1983).

11. Arthur Drewitz, *History of the German Branch of the Pentecostal Assemblies of Canada, 1940-1980* (Kitchener: for the German Branch, 1986), p. 3.

12. Horst Doberstein, managing editor, *Grace & Glory: the story of the German Branch of The Pentecostal Assemblies of Canada* (Published by the German Branch, 1990), pp. 30-41.

13. D. N. Buntain, "Challenge of the Northland," *The Pentecostal Testimony* (May 15, 1952), 10; see also Ken Gaetz, "Pentecostal Pioneers in Canada's Northwest Territories," *The Pentecostal Testimony* (June 15, 1950), 11, 17.

14. "Pentecostal Assemblies of Canada Opens New Hospital," *The Pentecostal Testimony* (January 1958), 12.

15. Grace Brown, "Introduction," *Top Of The World* (Saskatoon: Modern Press, 1973).

16. Individual Saskatchewan church histories may be consulted in Paul Hawkes, *Songs of the Reaper: The Story of Pentecostal Assemblies in Canada in Saskatchewan* (Saskatoon: Saskatchewan District, PAOC, 1985).

17. Watson Argue, "Calvary Temple Burns Mortgage," *The Pentecostal Testimony* (January 15, 1941), 7.

18. See W. J. Taylor, "History of the First 50 Years of Manitoba and NW Ontario District, 1927 - 1977," mimeographed, Manitoba and NW Ontario District, PAOC, 1977.

19. See Victor G. Brown, ed. and compiler, *Fifty Years of Pentecostal History, 1933-1983* (Burlington: Western Ontario District, PAOC, 1983), p. 179.
20. Ibid., pp. 167, 168.
21. Kulbeck, note 8, p. 135; and Richard A. Bombay, Sr., "Memoirs," typewritten copy, 1974.
22. William Kautz, "Richard Vineyard Healing Revival in Evangel Pentecostal Church," *The Pentecostal Testimony* (May 1954), 25.
23. G. Shaw, "Newfoundland News Report," World Pentecost, 2 (1974), 3-4; "Newfoundland Schools," *The Canadian Encyclopedia*, vol. 2, (Edmonton: Hurtig, 1985), 1244-1253.
24. "An Appraisal of the Pentecostal Movement by a Presbyterian Minister," *Pentecostal Evangel* (February 8, 1947), 2-3.
25. Dr. Robert P. Schuler, "A Tribute to Pentecostals," reprinted from *The Methodist Challenge* in *The Pentecostal Testimony* (February 1950), 7.
26. L. H. Fowler, "Salute to Pentecostals," *Toronto Daily Star*, May 2, 1959.
27. J. A. Synan, "The Purpose of God in the Pentecostal Movement for this Hour," in Donald Gee, ed., *Pentecostal World Conference Messages, Preached at the Fifth Triennial World Conference* (Toronto: Testimony Press, 1958), pp. 27-33.
28. Tom Johnstone, "Pentecostal Preaching," in Donald Gee, note 5, pp. 5-7.

Chapter 11

"CLASSICAL PENTECOSTALS" IN CANADA

"Third Force" Pentecostalism entered the 1960s with a new-found public acceptance and ecclesiastical respectability. The next 20 years would be a period of dramatic growth for the established Pentecostal organizations. Favorable assessments like that of Professor Van Dusen's prompted many mainline denominational leaders to take a less-hostile stance towards Pentecostalism. But it was the emergence of two renewal movements in North America which propelled the "Third Force" to international prominence.

The first of these catalysts was the "Jesus People Movement" which originated in the United States during the period of the Viet Nam War. It was an age of extreme social unrest among American youth — campus demonstrations, war protests, and denunciations of the "military-industrial complex." It also was a period of social rebellion against moral standards and traditional family lifestyles. A counter-culture arose based on "free sex," drug use, and communal living. College students "dropped out" of society, became "street people," or went underground to avoid the wartime military draft. There soon emerged a sub-culture known as the "hippie movement." It was in this environment that the Jesus People revolution began.

Various studies of its origins differ in detail, but it seems to have begun around 1966 in California. Ted Wise was a "hippie" in the Haight-Ashbury district of San Francisco when he became a born-again Christian. Other converts joined him in evangelizing their peers, often through the famous "coffee house" ministry. It has been estimated that by means of this novel ministry as many as 50,000 young people were touched with the gospel within two years. The technique was exported to other American states, to Canada, and to some European countries.

11 / "CLASSICAL PENTECOSTALS" IN CANADA

Rejecting traditional methods, the Jesus People devised new, sometimes bizarre, ways to win their friends to the Lord. They popularized the use of rock music with Christian lyrics. The professional rock scene reflected the influence of the Jesus People with the production of successful musicals like "Jesus Christ, Superstar," and "Godspell." In many areas they transformed communal-living houses to Christian communes where converts could find a haven to kick the drug habit and also be grounded in the Word of God. The old hippie terminology was employed in street witnessing so that phrases like "getting high on Jesus" became familiar. Parades, concerts, and demonstrations were organized to proclaim faith in Christ. Preaching took place in such unusual locations as a strippers' club in Texas. A number of popular entertainment idols professed to be born-again Christians. The old hymn "Amazing Grace" appeared on pop music charts as a number one hit.

The attention which the movement received was so remarkable that *Time* magazine featured the Jesus People on its June 1971 cover. Innovative methods, exuberant worship, zealous witnessing, and public notice all contributed to rapid growth among the adherents. The membership of the movement in 1972 was estimated to be as high as 300,000.[1] Although it was evangelical in theology and charismatic in worship, the Jesus People Movement did not merge with any one of the main branches of Christianity. It resembled in many respects early 20th-century Pentecostalism.

The key reason the Jesus People failed to blend with traditional Pentecostal groups arose from the confirmed attitudes on both sides. The Jesus People usually dressed in blue jeans and "grannie" dresses, the men wore long hair, and their viewpoints generally echoed those of their hippie peers. Canadian Pentecostals, by contrast, were mainly middle-class and wary of such an unusual form of religious renewal. Some leaders were suspicious of the Jesus People because they did not immediately adapt to the familiar modes of church worship. Fortunately, Christian charity and tolerance prevailed and many of these converts, with all their differences, were embraced in Pentecostal churches.[2] Soon some of the features, such as the coffee house and street-witnessing ministries, appeared on the streets of Canadian cities as independent groups, parachurch organizations, and denominational youth groups engaged in front-line evangelism.

By the early-70s, Vancouver had become the hub of the Jesus People Movement in Canada. Young Canadians were urged to "take a second look at Jesus" — hundreds liked what they saw. Many of these new believers had rejected their parents' values even though they had been privileged members of the best-dressed, best-educated, and most affluent segment of Canadian society. A large number had been to university where some of the really important issues of life had been ignored by their professors in favor of Eastern mysticism or Western materialism.

The success of Jesus People workers in Vancouver was emulated in other cities across Canada. In Saskatoon, for example, Pastor Michael Horban permitted the Jesus People to meet weekly in Elim Tabernacle where attendance rose to about 200 at times. Similar groups were formed in several Ontario cities and also Montreal, usually with the sympathetic support of local Pentecostal pastors and people. Indeed, the youth in PAOC assemblies found their own spiritual lives rejuvenated by association with the Jesus People. Many congregations were greatly enriched by trying out some of the new worship modes.

Responsible observers of the Christian scene had some positive things to say about the Jesus People. When Billy Graham wrote an analysis of this movement, he concluded that it was Jesus-centered, Bible-based, and experiential in emphasizing the Holy Spirit, Christian discipline, and social responsibility.[3] Pentecostal leaders like Vinson Synan considered the Jesus People to be closer to the Azusa Street type of Pentecostal than any of the "established" Pentecostal denominations. An Assemblies of God spokesman, J. R. Flower, wrote enthusiastically of the achievements of the Jesus People. Ken Birch of the PAOC commended them out of his personal acquaintance with their beliefs and conduct.[4]

The Jesus People revolution had a profound, though relatively brief, impact upon North American society and a somewhat longer effect on North American Pentecostalism. It counteracted the drug culture of the '60s, won thousands of rebellious youth to obedience to Jesus Christ, inaugurated new modes of worship, and developed new methods of evangelism. By the late 1970s many of the evangelical and Pentecostal churches in Canada had adopted much of the movement's techniques. Coffee houses and campus ministries were set up and new choruses — derived directly from the Scriptures — were the norm in congregational gatherings. A fusion of Jesus People culture and Pentecostalism resulted from the gradual merging of both groups, although the "Jesus Freaks" had never developed any clearly recognizable denominational or ecclesiastical structures. On the other hand, some sections of the movement remained isolated from any evangelical bodies and eventually founded their own independent, charismatic congregations. One such group, Calvary Chapel in Costa Mesa, California, at one stage boasted a membership of 15,000.

These two trends (merging with older groups or establishing separate church congregations) led to the eventual disappearance of the Jesus People as a distinct renewal force in North America. A retrospective survey by *Christianity Today* concluded that the movement had made a

11 / "CLASSICAL PENTECOSTALS" IN CANADA

lasting impact upon evangelicalism, especially in the musical realm.[5] The end of the "revolution" was brought about by the blending process described above, and by the fact that it never produced any distinctive theology or ecclesiastical innovations. Thus a gradual absorption was easily achieved, especially within the Pentecostal denominations. The Jesus People Movement brought new vitality in worship and new zeal for witnessing to Canadian Pentecostal congregations and left them with a permanent change in worship modes, especially in the predominance of choruses over hymn singing.

The second major force in the period to bring change to the churches was the Charismatic Movement. Although it had some affinities with the Jesus People Movement, the charismatic renewal progressed along very different lines. Where the former movement generally had a beneficial but limited influence on Pentecostalism, the impact of the latter has been the subject of an ongoing debate. The origins of the Charismatic Movement have been traced to the Holy Spirit infilling in 1960 of Dennis Bennett, an Episcopalian clergyman in California.

Bennett introduced many others to the experience and publicized his work in the book *Nine O'Clock in the Morning*. A Roman Catholic writer named John Sherrill investigated Bennett's meetings and wrote the bestseller entitled *They Speak With Other Tongues*. These books introduced the topic to thousands of Roman Catholics and members of older Protestant denominations. Large numbers of the readers experienced Pentecost for themselves. A third book, *The Cross and the Switchblade*, detailed David Wilkerson's exciting ministry among New York City street gangs. The exposure provided the burgeoning Charismatic Movement with a sympathetic introduction to the older Pentecostal groups. Wilkerson was an ordained minister with the largest Pentecostal denomination, the Assemblies of God of Springfield, Missouri.

Innovative Pentecostal ministries in the 1960's, like Oral Roberts' TV programs and Demos Shakarian's Full Gospel Businessmen's Fellowship International meetings, acquainted thousands of people to traditional Pentecostalism. There followed such charismatically-oriented ministries as Jim Bakker's PTL (Praise the Lord) and Pat Robertson's CBN television shows. Still later, Assemblies of God evangelist Jimmy Swaggart began an extensive television outreach from his Baton Rouge headquarters.

While the evaluation of some of the long-term influences of these ministries may be less than positive, there is little question that in their time they brought much attention to Pentecostalism.

The period under review also witnessed the launching of a number of charismatic publications such as Shakarian's *Voice* magazine, and others like *New Wine, Logos Journal,* and *Renewal.* Old-line denominations in North America began to give greater prominence in preaching and publications to the role of the Holy Spirit and viewed the traditional Pentecostal groups with a friendlier spirit. Harold Bredesen of the Dutch Reformed Church in America wrote favorably of the infant Charismatic Movement, as did Larry Christenson of the Lutheran Church of America. They announced that a "new wine" of greater spirituality was infusing the "old wineskins" of historic denominationalism. The influence of Sherrill's book among Catholics was reinforced by Kevin Ranaghan's volume, *Catholic Pentecostals.* In a remarkably short space of time the renewal movement had produced thousands of books, magazine articles, and sermons on the charismatic elements of Christianity.

The publication in 1975 of Cardinal Suenens book, *A New Pentecost?* seemed to give at least an air of official Roman Catholic approval. Charismatic teachings swept through Roman Catholic circles chiefly by means of the publications cited above and through the charismatic renewal meetings which began at Duquesne University in 1967. Conferences on the charismatic renewal were held each summer at Notre Dame, Indiana; attendance grew from the original 90 to over 30,000. The movement spread around the world with great rapidity and expanded in spite of an official attitude of caution and restraint. Nonetheless, by the 1970s the Roman Catholic hierarchy admitted that Catholic Pentecostalism had become one of the most vital forces in its ranks.

The Roman Curia expressed fear that Catholics were becoming "too Anabaptistic." To reinforce the point, Cardinal Suenens maintained that the "gifts" being exercised by the charismatics had been originally conferred on them by the Church at baptism. Only now, argued the Cardinal, were the faithful "actualizing" what had been given them at first by the Catholic Church. The call of Pope Paul VI, in the 1970s, for a congress on the charismatic renewal in the Church led to several papal pronouncements on the benefits of the charismata to believers. The next Pope, John XXIII, continued this emphasis at the Second Vatican Council. Thus it seemed the Catholic hierarchy maintained its ancient claim to be the only arbiter for Catholics in doctrine, discipline, and practice. The official position has not been altered since Vatican II.[6]

The tolerant attitude of the hierarchy to the charismatic renewal within its branch of Christianity was no doubt influenced by contacts with Pentecostal personalities such as David du Plessis. A South African Pentecostal, du Plessis began travelling the world in the 1950s to persuade the mainline denominations to view Pentecostalism more favorably. This self-appointed emissary attended many Protestant and Catholic gatherings and came to be know to them as "Mr. Pentecost."

11 / "CLASSICAL PENTECOSTALS" IN CANADA

Even the World Council of Churches (WCC) came to acknowledge the Charismatic Movement as a vital, growing force in the historic denominations. Curiously, it suggested that the renewal, because it was inter-denominational in character, had obvious affinities with the WCC.[7]

The traditional, or "classical," Pentecostals were encouraged by the emergence of a new exuberance in worship and a new emphasis on the charisms of the Spirit in the old-line denominations. Whereas the early Pentecostals had been forced to leave their former denominational affiliation by the official rejection of early 20th-century Pentecostalism, the new charismatics were permitted to remain. Indeed, Canadian Pentecostals looked on in wonder at the formation of grassroots groups of charismatics who exhibited the same manifestations of glossolalia, prophecies, and prayer for the sick as was familiar among their own churches. Anglican, Lutheran, Presbyterian, Baptist, Mennonite, Orthodox, and Roman Catholic lay people and clergy met in their own churches across the country to participate in the religious renewal.

But Pentecostals were also mystified by the continuation of these revived persons in denominations which, to the Pentecostals, were bound by human tradition and unscriptural doctrines. Many traditional Pentecostals were puzzled at the reluctance of the charismatics to abandon their "dead" churches. For their part, the majority of new Pentecostals wanted to have a relationship with the "classical" Pentecostals but did not necessarily want to join them. While they maintained a loyalty to their own denomination and its tenets, they expressed sincere appreciation for the older Pentecostal denominations who had been the keepers of the Spirit Baptism. Catholic scholar Kilian McDonell, for example, wrote of "The Ecumenical Significance of the Pentecostal Movement" in flattering terms. Another competent observer linked both the Pentecostal and the charismatic movements as revival/renewal movements and claimed the latter movement was "an extension of Pentecostalism to a new environment."[8]

The charismatics did not form sectarian groups as the early Pentecostals had been obliged to do, but stayed within their existing denominations.[9] Although the movement was ecumenical in character, it remained theologically diverse and showed no inclination to affiliate with the older Pentecostal groups. As these differences gradually became more apparent to both sides, the Pentecostals became less enamored with the Charismatic Movement, and the charismatics began to distinguish themselves from one another along denominational lines — "Catholic charismatics," "Lutheran charismatics," and so on. It was this kind of labelling which produced the designation "Classical Pentecostals" for all the early 20th-century Pentecostal groups.

One interesting side note is the observation that the charismatics differed from their predecessors in North America by showing no evidence of anti-intellectualism. This trait in early Pentecostalism often had been exaggerated by its critics. Unfortunately, a stereotype emerged which portrayed the first generation of Pentecostals as largely uneducated and uncultured. The undeniable element of anti-intellectualism in the early period was due chiefly to suspicion among Pentecostals that higher education had fostered Darwinian evolution and theological liberalism. By the 1960s, fear of advanced education was a memory, but Pentecostals remained very cautious about the relationship between theology and secular education. Academic degrees and advanced education were not significant issues among the new charismatics in the old-line denominations.

Throughout the '70s, the differences between the "classical" and the new Pentecostals gradually replaced the 1960s emphasis on their similarities. Catholic charismatics such as Kevin Ranaghan and Bishop Joseph rejected the Classical Pentecostal view that speaking in tongues is "the initial physical evidence" of the Baptism in the Holy Spirit. They, as well as many Protestant charismatics, argued that any gift of the Spirit constituted evidence of the Pentecostal Baptism. Some went so far as to allege that proof of the Baptism could be found in their new devotion to their churches, their new-found liberty in worship, or even in a greater veneration of the Virgin Mary.

Canadian Pentecostals rejected the Catholic Church's claim that the gift of the Spirit was merely a "flowering" or "actualization" of a gift conferred by a priest at the sacrament of baptism. Pentecostals also expected dramatic changes in lifestyle among those who professed the Baptism in the Holy Spirit. At the turn of the century, when Pentecostals were imbued with elements of the earlier Holiness Movement, they reflected the esteem in which they held the principles of holiness by emphasizing "holiness of life" and "separation from the world." In contrast, the charismatics seemed indifferent about such practices as smoking and drinking alcohol. Furthermore, Pentecostals could not understand why Bible studies did not prompt charismatics to modify their theology to make it more biblically sound. For these reasons, Canadian Pentecostalism moved from enthusiastic approval of the new Charismatic Movement in the 1960s to a more wary assessment of it by the end of the '70s.

This process may be followed in the published comments and evaluative articles which appeared in *The Pentecostal Testimony*. A report on Dennis Bennett and the Baptism in the Holy Spirit, experienced by about 1,300 Episcopalians, indicated that the news was received

11 / "CLASSICAL PENTECOSTALS" IN CANADA

enthusiastically by delegates at the 1961 Chicago conference of the Pentecostal Fellowship of North America. When the Second Vatican Council was convened, Canadian Pentecostal scholar Dr. J. Harry Faught noted that all Pentecostals rejoiced at the new emphasis in Catholicism on the person and work of the Holy Spirit. He also expressed the hope that the Council would bring a greater sense of unity to Christendom than had been known for centuries. Faith Campbell reported most favorably on a charismatic gathering at Yale University, under the leadership of Harold Bredesen, where many students were filled with the Spirit.[10]

When Kevin Ranaghan spoke in the Vancouver area and on the university campus, Pentecostal pastor and university chaplain Bernice Gerard cooperated with his ministry. About two-thirds of Ranaghan's audience was composed of members of the Anglican, Baptist, Mennonite, Presbyterian, and United churches. More than 100 responded to his message and were filled with the Spirit. Gerard reported that "although this breakthrough is heartening, a much greater stirring by the Holy Spirit can be expected."[11] Her attitude at that time reflected the view of the majority of Canadian Pentecostals who respected the gains which the Charismatic Movement had made in spiritual renewal.

The expectation of traditional Pentecostals, however, that many in the new movement would embrace more of the Classical Pentecostalism was made explicit in two articles in the *Testimony* written by a former Catholic priest. Armaro Todriguez, in "What is Happening in the Roman Catholic Church?" and "The Spirit of God is Moving," anticipated many changes as a result of Vatican II. But, in his opinion, the changes unfortunately would not be great enough to renew the Catholic Church. Since changes might occur in discipline and church life but not in doctrine, he urged Catholic charismatics to take the ultimate step and leave Rome.[12]

A considerable number of charismatics did leave Catholicism, as well as some of the Protestant charismatic groups, and joined the Classical Pentecostals. Many PAOC churches were enlarged by their admission. But this positive development was accompanied by a growing concern among PAOC leaders about the effect that fame and acceptance might have on the Fellowship. General Superintendent Walter E. McAlister issued a call in 1960 for a unanimous commitment by PAOC members to pray for a spiritual revival that would stoke the Pentecostal fires which had been lit earlier in the century.

Other clergymen issued warnings of spiritual decline in the PAOC. Pastor Ronald Reid welcomed the resurgence of interest in the Holy Spirit, but warned of "a lamentable indifference and coldness which is becoming evident in many places." Respected Bible college teacher and administrator Alvin C. Schindel observed that "our movement has lost some of its youthful exuberance, some of its standards have changed, and some of its goals have been modified." Another academic, William A. Griffin, noted the success the Pentecostal Movement was experiencing:

> National magazines are writing about us; religious periodicals are flattering us; major denominations are in consultation with us; former critics are being filled with the Holy Spirit and are speaking in tongues.[13]

But the title of Griffin's article expressed the basic concern, "Can We Stand Success?" He stated that Pentecostals "without fear and with more than a little pride" announce their religious affiliation, but they "no longer pray as they once did."

Much of the success which the Fellowship experienced in the 1960s related to its involvement in evangelism. *The Pentecostal Testimony* carried articles about the original vision to establish a Pentecostal assembly in every city and larger community in Canada. The magazine itself attempted to reach non-Christian readers by printing simple presentations of the gospel; several issues of the *Testimony* included articles by A. H. Townsend under the heading "A Word to the Unconverted." The 1960 General Conference at London provided PAOC leaders with the opportunity to reassess the achievements of the movement to that date and to chart the course for the future. Conference delegates were told that in the two-year period prior to their gathering some 90 new church buildings had been erected. The International Office in Toronto had received almost 2.4 million dollars for world missions. Circulation of the official national magazine, *The Pentecostal Testimony*, had reached 25,000 copies per month. That number represented nearly a three-fold increase over the 1950 statistics. Despite the record of progress, delegates were urged to give themselves to renewed and innovative methods of evangelism.

The '60s in Canada marked the decade when "bus ministries" made their appearance and dramatically increased attendance at Pentecostal Sunday schools and churches. The new method of outreach, which was developed first in the United States, became increasingly popular among the Canadian churches. Pastor Fred Spring of Sault St. Marie, Ontario, for example, first considered bus evangelism in 1972. By 1974, Spring and his church board had inaugurated their own program in the city and surrounding region. Within a year of mobilizing six buses, the average Sunday school attendance had risen from 159 to 375.[14]

Another example of evangelistic innovation occurred at the Hi-Way Pentecostal Church in Barrie, Ontario. In order to attract both local people

11 / "CLASSICAL PENTECOSTALS" IN CANADA

and some of the many thousands who drove past Barrie each weekend on their way to cottage country, the church erected a tent on a site beside the busy Highway 400 North. The first services, with evangelist Roy Davis, were so encouraging that the church continued the summer tent meetings for about 10 years.

A flexible approach to evangelism resulted in the emergence of a number of ministries new to Canadian Pentecostalism. Local assemblies in the Lower Mainland of British Columbia provided support for new programs of evangelism in the prisons at Abbotsford, Burnaby, Agazzis, and Ruskin, and at the regional psychiatric centre in Abbotsford. Late in the '70s these programs were expanded to include inmates at Haney and Mission City. A Vancouver pastor, Bernice Gerard, not only gave spiritual leadership to the Fraserview assembly in that city, but served as a city councillor and conducted a radio "hot line" show.[15] Gerard also served as a university chaplain. The effectiveness of her innovative ministry was acknowledged by her colleagues when she was invited to be one of the principal speakers at the 1976 General Conference of the PAOC.

The PAOC has always demonstrated a willingness to participate in joint efforts in evangelism. One such international program which attracted Pentecostals was Key '73. When the Billy Graham Evangelistic Association challenged the churches of North America to reach the masses in one year, the Pentecostals responded eagerly. Evangelist Roy Davis outlined in the *Testimony* the plans to make 1973 a year of effective evangelism in Canada. To assist pastors and congregations, the national office mailed packets of materials and a resource book on Key '73 to affiliated churches. The express aim was to have all lay people involved. A year later, the PAOC introduced its own nationwide evangelism scheme — Pentecostal Assemblies Church Extension (PACE). This program had two main goals: to re-emphasize the Great Commission and to prepare local believers for ministry. Some of the methods suggested for the local churches were

> drive-in services, witness meetings in parks and beaches, etc., literature distribution, youth ministries, fasting and prayer, opening branch SS, assisting sister churches and mothering new assemblies.[16]

The PACE scheme was phased out in 1976 when other forms of evangelistic activity came into prominence.

In a conscious attempt to highlight the ministry of the itinerant evangelist, the first "evangelists' seminar" was organized in Toronto in 1973 with 14 Canadian workers in attendance. Presentations were made,

"CLASSICAL PENTECOSTALS" IN CANADA / 11

followed by discussions, on such topics as "The Anointed Ministry," "The Supernatural in Evangelism," and "Effective Evangelistic Preaching."[17]

Television offered another form of ministry which was particularly suited to the entertaining style of Pentecostal evangelism. Because of stringent government regulations with reference to broadcasting, it was much more difficult in Canada than in the United States to engage in television ministries. A few of the larger Canadian churches, such as Calvary Temple in Winnipeg, Elim Tabernacle in Saskatoon, and Queensway Cathedral in Toronto, implemented TV ministries on public television channels as an outreach of the local assembly. Certainly the most influential and widely-viewed Pentecostal/charismatic television ministry has been the "100 Huntley Street" telecast under the leadership of David Mainse in Toronto.

After his graduation from Eastern Pentecostal Bible College, Mainse pastored in Ontario and ventured into the field of television. Out of his early labors came the "Crossroads" and "Circle Square" programs. But the culmination of Mainse's work has been a daily "talk show" telecast from Toronto. "100 Huntley Street" (the name was derived from the street address in Toronto) was the first daily television ministry of its type in the country. Although "100 Huntley Street" has operated as an independent, non-denominational ministry, Mainse has retained his personal ministerial credentials with the PAOC. The program has received much moral and financial support from PAOC members and adherents with whom it enjoys a unique relationship.[18]

An innovative evangelism/discipleship program in Edmonton provides evidence of the impact of the Jesus People Movement on Canadian Pentecostalism. Pastors Laurie and Iris Hueppelsheuser designed a building for their new congregation of former Jesus People. Since many of the converts had difficulties in developing social and inter-personal relationships, the Hueppelsheusers turned the new sanctuary into a multi-use facility which could provide for other needs of the people throughout the week. Among its services were a 24-hour "hotline" and a K-12 Christian day school. Within 10 years after its beginning, the congregation constructed a one-million-dollar sanctuary. It was just one of the more than 20 new congregations established in Alberta in the decade before 1978.

The related concepts of "mothering" and "planting" new assemblies through the cooperation of sponsoring churches and/or district executives had been used successfully throughout Canada for several decades. The increased use of these two methods, therefore, in the '60s and '70s was the result of a renewed emphasis on evangelism rather than a new departure. There are scores of examples from which to choose, but the following selections will suffice to illustrate PAOC church growth patterns in that period.

In northern Saskatchewan a church was founded in La Ronge through the involvement of the District Executive. Land was purchased, a parsonage erected, and a nucleus of believers gathered. In 1980, an enthusiastic group of Pentecostal laymen organized a Men's Fellowship retreat in the community. These men paid their own expenses, purchased materials for the church, and erected a new sanctuary during their holidays in La Ronge.

At Pickle Lake, Ontario, a layman named Wally Wood, who believed he and his wife were divinely called, came north in 1978 without any promise of financial support. When they arrived, they met Dale and Alberta Cummins, two workers who had just been sent out by the Western Ontario district to establish a Native Bible school at Pickle Lake. These people combined their resources and held meetings in a house trailer. Within a few months their congregation numbered between 30 and 40 each Sunday.

Another assembly was founded at Terrace Bay by two graduates of Eastern Pentecostal Bible College — John Laari and David Laakso. After beginning meetings in 1975, they gathered a stable congregation and constructed a church by 1980.

In London, Ontario, the London Gospel Temple sponsored another assembly — Royal View — in a suburb of the city. What was unique in this "mothering" process was that the Royal View Church itself some years later gave birth to a third London assembly — Glad Tidings. Throughout the Western Ontario district a renewed commitment to church planting had significant results. Within 20 years, some 30 new congregations had been established. Three of these were located in Hamilton — Parkdale, Southmont, and Westdale. Each new assembly was strategically located to meet the spiritual needs of the residents of these fast-growing suburbs.

A vision for reaching recent immigrants to Canada motivated the congregation of Danforth Gospel Temple in Toronto. With an estimated 15,000 Spanish-speaking people living in the city in 1973, Paul and Dorothy Sorensen (former missionaries to Argentina) began work among these new Canadians. The response was quite encouraging as attendance at the meetings grew from 50 to about 90. A Spanish Bible class attracted more people during the week. Within a short time 55 people had been converted to Christ.

The planting of a Pentecostal assembly in the Ottawa area was an excellent demonstration of the denomination's evangelistic outreach program. Demographic studies indicated that Orleans, a bedroom community on the east side of the city, was experiencing rapid growth and had a high proportion of young families. With the approval and support of the district office in Belleville, the Ottawa Bethel congregation initiated a church planting project in Orleans. Bethel released a number of families to form the nucleus of the new assembly. Bert Liira accepted the invitation to pastor the young church. He rented a suitable building and inaugurated activities and ministries geared to young families. The first Sunday school class had 47 in attendance when it began in April 1978.

In order to record the areas of voluntary work in which they were interested, a questionnaire was distributed to the adults who attended the first services in Orleans. The families who had transferred from Bethel assembly and other Pentecostal churches provided experienced leadership. In this manner, Liira quickly put together a Sunday school staff, a youth program, and a music ministry. After 21 months of meeting in a school gymnasium, the congregation launched a church building program. The funds required were over $40,000. The district provided $2,000, in addition to the debt-free grant of land; $7,000 came from a special "Penny Day" offering at Lakeshore Pentecostal Camp; and about $15,000 from the Ottawa Bethel assembly. The balance of the money was raised by the Orleans people. So successful was this evangelistic outreach that from 1978 to 1980 the new church returned about $40,000, by way of church tithes, to the district office.

By the time the new Community Pentecostal Church was completed, weekly attendance was averaging about 450 — a phenomenal growth rate for a pioneer endeavor which had begun with only 47 Sunday school students and a few adults. It had moved from what Bert Liira called a "suitcase operation" (because all the equipment had to be packed in boxes and suitcases and removed from the rented school facilities after each service) to a firmly established and vibrant Pentecostal assembly. The methods adopted for its numerical and spiritual development were both the traditional ones used by most pioneering preachers and also some innovative strategies. These included the fostering among the people of "a loving attitude" to each other and visitors alike; regular classes each winter on "Christian growth" so that all members were well grounded in the Bible; and a systematic program of home visitation to invite people in the community to the church services.

Liira's experience at Orleans was, in his own estimation, one of the most exciting in his years of ministry. Like other Pentecostal pastors, he had read many of the church growth books and magazine articles coming from the United States, but he found that the Canadian scene required

11 / "CLASSICAL PENTECOSTALS" IN CANADA

distinctive, flexible approaches. His "Christian growth" class was particularly effective in retaining new converts. If they remained in that class nine to ten months, few of them dropped out of the congregation.[19]

The merging of local church initiative and district financial support had been a feature of Maritime Pentecostalism in the '60s under the direction of superintendent Ivan Raymer. The district had supported tent meetings in a number of communities such as Fredericton, New Brunswick; Shelburne, Nova Scotia; and Summerside, Prince Edward Island. The meetings led to the formation of churches in several centres, including Shelburne where Robert Cross came in 1965 to pastor the young congregation. The next Maritime district superintendent, Don Moore, provided leadership and assistance in the erection of a new building for the congregation at Elmwood, Nova Scotia. A struggling work at Montague, on Prince Edward Island, received a boost with the arrival of Barry and Sharon Slauenwhite. Under their leadership the work progressed and a church building was put up with district support. The new building enhanced the ministry of Crossroads Pentecostal Tabernacle in the community.

The Maritime pastors also utilized the "mothering" concept of evangelism and church growth. One pastor in the community of Western Shore felt a God-given burden for the residents of nearby Mahone Bay. He started services among them in 1967 and witnessed the conversion of a number of people. After a new congregation was established, one of its first acts was to purchase an empty church building and renovate it for Pentecostal worship. Perhaps the most extraordinary evangelistic outreach of the '70s in the Maritimes was a revival which began midway through the decade at Edmundston, New Brunswick. The pastor at nearby Grand Falls, Denys Blackmore, concerned about the unevangelized residents in Edmundston, secured evangelist Peter Youngren for a crusade. The local Roman Catholic hierarchy appeared to be very much opposed to the evangelistic efforts. Sometimes the community halls which Blackmore had booked for their meetings would suddenly become unavailable. In spite of the obstacles, the services were held and attracted crowds of 1,000 and more.

A number of spectacular healings convinced the people that the whole thing was of God. During one particular series of meetings, there were 133 converts in just three days, and another 350 converts a short time later. Altogether, there were an estimated 700 new believers. Unfortunately, many who expressed interest in the gospel succumbed to clerical and family pressure and reneged on their professions of faith in Christ. A Pentecostal congregation of about 400 was established at Edmundston. Blackmore pastored both the church at Grand Falls and the new Edmundston assembly for some time. After a new church building was constructed with the assistance of national and district home missions funds, David Whittaker, a bilingual pastor, came from Montreal to lead the Edmundston congregation.[20]

Nowhere was the distinctive nature of PAOC expansion better demonstrated than in the province of Quebec. The ministry was a complex web of activity based on the local church, the French Conference, the district of Eastern Ontario and Quebec, and the national office. This multi-faceted relationship, familiar throughout the history of Pentecostalism in Canada, was made all the more complex in French Canada because of historical, governmental, ecclesiastical, and cultural differences. At times, there were repressive measures from both government and Catholic Church officials against the "cults," a category in which Pentecostalism was included.

In 1960, there were only about 5,700 PAOC adherents in the province and about 45 churches, 20 of which were composed exclusively of French-speaking members. These churches lacked the financial resources and the trained personnel to make any significant impact on the province. The Berea Bible Institute faculty and the French Conference superintendent were heroic in their sacrifices and labors, but there were simply not enough resources to carry on widespread evangelism. Historically, the district of Eastern Ontario and Quebec, because of its geographic jurisdiction in the province, gave supervision to the English-speaking churches while the French Conference coordinated the francophone assemblies. Subsequent decisions by the district and the national office to extend their efforts in evangelism and church planting to include the French-speaking majority of Quebec signalled a dramatic expansion of the Pentecostal presence in that province. As the number of French-speaking congregations under its supervision increased, the Eastern Ontario and Quebec district formalized the structure of its French Ministries wing and ultimately amended its constitution to become officially bilingual. This bilingual feature is unique among all seven districts of the PAOC.

The decade of the '70s witnessed further development of local assemblies in Quebec on all fronts. One interesting story relates to the origin of PAOC work among Chinese residents in Montreal. From an original group of only 19 baptized members, the Chinese Pentecostal Assembly steadily grew in this period until it became a self-supporting church with its own Chinese-speaking pastor. Another small group of believers was organized in the Montreal suburb of LaSalle in 1974. By the end of the decade this group of French-speaking Pentecostals, known as L'Assemblée du Plein Evangile, had increased from a few people to a membership of about 300. In St-Hubert, a small nucleus of believers, who gathered regularly for prayer and Bible study, initiated the "cell group" system and mushroomed into a congregation of about 500 believers within a short time.

A basic strategy in stimulating evangelism and church planting in Quebec was to produce more qualified leaders. To augment the work being done by Berea Bible Institute among francophone ministry candidates within the province, the national office launched a program, known as "French Language Intensive Training for Evangelism" (FLITE). The goal was to recruit graduates of the English Bible colleges and train them in French for evangelism in Quebec. Under the guidance of Robert Argue, Executive Director of Home Missions and Bible Colleges, dedicated men and women joined the FLITE plan and registered for special language instruction at Laval University in Quebec City. Since the FLITE program recruited only graduates of other PAOC Bible colleges, the students were qualified upon completion of their language studies to enter ministry immediately. By 1980, about 40 ministers had graduated from the FLITE program.[21]

Another important factor in the effective PAOC outreach in the province was the development of an English-speaking assembly in Quebec City. With financial support from the district office in Belleville, Verner and Marjorie O'Brien pioneered the English work in Quebec City in 1965. After the O'Briens resigned, Al Bowen, a bilingual minister, assumed pastoral duties. When an AIM team carried out an evangelism "blitz" in the city in 1972, a number of francophone young people were converted. This small group of believers formed the foundation of a new French church. Under the leadership of Al and Irene Bowen, the church became the strong French-speaking assembly known as Carrefour Chrétien De La Capitale. By 1990 about 900 worshippers attended services regularly in the large, well-equipped church complex.

The leadership of the work in Quebec City had a vision to impact the entire area with the full gospel. The basic requirement to initiate the task was a body of trained workers. Al Bowen and Don Martin played key roles in the formulation of a "Bible school" known as Formation Timothée. They secured some financial support from outside the province to launch the program. As Formation Timothée developed its unique curriculum, it recruited additional faculty members. Don and Betty Krohn played a significant role in the school for several years before they accepted a missions assignment in Mozambique. Larry and Doreen Broughton, another missionary couple, served for a brief stint in the Quebec City school.

Through the '70s there emerged an increasingly sophisticated academic program of studies for young pastors who could only leave their posts for brief periods of study. Students were mailed audio, and later video, cassettes for home study. Periodically, the students came to the Quebec City centre for short, intensive, in-class instruction. An evening study plan was also inaugurated. Formation Timothée was designed to be completed in three years.[22] Its ultimate success was achieved when the PAOC recognized its graduates as eligible for ministerial credentials.

No doubt Pentecostalism in the province benefited from the so-called "living room revolt against the clergy" of the 1970s. Television, especially gospel and charismatic programs then being telecast, was a powerful force in opening the eyes of the Québecois to the outside world. The emphases of the Charismatic Movement that swept through Roman Catholicism also had a powerful impact on spiritually hungry souls. The Catholic hierarchy in Quebec bemoaned the loss of members. It complained that only 25 per cent of Catholics regularly attended mass and only a small percentage of high school students went to church. While they were turning away from the traditional church, the people of Quebec were responsive to other groups entering the province. One example of the openness to the Pentecostal message was the great response in Sept-Iles during the winter of 1978 to the ministry of evangelist Don Schellenberg. Over 40 people professed healing from various illnesses and about 100 were converted.[23]

The number of French churches in the late-80s reached about 100 with approximately half of this number under the supervision of the French Conference and the other half related to the district of Eastern Ontario and Quebec. The progress was positive evidence of what could be accomplished when the different levels of the PAOC (local church, branch conference, district, and national office) engaged in singular and cooperative evangelism projects. While the results were quite impressive, bringing the Pentecostals to the forefront of Protestantism in the province, it must be reported that the presence of two parallel PAOC administrative structures — one exclusively French-speaking, the other involving both French and English churches, and each administration sponsoring a Bible college — created some tension.

Attempts to consolidate the two Pentecostal administrations into a single entity for the province did not succeed. A proposal for amalgamation, offered by a committee which was composed of representatives from both groups and from the General Executive, was considered at the respective spring conferences in 1989. The plan failed when the delegates of the French Conference decided to maintain their own structure. Although organizational unity was not accomplished, good will prevailed among the credential holders. Both groups continue to minister effectively and cooperate in joint ministries.

11 / "CLASSICAL PENTECOSTALS" IN CANADA

Dozens of other exciting success stories could be told if space permitted — about the expansion in the Yukon and Northwest Territories; the effectiveness of the gospel boat work on the Pacific coast; the multiplication of Native works in several districts, the two new Eskimo congregations at Coppermine and Nanisivik in the Arctic; the development among the Chinese, Korean, Spanish, and other ethnic groups; and the list goes on...

Concurrent with local church growth, Pentecostals maintained their affection for the camp meeting. At the beginning of the '60s there were twelve PAOC campgrounds in operation. The next two decades saw the establishment of several new campgrounds and the renovation and enlargement of many of the existing sites. Particularly significant was a five-day camp meeting which was organized in 1961 for Native Canadians at Fort Rupert, British Columbia. Wilson Waterhouse, the indefatigable lay evangelist from Parkside, Saskatchewan, was present and reported the dramatic results of the meetings. He considered the event to be the greatest move of God among the Natives he had ever witnessed. About 70 were saved and a number were healed of various ailments during the camp.[24]

A camp meeting facility in the Northwest Territories proved to be a source of much spiritual blessing in that area. During the 1961 camp, the first Slavey Indian received the Baptism in the Holy Spirit and spoke in tongues. Another campground was founded at Lake Nakamun in Alberta in 1963. It merged, in 1978, with the German Conference Camp at Alberta Beach and was renamed the Sunset Point Pentecostal Camp. Plans were made late in the '70s for a new type of church campground near Grande Prairie, Alberta. The "Inner Peace Camp" provided a wilderness setting for campers. After its opening in 1981, it attracted people from all parts of Canada.

The old campground at Living Waters Camp near Watrous in Saskatchewan was a source of blessing and inspiration to a generation of Pentecostals before it was relocated. A new site at Adamson Lake, in the north-central park lands of the province, was developed under the direction of District Superintendent Jim Tyler. Initially, a dining hall, chapel, cabins, and a kitchen were erected. In 1979, a new tabernacle was built. The first special speakers were Robert Taitinger and Robert Muir. About the same time, another campground was organized by the pastor and people of the Melville assembly on the shores of nearby Good Spirit Lake. The response to the first Plains Pentecostal Camp was so promising that it was relocated to a more suitable site at Echo Valley, in the southern part of the province.

Camps also played a significant role in the district of Manitoba and

Northwestern Ontario. During the tenure of Percy Munro as superintendent, the Manhattan Beach Camp was given a necessary legal survey to correct errors in property lines. The camp facilities were continually upgraded to meet the needs of increasing crowds of summer visitors. The largest Pentecostal church in the district, Calvary Temple in Winnipeg, maintained its own church camp for its children and youth. Over the years, the facility was improved to provide for various types of ministry to adults and senior citizens.

Pentecostal camps were in operation in Ontario from a relatively early date in the development of Pentecostalism. They proved so effective in evangelizing the unconverted, motivating and enriching church members, and promoting the cause of world missions that they have undergone continuous enlargement and improvement. Braeside, one of the oldest camps and situated in the Western Ontario district, was upgraded during District Superintendent Howard Honsinger's leadership. In the '70s a larger, more commodious tabernacle was erected and the camp water supply and electrical systems were modernized. The grounds were landscaped, cabins built, and innovative programs put in place to meet the changing needs of the Pentecostal people who attended the summer camp meetings. Under the direction of another district superintendent, Homer Cantelon, Braeside Camp moved gradually towards a fuller utilization of its facilities on a year-round basis. Similar improvement programs were undertaken in the 1970s at both the Spring Bay Camp on Manitoulin Island and Silver Birches Camp near Kirkland Lake. The latter built a new kitchen and dining facility in 1970. It was named the "Adams Hall" in honor of A. E. Adams, a pioneer pastor and camp manager for many years.

Lakeshore Camp, near Cobourg in the Eastern Ontario and Quebec district, began during the Great Depression and experienced steady development despite the hardships of that period and the difficulties caused by the Second World War. The '70s witnessed a program of extensive renovation under the leadership of District Superintendent Gordon Upton. The old tabernacle, which had been erected 30 years previously, was completely revamped and enlarged to seat 1,800 people. The impact of these expenditures could be measured in the lives of new converts and established believers. Cal Bombay, of "100 Huntley Street," serves as an example as he refers to his spiritual growth and call to the ministry:

> When I think of camp meetings, my whole life comes in review before my eyes. Cobourg Camp, especially, stands out in my mind, for it was there as a boy in Children's Camp that I was deeply touched by God . . . A few years later, during Youth Camp at

11 / "CLASSICAL PENTECOSTALS" IN CANADA

Cobourg, God gripped my heart and very clearly called me into full time Christian ministry.[25]

Bombay's acknowledgment of the spiritual benefits of the Pentecostal camp meeting could be multiplied among people who have attended PAOC camps.

The renovations and expansions of the Pentecostal campgrounds were accompanied by renewed emphasis on worship and praise. In this area, both the Jesus People Movement and the Charismatic Movement made permanent contributions to Pentecostal worship modes. Pentecostalism, from its origin in Canada, had been characterized by fervent and vigorous forms of church services. The pioneers adopted a worship style which was not encumbered with the rituals of their former liturgical traditions. The emphasis on the Baptism in the Holy Spirit, the openness to the gifts during the assembly of believers, and the joyous expression of praise produced a sometimes noisy, ebullient church service. Historically, Pentecostals were well conditioned for the acceptance of new forms of worship. The new choruses, with their lyrics based on Bible texts, were eagerly adopted and considered to be more "spiritual" than some of the older songs. Nowhere was the "freedom" in worship more evident than in the camp meetings.

The enthusiastic worship style was helpful in attracting people to occasional summer camp meetings designed for French-speaking people in Quebec. The praise format appealed strongly to a people encultured by a formal religious methodology, particularly the young. The renewed emphasis of the '60s and '70s on spiritual gifts, plus the re-discovered blessings of camp meetings, also contributed to rapid development of camp facilities in the Maritimes. Camp Evangeline at Debert, Nova Scotia, erected a new tabernacle in 1968 which was capable of seating about 1,000 people. A new dining room, cabins, and a trailer park were added later. This renewed emphasis on camp meeting evangelism was repeated in Newfoundland. The original PAON Camp near Conception Bay was relocated to Lewisporte in 1979. The results, as PAON historian John W. Hammond noted, amply justified the decision to expand the facilities:

> Camp Emmanuel . . . has been especially blessed of God. The story will never be told in full of the transformed lives, believers who have been baptized in the Holy Ghost, and the many believers who made the decision to enter the full-time ministry on the campgrounds.[26]

The ministry programs within the local church generally reflected the growth pattern of the PAOC. But success was not maintained in every area of ministry: the Sunday school, after growing dramatically with the bus ministry, regrettably showed signs of a decline by the beginning of the 1980's. There appears to have been a shift in emphasis from evangelism to Christian education which stressed the importance of quality training over reaching new children. The Sunday school was also the victim in some churches of scheduling conflicts as expanding Sunday morning worship services demanded two time slots.

In the late-50s there were 10,000 adults and 47,000 children in PAOC Sunday schools. Evidence of the effectiveness of the schools may be gleaned from the 1960 annual report which showed that nearly 4,000 children had been converted and about 1,400 had been filled with the Spirit. Throughout the '70s enrollment rose to 34,000 adults and 77,000 children. By 1980 the total enrollment had peaked around 100,000 and growth seemed to have come to an end. While the accuracy of the statistics may be questioned because of the formula used to estimate the numbers in Sunday schools which failed to submit annual reports, the trends and the capping of the growth cycle were quite evident. Although Pentecostal leaders took little consolation in the observation, studies revealed that the decline of Sunday school enrollment was reflected also in most other evangelical denominations. Donald Feltmate, Executive Director of the Christian Education and Youth Department, declared the Sunday school setback could be attributed to a lack of evangelism. He expressed a hope that the negative trend could be reversed in the 1980s by placing more emphasis on outreach to children.[27]

While the Sunday school has always been the basic agency for the Fellowship's ministry to children, the official mid-week programs also have played a significant role. Pentecostal Crusaders, directed by Dominion Commissioner Bernard Parkinson, had by 1960 enrolled 1,800 boys and girls. The "Advance Crusader Leadership Training" prepared lay men and women to work with the children. By 1980, there were nearly 6,700 children and 1,800 leaders registered in Crusaders. After Parkinson, other national directors were Murray Lincoln, Douglas Lindsay, and David McConnell. The Missionettes program, which was designed for girls and supervised by the Women's Missionary Council (later Women's Ministries), functioned in more than 100 churches. Evelyn Bowers gave national leadership to the program for most of its history. A program known as "Wee College" and aimed at children 4 to 6 years of age was borrowed from Central Tabernacle in Edmonton and made available by the national office for scores of churches.

PAOC youth programs have been very successful in recruiting teenagers through evangelism and in discipling them as believers. As the Christ's Ambassadors organization of the '50s was expanded and improved over the next two decades, membership increased steadily. One outgrowth of the C.A. program was the introduction of "Ambassadors In Mission" which employed young people in specific evangelism efforts, both in Canada and overseas. Pentecostal young people, for example, assisted with a literature distribution scheme in Quebec in 1971. Another team of young volunteers engaged in evangelism in Frobisher Bay in the Arctic and came home with reports of 54 conversions. A large number of PAOC youth participated in personal witnessing and other evangelistic activities during the 1976 Montreal Olympics. A practical result of these C.A. programs and outreaches was the call to Bible college which scores of young men and women experienced while they were involved in the youth evangelism ministries.

The rapid and continuing development of the PAOC Bible colleges promised a good supply of potential leaders for the Fellowship. In 1960 the schools were graduating about 100 students a year. Academic requirements were stiffened by a General Conference decision to require secondary school graduation as an entrance prerequisite, although exceptions could be made for those who were deemed to merit special consideration. Public interest in the schools was reflected by articles in the *Testimony* bearing such titles as "Are Bible Schools and Seminaries Doing the Job?" and "Bible Colleges Gain Status." By 1970, enrollment in the five Canadian Bible colleges was about 475. Ten years later the number had risen to nearly 800 students.[28]

Clearly Pentecostals were shaking off the vestiges of any anti-education feelings which may have been lingering. While there was a constant process of upgrading the academic qualifications of the teachers as well as the education standards in the colleges, there was little support for the establishment of a seminary when the subject was discussed at the 1970 General Conference. With the opening of the Assemblies of God graduate school of theology in Springfield two years later, some Canadian students were able to get the graduate training they sought within a Pentecostal academic environment.

A nationally-approved Bible correspondence course offered ministerial training for students unable to attend one of the Bible schools. The course was compiled and directed for many years by Charles Ratz, a teacher and academic dean at Eastern Pentecostal Bible College. When Ratz resigned in 1972, Paul Hawkes assumed leadership and moved the course administration to Central Pentecostal College in Saskatoon. Hawkes, in turn, handed the course over to Leslie T. Holdcroft, of Western Pentecostal Bible College, when he accepted an appointment as PAOC Regional Missions Director in the Far East. The correspondence course underwent significant alterations under both Hawkes and Holdcroft.[29]

The schools in Canada greatly benefited from the sacrificial labors of administrators and teachers who devoted major portions of their ministries to Bible college work. Among the many who could be singled out for long service in the period 1950 – 1980 were Leslie T. Holdcroft, John C. Cooke, Alvin C. Schindel, Grace M. Brown, Karel Marek, George B. Griffin, Gordon F. Atter, Norman E. Schlarbaum, William A. Griffin, C. Herbert Bronsdon, Beulah Smith, Emma Hann, and, of course, Charles Ratz whose entire period of service at EPBC totalled over 30 years. The Bible colleges were administered by their own boards and financially supported by the churches of each region.

The vital role of women in the establishment and spread of Pentecostalism from its beginnings early in the century needs to be underlined. The records give evidence of their commitment and success on the mission fields, in pioneer churches, in Bible colleges — indeed, in every area of ministry. Women were often regarded as partners with their husbands in pastoral and evangelism ministries. Many of these ministering couples met in Bible colleges (sometimes warmly referred to as "bridal colleges") where a large percentage of the student body was composed of females. The contribution of women also shows up very forcefully in the local church. The majority of the people working in the Sunday school and children's ministries were women. The same observation may be made about the gender of the "saints on their knees at the prayer meeting."

One of the most effective ministries in the church has been the women's group — first known as the "Women's Missionary Society." Traditionally, the women have demonstrated a great interest in missions, both at home and overseas. They have raised large amounts of money to "outfit" missionaries and sponsor projects. In the Western Ontario district during the '80s, for example, the women regularly contributed over $100,000 annually to assist home missions church building projects. In recognition of the widespread involvement of Pentecostal women in most of the programs of the local church, the delegates at the General Conference in 1978 approved a new name for the organization, "Women's Ministries."

While there was evident recognition and appreciation for the role of women, the Fellowship did not easily grant ordination status to female ministers. After operating for decades with a credential known as "Ministerial License For Women," which was said to be equivalent to "Ordained" for males, the PAOC dealt with the question of ordination for women at the 1974 General Conference in Regina. The motion to grant ordination to qualified women was defeated with 149 voting "yes," and 143 "no." The PAOC constitution required a two-thirds majority vote before any alteration could be made to the by-laws.

11 / "CLASSICAL PENTECOSTALS" IN CANADA

A similar proposal came to the 1978 General Conference and again was defeated. By 1980, the tally of votes on women's ordination had reached the level of 51 per cent in favor, still too small for legislative change. When the change finally came at the 1984 Conference in Saint John, the vote was overwhelmingly in favor of the new status for female ministers. Surprisingly, only a small number of women entered the ordained ranks. Since one of the qualifications for the ordination of both males and females was a minimum of two years of successful ministry, and since very few local churches called women as pastors, there were not many women who had acquired the ministry time-requirement for ordination eligibility.

The growing maturity and evangelistic effectiveness of the denomination was reflected in the choice of Canada for two international conferences in the '70s. Toronto was chosen as the site of the 1972 gathering of the Pentecostal Fellowship of North America, and Vancouver was the host of the 1979 World Pentecostal Conference (WPC). Canadians composed a substantial portion of the 10,000 delegates from 14 countries who were in attendance in Vancouver. PAOC leaders adopted the WPC themes as their own and publicized them in the *Testimony*. They urged all Canadian believers to praise God for past achievements, yield themselves to the Holy Spirit for still greater progress, and to expect continuing momentum in the worldwide Pentecostal Movement.

Not only did the PAOC catch the attention of the rest of the Pentecostal world but also the notice of other Canadian denominations. At the community level, especially, Pentecostal pastors played prominent roles in ministerial associations and led their people into joint ventures with other evangelical religious groups. Although there were opportunities for greater involvement in ecumenical activities with the larger, old-line denominations, the PAOC went on record as being "opposed to an ecumenicity based on organic or organizational unity rather than the biblical doctrine of spiritual unity in the Church of Jesus Christ."[30]

At the same time, the leaders of the movement demonstrated a sense of responsibility for involvement in some of the educational, ethical, and social issues of the day. A formal brief was presented to the Ontario government in 1973 which expressed concern about the directions taken by provincial education authorities. The PAOC argued that "the fundamental right in the education of children under God, lies with the parent." The position taken was that "theistic values and basic Christian moral teachings" should be retained and not diluted by government action.[31]

When abortion surfaced as a public medical and moral issue, the denomination made its opposition to the practice unmistakably clear. A series of articles in the *Testimony* reflected that position with such titles as "Therapeutic Abortion from the Medical Standpoint" and "Therapeutic Abortion from a Theological Viewpoint." Pentecostals recognized themselves to be part of a minority in society who were resisting the debilitating influences of secular humanism. At the 1976 General Conference the delegates acknowledged that the "critical point" of moral deterioration in the nation had arrived. In response, the conference approved the establishment of a committee to prepare and present PAOC views on major issues. By the 1978 General Conference, with committee reports in hand, the denomination dealt with abortion, sex education in public schools, homosexuality, and obscenity. The voting delegates went on record as being opposed to the legalization of prostitution, abortion, and lotteries in Canada. An important decision was made at the 1982 Winnipeg conference when the General Executive was requested to appoint a full-time person to address social concerns. Hudson Hilsden served in this capacity with great distinction until his retirement in 1991.

While evangelism and the topic of "eternal life" have always been the primary focus for Pentecostals, they have not been unmindful of human needs in this life. Although they were criticized for failing to engage in humanitarian works early in their history, the reality was that they were simply too few in number and too lacking in resources to make significant contributions in charitable endeavors. By the 1960s this situation had changed. PAOC credential holders and agencies launched a number of humanitarian projects. The original nursing station at Hay River in the Northwest Territories was expanded into a small hospital and later into a fully-modern institution known as the H. H. Williams Memorial Hospital. It was the only hospital of its kind in that remote region of Canada and proved to be a great blessing to the residents of the north. Shepherd Lodge in Toronto was founded in 1960 to care for the needs of elderly people, and a similar institution, Bethel Home, was established in New Brunswick. Retired Canadians in Quebec were assisted by the development of the Foyer Laurentian early in the '70s, and Shepherd Manor was erected in Toronto in 1976. These achievements heralded the interest of the PAOC in meeting social needs, and its enlarged financial capacity to do so.

During this period of growth and maturation, the Fellowship moved smoothly through administration changes and expansion. The staff of the national office, which numbered about 50 by the mid-60s, outgrew the old head office building on Euston Avenue. A new office was built on Overlea Boulevard in Toronto in 1966. The building was named the

11 / "CLASSICAL PENTECOSTALS" IN CANADA

International Office in recognition of the growing overseas missions operation but the name has not proven popular and is rarely used.

Walter McAlister retired as General Superintendent in 1962 and was succeeded by Tom Johnstone, the former Executive Director of Home Missions and Bible Colleges. C. H. Stiller moved into Johnstone's vacated position at the same conference. The long and illustrious careers of Charles M. Wortman and George R. Upton ended in 1966 with Stiller moving into Wortman's position as General Secretary-Treasurer and Carman W. Lynn into Upton's role in the Overseas Missions Department. Robert M. Argue was elected to take over Home Missions and Bible Colleges after Stiller. In 1968, James Montgomery stepped aside from his leadership position in Christian Education and Youth and was replaced by S. Donald Feltmate. In the same year Robert W. Taitinger was chosen to succeed Tom Johnstone.

When C. H. Stiller died while in office in 1971, the General Executive requested James Montgomery to come out of retirement and serve the remaining part of Stiller's term. At the next General Conference, in Halifax in 1972, the delegates voted to split the office of General Secretary-Treasurer. Montgomery was elected to be General Secretary and A. Graydon Richards the General Treasurer. Montgomery retired from the office after one term and was followed by Charles Yates. The six officers remained in place for the next six years. At the 1980 General Conference in Hamilton, Lynn and Feltmate resigned and were succeeded by William Cornelius and William Griffin respectively.

The national executive officers were accompanied on the legislative body known as the General Executive by the district superintendents and leaders of the various ethnic branches, plus another five men (members-at-large) elected from among the body of national PAOC clergymen.

Pentecostalism in Canada has followed the historic path of progress and structural development of other revival movements so well analyzed by sociologists and historians. But the PAOC has demonstrated a keen awareness of the dangers which accompany growth and success. Again and again leaders have warned of the tragic consequences if the movement should get disconnected from its roots. Of particular concern was the possibility of damage to its spirituality, or the loss of its evangelistic passion for the unconverted, or the weakening of its confidence in the power of the Holy Spirit. General Superintendent Robert Taitinger, in 1972, issued a call to prayer. He noted that a "National Call to Prayer" was essential for the continued development of the denomination. The significance of that appeal has not diminished.

"CLASSICAL PENTECOSTALS" IN CANADA / 11

Endnotes

1. Ronald M. Enroth and others, *The Jesus People* (Grand Rapids: Eerdmans, 1972), pp. 9-17; see also "The Jesus Revolution," *Time* (June 21, 1971).

2. The author recalls attending a service in Evangel Church in Montreal in the '60s in which a group of converted hippies, dressed in jeans, overalls and less formal attire, and with bare feet instead of shoes, joined in the worship. The congregation appeared to have a genuine affection for the unconventional worshippers.

3. Billy Graham, *The Jesus Generation* (Grand Rapids: Zondervan, 1971); see also H. Vinson Synan, "Pentecostal and The Jesus Revolution," *End Times Messenger* (September 1972), 8-9.

4. Kenneth B. Birch, "Can We Learn From The Jesus People?" *The Pentecostal Testimony* (December 1971), 24-25.

5. Edward E. Plowman, "Whatever Happened to the Jesus Movement?" *Christianity Today* (October 24, 1975), 46-47.

6. Leslie R. Keylock, "After 20 Years Vatican II Still Draws Mixed Reviews," *Christianity Today* (March 7, 1986), 48-49; see also Edward O'Connor, "The Hidden Roots of the Charismatic Renewal in the Catholic Church," in Vinson Synan, ed., *Aspects of Pentecostal-Charismatic Origins*, (Plainsfield: Logos, 1975).

7. See Arnold Bittlinger, ed., *The Church is Charismatic* (Geneva: World Council of Churches, 1981).

8. Kilian McDonnell, "The Ecumenical Significance of the Pentecostal Movement," reprinted in *The Pentecostal Testimony* (June 1968), 8; and Peter Hocken, "The Pentecostal-Charismatic Movement as Revival and Renewal," *Pneuma* (Spring 1981), 31-47.

9. Ronald Neufeldt, "Charismatic Renewal," *The Canadian Encyclopedia*, vol. 1 (Edmonton: Hurtig Publishers, 1988), 396.

10. Jean Stone, "More that 1,300 California Episcopalians Receive Pentecostal Baptism," *The Pentecostal Testimony* (June 1962), 8-9, 31-32; J. Harry Faught, "Evangelicals and the Vatican Council," *The Pentecostal Testimony* (January 1963), 7-8; and Faith Campbell, "The Holy Spirit Falls on Yale Students," reprinted in *The Pentecostal Testimony* (June 1963), 6, 32-34.

11. Bernice Gerard, "Charismatic Renewal in Vancouver," *The Pentecostal Testimony* (April 1968), 8-9,32; see also Jack Ozard, "Let's Stay on Course," and Peter Prosser, "Roman Catholic Charismatic Impact Increases," *The Pentecostal Testimony* (September 1973), 4-5, 26.

12. Armaro Rodriguez, "What is happening in the Roman Catholic Church?" *The Pentecostal Testimony* (April 1970), 6-7; and "The Spirit of God is Moving," *The Pentecostal Testimony* (August 1970), 8-9.

11 / "CLASSICAL PENTECOSTALS" IN CANADA

13. William Griffin, "Can We Stand Success?" *The Pentecostal Testimony* (January 1965), 4, 33; Ron Reid, "Pentecostal Power, *The Pentecostal Testimony* (March 1964), 6-7; and Alvin Schindel, "The Role of Bible Colleges in our Pentecostal Fellowship," *The Pentecostal Testimony* (July 1964), 5, 14.

14. B. T. Parkinson, "Sunday School Driving Power," *The Pentecostal Testimony* (April 1975), 4-7.

15. Helen Lescheid, "Bernice Gerard: Hotliner for Jesus," *The Pentecostal Testimony* (August 1976), 6-7.

16. "PACE," *The Pentecostal Testimony* (June 1974), 24.

17. R. W. Taitinger, "Evangelist's Seminar," *The Pentecostal Testimony* (February 1974), 17.

18. "100 Huntley Street," *The Pentecostal Testimony* (August 1977), 16-17,30-31. In 1992 when the lease on Mainse's Toronto building expired, he erected a 20-million-dollar production and broadcasting facility on a strategic property located between Burlington and Hamilton. A road on the new property was named Huntley Street to allow the ministry to maintain its name after the relocation.

19. Thomas Wm. Miller, taped interview with Bert Liira, April 9, 1986.

20. "Revival Brings Urgent Need for Building," *The Pentecostal Testimony* (July 1978), 11; additional information in author's correspondence with D. Blackmore.

21. "French Scholarship Program Continues," *The Pentecostal Testimony* (August 1971), 10; Kenneth B. Birch, "Taking FLITE for Ministry in Quebec," *The Pentecostal Testimony* (February 1974), 20-21; and Donald R. Martin, "FLITE Celebrates Anniversary," *The Pentecostal Testimony* (June, 1980), 24; see also Aubrey Wice, "The Pentecostals zero in on Quebec," *The Globe And Mail*, August 23, 1975.

22. Donald R. Martin, "Formation Timothée," *The Pentecostal Testimony* (August 1980), 10-12.

23. "What God Hath Wrought in Quebec," *The Pentecostal Testimony* (September 1964), 2, 32; and "Quebec Bishops Hope Their Dwindling Church Will Rebound," *Christianity Today* (January 13, 1984), 44; Don Krohn, "God Loves Quebec: Report on the Sept-Iles, Quebec, Crusade," *The Pentecostal Testimony* (February 1979), 6-7.

24. Wilson Waterhouse, "Great Move of God Among Saskatchewan Indians," *The Pentecostal Testimony* (October 1961), 10.

25. Cal Bombay, "Camp Meetings — What a Blessing," *The Pentecostal Testimony* (July 1983), 12.

26. John W. Hammond, *The Joyful Sound: A History of the Pentecostal Assemblies of Newfoundland and Labrador* (St. Stephen, NB, 1982), p. 167.

27. S. D. Feltmate, "Report of The Executive Director of Christian Education and Youth Department," *32nd Biennial General Conference, August. 21-26, 1980, Hamilton Ontario*, PAOC Archives, 23-28.

28. Statistical data from General Secretary Charles Yates to Thomas Wm. Miller, April 17, 1979.
29. Further changes in the correspondence course were made by Roger J. Stronstad, academic dean of WPBC, when he became the director in 1990. Although the Canadian Pentecostal Correspondence Course continues to be offered for interested lay people, the 1992 General Conference accepted the International Correspondence Course (ICI) of the Assemblies of God as the new official course for ministerial candidates.
30. "24th General Conference, Montreal," *The Pentecostal Testimony* (November 1964), 4-7, 31.
31. "Highlights of a Brief Presented to the Honorable T. L. Wells," *The Pentecostal Testimony* (August 1973), 6-7.

Chapter 12

THE "UNBELIEVABLE YEARS" IN OVERSEAS MISSIONS

The PAOC overseas missions program enjoyed a period of unprecedented expansion and development in the quarter-century after the Second World War. Despite the disruptions and shortages occasioned by the international conflict, the missions program steadily advanced. The election of George R. Upton in 1944 as full-time Missionary Secretary was a significant move. His promotion of overseas work among Canadian assemblies as well as his visits to each overseas field contributed much to this growth. At the end of the 1940s, there were nearly 80 Canadian missionaries, assisted by 800 national workers, who were active on 10 different fields. These missionaries and nationals gave leadership to over 700 churches and a number of Bible schools. About 20 of the Canadian missionaries were working in the Far East and the remainder were about equally divided between Africa and South America/West Indies. The amount of financial support provided by churches in the homeland averaged around $300,000 a year at the start of the '50s.

By the middle of the 1970s, there had been extraordinary growth in every area of PAOC overseas missions. The number of national churches had increased to 2,449 and the total of national ministers to 2,721. The membership roll had risen from about 70,000 to nearly 171,000. Statistics on membership always have been very conservative. The PAOC generally has not included in its enumeration those people who attend its local church services but who have not formally identified with the Fellowship. By the mid-70s, the PAOC had entered seven new countries and was maintaining a missions force of over 170 Canadian workers. The annual financial contributions to these foreign endeavors then totaled nearly 2.4 million dollars.

When these statistics were compiled and the spiritual progress on the

12 / THE "UNBELIEVABLE YEARS" IN OVERSEAS MISSIONS

various fields assessed, the period under review was described as "Twenty-five Unbelievable Years."[1] But they also were years of great sacrifice, much labor, and enormous cost in terms of the demands made on the health and strength of the Canadian missionaries. By its very nature, missions work cannot be analyzed and described in neat chronological sequences. Much of the accomplishments of the '60s and the '70s were possible only through the ground-breaking labors of earlier missionaries. And some growth was the product of particular ministries which had been developed over longer periods of time and bore fruit in those two decades. Sunday schools and women's ministries in Kenya, for example, benefited from the decades of input by women workers like Renata Siemens, Margaret Cantwell, June Deacon, and Iris Scheel.

Siemens arrived in the former British colony in 1939. She labored in Kenya at a time when it was very difficult to send out male missionary personnel. Otto Keller described her as "a talented, gifted, Holy Ghost-anointed preacher and teacher." Siemens began pioneer work among the Luo tribe, organized Sunday schools and women's work, translated a number of books, and supervised the construction of a mission station at Awasi. When completed, the station included a church, school, workshop, infirmary, missionary residence, and girls' dormitory. During her fifth term, Siemens took the Pentecostal message to new areas of Kenya and Tanganyika (now Tanzania). She also travelled to some of the still-backward tribes in the Gulu region of Uganda. In 1972, she was supervising women's church auxiliaries in nearly 300 churches when the military government of Idi Amin forced her to leave the country.

Margaret Cantwell arrived in Kenya from Ontario in 1950. Fulfilling a life-long ambition to serve God on the mission field, she was nearly 40 years of age when she started her career as a missionary. Cantwell used her professional training and experience to make a lasting impact on many young Africans during the 20 years she spent teaching in the mission schools. One of her former pupils was Michael Otanga who obtained further academic training and returned to Kenya to become the General Secretary, and later General Superintendent, of the Pentecostal Assemblies of God.

June Deacon was a teacher for nine years in Canada before going to Kenya in 1949. She taught for many years in mission schools sponsored by the PAOC. Deacon was also quite involved with evangelistic outreaches among the educated, English-speaking Kenyans. In the late-60s and '70s she was headmistress of the Kereri Girls' School.

Iris Scheel also was a teacher in Canada before taking up a similar ministry in Kenya. In 1953 she became the principal of Goibei Girls' School. Following her first furlough, Scheel directed both the Sunday school and the youth work for East Africa (Kenya, Uganda, Tanzania). She also helped to train young Kenyans to assist in the ministries of the Pentecostal churches. In 1976, Scheel supervised the erection of a Christian education centre at Goibei. Kenyan public school teachers attend sessions at this centre in preparation for teaching religious knowledge courses in the school system. Scheel has acted as advisor to the Christian education and the national missions departments of the Pentecostal Assemblies of God.

Although the missionaries ministered safely in Kenya for decades, there was an ever-present danger of tribal warfare. One very serious incident of this type erupted in the Nyang'ori district in 1962. Arnold Bowler was attempting to resolve a boundary dispute when a fight broke out among the people involved. He and a national assistant attempted to escape from the scene to the safety of a nearby police station. Suddenly, a mob of about 40 men with clubs and spears blocked their way and demanded they stop. Bowler, believing it would mean instant death if he stopped, maintained the vehicle's speed forcing the angry crowd to jump aside. A spear hurled at his car came within a few inches of Bowler's head.[2]

Arnold Bowler was a graduate of Eastern Pentecostal Bible College and a skilled printer when God called him and his bride Elsie to Africa. In Kenya, he spent 16 years in the publication of Christian literature which had a profound impact in the colony. Since Kenyans had been taught by earlier missionaries to read, they were likely targets for the vast amounts of evangelistic and discipleship literature which were produced under Bowler's direction at Evangel Press. The Bowlers also gave counsel to the national Pentecostal churches in three regions with a total of 200 congregations.

The Bowlers moved to Uganda in the mid-60s where the number of Pentecostal congregations increased by 500 per cent within two years. Bowler, with the assistance of missionary Robert Eames, organized a training centre to produce qualified national leaders for Uganda. But the rise to power of Idi Amin, and the atrocities committed by his troops, forced the missionaries to flee the country in 1972. Back in Kenya, the Bowlers were asked to assist the national leaders in the development of their own missions department. This objective was an unmistakable sign of the maturing of the Kenyan Pentecostal assemblies in the '70s. The goal they set for themselves was to motivate and organize the 1,600 Kenyan congregations in sending and supporting Kenyan gospel workers in needy regions.

Another sign of the rapid development of PAOC missions in Africa was the extensive expansion of the facilities of the Evangel Press (later renamed Evangel Publishing House). Under Cal Bombay's enterprising leadership a new 18,500 square foot building was acquired in 1979 in the capital city of Nairobi. The press was able to expand its annual output to nearly 170,000 periodicals and newspapers, 140,000 books and booklets, and 700,000 tracts. The publishing house also provided Bible correspondence courses and study guides to about 2,000 students enrolled in the Theological Education by Extension (TEE) program operated by the PAOC missions department.

TEE was designed in 1963 for use in a Presbyterian seminary in Guatemala. Its obvious benefits for the Third World countries were recognized by other religious groups. When PAOC missionaries adapted TEE to their own African fields, Evangel Press became the chief supplier of texts and study materials for many countries. By the end of the 1980s, Evangel Press had printed correspondence materials for more than 60 countries in over 100 languages. Ironically, the overseas publishing house has provided TEE materials for Canadian instructional programs among the Natives and Inuit of northern Canada.

The TEE program was constantly updated and improved to meet specific regional or national needs. Missionaries, such as Cal Ratz, Arnold Labrentz, Bruce Brand, and David Koop, carried on extensive revisions to keep this theological education scheme relevant. As Brand put it, TEE was "a powerful force for infiltrating the kingdoms of this earth with the message of the King of kings."[3] The use of this correspondence plan allowed hundreds of native pastors, teachers, and evangelists to study without leaving their homes or their native congregations. It was "learning-on-the-job" in the truest sense of that term.

The impact of Evangel Publishing House was broader than the religious community. It also published the textbooks for the religious knowledge courses taught in Kenyan public schools. The growing maturity of the Pentecostal national leadership in the decades after 1950 allowed the Canadian missionaries to carry out the PAOC mandate to develop indigenous churches overseas. John McBride was appointed field director of the East African work in 1956. That same year Mitia Alinogwa was elected the first national superintendent of the Pentecostal Assemblies of East Africa (later renamed Pentecostal Assemblies of God). He was succeeded in turn by Charles Gungu, Shem Irangi, and Michael Otanga.

When William and Lillian Cornelius came to Kenya in 1955, the mission's activities were governed by a body about equally composed of nationals and Canadians. After Cornelius became field director in 1965, he pressed for a reduction in Canadian representation. Eventually the composition changed in favor of the Africans until there was only one Canadian on the East African national executive. To expedite progress towards a self-governing national church, the PAOC negotiated with the

Kenyan leaders in 1966 to define the governing relationship between the nationals and the Overseas Mission Department. This document was one of the first of its kind in Africa to adapt to the aspirations for independence which swept over the national churches in the '60s.[4]

A vital contribution to the growing independence of the Kenyan Pentecostals was made by Jack and Edna Lynn. The Lynns served six terms in Africa following their arrival in Kenya in 1946. The first area of ministry was church planting and the supervision of schools. By the '60s, Jack Lynn was acting as a missionary advisor to the national leaders and district churches. He also provided a series of regional Bible refresher courses for the growing national church. In an effort to establish financial responsibility among the nationals, he held stewardship seminars throughout Kenya. Since Lynn's managerial skills were known to government officials, he was asked to supervise a number of state schools.

By the time the Lynns completed six terms in the land of their calling, the Kenyan Pentecostal Assemblies of God had emerged as an autonomous national body with over 1,700 affiliated churches, complete with their own leaders, and with total financial independence. When asked for his "missions philosophy," Lynn replied:

> If Jesus is Lord and made such a great sacrifice for me, there's nothing for me to do except serve Him with all my heart — whether it's at home or on the mission field . . . These national pastors and leaders are the joy and crown of our whole work for God.[5]

The work in Kenya benefited immeasurably from the establishment of Bible schools. The school at Nyang'ori, founded in 1949, underwent steady expansion and regular improvements in its curriculum. By 1974, the school had graduated 280 students — 210 of that number engaged in full-time ministry in East Africa. One of its graduates, Charles Gungu, later became the first superintendent of the national church. Despite the almost omnipresent "curse of Africa" — the fierce and unrelenting tribal enmities — the Kisumu college managed to eliminate such problems among its student body. By the late-70s, the school had over 70 men from almost 20 different tribes studying and working together in harmonious relationships. The faculty and staff were also from several different tribal and racial backgrounds.

The establishment of another institution of higher learning in Kenya came about in a curious fashion. The Pan Africa Christian College was founded in 1976 on a 20 acre site which originally had been used to train communists. Although the land and buildings were then estimated to be worth about 1.5 million dollars, the PAOC acquired it for a fraction of its appraised value and turned it into a Christian college. Pan Africa Christian College operates as a Pentecostal institution but accepts students of other denominations. The college effectively trains pastors for city churches and teachers for Bible schools. This institution was the first of its type on any PAOC overseas field to offer a BA degree in Christian theology. Students have come from most of the English-speaking countries in Africa.

One of the most successful innovations in PAOC overseas missionary work was the development of the large multi-racial, city church. John and Ella McBride held meetings in Nairobi in the 1950s. Ernest and Shirley Francis were also part of the early history of the work which later developed into the Valley Road Church. An evangelistic crusade with Clifton Erickson produced considerable growth. When the call went out for an experienced Canadian pastor to give administrative leadership to the growing Nairobi assembly, Richard and Olive Bombay of Oshawa, Ontario, responded. Bombay, referring to his search for suitable property for the church, declared that he was "wonderfully led of God to a very central location in the heart of the city, on its main traffic routes." At a bargain price, Bombay secured the Valley Road property which already had a large residence on it. The congregation with the assistance of the Overseas Missions Department built an evangelistic centre on the site. When the Canadian evangelist Lorne Fox preached at the centre, hundreds of Kenyans heard the gospel and scores were saved, healed, and filled with the Spirit. Although a variety of language groups attended the services, the preaching at the Valley Road Church was in English.

The congregation entered another period of significant growth when Mervyn and Sheila Thomas came to pastor in 1970. Eventually it became the largest church in Nairobi. Thomas introduced a host of programs for married couples, youth and children, and even an educational program for discipleship. The influence of the church extended to several Kenyan government leaders who often attended the services. The Valley Road model was later used by the PAOC in other parts of the world where a strong city church could have a healthy impact on the rural churches.

The enormous social, economic, and political changes which swept the world after the Second World War had an important effect on the work of the missionaries. Prior to that conflict, the usual practice was for the missionaries to make most of the decisions about the work of the church on the various fields. Although the missions objective of the PAOC had always been to establish an indigenous national church, this process often was hampered by the lack of leadership or political stability in the local culture. In the British colonies of East Africa, the switch to independence was generally carried out quite smoothly but not always without violence. Even in such an enlightened colony as Kenya, there was the Mau Mau terrorist movement. In many other colonies, the European ruling powers employed military repression which ultimately had to bow to nationalist forces. Eventually, a host of new African nations emerged with new names.

George Upton, Missionary Secretary from 1944 to 1966, summarized this eventful period as a time of gratifying advances on the PAOC mission fields but one that was difficult for both missionaries and native leaders:

> The war had ended and a mighty Spirit of nationalism was stirring many colonies. God enabled me to see that we could capitalize on that nationalism and encourage the development of national churches, under their own pastors and leaders, for which we must establish national Bible training schools, in various parts of the world, which we did with the Lord's help . . . The early field gradually changed. Sometimes it was painful for both missionaries and nationals.[6]

Other major problems during that era identified by Upton were the threat of communism, the opposition of Islam, and the rise of the Ecumenical Movement. All of these potential threats were present to some degree on the 17 fields then supervised by the PAOC.

When Carman Lynn became the new Executive Director of the Overseas Missions Department in 1967, one of his priorities was to provide training for national leaders and workers on each field. Despite the rise of intense nationalistic fervor in many countries, Canadian missionaries were urged by the nationals to remain and assist them in the work. Gradually, these Canadians moved into advisory roles as the nationals took over the leadership of churches for which they had been prepared. Even where the missionaries were forced to leave for a period, as in Uganda, the national leaders were able to provide direction and continue the work of evangelism. When the war in Uganda abated, PAOC missionaries were welcomed back by the national believers.

Early Pentecostal work in Uganda was initiated by Kenyans living across the border. William and Viola Brown were the first PAOC missionaries to live in the country. The work was hampered by the complications of communicating with people who spoke at least 15 languages. The missionary strategy was to train the national pastors who were best capable of reaching their own linguistic groups. Some of the more promising young men were sent to Kenya for training in the Bible school. In the '60s, Robert and Mabel Eames gave leadership in establishing a Bible training centre at Mbale in Uganda. A new church, the Mbale Evangelistic Centre, was opened in 1962. About the same time, a master plan for church planting was adopted which aimed at reaching every major Ugandan tribe with the gospel. Soon there were 70 congregations among the Teso people. With the work expanding, several missionary families arrived on the scene including Fred and Rhoda Clarke, Frank and Dorothy Holder, Lyle and Irene Horrill, and Alex and Janet Strong. By 1970 the number of Pentecostal churches in Uganda had increased to 265 with about 10,000 members. PAOC missions work in Uganda was strengthened by the assistance of the Vokesmission of Stuttgart, Germany — most notably through the ministry of Herbert and Christiane Ros.

The PAOC missions work began in Tanganyika when Renata Siemens held meetings among Kenyans who had migrated to that nation. A general missions outreach began with the arrival in 1956 of Gus and Doris Wentland, who were supported by the German Branch Conference of the PAOC. The city of Musoma became their headquarters. When growth in the work called for a second missionary family, Paul and Ida Schellert were sent out by the Overseas Missions Committee and supported by the German Branch. Having discovered a collection of unused mine buildings in a strategic location, the Schellerts set up Nyasirori Station. The work of the German missionaries went through a most difficult period when the nationals in Tanganyika and nearby Zanzibar engaged in a conflict with Britain to acquire political independence. But by 1964, the troubled times were past and Tanganyika and Zanzibar united and assumed the new name of Tanzania.

Through the 1970s, a stream of missionaries arrived to assist in the work — Immanuel and Ruth Mueller, Johann and Irmgard Haug, Bruno and Elizabeth Doberstein, Ron and Loudell Posein, and Rainer and Elizabeth Mittelstaedt. In one two-year period (1976-78) the Tanzanian field experienced phenomenal growth with 71 new churches established to care for the converts. Johann Haug became the head of a new Bible school, founded in 1974, which trained hundreds of young men for ministry among their own people. When evaluating the work in Tanzania up to 1980, German Branch Superintendent Gustav Kurtz declared that "the Bible school has proven to be the key to the phenomenal growth of the mission in that country."[7]

Pentecostalism gained a foothold in Northern Rhodesia (now Zambia) through the efforts of Jack and Winnie Muggleton. After Muggleton's conversion and release from military service in 1947, he and his wife began working with a missions organization in the Kabompo region of Northern Rhodesia where they learned the Luvale language and launched out in full-time evangelism. Their itineraries took them on long journeys through the bush to reach the tribes. After coming into contact with the Pentecostal message, and receiving the Baptism themselves, the Muggletons affiliated with the PAOC. With the advice and support of James Skinner, they founded a new mission station at Mwambashi, near Kitwe in the copperbelt.

Robert and Doris Skinner joined the Muggletons in 1962. Within a few years they had eight self-supporting national churches and a number of established preaching points. A large amount of literature was printed in 15 languages for the thousands of miners who came from all over Africa to work in the mines. The tract ministry proved productive in reaching souls. The need for workers led them to set up a Bible training institution. David and Margaret Purdie came from Canada to join the staff.

Northern Rhodesia changed its name to Zambia in the '60s. The mission work continued without interruption through the political changes under the direction of the Purdies and, later, Ray and Vivian Callahan of the Pentecostal Assemblies of Newfoundland. Two couples who worked with them were Glen and Ruth Kauffeldt and Ken and Marjorie MacGowan. Later arrivals from Canada included David and Carol Slauenwhite, Vern and Belva Tisdalle, David and Florence Way, Scott and Nancy Hunter, and also Winston and Gloria Broomes from the West Indies. In keeping with official PAOC missions policy, every effort was made to turn the Zambian mission into an indigenous work as soon as possible. Throughout the 1970s, the leadership became increasingly African and eventually the work emerged as "The Pentecostal Assemblies of God (Zambia)."

Several factors contributed significantly to the success of the work in Zambia. As in other countries, the PAOC's policy of establishing a Bible school program as quickly as possible produced excellent results. The school in Zambia attracted fine young people and sent them out on weekend ministry assignments in order to gain experience. The work of these young people from the school, in turn, helped to stabilize and to strengthen the assemblies. An emphasis on city churches, such as the one in Lusaka, as well as large evangelistic crusades by people like Don Schellenberg, resulted in the conversion of many nationals and subsequently an increase in the number of candidates for the ministry. The publication of Christian education literature was also very helpful in establishing Zambians in the faith.

The first Canadian missionaries in Southern Rhodesia [now Zimbabwe] were James and Lila Skinner. Within 15 years of their arrival, their mission work encompassed 45 churches, 50 national workers, and about 2,500 Pentecostal adherents. Working out of the main mission station at Umtali, they engaged in an extensive educational program for the

12 / THE "UNBELIEVABLE YEARS" IN OVERSEAS MISSIONS

Africans. After the Skinners were reinforced by the families of James and Vera Bush and Henry and Florence Koopman, other new mission sites were developed — one at Marhumbini and another at Fort Victoria. Later recruits who followed were Elmer and Sylvia Delport and Elmer and Edith Myers. A Bible school was established from which the first graduates of a three-year program of studies emerged in 1968. That also was the year that the mission was established as an independent entity as the Pentecostal Assemblies of Rhodesia (later Zimbabwe). The work then entered a period of consolidation and growth.

The missionaries had prepared for a move of God by scheduling a series of evangelistic tent meetings. The anticipated revival swept the field. Hundreds were converted — both black and white Rhodesians — and the impact was felt throughout the country in the '70s. One of the by-products of this revival was that much of the hostility which had been directed towards the Pentecostal Baptism in the Spirit — especially speaking in tongues — dissipated and a favorable public attitude emerged. Pentecostal congregations were established in the major urban centers. Bible school students were utilized in outreach evangelism and Christian education programs. The Kauffeldts transferred to Zimbabwe from Zambia and assumed the leadership role. Other Canadians who assisted included Danny and Sharon Curle, John and Betty Burrage, and Robert and Jean Peel.

The history of Pentecostal missions in Mozambique is forever associated with the name of Austin and Ingrid Chawner. The country had been especially difficult to penetrate while it remained a Portuguese colony. When it was first conquered, it was presented by Portugal as a gift to the Pope. The Roman Catholic Church, therefore, had sole control of the religious instruction of the nationals for generations. Despite this connection with Catholicism, many of the seven million inhabitants, which were divided into 44 tribes, remained bound by animism. Although the Chawners were obliged to establish their first mission station just outside the border, they persevered for years until they were finally granted permission to set up ministries in Lourenco Marques, the capital city, and in other locations in the colony. Within a few years, the Pentecostals had about 300 congregations in Mozambique. The Chawners later recruited José Pina, who had served on the police force, and his wife Maria as well as Hans and Evangeline Casqueiro as assistants.

One of the great aids to spreading the full gospel in Mozambique was the migration of mine workers to South Africa and their subsequent return to home areas with the Pentecostal message. Bernard Hunter was engaged in evangelism in the mining compounds near Johannesburg from 1948 to 1983. Of the thousands of Africans reached with the gospel and converted to Christ, there were many from Mozambique. Austin Chawner once told

Hunter that he estimated about 400 congregations had resulted from the return of these men following their conversion. These converted Mozambique citizens, having received at least a smattering of Bible instruction while in South Africa, became zealous witnesses for the Lord upon their return to their home villages.[8]

After a change in the colonial government, there was new freedom for missions work which permitted both evangelistic meetings and tract distribution in Lourenco Marques. By 1970 it was possible to bring in special speakers to hold large-scale evangelistic gatherings; one such event attracted crowds of 15,000 people. A large multi-racial church was developed in the capital and enjoyed rapid growth in membership. Much of the support for all forms of evangelism was provided by the believers in this new and vibrant assembly. The church itself was the outgrowth of much prayer and planning by both the PAOC missions department and the national Mozambique leaders. In spite of a great deal of political turmoil throughout the 1970s, the preparation for this great ministry with a planned multi-racial character was completed by 1975. The new church facility, which could seat 2,500, and its ancillary buildings were then valued at $900,000. Carman Lynn, the Executive Director of the Overseas Missions Department at the time, described the Lourenco Marques complex as "a vision fulfilled."[9]

The next year, when the Portuguese ceded control of the colony to a national government, the Pentecostal work entered a new era. Besides the large multi-racial complex, there were about 20 other African churches and prayer groups in the capital. Since the new government was "Maoist," hundreds of Pentecostals were forced to flee the country or to compromise with communism. As missionary Alex Strong explained, the Pentecostals were forced to choose God or Marxism.[10] For the next decade, the work in Mozambique had to be conducted under the most difficult of circumstances.

The Chawner name, so prominent in the Mozambique story, is also associated in fond memory with South Africa. The work of Charles and Emma Chawner, parents of Austin, has been described elsewhere in this book. One of the most fruitful forms of evangelism, which they established among the mining compounds, was carried on by many Canadian missionaries. Thousands of men with dozens of different languages and dialects were recruited in Mozambique, North and South Rhodesia, Malawi, Tanzania, and other countries to work in the mines. The missionaries gained access to the compounds where the men lived during their contracted period of employment. They shared the gospel with the miners and nurtured them in the Christian faith. These converts became the nucleus of new assemblies when they returned to their home territories. Robert Peel and Bernard Hunter spent the majority of their missionary careers in mine ministries.

12 / THE "UNBELIEVABLE YEARS" IN OVERSEAS MISSIONS

Hunter spent 35 years, until his retirement from the field in 1983, in South Africa. His method was to hold open air meetings in the compounds, assisted by a national evangelist, followed by teaching sessions each day. If many tribal groups were represented in his audience, he chose the language of the majority present. If he could not address the Africans, he preached in English and had an interpreter assist him. At one time, Hunter was blessed with a national associate who spoke seven African languages. Altogether, he ministered to miners from 23 different tribes. He endeavored to maintain contact with the converts and disciple them to some extent before their contract period ended.

When Bernard and Beth Hunter arrived in Johannesburg, there was no Sunday school for their children. Beth Hunter began one in her home. From an initial membership of 65 children, this work continually expanded, through the conversion of parents and other white South Africans, until a church congregation resulted. Then it underwent steady growth with national pastors until, by 1983, the congregation numbered about 1,100. One of the converts had been an alcoholic whose wife and seven children were ready to leave him. The man was wonderfully converted, delivered from drink, and became a stalwart member of this new assembly — the Roodispoort church. For many years this person served as the church secretary. All this from a humble beginning as a Sunday school!

Bernard Hunter served for several years as the chairman of the black African churches in the Johannesburg region. He was instrumental in building (literally, with his own hands) seven churches and four parsonages for native congregations. After his tent services in Soweto Township resulted in an assembly of believers, he was asked to help them build a church. Upon inquiry, he found the Africans had only about $60 for materials, but they professed a firm faith that the Lord would provide. So he began construction work and built the walls of the church to window height before the money ran out. Then, as he told the author, he prayed, "Oh, Lord, surely you have some man in Canada with the money to finish this job." He reported that the Lord told him to borrow his wife's legacy of $300 and buy a nearby house which was for sale. After renovating the house and selling it at a profit, Hunter secured enough money to finish the Soweto church.

In similar fashion, the Lord provided funds in supernatural ways for the erection of other national churches as well as for the large Orlando church in Soweto. While engaged in building this church, Hunter nearly died from an attack of yellow jaundice. An African evangelist who came to see Hunter prostrated himself on the floor and cried out to God to "spare our missionary for we need him." And from that moment Hunter's health began to improve.[11] Despite these strenuous tasks of church construction, he remained focused on his chief work – evangelism.

The literature distribution work in the mine compounds was the primary employment of Robert and Jean Peel. They were able to use their special talents in printing at both the Evangel Press in Kenya and the PAOC printing plant at Nelspruit in South Africa. In 1964, the direction of the Nelspruit Press was taken over by Robert and Doris Skinner.

One form of outreach that was novel for that era in South Africa was the holding of tent meetings. Lawrence and Lois Delport established themselves at Pietersburg, in the Transvaal, and used a large gospel tent to reach the tribespeople. They were assisted by a number of national workers whose expenses were covered by an innovative PAOC funding program known as "Pentecostal Evangelistic Pioneers (PEP)." The program raised funds in Canada for the specific purpose of supporting national evangelists in ministry among their countrymen. By the 1970s, Canadian Pentecostal missions was firmly established in the Johannesburg, Witwatersrand, and Nelspruit regions.

The political conditions prevailing in South Africa in that period were such that white and black believers could not meet together in official gatherings. Separate conferences had to be held. The limitation was overcome, to some extent, by the evangelistic ministry of Nicholas Benghu, a very effective black preacher. This evangelist was so successful in his public ministry that he was called "the Billy Graham of Africa." Benghu was connected closely with PAOC missionaries and worked together with them as much as circumstances permitted. Again, the presence of thousands of converts in the country revealed the need of a Bible training institution.

A Bible school was set up at Tzaneen with some 20 students in attendance by 1970. Jack and Winnie Muggleton were sent to give leadership to the Tzaneen training program. As in Canada and other PAOC mission fields, the students spent their weekends in outreach ministry as both a means of evangelism and an opportunity for gaining practical experience. Missionaries Carl and Ruth Verhulst ministered in the region around Shingwedzi and also Louis Trichardt. They held evangelistic meetings in a tent as a means of getting their message to the people. Tent evangelism also was used by Robert Skinner in the Nelspruit area. He was assisted there for a time by Ingrid Chawner (then widowed). Hundreds of people were led to the Lord and about 50 local congregations were established in the decade before 1980. Dr. Douglas Abbey and his wife Beatrice came in 1970 from the PAOC Hay River Hospital in Canada to open a medical mission in Lesotho, a tiny independent territory within South Africa. This medical work was not sponsored by the PAOC, but the Abbey's full gospel ministry in that desperately needy land had denominational approval.

Pentecostal foundations in Liberia had been laid by self-sacrificing pioneers like Sophie Nygaard early in the twentieth century. Annie Cressman arrived to work with Nygaard in evangelism and, later, in linguistic and literary ministries. In this latter task, Cressman was assisted by Joy Hansell. Other Canadian workers included Vernon and Laura Morrison, Immanuel and Isabel Jensen, William and Viola Brown, Ron and Laura White, Gerald and Ruth Morrison, Florence Hamilton, and Margaret Wadge. Gerald Morrison took over leadership of the Bible school at Tchien, Zwedru, and supervised an ambitious program of campus development. But the work was often impeded by events which, to a Canadian, were in themselves of little significance. On one occasion, while the workmen were transporting a large load of rocks, both the rocks and several assisting students accidently were thrown down a steep hill. Morrison feared that if the very superstitious local natives attributed the accident to evil spirits, they would be afraid to come to the gospel meetings. But God overruled. Not one of the students was injured and no negative associations were attached to the evangelistic outreach. Over a period of years, the Tchien school complex was expanded until it consisted of 19 buildings.

Morrison was both school principal and superintendent of the Liberian churches. In 1973, after having moved to Monrovia, the Morrisons began a specialized ministry for youth and for the hundreds of young families then migrating to the capital city. This career missionary couple encountered their share of difficulties. Before moving to Monrovia, their home in Tchien (Zwedru) was destroyed by fire because of a faulty propane connection. Along with many other dangers, Morrison reported that their home had been burglarized 12 times, but he was still able to testify, "I have no regrets at having given my life to God's work, and to the fulfilling of His call."

During the 1970s, the ranks of Canadian missionaries in Liberia were increased with the arrival of Larry and Doreen Broughton, Jesse and Virginia Lynn, Grace Sjokvist, and Herb and LaVerne Tisher. Jesse Lynn took over the training of pastors at the Tchien Bible school. Grace Sjokvist taught in the school and also was its accountant. A new high school was opened at Zwedru in 1976 with assistance from Ron Martin and Alf Janke, a construction specialist. At the opening ceremony, the Pentecostal workers were honored by the attendance of the president of Liberia, William Tolbert.

The scope of missionary ministries in Liberia included youth camps, Christ's Ambassadors, Women's Missionary Councils, Sunday schools, and Christian day schools. The mission also supervised a book store, a literature department, a recording studio, and a "drop-in" youth centre. Harvey Best organized a TEE department and set up educational classes in six communities. Gordon and Kathy Nelson joined the Monrovia Bible school faculty.

Annie Cressman's work had by that time shifted from village evangelism to linguistic labors and the publication of a simplified English-language Bible for Liberians. Joy Hansell assisted in the production of a hymnal and a primer in the Grebo dialect. Hansell also assisted Cressman with Bible translation. Later, Joy Hansell returned to Canada to work in the national office. When Earl Kulbeck retired as editor of *The Pentecostal Testimony*, Hansell was appointed to that position.

The Pentecostal awakening of the early 20th century reached Argentina in 1908. The first Canadian Pentecostals to work in the "land of silver" were Dr. and Mrs. C. M. Wortman, of London, Ontario. Their ministry which began in Buenos Aires in 1921 has already been described in an earlier chapter. After the Wortmans returned to Canada in 1939 they were replaced by other workers such as Erling and Alvina Andresen and Horst and Elvine Doberstein. Later recruits from Canada included Fred and Susan Clements, Howard and Katherine Kerr, Paul and Dorothy Sorensen, Joseph and Ellen Anonby, and Garry and Jean Fricker. Triggered by the Tommy Hicks crusade in Buenos Aires and extended through the faithful service of missionaries and nationals, revival swept the land. By the end of the 1950s, there were more than 100 Pentecostal churches with about 3,000 members. Most of these churches were pastored by 80 trained nationals. Thirty years later the number of members in Pentecostal churches had grown to about 80,000.

Since the level of literacy in Argentina was high, Christian literature was used with great effectiveness in reaching the masses. A radio ministry expanded outreach in the '60s. Perhaps the most important development with a long-lasting impact was the establishment of a Bible school. Howard Kerr directed the school. With the encouragement and support of both George Upton and his successor, Carman Lynn, of the Overseas Missions Department, the theological education programs were steadily expanded to provide the needed national workers in the country.

Evangelistic outreaches in the '70s were spearheaded by Fred and Kay Nerling, Horst and Elvine Doberstein, and Werner and Hedwig Kniesel, of the German Branch, as well as Garry and Jean Fricker. Significant events in the outreach were the founding of an orphanage in San Nicolas, the opening of a Christian book store in Buenos Aires, and the establishment of an evangelistic centre in that large capital city. Those were troubled times in Argentina because of unstable governments and economic uncertainties. An occasional military coup added to the political instability. Although the Canadian missionaries had relatively unhindered access to the people, it was difficult to get a hearing in a population which, in 1970, was as large as Canada's but had only about a half-million Protestants. For another decade, the full gospel work made slow progress. A sovereign move of the Spirit of God in the 1980's dramatically introduced a period of revival and rapid growth. The work achieved self-governing status, receiving only limited financial assistance and occasional counsel from Canada.

Canadian involvement in Brazil came through the initially independent ministry of Harold Matson. Matson was a Saskatchewan native (Canwood) who was called of God to Brazil. He and his first wife Ethel began by ministering to the 27,000 rubber workers employed by a major company in that region. After mastering Portuguese, the Matsons pioneered Pentecostal churches in a number of the major cities of Brazil. When they considered these new congregations to be strong enough to survive, the Matsons turned them over to the leadership of nationals while they went on to other pioneer ventures. At the city of Joao Pessoa, for example, the work they began steadily expanded until it consisted of three congregations pastored by nationals.

After the death of Ethel, Matson married Canadian Amy Milne. The couple returned to Brazil to establish a Bible school. By the early 1960s, as the growth in churches outpaced the supply of trained pastors, evangelists, and teachers, a Bible training program was imperative. Amy, who had been very active in PAOC Sunday school work and children's evangelism in Canada, conducted these ministries effectively on the field.

In 1965, when the Matsons applied for affiliation with the PAOC, the work came under Canadian direction. In the 1970s, James and Shirley Culham were sent out to assist them. The breadth of the work soon expanded to include congregations in Recife, Natal, Pessoa, Fortaleza, and Manaus. When the Matsons first began preaching near Manaus, they sometimes needed the protection of the local police from mobs who attempted to stone them. Among their earliest converts in this community were five men who later became ministers of the full gospel.

To conserve the work in the unsettled times which then prevailed in Brazil, Matson called a conference of workers for the purpose of creating a formal constitution for the young association of churches. That action proved to be a very wise move for the future of the Pentecostal Movement in the country. As new congregations were set up, they formed "regional councils" which ultimately came to be the basis for the Pentecostal Evangelical Mission of Brazil.

Evangelism took many forms. One strategy was to reach the children in special meetings where the gospel would be presented through flannelgraph lessons. As large crowds gathered, the parents were often converted along with their children. Another means was the use of a gospel tent. Most Brazilians felt too much religious and social pressure to enter an evangelical church, but they would attend gospel meetings in a tent. One account tells of a gang of young men who attended a service and were drawn by the Spirit of God to repentance — two of them later became Pentecostal pastors.

A whole range of evangelistic activities presented the claims of Christ to a population steeped in spiritism and almost totally ignorant of biblical content. One of the novel methods adopted by the Matsons was the operation of an orphanage. It was a laborious and heart-wrenching type of work, but it was also the means of reaching hundreds of children and youth with the gospel. As Amy Matson reported,

> We would never exchange those years when it was our privilege to do what we could for the Lord in Brazil. The work goes on by others that have heard the same call.[12]

The Pentecostal mission founded in the West Indies by Robert J. Jamieson expanded steadily with the contributions of later Canadian recruits. Charles and Myrtle Barker, Robert and Mabel Eames, Harry and Marguerite Eggleton, Ray and Lillian McKillop, Frank and Lenore Meyer, Jack and Aleta Piper, Larry and Esther Ulseth, Jack and Daisy Keys, Clara Siemens, Marion Parkinson, Ruth Pemberton, and Catherine Simpson all participated effectively in the full range of missions ministries.

Their consecrated labors resulted, by 1960, in the establishment of more than 80 churches on the scattered islands, plus some 300 Sunday schools with over 10,000 children enrolled. About 70 Women's Missionary Council and Men's Fellowship groups were formed to enable West Indians to participate directly in their own evangelistic programs. Christ's Ambassadors, Pentecostal Crusaders, and Pioneer Missionary Action Girls served the same functions in the islands as in Canada — instructional as well as social.

The West Indies School of Theology (WIST) was founded in 1947 to prepare young men and women for ministry to their own people. Abe and Verna Jacobson provided leadership and were assisted for various periods of time by Leroy and Marilyn Lebeck and Grace Sjokvist. Bonnie Hauser and Carol Perkins arrived later to work as vocational missionaries, using skills acquired in the homeland to advance the work on the islands. By 1970, the school had provided training to about 600 West Indian young men and women. Several of these graduates were recruited as faculty for the school and two of them, Tom Maginley and Dennis White, served later as president of the institution.

The work which Jamieson had begun progressed so well that by 1958 the mission's direction was turned over to the nationals. The official name became The Pentecostal Assemblies of the West Indies, with headquarters on Trinidad. Canadians continued to assist the nationals and were able to forge a harmonious working relationship which has existed into the '90s between the West Indies organization and the PAOC. Don and Janice Scheske were engaged for some years on Dominica and St. Lucia. John and Marilyn Dobroski also labored for a term on Dominica. Harold Skovmand made a unique contribution to the work by providing the services of his aircraft and engaging in evangelism wherever possible.

One of the ways Canadians assisted was in the setting up of a radio gospel broadcast which reached a potential audience of one million people. A remarkable revival began in 1961 in San Fernando where more than 1,500 were converted. The by-product of new members was an increase in applications for the school of theology. New school facilities were constructed near the town of Curepe, Trinidad. The PAOC provided $100,000 for this expansion at WIST.

The Canadians were able to enter Cuba when political disruptions obliged American Pentecostal missionaries to leave that island. When the Castro revolution embittered relationships between Cuba and the USA, the Americans were no longer welcome. The Pentecostals on the island, along with other evangelicals, had retained possession of their church buildings but were forbidden to hold house meetings or distribute literature on the streets. In 1976, there were about 80 Pentecostal congregations in Cuba with about 5,000 adherents. They sought affiliation with the PAOC but a formal connection was then impossible. The Canadian denominational leaders have provided encouragement and various forms of support.[13]

Alex and Gwendolyn Munroe were the first Canadian Pentecostals in 1920 to begin working in Japan. After their retirement, Jessie Gillespie labored there until the start of the Second World War. At the conclusion of that conflict, a second generation of Canadian missionaries, including Don and Irene Kauffman, Virgil and Della Gingrich, and Jean Latta, entered Japan. The obstacles they faced were enormous: racial animosities created by the war, a densely-packed population in war-ravaged cities, a difficult language, and a Japanese culture that long had despised Western ways. Despite the problems, these mission workers succeeded in ministering in seven cities and organizing six church groups. By combining their efforts with those of American Pentecostal missionaries, they raised the total to about 80 congregations. These assemblies, with assistance from the United States and Canada, sponsored a radio broadcast with a potential audience of 30 million people. Tract distribution and literature evangelism were used extensively, but the most fruitful form of outreach was the personal witnessing of lay workers. A Bible school, which was set up in Tokyo to train Japanese workers, averaged about 40 students a year.

In 1961, the PAOC elected to withdraw from Japan and to turn over their work to the Japan Assemblies of God. This body has maintained a close working relationship with the American Assemblies of God. It seemed expedient to PAOC leaders to place the direction of their churches and national workers in the hands of these two Pentecostal organizations. The plan was for the PAOC to relocate its missions resources to other newly opened or expanding fields such as Hong Kong, Macau, Taiwan, and Thailand. Some of the Canadians who moved into those areas had earlier been involved in Pentecostal missions in China. The Japanese conquest of China, the internment in prison camps of the missionaries, and the subsequent victory of Chinese communism over the Chiang Kai Shek nationalists left China closed to missionaries after 1949. Among Canadians who switched their fields of labor to Hong Kong were Clare and Lydia Scratch, Rutherford and Florence Spence, Sadie McLeod, and Blanche Pardo. The Chinese Bible school was relocated to Hong Kong where J. Elmor Morrison and his wife Laura gave direction to the training of Chinese nationals for the Pentecostal ministry. Both Hong Kong and Macau were colonies of European powers — Britain and Portugal respectively. The Chinese communist government permitted them to continue as colonies for its own economic interests. Thus Pentecostal missions work went on unimpeded by any hostile government.

Several factors played key roles in the establishment of a solid missions base in the Far East. Religious literature spread the good news of saving faith in Christ to the thousands of refugees, and residents alike, who crowded the two small territories. The Bible school, Ecclesia Bible Institute, was set up in Shatin and produced scores of competent young national workers. Another fruitful field of evangelism was on the rooftops of the densely packed, high-rise apartment buildings in Hong Kong where day schools were set up. The unlikely location was evidence of the ingenuity of the missionaries in an area where land shortage would never have permitted the erection of more conventional schools. The great veneration of the Chinese for education guaranteed a large supply of students who received the gospel with the "three Rs" — or the Chinese equivalent. By 1960, the PAOC had several day schools with over 3,400 children in attendance. By this means the parents were also touched with the Christian message.

Constant growth in the Hong Kong work required reinforcements from Canada. These included Ray and Verna Austin, Don and Irene Kauffman, Cal and Ruth Ratz, Louisa Barker, and Jean Latta. Some were put to work in the roof-top schools, which had become so popular in the '70s that it was necessary to schedule three shifts of students per day. The need for a secondary school was so great that one of the Chinese Pentecostal churches built a seven-storey building to house the school. It was named the Hebron English School. A second such institution was set up later in Shek Kip Mei.

Graduates of the Bible institute founded several new congregations in Hong Kong and its suburbs. Other zealous young workers went to mainland China. For years, it was almost impossible for news of their progress to filter back to the Pentecostal leaders in the crown colony. To meet still another need, Ecclesia Bible Institute inaugurated extension classes in theological education for Chinese who could not attend daytime classes. Much of the responsibility for training the young workers in the churches fell upon Don and Irene Kauffman. A radio broadcast was also begun which was capable of reaching the entire population of the city, as well as parts of mainland China.

Don Kauffman served as field director of PAOC work in Hong Kong. By 1974, Chinese national Siu Hoi Lei became General Superintendent of the Southeast Asia Assemblies of God. Lei paid tribute to the work of the Canadians:

> Despite obstacles and satanic attack . . . we have . . . the foundations laid for a strong Pentecostal Church in Hong Kong . . . I praise the Lord for those that the Pentecostal Assemblies of Canada sent out . . . The Lord has also called out many National Brethren (to) join hands with the Missionaries in preaching the Gospel and establishing churches.[14]

Protestant mission endeavors in Macau had always been opposed by the Portuguese colonial rulers. The surrender of control to the communist Chinese — although the Portuguese carried on day-to-day direction — made penetration by Pentecostalism somewhat easier after the Second World War. By the late 1970s, the two colonies had a combined total of 19 churches and 2,700 members. There also were in operation 13 schools (K-12) with 165 teachers and about 7,000 students. All told, the Hong Kong-Macau conference had more than 100 national pastors and lay workers. The size and wide range of the conference's many ministries were the products of decades of development. In addition to the churches and day schools, these ministries promoted Sunday schools, youth programs, Women's Missionary Council, Men's Fellowship, and a Home Missions/Benevolence department. Among Canadians who served in later years as missionaries in this conference were George and Barbara Grosshans, Henry and Janet Borzel, and Murray and Alida Lincoln.

One spectacular event in Hong Kong's religious history involved the miraculous preservation of a Pentecostal church from a raging fire. An official of the conference, Secretary Tsan Bing Woh, recalled a day when a massive fire swept over the community of Shek Kip Mei, burning every building in its path and leaving 60,000 people homeless. Miraculously, the fire raced past the Pentecostal church and left it untouched. When scores of Chinese came to the church to receive emergency aid, the miracle was evident to all and made a profound impression on the people.

Before his retirement as director of overseas missions, George Upton recommended that the PAOC commence mission work in Thailand. The first PAOC workers sent to this country, where the population was 95 per cent Buddhist, were William and Elsie Butcher. Their initial work in Bangkok among the Chinese residents was extremely difficult and slow in showing results. At times it seemed destined to fail. Spiritual darkness and an indifference among the people to a Western gospel hampered their efforts. When Butcher died in a car accident while on furlough in Canada in 1965, PAOC missions in Thailand appeared to have reached the end. But other workers came forward to replace Will Butcher as Canadian Pentecostals strengthened their resolve to maintain missions work in Thailand.

Two sisters from Canada, Jean and Marion Bolton, found jobs in the country and financed their own evangelistic activities among the people. Since Thai young people were very eager to learn English, the Bolton sisters founded the Sharon English Bible Learning Centre. They were assisted in the instructional program by Florence Hamilton. By 1969, large numbers of high school and university students had enrolled in the English classes which used the Bible as one of the text books. Among the Canadians to go to this new and challenging field were Don and Faye Schellenberg, Ron and Laura White, and Sterling and Bev Irvine. Additional personnel arrived in the persons of Sadie McLeod, Blanche Pardo, and Janice Loewen who came to help with a youth centre ministry. A tragic note involved the death of missionary Ron White in a car accident while serving on the field.

Other forms of evangelism included literature distribution, Bible correspondence courses, and tent crusades. Don Schellenberg held a crusade in 1976 in the city of Lamphuun which was attended by about 1,000 people each night. Despite much opposition and persecution of the converts, many became Christians and a number also experienced supernatural healings. At the end of the tent crusade, a Pentecostal church formed in that community. Don and Dorothy Raymer of Canada were instrumental in the founding of a new missions complex in Bangkok which included a church, a Bible school building, and other facilities. The Jai Saman church when finished seated 1,200 people. The Bible school enrolled many eager Thai students. A radio broadcast spread the gospel message in an effective manner. A printing operation was also established. These projects were funded by a gift of about $100,000 from Toronto's Stone Church in honor of the memory of missionary Robert Eames. After serving for many years in the West Indies, the Eames had transferred to Thailand. Robert Eames' death from a heart attack was another severe blow to the work in this difficult field.

One of the significant observations to emerge from a study of PAOC missions worldwide is the fact that several of the overseas ministries were "independent" operations before they were adopted by the Canadian Fellowship. This note should not be surprising, considering the great rapidity with which the Pentecostal awakening spread around the globe. The absence of organization and denomination structure forced many aspiring Pentecostal missionaries to begin on their own or with whatever support might be available. That is how the early work started in Mongolia through the labors of Ken and Wyn McGillivray.

McGillivray went to the Far East on behalf of the Elim Assemblies of Great Britain. Wyn went out from Canada with the China Inland Mission. After their marriage, they carried on a medical mission on the steppes of Mongolia. Their work ended with the communist Chinese conquest of that land. During the war, they were interned in a prison camp by the Japanese. At the war's end, the two missionaries went to Hong Kong where they heard an appeal by nationalist General Chiang Kai Shek for all former missionaries to China to come to Formosa (now Taiwan), an island about the size of Vancouver Island with a population of 20 million. The General was offering missionaries the opportunity to evangelize among his troops, who had come with him when the nationalist Chinese government fled the mainland. McGillivray, who had been born in China and spoke the Mandarin language like a national, decided to go to Taiwan for a brief visit. The couple stayed for 30 years. His ministry among the soldiers resulted in a a great number of conversions and Pentecostal Baptisms. After about five years of such fruitful work, the McGillivrays turned their attention to the native Taiwanese, who had been terribly oppressed during a half-century of Japanese occupation. Choosing the city of Ilan on the eastern coast of the country as a base, they began to evangelize in the cities on the seaboard.

The McGillivrays met George Upton, the PAOC director of overseas missions, in 1964 and applied for affiliation with the Canadians. This arrangement guaranteed the couple regular financial support as well as additional missionaries to assist them. The full gospel work on the island was blessed by God. Wyn McGillivray tells of the extraordinary beginning of the work in the village of Yuan Shan. McGillivray and his assistant preacher, wearing white suits and carrying Bibles, arrived in the village without ceremony. Two local men met them with astonishment. They told McGillivray that God had appeared to them and announced that "two men in white with Bibles" were His servants with the truth of salvation. The two locals were converted and a church was begun in that place. One of the new believers later contracted leprosy, but his triumphant testimony throughout his affliction led to the conversion of most of the residents in a leper colony.[15]

The Pentecostal work also benefited indirectly from a government policy to move their employees after two or three years service to other areas of the island. This practice provided core members for new Pentecostal congregations as government employees who were members of the central church were obliged to transfer to other areas. Wherever they went, they helped to found new churches.

An interesting story involved the McGillivrays holding meetings in Chao Hsi in the home of a local believer. A group of converts from these meetings bought and paid for a tract of land for a new church building. But local government officials forbade construction until the land had been raised about three feet. McGillivray could hardly imagine how they could move fill to the land. One day, while standing on a small mountain across the river from the church land, he believed that God assured him the He would give him "the land on which he stood." McGillivray was baffled, but understood the message three days later. A typhoon swept tons of earth and rock down the mountain into the river. Officials called on all residents to remove this material which had dammed up the river in order to avoid a disastrous flood. Thousands of people were obliged to haul the material to the nearby vacant church site. Within 24 hours the elevation of the lot rose considerably — three feet, to be specific! The church built on that site was one of 16 which the McGillivrays brought into the PAOC. They also established three day schools.

Ray and Verna Austin helped with the opening of a PAOC gospel centre in Taipei, the capital city of Taiwan. One effective means of establishing a relationship with the nationals was to offer courses which were attractive to them, such as English language and cooking. Children's meetings followed a more traditional evangelistic format. Austin acquired a high profile in the region with his appointment as principal of the Ming Tao United Bible School, an institution for the training of ministerial candidates for several denominations in Taiwan. He also acted as the PAOC field director for some years.

Ken McGillivray's life work ended while preaching at a camp meeting in Taiwan in 1983. Chinese believers who revered his memory arranged all aspects of the funeral ceremony and the interment. Banners appeared above the coffin — in Chinese style — reading, "He was born among us. He loved us. He served us. He is one of us." The funeral cortege, attended by thousands, moved from Taipei to Ilan, where a 15-foot monument was erected to mark the site of his grave.[16] The work he began and carried on for three decades was expanded throughout Taiwan by the dedicated PAOC missionaries and national pastors who followed in his footsteps.

The Overseas Missions Department in Toronto developed programs which could take advantage of the professional skills and commitment of Canadian lay people who wished to be involved on the front line of missions work. The "Volunteers in Missions" (VIM) programs was inaugurated in 1977. This ministry recruited lay people for short-term missions assignments — usually six months to one year — on various foreign fields. Men and women with needed technical skills — teachers, evangelists, musicians, and so on — volunteered their services and agreed to pay 50 per cent of their travel and living expenses while on the field. The Overseas Missions Department paid the balance.[17]

A year later, Carman Lynn, the Executive Director of the Overseas Missions Department, established another innovative lay ministry program for "seniors." The Seniors Overseas Service plan (SOS) was aimed at retired lay workers who could assist on the overseas fields with a variety of tasks and for flexible periods of time. The SOS volunteers paid almost all of the costs of travel to the field as well as their own expenses while overseas.[18]

The entire missionary program expanded so rapidly between 1960 and 1980 that the Executive Director of the OMD needed more help in the Toronto office. Clare Scratch was appointed Promotional Secretary for the Department in 1961. His responsibilities were further shared by the appointment of two field representatives in 1966: Ernest Francis in Western Canada and Robert Argue in Eastern Canada provided closer liaison with pastors and people. Others who later served in this capacity were Roy Upton, Robert Skinner, and Gordon Fulford. The 1978 General Conference in Calgary passed a resolution to appoint an executive assistant to work with the Executive Director of the department. William Cornelius, a veteran missionary, was the first person to fill this new post.

A very important move which increased efficiency in the operation of the PAOC missions program was the establishment of a "School of Missions" in 1961. James Skinner directed this annual school until his retirement at which time Keith Morrison assumed the oversight. All candidates for the overseas fields and all furloughing missionaries attended these sessions. The goals were to provide a realistic insight for novice missionaries into the problems and complexities of the field and to encourage and instruct experienced workers in the newest missions techniques. Significant changes in the late-80s involved changing the school to a biennial schedule and adding lay and clerical workers who were not planning on missionary careers but were interested in a better understanding of missions work. The School of Missions has been held at the Eastern Pentecostal Bible College campus in Peterborough.

Financial support of overseas missions was a very high priority among Canadian Pentecostals even before the inception of the PAOC in 1919. It was decided early in the history of the movement that all missions contributions would be divided on the basis of two-thirds for overseas work and one-third for home missions. That principle was reviewed at the request of some delegates at the 1966 General Conference. The decision was in favor of continuing the familiar distribution scheme, since it had "enjoyed considerable success" and had "proven to be equitable and workable."

One novel fund-raising method adopted in the '60s was the "offerama" at general conferences. By special arrangements, an offering for missions was taken by all participating churches in Canada and the tally phoned into a central reporting office. The sums raised have shown constant increase each time the "offerama" has been conducted at the biennial conference. In 1970 it reached a total of more than $160,000. The PAOC then had 158 active missionaries on 15 foreign fields, 11 overseas Bible schools with 444 students, plus some 2,000 churches with nearly 165,000 members. The number of native pastors and evangelists was 2,175.[19]

A decade later, the PAOC was taking in more than six million dollars a year for its missions work. The "offerama" of the 1980 General Conference was over $614,000. At that time the Fellowship had 209 missionaries in 18 overseas fields with over 5,000 churches and some 440,000 members and adherents. The rapidity of these increases was evident in the fact that 344 of the 5,000 churches had been established in the preceding two-year period. The number of Bible schools had risen to 17 and the number of teachers and national workers to nearly 4,000.[20]

By the 1980s The Pentecostal Assemblies of Canada had begun to look beyond the countries in which it had carried on the bulk of its missions outreach during the previous two generations. Executive Director Carman Lynn summarized the strategy of the PAOC, as it responded to the changing world missions environment, for the 1980 General Conference delegates . He highlighted the opportunities available and the need to end some PAOC involvement in mature mission fields as national leaders learned to chart their own course without dependence upon the direction of missionaries:

> Appealing opportunities are available on every continent, but there are financial limits to be reckoned with . . . Wisdom higher than the human level is needed to know where God would direct The Pentecostal Assemblies of Canada to become involved. There is also that pruning necessary to excise operations which have fulfilled their purpose . . . The time does come when the national church should draw sustenance through its own roots . . . Thus the parent body can direct its energies and genius to reproduce itself in another geographical area.[21]

With this perspective about its role in overseas work, the PAOC began to direct its interests to new fields. By 1980 it had re-established its work in India — a field entered early in the 20th century by Canadians, but left to other Pentecostal groups some years later. A long-planned entry to Europe was launched through contacts with Pentecostal groups in Iceland, Greece, and Eastern Europe. The European Pentecostal Fellowship was formed to promote ministry in Eastern European countries. In 1979 this new association sponsored a preaching/teaching seminar in Vienna. These exploratory initiatives were to be more fully developed in the next decade.

Endnotes

1. Robert Skinner, "Twenty-five Unbelievable Years," special insert in *The Pentecostal Testimony* (January 1974).
2. Keith Morrison, "Missionaries I know: Arnold and Elsie Bowler," *The Pentecostal Testimony* (April 1981), 18-19.
3. Bruce Brand, "Evangel's Worldwide Literature Ministry," *The Pentecostal Testimony* (February 1985), 38-39; Arnie Labrentz, "Theological Education by Extension — Worldwide," *The Pentecostal Testimony* (September 1980), 22; see also K. B. Birch, "Theological Education by Extension," a discussion paper, PAOC Archives.
4. Thomas Wm. Miller, interview with William C. Cornelius, Executive Director of the Overseas Missions Department of the PAOC, August 7, 1991.
5. Keith Morrison, "Missionaries I Know: John (Jack) and Edna Lynn," *The Pentecostal Testimony* (September 1981), 22-24.

THE "UNBELIEVABLE YEARS" IN OVERSEAS MISSIONS / 12

6. George R. Upton, letter to Thomas Wm. Miller, August 1, 1983.
7. Gustav Kurtz, quoted in Arthur Drewitz, *History of the German Branch of the Pentecostal Assemblies of Canada, 1940-1980*, (Printed by the German Branch, 1986), p. 51.
8. Thomas Wm. Miller, interview with Bernard Hunter, October 21, 1988.
9. C. W. Lynn, "Mozambique Church Complex: A Vision Fulfilled," *The Pentecostal Testimony* (August 1975), 8; see also George R. Upton, *The Miracle of Mozambique* (Clearbrook, B.C.: A. Olfert, 1980).
10. Alex Strong, "A New Era Begins in Mozambique," *Action* (January 1976), 4-5.
11. Thomas Wm. Miller, note 8.
12. Amy Matson, letter to Thomas Wm. Miller, November 13, 1988.
13. C. W. Lynn, "The Living Church in Cuba," *The Pentecostal Testimony* (January 1977), 16-17.
14. Siu Hoi Lei, "25th Anniversary of the PAOC in Hong Kong, 1949-1974," pamphlet, PAOC Archives.
15. Thomas Wm. Miller, interview with Wyn McGillivray, October 24, 1988.
16. Ibid.
17. C. W. Lynn, "Volunteers in Mission," *The Pentecostal Testimony* (December 1977), 20-21.
18. C. W. Lynn, "Senior's Overseas Service," *The Pentecostal Testimony* (June 1978), 8.
19. C. W. Lynn, "Report of the Executive Director of Overseas Missions," *27th Biennial General Conference, Victoria, B.C., August 20-25, 1970*, PAOC Archives, 13-23.
20. C. W. Lynn, "Report of the Executive Director of Overseas Missions," *32nd Biennial General Conference, Hamilton, Ontario, August 21-26, 1980*, PAOC Archives, 17-22.
21. Ibid., 21.

Chapter 13
ON TRACK!

The Congress On Pentecostal Leadership (COPL'87) was described officially as "the most significant congress" in the history of the PAOC. It was held in October 1987 in Toronto. The first announcement in the *Testimony* promoted COPL'87 as a gathering "for all church workers, pastors and wives with a desire for a clear vision of the future of the ministry in Canada." It was to have three specific objectives:

1. To determine our direction (where?)
2. To define our mission (why?)
3. To covenant our decision (how?)[1]

The conference was an extraordinary, Canada-wide gathering called to reassess the purposes and priorities of the Fellowship. It was largely the vision of General Superintendent James MacKnight, but it received keen support from denominational executives at the national and district levels as well as the leadership in the local church. The enthusiasm of the 2,500 delegates represented a ground swell of sentiment among Pentecostal leaders that it was time for an assessment of the past and the choosing of priorities for the future. A consensus for such a gathering had been building for a decade in Canadian Pentecostalism. Pastors, evangelists, lay leaders, missionaries, and administrators wanted to know if the PAOC was still "On Track" — the motto chosen for COPL'87.

Twelve plenary speakers addressed the delegates and over 100 workshop leaders dealt with the whole range of practical ministries which function in the local church as well as a variety of social concerns. Several prominent personalities from outside of the PAOC were invited to help the Fellowship understand its role in the context of world evangelism

13 / ON TRACK!

— people like Jimmy Swaggart, Jack Hayford, Tommy Barnett, and Tony Campolo.

Most of the workshops were presented by the Fellowship's own credential holders. The wide range of topics was designed to touch the areas represented by both clergy and lay leaders. For example, Herb Barber's focus was the Sunday school, one of the vital ministries which had helped Calvary Temple make such an impact on the city of Winnipeg. He warned delegates that the decline of this valuable ministry should be a cause of great concern; indeed, neglect could leave the Sunday school "one generation from extinction." Margaret Gibb, a pastor's wife and guest speaker at women's conferences, reminded her audience that Pentecostal women had shared fully in founding the PAOC and that women should again take their rightful place in worldwide evangelism. William Griffin, one of the national executive officers, dealt with a theological issue which was threatening to make inroads on the Canadian scene. The topic "Kingdom Now — New Hope or New Heresy?" addressed the issue of the time and manner for establishing the Lord's kingdom on the earth. Of particular concern for the PAOC was the similarities the "Kingdom Now" teaching appeared to have with the Latter Rain Movement of the late 1940s in the area of spiritual gifts.

Congress delegates participated in a unique "COPL Covenant" as a form of personal commitment to the Pentecostal distinctives and worldwide evangelism. An official summary of COPL'87 regarded the gathering as "successful beyond our greatest hopes:"

> It may well go down in history as a watershed in the history of the PAOC. After 80 years of history we all felt a need for renewal in our spirits and in our purpose. We sensed our need for the Holy Spirit to guide us . . . and to ensure that we are "on track." [2]

COPL'87 served its intended purpose in providing third and fourth generation Pentecostals with an honest appraisal of the present status of the PAOC and a confirmation of its mission. The process of critical self-evaluation manifest did not end with COPL'87. Both at national headquarters, and among PAOC people, there was an openness to a reexamination of Pentecostalism. General Superintendent James MacKnight's New Year's message for 1988 was essentially a call to return to the roots — the foundation upon which the PAOC was established. His theme was so firmly expressed as to verge on bluntness: it was that, above every other felt need, "We Need Another Pentecost." MacKnight reiterated the call at the General Conference in Hamilton in 1988 and again at Winnipeg in 1990.

While the decade of the '80s provided evidence of the PAOC's desire to relate to its spiritual roots, it also revealed that the organization was developing an awareness of its role as a significant evangelical body in Canadian culture. Pentecostals noted that the nation was in the throes of enormous changes in social mores. The federal and provincial governments seemed to be succumbing to pressures from such groups as radical feminists, advocates of publicly funded abortions, and outspoken homosexuals. Most Pentecostals were deeply disturbed by what they perceived to be an attack on traditional Judeo-Christian standards and a breakdown of public morality. Not surprisingly, the consequences of these trends surfaced in the form of broken marriages, single-parent families, teenage pregnancies, increased alcoholism, drug addiction, and child-runaways.

The PAOC took an aggressive stance throughout the '80s in opposition to these trends which were, cumulatively, the results of the progress of secular humanism in Canada. In addition to the grass roots resistance, the denomination decided upon a systematic presentation of its views to politicians and the public by means of an Ethics and Social Concerns Committee which it established in 1980.

In retrospect, the times were propitious for the PAOC: it had acquired a degree of maturity and a level of respectability which added authority to its publicized views. It also was the period in which the denomination became self-confident in relation to the accomplishments of over 60 years of progress, both at home and abroad. This awareness of "the end of an era" in its development from revivalistic sect to religious organization had become self-evident.

According to the 1981 federal census, there were 338,790 Pentecostals in the country, a figure representing 1.3 per cent of the population. While the PAOC was the largest Pentecostal entity in the nation, some of those listed as "Pentecostal" in the census were members of smaller organizations such as the Pentecostal Assemblies of Newfoundland, the Apostolic Church of Pentecost of Canada, the United Pentecostal Church, the Church of God, and independent charismatic churches. The PAOC, which counted only older teens and adults, used a different statistical measurement than the federal government. The latter included all children and relatives of a household in the count when the parents identified themselves by a particular religious label. By its own reckoning, based on returned questionnaires from pastors, the PAOC had 134,662 members and adherents in 1981. PAON membership in Newfoundland was approximately 30,000. A year later, PAOC numbers in Canada had increased by 12.5 per cent to a total of 155,257.[3] The PAOC had nearly 900 congregations and "preaching points," 2,800 credential-holders, 1,100 students in its Bible schools, and was handling in excess of 12 million dollars annually at the national office.

13 / ON TRACK!

The progress recorded by the denomination in the '70s was considered only to have laid the groundwork for a more ambitious evangelistic program in the next decade. General Superintendent Robert Taitinger called on delegates at the 1980 General Conference in Hamilton, Ontario, to increase their efforts to reach the masses for Christ. He declared,

> Canada must be evangelized. If we don't do it, who will? The PAOC must do its part. We must continue to plant churches, to support home missions projects, to identify with specific geographical needs . . . Our growing in the '80s will be of prime concern to the leadership of the PAOC.[4]

The decade was marked by substantial changes in denominational leadership. At the 1980 General Conference the delegates approved an expansion of the General Executive from three to five elected "members-at-large," presumably to ensure the practical input of more pastors in policy decisions. This increase raised the membership of the executive body to 22 — six national executive officers, seven district superintendents, the superintendent of the French Conference, three superintendents of ethnic Branch Conferences, and five pastors.

Two new executive officers began their tenures at the Hamilton General Conference. William Cornelius was chosen to give direction to the Overseas Missions Department when retiring Executive Officer Carman Lynn took a position on the faculty of Eastern Pentecostal Bible College. Cornelius, a long-time missionary in Kenya, had served as an assistant to Lynn before being elected to the top position in the department. The second new officer was William Griffin who had spent 17 years of his ministry as a Bible college teacher and academic dean. Griffin took on the newly created Church Ministries portfolio which combined the ministries of youth and Christian education with several other church programs. Don Feltmate, the former Executive Director of Christian Education and Youth, departed the national scene to accept the challenge of pioneering a church in Malvern, a community on the east side of metropolitan Toronto.

When Robert Taitinger chose to leave the national office in 1982 to become president of EPBC, James MacKnight succeeded him as General Superintendent. Prior to his election, MacKnight had been pastor of one of the PAOC's flagship churches, Central Tabernacle in Edmonton. He had also served in earlier years as a national evangelist with "Canada For Christ," an evangelistic thrust sponsored by the national office.

After 16 years as the Executive Director of Home Missions and Bible Colleges, Robert Argue retired from office in 1982 and assumed pastoral duties in Flemingdon Park Pentecostal Church, just a few blocks from the headquarters building. His successor was Gordon Upton, son of the distinguished missions leader, George Upton. Prior to his election to the national post, Gordon Upton served as district superintendent of Eastern Ontario and Quebec.

Two years later, Graydon Richards stepped down as PAOC General Treasurer. Richards had spent 40 years in the ministry, 12 of them in the national office. John Totafurno, who had served as chief accountant under Richards, was elected in his stead. In 1988, after completing two terms, Totafurno retired. His replacement was Reuben Schmunk, former British Columbia district superintendent. In less than a decade, the group of chief officers had undergone a complete change over in personnel, with one notable exception. Charles Yates continued to serve with distinction as the General Secretary throughout the complete transitional period.

The '80s witnessed many changes among the executive assistants who directed the departments under the general supervision of the six executive officers. There were also some new departments formed to meet the changing needs of the times. Doug Lindsay was appointed Dominion Commissioner of Pentecostal Crusaders, the midweek program for boys and girls, when incumbent Murray Lincoln received missionary appointment to Hong Kong. Rick Hiebert succeeded Ivan Gaetz as national director of Christian Education. Hiebert later moved into the newly created position of director of Family Ministries and editor of *Resource* magazine. William Hale then replaced Hiebert as national director of Christian education. Howard Honsinger, forced by failing health to resign as district superintendent of Western Ontario and later as senior pastor of Glad Tidings in Burlington, Ontario, refused to sit on the sidelines and became the first national director of Seniors Ministries.

Greg Foley followed David Johnston as national director of Youth Ministries. Charles Benn filled the vacancy in Spiritual Life and Evangelism which had been created by Sam Buick's move to the pastorate in Waterloo. David Boyd followed Gerald Harbridge as assistant to the Executive Director of Home Missions and Bible Colleges. George Grosshans, who had assisted Robert Argue in Home Missions and Bible Colleges for two years in the '70s, returned to the national office as director of World Missions Communications when Don Raymer shifted into the leadership of a new department, Emergency Relief and Development Overseas (ERDO). Don Niles became chief accountant when John Totafurno moved from that post to become the General Treasurer. Harry Anderson took over the management of Full Gospel Publishing House when Vic Smallridge ended his long and effective

13 / ON TRACK!

tenure in that position. Smallridge then played a major role in programming the mainframe computer as the national office plunged into the technological era. Two notable stalwarts who labored faithfully through the entire decade in their executive assistant roles were Keith Morrison in OMD and Wilf Klingspohn in Stewardship.

But the story cannot be rehearsed without some painful memories of loss. Joy Hansell, former missionary and first female editor of *The Pentecostal Testimony*, died in 1982. William Griffin, the Executive Director of Church Ministries, produced the magazine for a year until a permanent editor was appointed in the person of Robert Skinner. Terminal illnesses also brought about changes in the Women's Ministries and Men's Fellowship departments. Eileen Stewart assumed the leadership role which had been occupied so successfully by Elma Barber Scratch. Layman John Bernhardt took over the Men's Fellowship from another outstanding layman, Hank Roberts. And then Howard Honsinger died in full harness, bringing to an end a magnificent lifetime of service as senior pastor of both small and large churches, radio broadcaster, long-time member of the General Executive, and district superintendent. George Tunks, former pastor and evangelist, followed Honsinger as director of Seniors Ministries and editor of *The Senior Contact*.

With the appointment in 1982 of Hudson Hilsden as full-time head of the new Ethics and Social Concerns Committee, the PAOC spoke out on many controversial issues. The creation of this post was the culmination of a process which began at the 1978 General Conference in Calgary with the formation of a National Committee on Moral Standards. The next General Conference in Hamilton changed the committee's name to Ethics and Social Concerns and called on the General Executive to consider the appointment of a full-time chairman. The call was stronger two years later in Winnipeg where the General Conference delegates passed a resolution requesting "prompt action" in securing a suitable person to give leadership. Canadian Pentecostals have always held strong convictions about the traditional "vices" such as alcoholism and sexual immorality. But the '80s produced such a onslaught of ethical and moral issues that they felt obliged to enter the public forum in a new way. Hilsden's research led to the publication of many reports designed to inform pastors and people respecting the issues of the day.[5]

Another means to that end was a series of articles in the *Testimony* on such topics as "What Do We Mean By Secular Humanism?" "The Significance of the Charter of Rights," and "Sexual Orientation." The last-mentioned article was a summary of an earlier letter Hilsden sent to the prime minister and parliament of Canada on the government's "Equality For All" report. The range of concerns addressed was extraordinary: rock music in the church, secular humanism, euthanasia, abortion, divorce, abuse of wives and children, sexual orientation, separation of church and state, Christians in parliament, famine relief, the Charter of Rights, lotteries, family life, birth control, drug and alcohol addiction, capital punishment, AIDS, homosexuality, and pornography.

The editor of the *Testimony*, Robert Skinner, summarized the social ills of the 1980s as a threat to the nation's continued prosperity. In "Civilization On The Skids," Skinner advised his readers that only a spiritual revival sweeping across Canada could arrest the moral decline so evidently underway.[6] It was apparent that PAOC involvement in seeking solutions to society's evils had a religious motivation. Pentecostals were not adopting the "social gospel," but were identifying social disintegration and moral collapse as symptoms of a spiritual malaise.

Hilsden urged PAOC people to become more politically active. In the September 1986 "News Release" he declared,

> Christians must get involved! Democracy survives only if those who govern are required to be accountable to those who are governed.[7]

Such appeals to become involved in political and ethical issues marked a definite shift in the way Canadian Pentecostals viewed their place in society. By tradition, they had maintained an arms-length relationship with social activists and had resolutely refused to take sides politically. They still retained the latter position, but in the '80s acknowledged a need to share in seeking solutions to the country's social ills.

Another significant development, and perhaps also a reflection of the times, was the legislative provision in 1982 for a clarification of the denomination's disciplinary procedures in reference to its credential holders. In part, it was a response to a growing disposition among some professions to seek recourse in the courts when it was perceived that individual rights were not being observed and protected. Although the Fellowship regarded its system of hearing and responding to charges against clergy to be appropriate and fair, the climate of the '80s required a more sophisticated set of judicial processes. The revisions, which were designed to give the PAOC an ecclesiastical court which clearly demonstrated its commitment to justice, were drawn up with professional advice, incorporated in by-laws, duly published, and adopted by the constituency.[8]

The 1984 General Conference was notable for a major change with respect to the credential status of women in the PAOC ministry. The issue of the ordination of women had been vigorously debated at both the district and national levels after emerging as a contentious issue at the

13 / ON TRACK!

General Conference in Regina in 1976. While there had been significant support for women's ordination, sometimes a majority, the proponents had never been able to muster the necessary two-thirds majority at a General Conference to change the regulatory by-law regarding ordination. But at Saint John, New Brunswick, in 1984 the measure was overwhelmingly approved by a margin of more than 90 per cent. The decision was not easily received across the country by those whose opposition was based on their interpretation of certain biblical texts, but the long debate appeared finally to have come to an end. The Fellowship had travelled a long way from the position in its first constitution in 1919 which declared that "women may act as Evangelists, Missionaries, or Deaconesses, but not as Pastors or Elders."[9]

Within a few months of the Saint John decision, experienced female workers had been ordained in most of the districts. Among the earliest were evangelists Maud Ellis, Janet Rodger, and Hannah Price Richardson in the Eastern Ontario and Quebec District. In the West, the District of Saskatchewan ordained Grace Brown, for some 30 years a teacher at the Bible college in Saskatoon, and the McTaggart sisters, Margaret and Matilda, who had pastored for 28 years in that province.

Concurrent with the 10-year debate on women's ordination was an even more contentious issue — divorce and remarriage. Resolutions on the subject landed on General Conference agendas in a variety of forms. The results were the same. The denominational position was reinforced again and again: divorce was discouraged, divorced people were advised to stay single, and PAOC ministers were forbidden to officiate at a marriage where one of the persons had been previously married and whose former spouse was still living. While the PAOC was adamant in its opposition to divorce and remarriage, and while it declared divorced and remarried persons ineligible to serve as ministers or members of church boards, the denomination demonstrated its openness by extending membership and opportunities for involvement in Christian service. The incorporation of divorced and remarried people into the life of local churches provided evidence that although the PAOC had not changed its official position, it had moved a considerable distance from the earlier view that such remarriages were tantamount to "living in sin."

It may be noted that while the PAOC was showing considerable flexibility in its administrative structure and its responsiveness to the demands of the day, it did not make significant doctrinal shifts. The revised *Statement of Fundamental and Essential Truths*, approved at the 1980 Hamilton Conference, was a slimmed-down version of the basic doctrines.

Two deletions in the amended statement of faith are worth noting. The section titled "The Believer's Obedience To God," which spoke against the concept of "eternal security" for those who lived in moral disobedience, was dropped. An attempt was made on the conference floor to insert a section on "Continuance" which underlined the necessity of maintaining salvation by faith, but it was defeated. The second change related to a rather sensitive area and involved the deletion of the paragraph caption, "Our Distinctive Testimony," and also the deletion of the word "physical" from the phrase relating to "other tongues." There was no suggestion that the organization was altering its view that the Baptism in the Holy Spirit should be accompanied by tongues. To the contrary, and in opposition to some "charismatic" teachings, it was declaring that tongues was the first evidence of any kind that signified the Pentecostal immersion in the Spirit.

Noting the necessity of agreement on doctrinal matters, the 1982 General Conference delegates passed a resolution which expressed concern about the "questions" which were being raised about eschatology. Specifically, the motion requested the formation of a committee which would study the topic as presented in the *Statement of Fundamental and Essential Truths* and report its findings to the General Executive the following year. Subsequently, the General Executive sponsored an amendment at the 1984 General Conference in Saint John which made a minor concession to people who had some difficulty with the "pre-tribulation rapture." While the amendment maintained an emphasis on the imminent return of Christ for the Church before the wrath of God would be visited on the earth, it was worded in such a way that there was room for the so-called "mid-trib" rapture.

The steadfastness with which the PAOC held its theological positions may be illustrated by its opposition to "faddish" Pentecostal themes. Unquestionably, the PAOC had been more comfortable defending its views against non-Pentecostals than against its own ranks. The Latter Rain Movement of the late-40s, with its radical emphasis on the gifts of the Spirit, brought considerable division to the Fellowship because of the leadership's aversion to speak and act in a manner which might appear that it was resisting the Spirit. Similarly, there was reluctance to respond to the "Positive Confession" movement of the '80s which majored on faith and miracles. It was an emphasis which Pentecostals appreciated, and yet it was known that a proper emphasis on faith had to be balanced with respect for the sovereignty of God. The leadership of the Fellowship believed that it was necessary to warn the constituency of the danger inherent in the excesses.

In the same manner, the PAOC spoke against the extreme views of independent Pentecostals, sometimes known as the "Kingdom Now" movement, who visualized the concrete establishment of Christ's Kingdom on earth before His physical return. While the classic Pentecostals were quite familiar with "dancing in the spirit," many were uncomfortable with the "hopping" and choreographed dancing which became a standard mode of worship for the Restoration Movement. James MacKnight, in an article titled "Things Most Surely Believed Among Us," appealed for a concerted focus on the essential mandate of the Fellowship — to proclaim the gospel throughout the whole world. He warned that the emphases of the Restoration Movement would create difficulties:

> When this teaching of "the Kingdom" is examined in the light of the whole scripture, there is an evidence of error. . . . We must avoid dividing congregations by demanding of God's people an outward conformity to a certain type of praise . . . We must not be deceived into basing unity on experience rather than truth and developing a critical attitude which breeds disunity, the very opposite of the unity which the restoration movement avows.[10]

True to their revivalist roots, Canadian Pentecostals periodically have renewed their commitment to evangelism, both at home and abroad. General Superintendent MacKnight challenged leaders and lay people at the 1984 General Conference to redouble church planting efforts. The denomination set a goal of 75 new congregations in two years, and a total of 400 new assemblies within a decade. The first phase of the goal was surpassed with the establishment of 87 new churches by 1986. Space does not permit documentation for all the new assemblies, but random details about a few of them will illustrate the enthusiasm with which the project was launched and the effectiveness of the participants.

Particularly noteworthy was the growth among Canada's Native people. A Native assembly was established at Burns Lake, B.C. Another congregation was set up in a renovated building in Tumbler Ridge, B.C. A great advance in Native evangelism came with the organization of the first National Native Leadership Council in 1985 sponsored by the national Home Missions department. This first meeting proved so beneficial that a second was held the next year at Clayburn, B.C. Native pastors, evangelists, and lay workers gathered to worship and learn how to be more effective in reaching their own people. Speakers came from Prince Rupert, Alaska, Arizona, and Quebec. Among the delegates were members of a new Native Pentecostal church in Vancouver.[11]

A new church was built in Fort Providence, Northwest Territories, in the summer of 1986 by a group of men and women from Calgary. Workers in Hay River had laid the foundation and the "Work Force" team from the south completed the sanctuary in eight days.

Douglas Stiller had already pioneered one new church when he took up the challenge of forming a new congregation in Calgary in 1984. A nucleus of supporters from one of the older city congregations provided assistance. Within a few months there were over 120 people in the meetings and the church was self-supporting. Stiller, offering sage advice to other pastors considering similar projects, warned that church planters must guard against intimidation in the face of great obstacles; they also must guard against personal "kingdom building." Finally, he noted, pastors of older assemblies must not be threatened by the emergence of a new congregation in their vicinity.[12]

A new church in the Redwater-Gibbon area of Alberta was the outgrowth of pioneer workers who had just completed Bible school. Mr. and Mrs. Robert Hehl held services in both communities and by 1982 had a congregation of about 60 in one town and a promising assembly beginning in the other.

A novel approach to church planting saw the organization of the "Marketplace Chapel" in the West Edmonton Mall. This vast shopping concourse, with thousands of employees, opens seven days a week for about a half-million shoppers. The director of the chapel, Nelson Wolf, provided a variety of services to address the spiritual needs of many who attended. A significant number of converts were made right from its earliest stages.

The Pentecostal Sub-Arctic Mission opened a new church in the Inuit community of Holman Island in 1987. The pastor was Marilyn Smith, formerly an RNA at the Hay River Hospital. The tasks Marilyn faced in evangelizing the settlement can best be imagined by focusing on the problems of an arctic environment: Holman Island is only 1,300 miles from the North Pole.

In 1986 the goal of the Sub-Arctic Mission to provide more national leaders for the far North was given a boost. A residential facility was acquired in Fort Smith and a program of studies designed which won the approval of the government of the Northwest Territories, as well as the PAOC national accrediting committee. The Sub-Arctic Leadership Training program (SALT) began with a faculty of seven and a student enrollment of six, drawn from all across the North. Much of the funding for the Native training program and for the development of new congregations came from the dedicated professional staff at the H. H. Williams Memorial Hospital in Hay River. They were paid by the Territories government, but individual staff members voluntarily donated considerable portions of their salaries to finance northern missions.

One measure of the impact which the Sub-Arctic Mission had on northern communities was the recognition achieved by pioneer

13 / ON TRACK!

Eva Nichol as "Citizen of the Year." She had pastored for 28 years in the North and was responsible for the establishment of the Pentecostal church in Fort Smith.[13]

The hospital in Hay River grew both in number of beds and impact on the community. In 1987, James Tyler, the director of the hospital, began preparations to erect a 16-unit, multi-level, care home on a site next to the medical buildings.

Saskatchewan was one of the few PAOC districts to have a full-time director of its Native Ministries. Under the supervision of this department, Rodger Ratt and his wife pastored a new church at LaRonge and held meetings in two other outposts. In Saskatoon, the Native New Life Assembly, which had begun in the '70s, appointed Native Pat Linklater in 1987 as its resident evangelist. This move enabled the congregation to make a more effective outreach to the Native population of the city.

It was early in the '80s that pastor Vern Seabrook of Glaslyn began holding Sunday school and Bible studies at nearby Edam. The congregation at first consisted of only six women and five children. The women were determined to succeed. With the advice and support of the district office, they elected four of their number to a church board and outlined their goals. They wanted to see all the husbands converted, a church building erected, and a full-time pastor in place. With district help, a building 30 by 50 feet was built in Edam.[14] By 1984, all the goals the women had set were accomplished.

Growth continued in the province of Manitoba. Clare Rattai started a new congregation in north Winnipeg with about 20 people. Their number soon increased to over 70. Another assembly was launched in 1984 in Ameranth, Manitoba. Per Knudsen began services that summer in a school gymnasium. One of the oldest and largest PAOC churches, Calvary Temple, completed a two-million-dollar church ministries building in 1986. The new "A. H. Argue Building" provided additional facilities for the great Sunday school ministry in the church as well as office space for the more than 20 departments.

Another major re-development involved the construction of a new sanctuary by the congregation of Bethel Pentecostal Church in Ottawa. The new facilities were dedicated in 1986, a date that coincided with the assembly's 75th anniversary. The change of address from Ottawa to Kanata was a sign of the times as older assemblies moved to the suburbs.

The PAOC made further strides in the Ottawa area in the '80s when the district sponsored a pioneer assembly located in Kanata. A former Bible college instructor, Ron Kydd, began pastoring the fledgling congregation in 1984. From the first meetings, attendance totalled about 90 adults and 120 children in Sunday school. A beautiful new building was erected which later housed both the church and the district office when it relocated from Belleville in 1993.

The pastor and congregation of Kennedy Road Tabernacle in Brampton provided assistance and advice to Edward Bellsmith in the founding of an assembly at Malton in 1984. Soon, over 100 people were attending regularly. Another church-planter, John Mercer, pioneered an urban church in Toronto's Thornhill region. This work began with a Sunday school in rented premises and then drew together a nucleus of believers who erected a building with district assistance.

Pentecostal meetings were started by Buddy Burge in a meeting room of a large hotel in the Rexdale district of Metropolitan Toronto. With the assistance of the Western Ontario District, the work grew until about 200 adults, 30 young people, and 60 children attended weekly meetings. In a short while, the congregation leased space in a commercial complex and refurbished it to provide a sanctuary and office space.

Evangel Pentecostal Church in Brantford sponsored a "daughter" assembly in that city in late 1986. Pastor Lorrie Gibbons directed this outreach with the help of about 150 people who were willing to leave their former church and relocate to the New Life Church on Sherwood Drive. Subsequent to this bold step in church planting, both the new congregation and the original assembly recorded marked growth in attendance. The pastor of Evangel, Bruce Schwindt, reported that 50 to 60 new people were attending the mother church soon after the original members had departed to form the new church.

The decade of the '80s also witnessed steady growth in the Maritimes and Quebec. By 1984, a young church had been planted in Sussex, New Brunswick, and another six were on the drawing boards of the district office. Quebec with its predominantly Roman Catholic population had witnessed the spread of Pentecostalism at a slower pace than other parts of the country. However, with the accelerated input of personnel and finances from the Eastern Ontario and Quebec District, the French language training program (FLITE) sponsored by the national Home Missions department for graduates of English Bible Colleges, and the faithful labors of the French Conference, the work in that province made tremendous advances.

When Pierre Hébert became the director of French Ministries in 1983, he gave up his pastoral duties in Montreal to supervise about 40 churches in the province which were affiliated with the District of Eastern Ontario and Quebec. By 1990 the total had increased to 50. The need for more workers was obvious and pressing.

Randy Stewart, a pastor in Montreal, formed a group of 30 singers in an effort to communicate with Quebec youth. "Musicale '84," under

Stewart's leadership, travelled to many communities sharing the gospel and the Pentecostal message to appreciative audiences. A pastor in Jonquiere, Stu Burger, launched a religious tabloid in the French language, "Le Témoignage." About 50,000 copies of each edition of the paper were delivered to the French churches for distribution. The PAOC's Quebec Literature Crusade (QLC) had been active in the province for several years when it expanded in the mid-80s and printed religious literature in a wider range of languages. Some of this material was aimed at new immigrants to the province. The QLC was later renamed the Language Literature Ministries (LLM).

When David Wilkerson held evangelistic crusades in several Quebec centres in 1985, about 2,000 conversions were recorded. Obviously, new believers needed pastors and teachers, nearly all of whom had to come from the PAOC French-language training institutions in Quebec. By the middle of the '80s, there were some 250 students enrolled in full and part-time studies.

Graduates of the FLITE program, such as Robert and Candy Baldwin, were sent out to pioneer churches in needy areas as soon as they completed their studies in the French language. The Baldwins went to Pokemouche, a predominantly Roman Catholic region in northern New Brunswick. Despite some opposition, they formed a congregation of 25 adults and 12 children — plus about 50 contacts who showed an interest in the Pentecostal message.

Gerry and Marcia Plunkett and Paul Pattison, all FLITE graduates, began working in the North Shore community of La Malbaie in the Spring of 1983. The town, a popular tourist resort of about 4,000, is 90 miles east of Quebec City. The first members of the new assembly were a small group of believers who had been converted about six months earlier through the ministry of evangelist Raymond Bourgier. The first Plunkett-Pattison meetings in a rented hall were, in Gerry's estimation, lacking in any element of praise or worship. The converts out of Catholicism had not yet learned how to engage in Pentecostal worship. The three young workers fasted and prayed for a genuine move of the Spirit upon their small congregation. A weekend of services was planned to focus on the need of an outpouring of the Spirit. But the services on Friday, Saturday, and Sunday morning provided little encouragement. In the final service on the Sunday evening even the singing seemed dry and uninspiring. Suddenly, just before Plunkett started his sermon, a young woman openly began to worship God in the Spirit; soon the entire assembly was caught up in praise and joy. From that time forward, the congregation experienced Pentecostal-style worship.

The Plunketts lived in a mobile home and were financed by the national Home Missions department with assistance from the Eastern Ontario and

Quebec District. But the young church in La Malbaie began to assume some financial responsibilities as the new converts, some saved only three weeks, began to tithe and support the work.

Plunkett noted that the region seemed to have an inordinate number of people experiencing emotional depression. One young woman suffered from what the doctors called "panic syndrome" — a condition which inflicted great mental anguish, particularly at the thought of dying. She would curl up in a fetal position and break down emotionally. Her weight dropped to less than 40 kilograms. Responding to the call of the woman's mother, Plunkett came to pray for her and witnessed a remarkable deliverance from her affliction. Miraculously, the young woman soon returned to normal health, married, and became a mother.

Another remarkable case of deliverance involved a married couple, both of whom had been alcoholics for about 25 years. No amount of treatment at government detoxification centres could help them break free. When their children were delivered from drugs, this couple came to the Pentecostal church in search of help. After prayer, they both were converted and delivered completely from the bondage of alcohol. The Spirit of God had done what six treatments of electric-shock therapy had failed to accomplish.

While the Plunketts were witnessing from door to door in the community, they encountered a couple in their thirties who had been indoctrinated by a false cult. As they discussed theological questions with the couple, the husband demanded to know whether Jesus could save him "right now." The sincere inquiry was made by a needy individual — later he revealed that he had suffered from depression for 12 years and had contemplated shooting his wife and children and then turning the rifle on himself. But confession and prayer brought total deliverance.

Another convert became a joyful, faithful witness for the Lord in the local mill where he worked, despite intense ridicule and much persecution. Thus the work in Le Malbaie progressed. The members of the congregation enthusiastically supported outreach by means of street-witnessing and house-to-house visitation. As a result, the membership increased to about 70 and the work showed much promise in the estimation of the Plunketts.[15] All told, the PAOC's church planting program in Quebec averaged six new congregations a year.

While much has been said about the role of pioneer pastors in establishing new churches, Pentecostals have always been conscious of the valuable contribution of another ministry gift — the evangelist. In 1987, the need of evangelists to spread the full gospel was reaffirmed. The director of the National Spiritual Life and Evangelism department, Charles Benn, urged pastors and boards to "value the evangelistic gift and

13 / ON TRACK!

give place to the evangelist." He also published a list of some 100 experienced evangelists who were available to minister wherever they were needed.[16]

Some of these men and women, like Maud Ellis and Harold Chamberlain, were used by God in both evangelistic and healing ministries. Chamberlain's observation as an evangelist itinerating among the churches prompted him, in 1989, to call for a "return to basics" by Canadian Pentecostals. Without such a return to the Fellowship's revivalistic roots, he cautioned,

> We could possibly face extinction . . . Pentecostals . . . are a source of hope for a world where righteousness, morality and spirituality are almost a thing of the past. For anyone to think Pentecost can continue on its own merits, without any personal agony, struggling or endeavors is absurd . . . Never can the experience of Pentecost be preserved through adaptation to please men. Pentecost is the answer for Pentecost![17]

A host of inter-church ministries complemented the work of both pastors and evangelists. One novel means of evangelism was the dramatic presentation "Heaven's Gates and Hell's Flames" produced by the Reality Outreach Ministry of St. Catharines, Ontario. Its director, Rudy Krulik, put several drama teams on the road each year who confronted large crowds in hundreds of churches with the biblical perspectives on the eternal destiny of humanity. Literally, thousands of conversions were recorded through the 1980s.[18]

Innovative methods were used to take the gospel beyond the walls of the church. David Mainse of 100 Huntley Street constructed the "Pavilion of Promise" at Vancouver's Expo'86. Many thousands, both Canadians and visitors from overseas, had the claims of Christ presented to them at the Pavilion. Teenaged Pentecostal youth were mobilized to distribute tracts on Vancouver streets. Similar work was done by young people on the infamous "Yonge Street Strip" in Toronto. Large numbers of Pentecostal workers engaged in evangelism by personal witnessing and literature handouts at the 1988 Winter Olympics in Calgary. Several university campuses were targeted for chaplaincy ministries.

A unique pastoral/evangelistic form of ministry was launched by bank-robber-turned-preacher Ernie Hollands. Hollands sought to provide a nurturing environment for converted convicts. He set up the Hebron Farm near London, Ontario, where former prisoners were grounded in the faith. Some of these ex-convicts went on to Bible school and several into full-time ministry.

Women's Ministries, directed by Eileen Stewart, trained women for evangelism and mobilized a national prayer movement. A cross-Canada campaign endeavored to enlist 10,000 women in prayer for a harvest of souls. The first National Leadership Conference for Women was convened at Oakville, Ontario in 1985. About 400 delegates registered. The conference was so successful that a second was planned for Calgary two years later. This time over 600 delegates attended, including women from other denominations.

The women not only witnessed and prayed, they raised money too. One of the organization's effective programs was the annual "Penny Day." The funds collected by WM groups throughout the year were handed over to district officials on a specific day of the year to assist a variety of home missions projects. The women of Western Ontario, for example, assembled annually at Braeside Camp and contributed over $100,000 every year for the support of new churches in the district. Another interesting statistic was the record offering given by the WM group in Canning, Nova Scotia — $9,000 in July 1987. The total from WM groups across Canada that year was $265,000.

PAOC institutions involved in ministerial training continued to undergo improvements in curricula, faculty academic qualifications, and accreditation standards. Student enrollment by the mid-80s in the six Bible colleges showed a combined total of over 1,000, plus the students in attendance at specialized schools. The latter included the SALT Centre in Fort Smith, Northwest Territories, the Canwood Indian Bible School in Saskatchewan, the Northland Missions Bible College at Pickle Lake, Ontario, and the Native Pentecostal Bible College at Chibougamau, Quebec. In 1988, for example, the PAOC's affiliated schools and colleges had nearly 300 graduates, most of whom aimed at immediate full-time ministry. During the decade, about half of all ministerial students in Quebec attending evangelical schools were Pentecostal.

It was in the 1980s that several of the PAOC Bible colleges applied for accreditation with the American Association of Bible Colleges and worked at establishing relationships with Canadian universities and seminaries. Denominational commitment to the best possible program of ministerial training was reinforced by the National Bible College Committee (NBCC). But cautions were voiced in several quarters about placing academics above spirituality.[19] That was a concern often expressed even in the days when PAOC schools had relatively little interest in formal recognition from non-Pentecostal educational authorities.

Organization of the national Church Ministries department under the leadership of William Griffin led to a sharpened focus on the unique role of national departments as they worked in harmony with their counterparts on the district and local church levels. Griffin saw one of the basic responsibilities of the national departments to be the preparation and

13 / ON TRACK!

distribution of program materials in the areas of evangelism, discipleship, and missions.

The Church Ministries missions projects were extremely effective — producing about $500,000 annually. The Wing the Word program sponsored by the youth department took on new life as individual youth groups committed themselves to the task of "putting wheels under every missionary." In 1982, the Sunday School Missions Across Canada (MAC) program was launched at a cost of $75,000 — a shocking amount for those days. Over 100,000 of the egg-shaped plastic MAC banks were distributed among the Sunday school students for their use in saving coins for the monthly missions offering. The proceeds from the banks quickly covered the cost of production and promotion. The MAC program produced about two million dollars during the '80s for the support of missionary children, literature, and other Christian education projects.

Another strategy of Church Ministries was to communicate with the constituency through magazines such as *Source* (Christian Education), *Chivalry* (Pentecostal Crusaders), *Youth Profile* (Youth), *Family Talk* (Family Ministries), and *The Senior Contact* (Seniors Ministries).

Still another emphasis was on leadership training. In 1986, Church Ministries introduced the magazine *Resource* which was designed for all the leaders in the local church. The magazine was quite unique in that it was published in several versions, each version containing the general leadership material and a special eight-page insert prepared for a particular leadership group, such as Sunday school teachers or Crusader leaders. Rick Hiebert edited the magazine with the department directors serving as associate editors.

The youth department, under the direction of Greg Foley, produced an effective discipleship program known as "Team Canada." Several of the district youth directors assisted in the preparation of the material. James Craig, a PAOC minister and freelance writer in the Toronto area, wrote several manuals for the three-level ministry: Level I (Team Canada) prepared youth teams to evangelize in the local community and in district outreaches; Level II (Team Canada International) provided further training for groups who wished to engage in two to four weeks of missions activities in other countries; Level III (Team Canada Worldshakers) built on the previous levels of training and experience while preparing young adults for short-term missions stints up to one year in duration. Thousands of young people registered for the three levels of courses which were offered in the local churches.

Youth leadership conferences, called *Firehouse,* sponsored by the district youth departments, provided an effective means of schooling youth leaders in nationally approved programs. Several districts organized similar conferences for Christian education leaders. Some districts, which were not large enough to have annual leadership events for each category of ministry, sometimes organized general Church Ministries leadership conferences where the leaders from the various ministries, everything from Wee College to Seniors Ministries, would get together for training.

The Christian Education department introduced the "Teacher Certification" program for the approximately 10,000 workers who were involved in Sunday schools. Participating teachers studied the manual, *What Every Sunday School Teacher Should Know...*, over a six-hour period and then wrote an exam. By the end of the '80s about 5,000 Sunday school workers had received their certificates. Unfortunately, the emphasis on Sunday school was not sufficient to stem the decline in Sunday school attendance which most evangelical denominations experienced in the early-80s. In a series of reports to the General Executive as well as the church at large, Griffin warned that there was a growing tendency to devalue the Sunday school and that such a treatment would have very unfavorable consequences for the future of the movement. It was a known fact that the overwhelming majority of the leaders and pastors of the PAOC had come up through the ranks of the Sunday school.

There were warnings, too, from the national Home Missions director, Gordon Upton, concerning the spiritual needs of the burgeoning ethnic population of Canada. In 1984, he announced an emphasis known as "Mission Canada" which focused on reaching the large number of immigrants who were arriving in Canada from various parts of the world. Upton commended the Fellowship for its traditional passion for overseas missions but insisted that it was mandatory to also look closer to home when thinking about the mission of the church. Since in some respects it could now be said that the peoples and religions of the world had come to Canada, the PAOC now had the opportunity to evangelize these newcomers with the gospel on its own doorstep. And to reach these people required the establishment of many more PAOC assemblies, groups of ethnic believers, and organized fellowships of ethnic churches. As a proof of the need to "re-think missions," he noted that the success the PAOC experienced in Kenya, where there was one church for every 26,000 people, had not been matched in this country.[20]

The arrival of Spanish-speaking immigrants was a case in point which illustrated the opportunity for the PAOC to do missions at home. Their number was about 200,000 at the start of the 1980s but within the space of a very few years it had grown to an estimated 500,000. To assist the pastors working among these recent immigrants, the PAOC held its first National Spanish Conference in Toronto in 1989. Some 900 delegates

13 / ON TRACK!

were there to hear experts in evangelism and cross-cultural ministries present helpful advice. One of the prominent pastors was an Argentinian, Jorge Olea, who came to Canada seeking a better life, and was converted to Christ only 12 days after his arrival. The PAOC appointed Eusebio Perez of Toronto to act as the national coordinator of the Hispanic work in Canada. By the end of the decade there were 33 Hispanic congregations with about 2,500 members and adherents.

Work among the Korean immigrants got underway in the early-80s and by 1985 there were 10 congregations located in Vancouver, Toronto, Edmonton, and Montreal. Jong Moon Lee came from the United States to give leadership for this new community of Pentecostal believers. A Korean Bible school, the first of its kind for immigrant groups in Canada, was initiated in a local church and achieved affiliation with Eastern Pentecostal Bible College in Peterborough.

PAOC work among the Chinese of Canada has been carried on for decades, but it became increasingly important because of the large numbers of Orientals moving to this country in the '80s. Several National Chinese Leadership Councils were held to give support to this work and to help identify those groups of Chinese still unreached in Canadian cities. Other outreaches under the "Mission Canada" mandate were to Pakistanis and Punjabis in Toronto, and to Tamils in both Toronto and Montreal. These fields of ministry among recent immigrants offered the potential for what Upton called "explosive growth" in the near future.

In so many ways the decade of the '80s illustrated the growing maturity of the PAOC. Structurally, the Fellowship reshaped itself to address the needs of a changing world. New departments in Church Ministries, the introduction of the Social Concerns Committee, and the Missions Canada emphases were just a few of the organizational changes which equipped it for effective service. New leaders, steeped in the traditional values of the movement but also exposed to the mainstream educational institutions, demonstrated that there was a depth of qualified personnel who could assume the responsibility of carrying on with the mission.

Although the focus of this chapter has been on the domestic operation of the PAOC and its response to the Canadian cultural scene, similar observations can be made about the ministry which has always been at the heart of the Fellowship — overseas missions. The determination of the forefathers to ring the globe with the full gospel message continued to be the focal point of a unified vision.

Endnotes

1. "COPL'87," *The Pentecostal Testimony* (January 1987), 7.
2. R. J. Skinner, "Congress on Pentecostal Leadership," *The Pentecostal Testimony* (January 1988), 15-18.
3. *Canada Update from the 1981 Census of Canada* (Ottawa: Statistics Canada, April 26, 1983); Charles Yates, letter to Thomas Wm. Miller, September 1983.
4. R. W. Taitinger, "Address to General Conference," Hamilton, 1980.
5. For example, "News Release," by the Office of Information, Public Relations and Social Concerns, with titles such as "Abortion Update" and "Sunday Closing Controversy Rages On," 1986.
6. Bob Skinner, "Insight: Civilization On The Skids," *The Pentecostal Testimony* (February 1987), 2-3.
7. See "News Release," September 1986.
8. "Minutes of the 33rd Biennial General Conference, Winnipeg, Manitoba, August 26-31, 1982," 8-16.
9. "Combined Minutes of The Pentecostal Assemblies of Canada, Ltd., District Council of the General Council, Assemblies of God, U.S.A., 1919 - 1922," 3.
10. James M. MacKnight, "Things Most Surely Believed Among Us," *The Pentecostal Testimony (May* 1985), 14-16; see also William A. Griffin, "Kingdom Now: New Hope Or New Heresy?" Eastern *Journal of Practical Theology*, 2 (Spring 1988), 6-36; Scott Bullerwell, "Restorationism: A Contemporary Theological Extreme," *The Pentecostal Testimony* (May 1988), 32-35; and W. Robert Mercer, "The Kingdom: Now and Forever," *The Pentecostal Testimony* (June 1988), 40-42.
11. Gordon R. Upton, "Native Leadership in Canada, *The Pentecostal Testimony* (December 1986), 35.
12. Douglas Stiller, "Right Attitudes Toward Church Planting," *The Pentecostal Testimony* (August 1985), 14-15.
13. "Eva Inspires Other Workers," The *Slave River Journal*, reprinted in *The Pentecostal Testimony* (May 1988), 38.
14. Eileen Leasack, "Baby Church Achieves Goals," *The Pentecostal Testimony* (August 1985), 12-13.
15. Gerry Plunkett, taped commentary on La Malbaie ministry, La Malbaie, Quebec.
16. Charles K. Benn, "Directory of Evangelists," *The Pentecostal Testimony* (June 1987), 9-15.
17. Harold Chamberlain, letter to Thomas Wm. Miller, January 19, 1989.
18. Rudy Krulik, "Heaven's Gates And Hell's Flames," *The Pentecostal Testimony* (June 1987), 42-43.

13 / ON TRACK!

19. See R. M. Argue, "Degrees Granted by a PAOC College," *The Pentecostal Testimony* (July 1982), 26; K. B. Birch, "100 Years and Still Growing Strong," *The Pentecostal Testimony* (September 1982), 14; Thomas Wm. Miller, "Education vs. Spirituality — A Red Herring," *The Pentecostal Testimony* (April 1983), 17; and Carman W. Lynn, "The Centrality of Ministry Development in our Bible Colleges," *The Pentecostal Testimony* (April 1988), 22-23.

20. Gordon R. Upton, "Mission Canada," *The Pentecostal Testimony* (April 1984), 16-17; "Conference Communique," *The Pentecostal Testimony* (September 1984), 8-9; and "The Changing Face of Missions," *The Pentecostal Testimony* (November 1985), 28-30.

Chapter 14

EXPANDING THE VISION

In recognition of the maturity of many of its overseas fields in the early 1980s and the need to adjust its relationship with the growing national church, the PAOC adopted the world missions theme, "Teach to Reach." The slogan illustrated the changing role of the denomination on many of its long-established fields. Supportive and advisory became the key words. And that was exactly what the founders of the Canadian Fellowship had anticipated — the development of an indigenous national church in each country which would be fully self-governing, self-supporting, and self-propagating. That did not mean that the PAOC would abandon its involvement altogether, for in some cases war, famine, revolution, and economic disruptions made the national church dependent upon Canada for continued aid. But the overall emphasis in that decade was upon giving autonomy and handing over leadership to nationals in each country.

The national church organizations which emerged on PAOC missions fields maintained a cooperative relationship with the missionaries. But the roles were reversed: the missionaries took the secondary roles as the nationals assumed leadership. The PAOC continued to assist in areas such as church planting, Christian education, Bible schools, and literature publication.

The foreign missions policy of the PAOC underwent several important changes in the '80s. The new strategies had their origin in the departmental reviews and on-site evaluations which were carried out by missions personnel in the late 1970s. Some of the shifts were underway when Carman Lynn, the Executive Director of the Overseas Missions Department, suggested to General Conference delegates that the time had come to consider the reduction of PAOC personnel and resources on

14 / EXPANDING THE VISION

fields which had matured and were self-sufficient so that the Fellowship could set its sights on new fields.

The process of change began in earnest with the election in 1980 of William Cornelius as Executive Director of the Overseas Missions Department. During the next 10 years, the number of missionaries was decreased in the West Indies, Argentina, Kenya, South Africa, and Liberia. New and additional workers were deployed to places like Indonesia, Sri Lanka, Iceland, Thailand, India, Spain, Holland, Israel, Greece, Seychelles, Mozambique, and French West Africa.

One of the very significant strategies was to establish strong, centrally located Pentecostal churches in some of the major cities of the world. By the mid-80s, the PAOC had selected a number of target cities for concentrated evangelism — cities such as Harare, Zimbabwe; Kampala, Uganda; Lusaka, Zambia; and Nairobi, Kenya.[1] This new thrust into the world's great cities was fuelled by the realization that the greatest population growth around the world was in the "megacities." The rate of urban growth of these major urban centers had been phenomenal: in 1900 only 400 cities had populations over one hundred thousand, but by the mid-80s there were more than 280 cities with a million inhabitants each. The first and the most extensively developed of the PAOC's megacity outreaches was in Nairobi. Reference was made to the early years of this very significant assembly in chapter 12.

Despite a few difficult years in Nairobi, missionaries Mervyn and Sheila Thomas led a multi-racial congregation in a development program which resulted in the erection of an impressive facility. Kenyan government leaders often attended the services. In 1982 President Daniel Arap Moi asked the members of the Valley Road assembly to pray for the nation. The president reiterated this request on several subsequent occasions and often worshipped with the congregation.

A number of successful evangelistic campaigns resulted in substantial increases in the membership of the Nairobi church. Another effective means of evangelism was via radio programs, from the church's broadcasting facility, which reached the entire country and as far as Mogadishu in Somalia. The growth in members and adherents led to an expansion of church seating so that 1200 people could be accommodated, although at times many more packed the building.

After the Thomas family left Kenya to assume pastoral duties in Ontario, they were succeeded by Roy and Maisie Upton. The Uptons led in the construction of a new church complex on the Valley Road site. The new facility which seated 4,000 was officially opened in September 1986. President Moi cut the ribbon.[2] Dennis and Esther White followed the Uptons in 1987 when the latter finished their assignment and returned to

Canada. White, a product of PAOC missions in the West Indies and former General Superintendent of the Pentecostal Assemblies of the West Indies, was well qualified to build on the work of his predecessors.

Remarkable growth in attendance quickly stretched the church's facilities and necessitated multiple services on Sundays to handle the crowds. The Whites developed special programs for children and youth which caught the attention of the entire city.

The strategic location of Valley Road Church was illustrated by 1987 records which showed that 2,300 visitors from other countries attended church services. The church's progress since its founding 30 year earlier was a testament to the foresight and dedication of PAOC missions executives and missionary pastors.

Like Kenya, the country of Uganda had received Pentecostal missionaries for several decades. The country was racked by civil war for much of the '80s and gospel work had been attended by enormous difficulties. Gary and Marilyn Skinner arrived in Kampala in 1984 to begin missionary work in that metropolis. Services were begun in a local hotel but the congregation quickly outgrew those facilities. With the financial support of the Overseas Mission Department, an unused 1,200-seat theatre was leased. The cinema had reportedly been used as a "detention center" for enemies of the government. It was in a strategic location in the heart of Kampala. The acquisition, and later purchase, of the building was viewed as a marvel of God's intervention in response to prayer.

After a laborious cleanup of the premises, Skinner scheduled an evangelistic crusade with Ken Bombay, pastor of Trinity Church in LaSalle, Quebec. The crusade began with 600 people at the first meeting. Before it ended, a guerrilla army had overcome the government's forces and taken control of the city. In spite of the political turbulence, the church increased dramatically. One innovation which captured the interest of the Ugandans attending the Kampala Pentecostal Church was a series of all-night prayer meetings held on Fridays. As it became evident that the new converts needed to be trained for leadership roles, the upper balcony in the cinema was refitted to serve as the "Timothy School of Discipleship."

Paul and Gloria Willoughby served as interim pastors when the Skinners returned to Canada for furlough. The work continued to grow. At its third anniversary service at Easter in 1987, there were over 1,000 in attendance in the Kampala church. But missions work still faced special challenges in the countryside. Yet another guerrilla faction made it dangerous for the dedicated Bible school students to engage in evangelism throughout the area.

14 / EXPANDING THE VISION

After the Skinners returned from Canada to resume their responsibilities, they sought new ways of sharing the full gospel message. An outreach to prisoners took them into six penal institutions in the Kampala area. A group of young adults on a short-term assignment (Team Canada Worldshakers) from Queensway Cathedral in Toronto ministered so effectively in the prisons that an estimated 4,500 inmates indicated a desire to be saved. Other outreaches from the Pentecostal church focused on the city's schools. In one of the school meetings, over 60 individuals made commitments to Christ. The entire community was stirred by the remarkable healing of the 17-year-old daughter of a government official. The girl, suffering from cerebral malaria, was considered as good as dead, but she was restored to good health when prayer was offered on her behalf. The facts of her supernatural restoration were confirmed by a Canadian doctor who visited Uganda.[3]

The Pentecostal work in Lusaka, capital of Zambia, enjoyed steady advance during the ministry of Vern and Belva Tisdalle. Elmer and Sherry Komant took over the city's Northmead assembly in 1982. During one series of meetings in 1988 nearly 80 people were filled with the Spirit. Northmead mobilized its parishioners for evangelism work in the surrounding countryside. During one such outreach about 100 accepted Christ. Another evangelistic thrust by the Lusaka church resulted in the conversion of 400 Zambians in the city of Namwala. Komant, who was seriously ill with a brain tumor, experienced a miracle of healing in answer to prayer.[4] In 1987, the Komant family transferred to Kenya and established a strong work in the city of Mombasa.

Another major urban outreach, in accord with the 1980s emphasis by the PAOC on the world's megacities, was established in Zimbabwe. The PAOC purchased a large building in the heart of Harare, the capital city, which had commercial shops at street level and an auditorium on the second floor. Glenn and Ruth Kauffeldt pastored the Upper Room Ministries church. To increase its evangelistic outreach, the church set up a counselling center and a Christian bookstore. Another effective form of ministry was the practice of sending out teams of believers to carry on street-witnessing campaigns, often through short dramas which conveyed the gospel message. When Kauffeldt moved to a different ministry in Zimbabwe, the pastoral duties were assumed by Murray and Cindy Cornelius.

The PAOC launched similar programs for a number of other large cities in the Third World. While these efforts did not experience the same spectacular results, the Fellowship retained its strategy of building strong churches in major cities. The results have shown that a healthy urban church is able to impact whole regions by establishing a presence for the mission and acting as a sending centre for people who move into the outlying areas.

Early in the '80s, the Overseas Missions Department created a new ministry, known as Emergency Relief and Development Overseas (ERDO), to respond to the physical and social needs of the people it was attempting to reach with the gospel. Historically, the missions outreach had been involved with education, medical services, child care, and feeding programs, but never with the resources which became available through ERDO. Don Raymer, former missionary to Thailand and later director of Specialized Ministries for OMD, was assigned the task of organizing and directing ERDO.

The PAOC, through its ERDO wing, joined with six other church organizations to form the Canadian Foodgrains Bank for the purpose of moving Canadian produce to hungry areas of the world. Several federal and provincial government agencies channelled aid to these needy countries through the Foodgrains Bank by matching the donations, sometimes four to one, given by members of the founding church organizations. Quite often the government agencies responded to project requests made by ERDO on behalf of Third World countries. An important factor which helped ERDO gain the confidence of governments, both in Canada and overseas, was that it usually directed projects in cooperation with dedicated missions personnel stationed in the countries which were in need. The practical result of the ERDO program in relation to the gospel was that through the demonstration of concern for the people the missionaries earned "the right to be heard."

Throughout the decade of the '80s, ERDO sent thousands of tonnes of food to Mozambique, Kenya, India, the West Indies, and other needy areas. Food and other necessities were delivered also to hundreds of thousands of refugees in Ethiopia, Swaziland, Zambia, and Zimbabwe. Other projects included the placement of five PAOC nurses in remote regions of Kenya to operate three medical clinics with the help of ERDO funds. In Indonesia, ERDO gave assistance in a vocational project in Irian Jaya; in Thailand, a school for the blind; in India, a school for orphan boys; and numerous other projects of a similar nature. In Canada, ERDO set up a warehouse in Guelph, Ontario, manned by volunteers to assemble and organize overseas shipments of food, clothing, and medical supplies.

While the ERDO projects reflected very favorably the awareness of educational, physical, and social needs in the Third World, the primary purpose of the PAOC to present the gospel remained its top priority.

Still another part of the overseas missions blueprint for the '80s was the penetration of new fields. The freshness and excitement of the new challenges helped maintain the Fellowship's passion for missions. This

14 / EXPANDING THE VISION

limited narrative cannot present the details of the entrance into all of the new countries. A brief summary, however, of the achievements of some of the missionaries and their national co-workers will demonstrate the commitment of the PAOC missions team to take the whole gospel to the whole world.

Carl and Ruth Verhulst went to Windhoek, the capital of Namibia, in 1983 to pioneer a work in that city of 100,000 people. They held street meetings and home Bible studies and soon had a small congregation of about 70 adults and 40 children. The Overseas Missions Department loaned them $70,000 to build a church. Progress at first was slow as the Verhulsts labored with limited resources. Fresh volunteers from Canada arrived with some of the skills needed to erect the new building complex. For example, two Canadian bricklayers donated several weeks of their time to the project. The structure, which was 30 by 40 metres, consisted of an auditorium, offices, Sunday school rooms, and living quarters for the missionaries. While the building was under construction, the Verhulsts held meetings in a temporary sanctuary and found a good response to the full gospel message.

After many years with a closed-door policy, the West African Muslim nation of Guinea relaxed its rigid stance and allowed PAOC missionaries to move into the country. Eli and Elsa Chiarelli began working in June 1988 in Conakry, the capital city. Another new venture had begun a year earlier in Côte D'Ivoire (Ivory Coast), also in West Africa. Michel and Louise Charbonneau held meetings in the city of San Pedro and arranged special conferences for the leaders of the local churches. Charbonneau was the missionary advisor to about 125 Pentecostal churches in the San Pedro area, plus two Christian schools.

PAOC involvement in the islands of Malaysia and Indonesia began in the 1980s through an invitation from a national Pentecostal church body. After the superintendent of an association of churches in Irian Jaya, which numbered approximately 220, contacted the Overseas Missions Department, Wayne and Doreen Halliwell were sent to give assistance. Using Singapore as their base, the Halliwells travelled extensively, holding training seminars for pastors throughout the region. The Overseas Missions Department provided a boat and motor for Superintendent Ayomi which enabled him to travel to other islands for evangelism and supervision of the Pentecostal churches. Indonesia, with an estimated 1,640 "people groups" still untouched by the gospel, and Malaysia with another 240 presented the missionaries and the nationals with an incredible challenge as they endeavored to deliver the full gospel.

Despite the strong Hindu and Muslim influences, the Halliwells found many people eager to hear about Christianity. Furthermore, there was a hunger for the Pentecostal message. The large number of people who had embraced Christianity in a revival which had swept across this area in the 1970s, as well as the thousands of more recent converts, were ripe for the Baptism in the Holy Spirit. By the middle of the 1980s, there were large churches with wide- open doors for Pentecostal teachers.

A Bible school was established at Genyem in Irian Jaya. On the island of Java the national pastors requested PAOC assistance in providing teachers for their Bible school near Surabaya. A new Bible school was established in Sumatra. Church growth kept pace and a new congregation was planted in the city of Medan. PAOC involvement consisted primarily in assisting the national church and its leaders.

India received PAOC missionaries at the turn of the century, but after a few years the work was given over to the supervision of the American Assemblies of God. The Overseas Missions Department, however, had retained an involvement in India, partly through associate missionary Mark Buntain and the Christian Mission Hospital in Calcutta, but also by supporting periodic evangelistic ventures.

The PAOC supported the ministry of Dhruv Prasad. Dhruv was a 21-year-old Hindu when he became a Christian after reading the New Testament given to him by an itinerant evangelist. Forced to leave his home in Bokaro, he studied for the ministry and met Rita, a talented young Christian who became his wife. He then returned to his home area to preach the gospel. The state of Bihar, where he concentrated his efforts, was militantly Hindu and the progress of the Christian message was difficult in the face of such hostile opposition. Dhruv used Christian films quite effectively in attracting large crowds and sharing the Bible stories.

Rita played a very influential role in the establishment of the Pentecostal Assemblies School in Bokaro on land donated by the largest steel mill in Asia. The school, with 15 teachers working under principal Rita's supervision, made a powerful Christian witness in the heart of Hindu territory. The assembly hall of the school also served as a church auditorium.

Another outreach in India which received PAOC support was the boys' home in Nagpur founded by Canadian Frank Juelich. In the late '80s, the home was enlarged to care for 160 children. Juelich, a lay evangelist, ministered also to the needs of the nationals by translating the entire New Testament in Mawchi. All of these programs of outreach, from Singapore to India, were supervised by Asia regional coordinator Paul Hawkes from his office in Hong Kong.[5]

The PAOC became involved in missions in the Seychelles, a group of islands off the east coast of Africa, in an unusual way. A woman from the

14 / EXPANDING THE VISION

islands, May Fernandes, was converted to Christ in Pentecostal meetings in Nairobi, Kenya. In 1982, she felt led of the Lord to return home and tell about the changes which had come into her life when she received the full gospel message. Her witnessing was made all the more effective by a number of supernatural healings which followed her prayers for the sick. Soon she had a small congregation and appealed to the PAOC for help. Gerald Morrison, the regional coordinator for Africa, came to assist. During a short stay he baptized 240 converts in water and received government permission to send in Canadian missionaries.

Eli Chiarelli and his wife Elsa arrived in the Seychelles in late 1985 and gave oversight to a church congregation of about 200. The original facilities used for meetings were altered to provide space for Christian education. After the Chiarellis returned to Canada on furlough, Jocelyn and Carole Binette provided leadership. Following the traditional PAOC format, they began to train gifted Seychellois nationals to assist them in the work. During special evangelistic meetings held in 1986, there were 180 converts. Plans for a new sanctuary were approved by government officials and the building was dedicated in 1991. James and Colleen Guskjolen from Saskatchewan became the resident missionaries after the Binettes.

A somewhat similar report can be given about the origins of PAOC missions in Sri Lanka (formerly Ceylon), an island off the southern tip of India. A national named Preman Seresinhe was converted in Colombo before going to Canada for employment. After completing ministerial training in Canada and securing credentials from the Saskatchewan District, he returned to Sri Lanka to evangelize his countrymen. Soon there were several congregations with a total of about 600 members.

One of the effective forms of outreach was by means of a rehabilitation program for drug addicts. The program was begun by a young man who himself had been recently saved and delivered from drug dependency. Nurse Kim Taylor of Canada staffed the clinic and her husband Philip, an ordained PAOC minister, concentrated on evangelism.[6] Emese Lehotay also worked in various types of outreach in Sri Lanka following some years of ministry in Kenya. One of her more unusual activities was teaching in a Buddhist monastery.

Early in 1987, the work in Sri Lanka experienced some internal difficulties. Nevertheless, a series of meetings between PAOC representatives and national pastors resolved the contentious issues and provided a base for a new working relationship. One of the PAOC representatives, John Abraham, engaged in several weeks of evangelism while he was in the country. Since outdoor public meetings were illegal at the time, the religious services were conducted on private tea estates. The evangelist ministered with two interpreters translating into the Sinhala and Tamil languages. Abraham's theme was always the same — "I've come to tell you about my very good Friend — about Someone who loves you." Sri Lankan people knew about gods, but not about the God who died for their sins. To reinforce the need for a complete break with paganism and idolatry, the "sinner's prayer" was modified appropriately: "Living God, I accept You as Saviour. I turn my back on witchcraft, fetishes, idol-worship . . ." Huge crowds attended the meetings and large numbers made professions of salvation. The Christian workers secured the names of scores of seekers for further contact. Before he left the island, Abraham conducted discussions with government officials and helped to secure recognition for the national churches as the Pentecostal Assemblies of Sri Lanka.[7]

Missionaries Rainer and Elizabeth Mittelstaedt, who transferred from Tanzania in 1988, witnessed steady growth in the churches as well as a regular increase in the number of churches. Reporting on another Abraham crusade, the Mittelstaedts told the story of a particular man who was resisting the invitation of the Holy Spirit:

> He was bucking it all the way. He was led through the sinner's prayer all the while resisting in his spirit. Yet he continued to feel irresistibly drawn. When he went home, he felt driven to kneel down and again pray the sinner's prayer on his own. As he was praying he began to shake uncontrollably and to say things in a language he could not understand. He came back the next night and asked us: "What was it that happened to me?" We of course knew that 'Acts 2:4' had happened to him.[8]

The report closed with the triumphant declaration: "The God of Miracles is at work in Sri Lanka."

Canadian Pentecostal efforts at evangelism in Israel began with the inauguration of the Kibbutz Shalom program in 1981. Jim and Cathy Cantelon arranged for young Pentecostals from Canada to work on selected kibbutzim and to model true Christianity through service and compassion. The outreach was extended to include Campus Shalom which offered the opportunity for Canadian young people to study in Israel. The Cantelons were joined by Wayne and Ann Hilsden who later assumed leadership of the Jerusalem church which met regularly in the YMCA. The PAOC paid over $100,000 up front to the YMCA for alterations in the building, provided volunteer workmen from Canada to assist in the refurbishing, and entered into a long-term leasing arrangement. The Jerusalem Christian Assembly (since renamed King of

14 / EXPANDING THE VISION

Kings Assembly) soon became a healthy church of about 400 members and adherents. A discipleship program for local Israelis developed into a Bible college program known as King of Kings College.

The PAOC became involved in Greece in 1983 when the Overseas Missions Department granted Andreas Papadopoulos a missionary credential. Papadopoulos, with his wife Beverly, had returned to his homeland a year earlier to engage in evangelistic work. Calvary Temple in Winnipeg provided encouragement and some financial support. Papadopoulos determined that full gospel literature was the most effective means of communicating the good news of salvation. He also introduced a Christian newspaper which had a circulation of about 12,000. Religious services were begun in downtown Athens for interested seekers. Another effective means for promoting evangelism was through a series of leadership seminars for lay people. Perhaps the largest project undertaken was the translation of the Scriptures into modern Greek. The first completed portions, which included the Gospels, Acts, Romans, and Revelation, proved to be extremely popular. Bookstores were eager to stock each edition. One press run provided 15,000 copies which sold quickly. Even the Orthodox Church requested copies for use in its services.

There had been a series of PAOC contacts with Pentecostal pastors in Iceland starting in the 1970s. The full gospel work, which had languished in the country for various reasons, received a big boost when the PAOC sent affiliate missionaries Indridi and Carolyn Kristjansson in 1984. For Indridi, it was a return to his native land; for Carolyn, daughter of missionaries Bill and Linda Mercer, it was another missions challenge. Within a couple of years, the couple were able to report at least 12 congregations in Iceland in various stages of growth and development.

In Spain, the religious climate had become quite tolerant in the '80s. National Pentecostal pastors were experiencing significant success. The PAOC entered Spain through a relationship it developed with the leader of an indigenous Pentecostal organization. Alister and Lindy Belbin, who had spent a term in Argentina and were fluent in Spanish, went to Spain in 1985 as the Fellowship's first missionaries. After settling in the northern city of Bilbao, they began holding meetings in that city and other nearby communities. Belbin started a night Bible school which enrolled about 35 people at Bilbao. Similar schools were organized in other nearby communities where a number of people came to the Lord. In the summer of 1988, they opened another front and began meetings in the city of Alicante. An indicator of the development of the ministry showed up in a practical manner as the financial support raised among the Spanish people showed steady increases and made it possible to secure larger facilities.

EXPANDING THE VISION / 14

An evangelistic thrust into Eastern Europe was undertaken by sending financial support to several national Pentecostal pastors. The funds were used for literature publication and distribution, radio outreach, and church work. An important player in the outreach to Eastern Europe was an agency known as World Christian Ministries (WCM). George Derkatch, a Toronto Pentecostal pastor, had founded WCM for the express purpose of assisting Christian workers in communist countries and getting Bibles through the Iron Curtain. In the early-80s when Derkatch handed WCM over to the PAOC, the Overseas Missions Department appointed James Weller, former district superintendent in Eastern Ontario and Quebec, as director. WCM provided hundreds of thousands of Bibles and hymn books. Millions of tracts and booklets were distributed to hungry readers in communist lands. Pentecostal broadcasts from radio stations in Malta and Portugal elicited replies from 18 countries. Weller reported in 1987 that some 40,000 Russians had been won to Christ in the preceding five years; about 90 per cent of them were reached through the radio broadcasts.

The PAOC provided support for the believers in Eastern Europe by sending a crusade team of pastors and evangelists on a tour of several countries in 1988. This team conducted a youth convention in Yugoslavia, an almost-unheard-of-event in that land. Two Canadian Bible college teachers, Carman Lynn and Lyman Kulathungam, provided short-term support for the work in Poland by giving lectures in the new seminary and preaching in the churches. The effort was of great value to the Pentecostal believers as it addressed, at least in a limited way, the severe shortage of trained clergy and good theological literature. The decision of the Polish government to allow the construction of a new headquarters for the developing denomination, officially registered as the Pentecostal Church of Poland, was a landmark occasion for the Pentecostal Movement.

Again, space does not permit a comprehensive survey of the progress of the older PAOC missions fields. It is important to note, however, that although the PAOC passed control over to nationals and in many cases reduced the number of missionaries (sometimes removed all of them), the influence and impact of the Canadian body continued in a variety of ways. A survey of several selected fields where the PAOC had been involved for many years will illustrate the point.

The East African country of Kenya has received the largest number of PAOC missionaries of any overseas field. By 1990, there were over 2,500 congregations under the direction of the national church organization. The legacy of the PAOC missionaries can be measured in the effective institutions and programs which supported the burgeoning national church, not only in Kenya but throughout Africa and in other parts of the world.

Two Bible schools provided trained pastors, evangelists, and teachers. The Bible College at Nyang'ori, for example, turned out 19 graduates from its four-year course in 1987. Another 50 graduated from the annual six-week Swahili course over a five-year span. The Pan Africa Christian College in Nairobi reached its maximum capacity in the 1987-88 term with 70 students from 11 countries. Life-time missionary Iris Scheel at her Goibei training centre initiated the CREATE program — "Christian Religious Education and Training for Evangelism." The program provided instruction for school teachers with at least five years experience in the classroom.

The Evangel Publishing House in Nairobi produced vast amounts of Christian literature throughout the '80s. In one particular year, 55 book titles were published, plus 100,000 tracts in a number of vernacular languages. Books and tracts were shipped to more than 30 countries in Africa as well as many other nations. About 15,000 people were enrolled in correspondence courses.

Missionaries performed many vital roles in assisting the nationals in evangelizing their own countries. One unique form of assistance arrived in Africa in the person of Winston Broomes from Barbados. Broomes was a product of PAOC missions work in the West Indies. With some PAOC assistance, the Pentecostal Assemblies of the West Indies in turn became a missionary-sending church and sent the Broomes family to be missionaries in Zambia and later in Kenya. The leaders of the national church in Kenya, the Pentecostal Assemblies of God, appreciated Broomes' talents and designated him the head of their Kenyan evangelistic program. Further proof of the maturity of the national church in Kenya was their own missions/evangelism strategy to send out national workers to unreached tribes and peoples in their own country. By late 1988, they had sent 11 national workers and their wives to remote regions still unevangelized.

Uganda is another area where PAOC evangelism has had a long record of success in spite of the political warfare. Most of the mission facilities in Mbale, including the Bible college and houses, had been destroyed or severely damaged by bombardment and street-fighting in the early-80s When the situation became life-threatening, the Canadian missionaries were forced to flee to Kenya. However, when it became relatively safe to do so, the missionaries returned and discovered with joy that the churches were still active and functioning well in the face of great disadvantages.

Missionary Gloria Willoughby, recounting some of the hardships the Christians endured, noted that the people had few Bibles, fewer hymnals, no Sunday school materials, audio-visuals or even note paper, pens or pencils. Only one Bible school served a nation of some 15 million people.[9] Despite the lack of resources and the horrendous problems related to the civil strife, the return of PAOC workers in 1986, and the response of the people to the gospel, resulted in some 4,000 conversions that same year. There were five vernacular churches in the city of Kampala plus an English speaking assembly which projected a very positive Pentecostal witness. By 1990 there were over 700 churches in the country.

Mozambique, another troubled nation in Africa, was the scene of continuous growth in churches and membership despite enormous obstacles caused by governmental instability, poverty, and occasional famine. As in Uganda, the country also suffered from an internal war. The extent of the negative impact upon missions work can scarcely be imagined. Prominent national pastor Laurentino Mulungu was imprisoned in 1975 and not released until 1981. Undaunted by the years of unjust incarceration, Mulungu resumed his ministry to literally thousands of parishioners. In 1986 missionaries Bill and Linda Mercer attended a service in Mulungu's church during which more than 1,700 people were baptized in water.

In spite of prolonged opposition, the national church continued to evangelize Mozambique. The number of congregations rose to 300 with about 40 of that number in the urban centre of Maputo.[10] Altogether the Pentecostal churches in Maputo fed over 40,000 children three times each week. Much of the food was provided by the Emergency Relief and Development Organization (ERDO) of the PAOC.

Bill and Linda Mercer, having learned the Portuguese language in Brazil, transferred to Mozambique and started a Bible school to train nationals to reach their countrymen with the full gospel. About 100 enrolled for the first semester. Some students walked many miles to attend the classes which were held each evening. Don and Betty Krohn arrived from Quebec in 1986 to help in the growing ministry. Don had been involved previously in the Formation Timothée program in Quebec City. An anglophone, who learned French to minister in Quebec, Krohn soon mastered Portuguese and made an important contribution to the Maputo Bible school.

Enrollment at the school remained relatively high. Many students engaged in village evangelism in spite of the fact that some areas visited were dangerous due to the internal strife. The 1988 school statistics reported 60 graduates who joined the team of national workers committed to the task of evangelism. The largest Pentecostal church in Maputo reported 13,000 members and the total membership of the Assemblies of God of Mozambique was estimated at 250,000.

14 / EXPANDING THE VISION

The story of Pentecostal missionary work in Liberia spans the entire history of the PAOC. Enormous problems were posed by the illiteracy of the African tribes and their isolation in the interior. Previous chapters have outlined the heroic efforts of missionaries to get the gospel in a written form which the people could learn to read. The task was colossal. Dorothy Hurd, a volunteer lay missionary who worked in Liberia for some years in the '80s, found people who were still pre-literate and had never handled books, paper, or pencils. A new Tchien translation of the New Testament appeared in 1984. Doris Sauder was engaged in producing Tchien primers and teaching the nationals to read.

The focal point of the PAOC work for many years was the Tchien Mission Station and its Bible school. A higher-level Bible school had also been under constant development in Monrovia, the capital. It enrolled 31 pupils in 1985.

Field director Herb Tisher expressed concern about a strong Muslim threat to turn Liberia into an Islamic state. But he and his wife LaVerne reported to the home constituency in 1988 that there had been a gracious move of the Holy Spirit in that land. Prayers of many years were being answered and five new churches had been established in the capital city. One of these, the Sinkor assembly, had between 600 and 900 people in their weekly meetings. The church revealed plans to erect a building which would seat 2,000 people.

Unfortunately, the political situation in the country deteriorated in 1989 and civil war the next year forced all Canadian missionaries to flee. During the conflict, hundreds of Christians belonging to the Krahn tribe were killed, including the assistant superintendent and his wife. Tisher and other PAOC missionaries invested years in the translation of the New Testament in the Krahn language.

Pentecostal missions strategy in the '80s in southern Africa was to increase the number of churches in the rapidly growing cities of Malawi, Zambia, and Zimbabwe.

In Malawi, a Bible school and two churches were established in the city of Lilongwe where Harold and Maryella Minor had settled. A congregation was developed also in the city of Mzuzu. Extra personnel from Canada included Gordon and Rita Dyck, James and Gladys Nippard, and Herb and Christine Krusch. Arnold and Elsie Bowler moved in 1989 from Kenya to Malawi where Arnold assumed the responsibilities of field director. Carl and Ruth Verhulst, after establishing the new church in Namibia, transferred to Malawi and accepted another church planting role in the northern part of the country. Another exciting development was the opportunity for Bible school students to hold meetings in Malawi's National Resource College.

EXPANDING THE VISION / 14

Zimbabwe had a strong Pentecostal presence in the church founded by Glenn and Ruth Kauffeldt in Harare, the capital. That city was the site of a huge Pentecostal conference in 1987 attended by 4,000 delegates from five continents. Evangelist Reinhard Bonnke ministered on the theme of African evangelism. The Bible school in Harare graduated 16 students that same year. James Seymour, an American Assemblies of God missionary, joined forces with the PAOC missions team early in the decade and served as principal of the Bible school. Not only did the school train the pastors for the Pentecostal churches, it also provided national leaders for at least five different evangelical denominations in Zimbabwe. Missionaries Brian and Helen Jarvis arrived in the country in 1981. Brian began his effective career as a teacher in the Bible school at that time and later assumed leadership responsibilities.

Pentecostal prospects in Zambia were bright as the 1980s began. A series of evangelistic campaigns conducted by graduates of the Zambian Bible school brought many converts into the churches. A new financial plan was adopted by the national workers in 1981 which proved to be effective in creating stability in the national church. The largely urbanized society in Zambia indicated to PAOC leaders that the missionaries should most profitably devote their energies to the cities. Eventually, the main city church in Lusaka was turned over to national pastors. Growth had been so dramatic in the Northmead assembly that they had to hold two morning services on Sundays to accommodate the crowds.

A number of Canadian couples made an impact on the PAOC work in the country. Gerald and Grace Cressman transferred from South Africa to teach in the Bible school at Kitwe, a facility located on the site of a former race track. Brian and Valerie Rutten and Gerald and Susan Jeske came to assist in this school. Brian and Colleen Rennick and Don and Jessie Oldford engaged in general missionary assignments. By 1987, George Mbulo, a Zambian trained by the missionaries, had been named principal of the Bible school.

There were about 40 churches in the Pentecostal national organization. The entire organization came under the direction of a general executive composed of national leaders. The zeal of the believers for evangelism resulted in new churches along the Zambian borders with Zaire and Angola. A layman named Julius Mukenzu started five new churches between 1983 and 1988. One of his congregations began with nine people and grew to over 100 in that period — all that before this church planter had even gone to Bible school! At the end of the decade, the executive of the national fellowship of churches in Zambia launched its own Decade of Destiny plan.

By the late-80s the PAOC mission in Tanzania had over 460 churches in the northern region of the country with workers planning an invasion of the south. Dodoma, the new capital city, was a special target for outreach. Most of the Canadians active in Tanzania (names like Doberstein, Mittelstaedt, Mueller, Paluch, Posein, and Rutten) were drawn from the German Branch of the PAOC.

South Africa had been a target of Pentecostal missionaries from Canada since 1908. The internal difficulties caused by the struggles over apartheid in the 1980s did not seriously disrupt the PAOC missionary effort as the denomination scrupulously avoided political entanglements. Elmer and Sylvia Delport provided leadership to the Bible school at Tzaneen. Expanded opportunities were developed for evangelism in the mine compounds and a literature ministry through tracts was maintained among the miners who came from many different regions of the continent. Wilbur and Ruby Morrison worked in the district around Tzaneen supervising church construction.

PAOC missions in Asia received a great deal of attention during the '80s. Much of the credit for the emphasis must be given to Paul Hawkes who reminded the PAOC constituency at every opportunity that there must be a new focus on the Far East. Hawkes resigned as district superintendent of Saskatchewan to move to Hong Kong and serve as Regional Coordinator in that part of the world. With more than 50 per cent of the world's population of 5.5 billion living in Asia, the Overseas Missions Department endeavored to increase its missionary force.

Hong Kong, a Far East field which had been well established since the end of the Second World War, was under effective national leadership. Murray and Alida Lincoln did evangelistic work and pioneered a new church in the Kowloon district in 1984. The congregation at West Point moved into large facilities and attracted new people. The school at Shek Kip Mei continued its program of relocation to Tuen Mun with a target for completion in 1993. Outreach in Macau continued with new buildings acquired for religious meetings and a new work was launched in 1988.

Taiwan and China have had PAOC missionaries for many years, though work in China by Canadians ended with the communist takeover. Foreign missionaries were not permitted to work in any part of that vast land, but estimates of believers in "house churches" ranges into the millions. One late 1980s report from Shanghai listed 4,000 Protestant churches and meeting places, 6,000 clergymen, and 10 theological seminaries with an enrollment of some 500 students.[11] Beyond those statistics were an undetermined number of Christians in the "underground" churches who manage to avoid government restrictions on religion. Verent Mills, a former missionary in China, made a tour of parts of the country recently and renewed acquaintances with many pastors who had been released after years in prison. He reported his assessment of the situation:

> In my opinion, never again will we see in China, missionaries as we think of them. Nevertheless, I believe dedicated Christian "tentmakers," with varying professions . . . (who) have the opportunity to fill technical positions . . . can be strength and encouragement to the leadership of the Church.[12]

Some evangelism has been possible in mainland China by radio broadcasting from Hong Kong, but with what effectiveness has remained unknown.

Derek and Sue Le Page ministered for several years in Taiwan with occasional help from workers in Hong Kong. They began a new work in 1986 in Lotung, a community of about 100,000 people, by distributing literature which caught the interest of a number of people. A week-long crusade featuring a group of young people from Hong Kong was also effective in attracting new converts. The 11 churches that in 1987 constituted The Pentecostal Assemblies of China in Taiwan were still small in membership and faced considerable difficulty in reaching the very materialistic Taiwanese. Another obstacle to the gospel was the strong grip on the people of the ancient system of idol worship. Still, progress was made: on one Easter Sunday, some 40 individuals were baptized in water in the Pentecostal churches throughout the island.

Gary and Eva Winsor pastored a storefront church in the capital, Taipei. They were assisted by Millie Toppings, a VISA (Volunteers in Special Assignments) worker, who taught English Bible studies. Don and Marieve Young labored in Kaohsiung in the south and engaged in evangelism as much as time and opportunity would allow. Bill and Diane Kelly ministered in the same area. The Roy Davis evangelistic team arrived in the island in 1987 for a year-long program of evangelism in Taipei. The work in Taiwan has been described by a PAOC official as "one of the most difficult mission fields in which to win souls."[13]

The work in Thailand faced many difficulties in the early years of its development, not the least being the untimely deaths of men like Will Butcher, Ron White, and Bob Eames. Although the OMD experienced more than a few reasons for discouragement along the way, one important sign of success emerged in 1974 with the formation of The Full Gospel Assemblies of Thailand with its own national superintendent, Nirut Chandkorn. The PAOC continued to provide support staff and teachers for the Bible school in Bangkok, for church planting, for rural and urban evangelism, and for radio and TV ministries.

Carl and Dorothy Young pastored a church in Korat and Tony and Ursula Wilson planted a new church in the same district. John and

Jennifer Churchill supervised the construction of a training centre and hostel in Chiang Mai. Sam and Noella Winsor began a new work in Bangkok in 1984. John and Debbie Edwards engaged in evangelistic work. Debbie used English-language teaching as a tool to reach her students with the gospel. Young Thais who were eager to learn English enrolled in courses at the local Pentecostal church where the Bible was used as textbook. The Edwards worked first at Khon Kaen and then moved to hold teaching classes at Lamphun and San Ba Thong in the north of Thailand.

Bangkok and its suburbs offered numerous evangelistic opportunities. New churches were set up in Rangsit and Bang Phlee, in addition to the large assembly in Bangkok which numbered over 1,000 members and adherents. Missionary Cavell Rowsell prepared suitable papers and study quarterlies in Thai for the rapidly growing Sunday schools in the churches.

Pentecostal evangelism in Thailand aimed at all classes of society, including those living in temple communities. Those otherwise unreachable elements of the population, such as the priests of Buddha, were contacted and instructed through English language lessons, often taught by VIM (Volunteers in Missions) personnel. A radio gospel broadcast from Bangkok received a very positive acceptance with thousands of response letters and many thousands more enrolled in the Bible correspondence program. Another outreach was by means of a camp meeting in the Spring of 1987, a first for the nationals. It was a time of real blessing for the believers with about 600 people in attendance.

A significant milestone was reached on February 29, 1990 when the new Thailand Pentecostal Bible College was dedicated. Missionary Scott Doggart, reporting on the opening ceremonies, stated that "what had once been a dead, putrid swamp had been transformed into a facility fit to train ministers of the gospel."[14] The new school, which is capable of housing 100 students, awards diplomas and degrees to graduates of the four-year program.

The West Indies have been evangelized by two generations of Canadian Pentecostals, starting with R. J. Jamieson. Missionary Larry Ulseth, who ministered in the islands for over 30 years, rejoiced over the results of a 1984 crusade of Trinidad and the neighboring island of Tobago. Several well known American evangelists came to minister, as well as a national evangelist named Jeremiah Prescod. God so moved upon the people that in just four offerings more than $100,000 in Canadian-equivalent funds was received for costs of the crusade. That was, in Ulseth's opinion, a miracle in itself. The work in Curepe, Trinidad, which had a membership in 1963 of 40, had increased by 1986 to over 1,000. Crowds of 1,700 regularly attended the meetings. Missionary Harold Skovmand on Montserrat was much encouraged with meetings that seemed to portend a revival.

In the summer of 1987 a missionary convention was held in Bridgetown, Barbados, which was a first for Abundant Life Assembly and pastor William Cuke. This convention proved immensely successful in highlighting for West Indians the cause of missions and in raising funds for overseas ministries. The Winston Broomes were the first to be sent from the West Indies to another country to serve as missionaries.

"Team Canada International" and "Task Force" teams of Canadians, at various times, travelled to Dominica, St. Lucia, Grenada, Trinidad, Montserrat, and St. Vincent to erect new church buildings. These teams also engaged in other helpful tasks that improved the evangelistic outreach of both the nationals and the missionaries.

Pentecostalism in Brazil can be dated to the arrival of Swedish missionaries in 1911. The congregations they founded then grew over the decades to become part of a denomination with millions of members. One of the great hindrances to evangelism, however, continued to be the all-pervading presence of spiritism, sometimes masked under Roman Catholic liturgy.

PAOC involvement in Brazil began with the ministry of Harold and Amy Matson in 1965. The Matsons started a Bible school in Recife. A number of other Canadians missionaries responded to the call for assistance in preparing Brazilians for leadership in the local churches: the group included Reg and Mary Hoover, Bill and Linda Mercer, Tom and Laura Fodor, Rex and Rita Stuckless, Stephen and Heather Chaloner, and John and Sirpe Polkki, to name a few. The assessment of the PAOC Overseas Missions Department was that the greatest need of the burgeoning Pentecostal Movement in Brazil was trained pastors. By the close of the '80s two more Bible colleges had been established — in Fortaleza in the north and in Sao Paulo in the south. The missionaries also administered a Theological Education by Extension (TEE) program with over 1,000 pupils registered.

Canadians Kurt and Gudrun Redmann were honored in the summer of 1988 by dignitaries at Boa Vista for their contributions to that community. The Redmanns operated a boys' vocational school as part of their evangelistic outreach to Brazilians. Other missionaries sent to that field by the German branch of the PAOC include Waldemar and Herta Hirch, and Herman and Irmgard Sasse.

The fellowship of churches with which the PAOC identified most directly numbered more than 80 with nearly 5,000 members. Reg Hoover observed that after 30 years in Brazil the Pentecostals are "possibly 40

14 / EXPANDING THE VISION

years behind in regard to Bible schools and there is much catching up that needs to be done." Nonetheless, he was convinced that within a few years Brazil would become a "missions-sending" country.[15]

Argentina is the last in this short survey of the older fields in which the PAOC has been active for many years. That land was blessed by a mighty, nation-wide revival of religion in the 1980s. The move of God had been so spontaneous, so wide-ranging in its impact, and so productive in terms of the number of converts that even at the end of the decade it was difficult to assess. Argentina is a modern illustration of the biblical principle of sowing in tears and reaping in joy. Following the nation's humiliating defeat in a brief war with Britain, there swept over the land in 1985 a mighty move of the Holy Spirit. After PAOC missions director William Cornelius visited the land, his report was titled "You're Not Going To Believe This." Although the PAOC no longer had missionaries in Argentina, it was a source of great satisfaction that the foundation laid by early Canadian pioneers had helped prepare the country for the sovereign move of God.

The Argentina revival actually began in 1984 after pastor Alberto Scataglini and his people committed themselves to intercessory prayer. That summer, a series of outdoors crusades with evangelist Carlos Annacondia brought crowds of 15,000 each night and soon there were 40,000 converts. Later, attendance at his meetings increased until at times there were 70,000 people in attendance. The evangelist's ministry was marked by confirming signs of healings and deliverances from demon possession. In his own city of La Plata, Pastor Scataglini had no room for all the converts and had to rent a nightclub to hold instruction sessions for the new Christians. Daniel Grasso, the superintendent of the Argentina work, stated,

> We believe we are seeing a special time of visitation of God in Argentina . . . His mercy has remembered Argentina. Evidences of this revival are, apart from the signs, healings and miracles, the multitudes of people who are accepting the Lord as Saviour.[16]

When Grasso made this statement, he was referring to estimates of 85,000 conversions in Mar del Plata, 60,000 in San Justo, 15,000 in Monte Grande, and 56,000 in San Martin. Everywhere, the Pentecostal churches as well as other denominations were forced into emergency building programs to accommodate the huge congregations. In some cases, groups of 40 or fewer members were suddenly increased to congregations of 600 to 1,000 and more. One pastor in Buenos Aires started a church in a rented parking garage and in two years had some 700 people in the meetings. These tremendous increases continued to be achieved through 1986 and 1987. Mass crusades reached thousands as previously unknown national evangelists were raised up by God. Canadian Pentecostal evangelist Otto Kakoschke from Kelowna, British Columbia, visited the country in 1986 and participated in reaping a large number of souls. Kakoschke also was present at the Carlos Annacondia meetings in Cordoba when, after 58 days of meetings, about 85,000 decision cards were signed. In addition, hundreds of demon-possessed individuals and thousands of sick people were delivered and healed.[17]

The pastor of the San Nicholas church reported a doubling in attendance in late 1988 from 1,000 to 2,000 people. He also had five branch churches to supervise as a result of the revival. The national church in Argentina directed the outreach with wisdom and much gratitude to God for the glorious work of His Spirit. The organization related to the PAOC numbered over 800 churches and preaching points and 26 Bible training centres in Argentina. The revival resulted in hundreds of new applications for admission to these schools.

As the decade of consolidation and expansions drew to a close, the varied home and overseas missions programs absorbed the energies of many hundreds of dedicated workers. Financial and prayer support remained strong among the churches across the nation. There was one disconcerting word, however, which was showing up in various reports — "plateau." After decades of continual growth, there were some indications that missions offerings and the number of missions personnel were levelling off. The dawning of the '90s brought with it a new realization in the PAOC that still greater efforts were required for successful evangelism at home and abroad. The final 10 years of the century, of the millennium, would be the "Decade of Destiny."

Endnotes

1. George W. Grosshans, "Who Wants To Live In Babylon?" *The Pentecostal Testimony* (November 1985), 4-7; William C. Cornelius, "You're Not Going To Believe This!" *The Pentecostal Testimony* (November 1985), 9.

2. R. J. Skinner, "Nairobi Pentecostal Church Opening," *The Pentecostal Testimony* (January 1987), 20-21.

3. Gary M. Skinner, "Triumph in Kampala," *The Pentecostal Testimony* (January 1987), 22-23; "Many Prisoners Saved," *The Pentecostal Testimony* (August 1988), 14; see also references to Uganda in *Action*, official voice of Overseas Missions Department, from 1984-1987.

4. *World-View Up-Date* (October 1986).

14 / EXPANDING THE VISION

5. Paul Hawkes, "The People Time Forgot," *The Pentecostal Testimony* (October 1988), 36.
6. Preman Seresinhe, "The Cry of Colombo," *The Pentecostal Testimony* (November 1985), 13.
7. Thomas Wm. Miller, interview with John Abraham, Clearbrook, B.C., November 8, 1988; and "Phenomenal Response in Sri Lanka," *The Pentecostal Testimony* (November 1988), 15.
8. Rainer and Elizabeth Mittelstaedt, "God has a Miracle for You!" *Sri Lanka Mission News*, 4 (May 1991).
9. Gloria Willoughby, "The Fat and The Lean," *The Pentecostal Testimony* (August 1987), 5-7.
10. Kate Rafferty, "Impact: Samora Machel's Death Shocks Mozambique," *The Pentecostal Testimony* (April 1987), 42-43; Jack and Edna Lynn, "World Missions The Way I See It," *Action* (Fall 1985).
11. E. Ruth Peever, "The Christian Church in China," *The Pentecostal Testimony* (May, 1987), 36-37.
12. Verent Mills, "The Incredible Church In China," *Action* (Summer 1988), 2-3.
13. G. W. Grosshans, "Ten Thousand And One Gods," *The Pentecostal Testimony* (November 1988), 8-9.
14. Scott Doggart, "Transforming Swamps and Lives in Thailand," *The Pentecostal Testimony* (July 1990), 4.
15. T. R. Hoover, "Brazil '77," *The Pentecostal Testimony* (November 1988), 34-38.
16. William C. Cornelius, "You're Not Going to Believe This," *The Pentecostal Testimony* (November 1985), 8-10.
17. Several brief reports on the Argentina Revival appeared in *The Pentecostal Testimony;* see Wayne Parks, "Argentina's Great Harvest," *The Pentecostal Testimony* (October 1988), 37-38; "Tremendous Growth in Argentina," *The Pentecostal Testimony* (October 1988), 35.

Chapter 15

THE DECADE OF DESTINY

The end of the second millennium of the church age moved into sight. The dawning of the final decade had a significant impact on many Christian organizations. The awareness that there were only "10 years to go" before the calendar would reach the last page of a thousand-year period stimulated some deep reflection as well as some aggressive goal-setting. Could the mandate to take the gospel to every nation be accomplished by the year 2000? One thing was clear — evangelism had to take precedence over all other activities of the church.

One of the models for systematic evangelism during the 1990s which emerged for consideration was the one crafted by the Assemblies of God (USA). At its 1987 General Council in Oklahoma the AG announced its Decade of Harvest program, a 10-year strategy for reaching the United States and AG missions fields before the year 2000. In Canada, a year later, the General Executive authorized James MacKnight to form the Total Church Evangelism Strategy Committee (TCESC) to define the PAOC's general plans for the final decade. The name of the committee told the story — it was to design a strategy which would involve the total church in evangelism. The choice of the members for the committee captured the experience of the Fellowship in men like Herb Barber, Don Cantelon, and Roy Upton; younger ministers such as Keith Smith and Doug Stiller brought the perspective of a new generation; James MacKnight and George Grosshans represented the International Office where the support materials would be developed and the themes communicated. The PAOC's "Decade of Destiny" was born.

Much of the first sessions of the committee were devoted to prayer. MacKnight summarized those meetings:

15 / THE DECADE OF DESTINY

> As we began to open our hearts before God, the enormity of the need we are facing in this crucial time of history, coupled with a deep awareness of our own spiritual need, brought us quickly to a place of brokenness before Him. . . . A heart's cry of desperation for a fresh move of the Holy Spirit rose from each member . . . Consequently, as deliberations drew to a close, there was a unanimous consent and decision that the Decade of Destiny must begin with a movement of prayer that starts with the leadership and flows down to every member of our congregations.[1]

PAOC pastors were urged to make 1989 a special year of prayer for revival. National executive members committed themselves to a period of united prayer each Tuesday from 9 to 10 a.m. Canadian Pentecostals were urged to take action at the local church level and begin to "build a prayer network." To assist with the organization and promotion of the themes, a new national office post was instituted: Coordinator of the Decade of Destiny. George Grosshans, who was already serving as Coordinator of Spiritual Life and Evangelism, added this portfolio to his duties. Throughout 1989, the "Decade of Destiny" was presented as "a vision rather than a structured plan of action." The first need was for "powerful, intercessory prayer by all who want to see and experience a fresh Pentecostal outpouring." The strategy was quite different from the AG's Decade of Harvest in that there was little attempt to offer the constituency concrete objectives, methodologies, or programs. There was just one goal — get God's people on their knees.

One of the means of encouraging local churches to become involved in the renewed prayer emphasis was a "first" for the PAOC: General Superintendent MacKnight mailed a videotaped message to each congregation. Further mailings from the coordinator's office included a list of suggestions for pastors on enlisting people to pray. Pastors were also invited to write reports about the prayer events which were happening in their areas and the results of prayer.

Pastor Guy Alfieri of Marathon, Ontario, submitted an enthusiastic account of spiritual renewal and local evangelism in his community. Late in 1989, the church began its outreach by having the members list on a chalkboard in the sanctuary the names of people they hoped to see converted to Christ. The congregation scheduled special meetings and prayed fervently throughout 1990, the first year of the Decade of Destiny. Souls were saved and incorporated in the assembly. As the people whose names were listed on the chalkboard came to Christ, other names appeared. Evangelistic campaigns throughout the year complemented the prayer emphasis. Attendance on Sundays in the small Marathon assembly increased to approximately 100. On one notable Sunday, a total of nine

THE DECADE OF DESTINY / 15

adults were converted. The emphasis remained on prayer, and people were drawn to the church by the Holy Spirit. Pastor Alfieri reported that in 1991 more than 20 people had been brought to the Lord by Easter Sunday.[2]

One of the basic strategies of the TCESC as it worked on the annual themes during the Decade of Destiny was to make them cumulative — that is, the prayer emphasis of the first year should be carried through the entire decade; similarly, subsequent annual themes would be carried over. The slogan for 1991 focused on a Pentecostal emphasis: "Prepared with Power." The official minutes recorded the rationale of the committee:

> The emphasis should focus on being prepared with prayer and with power, praying for the power, preparing for the harvest and believing God for the power to witness.[3]

The 1992 theme called for evangelism among children and youth. The national Church Ministries department was requested to develop a strategy for the implementation of the theme by all the ministries in the local church. The slogan caught the attention of the entire constituency — "Kids Do Pay." The theme for 1993 was "As You Go, Make Disciples" and for 1994 "Families Focused on Jesus."

The timely spiritual emphasis on evangelism did not remove one of the growing concerns of the Fellowship — not only were the growth statistics slowing down but the income for world missions had levelled off, "plateaued" was the delicate way of putting it. The word was heard clearly in General Superintendent MacKnight's message to the delegates at the 1990 conference in Winnipeg:

> All is not well. We have seriously plateaued in our growth in the last decade, and especially in the last couple of years.[4]

It was an ominous signal which called for a serious response.

A major change occurred in 1990, when the PAOC adopted a new financial plan. For most of its history the Fellowship had supported its operation through the "undesignated" offerings remitted on a monthly basis by the local churches. A special finance committee recommended a shift to "directed" giving which would help the donor identify with specific mission fields, ministries, and projects which were of particular interest. It was a dramatic shift and one which would take some time to implement. By early 1991, George Grosshans had been appointed to the new position of Director of Advancement with the job of facilitating the new financial plan. Grosshans' challenge was to coordinate "directed

15 / THE DECADE OF DESTINY

giving" with his other leadership roles in the Spiritual Life and Evangelism department and the Decade of Destiny emphases.[5] It was a formidable assignment.

The Fellowship had long held the conviction that it had a mandate from God to engage in worldwide evangelism. And it had been notably successful, when compared with other denominations in Canada, in spreading the gospel both at home and overseas. A realistic assessment of PAOC accomplishments by the Research Task Force of Vision 2000 Canada presented a very favorable report on the denomination.[6] But the mood of the leadership was to refocus. The constituency was invited to submit suggestions for a "mission statement" which would capsulize the essential business of the PAOC.

After a probing re-examination of the basic purposes of the Fellowship and a consideration of the submissions of interested members, the leadership verbalized the "mission:"

> To make disciples everywhere by the proclamation and practice of the gospel of Christ in the power of the Holy Spirit; to establish local congregations and to train spiritual leaders.[7]

Commenting on the new "Mission Statement," MacKnight expressed confidence that, under God, the Pentecostal Assemblies of Canada would move forward and accomplish its objectives during its Decade of Destiny.

The '90s brought an important change in the office of Social Concerns with the retirement of its national coordinator, Hudson Hilsden. During his busy tenure, Hilsden produced a monthly News Release for pastors and other leaders. He represented the PAOC on numerous interdenominational committees and at many conferences dealing with controversial social issues. With the help of informed contributors which he recruited, he produced position papers and made presentations to provincial and federal officials and politicians. Counterparts in each district served with Hilsden on a national social concerns committee.

Although Hilsden's pioneering efforts in the field had been very effective in raising the consciousness of Pentecostals on many issues, the General Executive decided that it was time for an additional emphasis.[8] Hilsden was lauded for having confronted activists and legislators who seemed determined to prove that Canada was no longer a "Christian country" through their attacks on traditional moral standards and family values. While the PAOC would continue to declare itself on essential issues which were being debated in public, the new direction was to target Pentecostals and persuade them to act out their social concern in the ministries of the local church. To put it succinctly and in the language of the Mission Statement, it was time for the "practice of the Gospel of Christ in the power of the Holy Spirit." MacKnight described it as a concentration "on social *concerns*, rather than social *issues*".[9]

In 1992, the General Executive formally added "social concerns" to "evangelism" and "missions" in a resolution which defined the essential emphases of the different ministries of the church.[10] The same year, a successful motion from the floor of the General Conference in Ottawa officially placed the Social Concerns department in the *General Constitution and By-Laws*.[11] The new direction was labelled as "pre-evangelism" because it gave a practical demonstration of the compassion of Christ to accompany the good news of salvation.

Evangelism occupied centre stage at the Congress on Pentecostal Leadership (COPL) held at the Constellation Hotel on Toronto's airport strip in October 1993. The first COPL, which had such a positive impact on the Fellowship, had taken place six years earlier at the same location. The theme of the second COPL was simple — and dramatic: "Just Go!" Nearly 2,000 credential holders, lay delegates, and visitors from other organizations registered to deal with the "Go".

There was no doubt about the necessity of the "Go" but there were some questions which related to "how to go." Pentecostals, like many evangelicals, had never been reluctant to employ secular methods for sacred purposes. School buses, for example, were necessary to get children to school, but they were also useful in getting them to *Sunday school*. Thousands of the kids who were picked up during the "bus ministry" days of the '70s later became leaders in the church. An interesting statistic from a recent survey of PAOC ministers revealed that a large majority grew up in a Christian home; even more revealing was the fact that a *larger* majority attended Sunday school.[12] One interpretation of these statistics is that many of today's Pentecostal preachers were reached as children in non-Christian homes by dedicated bus workers and Sunday school teachers — bussing, as a methodology, certainly had spiritual results. Less spectacular claims could be made for "coffee house" ministries, "all-night" sings, and even "Wing the Word car washes."

When the organizers started to work on COPL'93, one of the methodologies in vogue was the "seeker sensitive" church service. The basic approach called for a study of the characteristics and interests of non-churchgoers and then creative planning of church events which would attract them. The gospel was to be packaged in such a way that a generation unfamiliar with even the most fundamental Bible themes would clearly hear and understand the claims of Christ. Drama, overhead transparencies, dressed-down worship leaders, and short services were

15 / THE DECADE OF DESTINY

"with it;" long sermons, theological jargon, hymn books, and choir gowns were "out." The manuals written by people like George Barna, Bill Hybels, and Canadian Reginald Bibby called upon the church to be sociologists and psychologists, among other learned pursuits. Pentecostal pastors were interested in any means which would help them reach lost souls and that included learning about the baby boomers, busters, yuppies, and church hoppers and shoppers. The subject demanded a very positive examination.

One of the sub-themes of the congress was "Go With Preparation." Guest speakers Leith Anderson and Rich Buhler lectured on the importance of understanding the times and the people-needs so that the gospel could be communicated in a meaningful way. A few sessions offered models of "seeker sensitive" services. Frank Patrick, a PAOC pastor in Peterborough, demonstrated how a "Pentecostal version" of the emphasis was working in his church.

It goes without saying that for the congress to qualify as "Pentecostal," there had to be a strong emphasis on the person and work of the Holy Spirit. The distinctive genius of Pentecostalism has been that any methodology, whether old or new, must be saturated with the presence of the Holy Spirit. The climactic theme of the congress was "Go In Power." Evangelist Reinhard Bonnke reminded 4,000 delegates and visitors in the closing session at Queensway Cathedral that what the church needs most is the fire of Pentecost accompanied by the signs and wonders promised by the Lord.

The urgency to go with the gospel has from the beginnings of the PAOC meant to go *into all the world*. The early pioneers of the movement worked diligently to make the church in Canada strong. But what fired their imagination was the challenge to get the gospel over the seas to those who had never heard. It was the task that united the Fellowship: some could go, many could give, all could pray. The ongoing success of the missions program can only be described as miraculous. The Overseas Missions Department compiled statistics for the report to the 1992 General Conference Report which showed that 60,000 people had been converted and 47,171 had been baptized in water during the previous year. Furthermore,

> On any given Sunday nearly ten thousand (9,671) sister churches worship God in 38 countries around the world. . . . Total members and adherents number over one million, not counting the thousands of churches in Brazil and Argentina with whom we fellowship. . . . Thirty-one Bible schools and training institutes teach more than 2,656 future pastors and leaders.[13]

Although full-time ministerial missionaries compose the major group serving overseas, the PAOC demonstrated versatility in the deployment of lay and short-term missionaries. In earlier years some missionaries offered professional skills in areas like health care and education. Later, a number of programs were developed to provide opportunities for lay people to get involved in front-line missions. With the arrival of the '90s there was a noticeable trend among North American missions agencies to send lay people on missions assignments. The PAOC kept pace with this trend and appointed Keith Parks as director of Short-Term Missions.

An Overseas Missions Department report listed the short-term programs and the number of teams and individuals involved during 1990:

Type of Ministry	Number of Teams	Number of People
TASK FORCE (a volunteer program for men to assist in overseas building projects)	11	260
TEAM CANADA INTERNATIONAL (TCI) (three-week outreaches for youth teams on missions fields)	29	434
TEAM CANADA WORLDSHAKERS (TCW) (three months to one year missions assignments for teams of young adults with previous TCI experience)	2	12
VOLUNTEERS IN MISSION (VIM) (one to two year vocational assignments for singles and young couples)		16
VOLUNTEERS IN SPECIAL ASSIGNMENT (VISA) Formerly, SENIORS ON ASSIGNMENT - SOS (opportunities for mature adults to use their gifts overseas)		14
KIBBUTZ SHALOM (three-month labor stints for young adults on a kibbutz in Israel)	2	7
BIBLE COLLEGES (internships for missions majors and also discipleship teams)	2	55
TOTALS	**46**	**798**[14]

15 / THE DECADE OF DESTINY

For the most part, the Short-Term Missions people paid their own expenses while engaged on various PAOC overseas fields. Many of them utilized their vacation periods to minister in other countries. Their usual reaction, upon returning home, was that involvement in short-term missions had opened their eyes to the needs of the mission fields and the cultural problems encountered by missionaries. A number expressed keen interest in full-time missionary service as a result of their initial overseas experience. Another factor, the value of which can hardly be estimated, was that literally thousands of family members and friends of the short-term missionaries, who stayed at home and prayed, developed a new interest in missions.

The 1992 General Conference elected a team of executive officers which had some new faces. Prior to the conference three of the incumbents indicated that they would not be available for re-election to their posts. Charles Yates had served as General Secretary for 18 years; Gordon Upton as Executive Director of Home Missions and Bible Colleges for 10 years; and William Griffin as Executive Director of Church Ministries for 12 years. At the conference, Griffin was chosen to be General Secretary. Keith Parks was elected to the Church Ministries position and Ken Birch to Home Missions and Bible Colleges. Parks had been serving in OMD as the director of World Christian Ministries, a missions outreach which focused on Eastern Europe, as well as coordinator of the short-term missions program. Birch, who was pastor of Mississauga Gospel Temple at the time of his election, brought with him considerable Bible college experience. He had served for 10 years as president of Central Pentecostal Bible College in Saskatoon and also a one-year term at Pan African Christian College in Nairobi.

The final change in the slate of officers involved the sudden loss of William Cornelius, Executive Director of Overseas Missions for 12 years. Cornelius had been re-elected to his post at the General Conference, but suffered a fatal brain aneurism in December 1992. The Executive Officers' Committee asked Charles Yates to direct the Overseas Missions Department until the constitutional requirement of an appointment of a new officer within 60 days could be fulfilled. The General Executive chose Lester Markham, former missionary and district superintendent of British Columbia and Yukon, to serve the remainder of the term.

A "bricks-and-mortar" change took place when the PAOC took steps to improve its administrative efficiency by moving the International Office to new facilities in Mississauga. The former building at 10 Overlea had served the Fellowship well for 30 years but it was time to prepare for the future. The new office building, located only 10 minutes from the airport

THE DECADE OF DESTINY / 15

and in proximity to economical housing for personnel, was dedicated on October 27, 1990.

There were three long-standing topics which accompanied the Fellowship into the '90s: divorce and remarriage, ministerial training, and the administrative structure of the national office. Obviously, they were quite diverse, quite controversial, but each very important.

After having been debated at the national level on several occasions, the issue of divorce and remarriage surfaced at the Western Ontario District Conference in 1990. The delegates passed a motion which requested that the question be placed on the agenda of the upcoming General Conference in Winnipeg. The essence of the motion was that the *General Constitution and By-Laws* be amended to permit the remarriage of divorced individuals whose divorce took place prior to Christian conversion. A technical difficulty arose when the district motion was not processed in time for the required 60-day notice of a by-law amendment to be mailed to the constituency.

Although the motion could not be debated at the Winnipeg conference, it was brought on the floor as a request for a study and a preparation of the related by-law amendments for presentation to the next General Conference in 1992. An amendment to the motion on the floor expanded the study to include "the biblical, social, and pastoral implications of divorce and remarriage and, further, a definition of marriage, divorce, and remarriage, and that this be presented by February 1, 1992 to all credential holders." The document produced by a special committee was the most thorough study the PAOC had done on the subject.

The issue was brought back to the 1992 General Conference in Ottawa in the form of two resolutions. One resolution was the product of the committee's work on the "biblical, social, and pastoral implications of divorce and remarriage" and the other one related to divorce prior to conversion. The General Executive determined that since the former would offer the best opportunity for the delegates to express themselves on the issue, it would be brought to the floor first. Basically, it stated that PAOC ministers would be able to officiate at a marriage where either the man or the woman, or both, had been married previously with the former spouse still living and where the following three conditions exist:

1. all reasonable efforts at reconciliation with the former partner have been exhausted;

2. a legal divorce has been obtained;

3. the sexual immorality of the former partner has been established or one of the partners has remarried.

15 / THE DECADE OF DESTINY

The key argument in favor of the resolution, which meant a change in position for the PAOC, was based on the interpretation of the "exception" clause in Matthew 19 which suggested that sexual immorality (*porneia*) could break the marriage bond. Thirty-nine delegates spoke for and against the resolution. When the secret ballot was taken, 55 per cent voted in favor of the resolution. Since the requirement for a by-law change was a 66.66 per cent majority, the resolution was defeated. When the other resolution with the "prior to conversion" phrase was voted on, it failed to get even a simple majority.

When at least two districts indicated that credential holders were preparing new resolutions on the divorce and remarriage issue for the 1994 General Conference in Calgary, the General Executive decided to offer its own resolution. A small committee was formed to study the transcript of the debate on the first resolution on divorce and remarriage at the '92 conference. The purpose was to discover whether the resolution could be clarified with reference to legal ramifications which had been raised previously.

The resolution for the Calgary conference was similar to the one previously offered except it stressed that the individual PAOC minister could "choose" to officiate if "to his satisfaction" specific conditions existed. This emphasis on the pastor's judgment removed the ambiguity concerning the condition in the previous resolution which stated that the sexual immorality of the former spouse "had been established." In the debate on the resolution at the '92 conference, the question was raised by several speakers, " How is the sexual immorality to be established and by whom?" The intent of the General Executive with the '94 resolution was to present the issue to the conference in Calgary in such a form that it would be decided in terms of Biblical interpretation alone.

The second major topic which remained in front of the Fellowship related to ministerial training. Discussions about the need of a PAOC seminary date back to the '60s. The subject was set aside in the early-80s when the Bible colleges began to grant degrees to their graduates. As it became more apparent, however, that a growing number of ministerial candidates were engaging in graduate work in non-Pentecostal colleges and seminaries, there was renewed interest in establishing a seminary.

As the General Executive grappled with the need to train the students who would become the Bible college teachers and leaders of the Fellowship, it brought to light a number of related questions about such subjects as the number of Bible colleges and the number of students, diversified training for non-traditional ministries, debt-load of graduates, discipleship programs, nature of training in relation to the needs of the

Fellowship, and the effects of subsidies to Bible colleges on church planting and missions resources. The course of action was to ask the delegates at the '92 General Conference to approve a study commission "for the purpose of reassessing our entire philosophy of ministerial training in Canada."

Although the work of the commission is still in progress, the general principles of the philosophy of ministerial training have been defined on three levels:

> Level I — Discipleship Schools — a major part of the PAOC Mission Statement is "to make disciples everywhere" — primarily the responsibility of the local church;
>
> Level II — Bible Colleges — the historic training agency of PAOC pastors and missionaries would maintain its basic mandate — primarily the responsibility of the supporting districts;
>
> Level III — Seminary — a new training agency for University graduates who wish to enter PAOC ministry — primarily the responsibility of the national General Executive.

National committees would set the academic and ministry standards for all three levels.

The matter of "responsibilities" among the local church, the district, and the national office triggered another round of restructure studies at the national level. It was the fourth time in the space of 14 years that a major review of the executive positions and the functions of the national office was undertaken. Previous restructure committees had only limited success in getting General Conference approval for their recommendations. The attempt, for example, to combine the offices of the General Secretary and the General Treasurer failed at the 1986 conference in Edmonton and the 1992 conference in Ottawa.

The announced rationale for the most recent restructure study was to achieve maximum efficiency. The simple question was where and how could the basic functions related to administration, missions, and church ministries be performed for the Fellowship. About 100 credential holders, including the members of the General Executive and people associated with the national and district offices, were asked to express their opinions concerning the functions at the three levels — national, district, and local church.

The General Executive concluded that the number of executive officers could be reduced from six to four by combining the offices of the General Secretary and the General Treasurer and also the offices of the Executive

15 / THE DECADE OF DESTINY

Director of Church Ministries and the Executive Director of Home Missions and Bible Colleges. The merging of the two administrative offices would permit an officer to devote himself to the ministerial business of the Fellowship while individuals with special training or experience in accounting or legal matters could address those areas.

The recommendation to combine the other two offices was based on the view that the national office could best serve as a facilitator or coordinator. With the increase of personnel and resources in the district offices and the development of strong Church Ministries departments in geographical proximity to the churches, it was thought that the national office staff could be reduced in these areas. The national and district leaders determined to act as partners in focusing on the challenges and opportunities related to ethnic ministries and church planting.[15]

The Fellowship has taken very seriously the part of its "Mission Statement" which says, "to establish local congregations." Douglas Stiller was appointed first National Coordinator of Church Planting in 1993. His task was to communicate the necessity of "growing" churches and to assist the districts wherever needed in their church planting ventures. In the early years of the '90s the most significant increase in the number of PAOC churches took place among the ethnic groups who had recently emigrated to Canada. During 1993, 28 of the 40 new churches which were born were non-English. At last count, there were 39 Spanish assemblies, 14 Korean, 12 Chinese, and several among other groups such as Arabic, Estonian, Ethiopian, Fijian, Filipino, Hungarian, Portuguese, Romanian, Tamil, West Indian, and Yugoslavian.[16]

So rapid was the development of ministries among ethnic groups that a steady supply of ethnic pastors became a critical requirement. One response to this need was the founding of Korean and Spanish Bible colleges in the Toronto area in 1989 and 1990 respectively. The colleges were modeled on the PAOC standard Bible college curriculum. Another strategy involved a "missions in reverse" tactic which imported ethnic leaders to Canada from foreign mission fields.

While the number of Native congregations has remained around the 90 mark for a number of years, the three Native Bible colleges continue to prepare Native leaders who will make an impact among their own people. The PAOC named James Kalappa as first National Coordinator of Native Ministries in June 1994.

Pentecostalism in French Canada has not maintained the rate of growth which it experienced in the early-80s. While the PAOC can claim almost one-third of all evangelical Protestant churches in that province, this still represents only 100 congregations. Less than one percent of all Quebecers belong to an evangelical denomination. Quebec continues to be Canada's "mission field."

Several "deaf" congregations have affiliated with the PAOC. The national Home Missions department organized a National Deaf Conference in Calgary early in 1991, a "first" for the denomination. A year earlier, the Fellowship had ordained its first deaf credential holder — John Graham, pastor of Bethel Deaf Tabernacle in Hamilton.

The PAOC celebrated its 75th anniversary in May 1994. Its progress must be regarded as phenomenal. At the time of incorporation as a religious body in 1919, the Fellowship had 27 assemblies and 31 clergy and lay leaders. Its membership numbered in the hundreds with budgets which totalled only a few thousand dollars. By 1994, the PAOC had 1,064 congregations with over 231,000 members and adherents. There were 3,690 credential holders, including a total of 298 missionaries.[17] Annual giving by PAOC people to world missions was around the 12 million dollar mark. Impressive statistics for a revivalistic group whose beginnings were clouded with persecution and allegations of being a fanatical sect.

As the Fellowship observed its 75th birthday, there was obvious reason for thanksgiving but also need for thoughtful reflection and self-examination. In his monumental study of Pentecostalism, W. J. Hollenweger concluded that the first generation of preachers left church organizations which perpetuated institutions for their own sake. In the early 20th-century outpouring of the Holy Spirit, these ministers created a flexible structure which met their need for worship and which positioned the Bible as final authority. It was a living faith that was, in Hollenweger's view, both rationally and emotionally satisfying.[18] At a significant milestone in its history, the key question for the PAOC was whether the purposes which inspired the early Pentecostals to incorporate the Fellowship were still relevant and being honored?

David Moberg's analysis of the development of a typical movement from sect to denominational status provides a useful measuring device. Along with its extraordinary spiritual, organizational, and missionary accomplishments, Canadian Pentecostalism has undergone another obvious development: it has become respectable! Indeed, the 1991 federal census listed Pentecostals as the sixth largest Protestant group in the nation – and the only one of the six that had grown during the decade (28 per cent). Moberg's five natural stages in an institution's life-cycle may be summarized as incipient association, formal organization, maximizing efficiency, bureaucratic growth, and disintegration.[19] PAOC commentators have expressed quite clearly their awareness that the Fellowship can be located on the Moberg continuum.

15 / THE DECADE OF DESTINY

Understandably, the leadership is determined to avoid the latter stages outlined by Moberg. The energy devoted to restructuring reveals the concern about "bureaucratic growth." Even more significant, both the veterans of Canadian Pentecostalism and the current leaders regularly insist on the maintenance of the thirst for revival which has been the dominant characteristic of the Fellowship. For Pentecostals, revival means a fresh awareness of the presence of God which results in lost souls coming to Christ and the manifest activity of the Holy Spirit with signs and wonders. It is the visible moving of the Spirit which characterizes a Pentecostal revival.

This writer had the privilege of being the first PAOC author to produce a book on the revival theme — *Ripe for Revival*. Former PAOC General Superintendent Walter McAlister, who often expressed his personal desire for revival and the need to keep Pentecostal priorities in place, generously gave the book a glowing tribute and recommended it as timely reading for Pentecostals. In a conversation with the writer, McAlister shared his concerns:

> I ask myself, "In what direction are we going?" We need a revival across our Fellowship. Canada needs a mighty revival. We have the potential for revival if our churches across Canada will catch the vision . . . We are in danger of gradually losing our Pentecostal heritage by neglect . . . We must take appropriate action today to make sure that our people receive the Pentecostal baptism.

Other leaders have mentioned similar sentiments:

> **George B. Griffin**: Today we are accepted, whereas in the early days people questioned our right to be around. After 50 years I see some little loosening of doctrine — if it continues, there is trouble down the road. I advise our leaders to be wary of trends that may prove detrimental.

> **Tom Johnstone**: I would like the Pentecostal Movement to go forward to fulfil its mission under God, and that is to have a genuine, biblical, spiritual evangelicalism to meet the needs . . . I believe that we could have a revival, a visitation . . . God can crowd in a short period what man might expect would take a thousand years.

> **Gordon F. Atter**: We were known as praying folk. We spent far more time in praying in the early days than teaching and preaching. If neglected (prayer) will lead to a change of philosophy and then of conduct. I am disturbed by the lack of prayer at the altars of our camps . . . A. H. Argue told us when students at the Winnipeg Bible school, "When you become a pastor, keep you altar service alive."

George R. Upton: In the earlier years I knew a number of men and women, both ministers and layman, who became effective intercessors . . . They are not easy to replace. We are much too busy for protracted intercession. With increased efficiency, I see a trend to organize, rather than agonize, to talk of revival without repentance, to major on numbers rather than godliness, loyalty to a church's program rather than on personal loyalty to Christ. Happy the spiritual movement that can go on to the third and fourth generation, retaining the original simplicity of faith, dependence on God's Word, and the Lordship of Jesus.[20]

The historian may slice into PAOC history in any one of its eight decades and hear the prayer for revival. But perhaps one of the major reasons for the success of the Fellowship is that the call to recover and retain the emphases of the past is usually accompanied by the appeal for a spiritual vision of the future.

George Chambers, the first national leader of The Pentecostal Assemblies of Canada, verbalized the cry of his heart in a booklet which he addressed to his fellow-preachers and lay workers around 1930, *Spiritual Vision is the Greatest Need of the Hour.*[21] The title summarized the powerful message! A succession of leaders have had the same kind of heart.

James MacKnight, the current General Superintendent, perpetuates the call. In a brochure circulated among the churches, entitled "Renewing Our Passion / Fulfilling Our Vision," MacKnight declared,

> A fresh wind of the Spirit is blowing across Canada and around the world! The Lord is initiating a vision and we are receiving it! . . . We are being spiritually rekindled for a great final harvest.[22]

And so, let the next chapter unfold.

Endnotes

1. James MacKnight, two letters to credential holders, January 1989 and May 1989.
2. See "Prayer Emphasis Brings Results in Marathon," Decade of Destiny pamphlet (April 1991).
3. "Minutes of the Total Church Evangelism Strategy Committee," February 19-22, 1990.
4. James M. MacKnight, "Continuing the Process of the Decade of Destiny," *The Conference*, a publication in newspaper format presented at the 1990 General conference in Winnipeg (August 23-28, 1990), 1, 13.

15 / THE DECADE OF DESTINY

5. See "The Challenge," letter of the General Superintendent to credential holders, January 1991; and "Report of the General Superintendent to the District Conferences," Spring 1991.
6. See Arnell Motz, ed., *Reclaiming a Nation: the Challenge of Re-evangelizing Canada by the Year 2000* (Richmond: Church Leadership Library, 2nd ed., 1990).
7. James M. MacKnight, "A Special Announcement From The General Superintendent," March 20, 1991.
8. See the paper commissioned by the General Executive for consideration at its pre-conference meeting in Winnipeg 1990: William Griffin, "Practicing The Gospel In A Pagan Age," *Resource* (May-June 1991), 3, 6-8.
9. See MacKnight's comments, "Report of the General Superintendent to the District Conferences," Spring 1991.
10. "Minutes of the General Executive," February 1992.
11. "Minutes of the 40th Biennial General Conference," August 19-23, 1992, 46.
12. W. A. Griffin, "Report of the General Secretary," *41st Biennial General Conference, Calgary, Alberta, August 23-28, 1994.*
13. "Report of the Executive Director of Overseas Missions," *40th Biennial General Conference, Ottawa, Ontario, August 19-23, 1992*, PAOC Archives, 20, 21.
14. *World-View Up-Date* (March 1991).
15. As this volume goes to press, the constitutional and by-law amendments to bring about the restructuring are being mailed to the constituency for consideration at the 1994 General Conference.
16. W. A. Griffin, "Report of the General Secretary to the District Conferences," Spring 1994.
17. Ibid.
18. Walter J. Hollenweger, *The Pentecostals: the Charismatic Movement in the Churches*, trans. by R. W. Wilson from 1969 German edition (Minneapolis: Augsburg, 1972 ed.), pp. 63-74.
19. David O. Moberg, *The Church as a Social Institution: The Sociology of American Religion* (Grand Rapids: Baker Book House, 2nd ed. rev., 1984), pp. 118-123.
20. These selected quotations came from taped interviews and correspondence with the author. All have been used with permission.
21. George A. Chambers, *Spiritual Vision: The Greatest Need of the Hour"* (Kitchener: for the author, [1930]).
22. "Renewing Our Passion / Fulfilling Our Vision," November 1993.

A Note on the Sources

Every effort has been expended to make this history of Canadian Pentecostals both a scholarly record and an inspiring account for the reader. The search for original source materials and documents has lasted some twenty years. Countless hours and days have been devoted to searches in the libraries of universities and colleges both in Canada and the United States. The libraries of all Canadian Pentecostal Bible colleges have been included in these research travels.

Over the years, valuable rare books on 18th and 19th century revivalism have been added to my personal collection. Of special value in this group are the histories of the Baptists in the Maritime provinces and the Methodists in "Upper Canada" (now Ontario). Other volumes dealing with the 19th century Holiness Movement have been useful in tracing the roots of the distinctive theology of the PAOC.

In the past twenty-five years, a small number of Canadian denominational histories have been published. I have drawn some data from the accounts of the Pentecostal Assemblies of Newfoundland, the Apostolic Faith (headquarters in Portland, Oregon, but with churches in Canada), The Apostolic Church of Pentecost of Canada, and the Mennonites. Much more numerous and more readily accessible have been the scores of periodicals published by evangelical and Pentecostal organizations in North America. Of particular significance in my research have been the monthly issues of *The Pentecostal Testimony*.

Two serious attempts have been made since 1955 to provide an historical framework for Canadian Pentecostalism. The first of these was the 1958 publication of *What God Hath Wrought* by Gloria G. Kulbeck. This volume was essentially a compilation of data assembled from materials solicited from pioneer PAOC workers. While serving as General Superintendent, Walter E. McAlister requested numerous colleagues and friends to write accounts of personal experiences and observations. These letters formed the bulk of Kulbeck's sources. Regrettably, the originals have disappeared and only typescript copies remain. Another data source was a large collection of Pentecostal periodicals loaned to the PAOC by historian Gordon F. Atter. Kulbeck made some use of these materials, but the collection of magazines seems to have disappeared.

One reason for the loss of such valuable data was the lack of any systematic filing system at the national headquarters of the PAOC in the earlier years. Since the first-generation Pentecostals expected the imminent return of Christ, record-keeping had little attraction for them. And their rapid progress as a revival movement militated against historical and reflective analysis. When I began my research, there was no archives department at the national office in Toronto; the records and files on hand were simply stored in cardboard boxes. Consequently my labors had to be expanded into a search for documents before any data could be acquired or any analysis carried out.

There were in print at that time a small number of biographies and autobiographies of early Pentecostals, but no copies were found in the head office collection. I have acquired a personal collection of these sources. Kulbeck was not as fortunate in this regard. Nonetheless, *What God Hath Wrought* was a commendable first effort at recounting the history of the PAOC. The book is chiefly anecdotal and does not attempt to offer a serious analysis or interpretation of trends. I have been informed also by W. E. McAlister and other PAOC leaders that there are some errors in dates, events, and processes related to PAOC development.

A more professional account of Canadian Pentecostalism is available in Gordon F. Atter's book, *The Third Force*. Atter, the son of one of the first Pentecostal/Latter Rain leaders in Canada, was himself a Pentecostal preacher for over 50 years. Thus he was in a unique position to record the development of the "Fellowship," as the members of the PAOC refer to their organization. He personally knew many of the first-generation Pentecostals and had a life-long interest in documenting their ministries. However, he never attempted a specifically PAOC history: his *Third Force* was a survey of many Pentecostal organizations around the world. PAOC historical accounts formed only a small portion of the entire book.

Atter's book was published in 1962 and was revised several times. Much of his material was derived from his personal collection of Pentecostal magazines to which he subscribed. But the information he supplied on the PAOC was from Canadian sources and his own personal recollections. Besides this valuable volume, Atter had written a number of "statements of faith" and "histories" for the PAOC. These were chiefly informational in nature and were published as booklets and pamphlets for public distribution. In addition, he has published several volumes of personal reminiscences and memoirs. All of these sources have been provided for me by Atter with permission to use them in any appropriate manner.

The fact that such materials as were used by Atter and Kulbeck were not systematically filed made my task rather difficult. Letters unearthed from the boxes had to be checked and cross-checked for reliability. On a few occasions dates, or personalities involved, or events described, were not in total agreement with other sources. However, in the main, the "letters" have proven to be very reliable. They have enabled this author to "soak" himself in the culture, philosophy, and dogmas of the early Pentecostals in Canada.

A modified form of the letters sent in response to the solicitations of W. E. McAlister were hand-written "histories" from the pioneers. Some were accounts of personal ministries over a period of years, others were attempts to delineate the progress of Pentecostalism within narrow confines. One example is the account of Winifred Barnes concerning the ministries of herself and her husband John in establishing numerous PAOC congregations in British Columbia prior to 1935. A few of these "histories" covered the period from 1907 to 1956.

A limited number of autobiographical accounts have been collected and analyzed for their contributions to this book. It is difficult to categorize these sources for the same reasons as listed above. The most valuable personal accounts were those by such first-generation Pentecostals as Charles Chawner, Marion Keller, George Chambers, and Zelma Argue. Just a little later in time, some helpful accounts of Pentecostalism in individual provinces were produced, such as that by Percy S. Jones. These sources may be referred to as "memoirs," although most of them cover only brief periods in the authors' lives.

To this list there may be added a number of local "church histories," usually compiled by volunteer historians or "church history committees." In this category are histories for PAOC churches in Kitchener, Vineland, Victoria, and others. More extensive histories have appeared in recent years, issued by officials in the district offices or by some of the Bible colleges. Among these are publications from the Alberta and N.W.T., Saskatchewan, and Western Ontario districts, as well as the accounts from the Western Pentecostal Bible College and the Eastern Ontario Bible College.

This writer has had complete access to all the official *Records, Minutes,* and *General Conference Reports* of the PAOC, dating from 1919 to the present. Indeed, the whole range of PAOC publications have been provided me whenever requested. Another official source has been the *Minutes of the British Columbia District.* The German Branch of the PAOC has provided me with an English translation of its Conference history. This document has proven particularly helpful in tracing the spread of Pentecostalism in Western Canada. The many issues of *The Pentecostal Testimony,* dating from 1920, have been a gold mine of information. I also have been able to utilize the information and insights incorporated in a small number of published academic theses. These studies usually focused on specific aspects of Pentecostalism rather than any comprehensive overview. There have been a number of well-researched papers on the development of the movement published in Pentecostal magazines such as *Paraclete* and *Pneuma*. Some of the material that the author has presented previously in articles published in these magazines has been repeated in this narrative.

A final category of sources includes "taped interviews" with prominent pioneers as well as current PAOC leaders. A number of additional interviews were conducted in situations where taping was not possible. Finally, there has been a considerable collection of letters from Pentecostals across Canada who have volunteered personal reminiscences or provided information on specific features of PAOC development. Numerous phone calls have helped to elicit further data and confirm facts already in hand.

The sources have been identified in the text by numerous footnotes. For convenience, these have been incorporated in a section at the end of each chapter. Thus the reader whose chief interest is in the spiritual development of the PAOC can bypass the critical apparatus which is included for those interested in further research.

It is common for books to be published based on an author's former academic studies. That is not the case with this volume. Nonetheless, it is hoped that the book will prove to be a gold mine of information for scholars undertaking a serious examination of the origins of Pentecostalism in Canada and for readers in general who have a particular interest in The Pentecostal Assemblies of Canada.

Appendix A

National Officers of The Pentecostal Assemblies of Canada

George A. Chambers	General Superintendent	1919-1934
Robert M. McAlister	General Secretary-Treasurer	1919-1932
	Missionary Secretary	1919-1932
Alfred G. Ward	General Secretary-Treasurer	1932-1938
	Missionary Secretary	1932-1938
James Swanson	General Superintendent	1935-1936
Daniel Buntain	General Superintendent	1937-1944
Charles M. Wortman	Secretary-Treasurer	1939-1966
	Missionary Secretary	1939-1944
Campbell B. Smith	General Superintendent	1945-1952
George R. Upton	Missionary Secretary	1945-1966
James Montgomery	Christian Education and Youth	1947-1968
	General Secretary-Treasurer	1971-1972
	General Secretary	1973-1974
Walter E. McAlister	General Superintendent	1953-1962
Tom Johnstone	General Superintendent	1963-1968
C. Hilmer Stiller	Home Missions and Bible Colleges	1963-1966
	General Secretary-Treasurer	1967-1971
Carman W. Lynn	Overseas Missions	1967-1980
Robert M. Argue	Home Missions and Bible Colleges	1967-1982
S. Donald Feltmate	Christian Education and Youth	1969-1980
Robert W. Taitinger	General Superintendent	1969-1982
A. Graydon Richards	General Treasurer	1973-1984
Charles Yates	General Secretary	1975-1992
William C. Cornelius	Overseas Missions	1981-1992
Gordon R. Upton	Home Missions and Bible Colleges	1983-1992
John Totafurno	General Treasurer	1985-1988
William A. Griffin	Church Ministries	1981-1992
	General Secretary	1993-
James M. MacKnight	General Superintendent	1983-
Reuben L. Schmunk	General Treasurer	1989-
Kenneth B. Birch	Home Missions and Bible Colleges	1993-
Keith H. Parks	Church Ministries	1993-
Lester E. Markham	Overseas Missions	1993-

Appendix B

District Superintendents of The Pentecostal Assemblies of Canada

British Columbia and Yukon

J. E. Barnes	1929 - 1934	E. A. Hornby	1966 - 1972
A. J. Hughes	1935 - 1937	J. M. House	1972 - 1982
Tom Johnstone	1938 - 1940	R. L. Schmunk	1982 - 1988
C. A. Story	1941 - 1943	L. E. Markham	1988 - 1993
P. S. Jones	1944 - 1952	W. R. Gibson	1993 -
C. W. Lynn	1953 - 1965		

Alberta and Northwest Territories (Mackenzie)

John McAlister	1929 - 1933	A. A. Lewis	1948 - 1950
C. C. Scratch	1933 - 1934	D. N. Buntain	1950 - 1952
George R. Upton	1934 - 1943	S. R. Tilton	1952 - 1968
W. S. Frederick	1943 - 1944	Charles Yates	1968 - 1974
A. A. Lewis	1944 - 1946	I. A. Roset	1974 - 1985
D. N. Buntain	1946 - 1948	J. A. Keys	1985 -

Saskatchewan

W. E. McAlister	1926 - 1930	E. A. Hornby	1944 - 1948
C. B. Smith	1930	C. H. Stiller	1948 - 1962
J. W. McKillop	1930 - 1936	G. N. Fulford	1962 - 1971
Ernest Clemens	1936	J. C. Tyler	1971 - 1981
W. H. Found	1936 - 1942	Paul Hawkes	1981 - 1985
J. T. Brooks	1942 - 1944	L. C. King	1985 -

Manitoba and Northwestern Ontario

D. N. Buntain	1928 - 1936	P. M. Munro	1962 - 1972
T. T. Latto	1937 - 1938	W. G. Reinheimer	1972 - 1982
W. C. Nelson	1939 - 1943	V. W. Taylor	1982 - 1989
W. J. Taylor	1944 - 1949	G. V. Peters	1989 -
C. Walker	1950 - 1961		

Western Ontario

W. L. Draffin	1927 - 1933	H. J. Cantelon	1978 - 1987
J. H. Blair	1933 - 1966	E. K. Young	1987 - 1990
D. A. Emmons	1966 - 1972	W. D. Morrow	1990 -
H. D. Honsinger	1972 - 1978		

Eastern Ontario and Quebec

A. E. Adams	1932 - 1934	K. M. Haystead	1948
G. A. Chambers	1936 - 1937	W. B. Greenwood	1949 - 1964
C. B. Smith	1938 - 1942	R. A. Bombay	1964 - 1972
H. J. McAlister	1942 - 1945	Gordon R. Upton	1973 - 1982
W. G. McPherson	1945 - 1946	J. P. Weller	1983 - 1985
W. B. Greenwood	1947 - 1948	E. S. Hunter	1985 -

Maritime

James Montgomery	1931 - 1936	I. D. Raymer	1948 - 1974
M. S. Winger	1936 - 1947	A. D. Moore	1974 - 1988
C. W. Jones	1947 - 1948	D. C. Slauenwhite	1988 -

Appendix C

Hundreds of committed Pentecostals have been involved overseas with the PAOC Missions Department. The list below records the name of each missionary, the name of the first foreign country where each served, and the year of the first appointment. Some labored for their entire ministry on the field mentioned; others served in several different parts of the world; still others accepted special assignments which may have been only six months in duration. Together they proclaimed and practised the gospel of Christ in the power of the Spirit and helped to establish the Church in scores of countries.

Name	Country	Year
Abbey, Beatrice	Lesotho	1963
Abbey, Douglas	Lesotho	1963
Abraham, John	Hong Kong	1989
Abraham, Shirley	Hong Kong	1989
Adams, Barbara	Kenya	1992
Ahlberg, Klas	Chile	1992
Ahlberg, Victoria	Chile	1992
Aldworth, John	Namibia	1986
Aldworth, Lois	Namibia	1986
Allaire, Lise	Thailand	1987
Allen, Henry	Kenya	1978
Allum, Rita	Hong Kong	1987
Anchieri, Maria	Uruguay	1990
Anchieri, Mario	Uruguay	1990
Anderson, Daniel	S. Africa	1961
Anderson, Valborg	S. Africa	1961
Andersson, Carl	Kenya	1980
Andersson, Elizabeth	Kenya	1980
Andresen, Alvina	Argentina	1926
Andresen, Erling	Argentina	1926
Andresen, John	Argentina	1953
Andresen, Lois	Argentina	1953
Angus, Lillian	Kenya	1979
Anonby, Ellen	Argentina	1970
Anonby, Joseph	Argentina	1970
Anonby, Elizabeth	Kenya	1984
Anonby, John	Kenya	1984
Anstey, Andy	Uganda	1990
Anstey, Catherine	Uganda	1990
Arbour, Suzanne	Kenya	1988
Arva, Jean	Liberia	1983
Atter, Arthur	China	1908
Atter, Jessie	China	1908
Augustine, Lena	West Indies	1981
Augustine, Samuel	West Indies	1981
Austin, Raymond	Taiwan	1968
Austin, Verna	Taiwan	1968
Baker, Kris	Macau	1991
Baldwin, Candace	Indonesia	1989
Baldwin, Robert	Indonesia	1989
Balfour, Bruce	Israel	1982
Barber, Charlene	Liberia	1987
Barber, James	Liberia	1987
Barker, Charles	West Indies	1946
Barker, Myrtle	West Indies	1946
Barker, Louisa	Hong Kong	1964
Barrett, Diane	Kenya	1983
Barron, Don	Uganda	1984
Barron, Kathy	Macau	1987
Bateman, Doris	Liberia	1964
Battermann, Edelgard	Kenya	1960
Battermann, Heinz	Kenya	1956
Bear, Holly	Zimbabwe	1986
Bear, Betty	Kenya	1987
Bear, Robert	Kenya	1987
Belbin, Alister	Argentina	1976
Belbin, Lindy	Argentina	1976
Benjamin, Shanty	Kenya	1984
Bennett, Dan	Kenya	1988
Berg, Lorraine	Kenya	1985
Bergman, Gordon	Kenya	1991
Bergman, Jennie	Kenya	1991
Bespoyasny, Doreen	Thailand	1990
Best, Harvey	Liberia	1972
Best, Patsy	Liberia	1972
Binette, Carole	Seychelles	1987
Binette, Jocelyn	Seychelles	1987
Bingeman, Ethel	Liberia	1915
Birch, Kenneth	Hong Kong	1968
Birch, Shirley	Hong Kong	1968

Biro, Janice	Hong Kong	1988
Bishop, Lori	Netherlands	1990
Bjurling, Patrick	Kenya	1991
Black, Cynthia	Kenya	1985
Black, Philip	Kenya	1985
Blackborow, Elizabeth	Israel	1984
Bolton, Jean	Zimbabwe	1955
Bolton, Marion	Zimbabwe	1955
Bombay, Olive	Kenya	1959
Bombay, Richard	Kenya	1959
Bombay, Calvin	Kenya	1962
Bombay, Mary	Kenya	1962
Bombay, Deborah	Hong Kong	1983
Bond, Margaret	Kenya	1976
Bond, William	Kenya	1976
Bonnell, Crystal-Ann	Hong Kong	1990
Boris, Irene	Kenya	1952
Borzel, Henry	Macau	1976
Borzel, Janet	Macau	1976
Bourgier, Andree	Fr. Polynesia	1986
Bourgier, Raymond	Fr. Polynesia	1986
Bowering, Joy	Kenya	1979
Bowler, Arnold	Kenya	1955
Bowler, Elsie	Kenya	1955
Bowler, Stephen	Ethiopia	1988
Bowler, Kathy	Botswana	1993
Bowman, Mark	Zambia	1987
Brand, Bruce	Kenya	1977
Brand, Martha	Kenya	1977
Bridle, Ginny	Europe	1984
Bridle, Terence	Europe	1984
Brndjar, Rodger	Kenya	1978
Brooks, Carey	Hong Kong	1986
Broomer, Michael	Zimbabwe	1984
Broomer, Sharon	Zimbabwe	1984
Broomes, Gloria	Zambia	1976
Broomes, Winston	Zambia	1976
Brotton, Karen	Taiwan	1972
Brotton, Kevin	Taiwan	1968
Broughton, Doreen	Liberia	1968
Broughton, Larry	Liberia	1968
Brown, Viola	Liberia	1940
Brown, William	Liberia	1940
Brown, Bruce	Taiwan	1989
Brown, Karen	West Indies	1989
Buchwalter, Frances	China	1917
Buntain, Huldah	India	1954
Buntain, Mark	India	1954
Burrage, Betty	Zimbabwe	1971
Burrage, John	Zimbabwe	1971
Burry, Barbara	Kenya	1983
Bush, James	Zimbabwe	1951
Bush, Vera	Zimbabwe	1951
Bush, Marilyn	Kenya	1974
Buss, Beverley	China	1989
Buss, Erhard	China	1989
Buss, Manfred	West Indies	1983
Butcher, Elsie	Thailand	1961
Butcher, William	Thailand	1961
Butler, Elsie	Zaire	1951
Butler, Horace	Zaire	1950
Cadorette, Maxine	Singapore	1986
Cadorette, Nicolas	Singapore	1986
Callahan, Raymond	Zambia	1968
Callahan, Vivian	Zambia	1968
Campeau, Guy	China	1991
Cantelon, James	Israel	1981
Cantelon, Kathryn	Israel	1981
Cantwell, Margaret	Kenya	1950
Cardinal, Johanna	China	1989
Cardinal, Robert	China	1989
Carle, Juanita	Mozambique	1988
Carlson, Allan	Kenya	1968
Carlson, Joanne	Kenya	1968
Casqueiro, Evangeline	Mozambique	1961
Cassidy, Douglas	Thailand	1987
Cassidy, Katherine	Thailand	1987
Cawston, Alfred	India	1928
Cawston, Elizabeth	India	1928
Cechetto, Esther	Kenya	1986
Chalmers, Audrey	Kenya	1975
Chalmers, Kervan	Kenya	1975
Chaloner, Heather	Brazil	1983
Chaloner, Stephen	Brazil	1983
Chambers, Bernietta	Malawi	1982
Chambers, Brian	Malawi	1982
Charbonneau, Louise	Ivory Coast	1986
Charbonneau, Michel	Ivory Coast	1986
Chawner, Charles	S. Africa	1908
Chawner, Emma	S. Africa	1908
Chawner, Austin	S. Africa	1925
Chawner, Carrie	Mozambique	1927
Chawner, Ingrid Lokken	Mozambique	1920
Chiarelli, Eli	Kenya	1964
Chiarelli, Elsa	Kenya	1964
Christianson, Jackie	Taiwan	1987
Christink, Blair	Zimbabwe	1984
Christink, Maribeth	Zimbabwe	1984
Churchill, Jennifer	Thailand	1980
Churchill, John	Thailand	1980
Clarke, Fred	Kenya	1939
Clarke, Rhoda	Kenya	1939
Clarke, Elizabeth	Liberia	1978
Clarke, Ronald	Liberia	1978
Clarke, Brian	Kenya	1981
Clarke, Shelley	Kenya	1992
Clements, Frederick	Argentina	1927
Clements, Susan	Argentina	1927

Name	Country	Year
Clements, Donald	Japan	1951
Clements, Evelyne	Japan	1951
Code, Margaret	Taiwan	1980
Code, Ronald	Taiwan	1980
Coneybeare, Lori	Thailand	1989
Cornelius, Lillian	Kenya	1955
Cornelius, William	Kenya	1955
Cornelius, Ethel	Kenya	1984
Cornelius, Myrrl	Kenya	1984
Cornelius, Cindy	Zimbabwe	1987
Cornelius, Murray	Zimbabwe	1987
Cox, Barbara	China	1993
Cox, James	China	1993
Crawford, Ruth	Taiwan	1981
Cressman, Annie	Liberia	1940
Cressman, Gerald	Zambia	1979
Cressman, Grace	Zambia	1979
Culham, James	Brazil	1968
Culham, Shirley	Brazil	1968
Cummins, Alberta	Kenya	1959
Cummins, Dale	Kenya	1959
Curle, Daniel	Liberia	1962
Curle, Sharon	Liberia	1962
Curr, Andrea	Kenya	1981
Daly, Dean	Thailand	1986
Daly, Mary-Anne	Thailand	1986
Davidson, Richard	Kenya	1975
Davis, Gerda	Taiwan	1987
Davis, Roy	Taiwan	1987
Davy, Joy	Zimbabwe	1980
Davy, Lorne	Zimbabwe	1980
Dawson, Arleen	Kenya	1987
Dawson-North, Elizabeth	Kenya	1980
Dawson-North, George	Kenya	1980
De Vries, Margaret	Uganda	1994
Deacon, June	Kenya	1949
Delport, Lawrence (J.H.)	S. Africa	1942
Delport, Lois	S. Africa	1942
Delport, Elmer	S. Africa	1969
Delport, Sylvia	S. Africa	1969
Delviken, Evangelene	Kenya	1987
Dergousoff, Debbie	Hong Kong	1980
Detheridge, Heather	Israel	1983
Dewald, Lisa	Kenya	1991
DeWit, Patricia	Thailand	1991
DeWit, Peter	Thailand	1991
Doberstein, Elvine	Argentina	1960
Doberstein, Horst	Argentina	1960
Doberstein, Bruno	Tanzania	1970
Doberstein, Elizabeth	Tanzania	1970
Dobroski, John	Taiwan	1976
Dobroski, Marilyn	Taiwan	1976
Dodding, Arlene Embree	Kenya	1964
Dodding, Richard	Kenya	1966
Doggart, Catharine	Thailand	1985
Doggart, Scott	Thailand	1985
Doner, Lynn	China	1992
Douglas, Melvin	Kenya	1985
Dowler, Marion	China	1989
Dudgeon, Emily	Kenya	1955
Duncalfe, Anne	Kenya	1965
Duncalfe, Jack	Kenya	1965
Duncalfe, Jillian	Hong Kong	1987
Duncalfe, Alan	Greece	1988
Duncalfe, Gloria	Greece	1988
Dyck, Hilda	Zambia	1984
Dyck, Gordon	Malawi	1990
Dyck, Rita	Malawi	1990
Dykema, Donna-Lynn	Thailand	1994
Eames, Mabel	West Indies	1955
Eames, Robert	West Indies	1955
Edler, Mary	Kenya	1957
Edwards, Eileen	India	1934
Edwards, Deborah	Thailand	1980
Edwards, John	Thailand	1980
Eggleton, Harry	West Indies	1927
Eggleton, Marguerite	West Indies	1927
Eling, Clarice	Kenya	1987
Ellsmore, Karen	Taiwan	1983
Embree, Bernard	Hong Kong	1953
Embree, Elsie	Hong Kong	1953
Embree, James	Kenya	1987
Emde, Mark	Thailand	1985
Emde, Nancy	Thailand	1985
Enos, Shirley	Taiwan	1981
Errington, Ellen	Philippines	1987
Errington, Ross	Philippines	1987
Evers, Connie	Kenya	1981
Faa, Allon	China	1993
Faa, Betty-Lou	China	1993
Faa, Ronald	Sri Lanka	1991
Farrow, Heather	Kenya	1978
Faught, Barbara	Kenya	1993
Faught, Harry	Kenya	1993
Faulkner, Betty	Thailand	1975
Faulkner, Ray	Thailand	1975
Finn, Marcia	China	1993
Fitz, Audrey	Tanzania	1977
Fitz, Stanley	Tanzania	1977
Fodor, Laura	Brazil	1975
Fodor, Thomas	Brazil	1975
Ford, Duane	Hong Kong	1988
Ford, Lesli	Hong Kong	1988
Foreman, Garry	Kenya	1971
Foreman, Margaret	Kenya	1971
Forsythe, Denise	Zambia	1978
Fortune, Betty Ann	Zambia	1983
Fortune, David	Zambia	1988

Francis, Ernest	Kenya	1950
Francis, Shirley	Kenya	1950
Franz, Hilde	Kenya	1960
Franz, Martin	Kenya	1960
Franz, Peter	Kenya	1988
Franz, Rebekka	Kenya	1988
Frey, Cornelia	Kenya	1988
Fricker, Garry	Argentina	1969
Fricker, Jean	Argentina	1969
Friesen, Duff	Kenya	1984
Friesen, Therese	Kenya	1984
Froelich, Martin	Thailand	1993
Froelich, Paula	Thailand	1993
Funk, Betty	Kenya	1971
Gaglardi, Eunice	Liberia	1972
Gaglardi, Kenneth	Liberia	1972
Galessiere, Mary	Zimbabwe	1991
Gannon, Kassiani	Israel	1989
Gannon, Raymond	Israel	1989
Garrard, David	Zaire	1973
Garrard, Ruth	Zaire	1973
Garratt, Julia	China	1988
Garratt, Kevin	China	1988
Geisberger, Heather	China	1993
Georgeson, Mary Ellen	Thailand	1984
Gerke, Audrey	China	1989
Gerke, Kenneth	China	1989
Giesbrecht, Mary	Liberia	1945
Gillespy, Jessie	Japan	1949
Gilmour, Nigel	Israel	1987
Gingrich, Della	Japan	1954
Gingrich, Virgil	Japan	1954
Glover, Ruth	Hong Kong	1983
Golbeck, Gerald	Tanzania	1989
Goodman, Victor	Kenya	1986
Gordon, Glen	Mozambique	1993
Gordon, Karen	Mozambique	1993
Goshinmon, Cary	Guatemala	1990
Goshinmon, Karen	Guatemala	1990
Graham, Robert	Liberia	1974
Greig, Colin	Zimbabwe	1991
Greig, Susan	Zimbabwe	1991
Grosshans, Barbara	Hong Kong	1971
Grosshans, George	Hong Kong	1971
Guskjolen, Colleen	Seychelles	1992
Guskjolen, James	Seychelles	1992
Haberstock, Ruth	Hong Kong	1986
Hacker, Jeannine	Kenya	1971
Hacker, Paul	Kenya	1968
Haist, Coralee	China	1917
Haist, Idella	China	1938
Halliwell, Doreen	Singapore	1982
Halliwell, Wayne	Singapore	1982
Halliwell, Kerry	Malawi	1992
Halliwell, Glen	Malawi	1992
Hamilton, Florence	Liberia	1960
Hamman, Bryan	Thailand	1990
Hamman, Janice Loewen	Thailand	1966
Hansell, Joy	Liberia	1953
Hardy, David	Liberia	1973
Hardy, Marilyn	Liberia	1973
Haug, Irmgard	Tanzania	1968
Haug, Johann	Tanzania	1968
Hawkes, Mary Ann	Kenya	1958
Hawkes, Paul	Kenya	1958
Hazzard, David	Kenya	1985
Hazzard, Stacey	Kenya	1985
Hazzard, Margaret	Sri Lanka	1989
Hazzard, Russ	Sri Lanka	1989
Hearn, Gail	Kenya	1978
Hearn, Judi	Angola	1992
Hearn, Kenneth	Angola	1992
Hedding, Malcolm	Israel	1987
Hendrickson, Nellie	Kenya	1930
Hern, Louise	Kenya	1984
Hertzwall, Carina	Guinea	1990
Hesp, Harry	Kenya	1994
Hesp, Irene	Kenya	1994
Higgins, Grace	Kenya	1980
Higgins, Patrick	Kenya	1980
Hildebrandt, Lillian	Kenya	1989
Hildebrandt, Wilfred	Kenya	1989
Hilsden, Ann	Israel	1983
Hilsden, Wayne	Israel	1983
Hirch, Herta	Argentina	1971
Hirch, Waldemar	Argentina	1971
Hoekstra, Yvonne	Taiwan	1981
Holder, Dorothy	China	1938
Holder, Frank	China	1936
Holmes, Coralie	Singapore	1967
Holmes, Miriam	Kenya	1977
Holmquist, Diane	Zambia	1978
Holmquist, Harry	Zambia	1978
Hoover, Mary	Brazil	1957
Hoover, Reginald	Brazil	1957
Horban, Rose	Kenya	1965
Horrill, Beverley	Uganda	1984
Horrill, Irene	Uganda	1968
Horrill, Lyle	Uganda	1968
Houghton, Audrey	Kenya	1963
Houghton, Philip	Kenya	1963
Hunter, Bernard	S. Africa	1948
Hunter, Elizabeth	S. Africa	1948
Hunter, Mary	S. Africa	1979
Hunter, Nancy	Zambia	1972
Hunter, Scott	Zambia	1972
Hunter, David	Zambia	1973
Hunter, Ruth	Zambia	1973

Name	Location	Year	Name	Location	Year
Hurd, Dorothy	Liberia	1980	Kennedy, Terry	Kenya	1978
Hyponnen, Hannu-Heikki	E. Europe	1990	Kerr, Howard	Argentina	1941
Hypponen, Anne	E. Europe	1990	Kerr, Katherine	Argentina	1941
Irvine, Beverley	Thailand	1972	Kerr, Susan	Thailand	1981
Irvine, Sterling	Thailand	1972	Keys, Daisy	West Indies	1961
Irwin, Mary Lou	Kenya	1994	Keys, John	West Indies	1961
Jacobson, A.T.	West Indies	1943	Killby, Katherine	Hong Kong	1987
Jacobson, Verna	West Indies	1943	King, Earley	S. Africa	1938
Jailos, Liisa	Liberia	1976	King, Pearl	S. Africa	1938
James, David	S. Africa	1983	King, Linda	Zimbabwe	1983
Jamieson, Elizabeth	West Indies	1907	King, Terry	Zimbabwe	1983
Jamieson, Robert J.	West Indies	1907	Kipling, Kim	Thailand	1984
Janes, Karen	Liberia	1979	Kipp, Shelley	Kenya	1994
Janke, Alfons	Kenya	1972	Kipp, Stuart	Kenya	1994
Jardine, Edith	Kenya	1985	Kirsch, Bonnie	Uganda	1972
Jarvis, Brian	Zimbabwe	1981	Kirsch, Ivan	Uganda	1972
Jarvis, Helen	Zimbabwe	1981	Kitts, John	Kenya	1940
Jeffery, Nicki	Israel	1992	Kitts, Sophia	Kenya	1940
Jensen, Immanuel	Liberia	1944	Klammer, Esther	S. Africa	1979
Jensen, Isabel	Liberia	1944	Kniesel, Hedwig	Argentina	1963
Jeske, Gerald	Zambia	1986	Kniesel, Werner	Argentina	1963
Jeske, Susan	Zambia	1986	Knott, Jeffrey	Macau	1990
Jiang, Andrew	Singapore	1994	Knott, Shelley	Macau	1990
Jiang, Isabele	Singapore	1994	Kohls, Lynn	Kenya	1981
Johnas, Lois	West Indies	1990	Kohls, Paul	Kenya	1979
Johnas, Volker	West Indies	1990	Kolba, Wanda	Kenya	1983
Johnson, Eugene	Kenya	1968	Komant, Elmer	Zambia	1980
Johnson, Lois	Kenya	1968	Komant, Sherry	Zambia	1980
Johnson, Betty Lou	Kenya	1981	Koop, David	Kenya	1984
Johnson, Cheryl Ann	Liberia	1981	Koop, Donna	Kenya	1984
Johnston, Joy	China	1989	Koopman, Florence	Zimbabwe	1954
Juelich, Frank	India	1976	Koopman, Henry	Zimbabwe	1954
Kampulainen, Liisa	Papua N.G.	1971	Korhonen, Elja	Papua N.G.	1994
Kampulainen, Matti	Papua N.G.	1971	Korpela, Marja	Kenya	1984
Karr, Cathaleen	Thailand	1982	Korpela, Paavo	Kenya	1984
Karr, James	Thailand	1982	Koster, Bernice	Netherlands	1989
Kauffeldt, Glenn	Zambia	1967	Koster, Bill	Netherlands	1989
Kauffeldt, Ruth	Zambia	1967	Kovac, Kathy	Europe	1981
Kauffman, Frances	Tibet	1907	Kovac, Paul	Europe	1974
Kauffman, Ivan	Tibet	1907	Kristjansson, Carolyn	Iceland	1984
Kauffman, Donald	China	1947	Kristjansson, Indridi	Iceland	1984
Kauffman, Irene	China	1947	Kroeker, Anna	Japan	1950
Kauffman, Janet	Hong Kong	1960	Kroeker, Valerie	Kenya	1982
Kauffman, Paul	Hong Kong	1960	Krohn, Betty	Mozambique	1987
Keddy, James	Hong Kong	1992	Krohn, Donald	Mozambique	1987
Keddy, Susan	Hong Kong	1992	Krusch, Christine	Malawi	1989
Keller, Marian Wittich	Tanzania	1914	Krusch, Herbert	Malawi	1989
Keller, Otto	Kenya	1918	Krymusa, Deborah	Liberia	1975
Kells, Linda	West Indies	1989	Krymusa, Paul	Liberia	1975
Kelly, Brenda	Israel	1989	Kubicek, Mary	Kenya	1987
Kelly, Diane	Taiwan	1987	Kumpulainen, Liisa	Papua N.G.	1991
Kelly, William	Taiwan	1987	Kumpulainen, Matti	Papua N.G.	1991
Kelsey, Esther	West Indies	1956	Kurtz, Robert	Kenya	1976
Kemp, Caralee	Thailand	1989	Kurtz, Sally	Kenya	1976

Labrentz, Arnold	Kenya	1966		Lund, Wilda	Liberia	1978
Labrentz, Doreen	Kenya	1966		Lynn, Edna	Kenya	1946
Labrentz, Norman	Malawi	1985		Lynn, John	Kenya	1946
Labrentz, Phyllis	Malawi	1985		Lynn, Jesse	Liberia	1968
Laing, Carol-Leah	Hong Kong	1989		Lynn, Virginia	Liberia	1968
Laing, Stephen	Hong Kong	1989		Lynn, Douglas	Kenya	1973
Laing, Gerald	Kenya	1991		Lynn, Lowana	Kenya	1973
Laing, Grace	Kenya	1991		MacGowan, Kenyon	Zambia	1970
Laity, David	Zambia	1993		MacGowan, Marjorie	Zambia	1970
Laity, Teresa	Zambia	1993		Mackey, Carol	Belize	1987
Lalonde, David	Kenya	1983		Mackey, Garry	Belize	1987
Lalonde, Mary	Kenya	1983		MacLean, Jordon	Liberia	1974
Lambier, Douglas	Kenya	1987		MacMinn, Helen	Kenya	1974
Langdon, Lynnette	Kenya	1984		MacTavish, Daniel	Spain	1986
Lappalainen, Anne	Ethiopia	1975		MacTavish, Mardell	Spain	1986
Lappalainen, Aulis	Ethiopia	1975		Madden, Maxine	Senegal	1992
Larkin, Deborah	Kenya	1987		Mann, Bruce	Israel	1982
Larson, Ethel	Hong Kong	1973		Mann, Wanda	Israel	1982
Lashley, Wendy	Kenya	1979		Marek, Herma	Kenya	1977
Latta, Jean	Japan	1950		Marek, Karel	Kenya	1977
Lau, Patrick	Macau	1991		Markham, Lester	Thailand	1974
Laundry, Grant	Zambia	1985		Markham, Patricia	Thailand	1974
Laur, Allan	Estonia	1991		Marsdin, George	Kenya	1979
Laur, Rael	Estonia	1991		Marsdin, Jennie	Kenya	1979
Lavigne, Jody	Zimbabwe	1991		Martin, Donald	France	1989
Lawrence, Geraldine	Kenya	1976		Martin, Johanna	France	1989
Layman, Louise	Argentina	1934		Mascher, Elsie	Kenya	1962
Le Page, Derek	Taiwan	1972		Mascher, Hellmut	Kenya	1962
Le Page, Susan	Taiwan	1972		Mast, Bernhard	Kenya	1980
Le Pers, Ruth	Liberia	1926		Mast, Elisabeth	Kenya	1980
Lebeck, Leroy	West Indies	1966		Matson, Amy	Brazil	1965
Lebeck, Marilyn	West Indies	1966		Matson, Harold	Brazil	1965
Lees, Roxanne	China	1991		Mattheis, Reinhard	Mozambique	1989
Legge, Caroline	Liberia	1945		Mattheis, Sieglinde	Mozambique	1989
Lehotay, Emese	Kenya	1975		Maxwell, Beyrl	Zimbabwe	1983
Leier, Joe	Israel	1982		Maxwell, Brent	Zimbabwe	1983
Leonard, Martha	Kenya	1987		Mayer, Margaret	Kenya	1975
LeShana, Mrs. N	India	1929		McAllister, Mamie	Kenya	1983
LeShana, Newman	India	1929		McBride, Ella	Kenya	1943
Liira, John	Kenya	1987		McBride, John	Kenya	1943
Lincoln, Alida	Hong Kong	1981		McBride, Bruce	Kenya	1977
Lincoln, Murray	Hong Kong	1981		McBride, Pamela	Kenya	1977
Lingren, Sandra	Kenya	1979		McGarrell, Gladys	Zimbabwe	1985
Lister, Rhonda	Taiwan	1984		McGillivray, Ken	China	1940
Livingstone, Katherine	Kenya	1981		McGillivray, Winnie	China	1940
Logan, Avis	Macau	1983		McGillivray, Vera	China	1940
Logan, Bryan	Macau	1983		McGowan, Hugh	Europe	1986
Longman, Clarence	Kenya	1985		McGowan, Iris	Europe	1986
Loyley, Martin	Kenya	1981		McKillop, Lillian	West Indies	1956
Loyley, Sharon	Kenya	1981		McKillop, Raymond	West Indies	1956
Loyst, Hazel	Kenya	1976		McLeod, Sadie	Hong Kong	1947
Ludwick, James	Taiwan	1982		McMillan, Donald	Thailand	1971
Luinstra, Marilyn	S. Africa	1992		McMillan, Patricia	Thailand	1971
Luinstra, Ray	S. Africa	1992		McNeill, Karen	China	1993

McNeill, Stephen	China	1993
McQuarrie, Gordon	Kenya	1956
McQuarrie, Minnie	Kenya	1956
McQuarrie, Eleda	Kenya	1976
McQuarrie, Ross	Kenya	1976
Meier, Elsbeth	Kenya	1983
Meikle, Jean	Kenya	1958
Melin, Lillian	Israel	1982
Mercer, Linda	Brazil	1972
Mercer, William	Brazil	1972
Meyer, Frank	West Indies	1946
Meyer, Lenore	West Indies	1946
Middlebrook, Michael	Liberia	1989
Middlebrook, Sheila	Liberia	1989
Miller, Claude	Kenya	1908
Miller, Gloria	Kenya	1958
Miller, Jim	Kenya	1958
Miller, Penny	Kenya	1984
Mills, Alma	China	1932
Mills, Verent	China	1932
Minor, Harold	Kenya	1971
Minor, Maryella	Kenya	1971
Mitchell, Muriel	Zambia	1976
Mitchell, Peter	Zambia	1976
Mittelstadt, Caroline	Brazil	1992
Mittelstadt, Peter	Brazil	1992
Mittelstaedt, Elizabeth	Tanzania	1977
Mittelstaedt, Rainer	Tanzania	1977
Mittelstaedt, Leonard	Tanzania	1983
Mittelstaedt, Marilyn	Tanzania	1983
Moffat, Shirley	Kenya	1984
Molin, Elvir	Kenya	1972
Molin, Lilly	Kenya	1972
Moore, Lynn	Israel	1983
Morrison, Louella	China	1919
Morrison, Elmor	China	1923
Morrison, Laura	China	1923
Morrison, Wilbur	Kenya	1948
Morrison, Ruby	Kenya	1949
Morrison, Eleanor Malhus	Kenya	1950
Morrison, Leroy	Kenya	1951
Morrison, Eleanor	Kenya	1963
Morrison, Keith	Kenya	1963
Morrison, Gertrude	S. Africa	1921
Morrison, Vernon	Liberia	1926
Morrison, Gerald	Liberia	1960
Morrison, Ruth	Liberia	1960
Moss, Don	Zambia	1987
Moss, Phyllis	Zambia	1987
Mott, Fredrick	Taiwan	1974
Mott, Lois	Taiwan	1974
Mueller, Immanuel	Tanzania	1964
Mueller, Ruth	Tanzania	1964
Mueller, Esther	Hong Kong	1981
Muggleton, Jack	S. Africa	1964
Muggleton, Winsome	S. Africa	1964
Muir, Jennie	West Indies	1954
Munro, Marion	Kenya	1939
Myers, Edith	Zimbabwe	1956
Myers, Elmer	Zimbabwe	1956
Myers, Rae Garden	Kenya	1967
Naylor, Randall	Hong Kong	1988
Nelson, Brenda	Taiwan	1984
Nelson, Gordon	Liberia	1974
Nelson, Kathleen	Liberia	1974
Nerling, Fred	Argentina	1966
Nerling, Kay	Argentina	1966
Neuenburg, Bonnie	Zambia	1983
Neuenburg, Duane	Zambia	1983
Newman, Janice Rideout	Kenya	1981
Newman, Norman	Kenya	1981
Newsham, Loretta	Hong Kong	1984
Nieuwolt, Simone	Kenya	1984
Nippard, Gladys	Malawi	1985
Nippard, James	Malawi	1985
Nishimoto, Clara	Thailand	1991
Nishimoto, Robert	Thailand	1991
Nolet, Janice	Zimbabwe	1989
Nolet, Paul	Zimbabwe	1989
Nowen, Lars	Uganda	1993
Nygaard, Sophia	Liberia	1919
Oldford, Don	Kenya	1981
Oldford, Jessie	Kenya	1981
Olson, Elaine	Uganda	1992
Olson, Greg	Uganda	1992
Oskarsdottir, Lilja	Ethiopia	1992
Oxford, Debra	Thailand	1985
Paluch, Arlene	Tanzania	1983
Paluch, Peter	Tanzania	1983
Papadopoulos, Andreas	Greece	1983
Papadopoulos, Beverly	Greece	1983
Pardo, Blanche	Hong Kong	1947
Parkinson, Marion	West Indies	1942
Parks, Carol	Argentina	1973
Parks, Wayne	Argentina	1973
Payne, Shivonne	Kenya	1989
Peel, Jean	Zimbabwe	1947
Peel, Robert	Zimbabwe	1947
Peever, Ruth	Thailand	1972
Pemberton, Ruth	West Indies	1918
Pennoyer, Greg	West Indies	1980
Perkins, John	Liberia	1908
Peters, Erna	Liberia	1979
Pettersen, Cynthia	Kenya	1989
Pharand, Beverley	Guinea	1991
Pharand, William	Guinea	1991
Phoenix, Joan	Kenya	1989
Phoenix, Kelvin	Kenya	1989

Name	Country	Year	Name	Country	Year
Pieniniemi, Hilkka	Philippines	1987	Richards, James	Kenya	1978
Pieniniemi, Osmo	Philippines	1987	Richardson, Donna	Kenya	1987
Pierce, Allan	Senegal	1989	Rideout, Avis	Thailand	1978
Pierce, Joan	Senegal	1989	Rideout, Roy	Thailand	1978
Pina, Jose	Mozambique	1959	Rideout, Sheila	Taiwan	1985
Pina, Maria	Mozambique	1959	Robillard, Keilani	China	1992
Piper, Aleta	West Indies	1944	Rogers, Patricia	Taiwan	1982
Piper, Jack	West Indies	1944	Roller, Egan	Zambia	1981
Polkki, John	Brazil	1986	Roller, Lena	Zambia	1981
Polkki, Sirpa	Brazil	1986	Ros, Christiane	Kenya	1965
Posein, Loudell	Tanzania	1973	Ros, Herbert	Kenya	1965
Posein, Ronald	Tanzania	1973	Rosborough, Dale	Kenya	1982
Poultney, June	Thailand	1987	Rosborough, Daniel	Kenya	1982
Poultney, Ron	Thailand	1987	Rosenau, Arthur	Kenya	1951
Powell, Anna	Taiwan	1991	Rosenau, Edna	Kenya	1951
Powell, Ron	Taiwan	1991	Roth, Kathryn	Kenya	1958
Pratt, James	Europe	1991	Rowsell, Cavell	Thailand	1977
Pratt, Mildred	Europe	1991	Rowsell, Joan	Zambia	1988
Prince, Derek	Kenya	1957	Rowsell, Ralph	Zambia	1988
Prince, Lydia	Kenya	1957	Rumball, Carolyn	Kenya	1984
Prosser, Erika	Kenya	1976	Ruthven, Jon	Kenya	1980
Prosser, Paul	Kenya	1976	Rutten, Leonard	Tanzania	1981
Pruden, Nancy	Kenya	1983	Rutten, Lorie	Tanzania	1981
Purdie, David	Zimbabwe	1964	Rutten, Brian	Zambia	1983
Purdie, Margaret	Zimbabwe	1964	Rutten, Valerie	Zambia	1983
Pyykkonen, Saara	Taiwan	1985	Sackett, Shelley	China	1993
Quigley, Brenda	Zambia	1983	Sader, Dean	China	1993
Randall, Arthur	Japan	1929	Sader, Patricia	China	1993
Randall, Sarah	Japan	1929	Salton, Douglas	West Indies	1946
Rathjen, David	Europe	1992	Salton, Sadie	West Indies	1946
Rattai, Edwin	Tanzania	1991	Sasse, Hermann	Brazil	1975
Ratz, Calvin	Hong Kong	1964	Sasse, Irmgard	Brazil	1975
Ratz, Ruth	Hong Kong	1964	Sauder, Doris	Liberia	1980
Ratz, Barbara	Hong Kong	1989	Schaaf, Frieda	Kenya	1972
Rawlinson, Jacqueline	Spain	1990	Schaaf, Richard	Kenya	1972
Raymer, Don	Thailand	1970	Scheel, Iris	Kenya	1954
Raymer, Dorothy	Thailand	1970	Schellenberg, Donald	Thailand	1965
Raymer, Bonnie	Thailand	1972	Schellenberg, Faye	Thailand	1965
Raymer, Marilyn	Kenya	1973	Schellert, Ida	Tanzania	1959
Raymer, Robert	Kenya	1973	Schellert, Paul	Tanzania	1959
Raymer, Ada	Kenya	1975	Scheske, Donald	West Indies	1973
Raymer, Ivan	Kenya	1975	Scheske, Janice	West Indies	1973
Raymer, Ambrose	Uganda	1983	Schindel, Margaret	Kenya	1987
Raymer, Irene	Uganda	1983	Schindel, Reuben	Kenya	1987
Reath, James	Kenya	1968	Schmale, Eleanor	Kenya	1983
Reath, Judy	Keny	1968	Schmale, John	Kenya	1983
Redmann, Gudrun	Brazil	1970	Schmidt, Arlene	Liberia	1977
Redmann, Kurt	Brazil	1970	Schmidt, Douglas	Kenya	1985
Reed, Dudley	S. Africa	1978	Schneider, Eleanor Strom	Kenya	1970
Regehr, Frieda	Kenya	1968	Schrader, Leslie	Liberia	1977
Reid, Janel	Kenya	1984	Schrader, Pauline	Liberia	1977
Rennick, Brian	Zambia	1981	Sciacca, Berthe	West Indies	1970
Rennick, Colleen	Zambia	1981	Sciacca, Vito	West Indies	1970
Richard, Jeannette	Guinea	1991	Scott, Thomas	Zambia	1985

Scott, Thomas	Zambia	1985		Sowerby, Harold	Guinea	1990
Scratch, Clare	China	1935		Sowerby, Ruth	Guinea	1990
Scratch, Lydia	China	1935		Spence, Phoebe	China	1919
Scratch, Elma	Hong Kong	1963		Spence, Rutherford	China	1919
Scully, Georgette	Brazil	1980		Spence, Florence	China	1946
Seaboyer, Amy	Kenya	1969		Spengler, Denise	Kenya	1969
Seaboyer, Robert	Kenya	1969		Spengler, Ernst	Kenya	1969
Seresinhe, Kanthinie	Sri Lanka	1982		Stafford, Gloria	Malawi	1985
Seresinhe, Preman	Sri Lanka	1982		Starrett, Evelyn	Zambia	1980
Seward, Anthony	China	1990		Starrett, Robert	Zambia	1980
Seward, Beverley	China	1990		Stevens, Fred J	Kenya	1954
Seymour, Dawn	Zimbabwe	1980		Stevenson, Edith	Liberia	1928
Seymour, James	Zimbabwe	1980		Stevenson, Kenneth	Liberia	1928
Shank, Clare	Kenya	1988		Stevenson, Ellen	Kenya	1968
Shank, Edna	Kenya	1988		Stevenson, Gerald	Kenya	1968
Sharp, Carol	Kenya	1962		Stevenson, Kathy	Israel	1982
Sharp, William	Kenya	1962		Stoik, Ruth	Kenya	1982
Shaw, Geoffrey	Kenya	1954		Strelau, Anita	Kenya	1989
Shaw, Pauline Vaters	Kenya	1954		Strong, Alexander	Uganda	1969
Shew, Dorcas	Hong Kong	1992		Strong, Janet	Uganda	1969
Shew, Eugene	Hong Kong	1992		Stuckless, Rex	Brazil	1976
Shorrocks, Phyllis	Hong Kong	1985		Stuckless, Rita	Brazil	1976
Siemens, Clara	West Indies	1918		Suomela, Kaarlo	Nepal	1992
Siemens, Renata	Kenya	1939		Suomela, Maija	Nepal	1992
Simard, Giselle	China	1989		Swartz, Frank	Liberia	1930
Sirett, Carol	Kenya	1968		Swartz, Winnifred	Liberia	1930
Sirjoosingh, Deborah	Kenya	1983		Takkunen, Anni	Ethiopia	1974
Sjokvist, Grace	West Indies	1965		Takkunen, Smertsi	Ethiopia	1974
Skinner, James	Kenya	1936		Tatge, Agatha	India	1911
Skinner, Lila	Kenya	1936		Taylor, Kimberley	Sri Lanka	1985
Skinner, Robert	S. Africa	1954		Taylor, Philip	Sri Lanka	1985
Skinner, Doris	S. Africa	1954		Terveld, David	Netherlands	1990
Skinner, Gary	Zambia	1979		Thibault, Denis	Ivory Coast	1993
Skinner, Marilyn	Zambia	1979		Thibeault, Manon	Ivory Coast	1993
Skovmand, Harold	West Indies	1983		Thomas, Mervyn	Tanzania	1957
Slauenwhite, Carol	Zambia	1972		Thomas, Sheila	Tanzania	1959
Slauenwhite, David	Zambia	1972		Thunberg, Patricia	Liberia	1977
Smith, Ethel	China	1947		Thunberg, Paul	Liberia	1977
Smith, Leslie	China	1947		Tippel, Henry	Rhodesia	1964
Smith, Sandra	Hong Kong	1981		Tippel, Marilyn	Rhodesia	1964
Smith, Grace	Hong Kong	1985		Tisdalle, Belva	Zambia	1972
Smith, Jerry	Hong Kong	1985		Tisdalle, Vernon	Zambia	1972
Smith, Clayton	Kenya	1986		Tisher, Herbert	Liberia	1973
Smith, Marilyn	Kenya	1986		Tisher, LaVerne Lynn	Kenya	1973
Soetopo, Darlene	Indonesia	1990		Tollefson, Doris	Kenya	1989
Soetopo, Paul	Indonesia	1990		Tollefson, Gordon	Kenya	1989
Sohnchen, Ernst	Kenya	1981		Toman, Deborah	Kenya	1990
Sohnchen, Lydia	Kenya	1981		Toppings, Mildred	Taiwan	1986
Sorensen, Annina	Argentina	1913		Tracey, Janice	Kenya	1982
Sorensen, Niels	Argentina	1913		Tuck, Deborah	Kenya	1990
Sorensen, Esther	Argentina	1941		Tuomi, Airi	Ethiopia	1965
Sorensen, Samuel	Argentina	1941		Tuomi, Helmi	Ethiopia	1958
Sorensen, Dorothy	Argentina	1947		Tuomi, Aulis	Ethiopia	1958
Sorensen, Paul	Argentina	1947		Twigg, Marjorie	Kenya	1968

Name	Country	Year	Name	Country	Year
Twigg, Paul	Kenya	1968	White, Esther	Kenya	1987
Ulseth, Esther	West Indies	1954	White, Laura	Thailand	1962
Ulseth, Lawrence	West Indies	1954	White, Ronald	Thailand	1962
Underhill, Harold	India	1946	White, John	Zimbabwe	1984
Underhill, Verna	India	1946	White, June	Zimbabwe	1984
Underhill, Pamela	Kenya	1979	Whitelaw, Douglas	Kenya	1991
Upton, Catherine Simpson	West Indies	1944	Whitelaw, Gloria	Kenya	1991
Upton, Maisie	Kenya	1983	Whitt, Irving	Kenya	1970
Upton, Roy	Kenya	1983	Whitt, Ruth	Kenya	1970
Upton, Valerie	Hong Kong	1987	Whitt, Morley	Liberia	1979
Uttaro, Bethany	Malawi	1988	Whitt, Sharon	Liberia	1979
Vahakuopus, Seija	Ethiopia	1986	Wiebe, Mary	Kenya	1979
VanderStoel, Lorna	Europe	1987	Wiebe, Catherine	Tanzania	1987
VanderStoel, Rudy	Europe	1987	Wiebe, Gordon	Tanzania	1987
Veale, Lori	Thailand	1983	Wiley, Gloria	Israel	1985
Veldhuizen, Linda	Philippines	1992	Williams, Florence	Kenya	1979
Verhulst, Carl	S. Africa	1969	Williams, Leslie	Kenya	1979
Verhulst, Ruth	S. Africa	1969	Williams, Joyce	Thailand	1987
Vestrocy, Jo-Ann	Hong Kong	1986	Williams, Vaden	Thailand	1987
Vines, Doug	Israel	1984	Willingshofer, Pamela	Kenya	1984
Vogt, Maria	Kenya	1985	Willoughby, Gloria	Uganda	1981
Vogt, Peter	Kenya	1985	Willoughby, Paul	Uganda	1981
Vuorinen, Sirkka	Tanzania	1980	Wills, Jill	Netherlands	1991
Wabischewich, Linda	Malawi	1985	Wilson, John	Thailand	1982
Wadge, Margaret	Liberia	1937	Wilson, Ursula	Thailand	1982
Waine, Bruce	Hong Kong	1988	Wilson, Robert	Brazil	1990
Waine, Sylvia	Hong Kong	1988	Wilton, Brenda	West Indies	1986
Waine, Cherilyn	Malawi	1988	Wilton, Craig	West Indies	1986
Wall, Susan	Kenya	1994	Winnett, Joan	Indonesia	1992
Walters, Elaine	Kenya	1991	Winnett, Stephen	Indonesia	1992
Walters, Timothy	Kenya	1991	Winsor, Noella	Thailand	1977
Wang, Johanna	Hong Kong	1988	Winsor, Samuel	Thailand	1977
Ward, Letitia	China	1914	Winsor, Eva	Taiwan	1978
Wark, Mary Ann	Zambia	1984	Winsor, Gary	Taiwan	1978
Warkentin, Evelyn	Kenya	1975	Wolf, Nelson	Zambia	1980
Warkentin, Peter	Kenya	1975	Woods, Karen	Hong Kong	1981
Warkentin, Eunice	Kenya	1985	Wortman, Charles	Argentina	1921
Warkentin, Jack	Kenya	1985	Wortman, Margaret	Argentina	1921
Watkins, Lewis	Kenya	1979	Wright, Cyril	Kenya	1983
Watkins, Ruth	Kenya	1979	Wright, Leona	Kenya	1983
Way, David	Zambia	1975	Yeung, Anthony	Macau	1988
Way, Florence	Zambia	1975	Yewchuk, Scott	Kenya	1987
Weiland, Larry	Taiwan	1988	Young, Carl	Thailand	1970
Weiler, Steven	Kenya	1982	Young, Dorothy	Thailand	1970
Wentland, Doris	Tanzania	1956	Young, Annetta	Kenya	1983
Wentland, Gustav	Tanzania	1956	Young, Cecil	Kenya	1983
Werbiski, Albert	Kenya	1961	Young, Don	Taiwan	1985
Werbiski, Lillian	Kenya	1961	Young, Marieve	Taiwan	1985
Werbiski, Patricia	Sudan	1985	Zamir, Cheryl	Israel	1991
Werbiski, Tim	Kenya	1979	Zamir, Ilan	Israel	1991
Weslosky, Eunice	Kenya	1983	Zinkieu, Mark	Hong Kong	1984
Weston, Deborah	Kenya	1986	zum Felde, Barbel	Kenya	1980
White, Dennis	Kenya	1987			

Subject Index

Abbey, Beatrice, 337 (see Purdy, Beatrice)
Abbey, Dr. Douglas, 337
Abraham, John, 382, 383
Abundant Life Assembly, Toronto, 284
Ackroyd, W, 273
Adams, A. E., 52, 111, 114, 197, 313, 418
Adams, Leslie, 95
Adams, O., 41
Ahenakew, Burton, 214
Alberta Medical Association (AMA), 131, 132
Alexanian, Sarkis, 179
Alfieri, Guy, 398, 399
Alinogwa, Mitia, 328
Allen, A. A., 260
Alliance Mission (CMA), Winnipeg, 73
Alline, Henry, 23, 24, 166
Ambassadors In Mission (AIM), 310, 316
American Association of Bible Colleges, 369
American Revivalism, 25, 82, 100
Anderson, Bennie, 142
Anderson, Harry, 357
Anderson, Leith, 402
Anderson, Paul, 89
Anderson, Robert. 122
Andreasen, Olga, 237
Andreasen, Paul, 237
Andresen, Alvina, 238, 339
Andresen, Erling, 238, 339
Angelus Temple, Los Angeles, 129, 135
Anglican(s), 17, 25, 46, 73, 85, 86, 99, 101, 139, 166, 203, 213, 258, 290, 300, 302
Annacondia, Carlos, 394-5
Anonby, Ellen, 339
Anonby, Joseph, 339
Apostolic Church of Pentecost of Canada, The, 96, 97, 111, 123, 355
Apostolic Faith, 13, 19, 37, 45, 63, 64, 79, 99, 104, 123

Apostolic Faith Mission, 32, 39 (see Azusa Street Mission)
Apostolic Faith Movement, 29, 30
Apostolic Faith of Portland, Oregon, 35, 38, 77, 79, 93, 98
Apostolic Faith, The, 30, 32, 33, 35, 38, 41, 67, 96, 97, 101, 107, 112, 122, 123, 219
Apostolic Messenger, The, 78
Apostolic Movement, 1830, 37
Appleman, Hyman, 282
Argue Mission, 44, 62, 76, 77, 81, 103, 111, 136
Argue, Andrew Harvey, 26, 27, 35, 44, 50, 53, 62, 63, 71-81, 88, 91, 93, 96, 99, 104, 107, 108, 115, 116, 118, 126, 127, 133-136, 147, 151, 158, 187, 189, 191, 194, 216, 237, 260, 281, 410
Argue, Beulah, 133, 136 (see Smith, Beulah)
Argue, Eva, 73, 75
Argue, Harvey, 73
Argue, John, 72
Argue, Robert M., 209, 212, 261, 288, 310, 320, 348, 357, 374, 417
Argue, Watson, 50, 73, 78, 132, 133, 135, 136, 144, 147, 193, 282, 292
Argue, Zelma, 37, 50, 73-75, 78, 96, 97, 133-136, 147, 151, 189
Armstrong, Maurice W., 37
Arnold, Laura, 229, 230
Arroyo Seco, 65
Assemblée du Plein Evangile, LaSalle, 309
Assemblies of God (USA), 19, 28, 35, 36, 38, 54, 76, 79, 83, 88, 109-111, 113, 118, 122, 123, 124, 135, 161, 196, 198, 199, 200, 206, 235, 237, 238, 247, 253, 258, 259, 262, 266, 272, 297, 298, 316, 323, 343, 373, 381, 389, 397
Assemblies of God of Mozambique, 388
Atter, Arthur M., 43, 52, 105, 114, 143
Atter, Jessie, 43, 68, 231
Atter, Gordon F., 13, 15, 18, 37, 40, 45, 65, 68, 70, 77, 96, 111, 113, 115, 118, 120, 122-124, 143, 151, 153, 190, 193, 202,

429

208, 215-217, 220, 231, 241, 242, 266, 285, 291, 298, 317, 343, 410
Auburn Affirmation, 125
Austin, Ed, 209
Austin, Ray, 344, 347
Austin, Verna, 344, 347
Australia, Dr. J., 147
Awakening, First Great, 22, 24
Awrey, Daniel, 27, 41, 188
Azusa Street Mission, 17, 28-30, 32, 34, 35, 41, 62, 66, 71, 77, 90, 95, 102, 103, 107, 112, 113, 126, 187, 297 (see Apostolic Faith Mission)
Azusa Street Revival of 1906-09, 28, 74
Baird, R. G., 157
Baker, A. D., 77
Baker, Annie, 64, 70, 157
Baker, Charles E., 64, 112, 115, 129, 133, 151, 157-163, 175, 178, 181, 197, 288,
Baker, Daniel, 278
Bakker, Jim, 296, 298
Baldwin, Candy, 366
Baldwin, Robert, 366
Ball, John T., 44, 49, 50, 51, 56, 61, 69, 134, 142, 144
Baptism in the Holy Spirit (19th century), 26
Baptism in the Holy Spirit (Pentecostal), 17, 26, 28, 31, 75, 92, 95, 99, 107, 108, 112, 113, 130, 132, 133, 135, 175, 197 (see Full Gospel)
Baptist Ministeral Association of Vancouver, 131
Baptist(s) denomination, 17, 22, 24, 25, 101, 104, 121, 131, 166, 185, 300
Baptistic-Pentecostal, 108
Barber, Elma, 235 (see Scratch, Elma)
Barber, Herbert H., 50, 151, 256, 354, 397
Barker, Charles, 341
Barker, Myrtle, 243, 341
Barker, Louisa, 344
Barna, George, 402
Barnes, J. E., 146, 148, 153, 203, 272, 415, 418
Barnes, Winifred, 148, 415
Barnett, Tommy, 354
Barratt, T. B., 34

Barres, Gordon, 247
Barry, Sgt. E. B., 248
Bartleman, Frank, 29, 38, 41, 102, 123, 188
Baxter, M., 97
Beardi, Samuel, 213
Belbin, Alister, 384
Belbin, Lindy, 384
Bell, Art, 275
Bell, E. N., 79, 124, 196
Bellemare, L., 212
Bellsmith, Edward, 365
Benghu, Nicholas, 337
Benham, C. Orville, 80, 135, 147
Benn, Charles K., 357, 367, 373
Bennett, Dennis, 298, 301
Berea Bible Institute, Montreal (Institut Biblique Bérée), 165, 166, 211, 212, 287, 309, 310
Bergeron, Cecile, 289
Bergeron, Roland, 164, 165, 289
Bergerson, Ovila, 165
Bernhardt, John, 358
Bethel Bible Institute, Saskatoon, 208, 260, 261, 266, 280 (see Central Pentecostal College)
Bethel Bible Training School, Newark, New Jersey, 222
Bethel College, Topeka, 28, 112
Bethel Deaf Tabernacle, Hamilton, 409
Bethel Gospel Tabernacle, Hamilton, 285
Bethel Home for Girls, Toronto, 253, 256, 286
Bethel Home, New Brunswick, 319
Bethel Pentecostal Church, Ottawa, 307, 364
Bethel Pentecostal Tabernacle, Toronto, 207 (see Danforth Gospel Temple)
Bethesda Mission, St. John's, Nfld., 173, 174, 175, 178, 199
Beulah Mission, 87
Beverly, James, 36
Bibby, Reginald, 402
Billy Graham Evangelistic Association, 304 (see Graham, Billy)
Binette, Carole, 382
Binette, Jocelyn, 382

430

Bingeman, Ethel, 229, 230, 255
Bingham, Helen E., 69
Birch, Kenneth B., 209, 297, 321, 322, 350, 374, 404, 417
Biro, Sam, 214
Bittlinger, Arnold, 321
Bjorgan, Gordon, 208
Black, Rev. and Mrs. Billie, 147
Blackmore, Denys, 308, 322
Blair, J. Harold, 50, 65, 70, 126, 144, 153, 188-190, 207, 283, 285, 418
Blakely, John, 247
Blakeney, J. K., 224
Blumhofer, Edith L., 19
Boddy, A. A., 34, 105, 107, 113, 187
Boddy, J. T., 43
Boles, John B., 36
Bolton, Jean, 345
Bolton, Marion, 345
Bombay, Cal, 313, 314, 322, 327
Bombay, Ken, 377
Bombay, Olive, 330
Bombay, Richard A., 191, 263, 266, 286, 287, 293, 330, 418
Bonnke, Reinhard, 389, 402
Booth, Bramwell, 26, 37
Booth, General, 26, 27, 173, 174
Borzel, Henry, 345
Borzel, Janet, 345
Bosworth, F. F., 113
Bouchard, W. L., 165, 212, 288
Bourgier, Raymond, 366
Bowen, Al, 310
Bowen, Irene, 310
Bowler, Arnold, 327, 350, 388
Bowler, Elsie, 327, 350, 388
Bowers, Evelyn, 315
Boyd, David, 208, 218, 357
Boyd, Frank, 54
Braeside Camp, 136, 144, 189, 190, 207, 284, 313, 369
Brand, Bruce, 328, 350
Branham, William, 260
Bredesen, Harold, 292, 299, 302
British and Foreign Bible Society, 224

British Columbia Bible Institute (BCBI) 210, 211 (see Western Pentecostal Bible College)
Broadfoot, Barry, 242
Bronsdon, C. Herbert, 208, 317
Bronsdon, Edith, 230
Brooks, Elsie, 131
Brooks. J. T., 418
Broomes, Gloria, 333
Broomes, Winston, 333, 386, 393
Broughton, Doreen, 310, 338
Broughton, Larry, 310, 338
Brown, Annie, 93
Brown, Grace, 209, 243, 279, 292, 317, 360
Brown, Victor G., 285, 293
Brown, Viola, 230, 271, 331, 338
Brown, W. J., 221
Brown, William E., 271, 331, 338
Brumback, Carl, 38, 111, 122, 123, 266
Buhler, Rich, 402
Buick, Samuel, 357
Bullerwell, Scott, 373
Bumstead, J. M., 36, 182
Buntain, D. N., 26, 84, 200, 201, 205, 206, 207, 209, 210, 218, 250, 272, 276, 279, 292, 417, 418
Buntain, Kathleen, 210
Buntain, Mark, 98, 247, 381
Burge, Buddy, 365
Burger, Stu, 366
Burns, Will, 231
Burrage, Betty, 334
Burrag, John, 334
Bursey, A. Stanley, 178, 180, 183
Bush, James, 334
Bush, Vera, 334
Butcher, Elsie (Welsteed), 236, 237, 345
Butcher, William F., 236, 237, 345, 391
Butler, Mrs. E., 92
Butt, Philip, 177
Byng Avenue Church, Oshawa, 287
Cadwalder, Hugh M., 83, 88, 90, 118, 124, 192, 200, 216
Cairns, E. Earle, 206

Calderbank, Mrs. William, 86
Callahan, Ray, 333
Callahan, Vivian, 333
Calmer Christian Assembly, 276
Calvary Chapel, Costa Mesa, California, 297
Calvary Temple, Winnipeg, 50, 132, 136, 256, 281, 282, 283, 305, 313, 364, 384
Camp Emmanuel, Long Pond, Newfoundland, 289
Camp Evangeline, Debert, Nova Scotia, 314
Campbell, Faith, 302, 321
Campeau, Guy, 213
Campolo, Tony, 354
Canada for Christ, 356
Canadian Bible Society, Saskatoon, 142
Canadian District Councils of the Assemblies of God, 198
Canadian Foodgrains Bank, 379
Canadian Pentecostal Bible College, 85, 204, 205 (see Western Bible College and Winnipeg Bible school)
Cane Ridge, Kentucky, Camp Meetings of 1801, 23, 185
Cantelon, Cathy, 383
Cantelon, James, 383
Cantelon, Don, 397
Cantelon, Elmer, 81, 97, 191, 216, 255
Cantelon, Homer J., 313, 418
Cantelon, Todd, 142
Cantwell, Margaret, 326
Canwood Indian Bible School, Saskatchewan, 369
Carlson, G. Raymond, 206
Carrefour Chrétien De La Capitale, Quebec City, 310
Carrothers, W. F., 112
Carter, Ed, 161
Carter, Fred, 161
Cashwell, G. B., 35
Casqueiro, Evangeline, 334
Casqueiro, Hans, 334
Catholic Apostolic Church, 26
Catholic Pentecostalism, 299-302, 321
Catholicism (Catholics), 16, 55, 137, 156, 162, 300, 311, 334

Caughey, James, 24, 181
Cawson, Alfred A., 237
Cawson, Mary, 237
Central Bible Institute (CBI) Springfield, Missouri, 198, 202
Central Pentecostal College (CPC), Saskatoon, 208, 209, 316, 404 (see Bethel Bible Institute)
Central Tabernacle, Edmonton, 210, 315, 356
Centre Evangélique de St-Hyacinthe, 165
Challenge, The, 285
Chaloner, Heather, 393
Chaloner, Stephen, 393
Chamberlain, Harold, 368, 373
Chambers, George A., 41-44, 46-49, 53, 56-61, 66, 67-70, 88, 101, 108, 112-115, 118, 119, 121-124, 126, 127, 134, 139, 140, 151, 152, 170, 173, 181, 183, 187, 188, 190, 192, 194-197, 199, 203, 207, 215-216, 219, 220, 237, 241, 411-412, 417-418
Chambers, Ida, 55-58, 62, 70
Chandkorn, Nirut, 391
Chandler, Russell, 291
Charbonneau, Louise, 380
Charbonneau, Michel, 380
Charismatic Movement, 16, 298-302, 311, 314, 321, 412 (see Neo-Pentecostals)
Chawner, Austin, 222-225, 241, 242, 270, 334, 335
Chawner, Carrie, 222, 223
Chawner, Charles W., 43, 219-222, 241, 335
Chawner, Emma, 43, 219-221, 241, 335
Chawner, Ingrid, 224, 241, 242, 270, 334, 337 (see Lokken, Ingrid)
Chiarelli, Eli, 380, 382
Chiarelli, Elsa, 380, 382
China Inland Mission, 346
Chivalry, 370
Chorley, F., 211
Chouinard, Lucien, 165
Christ's Ambassadors (C.A.s), 172, 253, 256, 285, 289, 315, 338, 341
Christenson, Larry, 37, 299
Christian and Missionary Alliance, 17, 22, 46, 71, 73, 101, 105, 113, 121, 201, 219, 234

Christian Children's Fund, Travancore, India, 235
Christian Guardian, The, 24
Christian Mission Hospital, Calcutta, 381
Christian Religious Education and Training for Evangelism (CREATE), Goibei, Kenya, 386
Christianity Today, 297
Christianson, Mae, 280
Church Army (Anglican), 25
Church as a Social Institution, 248
Church of God, The, 355
Church of the Foursquare Gospel, California, 187
Churchill, Emma, 173
Churchill, Jennifer, 392
Churchill, John, 392
Clark, E. T., 265
Clark, S. D., 37, 265
Circle Square, 305 (see Crossroads Communications)
Clarke, Fred, 148, 225, 270, 332
Clarke, Rhonda, 148, 225, 332
Classical Pentecostals(ism), 16, 300-302
Clemens, Ernest, 418
Clements, Donald, 278
Clements, Evelyne, 278
Clements, Fred, 238, 339
Clements, Susan, 238, 339
Clemo, Frances, 274
Coates, Thomas F. G., 38
Collings, W. R., 148
Columbia Street Mission, Vancouver, 11
Community Pentecostal Church, Orleans, Ontario, 307
Concerning the Faith, 258
Congregational Church, 17
Congress On Pentecostal Leadership, (COPL), 353, 354, 373, 401
Cooke, J. C., 206, 210, 317
Cooke, Ida, 210
Cooksey, H. Wesley, 203
Copley, A. S., 41, 68
Cornelius, Cindy, 378
Cornelius, Murray, 378
Cornelius, Lillian, 14, 328
Cornelius, William C., 209, 320, 328, 348, 350, 356, 376, 394, 395, 396, 417
Coughlan, Lawrence, 172
Craig, James, 370
Crawford, Florence, 35, 77, 79, 92, 93, 102, 194
Crawford, Mattie, 167
Crawford, Percy, 146
Cressman, Annie, 230, 242, 271, 338, 339
Cressman, Gerald, 389
Cressman, Grace, 389
Cressman, Salome, 181, 182, 212, 287
Cross, C. L., 92, 115
Cross, Robert, 306
Crossley, H. T., 25, 37
Crossroads Christian Communications, 284 (see 100 Huntley Street, Circle Square, and Pavilion Of Promise)
Crossroads Pentecostal Tabernacle, Montague, 308
Cucheron, Dan, 247
Cuke, William, 393
Culham, James, 340
Culham, Shirley, 340
Cummins, Alberta, 213, 306
Cummins, Dale, 213, 306
Cunningham, Mabel, 139, 169, 240
Curle, Danny, 334
Curle, Sharon, 334
Czar Lake Camp, Alberta, 146, 193
Daigneault, Roger, 165
Dallimore, Arnold, 37
Dalby, A., 193
Danforth Gospel Temple, Toronto 207 (see Bethel Pentecostal Tabernacle)
Danzey, Frank, 287
Davis, Carro, 167
Davis, Harold, 69, 153, 215
Davis, Roy, 303
Davis, Susan, 167
Day, Charles F., 162, 189
Day, Margaret, 162
Deacon, June, 326
Decade of Destiny, 397, 398
Decade of Harvest, (AG), 397

Delport, Elmer, 334, 390
Delport, Sylvia, 334, 390
Delport, Lawrence (J.H.), 270, 337
Delport, Lois, 270, 337
Dent, George, 138
Derkatch, George, 385
Dickinson, Lila, 210
Dieter, Melvin, 37, 122
Dimmick, Ruby, 130
Disciples (denomination), 185
Dispensational(ism), 31, 32
Distaulo, G. A., 162
Divine Healing, 17, 26, 28, 75, 92, 95, 99, 102, 107, 130-131, 134, 137, 149 (see Full Gospel)
Doberstein, Bruno, 332
Doberstein, Elizabeth, 332
Doberstein, Elvine, 339
Doberstein, Horst, 292, 339
Dobroski, Marilyn, 342
Dobroski, John, 342
Doggart, Scott, 392, 396
Door of Hope Mission, China, 74
Dowie Mission, Toronto, 28
Dowie, John Alexander, 27-29
Draffin, William L., 59-61, 81, 88, 112, 114, 115, 195, 196, 197
Dresch, Mary, 71
Drewitz, Arthur, 292, 351
Drisner, E., 145
Drisner, Reuben, 276
du Plessis, David, 269, 299
Dublin Street Church, Peterborough, 118, 206, 208
Durham, W. H., 39, 43, 52, 53, 74, 79, 107-109
Dutaud, L. R., 163, 164
Dutch Reformed Church in America, 299
Dyck, Gordon, 388
Dyck, Rita, 388
Dyer, Helen S., 37
Dynna, Marvin, 209, 210
Eames, Mabel, 331, 341
Eames, Robert, 327, 331, 341, 346, 391
East End Mission, 39, 41, 43, 44, 101, 219, 220 (see Hebden Mission)

Eastern Canada District Council, 118
Eastern Pentecostal Bible College (EPBC), 204, 206-209, 213, 290, 305, 306, 316, 317, 327, 356, 372 (see Ontario Pentecostal Bible College)
Eby, Amos, 54
Eby, M. F., 63
Eby, Solomon, 25, 26, 45, 54
Ecclesia Bible Institute, Hong Kong, 232, 233, 343, 344
Eddy, Herbert, 175-177
Edwards, Debbie, 392
Edwards, John, 392
Edwards, Ilene, 237
Edwards, Jonathan, 21-23, 100, 392
Eggleton, Harry, 94, 95, 98, 147, 153, 240, 241, 341
Eggleton, Marguerite, 95, 98, 240, 341
Elim Assemblies of Great Britain, 346
Elim Bible school (Rochester Bible and Missionary Training School), 48, 52, 178, 226
Elim Pentecostal Evangel, 180
Elim Tabernacle, Saskatoon, 208, 297, 305
Ellis, Maud, 360, 368
Embree, Bernard, 206, 208
Emde, Adeline, 145
Emergency Relief and Development Organization (ERDO), 379, 387
Emmanuel Press, South Africa, 270
Emmons, Don, 208, 418
English, May, 209
English, Robert, 175
Enroth, Ronald J., 321
Entire Santification, 23, 25, 186 (see Sanctification)
Epp, Frank, 37
Erickson, Arthur, 89
Erickson, Clifton, 330
Erickson, Leif, 89
Erickson, Walter, 89
Ethics and Social Concerns Committee, 355 (see Social Concerns)
European Pentecostal Fellowship, 350
Evangel Church, Montreal, 160, 161, 288
Evangel Pentecostal Church, Brantford, 365

Evangel Press, Kenya, Nairobi (Evangel Publishing House), 225, 327, 328, 337, 386
Evangel Tabernacle, Bathurst, New Brunswick, 168
Evangel Temple, Toronto, 133, 207
Evangelical United Brethren, 277
Evans, Morley, 247
Evans, William (Moody Bible Institute), 85
Evans, William I., 54, 191
Evening Light Pentecostal, Bermuda, 172
Ewart, Frank J., 65, 108, 110, 123
Faith Bible School, Victoria, B.C., 210
Faith Tabernacle, Halifax, 288, 289
Faith to Live By, 283
Family Talk, 370
Faught, J. Harry, 302, 321
Fehr, Jake, 247
Feltmate, S. Donald, 315, 320, 323, 356, 417
Fernandes, May, 382
Findley *Courier, The*, 135
Finished Work, 107-109
Finney, Charles G., 13, 21, 23-25, 36, 100, 113
Finnish Conference (1939), 201
Fire-Baptized Holiness Church, 73
Firehouse, 370
Fisher Reserve, 81
Fisher, George, 42, 43
Fleming, Florence, 270 (see Koopman, Florence)
Flemingdon Park Pentecostal Church, Toronto, 357
Flower, J. Roswell, 28, 54, 123, 297
Fodor, Laura, 393
Fodor, Tom, 393
Foley, Greg, 357, 370
Fordham, Grace, 219
Fordham, Hindle, 219
Formation Timothée, 212, 213, 310, 311, 387
Forsey, Evelyn, 176, 183
Fosdick, H. E., 100
Found, W. H., 207, 208, 211, 288, 418
Foursquare Church, North Battleford, 261

Fowler, L. H., 290, 293
Fox, Ethel, 132, 151
Fox, Lorne F., 132, 151, 193, 330
Foyer Laurentian, 319
Francis, Ernest, 210, 336, 348
Francis, Shirley, 336, 348
Franklin, Gordon, 96, 152, 209, 210, 217
Fraser, Hugh, 146
Fredrick, W. S., 195, 276, 418
French Conference, 201, 288, 309, 311
French Language Intensive Training for Evangelism (FLITE), 212, 310, 365, 366
Fretz, David, 45
Fricker, Garry, 339
Fricker, Jean, 339
Friesen, W. J., 211
Frodsham, Stanley H., 41, 67
Fulford, Gordon, 208, 348, 418
Fulford, T., 157
Full Gospel Assemblies, Thailand, 391
Full Gospel Businessmen's Fellowship International (FGBMFI), 268, 298
Full Gospel Publishing House (FGPH), 199, 258, 357
Full Gospel (four cardinal doctrines), 17, 28, 39, 54, 67, 75, 95, 99, 130, 135, 174, 197 (see Salvation, Baptism in the Holy Spirit, Divine Healing, Second Coming)
Fundamentalist(s) (ism), 125, 133
Fundamentals: A Testimony to the Truth, The, 125
Funk, Betty, 208
Gaetz, Ivan, 357
Gaetz, Ken, 210, 278, 279, 280, 292
Gagné, Armand, 165
Gagnon, Marie-Paule, 212, 287
Gagnon, G., 181
Gamble, W. J., 282
Garr, A. G., 92, 105, 187
Garr, Lillian, 92, 105, 187
Garrigus, Alice Belle, 151, 173-181, 183, 199, 240, 289
Gaston, W. T., 191
Geddes, Howard, 203
Gee, Donald, 143, 191, 193, 225, 242, 267, 269, 293

Geiger, Ida, 142
Geiger, Sam, 142
Gerard, Bernice, 302, 304, 321, 322
German Branch Conference, 201, 312
German Conference Camp, Alberta 312 (see Sunset Point Pentecostal Camp),
Gibb, Margaret, 354
Gibbons, Lorrie, 365
Gibson, William, 71, 418
Gideon, Joseph, 292
Giesbrecht, Peter, 281
Gigliotti, Dr. Frank, 290
Gilchrist, H., 157
Gillespie, Jessie, 342
Gillespie, Robert, 95, 147
Gillett, Matilda, 175
Gillett, William, 175-177
Gingrich, Della, 342
Gingrich, Virgil, 342
Glad Tidings Tabernacle, Victoria, B.C., 211
Glad Tidings, Burlington, 357
Glad Tidings, London, 306
Gleaner, The, 179, 248
Goibei Girls' School, Training Centre, Kenya, 227, 270, 326, 327, 386
Good Report, The, 63, 64
Good Tidings, 180, 290
Gospel Light Boat, B.C., 148, 149, 214, 273
Gospel Messenger (Gospel Boat, Newfoundland), 176
Goss, Ethel, 97, 122
Goss, Howard, 28, 29, 99, 107, 111, 115, 117
Graham, Billy, 297, 321, 337 (see Billy Graham Evangelistic Association)
Graham, John, 409
Grainger, Joseph, 82
Gram, Frank, 95
Grasso, Daniel, 394
Graves, John, 72
Gray, James, 130, 151, 242
Great Depression, The, 17, 103, 127, 140-143, 162, 164, 170-171, 179, 189, 207, 223, 237-238, 242, 245, 275, 280, 283, 313

Great Revival of 1830, 166
Great Union Camp Meeting, Spencerville, 186
Great Unity Conference of the Pentecostal Movement of North America, St. Louis 1922, 198
Greenfield, John, 36
Greenwood, Wilbert B., 145, 191, 206, 286, 418
Grenfell, Wilfred, 173, 182
Gresham, John L., 36
Grierson, Elsie, 169
Griffin, George B., 69, 129, 151, 161, 202, 208, 317, 410
Griffin, William A., 11, 14, 18, 191, 208, 209, 303, 317, 320, 322, 354, 356, 358, 369, 371, 373, 404, 412, 417
Griffin, Patti, 14
Grosshans, Barbara, 345
Grosshans, George, 345, 357, 395, 396, 397-399
Grothaus, Clarence, 226, 242
Guide to Holiness, 85
Gullackson, George, 276
Gungu, Charles, 328, 329
Guskjolen, Colleen, 382
Guskjolen, James, 382
Guthrie, Georgie, 221
Guthrie, J., 221
H. H. Williams Memorial Hospital, Hay River, N.W.T., 210, 279, 319, 363, 364 (see Williams, H. H.)
Hagenback, K. R., 37
Haist, Coralee, 242, 252
Hale, William, 357
Hall, Dr. E. E., 147
Halliwell, Doreen, 380
Halliwell, Wayne, 380
Hamilton, Beulah, 169
Hamilton, Florence, 338, 345
Hamilton, Freeman, 192
Hammond, John W., 183, 314, 322
Hann, Emma, 208, 217, 265, 317
Hansell, Joy, 230, 271, 338, 339, 358
Harbarenko, J. D., 277
Harbridge, Gerald, 357

Harford, Frank, 148, 153, 273
Harford, Mabel, 148, 273
Harrow, Mrs. J. M. L., 229
Hart, J. L., 157
Harvey, Van A., 122
Hasking, Viola, 69
Haug, Irmgard, 332
Haug, Johann, 332
Hauser, Bonnie, 341
Hawkes, Paul, 97, 216, 266, 292, 316, 381, 390, 396, 418
Hawtin, Ernest, 145, 261
Hawtin, George R., 208, 209, 260, 261
Haycank, K., 277
Hayford, Jack, 354
Haystead, K. M., 418
Haywood, G. T., 157
Hazlett, James H., 276
Heaven's Gates and Hell's Flames, 368 (see Krulik, Rudy)
Hebden Mission, 40, 41-44, 46, 53, 66, 74, 82, 103 (see East End Mission)
Hebden, Ellen K., 9, 26, 35, 39-44, 48, 53, 56, 63, 67, 74, 101, 102, 106, 113, 187, 221, 231
Hebden, James, 9, 35, 40, 42-44, 48, 106
Hébert, Pierre, 365
Hebron English School, Hong Kong, 344
Hebron Farm, London, 368
Hehl, Robert, 363
Henderickson, Nellie, 143, 209, 228
Heritage, Brampton, 285 (see Kennedy Road Tabernacle)
Herron, C. B., 237
Hetherington, Orville, 84, 86
Hi-Way Pentecostal Church, Barrie, 303
Hicks, Tommy, 339
Hiebert, Rick, 357, 370
Hilsden, Ann, 383
Hilsden, Wayne, 383
Hilsden, Hudson, 319, 358, 359, 400
Hirch, Herta, 393
Hirch, Waldemar, 393
Hisey, Martha, 71, 229
Hocken, Peter, 321

Holdcroft, Leslie Thomas, 206, 211, 260, 263, 266, 316, 317
Holder, Dorthy, 332
Holder, Frank, 332
Holiness Movement, 13, 17, 21, 22, 25, 26, 73, 82, 85, 92, 101, 104, 107, 121, 259
Hollands, Ernie, 368
Hollenweger, W. J., 123, 409, 412
Holmes, Phoebe, 232, 233 (see Spence, Phoebe)
Holt, Herrick, 261
Home and Foreign Mission (Alliance, CMA), 72
Honderick, L. C., 252
Honsinger, Howard D., 209, 313, 357, 358
Hoover, Mary, 393
Hoover, Reg, 393
Hoover, Robert, 248
Hoover, T. R., 396
Horban, Michael P., 297
Hornby, Eric, 142, 418
Horner, A. G., 37
Horner, Ralph C., 37, 256
Horril, Irene, 332
Horril, Lyle, 332
Horton, Harry, 76
Horton, Stanley, 76, 96
Hostetler, Emma, 71
House of Welcome, Montford, 165
House, James, 274, 418
House, Marion, 274
Howey, Charles, 276
Hueppelsheuser, Iris, 305
Hueppelsheuser, Laurie, 305
Hughes, A. J., 272, 418
Hunt, Percy, 208, 209, 261
Hunter, Bernard, 334-336, 351
Hunter, Beth, 336
Hunter, E. Stewart, 418
Hunter, J. E., 25
Hunter, Scott, 333
Hunter, Nancy, 333
Huntley Street, 100 Huntley Street, 284, 305, 313 (see Crossroads Christian Communications)

Hurd, Dorthy, 288
Hurlbut, Charles, 89
Hurlbut, Mabel, 89
Hurst, J. F., 37
Hussite Movement, 22
Hutchinson, Mabel, 253
Hutchinson, Pearl, 253
Hutchisin, Joseph, 253
Hybels, Bill, 402
Independent Communion, The, 180
Ingersoll, Robert, 126
Initial Evidence, 28, 104, 107, 112, 113, 361
Inner Peace Camp, Grande Praire, Alberta, 312
International Missionary Council, 269
Interstate Camp Meeting, Eureka Springs, Arkansas, 1913, 79
Irangi, Shem, 328
Irvine, Bev, 345
Irvine, Sterling, 345
Irvin, R. J., 69
Irving, Edward, 26
Irvingites, 26, 54
Jackson, Mervil C., 142
Jackson, William, 93
Jacobson, A. T., 272, 341
Jacobson, Verna, 341
Jaenen, Cornelius J., 215, 263, 266
Jamieson, Elizabeth, 238, 239, 241, 243
Jamieson, Robert J., 175, 238-241, 243, 255, 271, 341, 342, 392
Janes, Burton, 183
Janke, Alf, 338
Japan Assemblies of God, 343
Jarvis, Brian, 389
Jarvis, Helen, 389
Jeffreys, George, 171
Jehovah's Witness, 56
Jenson, Immanuel, 214, 230, 271, 283, 338
Jenson, Isabel, 230, 271, 338
Jeske, Gerald, 389
Jeske, Susan, 389
Jeske, Oskar, 278
Jesus Only, 65, 66, 76, 79, 80, 107-109, 111, 112, 115, 117 (see New Issue and Oneness Pentecostalism)
Jesus People Movement, 295-297
Johnson, E. W., 83
Johnson, Gerald, 210
Johnson, Kevin, 13
Johnston, David, 357
Johnston, Maurice, 247
Johnstone, Doris, 162, 168, 170
Johnstone, Tom, 103, 120, 146, 162, 168, 170, 182, 189, 207, 211, 256, 257, 263, 266, 272, 291, 293, 320, 410, 417, 418
Jones, Claude W., 169, 288, 418
Jones, Percy S., 149, 150, 153, 195, 200, 203, 210, 216, 217, 272, 273, 418
Jordan Valley Camp, 49, 188, 237
Juelich, Frank, 381
Kadyschuk, Ronald, 209
Kakoschke, Otto, 395
Kalamen, Arnold, 161, 288
Kalappa, James, 408
Kampala Pentecostal Church, Uganda, 377
Kauffeldt, Glenn, 333, 334, 378, 389
Kauffeldt, Ruth, 333, 334, 378, 389
Kauffman, Don, 234, 243, 342, 344
Kauffman, Irene, 342, 344
Kauffman, Frances, 234
Kauffman, Ivan, 234, 243
Kauffman, Paul, 161, 234
Kautz, William H., 161, 288, 293
Keller, Marian, 227, 228, 242 (see Weller, Marian and Wittich, Marian)
Keller, Otto, 225, 227, 228, 326
Kelly, Bill, 391
Kelly, Diane, 391
Kennedy Road Tabernacle (KRT), Brampton, 284, 285, 365
Kennedy, Aimee (see Semple, Aimee and MacPherson, Aimee), 43, 52
Kenya Pentecostal Assemblies of God, 329
Kereri Girls' School, Kenya, 326
Kerr, D. W., 43, 192, 202
Kerr, Howard, 271, 339
Kerr, Katherine, 339
Kewley, Arthur, 215
Keylock, Lesley R., 321

Keys, Daisy, 277, 341
Keys, Jack, 210, 277, 341, 418
Kibbutz Shalom, 383, 403
Kiddies Kollege, Brampton, 285 (see Kennedy Road Tabernacle)
Kilburn, W. M., 266
King of Kings Assembly, Jerusalem, 384
King of Kings College, Jerusalem, 384
King Street Pentecostal Church, Oshawa, 287
King, L. Calvin, 418
King, Earley, 50, 206, 225, 271
King, Pearl, 225
King, J. H., 73, 74, 107
Kingdom Now Movement, 361, 362
Kirkpatrick, M. E., 253
Kitts, John, 270
Kitts, Sophia, 270
Klan, Donald, 92, 94, 98, 108, 123, 151, 292
Klingspohn, Wilf, 358
Klink, Otto, 190
Kniessel, Hedwig, 339
Kniessel, Werner, 339
Knight, John W., 148, 217
Knoll, Fred, 229
Knott, W. J., 130
Knudsen, Per, 364
Komant, Elmer, 378
Komant, Sherry, 378
Koop, David, 328
Koopman, Florence, 270, 334 (see Fleming, Florence)
Koopman, Henry, 270, 334
Kowalski, Wilhelm, 249, 278
Kreiger, Lila, 279, 280
Kristjansson, Carolyn, 384
Kristjansson, Indridi, 384
Krohn, Betty, 310, 387
Krohn, Don, 310, 322, 387
Krulik, Rudy, 368, 373
Krusch, Christine, 388
Krusch, Herbert, 388
Kulathungam, Lyman, 385
Kulbeck, Earl N. O., 206, 339

Kulbeck, Gloria G., 97, 98, 106, 115, 122, 124, 153, 241, 266, 286, 292, 293
Kurtz, Gustav, 332, 351
Kydd, Ronald N., 208, 217, 264
Laakso, David, 306
Laari, John, 306
Labrentz, Arnold, 328, 350
Lakeshore Pentecostal Camp, Cobourg (Cobourg Camp), 19, 307, 313
Lamalice, Chief, 280
Lamont, Ewen, 36
Lamount, M., 36
Lang, Mrs. E., 132
Language Literature Ministries (LLM), 366
Lankin, A. J., 81, 89
Larden, Robert A., 96, 97, 123
Lassègues, E. L., 155, 165, 181, 182, 212, 218, 287, 288
Latimer, Carson, 214
Latta, Jean, 342, 344
Latter Rain, 30, 31, 39, 41, 42, 44, 45, 72, 74, 75, 77, 78, 79, 99, 101, 104, 106, 129, 151, 157, 159, 181
Latter Rain Movement, 208, 261, 262, 266, 354, 360 (see New Order of the Latter Rain)
Latto, T. T., 418
Laughlin, Wm., 157
Lawler, H. L., 41, 63, 78, 219, 220
Lawrence, B. F., 37, 38, 99, 122, 123
Layman, Louise, 238
Laymen's Revival of 1857-59, 22
Leasack, Eileen, 373
Lee, Siu Hoi, 351
Le Page, Derek, 391
Le Page, Sue, 391
Le Pers, Ruth, 230, 242
LeShana, Newman J., 179, 237
Lebeck, Leroy, 341
Lebeck, Marilyn, 341
Lebrocq, Bertha (Smiley), 163
Lebrocq, Philip, 163, 164
Lee, John Moon, 372
Leggate, Allan, 14
Lehotay, Emese, 382
Lei, Siu Hoi, 344

Lemmert, Arthur, 213
Lemon, Gladys, 206, 255, 266
Lescheid, Helen, 322
Lessard, Dan, 14
Lewis A. A., 276, 418
Liberalism, 103, 126
Liberia Assemblies of God, 231
Life, 268
Liira, Bert, 307, 322
Lincoln, Arthur, 86
Lincoln, Alida, 345, 390
Lincoln, Murray, 315, 345, 357, 390
Lindsay, Alex, 237
Lindsay, Douglas, 315, 357
Lindsay, Gordon, 260
Linklater, Pat, 364
Living Waters Camp, Saskatchewan, 281, 312
Loetscher, Leffert A., 122
Loewen, Janice, 345
Logan, Ethel, 181
Logos Journal, 299
Lokken, Ingrid, 223 (see Chawner, Ingrid)
London Free Press, 138
London Gospel Temple, 306
Loney, John, 40, 41
Louis Trichardt, 225, 337
Lower, A. R. N., 181
Lutheran charismatics, 300
Lynn, Carman W., 14, 217, 228, 242, 292, 320, 331, 335, 339, 349, 350, 351, 356, 374, 375, 385, 417, 418
Lynn, Edna, 329
Lynn, John, 50, 329
Lynn, Jesse, 338
Lynn, Virginia, 338
MacArthur, General, 272
MacDonald, Donald, 23
MacGowan, Ken, 333
MacGowan, Marjorie, 333
MacKnight, James M., 9, 15, 18, 124, 169, 353, 354, 356, 362, 373, 397-401, 411, 412, 417
Maddaford, Frank R., 93, 147, 200
Maddaford, Lionel, 98, 153

Maginley, Tom, 342
Mahan, Asa, 24, 36
Mainse, David, 284, 305, 322, 368
Mallory, Allen, 144, 190
Manhattan Beach Camp, Pelican Lake, Manitoba, 192, 313
Manley, Ruth, 91, 141 (see McAlister, Ruth)
Manley, William, 231
Manson, John, 60
March, C. L., 175-177
Marek, Karel, 209, 317
Maritimes Bible School, Halifax, 172
Marketplace Chapel, Edmonton, 363
Markham Camp Meeting, 106, 187
Markham, Lester, 404, 417, 418
Marr, Martha, 229
Marshall, Susan, 51
Martin, Don, 310, 322
Martin, Edwin, 284
Martin, John, 141
Martin, Ron, 338
Mathews, Shailer, 100
Matson, Amy, 340, 341, 351, 383 (see Milne, Amy)
Matson, Ethel, 340
Matson, Harold, 340, 341, 393
Mayo, Dr. Charles H., 132
Mbale Evangelistic Centre, Uganda, 332
Mbale Training Centre, Uganda, 386
Mbulo, George, 389
McAlister, Clarence, 145
McAlister, Harvey C., 63, 114, 115, 144, 145, 196
McAlister, Hugh J., 88, 140, 286, 418
McAlister, Jessie, 62
McAlister, John, 62, 72, 80, 81, 87, 88, 90, 118, 128, 143, 151, 192, 200, 203, 418
McAlister, Lila, 62 (see Skinner, Lila)
McAlister, Laura, 119, 232
McAlister, Robert Edward, 15, 18, 25, 35, 43, 44, 50, 53, 56, 62-67, 79, 87, 99, 104, 109, 110, 112, 114, 115, 118-121, 122, 124, 126, 134, 138-140, 144, 157, 169, 187, 188, 194, 196, 197, 199, 201-203, 207, 215, 232, 234, 251, 258, 264, 417

McAlister, Ruth, 91 (see Manely, Ruth)
McAlister, Walter E., 13, 18, 62, 67, 69, 76, 86, 87, 88, 91, 96, 108, 112, 120, 121, 123, 136, 140, 142, 147, 152, 168, 181, 192, 195, 200, 216, 222, 241, 250, 269, 272, 286, 302, 320, 410, 417, 418
McBride, Ella, 228, 270
McBride, John, 228, 270, 328
McClung, Grant, 16
McConnell, David, 315
McConnell, John, 138, 143
McCorkle, Marcia, 213
McDonald, Donald, 24, 166
McDonell, Kilian, 300, 321
McFarlene, Lloyd, 247
McGie, Allan, 281
McGillivray, Ken, 346, 347, 348
McGillivray, Wyn, 346, 347, 351
McGready, James, 23
McKillop, J. W., 142, 418
McKillop, Lillian, 211
McKillop, Raymond, 211
McLeod, Sadie, 343, 345
McNair, Tom, 144, 145
McNaughton, Ray, 148
McNaughton, Jean, 148
McPherson, A. V., 93
McPherson, Aimee Semple, 26, 69, 102, 122, 126, 127, 130, 133, 135, 136, 139, 151, 159, 162, 163, 167, 203, 215, 260 (see Kennedy, Aimee and Semple, Aimee)
McPherson, Mamie, 48, 69
McPherson, W. G., 286, 418
McTaggart, Margaret, 360
McTaggart, Matilda, 360
Melnychuck, William, 277
Men's Fellowship, 162, 256, 274, 306, 341, 345
Mennonite Brethren in Christ (MBC), 26, 42, 45, 46, 48, 49, 53, 54, 72, 101
Mennonites, 17, 25, 55, 121, 134, 277, 300
Menzies, William W., 123
Mercer, Linda, 384, 393
Mercer, William, 384, 387
Mercer, John, 365

Mercer, W. Robert, 393
Methodist (ism), 17, 21, 22, 24, 25, 27, 33, 46, 48, 60, 73, 74, 81, 92, 100, 101, 104, 105, 121, 166, 172, 178, 185, 186, 189, 196, 196, 197, 290
Methodist Episcopal Church, 27
Metropolitan Methodist Church, Victoria, B.C., 129, 131
Meyer, Frank, 341,
Meyer, Lenore, 341
Michaelis, Dan, 51
Michaelis, Fred, 51
Michaelis, Martha, 51
Miline, Amy, 340 (see Matson, Amy)
Miller, Asa, 189
Miller, C. R., 54
Miller, Mary T., 147
Miller, Thomas William, 18, 67-70, 96, 97, 122-124, 151-153, 181-183, 208, 209, 215-217, 230, 241-243, 265-266, 321-323, 336, 350-351, 373-374, 396, 412, 415, 416
Milley, E. R., 180
Milley, Garry E., 183
Mills, Verent, 390
Ming Tap United Bible School, Taiwan, 348
Minor, Harold, 388
Minor, Maryella, 388
Mission Canada, 371
Mission Statement (PAOC), 408
Missionary Church, 45
Missionettes (Missionary Action Girls), 252, 274, 290, 315
Missions Across Canada (MAC), 370
Mississauga Gospel Temple, 404
Mistewassis Reserve, 192
Mittelstaedt, Elizabeth, 332, 383, 396
Mittelstaedt, Rainer, 332, 383, 396
Mitchell, E. C., 283
Mitchell, Thomas, 176, 177, 179
Moberg, David O., 15, 18, 248, 249, 265, 409, 412
Modernism (Modernists), 100, 103, 126, 129, 130, 131, 178 (see Liberals)
Moi, Daniel Arap, 376
Monrovia Bible School, Liberia, 388

Montgomery Pentecostal Tabernacle, Calgary, 276
Montgomery, Carrie Judd, 89
Montgomery, James, 68, 126, 169, 170, 171, 182, 200, 201, 217, 252, 256, 266, 320, 417, 418
Montgomery, Mabel, 285
Montreal Christian Academy, 165
Moody, Barry, 36
Moody Bible Institute, 85
Moody, D. L., 13, 25, 26, 27, 173
Moody, W. E., 43, 127, 191
Moody, W. H., 285
Moore, A. Donald, 308, 418
Moravians, 22
Morgan, G. Campbell, 85
Morning Star, The, 64
Morris, Eunice, 69
Morris, Gerald, 212
Morris, Irene, 179
Morris, Ruby, 148
Morris, Wilfred, 148
Morrison, Elmor J., 161, 235, 236, 343
Morrison, Laura, 161, 235, 338, 343
Morrison, Gerald, 230, 338, 382
Morrison, Ruth, 230, 338
Morrison, Keith, 235, 349, 350, 351, 358
Morrison, Leroy, 225
Morrison, Ruby, 390
Morrison, Wilbur, 390
Morrison, Gertrude, 225
Morrison, Vernon, 211, 225, 230, 338
Morrow, William D., 418
Morton, C. M., 182
Motz, Arnell, 412
Moyer, Effie, 48, 69
Moyles, R. G., 37, 183
Mueller, Immanuel, 332
Mueller, Ruth, 332
Muggleton, Jack, 332, 333, 337
Muggleton, Winnie, 332, 333, 337
Muir, Robert, 312
Mukenzu, Julius, 389
Mulungu, Laurentino, 387
Munro, Marion, 229

Munro, Percy, 313, 418
Munroe, Alex, 148, 342
Munroe, Gwendolyn, 148, 342
Murray, George, 43
Mussen, Mrs E. Hazel, 130, 151
Myers, Edith, 334
Myers, Elmer, 334
Myers, Agnus, 289
Myers, Sheldon, 289
Myhre, Cyrus, 211
Myrah, Eunice, 280
Nanoose Bay Camp, Nanaimo, B.C., 275
National Association of Evangelicals, 268
National Association of Religious Broadcasters, 269
National Bible College Committee (NBCC), 256, 264, 369
National Deaf Conference, Calgary, 409
National Leadership Conference For Women, Oakville (1985), 369
National Spanish Conference, Toronto (1981), 371
National Sunday School Convention, Toronto (1949), 252
National Sunday School Department (1940), 252
Native New Life Assembly, Saskatoon, 364
Native Pentecostal Bible College, Chibougamau, Quebec, 369
Nelson, Gordon, 339
Nelson, Kathy, 339
Nelson, W. Clifford, 142, 143, 144, 146, 147, 153, 192, 193, 216, 282, 418
Neo-Pentecostals, 16
Nerling, Fred, 339
Nerling, Kay, 339
Ness, Ken, 277
Ness, Velma, 277
Nettleton, Harry, 276
Nettleton, Mildred, 276
Neufeldt, Ronald, 321
Neve, C. M., 91
New Birth, 23, 24, 166
New Brethren in Christ, 17
New Issue, 79, 110, 111, 112, 118 (see Jesus Only and Oneness Pentecostalism)

New Life Church, Brantford, 365
New Life Community Church, Ogden, 276
New Light, 23, 100
New Order of the Latter Rain, 259, 260, 262-265, 281 (see Latter Rain Movement)
New Wine, 299
Nichol, Eva, 286, 364
Nichol, John T., 38, 122
Niles, Don, 357
Ninth Line Tabernacle of the Assembly of God, Kinburn, 157
Nippard, Gladys, 388
Nippard, James, 388
Noble, G. E., 177
Noble, Jonas, 177
North Avenue Mission, Chicago (Durham), 74, 107
Northland Missions Bible College, Pickle Lake (Sioux Lookout), 369
Northwest Bible College (NBC), Edmonton, 209, 210, 280
Nortons, Barbara, 237
Nortons, J., 237
Nyack Bible College, New York, 54
Nyang'ori Mission Station, 227, 328
Nygaard, Elizabeth, 273
Nygaard, John, 273
Nygaard, Sophie, 229, 230, 242, 338
Nystedt, Victor, 91
Oberlin Evangelist, The, 24, 26
O'Brien, Edgar, 252
O'Brien, Marjorie, 310
O'Brien, Verner, 310
O'Brien, Wesley, 193
Odegaard, S. T., 44, 52
Ohio Bible School, 48
Oldford, Don, 389
Oldford, Jessie, 389
Olea, Jorge, 372
Olson, Paul, 277
Oneness Pentecostalism, 65, 79, 108, 109, 111, 115, 117 (see Jesus Only and New Issue)
Ontario Pentecostal Bible College, 207 (see Eastern Pentecostal Bible College)

Ordination of women, 317-318, 359-360
Orwig, A. W., 29, 102, 122
Osborn, T. L., 260
Otanga, Michael, 326, 328
Otto, A. W., 158, 181
Ozard, Jack, 321
Ozman, Agnes, 28
Pacific Coast Missionary Society, 93, 94
Palmer, Phoebe, 25, 85 (see Spence, Phoebe)
Pan Africa Christian College, Nairobi, 329, 330, 386, 404
Papadopoulos, Andreas, 384
Papadopoulos, Beverly, 384
Pardo, Blanche, 343, 345
Parham, Charles F., 28-30, 107, 112
Parker, Ernie, 142
Parkhurst, Louis G., 36
Parkinson, Bernard, 252, 315, 322
Parkinson, Marion, 271, 272, 292, 341
Parkinson, Robert, 271
Parks, Keith H., 402, 404, 417
Parks, Wayne, 396
Parkside Assembly, Saskatchewan, 88, 141-142, 192, 228, 312
Parlee, Fred, 182, 208
Parsons, Bert, 176
Patrick, Frank, 131, 402
Pattison, Arthur Miles, 114, 115, 196
Pattison, Paul, 366
Paul, George S., 92-94, 108, 109
Pavilion of Promise,, 368 (see Crossroads Christian Communications)
Peel, Jean, 334, 337
Peel, Robert, 334, 335, 337
Peever, A., 157
Peever, E. Ruth, 396
Peever, Howard, 279
Peever, Wilma, 279
Pelly, Captain E. R., 180
Pemberton, Ruth, 240, 341
Pennington, Edith, 282
Pennoyer, Jean, 274
Penny Day, 284, 307
Pentecostal Assemblies Church Extension (PACE), 304

Pentecostal Assemblies of East Africa, 328
Pentecostal Assemblies of God, Zambia, 333
Pentecostal Assemblies of God, Kenya, 228, 326-329, 386
Pentecostal Assemblies of Newfoundland (PAON), 36, 180, 181, 199, 207, 258, 289, 290, 355
Pentecostal Assemblies of Rhodesia, 334
Pentecostal Assemblies of Sri Lanka, 338
Pentecostal Assemblies of the West Indies, 342, 386
Pentecostal Assemblies of the World, 114
Pentecostal Assemblies School (India), 381
Pentecostal Benevolent Association, 253, 286
Pentecostal Church of Poland, 385
Pentecostal Crusaders, 252, 253, 290, 341, 315
Pentecostal Evangelical Mission of Brazil, 340
Pentecostal Evangelistic Pioneers (PEP), 337
Pentecostal Fellowship of North America,
Pentecostal Herald, The, 180
Pentecostal Mission at Berlin (Kitchener), 53, 55, 158, 232
Pentecostal Missionary Union (P.M.U.), 105-107, 113
Pentecostal Testimony, The, 64, 82, 108, 119-121, 131, 140, 180, 189, 191, 196, 199, 202, 204, 230, 247, 252, 254, 258, 262, 271, 302, 302, 303, 304, 316, 318, 319, 339
Pentecostal Workers' Convention (1908), 43
Pentecostal Workers' Home, Toronto, 43
Perez, Eusebio, 372
Perkins, Carol, 341
Perkins, J., 229
Perks, Cecil, 146
Perks, Molly, 146
Perry, Martha, 51
Peterkin, Olive, 51
Peters, Erna Alma, 217, 218
Peters, G. V., 418
Peterson, C., 146
Phair, Archdeacon, 71, 73, 77, 81

Philpott, P. W., 25
Pierce, Christine, 81
Pierce, Willard C., 81, 147, 206, 217
Pietism, 22, 25
Pina, José, 334
Pina, Maria, 334
Piper, Aleta (Sternall), 54, 152, 341
Piper, Jack, 341
Plains Pentecostal Camp, Saskatchewan, 312
Plastow, Dorothy, 210
Playter, George F., 215
Plowman, Edward E., 321
Plunkett, Gerry, 366, 367, 373
Plunkett, Marcia, 366, 367
Polkki, John, 393
Polkki, Sirpe, 393
Pope John XXIII, 299
Pope Paul VI, 299
Posein, Loudell, 332
Posein, Ronald Ludwig, 278, 332, 390
Positive Confession movement, 361
Praise the Lord (PTL), 298
Prasad, Dhruv, 381
Prasad, Rita, 381
Presbyterian(s), 17, 22, 121, 300
Prescod, Jeremiah, 392
Presley, Gordon, 161
Presley, Ian, 274
Preston, Holy Ann, 48
Price, Dr. Charles S., 84, 96, 126, 129-133, 144, 147, 149, 151, 152, 190, 193, 241, 260, 276, 281
Priest, Dan, 280
Priest, Grace, 280
Promise of Pentecost, The, 78
Promise, The, 40, 42, 63, 106
Prosser, Peter, 321
Purdie, David, 333
Purdie, Margaret, 333
Purdie, J. Eustace, 24, 84-87, 96, 101, 107, 166, 169, 182, 201-207, 210-212, 217, 256, 258, 282
Purdy, Beatrice, 279 (see Abbey, Beatrice)
Purse, James, 211

Quakers, 33, 55
Queensway Cathedral, Toronto, 305, 378, 402
Rafferty, Kate, 396
Rafuse, Leslie, 247
Raines, Lucy, 175
Ramabai, Pandita, 27, 74, 232
Ranaghan, Kevin, 299, 301, 302
Randall, Herbert E., 41, 63, 64, 78, 219, 220
Ratt, Rodger, 364
Rattai, Clare, 364
Ratz, Cal, 344
Ratz, Dr. Charles A., 204-208, 256, 316, 317, 328
Ratz, Ruth, 344
Raymer, Don, 346, 357, 379
Raymer, Dorthy, 346
Raymer, Ivan D., 172, 211, 288, 308, 418
Reality Outreach Ministry, St. Catherines, 368 (see Krulik, Rudy)
Redmann, Gudrun, 393
Redmann, Kurt, 393
Reid, David A., 123
Reid, K. I., 205
Reid, Ronald, 302, 322
Reinheimer, W. G., 418
Renewal, 299
Rennick, Brian, 389
Rennick, Collen, 389
Research Task Force of Vision 2000 Canada, 400
Resource, 357, 370
Restoration Movement, 362
Reynolds, Joshua, 37
Richards, A. Graydon, 284, 320, 357, 417
Richards, James, 211
Richardson, Bishop, 85
Richardson, Hannah (Price), 360
Richmond, Beatrice, 275
Richmond, Gordon, 275
Richmond, Rolla, 141, 142, 152
Richmond, Elsie, 152
Ripe for Revival, 249, 410
Riss, Richard, 260, 266

Robert, René, 212, 287, 288
Roberts, Evan, 29, 34
Roberts, Hank, 358
Roberts, Oral, 260, 298
Robertson, Pat, 298
Robinson, Eva (Argue), 96, 97
Robinson, E. W., 146, 193, 206, 210, 211, 268
Robinson, H. E., 81
Rock Lake Camp, Manitoba, 136, 191, 192
Rodger, Janet, 360
Rodriguez, Arnaro, 321
Rogers, H. G., 79
Ros, Christine, 332
Ros, Herbert, 332
Rosenau, Art, 276
Roset, Ivar, 214, 418
Roulston, Don, 248
Rourke, Elizabeth, 162, 170, 182
Rourke, W. F., 162, 170, 288
Routley, Jim, 142
Rowsell, Cavell, 392
Royal View Church, London, 306
Royce, J. H., 226
Rudd, Douglas, 14
Rumble, George, 81
Rutten, Brian, 389, 390
Rutten, Valerie, 389
Ryan, Thomas, 71
Sadler, Dave, 248
Salmon, John, 43
Salvation, 17, 28, 75, 92, 95, 99, 107, 108, 130, 131, 132, 135, 137, 197 (see Full Gospel)
Salvation Army, 17, 25-27, 73, 173-175, 180, 232
Samson, Arthur, 165
Sanders, Florence, 233 (see Spence, Florence)
Sanderson, J. E., 182
Santification, 22-24, 30-32, 92, 100, 104, 107-109, 130, 186 (see Entire Sanctification)
Sasse, Herman, 393
Sasse, Irmgarde, 393
Sauder, Doris, 388

Saunders, Allan, 144
Saunders, Edward M., 36
Saunders, Jack D., 26, 79, 126, 136-139, 147, 151, 188, 191, 193
Scataglini, Alberto, 394
Schaff, Philip, 26, 37
Schatkoske, Julius, 145, 278
Scheel, Iris, 326, 327, 386
Schellenberg, Don, 311, 333, 345
Schellenberg, Faye, 345
Schellert, Ida, 332
Schellert, Paul, 332
Scheppe, John, 80, 110, 342
Scheske, Don, 342
Scheske, Janice, 342
Schindel, Albert, 145
Schindel, Alvin C., 206, 208, 209, 302, 317, 322
Schindel, Arthur J., 211
Schindel, Betty, 211
Schlarbaum, Norman E., 208, 317
Schmunk, Reuben L., 357, 417, 418
Schneider, George, 91, 200, 203, 277
Schneider, Robert, 280
Schoen, Ruth, 210
School of Missions, 349
Schuler, Dr. Robert P., 293
Schwab, Emil, 75, 81, 203, 256
Schwartz, Frank, 230
Schwarz, Winnifred, 230
Schwindt, Bruce, 365
Scott, Charles W. H., 161
Scott, R. J., 71, 72
Scratch, Clare, 143, 168, 234, 235, 243, 343, 348, 418
Scratch, Lydia, 168, 234, 343
Scratch, Elma, 235, 358 (see Barber, Elma)
Scratch, Gordon, 234
Scratch, Lorraine, 234
Scurrah, Edgar, 219, 221
Seabrook, Vera, 364
Second Coming, 17, 19, 28, 75, 92, 95, 99, 102, 107, 135, 197 (see Full Gospel)
Selbie, W. B., 36
Sellin, H. H., 91

Semple, Aimee, 43, 52, 53, 55, 187, 232 (see Kennedy, Aimee and McPherson, Aimee)
Semple, Robert, 43, 52, 53, 232
Semple, Neil, 215
Senior Contact, The, 358, 370
Seniors Overseas Service (SOS), 348
Seresinhe, Preman, 382, 396
Seymour, James, 389
Seymour, William, 29, 38, 67
Shakarian, Demos, 268, 298
Shanahan, Kevin, 18
Shannon, John, 273
Shannon, Mary, 273
Sharon Bible School, 261
Sharon English Bible Learning Centre, Hong Kong, 345
Shaw, Geoffry, 180, 293
Shek, General Chiang Kai, 346
Shepherd Lodge, Toronto, 286, 319
Shepherd Manor, Toronto, 286, 319
Sherrill, John, 298
Shevkenek, Alice, 276
Shipton, Olive, 211, 218
Shrier, Jack, 284
Siegrist, Clara, 209
Siemens, Clara, 232, 240, 333, 341
Siemens, Renata, 229, 326, 332
Silver Birches Camp Ground, Kirkland Lake, 190, 313
Simpson, A. B., 28, 54, 73, 201, 219
Simpson, Catherine, 341
Sims, Beatrice, 81, 161
Sipprell, W. J., 129, 130
Sirett, Carol, 208
Sixth Avenue Tabernacle, Vancouver, 146-148
Sjokvist, Grace, 338, 341
Skinner, Doris, 333, 337
Skinner, Robert, 333, 337, 348, 350, 358, 359, 373, 395
Skinner, Gary, 377, 378, 395
Skinner, Marilyn, 377, 378
Skinner, James, 63, 228, 229, 238, 242, 243, 270, 333, 334, 349
Skinner, Lila, 62, 63, 70, 97, 228, 229, 242,

333, 334 (see McAlister, Lila)
Skovmond, Harold, 342, 393
Slager, George C., 41-43, 67, 219, 241
Slauenwhite, Carol, 333
Slauenwhite, David, 333, 418
Slauenwhite, Barry, 308
Slauenwhite, Sharon, 308
Slavic Conference (Eastern and Western) 277,
Slavic Conference (1931), 201
Sly, Peter, 248
Sly, Valone, 69, 242
Small, Franklin, 65, 76, 78, 80, 83, 108, 110, 111, 114, 115, 117, 196
Smallridge, Vic, 357, 358
Smallwood, Joseph, 174
Smith, Beulah, 96, 97, 208, 317 (see Argue, Beulah)
Smith, C. B., 120, 136, 145, 205-208, 250, 262, 266, 268, 272, 273, 417, 418
Smith, Keith, 397
Smith, Marilyn, 363
Smith, Robert, 80, 97
Smythe, Ernest, 284
Snyder, Mrs. Henry, 45
Social Concerns, 253, 319, 353, 355, 358, 372, 373, 400, 401 (see Ethics and Social Concerns Committee)
Sod-Buster, 146
Solomonson, Sarah, 279
Sorensen, Annina, 238
Sorensen, Niels, 238, 271
Sorensen, Esther, 271
Sorensen, Samuel, 271
Sorensen, Dorothy, 271, 306, 339
Sorensen, Paul, 271, 306, 339
Sorrell, Mark, 38
Source, 370
Southeast Asia Assemblies of God, 344
Spaetzel, Roy Clifford, 68, 124, 243
Spaetzel, Viola (Chambers), 56, 70
Speed the Light, 253
Spence, Florence, 211, 233, 343 (see Sanders, Florence)
Spence, John Rutherford, 80, 141, 232, 233, 234, 243, 343

Spence, Phoebe, 233, 243 (see Holmes, Phoebe)
Spillenaar, John, 213, 283, 284
Spillenaar, R., 42
Spring Bay Camp, Manitoulin Island, 313
Spring, Fred, 303
Spurrell, Reuben P., 129, 151, 159, 181
St. Andrew's Church, Montreal, 129, 133, 159
St. James Anglican, Saskatoon, 84, 85, 87, 203
St. John's College, Winnipeg, 77
St. John's Mission, Newfoundland, 175
Stacey, C. P., 265
Stanley, Bill, 247
Starrett, Evelyn, 273
Starrett, Robert, 273
Statement of Faith (Seymour), 30
Statement of Fundamental and Essential Truths, 109, 120, 360, 361
Steed, Brian, 213
Steele, Katie, 138
Stephens, Commander R. M. T., 134
Sternall, Ella (Hostetler), 54
Sternall, Reuben Eby, 26, 44, 49, 53-55, 69, 114, 115, 139, 152, 196, 197, 216
Stevens, Ron, 284
Stevenson, Edith, 241
Stevenson, Kenneth. K., 230, 241
Stevenson, S. G., 157
Stewart, Eileen, 358, 368
Stewart, Mrs. George, 45
Stewart, Rae, 285
Stewart, Randy, 365, 366
Stiller, Brian, 209
Stiller, Carl H., 209, 261, 281, 320, 417, 418
Stiller, Douglas, 363, 373, 397, 408
Stone Church, Toronto, 283, 346
Stone, Jean, 321
Story, C. A. C., 83, 84, 97, 217, 272, 418
Story, F. G. M. (Gus), 83, 84, 142
Strachan, Gordon, 37
Strong, Alex, 332, 335
Strong, Janet, 332

Stronstad, Roger J., 211, 323
Stuckless, Rex, 393
Stuckless, Rita, 393
Sturliff, Miles, 248
Sub Artic Leadership Training Program (SALT), 363, 369
Sub Artic Mission, 363
Suenens, Cardinal, 299
Sunnyside Camp, Alberta, 193
Sunset Point Pentecostal Camp, 312 (see German Conference Camp)
Sunshine Evangel Hour, The, 143
Sutherland, Alexander, 182
Sutherland, Mrs. William, 140
Swaggart, Jimmy, 298, 354
Swallow, S. C., 185, 215
Swann, R. B., 27
Swanson, James, 207, 417
Swanson, May, 207
Swedish Mission Church, Moorhead, Minnesota, 27
Sweet, H. C., 207
Sylvan Lake Camp, Alberta, 276
Synan, J. A., 291, 293
Synan, Vinson, 108, 297, 122, 123, 321
Taitinger, Robert, 210, 312, 320, 356, 373, 417
Tarling, Edith, 282
Tarling, Peter, 282
Task Force, 393, 403
Tassé, Louis, 164
Tassé, Madame, 164
Taylor, George, 81, 91
Taylor, Kim, 382
Taylor, Philip, 382
Taylor, V. W., 418
Taylor, W. J., 74, 96, 282, 292, 418
Team Canada, 370, 378, 393, 403
Teen Challenge, Toronto, 286
Témoignage, Le, 366
Tannant, Lynda, 98, 153
Tchien Mission Station, Liberia, 388
Tennent, Gilbert, 21
Thailand Pentecostal Bible College, 392
Thaler, Carolyn, 169

Theological Education by Extension (TEE), 328, 339, 393
Third Force. 268, 291, 295
Third Force, The, 13, 123, 124, 414
Thiessen, Katherine, 276
Thomas, Emily, 172
Thomas, Gertrude, 172
Thomas, Harold, 172
Thomas, Mervyn, 330, 376
Thomas, Shelia, 330, 376
Tilton, S. R., 276, 418
Timothy School of Discipleship, Kampala, 377
Tingstad, Ingemar, 273
Tisdalle, Belva, 333, 378
Tisdalle, Vern, 333, 378
Tisher, Herb, 338, 388
Tisher, LaVerne, 338, 388
Todriguez, Armaro, 302
Tolbert, William, 338
Toppings, Millie, 391
Torrey, Reuben A., 85, 203
Torvegadon Mission Room, 34
Totafurno, John, 357, 417
Total Church Evangelism Strategy Committee (TCESC), 397, 399
Townsend, Arthur H., 146, 153, 303
Tunks, George, 284
Tunks, Ruth, 284
Tyler, Doris, 279
Tyler, James, 279, 312, 364, 418
Ulseth, Esther, 341
Ulseth, Larry, 341, 392
Underhill, Harold, 237
Underhill, Verna, 237
Unitarian-Pentecostal, 108
United Pentecostal Church, Canada, 355
United Pentecostal Church of the USA, 111
Upper Room Ministries Church, Harare, 378
Upper Room Mission, Montreal, 161, 162, 171, 189
Upton, George R., 89, 143, 152, 193, 216, 242, 251, 255, 276, 292, 320, 325, 331, 339, 345, 347, 348, 351, 357, 411, 417, 418

Upton, Marie (Larson), 143
Upton, Gordon R., 97, 181, 191, 193, 313, 357, 371, 372, 373, 374, 404, 417, 418
Upton, Maisie, 376
Upton, Roy E., 151, 193, 376, 397
Urshan, Andrew, 79
Valley Road Church, Kenya, 330, 376, 377
Van Dusen, Henry P. 268, 269, 291, 295
Van Kleek, Lawrence, 218
Vaters, Eugene, 161, 162, 174, 177-180, 181, 183, 201, 289
Vaters, Sarah, 178
Veale, Grace, 279, 280
Verge, Carl, 208
Verhulst, Carl, 337, 379, 388
Verhulst, Ruth, 337, 379, 388
Victoria Daily Colonist, 130
Victoria Ministerial Association, 131
Voice, 298
Voice of Healing, The, 260
Volunteers in Mission (VIM), 348, 392, 403
Volunteers in Special Assignment (VISA), 391, 403
Wachnuik, Gloria, 275
Wadge, Margaret, 230, 338
Walker, Alva, 94, 146, 14
Walker, Clarence, 282, 418
Walker, Peter, 208
Walsh, H. H., 37
Walthall, W. Jethro, 27
War Cry, 27
Ward, A. G., 26, 43-47, 67, 68-72, 76, 92, 96, 101, 104-106, 113, 119, 121, 122, 140, 179, 215, 417
Ward, Mary (Markle), 71
Ward, C. M., 46, 69, 96, 193
Ward, Clinton, 142
Ward, Lettie, 53, 231, 232
Waterhouse, Wilson, 214, 281, 312, 322
Watson, Essie. 182
Watson, George, 73
Watson, Joyce, 139, 167-170
Watson, Ray, 139, 167-170, 200
Watts, John M., 256, 276

Way, David, 333
Way, Florence, 333
Weale, David E., 182
Wee College, 315
Wellard, David, 139
Weller, James, 385, 418
Weller, Marion, 52, 226 (see Wittich, Marian and Keller, Marian)
Weller, Peter, 52
Weller, Sarah, 51, 52, 226, 237
Wells, T. L., 323
Welsh Revival (1904), 74, 173
Wendelbo, Ivar, 247, 248
Wentland, Doris, 278, 332
Wentland, Gus, 278, 332
Wesley, Charles, 21
Wesley, John, 21, 22, 24, 31, 78, 99, 390, 291
Wesleyan, 22, 25, 108, 109
Wesleyan Awakening, 99
West Coast Indian Pentecostal Bible School, Vancouver, 214
West Indies School of Theology (WIST), 272, 341, 342
West, Jack, 69, 144, 153, 215
Western Bible College, 206, 208, 248, 255 (see Canadian Pentecostal Bible College and Winnipeg Bible school)
Western Canada District Council of the Assemblies of God, 118
Western Pentecostal Bible College (WPBC), 211 (see British Columbia Bible Institute)
Whaley, Charles, 214
Wheaton College, 206
White, Dennis, 342, 376, 377
White, Esther, 376
White, Laura, 338, 345
White, Ron, 338, 345, 391
Whitfield, George, 21, 100
Whittaker, David, 309
Wice, Aubrey, 322
Wieman, H. N., 100
Wigglesworth, Smith, 147
Wilkerson, David, 298, 366
Will, George, 51

Williams, E. S., 54
Williams, H. H., 279 (see H. H. Williams Memorial Hospital, Hay River)
Willoughby, Gloria, 377, 386, 396
Willoughby, Paul, 377
Wilson, A. A., 189
Wilson, Alice, 141, 148
Wilson, Bryon R., 265
Wilson, Bob, 247
Wilson, Robert S., 37
Wilson, Sammy, 83, 144
Wilson, Tony, 391
Wilson, Ursula, 391
Wilson, Viola, 179
Winehouse, Irwin, 123
Wing the Word, 228, 254, 285 370, 401
Winger, M. S, 168, 172, 211, 288, 418
Winnipeg Bible Institute, 207
Winnipeg Bible school, 85, 168, 169, 179, 193, 228, 247 (see Canadian Pentecostal Bible College and Western Bible College)
Winslow, Ola E., 36
Winsor, Arthur S., 175-177, 179, 183
Winsor, Eva, 391
Winsor, Gary, 391
Winsor, Noella, 392
Winsor, Sam, 392
Winter, Ian, 213
Wise, Ted, 295
Withrow, W. H., 215
Wittich, Karl, 52, 226, 242
Wittich, Marian, 52, 226, 227 (see Weller, Marian and Keller, Marian)
Wittich, Philip, 90
Wolf, Nelson, 363
Women's Ministries (WM), 255, 315, 317
Women's Missionary Council (WMC), 172, 255, 256, 288, 315, 338, 341, 345
Women's Missionary Society, 254, 255, 317

Wood, Everett, 269
Wood, Wally, 306
Woodworth-Etter, Maria, 27, 38, 72, 78, 96, 102, 109, 123
Work Force, 256, 362
World Christian Ministries, 385
World Council of Churches (WCC), 269, 300
World Pentecostal Conference (WPC), 267, 268, 291, 318
World-Wide Camp Meeting of 1913, 72, 78-79, 109, 111
Wortman, Charles M., 65, 70, 188, 237, 238, 251, 265, 320, 339, 417
Wortman, Margaret, 237-238
Wortman, W. H., 53
Wragg, Phil, 247
Wragg, Walter, 247
Wright, Mrs. John, 138
Wycliffe College, Toronto, 85, 203, 204
Yates, Charles, 276, 320, 323, 357, 373, 404, 417, 418
Yeomans, Lillian, 90, 97, 98
Young, Arminius, 182
Young, Carl, 391
Young, Dorthy, 391
Young, Claude, 176, 183
Young, Earl K., 418
Young, Don, 391
Young, Marieve, 391
Young, Fred, 59
Youngren, Peter, 308
Youth For Christ, 268
Youth Profile, 370
Zabriskie, R., 213
Zeidman, Morris, 208
Zinzendorf, Count, 22
Zulus, The, 222